# Social Interaction

## READINGS IN
## SOCIOLOGY

### THIRD EDITION

# Social Interaction

## READINGS IN SOCIOLOGY

### THIRD EDITION

Edited by CANDACE CLARK
*Montclair State College*
HOWARD ROBBOY
*Trenton State College*

St. Martin's Press    New York

# In Memory of Herbert Blumer

Library of Congress Catalog Card Number: 87-060527
Copyright © 1988 by St. Martin's Press, Inc.
All Rights Reserved.
Manufactured in the United States of America.
1098
fedcb

For information, write St. Martin's Press, Inc.,
175 Fifth Avenue, New York, New York 10010

book design: Judith Woracek
cover: Darby Downey

ISBN: 0-312-733011

## Acknowledgments

Lynn Atwater: "Women and Marriage: Adding an Extramarital Role" was written for the first edition of *Social Interaction*.

Howard S. Becker: *Whose Side Are We On?* © by The Society for the Study of Social Problems. Reprinted from *Social Problems* 14, Winter, 1967, pp. 239–247, by permission.

Howard S. Becker, Blanche Geer, and Everett Hughes: Excerpt from *Making The Grade: The Academic Side of College Life*, 1968, John Wiley & Sons. Copyright © 1968 by Howard S. Becker. Reprinted by permission of the authors.

*Acknowlegments and copyrights continue at the back on pages 578-579, which constitute an extension of the copyright page.*

# Contents

## Correlation Chart for Social Interaction and Standard Sociology Texts

| Part (part #) | Conklin 2/e Macmillan (1987) | Coser, Lewis, Nock, Bufford Steffan 2/e [HBJ] (1987) | Hebding & Leonard/Intro to Sociology Random House (1987) | Hess, Markson, & Stein/Sociology 3/e Macmillan N.Y. (1988) | Karp, Yoels Peacock (1986) | Landis 6/e Sociology Concepts & Characteristics Wadsworth (1986) | Light & Keller 6/e Random House (1988) | Macionis/Sociology Prentice-Hall (1987) | Persell Harper & Row (1987) | Popenoe 6/e Prentice-Hall (1988) | Ritzer, Kemmeyer, & Yetman 3/e Allen & Bacon (1986) | Robertson Worth Publishing Co. (1987) | Shepard 3/e West Publishing Co. (1987) | Stark 2/e Wadsworth (1987) | Thio/Sociology: An Intro. Harper & Row (1986) | Tischler, Whitten & Hunter/Intro to Sociology Holt Rinehart & Winston (1986) | Van der Zanden Sociology: The Core Knopf (1986) |
|---|---|---|---|---|---|---|---|---|---|---|---|---|---|---|---|---|---|
| INTRODUCTION (I) | 1, 2 | 1, 2 | 1, 2 | 1, 2 | 1, 2 | 1, 14 | 1, 2 | 1, 2 | 1, 2 | 1, 2 | 1, 2, 3 | 1, 2 | 1, 2 | 1 | 1, 2 | 1, 2 | 1 |
| CULTURE (II) | 3 | 3 | 3 | 3 | 1 | 3 | 3 | 3 | 5 | 5 | 4 | 3 | 2 | 2, 5 | 3 | 3 | 2 |
| TRANSMISSION OF CULTURE: SOCIALIZATION (III) | 4 | 5 | 4 | 5 | 2, 3 | 2 | 5 | 6 | 6 | 6 | 7 | 5 | 5 | 6 | 6 | 4 | 3 |
| INTERACTION IN EVERYDAY LIFE (IV) | 6 | 1 | | 5 | 3 | | | 5 | 4 | 3 | 5 | 6 | | 3 | | 5 | 3 |
| SOCIAL ORGANIZATION: LIFE IN GROUPS (V) | 7 | 4, 6 | 5, 6 | 4 | 7 | 4 | 4, 7, 8, 16 | 5 | 7 | 4, 10, 17 | 5, 6 | 7 | 6 | 4 | 5 | 6 | 4 |

viii

# Preface

THE THIRD EDITION OF *SOCIAL INTERACTION* IS SUBSTANTIALLY REVISED. About a third of the articles here are newcomers, joining the the ranks of classics such as William Foote Whyte's study of streetcorner boys, Erving Goffman's analysis of self-presentations in everyday life, and D.L. Rosenhan's look inside a mental hospital.

We have remained loyal to two themes that cross-cut both previous editions. First, the majority of our selections come from the symbolic interactionist school of sociological theory and research. Second, we have purposefully chosen, for all sections of the book, articles that recognize women's roles in society and articles written by women sociologists. Further, we sought materials that were readable yet substantive and insightful—more than mere journalistic illustrations of concepts introduced in sociology texts.

Our goal is to engage both sociology students and their professors. We hope students will find that these articles strike familiar chords and offer ideas, concepts, and theories that help them make sense of their social worlds. We hope faculty members also will be excited by the new material and re-excited by the old. We still feel the fascination of sociology after twenty years in the field, and we hope this book conveys that fascination and inspires it in others.

In preparing this edition of *Social Interaction*, we relied on many people. Mark Hutter of Glassboro State College repeatedly suggested, criticized, reviewed, and encouraged. Judith Gerson of Rutgers University provided advice, perspective, and humor. Our editors at St. Martin's Press, first Michael Weber and later Andrea Guidoboni, were supportive and helpful. Beverly Hinton contributed greatly by securing publishing permissions for the articles. Finally, a team of sociologists assisted us by reviewing each of the articles in the second edition and suggesting deletions and additions. They are: Brian Berry, Rochester Institute of Technology; Saul Feinman, The University of Wyoming; James William Jordon, Longwood College; M. Ruggie, Barnard College; Glenn A. Goodwin, Pitzer College; Michael Klausner, University of Pittsburgh; Roslyn Bologh, St. John's University; Diane Sachs, Rhodes College; Regina Kenen, Trenton State College; Kathleen Daly, Yale University; Robert P. Stuckert, Berea College; Elizabeth Watson, University of Redlands;

S. Varmette, Southern Connecticut State University; Christian Ritter, Kent State University; Andrew Twaddle, University of Missouri, Columbia; Buford Farris, St. Louis University; Earl C. Nance, Rock Valley College; Theo Majka, University of Dayton; Robert H. West, Temple University; A. Pilkinston, California Polytechnic State University; Ray R. Canning, University of Utah; and G. Thomas Behler, Moravian College.

We also want to thank the many previous users of this book who on their own initiative have offered suggestions, comments, and praise. They have made the third edition possible.

As with previous editions, this work represents the joint contributions of the editors. For reasons of equity, for this edition, the names of the editors have been reversed from Howard Robboy and Candace Clark, to Candace Clark and Howard Robboy.

Candace Clark
Howard Robboy

# Social Interaction

## READINGS IN SOCIOLOGY

### THIRD EDITION

# Part I. Introduction

## THE SOCIOLOGICAL PERSPECTIVE

As participants in the give and take, ebb and flow of human interaction, we take much of our social experience for granted. We move from group to group—family, friends, strangers; in classrooms, in stores, in the workplace—unconcerned with the amazing complexity of human activity. We pay as little attention to what goes on beneath the surface of social activity as we do to the inner workings of the telephone or the automobile.

But the electronics technician and the automobile mechanic know that inside the telephone or under the hood of the car lies intricate machinery. In much the same way, the student of sociology learns to peer beneath the veneer of conventional understanding to look systematically at the patterns and the processes of our daily lives and the shared meanings and symbols that make the "social dance" possible. Sociology is, then, a unique way of viewing the human world. It is the study of the complexities of social life and interaction that we normally take for granted.

In this volume we have collected readings from articles and books that we, our colleagues, and especially our students have found to be exciting and challenging explorations beneath the surface of social life. The readings analyze human relationships taking place in small groups and huge bureaucracies. They report on investigations set in private homes, public offices, and street corner shops. They also consider important social processes—cooperation, conflict, socialization, and social change.

In the first selection, Peter Berger welcomes us to the sociological perspective. He examines the special meanings to sociology of the terms *society* and *social*. *Society*, according to Berger, can be defined as "a large complex of human relationships," "a system of interaction." A society does not necessarily comprise large numbers of interacting people; rather, a society is any relatively self-contained, autonomous system. The term *social* as used by sociologists refers to actions oriented toward others. Thus *social interaction* refers to those aspects of all types of human behavior that involve an awareness of other human beings.

1

## BERGER'S FOUR SOCIOLOGICAL MOTIFS

Furthermore, Berger delineates four major sociological themes, or motifs. When used together, these motifs allow us to view the world through sociological "lenses," thereby gaining insight into the workings of the social world. The first theme is that of debunking many myths that people hold about their societies. Social scientists cannot be so naïve as to accept at face value the common explanations of how things work. They must question these very explanations and try to understand how they are produced. They must gather evidence to determine whether or not they are accurate.

The second motif that Berger describes is that of paying attention to aspects of the social world that would be considered unrespectable by many middle-class members of society. Only by looking at criminals, the poor, minorities, and the like can we gain a complete picture of our world. "Respectable" citizens often describe the world in ways that protect and justify their own behavior. Also, their experiences with the system are not the same as the experiences of the "unrespectable." We need both viewpoints. For instance, a presidential commission studying the causes of widespread rioting in the mid-1960s included testimony of city officials *and* interviews with the residents of poor neighborhoods where rioting  occurred. Their conclusion was that, contrary to the officials' views, societal racism (in which the officials themselves played a part) was responsible for the conditions that sparked the violence. In another vein, sociologists who have attempted to understand the failure of our prison system to rehabilitate criminals have paid as much attention to the prisoners' descriptions of prison life and how it affects them as to the statements of guards and wardens.

Third, sociologists must always keep in mind the relativity of social values and beliefs. By this we mean that standards of "right" and "wrong," as well as opinions and even "knowledge," can be understood fully only within the context of a given society at a given point in time. What is considered appropriate behavior or truth or evil in one society at one historical moment may be considered inappropriate behavior or falsehood or good in another. Values are, therefore, relative to the society under study, rather than being absolute or universal. Sociologists will not be able to understand what a value or belief means to those who hold it unless they maintain awareness of the principle of relativity.

Fourth, Berger discusses the cosmopolitan motif in sociological thought. What he means here is that, rather than being oriented strictly toward local issues and concerns, sociologists have generally been oriented toward other lands, other peoples, other ways of life and world views.

Of course, these four motifs are interrelated and mutually reinforcing. They are the essence of the "sociological imagination." As you read

Berger's explanations of them, and the articles that follow, you too will start to view human interaction from the sociological perspective. Berger also notes that the sociologist works by making "inquisitive intrusions" beyond the facades of social life. Above all, sociology is an *empirical* study of human interaction, which means that it rests on research and observation of people working, relaxing, learning, thinking about their concerns—in short, how they are living their lives—rather than on prior assumptions or hunches about how society works.

## HOW SOCIOLOGISTS GATHER DATA

Research takes many forms for sociologists, but all forms involve searching for evidence that will help us discover the abstract patterns operating beneath the facades. These forms include the survey, in which a series of predetermined questions is put to a large sample of people. A survey can be very short and focused—as with Gallup polls of voters' intentions—or longer and more encompassing—as with studies of life-styles, aspirations, attitudes, and the like.

Participant observation is another commonly used method of getting information about social behavior. The researcher actually becomes involved as a member of the group or situation under study in order to gain clearer insights into the meanings that people give to their behavior and to absorb more of the flavor of the lives of those under study.

With intensive interviews, sociologists begin with a brief, open-ended interview schedule that allows them to delve and probe into the life situations of those chosen for research. At the same time respondents can answer in their own words and explain their answers in detail.

The classical experiment is seldom used in sociology, because many human characteristics and patterns of behavior cannot be dictated or altered by the researcher. In a true experiment, the researcher must begin with at least two groups—the *experimental* group and the *control* group—that are identical in all ways considered relevant for the study. The experimental group must then be manipulated by the experimenter; that is, some "treatment," such as an educational program, a frightening film, or additional income, must be administered to the experimental group only. Any changes found within this group are then compared with developments within the control group. If the groups were in fact identical to begin with, and if the experimental group changed more than the control group, we then infer that the treatment caused those changes. In reality, it is often difficult to say that the two groups were identical. Furthermore, many of the factors that we might expect to cause differences in people's lives—for instance, being born poor or black—cannot easily or ethically be introduced by the experimenter as treatments. Thus we rely often on other research methods, such as the survey or participant observation. With these methods, we can look at existing differences among people (whether they are poor or well-off, for example) to see if these differences are related to other factors (such as whether they can afford to attend college).

Using unobtrusive measures involves looking for traces of human actions and interactions without having to deal directly with those people under study. For example, one way of getting evidence about drinking patterns without asking people how much they drink is to observe the number of empty bottles thrown away. Researchers have determined which museum exhibits are the more popular by counting noseprints that accumulates on the glass enclosures of the exhibits. Documentary evidence of how people feel and act can be found in magazine stories, advertisements, newspaper editorials, telephone directories, and the like.

All the methods listed here except unobtrusive measures are reactive. By this we mean that the researcher must interact with those being studied, and the researcher's mere presence may cause others to react in ways that are not typical or completely truthful. Research involving humans is, therefore, necessarily subject to unique problems that chemists and physicists do not face. The research encounter itself is a type of interaction, and that interaction is based on informal, unwritten rules for how to act as, say, an "interviewer" and an "interviewee." Of course, this fact may cause us to question the validity, or accuracy, of research findings. No research method or technique is perfect, and we should be aware of likely flaws of various methods so that we can become critical consumers of information.

## ACCUSATIONS OF BIAS IN SOCIOLOGICAL RESEARCH

Some critics of sociological research claim that sociologists sympathize with some of the people they study more than others and that these sympathies get in the way of accuracy. That is, no matter how carefully they select their samples or design their survey questionnaires, sociologists are biased in favor of unrespectable "underdogs" and, therefore, present distorted pictures of the social world.

In the second article in this section, Howard Becker writes about this common (but not universal) sociological bias toward the underdog. He points out that studies sympathetic to the underdog's viewpoint are striking to the reader, *not* because they are heavily distorted, but because most other writing in our society is biased toward the "upperdogs" and "middledogs." We are, for the most part, unaware of upperdog bias because we are so used to it. Underdog bias explodes some of our culture's myths and balances our picture of the social world.

Is it possible to conduct research in a given setting without having a bias, without looking at the situation from the vantage point of one group or another? Becker says no. One must either accept the "official" view of a social setting or take an unofficial view—what Berger would call the "unrespectable" view. Those, Becker says, are the choices. And given those choices, the underdog position is probably more in need of study and *less* biased than the official story.

## RECURRING THEMES

This section introduces several themes that will recur again and again. First, as we noted earlier, societal members are generally unaware of patterned regularities and processes of beliefs and behavior that exist in their society. Second, when members of a society attempt to make sense of their social world, creating explanations for various events and phenomena, their explanations are often wrong. This is so because they do not have the time, the inclination, or the expertise to gather information appropriate for making valid observations and interpretations. Thus myths continue to exist in abundance.

A third theme that you will encounter here many times is the importance of social interaction for determining how we define the world, what we think of ourselves, and how we behave. By learning the symbols of our culture from those with whom we interact, we come to share in a common understanding of reality. Despite the fact that we in the United States have learned to think of ourselves as unique individuals who exercise "free will" to determine our own thoughts and behavior, in reality our interactions with others in various settings and situations are constantly constraining and limiting both our thoughts and actions. All you need to do to convince yourself of the validity of this point is to imagine what your thoughts, values, opinions, and actions would be if you had been born in a different society—say, in Japan, in Iran, or in Argentina. All these societies allow for some personal discretion in thought and behavior; but at the same time, all have definitions of reality, values, symbolic universes, and mechanisms of social control that shape those who happen to be born there (or who migrate there) at almost every turn. The very alternatives available to us are limited in number. And our "choices" among these alternatives are influenced by others with whom we interact, from parents to teachers to co-workers to police.

# SOCIOLOGY AS A FORM OF CONSCIOUSNESS

## Peter L. Berger

. . . Sociology is neither a timeless nor a necessary undertaking of the human mind. If this is conceded, the question logically arises as to the timely factors that made it a necessity to specific men. Perhaps, indeed, no intellectual enterprise is timeless or necessary. But religion, for instance, has been well-nigh universal in provoking intensive mental preoccupation throughout human history, while thoughts designed to solve the economic problems of existence have been a necessity in most human cultures. Certainly this does not mean that theology or economics . . . are universally present phenomena of the mind, but we are at least on safe ground if we say that there always seems to have been human thought directed towards the problems that now constitute the subject matter of these disciplines. Not even this much, however, can be said of sociology. It presents itself rather as a peculiarly modern and Western cogitation. And, as we shall try to argue [here], it is constituted by a peculiarly modern form of consciousness.

The peculiarity of sociological perspective becomes clear with some reflection concerning the meaning of the term "society," a term that refers to the object *par excellence* of the discipline. Like most terms used by sociologists, this one is derived from common usage, where its meaning is imprecise. Sometimes it means a particular band of people (as in "Society for the Prevention of Cruelty to Animals"), sometimes only those people endowed with great prestige or privilege (as in "Boston society ladies"), and on other occasions it is simply used to denote company of any sort (for example, "he greatly suffered in those years for lack of society"). There are other, less frequent meanings as well. The sociologist uses the term in a more precise sense, though, of course, there are differences in usage within the discipline itself. The sociologist thinks of "society" as denoting a large complex of human relationships, or to put it in more technical language, as referring to a system of interaction. The word "large" is difficult to specify quantitatively in this context. The sociologist may speak of a "society" including millions of human beings (say, "American society"), but he may also use the term to refer to a numerically much smaller collectivity (say, "the society of sophomores on

Peter L. Berger, *Invitation to Sociology: A Humanist Perspective.* (Garden City, N.Y.: Anchor Books, 1963), pp. 25–53.

this campus"). Two people chatting on a street corner will hardly constitute a "society," but three people stranded on an island certainly will.
The applicability of the concept, then, cannot be decided on quantitative
grounds alone. It rather applies when a complex of relationships is sufficiently succinct to be analyzed by itself, understood as an autonomous
entity, set against others of the same kind.

The adjective "social" must be similarly sharpened for sociological
use. In common speech it may denote, once more, a number of different
things—the informal quality of a certain gathering ("this is a social meeting—let's not discuss business"), an altruistic attitude on somebody's
part ("he had a strong social concern in his job"), or, more generally,
anything derived from contact with other people ("a social disease").
The sociologist will use the term more narrowly and more precisely to refer to the quality of interaction, interrelationship, mutuality. Thus two
men chatting on a street corner do not constitute a "society," but what
transpires between them is certainly "social." "Society" consists of a
complex of such "social" events. As to the exact definition of the "social," it is difficult to improve on Max Weber's definition of a "social"
situation as one in which people orient their actions towards one another. The web of meanings, expectations and conduct resulting from
such mutual orientation is the stuff of sociological analysis.

Yet this refinement of terminology is not enough to show up the dis-
tinctiveness of the sociological angle of vision. We may get close by comparing the latter with the perspective of other disciplines concerned with
human actions. The economist, for example, is concerned with the analyses of processes that occur in society and that can be described as social. These processes have to do with the basic problem of economic activity—the allocation of scarce goods and services within a society. The
economist will be concerned with these processes in terms of the way in
which they carry out, or fail to carry out, this function. The sociologist,
in looking at the same processes, will naturally have to take into consideration their economic purpose. But his distinctive interest is not necessarily related to this purpose as such. He will be interested in a variety of
human relationships and interactions that may occur here and that may
be quite irrelevant to the economic goals in question. Thus economic activity involves relationships of power, prestige, prejudice or even play
that can be analyzed with only marginal reference to the properly economic function of the activity.

The sociologist finds his subject matter present in all human activities,
but not all aspects of these activities constitute this subject matter. Social
interaction is not some specialized sector of what men do with each
other. It is rather a certain aspect of all these doings. Another way of putting this is by saying that the sociologist carries on a special sort of abstraction. The social, as an object of inquiry, is not a segregated field of
human activity. Rather (to borrow a phrase from Lutheran sacramental

theology) it is present "in, with and under" many different fields of such activity. The sociologist does not look at phenomena that nobody else is aware of. But he looks at the same phenomena in a different way.

As a further example we could take the perspective of the lawyer. Here we actually find a point of view much broader in scope than that of the economist. Almost any human activity can, at one time or another, fall within the province of the lawyer. This, indeed, is the fascination of the law. Again, we find here a very special procedure of abstraction. From the immense wealth and variety of human deportment the lawyer selects those aspects that are pertinent (or, as he would say, "material") to his very particular frame of reference. As anyone who has ever been involved in a lawsuit well knows, the criteria of what is relevant or irrelevant legally will often greatly surprise the principals in the case in question. This need not concern us here. We would rather observe that the legal frame of reference consists of a number of carefully defined models of human activity. Thus we have clear models of obligation, responsibility or wrongdoing. Definite conditions have to prevail before any empirical act can be subsumed under one of these headings, and these conditions are laid down by statutes or precedent. When these conditions are not met, the act in question is legally irrelevant. The expertise of the lawyer consists of knowing the rules by which these models are constructed. He knows, within his frame of reference, when a business contract is binding, when the driver of an automobile may be held to be negligent, or when rape has taken place.

The sociologist may look at these same phenomena, but his frame of reference will be quite different. Most importantly, his perspective on these phenomena cannot be derived from statutes or precedent. His interest in the human relationships occurring in a business transaction has no bearing on the legal validity of contracts signed, just as sociologically interesting deviance in sexual behavior may not be capable of being subsumed under some particular legal heading. From the lawyer's point of view, the sociologist's inquiry is extraneous to the legal frame of reference. One might say that, with reference to the conceptual edifice of the law, the sociologist's activity is subterranean in character. The lawyer is concerned with what may be called the official conception of the situation. The sociologist often deals with very unofficial conceptions indeed. For the lawyer the essential thing to understand is how the law looks upon a certain type of criminal. For the sociologist it is equally important to see how the criminal looks at the law.

To ask sociological questions, then, presupposes that one is interested in looking some distance beyond the commonly accepted or officially defined goals of human actions. It presupposes a certain awareness that human events have different levels of meaning, some of which are hidden from the consciousness of everyday life. It may even presuppose a measure of suspicion about the way in which human events are officially interpreted by the authorities, be they political, juridical or religious in character. If one is willing to go as far as that, it would seem evident that not all historical circumstances are equally favorable for the development of sociological perspective.

It would appear plausible, in consequence, that sociological thought would have the best chance to develop in historical circumstances marked by severe jolts to the self-conception, especially the official and authoritative and generally accepted self-conception, of a culture. It is only in such circumstances that perceptive men are likely to be motivated to think beyond the assertions of this self-conception and, as a result, question the authorities. . . . It was with the disintegration of [Christendom and feudalism and the emergence of urban, industrial states] that the underlying frame of "society" came into view—that is, a world of motives and forces that could not be understood in terms of the official interpretations of social reality. Sociological perspective can then be understood in terms of such phrases as "seeing through" "looking behind," very much as such phrases would be employed in common speech—"seeing through his game," "looking behind the scenes"—in other words, "being up on all the tricks."

We will not be far off if we see sociological thought as part of what Nietzsche called "the art of mistrust." Now, it would be a gross oversimplification to think that this art has existed only in modern times. "Seeing through" things is probably a pretty general function of intelligence, even in very primitive societies. The American anthropologist Paul Radin has provided us with a vivid description of the skeptic as a human type in primitive culture. We also have evidence from civilizations other than that of the modern West, bearing witness to forms of consciousness that could well be called protosociological. We could point, for instance, to Herodotus or to Ibn-Khaldun. There are even texts from ancient Egypt evincing a profound disenchantment with a political and social order that has acquired the reputation of having been one of the most cohesive in human history. However, with the beginning of the modern era in the West this form of consciousness intensifies, becomes concentrated and systematized, marks the thought of an increasing number of perceptive men. This is not the place to discuss in detail the prehistory of sociological thought. . . . Suffice it to stress once more that sociological thought marks the fruition of a number of intellectual developments that have a very specific location in modern Western history.

Let us return instead to the proposition that sociological perspective involves a process of "seeing through" the facades of social structures. We could think of this in terms of a common experience of people living in large cities. One of the fascinations of a large city is the immense variety of human activities taking place behind the seemingly anonymous and endlessly undifferentiated rows of houses. A person who lives in such a city will time and again experience surprise or even shock as he discovers the strange pursuits that some men engage in quite unobtrusively in houses that, from the outside, look like all the others on a certain street. Having had this experience once or twice, one will repeatedly find oneself walking down a street, perhaps late in the evening, and wondering what may be going on under the bright lights showing through a line of drawn curtains. An ordinary family engaged in pleasant talk with guests? A scene of desperation amid illness or death? Or a scene of debauched pleasures? Perhaps a strange cult or a dangerous conspiracy? The facades of the houses cannot tell us, proclaiming nothing but an architectural conformity to the tastes of some group or class that may not even inhabit the street any longer. The social mysteries lie behind the facades. The wish to penetrate to these mysteries is [analogous] to sociological curiosity. In some cities that are suddenly struck by calamity this wish may be abruptly realized. Those who have experienced wartime bombings know of the sudden encounters with unsuspected (and sometimes unimaginable) fellow tenants in the air-raid shelter of one's apartment building. Or they can recollect the startling morning sight of a house hit by a bomb during the night, neatly sliced in half, the facade torn away and the previously hidden interior mercilessly revealed in the daylight. But in most cities that one may normally live in, the facades must be penetrated by one's own inquisitive intrusions. Similarly, there are historical situations in which the facades of society are violently torn apart and all but the most incurious are forced to see that there was a reality behind the facades all along. Usually this does not happen and the facades continue to confront us with seemingly rocklike permanence. The perception of the reality behind the facades then demands a considerable intellectual effort.

A few examples of the way in which sociology "looks behind" the facades of social structures might serve to make our argument clearer. Take, for instance, the political organization of a community. If one wants to find out how a modern American city is governed, it is very easy to get the official information about this subject. The city will have a charter, operating under the laws of the state. With some advice from informed individuals, one may look up various statutes that define the constitution of the city. Thus one may find out that this particular community has a city-manager form of administration, or that party affiliations do not appear on the ballot in municipal elections, or that the city government participates in a regional water district. In similar fashion, with the help of some newspaper reading, one may find out the officially recognized political problems of the community. One may read that the city plans to annex a certain suburban area, or that there has been a change in the zoning ordinances to facilitate industrial development in another area, or even that one of the members of the city council has been accused of using his office for personal gain. All such matters still occur on the, as it were, visible, official or public level of political life.

However, it would be an exceedingly naive person who would believe that this kind of information gives him a rounded picture of the political reality of that community. The sociologist will want to know above all the constituency of the "informal power structure" (as it has been called by Floyd Hunter, an American sociologist interested in such studies), which is a configuration of men and their power that cannot be found in any statutes, and probably cannot be read about in the newspapers. The political scientist or the legal expert might find it very interesting to compare the city charter with the constitutions of other similar communities. The sociologist will be far more concerned with discovering the way in which powerful vested interests influence or even control the actions of officials elected under the charter. These vested interests will not be found in city hall, but rather in executive suites of corporations that may not even be located in that community, in the private mansions of a handful of powerful men, perhaps in the offices of certain labor unions or even, in some instances, in the headquarters of criminal organizations. When the sociologist concerns himself with power, he will "look behind" the official mechanisms that are supposed to regulate power in the community. This does not necessarily mean that he will regard the official mechanisms as totally ineffective or their legal definition as totally illusionary. But at the very least he will insist that there is another level of reality to be investigated in the particular system of power. In some cases he might conclude that to look for real power in the publicly recognized places is quite delusional.

•　　•　　•

Or take an example from economic life. The personnel manager of an industrial plant will take delight in preparing brightly colored charts that show the table of organization that is supposed to administer the production process. Every man has his place, every person in the organization knows from whom he receives his orders and to whom he must transmit them, every work team has its assigned role in the great drama of production. In reality things rarely work this way—and every good personnel manager knows this. Superimposed on the official blueprint of the organization is a much subtler, much less visible network of human groups, with their loyalties, prejudices, antipathies and (most important) codes of behavior. Industrial sociology is full of data on the operations of this informal network, which always exists in varying degrees of accommodation and conflict with the official system. Very much the same coexistence of formal and informal organization are to be found wherever large numbers of men work together or live together under a system of discipline—military organizations, prisons, hospitals, schools, going back to the mysterious leagues that children form among themselves and that their parents only rarely discern. Once more, the sociologist will seek to penetrate the smoke screen of the official versions of reality (those of the foreman, the officer, the teacher) and try to grasp the signals that come from the "underworld" (those of the worker, the enlisted man, the schoolboy).

Let us take one further example. In Western countries, and especially in America, it is assumed that men and women marry because they are in love. There is a broadly based popular mythology about the character of love as a violent, irresistible emotion that strikes where it will, a mystery that is the goal of most young people and often of the not-so-young as well. As soon as one investigates, however, which people actually marry each other, one finds that the lightning-shaft of Cupid seems to be guided rather strongly within very definite channels of class, income, education, racial and religious background. If one then investigates a little further into the behavior that is engaged in prior to marriage under the rather misleading euphemism of "courtship," one finds channels of interaction that are often rigid to the point of ritual. The suspicion begins to dawn on one that, most of the time, it is not so much the emotion of love that creates a certain kind of relationship, but that carefully predefined and often planned relationships eventually generate the desired emotion. In other words, when certain conditions are met or have been constructed, one allows oneself "to fall in love." The sociologist investigating our patterns of "courtship" and marriage soon discovers a complex web of motives related in many ways to the entire institutional structure within which an individual lives his life—class, career, economic ambition, aspirations of power and prestige. The miracle of love now begins to look somewhat synthetic. Again, this need not mean in any given instance that the sociologist will declare the romantic interpretation to be an illusion. But, once more, he will look beyond the immediately given and publicly approved interpretations. Contemplating a couple that in its turn is contemplating the moon, the sociologist need not feel constrained to deny the emotional impact of the scene thus illuminated. But he will observe the machinery that went into the construction of the scene in its nonlunar aspects—the status index of the automobile from which the contemplation occurs, the canons of taste and tactics that determine the costume of the contemplators, the many ways in which language and demeanor place them socially, thus the social location and intentionality of the entire enterprise.

It may have become clear at this point that the problems that will interest the sociologist are not necessarily what other people may call "problems." The way in which public officials and newspapers (and, alas, some college textbooks in sociology) speak about "social problems" serves to obscure this fact. People commonly speak of a "social problem" when something in society does not work the way it is supposed to according to the official interpretations. They then expect the sociologist to study the "problem" as they have defined it and perhaps even to come up with a "solution" that will take care of the matter to their own satisfaction. It is important, against this sort of expectation, to understand that a sociological problem is something quite different from a "social problem" in this sense. For example, it is naive to concentrate on crime as a "problem" because law-enforcement agencies so define it, or on divorce because that is a "problem" to the moralists of marriage. Even more clearly, the "problem" of the foreman to get his men to work efficiently or of the line officer to get his troops to charge the enemy more enthusiastically need not be problematic at all to the sociologist (leaving out of consideration for the moment the probable fact that the sociologist asked to study such "problems" is employed by the corporation or the army). *The sociological problem is always the understanding of what goes on here in terms of social interaction.* Thus the sociological problem is not so much why some things "go wrong" from the viewpoint of the authorities and the management of the social scene, but *how the whole system works in the first place,* what are its presuppositions and by what means it is held together. The fundamental sociological problem is not crime but the law, not divorce but marriage, not racial discrimination but racially defined stratification, not revolution but government.

This point can be explicated further by an example. Take a settlement house in a lower-class slum district trying to wean away teen-agers from the publicly disapproved activities of a juvenile gang. The frame of reference within which social workers and police officers define the "problems" of this situation is constituted by the world of middle-class, respectable, publicly approved values. It is a "problem" if teen-agers drive around in stolen automobiles, and it is a "solution" if instead they will play group games in the settlement house. But if one changes the frame of reference and looks at the situation from the viewpoint of the leaders of the juvenile gang, the "problems" are defined in reverse order. It is a "problem" for the solidarity of the gang if its members are seduced away from those activities that lend prestige to the gang within its own social world, and it would be a "solution" if the social workers went way the hell back uptown where they came from. What is a "problem" to one social system is the normal routine of things to the other system, and vice versa. Loyalty and disloyalty, solidarity and deviance, are defined in contradictory terms by the representatives of the two systems. Now, the sociologist may, in terms of his own values, regard the world of middle-class respectability as more desirable and therefore want to come to the assistance of the settlement house, which is its missionary outpost *in partibus infidelium.* This, however, does not justify the identification of the director's headaches with what are "problems" sociologically. The "problems" that the sociologist will want to solve concern an understanding of the entire social situation, the values and modes of action in *both* systems, and the way in which two systems coexist in space and time. Indeed, this very ability to look at a situation from the vantage points of competing systems of interpretation is, as we shall see more clearly later on, one of the hallmarks of sociological consciousness.

We would contend, then, that there is a *debunking* motif inherent in sociological consciousness. The sociologist will be driven time and again, by the very logic of his discipline, to debunk [or show that myths are not true regarding] the social systems he is studying. This unmasking tendency need not necessarily be due to the sociologist's temperament or inclinations. Indeed, it may happen that the sociologist, who as an individual may be of a conciliatory disposition and quite disinclined to disturb the comfortable assumptions on which he rests his own social existence, is nevertheless compelled by what he is doing to fly in the face of what those around him take for granted. In other words, we would contend that the roots of the debunking motif in sociology are not psychological but methodological. The sociological frame of reference, with its built-in procedure of looking for levels of reality other than those given in the official interpretations of society, carries with it a logical imperative to *unmask the pretensions* and the propaganda by which men cloak their actions with each other. This unmasking imperative is one of the characteristics of sociology particularly at home in the temper of the modern era.

• • •

The debunking tendency of sociology is implicit in all sociological theories that emphasize the autonomous character of social processes. For instance, Émile Durkheim, the founder of the most important school in French sociology, emphasized that society was a reality . . . that could not be reduced to psychological or other factors on different levels of analysis. . . . This is perhaps most sharply revealed in his well-known study of suicide, in the work of that title, where individual intentions of those who commit suicide are completely left out of the analysis in favor of statistics concerning various social characteristics of these individuals. In the Durkheimian perspective, to live in society means to exist under the domination of society's logic. Very often men act by this logic without knowing it. To discover this inner dynamic of society, therefore, the sociologist must frequently disregard the answers that the social actors themselves would give to his questions and look for explanations that are hidden from their own awareness. This essentially Durkheimian approach has been carried over into the theoretical approach now called functionalism. In functional analysis society is analyzed in terms of its own workings as a system, workings that are often obscure or opaque to those acting within the system. The contemporary American sociologist Robert Merton has expressed this approach well in his concepts of "manifest" and "latent" functions. The former are the conscious and deliberate functions of social processes, the latter the unconscious and unintended ones. Thus the "manifest" function of antigambling legislation may be to suppress gambling, its "latent" function to create an illegal empire for the gambling syndicates. Or Christian missions in parts of Africa "manifestly" tried to convert Africans to Christianity, "latently" helped to destroy the indigenous tribal cultures and thus provided an important impetus towards rapid social transformation. Or the control of the Communist Party over all sectors of social life in Russia "manifestly" was to assure the continued dominance of the revolutinary ethos, "latently" created a new class of comfortable bureaucrats uncannily bourgeois in its aspirations and increasingly disinclined toward the self-denial of Bolshevik dedication. Or the "manifest" function of many voluntary associations in America is sociability and public service, the "latent" function to attach status [indicators] to those permitted to belong to such associations.

•    •    •

It has been suggested above that sociological consciousness is likely to arise when the commonly accepted or authoritatively stated interpretations of society become shaky. As we have already said, there is a good case for thinking of the origins of sociology in France (the mother country of the discipline) in terms of an effort to cope intellectually with the consequences of the French Revolution, not only of the one great cataclysm of 1789 but of what De Tocqueville called the continuing Revolution of the nineteenth century. In the French case it is not difficult to perceive sociology against the background of the rapid transformations of modern society, the collapse of facades, the deflation of old creeds and the upsurge of frightening new forces on the social scene. In Germany, the other European country in which an important sociological movement arose in the nineteenth century, the matter has a rather different appearance. If one may quote Marx . . ., the Germans had a tendency to carry on in professors' studies the revolutions that the French performed on the barricades. At least one of these academic roots of revolution, perhaps the most important one, may be sought in the broadly based movement of thought that came to be called "historicism." This is not the place to go into the full story of this movement. Suffice it to say that it represents an attempt to deal philosophically with the overwhelming sense of the *relativity of all values in history.* [The term "relativity of values" refers to the fact that events and objects considered "good" or "bad" in one society may not be valued in the same way in other societies. Values are, thus, relative to the society in question at a given time.] This awareness of relativity was an almost necessary outcome of the immense accumulation of German historical scholarship in every conceivable field. Sociological thought was at least partly grounded in the need to bring order and intelligibility to the impression of chaos that this array of historical knowledge made on some observers. Needless to stress, however, the society of the German sociologist was changing all around him just as was that of his French colleague, as Germany rushed towards industrial power and nationhood in the second half of the nineteenth century. We shall not pursue these questions though. If we turn to America, the country in which sociology came to receive its most widespread acceptance, we find once more a different set of circumstances, though again against a background of rapid and profound social change. In looking at this American development we can detect another motif of sociology, closely related to that of debunking but not identical with it—its fascination with the *unrespectable* view of society.

In at least every Western society it is possible to distinguish between respectable and unrespectable sectors. In that respect American society is not in a unique position. But American respectability has a particularly pervasive quality about it. This may be ascribed in part, perhaps, to the lingering aftereffects of the Puritan way of life. More probably it has to do with the predominant role played by the bourgeoisie [or middle class] in shaping American culture. Be this as it may in terms of historical causation, it is not difficult to look at social phenomena in America and place them readily in one of these two sectors. We can perceive the official, respectable America represented symbolically by the Chamber of Commerce, the churches, the schools and other centers of civic ritual. But facing this world of respectability is an "other America," present in every town of any size, an America that has other symbols and that speaks another language. This language is probably its safest identification tag. It is the language of the poolroom and the poker game, of bars, brothels and army barracks. But it is also the language that breaks out with a sigh of relief between two salesmen having a drink in the parlor car as their train races past clean little Midwestern villages on a Sunday morning, with clean little villagers trooping into the whitewashed sanctuaries. It is the language that is suppressed in the company of ladies and clergymen, owing its life mainly to oral transmission from one generation of Huckleberry Finns to another (though in recent years the language has found literary deposition in some books designed to thrill ladies and clergymen). The "other America" that speaks this language can be found wherever people are excluded, or exclude themselves, from the world of middle-class propriety. We find it in those sections of the working class that have not yet proceeded too far on the road of *embourgeoisement*, in slums, shantytowns, and those parts of cities that urban sociologists have called "areas of transition." We find it expressed powerfully in the world of the American Negro. We also come on it in the subworlds of those who have, for one reason or another, withdrawn voluntarily from Main Street and Madison Avenue—in the worlds of hipsters, homosexuals, hoboes and other "marginal men," those worlds that are kept safely out of sight on the streets where the nice people live, work and amuse themselves. . . .

American sociology, accepted early both in academic circles and by those concerned with welfare activities, was from the beginning associated with the "official America," with the world of policy makers in community and nation. Sociology today retains this respectable affiliation in university, business and government. The appellation hardly induces eyebrows to be raised, except the eyebrows of such Southern racists sufficiently literate to have read the footnotes of the desegregation decision of 1954. However, we would contend that there has been an important undercurrent in American sociology, relating it to that "other America" of dirty language and disenchanted attitudes, that state of mind that refuses to be impressed, moved or befuddled by the official ideologies.

This unrespectable perspective on the American scene can be seen most clearly in the figure of Thorstein Veblen, one of the early important sociologists in America. His biography itself constitutes an exercise in marginality: a difficult, querulous character; born on a Norwegian farm on the Wisconsin frontier; acquiring English as a foreign language; involved all his life with morally and politically suspect individuals; an academic migrant; an inveterate seducer of . . . women. The perspective on America gained from this angle of vision can be found in the unmasking satire that runs like a purple thread through Veblen's work, most famously in his *Theory of the Leisure Class*, that merciless look from the underside at the pretensions of the American [newly rich]. Veblen's view of society can be understood most easily as a series of non-Rotarian insights—his understanding of "conspicuous consumption" as against the middle-class enthusiasm for the "finer things," his analysis of economic processes in terms of manipulation and waste as against the American productivity ethos, his understanding of the machinations of real estate speculation as against the American community ideology, most bitterly his description of academic life (in *The Higher Learning in America*) in terms of fraud and flatulence as against the American cult of education. We are not associating ourselves here with a certain neo-Veblenism that has become fashionable with some younger American sociologists, nor arguing that Veblen was a giant in the development of the field. We are only pointing to his irreverent curiosity and clear-sightedness as marks of a perspective coming from those places in the culture in which one gets up to shave about noon on Sundays. Nor are we arguing that clear-sightedness is a general trait of unrespectability. Stupidity and sluggishness of thought are probably distributed quite fairly throughout the social spectrum. But where there is intelligence and where it manages to free itself from the goggles of respectability, we can expect a clearer view of society than in those cases where the oratorical imagery is taken for real life.

A number of developments in empirical studies in American sociology furnish evidence of this same fascination with the unrespectable view of society. For example, looking back at the powerful development of urban studies undertaken at the University of Chicago in the 1920s we are struck by the apparently irresistible attraction to the seamier sides of city life upon these researchers. The advice to his students of Robert Park, the most important figure in this development, to the effect that they should get their hands dirty with research often enough meant quite literally an intense interest in all the things that North Shore residents would call "dirty." We sense in many of these studies the excitement of discovering the picaresque undersides of the metropolis—studies of slum life, of the melancholy world of rooming houses, of Skid Row, of the worlds of crime and prostitution. One of the offshoots of this so-called "Chicago school" has been the sociological study of occupations, due very largely to the pioneering work of Everett Hughes and his students. Here also we find a fascination with every possible world in which human beings live and make a living, not only with the worlds of respectable occupations, but with those of the taxi driver, the apartment-house janitor, the professional boxer or the jazz musician. The same tendency can be discovered in the course of American community studies following in the wake of the famous *Middletown* studies of Robert and Helen Lynd. Inevitably these studies had to bypass the official versions of community life, to look at the social reality of the community not only from the perspective of city hall but also from that of the city jail. Such sociological procedure is *ipso facto* a refutation of the respectable presupposition that only certain views of the world are to be taken seriously.

We would not want to give an exaggerated impression of the effect of such investigations on the consciousness of sociologists. We are well aware of the elements of muckraking and romanticism inherent in some of this. We also know that many sociologists participate as fully in the respectable [outlook] as all the other PTA members on their block. Nevertheless, we would maintain that sociological consciousness predisposes one towards an awareness of worlds other than that of middle-class respectability, an awareness which already carries within itself the seeds of intellectual unrespectability. In the second *Middletown* study the Lynds have given a classic analysis of the mind of middle-class America in their series of "of course statements"—that is, statements that represent a consensus so strong that the answer to any question concerning them will habitually be prefaced with the words "of course." "Is our economy one of free enterprise?" "Of course!" "Are all our important decisions arrived at through the democratic process?" "Of course!" "Is monogamy the natural form of marriage?" "Of course!" The sociologist, however conservative and conformist he may be in his private life, knows that there are serious questions to be raised about every one of these "of course statements." In this knowledge alone he is brought to the threshold of unrespectability.

This unrespectable motif of sociological consciousness need not imply a revolutionary attitude. We would even go further than that and express the opinion that sociological understanding is inimical to revolutionary ideologies, not because it has some sort of conservative bias, but because it sees not only through the illusions of the present *status quo* but also through the illusionary expectations concerning possible futures, such expectations being the customary spiritual nourishment of the revolutionary. This nonrevolutionary and moderating soberness of sociology we would value quite highly. More regrettable, from the viewpoint of one's values, is the fact that sociological understanding by itself does not necessarily lead to a greater tolerance with respect to the foibles of mankind. It is possible to view social reality with compassion or with cynicism, both attitudes being compatible with clear-sightedness. But whether he can bring himself to human sympathy with the phenomena he is studying or not, the sociologist will in some measure be detached from the taken-for-granted postures of his society. Unrespectability, whatever its ramifications in the emotions and the will, must remain a constant possibility in the sociologist's mind. It may be segregated from the rest of his life, overlaid by the routine mental states of everyday existence, even denied ideologically. Total respectability of thought, however, will invariably mean the death of sociology. This is one of the reasons why genuine sociology disappears promptly from the scene in totalitarian countries, as is well illustrated in the instance of Nazi Germany. By implication, sociological understanding is always potentially dangerous to the minds of policemen and other guardians of public order, since it will always tend to [question the universality of] the claim to absolute rightness upon which such minds like to rest.

Before concluding this chapter, we would look once more on this phenomenon of *relativization* that we have already touched upon a few times. We would now say explicitly that sociology is so much in tune with the temper of the modern era precisely because it represents the consciousness of a world in which values have been radically relativized. This relativization has become so much part of our everyday imagination that it is difficult for us to grasp fully how closed and absolutely binding the world views of other cultures have been and in some places still are. . . . For the traditional mind one is what one is, where one is, and cannot even imagine how one could be anything different. The modern mind, by contrast, is mobile, participates vicariously in the lives of others differently located from oneself, easily imagines itself changing occupation or residence. Thus [a sociologist working in the contemporary Middle East] found that some of the illiterate respondents to his questionnaires could only respond with laughter to the question as to what they would do if they were in the position of their rulers and would not even consider the question as to the circumstances under which they would be willing to leave their native village. Another way of putting this would be to say that traditional societies assign definite and permanent identities to their members. In modern society identity itself is uncertain and in flux. One does not really know what is expected of one as a ruler, as a parent, as a cultivated person, or as one who is sexually normal. Typically, one then requires various experts to tell one. The book club editor tells us what culture is, the interior designer what taste we ought to have, and the psychoanalyst who we are. To live in modern society means to live at the center of a kaleidoscope of everchanging roles.

Again, we must forego the temptation of enlarging on this point, since it would take us rather far afield from our argument into a general discussion of the social psychology of modern existence. We would rather stress the intellectual aspect of this situation, since it is in that aspect that we would see an important dimension of sociological consciousness. *The unprecedented rate of geographical and social mobility in modern society means that one becomes exposed to an unprecedented variety of ways of looking at the world.* The insights into other cultures that one might gather by travel are brought into one's own living room through the mass media. Someone once defined urbane sophistication as being the capacity to remain quite unperturbed upon seeing in front of one's house a man dressed in a turban and a loincloth, a snake coiled around his neck, beating a tom-tom as he leads a leashed tiger down the street. No doubt there are degrees to such sophistication, but a measure of it is acquired by every child who watches television. No doubt also this sophistication is commonly only superficial and does not extend to any real grappling with alternate ways of life. Nevertheless, the immensely broadened possibility of travel, in person and through the imagination, implies at least potentially the awareness that one's own culture, including its basic values, is relative in space and time. Social mobility, that is, the movement from one social stratum to another, augments this relativizing effect. Wherever industrialization occurs, a new dynamism is injected into the social system. Masses of people begin to change their social position, in groups or as individuals. And usually this change is in an "upward" direction. With this movement an individual's biography often involves a considerable journey not only through a variety of social groups but through the intellectual universes that are, so to speak, attached to these groups. Thus the Baptist mail clerk who used to read the *Reader's Digest* becomes an Episcopalian junior executive who reads *The New Yorker*, or the faculty wife whose husband becomes department chairman may graduate from the best-seller list to Proust or Kafka.

In view of this overall fluidity of world views in modern society it should not surprise us that our age has been characterized as one of conversion. Nor should it be surprising that intellectuals especially have been prone to change their world views radically and with amazing frequency. The intellectual attraction of strongly presented, theoretically closed systems of thought such as Catholicism or Communism has been frequently commented upon. Psychoanalysis, in all its forms, can be understood as an institutionalized mechanism of conversion, in which the individual changes not only his view of himself but of the world in general. The popularity of a multitude of new cults and creeds, presented in different degrees of intellectual refinement depending upon the educational level of their clientele, is another manifestation of this proneness to conversion of our contemporaries. It almost seems as if modern man, and especially modern educated man, is in a perpetual state of doubt about the nature of himself and of the universe in which he lives. In other words, the awareness of relativity, which probably in all ages of history has been the possession of a small group of intellectuals, today appears as a broad cultural fact reaching far down into the lower reaches of the social system.

We do not want to give the impression that this sense of relativity and the resulting proneness to change one's entire [world view] are manifestations of intellectual or emotional immaturity. Certainly one should not take with too much seriousness some representatives of this pattern. Nevertheless, we would contend that an essentially similar pattern becomes almost a destiny in even the most serious intellectual enterprises. It is impossible to exist with full awareness in the modern world without realizing that moral, political and philosophical commitments are relative, that, in Pascal's words, what is truth on one side of the Pyrenees is error on the other. Intensive occupation with the more fully elaborated meaning systems available in our time gives one a truly frightening understanding of the way in which these systems can provide a total interpretation of reality, within which will be included an interpretation of the alternate systems and of the ways of passing from one system to another. Catholicism may have a theory of Communism, but Communism returns the compliment and will produce a theory of Catholicism. To the Catholic thinker the Communist lives in a dark world of materialist delusion about the real meaning of life. To the Communist his Catholic adversary is helplessly caught in the "false consciousness" of a bourgeois mentality. To the psychoanalyst both Catholic and Communist may simply be acting out on the intellectual level the unconscious impulses that really move them. And psychoanalysis may be to the Catholic an escape from the reality of sin and to the Communist an avoidance of the realities of society. This means that the individual's choice of viewpoint will determine the way in which he looks back upon his own biography. American prisoners of war "brainwashed" by the Chinese Communists completely changed their viewpoints on social and political matters. To those that returned to America this change represented a sort of illness brought on by outward pressure, as a convalescent may look back on a delirious dream. But to their former captors this changed consciousness represents a brief glimmer of true understanding between long periods of ignorance. And to those prisoners who decided not to return, their conversion may still appear as the decisive passage from darkness to light.

Instead of speaking of conversion (a term with religiously charged connotations) we would prefer to use the more neutral term of *"alternation"* to describe this phenomenon. The intellectual situation just described brings with it the possibility that an individual may alternate back and forth between logically contradictory meaning systems. Each time, the meaning system he enters provides him with an interpretation of his existence and of his world, including in this interpretation an explanation of the meaning system he has abandoned. Also, the meaning system provides him with tools to combat his own doubts. Catholic confessional discipline, Communist "autocriticism" and the psychoanalytic techniques of coping with "resistance" all fulfill the same purpose of preventing alternation out of the particular meaning system, allowing the individual to interpret his own doubts in terms derived from the system itself, thus keeping him within it. On lower levels of sophistication there will also be various means employed to cut off questions that might threaten the individual's allegiance to the system, means that one can see at work in the dialectical acrobatics of even such relatively unsophisticated groups as Jehovah's Witnesses or Black Muslims.

If one resists the temptation, however, to accept such [narrow world views], and is willing to face squarely the experience of relativity brought on by the phenomenon of alternation, then one comes into possession of yet another crucial dimension of sociological consciousness—the awareness that not only identities but ideas are relative to specific social locations. . . . Suffice it to say here that this relativizing motif is another of the fundamental driving forces of the sociological enterprise.

In this chapter we have tried to outline the dimensions of sociological consciousness through the analysis of three motifs—those of debunking, unrespectability and relativizing. To these three we would, finally, add a fourth one, much less far-reaching in its implications but useful in rounding out our picture—the *cosmopolitan* motif. Going back to very ancient times, it was in cities that there developed an openness to the world, to other ways of thinking and acting. Whether we think of Athens or Alexandria, of medieval Paris or Renaissance Florence, or of the turbulent urban centers of modern history, we can identify a certain cosmopolitan consciousness that was especially characteristic of city culture. The individual, then, who is not only urban but urbane is one who, however passionately he may be attached to his own city, roams through the whole wide world in his intellectual voyages. His mind, if not his body and his emotions, is at home wherever there are other men who think. We would submit that sociological consciousness is marked by the same kind of cosmopolitanism. This is why a narrow parochialism in its focus of interest is always a danger signal for the sociological venture (a danger signal that, unfortunately, we would hoist over quite a few sociological studies in America today). The sociological perspective is a broad, open, emancipated vista on human life. The sociologist, at his best, is a man with a taste for other lands, inwardly open to the measureless richness of human possibilities, eager for new horizons and new worlds of human meaning. It probably requires no additional elaboration to make the point that this type of man can play a particularly useful part in the course of events today.

# Review Questions

1. Briefly summarize the four major sociological themes, or motifs, that Berger sets forth.
   a. debunking
   b. unrespectability
   c. cultural relativism
   d. cosmopolitanism

2. How would the "sociological consciousness" lead you to study the power structure of a city that is a gambling center (e.g., Atlantic City, New Jersey, or Las Vegas, Nevada)? How would your approach differ from the economist's approach or the lawyer's approach?

3. Berger claims that most of us are unaware of the patterned regularities in the phenomenon of love. What are our myths about love? What are some of the patterned regularities that show our myths to be partly or entirely false?

4. Why is it important to understand that a "sociological problem" is quite different from a "social problem"?

# WHOSE SIDE ARE WE ON?

## Howard S. Becker

To HAVE VALUES OR NOT TO HAVE VALUES; THE QUESTION IS ALWAYS WITH us. When sociologists undertake to study problems that have relevance to the world we live in, they find themselves caught in a crossfire. Some urge them not to take sides, to be neutral and do research that is technically correct and value free. Others tell them their work is shallow and useless if it does not express a deep commitment to a value position.

This dilemma, which seems so painful to so many, actually does not exist, for one of its horns is imaginary. For it to exist, one would have to assume, as some apparently do, that it is indeed possible to do research that is uncontaminated by personal and political sympathies. I propose to argue that it is not possible and, therefore, that the question is not whether we should take sides, since we inevitably will, but rather whose side we are on.

I will begin by considering the problem of taking sides as it arises in the study of deviance. . . .[1] When do we accuse ourselves and our fellow sociologists of bias? I think an inspection of representative instances would show that the accusation arises, in one important class of cases, when the research gives credence, in any serious way, to the perspective of the subordinate group in some hierarchical relationship. In the case of deviance, the hierarchical relationship is a moral one. The superordinate parties in the relationship are those who represent the forces of approved and official morality; the subordinate parties are those who, it is alleged, have violated that morality.

Though deviance is a typical case, it is by no means the only one. Similar situations, and similar feelings that our work is biased, occur in the study of schools, hospitals, asylums and prisons, in the study of physical as well as mental illness, in the study of both "normal" and delinquent youth. In these situations, the superordinate parties are usually the official and professional authorities in charge of some important institution, while the subordinates are those who make use of the services of that institution. Thus, the police are the superordinates, drug addicts are the subordinates; professors and administrators, principals and teachers, are the superordinates, while students and pupils are the sub-

Howard S. Becker, "Whose Side Are We On?" *Social Problems* 14 (winter 1967) :239–247.

ordinates; physicians are the superordinates, their patients the subordinates.

All of these cases represent one of the typical situations in which researchers accuse themselves and are accused of bias. It is a situation in which, while conflict and tension exist in the hierarchy, the conflict has not become openly political. The conflicting segments or ranks are not organized for conflict; no one attempts to alter the shape of the hierarchy. While subordinates may complain about the treatment they receive from those above them, they do not propose to move to a position of equality with them, or to reverse positions in the hierarchy. Thus, no one proposes that addicts should make and enforce laws for policemen, that patients should prescribe for doctors, or that adolescents should give orders to adults. . . .

We provoke the suspicion that we are biased in favor of the subordinate parties . . . when we tell the story from their point of view. We may, for instance, investigate their complaints, even though they are subordinates, about the way things are run just as though one ought to give their complaints as much credence as the statements of responsible officials. We provoke the charge when we assume, for the purposes of our research, that subordinates have as much right to be heard as superordinates, that they are as likely to be telling the truth as they see it as superordinates, that what they say about the institution has a right to be investigated and have its truth or falsity established, even though responsible officials assure us that it is unnecessary because the charges are false.

## HIERARCHY OF CREDIBILITY

We can use the notion of a *hierarchy of credibility* to understand this phenomenon. In any system of ranked groups, participants take it as given that members of the highest group have the right to define the way things really are. In any organization, no matter what the rest of the organization chart shows, the arrows indicating the flow of information point up, thus demonstrating (at least formally) that those at the top have access to a more complete picture of what is going on than anyone else. Members of lower groups will have incomplete information, and their view of reality will be partial and distorted in consequence. Therefore, from the point of view of a well-socialized participant in the system, any tale told by those at the top intrinsically deserves to be regarded as the most credible account obtainable of the organizations' workings. And since, as Sumner pointed out, matters of rank and status are contained in the mores,[2] this belief has a moral quality. We are, if we are proper members of the group, morally bound to accept the definition imposed on reality by a superordinate group in preference to the definitions espoused by subordinates. (By analogy, the same argument holds for the social classes of a community.) Thus, credibility and the right to be heard are differentially distributed through the ranks of the system.

As sociologists, we provoke the charge of bias, in ourselves and others, by refusing to give credence and deference to an established status order, in which knowledge of truth and the right to be heard are not equally distributed. "Everyone knows" that responsible professionals know more about things than laymen, that police are more respectable and their words ought to be taken more seriously than those of the deviants and criminals with whom they deal. By refusing to accept the hierarchy of credibility, we express disrespect for the entire established order.

We compound our sin and further provoke charges of bias by not giving immediate attention and "equal time" to the apologies and explanations of official authority. If, for instance, we are concerned with studying the way of life inmates in a mental hospital build up for themselves, we will naturally be concerned with the constraints and conditions created by the actions of the administrators and physicians who run the hospital. But unless we also make the administrators and physicians the object of our study (a possibility I will consider later), we will not inquire into why those conditions and constraints are present. We will not give responsible officials a chance to explain themselves and give their reasons for acting as they do, a chance to show why the complaints of inmates are not justified.

It is odd that, when we perceive bias, we usually see it in these circumstances. It is odd because it is easily ascertained that a great many more studies are biased in the direction of the interests of responsible officials than the other way around. We may accuse an occasional student of medical sociology of having given too much emphasis to the complaints of patients. But is it not obvious that most medical sociologists look at things from the point of view of the doctors? A few sociologists may be sufficiently biased in favor of youth to grant credibility to their account of how the adult world treats them. But why do we not accuse other sociologists who study youth of being biased in favor of adults? Most research on youth, after all, is clearly designed to find out why youth are so troublesome for adults, rather than asking the equally interesting sociological question: "Why do adults make so much trouble for youth?" Similarly, we accuse those who take the complaints of mental patients seriously of bias; what about those sociologists who only take seriously the complaints of physicians, families and others about mental patients?

Why this disproportion in the direction of accusations of bias? Why do we more often accuse those who are on the side of subordinates than those who are on the side of superordinates? Because when we make the former accusation, we have, like the well-socialized members of our society most of us are, accepted the hierarchy of credibility and taken over the accusation made by the responsible officials.

The reason responsible officials make the accusation so frequently is precisely because they are responsible. They have been entrusted with the care and operation of one or another of our important institutions: schools, hospitals, law enforcement, or whatever. They are the ones who, by virtue of their official position and the authority that goes with it, are in a position to "do something" when things are not what they should be and, similarly, are the ones who will be held to account if they fail to "do something" or if what they do is, for whatever reason, inadequate.

Because they are responsible in this way, officials usually have to lie. That is a gross way of putting it, but not inaccurate. Officials must lie because things are seldom as they ought to be. For a great variety of reasons, well-known to sociologists, institutions are refractory. They do not perform as society would like them to. Hospitals do not cure people; prisons do not rehabilitate prisoners; schools do not educate students. Since they are supposed to, officials develop ways both of denying the failure of the institution to perform as it should and explaining those failures which cannot be hidden. An account of an institution's operation from the point of view of subordinates therefore casts doubt on the official line and may possibly expose it as a lie.

For reasons that are a mirror image of those of officials, subordinates in an apolitical hierarchical relationship have no reason to complain of the bias of sociological research oriented toward the interests of superordinates. Subordinates typically are not organized in such a fashion as to be responsible for the overall operation of an institution. What happens in a school is credited or debited to the faculty and administrators; they can be identified and held to account. Even though the failure of a school may be the fault of the pupils, they are not so organized that any one of them is responsible for any failure but his own. If he does well, while others all around him flounder, cheat and steal, that is none of his affair, despite the attempt of honor codes to make it so. As long as the sociological report on his school says that every student there but one is a liar and a cheat, all the students will feel complacent, knowing they are the one exception. More likely, they will never hear of the report at all or, if they do, will reason that they will be gone before long, so what difference does it make? The lack of organization among subordinate members of an instutionalized relationship means that, having no responsibility for the group's welfare, they likewise have no complaints if someone maligns it. The sociologist who favors officialdom will be spared the accusation of bias.

And thus we see why we accuse ourselves of bias only when we take the side of the subordinate. It is because, in a situation that is not openly political, with the major issues defined as arguable, we join responsible officials and the man in the street in an unthinking acceptance of the hierarchy of credibility. We assume with them that the man at the top knows best. We do not realize that there are sides to be taken and that we are taking one of them.

The same reasoning allows us to understand why the researcher has the same worry about the effect of his sympathies on his work as his uninvolved colleague. The hierarchy of credibility is a feature of society whose existence we cannot deny, even if we disagree with its injunction to believe the man at the top. When we acquire sufficient sympathy with subordinates to see things from their perspective, we know that we are flying in the face of what "everyone knows." . . .

•   •   •

## TAKING SIDES

What I have said so far is all sociology of knowledge, suggesting by whom, in what situations and for what reasons sociologists will be accused of bias and distortion. I have not yet addressed the question of the truth of the accusations, of whether our findings are distorted by our sympathy for those we study. I have implied a partial answer, namely, that there is no position from which sociological research can be done that is not biased in one or another way.

We must always look at the matter from someone's point of view. The scientist who proposes to understand society must, as Mead long ago pointed out, get into the situation enough to have a perspective on it. And it is likely that his perspective will be greatly affected by whatever positions are taken by any or all of the other participants in that varied situation. Even if his participation is limited to reading in the field, he will necessarily read the arguments of partisans of one or another side to a relationship and will thus be affected, at least, by having suggested to him what the relevant arguments and issues are. A student of medical sociology may decide that he will take neither the perspective of the patient nor the perspective of the physician, but he will necessarily take a perspective that impinges on the many questions that arise between physicians and patients; no matter what perspective he takes, his work either will take into account the attitude of subordinates, or it will not. If he fails to consider the questions they raise, he will be working on the side of the officials. If he does raise those questions seriously and does find, as he may, that there is some merit in them, he will then expose himself to the outrage of the officials and of all those sociologists who award them the top spot in the hierarchy of credibility. Almost all the topics that sociologists study, at least those that have some relation to the real world around us, are seen by society as morality plays and we shall find ourselves, willy-nilly, taking part in those plays on one side or the other.

• • •

We can never avoid taking sides. So we are left with the question of whether taking sides means that some distortion is introduced into our work so great as to make it useless. Or, less drastically, whether some distortion is introduced that must be taken into account before the results of our work can be used. I do not refer here to feeling that the picture given by the research is not "balanced," the indignation aroused by having a conventionally discredited definition of reality given priority or equality with what "everyone knows," for it is clear that we cannot avoid that. That is the problem of officials, spokesmen and interested parties, not ours. Our problem is to make sure that, whatever point of view we take, our research meets the standards of good scientific work, that our unavoidable sympathies do not render our results invalid.

We might distort our findings, because of our sympathy with one of the parties in the relationship we are studying, by misusing the tools and techniques of our discipline. We might introduce loaded questions into a questionnaire, or act in some way in a field situation such that people would be constrained to tell us only the kind of thing we are already in sympathy with. All of our research techniques are hedged about with precautionary measures designed to guard against these errors. Similarly, though more abstractly, every one of our theories presumably contains a set of directives which exhaustively covers the field we are to study, specifying all the things we are to look at and take into account in our research. By using our theories and techniques impartially, we ought to be able to study all the things that need to be studied in such a way as to get all the facts we require, even though some of the questions that will be raised and some of the facts that will be produced run counter to our biases.

But the question may be precisely this. Given all our techniques of theoretical and technical control, how can we be sure that we will apply them impartially and across the board as they need to be applied? Our textbooks in  methodology are no help here. They tell us how to guard against error, but they do not tell us how to make sure that we will use all the safeguards available to us. We can, for a start, try to avoid sentimentality. We are sentimental when we refuse, for whatever reason, to investigate some matter that should properly be regarded as problematic. We are sentimental, especially, when our reason is that we would prefer not to know what is going on, if to know would be to violate some sympathy whose existence we may not even be aware of. Whatever side we are on, we must use our techniques impartially enough that a belief to which we are especially sympathetic could be proved untrue. We must always inspect our work carefully enough to know whether our techniques and theories are open enough to allow that possibility.

Let us consider, finally, what might seem a simple solution to the problems posed. If the difficulty is that we gain sympathy with underdogs by studying them, is it not also true that the superordinates in a hierarchical relationship usually have their own superordinates with whom they must contend? Is it not true that we might study those superordinates as subordinates, presenting their point of view on their relations with their superiors and thus gaining a deeper sympathy with them and avoiding the bias of one-sided identification with those below them? This is appealing, but deceptively so. For it only means that we will get into the same trouble with a new set of officials.

It is true, for instance, that the administrators of a prison are not free to do as they wish, not free to be responsive to the desires of inmates, for instance. If one talks to such an official, he will commonly tell us, in private, that of course the subordinates in the relationship have some right on their side, but they fail to understand that his desire to do better is frustrated by his superiors or by the regulations they have established. Thus, if a prison adminstrator is angered because we take the complaints of his inmates seriously, we may feel that we can get around that and get a more balanced picture by interviewing him and his associates. If we do, we may then write a report which *his* superiors will respond to with cries of "bias." They, in their turn, will say that we have not presented a balanced picture, because we have not looked at *their* side of it. And we may worry that what they say is true.

The point is obvious. By pursuing this seemingly simple solution, we arrive at a problem of infinite regress. For everyone has someone standing above him who prevents him from doing things just as he likes. If we question the superiors of the prison administrator, a state department of corrections or prisons, they will complain of the governor and the legislature. And if we go to the governor and the legislature, they will complain of lobbyists, party machines, the public and the newspapers. There is no end to it and we can never have a "balanced picture" until we have studied all of society simultaneously. I do not propose to hold my breath until that happy day.

We can, I think, satisfy the demands of our science by always making clear the limits of what we have studied, marking the boundaries beyond which our findings cannot be safely applied. Not just the conventional disclaimer, in which we warn that we have only studied a prison in New York or California and the findings may not hold in the other forty-nine states—which is not a useful procedure anyway, since the findings may very well hold if the conditions are the same elsewhere. I refer to a more sociological disclaimer in which we say, for instance, that we have studied the prison through the eyes of the inmates and not through the eyes of the guards or other involved parties. We warn people, thus, that our study tells us only how things look from that vantage point—what kinds of objects guards are in the prisoners' world—and does not attempt to explain why guards do what they do or to absolve the guards of what may seem, from the prisoners' side, morally unacceptable behavior. This will not protect us from accusations of bias, however, for the guards will still be outraged by the unbalanced picture. If we implicitly accept the conventional hierarchy of credibility, we will feel the sting in that accusation.

It is something of a solution to say that over the years each "one-sided" study will provoke further studies that gradually enlarge our grasp of all the relevant facets of an institution's operation. But that is a long-term solution, and not much help to the individual researcher who has to contend with the anger of officials who feel he has done them wrong, the criticism of those of his colleagues who think he is presenting a one-sided view, and his own worries.

What do we do in the meantime? I suppose the answers are more or less obvious. We take sides as our personal and political commitments dictate, use our theoretical and technical resources to avoid the distortions they might introduce into our work, limit our conclusions carefully, recognize the hierarchy of credibility for what it is, and field as best we can the accusations and doubts that will surely be our fate.

## NOTES

1. In the longer article from which this piece is excerpted, Becker also discusses accusations of bias made against sociologists who study one side in an organized, political situation (such as a political campaign or a management-worker dispute). We have omitted this discussion here because (1) none of the articles that follow in this volume is expressly political as Becker uses this term; (2) accusations of bias in political research is merely a special case of the more general phenomenon presented here; and (3) as Becker notes, sociologists who study political issues and cases are probably less likely to be accused of bias than those studying "apolitical" situations involving social hierarchies.

2. William Graham Sumner, "Status in the Folkways," *Folkways* (New York: New American Library, 1960), pp. 72–73.

# Review Questions

1. If sociologists describe the point of view of subordinates in a social system (e.g., prisoners, patients, students), they are likely to be accused of bias. Why?

2. If sociologists describe the point of view of people in positions of authority (e.g., prison officials, physicians, teachers), they are not likely to be accused of bias? Why not?

3. What does Becker conclude about the possibilities for eliminating bias from descriptions of the social system? What is the problem of "infinite regress"?


## Suggested Readings: Introduction

Berger, Peter L. *Invitation to Sociology: A Humanist Perspective.* Garden City, N.Y.: Anchor Books, 1963.

_____, and Hansfried Kellner. *Sociology Reinterpreted: An Essay on Method and Vocation.* Garden City, N.Y.: Anchor Books, 1981.

Mills, C. Wright. *The Sociological Imagination.* New York: Oxford University Press, 1959.

Simmel, Georg. "The Problem of Sociology," trans. Albion W. Small, *The American Journal of Sociology* 15, 3 (1909): 290–316.

# Part II. Culture

A PRIMARY REASON FOR THE COMPLEXITY OF SOCIAL INTERACTION IS THAT our species has no instinctive patterns of behavior. While we do have biological drives and needs, we have no instincts that force us to meet these needs in patterned ways. Unlike other species, humans must create and learn their own ways of coping with the environment, which includes their fellow beings. Such strategies for coping and interacting are, to a large extent, shared with others. They make up a way of life, or *culture*. A culture comprises all the objects, ideas, beliefs, norms, and values of a group of people—and the meanings that the group applies to its cultural elements. From the culture, we learn what to define as good and bad, which animals to consider suitable for food and which to consider inedible, and even which smells are pleasant and which are not.

Cultures vary a great deal, according to both time and place. The way people earn their living, rear children, and clean their homes in Bolivia, for instance, is different from the way people in Iceland or even in Mexico carry out these tasks. But all cultures are alike in that they are *ethnocentric* (culture-centered). That is, the members of every society come to believe that their culture is best and natural and that societies which do things differently are inferior. Imagine that you are traveling in the Far East. There you learn that it is a common practice for people to eat dog meat—but because you have learned not to consider the dog as a source of food, you are likely to react very negatively. In India, you might consider it strange that people your own age marry partners selected by their parents. Upon questioning, you discover that the mates hadn't met until the wedding day. Your immediate reaction may be that the American way is superior. But why? Because it is the way that you know. Of course, current American dating practices are seen as strange and unnatural by people from India.

As we go through our daily routines we are usually unaware of the influence that culture has on human behavior. We eat with knives and forks, believe that one type of car is better than another, make assumptions about "human nature," pay bills printed by computers, and fall in love—oblivious of the fact that such behavior is *not* typical of people in every other society.

It is relatively easy to recognize the influence of culture by examining societies other than our own. When we read of the eating of dog meat or arranged marriages, we become aware that people's behavior depends upon the culture in which they are reared. It is more difficult, though, for us to step outside our own society to analyze the elements of American culture and to see their effects on *us*. When we do, however, we reduce the tendency to assume that other cultures are peculiar and wrong, and that ours is normal and good.

In a classic article, "Body Ritual Among the Nacirema," the anthropologist Horace Miner helps us to stand apart from our culture and observe it in a more objective light. Miner originally wrote this article as a spoof on ethnocentric American anthropologists; the portion that is reprinted here humorously and imaginatively induces us to view components of our daily bathroom behavior from a new, and quite different, perspective. Miner's description is valuable just because it makes us realize how odd our behavior might seem to someone from another culture. We are so used to doing things in certain ways that we are often unaware of much of our own behavior and fail to consider that alternative behavior patterns (called *functional alternatives*) exist.

The second selection alerts us to the importance of *subcultural* norms, beliefs, and behavior patterns. A subculture is a somewhat, but not totally, unique way of life that exists within a larger culture. That is, members of a subsociety—such as an ethnic, religious, occupational, or even a deviant group, whose members choose and/or are forced to interact largely within that group—are affected both by the larger culture and by their subculture. In addition, subcultural patterns may exert an influence on the larger culture, as happened when the style of dress of 1960s youth spread to the fashion industry as a whole.

In the second selection, Mark Zborowski focuses on definitions of and reactions to the biologically based phenomenon of pain among members of several subsocieties—Jews, Italians, and "Old Americans." From his research, we learn that it is a mistake to assume that every group attaches the same meaning to pain or that every group deals with pain in the same way. Zborowski's findings are useful in medical settings, where professionals need to be sensitized to the subtleties of ethnic subcultures. We also see that the social meaning attached to pain is *learned* through *socialization*, rather than being a biological given. (The process of socialization will be examined in more detail in Part III.)

Sometimes cultures meet head on. When they do, sparks can fly—and wars can even start—because each group ethnocentrically believes that its ways and beliefs are superior. Benjamin D. Paul, in "The Role of Beliefs and Customs in Sanitation Programs," gives us examples of what has happened when public health workers from the United States and other Western nations have tried to implement sanitation programs in the developing countries of the Third World. Westerners are often quite surprised that cultural values and practices keep people from adopting the new scientific recommendations. At the same time, people from the Third World are struck by how tenaciously Westerners hold to their limited and flawed scientific belief system. What Paul illustrates is the powerful grip that culture can have over people's behavior and views of reality. He also shows how fragile and easily challenged our most cherished beliefs can be.

# BODY RITUAL AMONG THE NACIREMA

## Horace Miner

THE ANTHROPOLOGIST HAS BECOME SO FAMILIAR WITH THE DIVERSITY OF ways in which different peoples behave in similar situations that he is not apt to be surprised by even the most exotic customs. In fact, if all of the logically possible combinations of behavior have not been found somewhere in the world, he is apt to suspect that they must be present in some yet undescribed tribe. This point has, in fact, been expressed with respect to clan organization by Murdock (1949:71). In this light, the magical beliefs and practices of the Nacirema present such unusual aspects that it seems desirable to describe them as an example of the extremes to which human behavior can go.

Professor Linton first brought the ritual of the Nacirema to the attention of anthropologists years ago (1936:326), but the culture of this people is still very poorly understood. They are a North American group living in the territory between the Canadian Cree, the Yaqui and Tarahumare of Mexico, and the Carib and Arawak of the Antilles. Little is known of their origin, although tradition states that they came from the east. According to Nacirema mythology, their nation was originated by a cultural hero, Notgnihsaw, who is otherwise known for two great feats of strength—the throwing of a piece of wampum across the river Pa-To-Mac and the chopping down of a cherry tree in which the Spirit of Truth resided.

Nacirema culture is characterized by a highly developed market economy which has evolved in a rich natural habitat. While much of the people's time is devoted to economical pursuits, a large part of the fruits of these labors and a considerable portion of the day are spent in ritual activity. The focus of this activity is the human body, the appearance and health of which loom as a dominant concern in the ethos of the people. While such a concern is certainly not unusual, its ceremonial aspects and associated philosophy are unique.

The fundamental belief underlying the whole system appears to be that the human body is ugly and that its natural tendency is to debility and disease. Incarcerated in such a body, man's only hope is to avert these characteristics through the use of the powerful influences of ritual

Horace Miner, ''Body Ritual Among the Nacirema,'' *American Anthropologist* 58 (1955): 503–507.

and ceremony. Every household has one or more shrines devoted to this purpose. The more powerful individuals in the society have several shrines in their houses and, in fact, the opulence of a house is often referred to in terms of the number of such ritual centers it possesses. Most houses are of wattle and daub construction, but the shrine rooms of the more wealthy are walled with stone. Poorer families imitate the rich by applying pottery plaques to their shrine walls.

While each family has at least one such shrine, the rituals associated with it are not family ceremonies but are private and secret. The rites are normally only discussed with children, and then only during the period when they are being initiated into these mysteries. I was able, however, to establish sufficient rapport with the natives to examine these shrines and to have the rituals described to me.

The focal point of the shrine is a box or chest which is built into the wall. In this chest are kept the many charms and magical potions without which no native believes he could live. These preparations are secured from a variety of specialized practitioners. The most powerful of these are the medicine men, whose assistance must be rewarded with substantial gifts. However, the medicine men do not provide the curative potions for their clients, but decide what the ingredients should be and then write them down in an ancient and secret language. This writing is understood only by the medicine men and by the herbalists who, for another gift, provide the required charm.

The charm is not disposed of after it has served its purpose, but is placed in the charm-box of the household shrine. As these magical materials are specific for certain ills, and the real or imagined maladies of the people are many, the charm-box is usually full to overflowing. The magical packets are so numerous that people forget what their purposes were and fear to use them again. While the natives are very vague on this point, we can only assume that the idea in retaining all the old magical materials is that their presence in the charm-box, before which the body rituals are conducted, will in some way protect the worshipper.

Beneath the charm-box is a small font. Each day every member of the family, in succession, enters the shrine room, bows his head before the charm-box, mingles different sorts of holy water in the font, and proceeds with a brief rite of ablution. The holy waters are secured from the Water Temple of the community, where the priests conduct elaborate ceremonies to make the liquid ritually pure.

In the hierarchy of magical practitioners, and below the medicine men in prestige, are specialists whose designation is best translated "holy-mouth-men." The Nacirema have an almost pathological horror of and fascination with the mouth, the condition of which is believed to have a supernatural influence on all social relationships. Were is not for the rituals of the mouth, they believe that their teeth would fall out, their gums bleed, their jaws shrink, their friends desert them, and their lovers reject them. They also believe that a strong relationship exists between oral and moral characteristics. For example, there is a ritual ablution of the mouth for children which is supposed to improve their moral fiber.

The daily body ritual performed by everyone includes a mouth-rite. Despite the fact that these people are so punctilious about care of the mouth, this rite involves a practice which strikes the uninitiated stranger as revolting. It was reported to me that the ritual consists of inserting a small bundle of hog hairs into the mouth, along with certain magical powders, and then moving the bundle in a highly formalized series of gestures.

In addition to the private mouth-rite, the people seek out a holy-mouth-man once or twice a year. These practitioners have an impressive set of paraphernalia, consisting of a variety of augers, awls, probes, and prods. The use of these objects in the exorcism of the evils of the mouth involves almost unbelievable ritual torture of the client. The holy-mouth-man opens the client's mouth and, using the above mentioned tools, enlarges any holes which decay may have created in the teeth. Magical materials are put into these holes. If there are no naturally occurring holes in the teeth, large sections of one or more teeth are gouged out so that the supernatural substance can be applied. In the client's view, the purpose of these ministrations is to arrest decay and to draw friends. The extremely sacred and traditional character of the rite is evident in the fact that the natives return to the holy-mouth-men year after year, despite the fact that their teeth continue to decay.

It is to be hoped that, when a thorough study of the Nacirema is made, there will be careful inquiry into the personality structure of these people. One has but to watch the gleam in the eye of a holy-mouth-man, as he jabs an awl into an exposed nerve, to suspect that a certain amount of sadism is involved. If this can be established, a very interesting pattern emerges, for most of the population shows definite masochistic tendencies. It was to these that Professor Linton referred in discussing a distinctive part of the daily body ritual which is performed only by men. This part of the rite involves scraping and lacerating the surface of the face with a sharp instrument. Special women's rites are performed only four times during each lunar month, but what they lack in frequency is made up in barbarity. As part of this ceremony, women bake their heads in small ovens for about an hour. The theoretically interesting point is that what seems to be a preponderantly masochistic people have developed sadistic specialists.

The medicine men have an imposing temple, or *latipso*, in every community of any size. The more elaborate ceremonies required to treat very sick patients can only be performed at this temple. These ceremonies involve not only the thaumaturge [or miracle worker] but a permanent group of vestal maidens who move sedately about the temple chambers in distinctive costume and headdress.

The *latipso* ceremonies are so harsh that it is phenomenal that a fair proportion of the really sick natives who enter the temple ever recover. Small children whose indoctrination is still incomplete have been known to resist attempts to take them to the temple because "that is where you go to die." Despite this fact, sick adults are not only willing but eager to undergo the protracted ritual purification, if they can afford to do so. No matter how ill the supplicant or how grave the emergency, the guardians of many temples will not admit a client if he cannot give a rich gift to the custodian. Even after one has gained admission and survived the ceremonies, the guardians will not permit the neophyte to leave until he makes still another gift.

The supplicant entering the temple is first stripped of all his or her clothes. In everyday life the Nacirema avoids exposure of his body and its natural functions. Bathing and excretory acts are performed only in the secrecy of the household shrine, where they are ritualized as part of the body-rites. Psychological shock results from the fact that body secrecy is suddenly lost upon entry into the *latipso*. A man, whose own wife has never seen him in an excretory act, suddenly finds himself naked and assisted by a vestal maiden while he performs his natural functions into a sacred vessel. This sort of ceremonial treatment is necessitated by the fact that the excreta are used by a diviner to ascertain the course and nature of the client's sickness. Female clients, on the other hand, find their naked bodies are subjected to the scrutiny, manipulation and prodding of the medicine men.

Few supplicants in the temple are well enough to do anything but lie on their hard beds. The daily ceremonies, like the rites of the holy-mouth-men, involve discomfort and torture. With ritual precision, the vestals awaken their miserable charges each dawn and roll them about on their beds of pain while performing ablutions, in the formal movements of which the maidens are highly trained. At other times they insert magic wands in the supplicant's mouth or force him to eat substances which are supposed to be healing. From time to time the medicine men come to their clients and jab magically treated needles into their flesh. The fact that these temple ceremonies may not cure, and may even kill the neophyte, in no way decreases the people's faith in the medicine men.

There remains one other kind of practitioner, known as a "listener." This witch-doctor has the power to exorcise the devils that lodge in the heads of people who have been bewitched. The Nacirema believe that parents bewitch their own children. Mothers are particularly suspected of putting a curse on children while teaching them the secret body rituals. The counter-magic of the witch-doctor is unusual in its lack of ritual. The patient simply tells the "listener" all his troubles and fears, beginning with the earliest difficulties he can remember. The memory displayed by the Nacirema in these exorcism sessions is truly remarkable. It is not uncommon for the patient to bemoan the rejection he felt upon being weaned as a babe, and a few individuals even see their troubles going back to the traumatic effects of their own birth.

In conclusion, mention must be made of certain practices which have their base in native esthetics but which depend upon the pervasive aversion to the natural body and its functions. There are ritual fasts to make fat people thin and ceremonial feasts to make thin people fat. Still other rites are used to make women's breasts larger if they are small, and smaller if they are large. General dissatisfaction with breast shape is symbolized in the fact that the ideal form is virtually outside the range of human variation. A few women afflicted with almost inhuman hyper-mammary development are so idolized that they make a handsome living by simply going from village to village and permitting the natives to stare at them for a fee.

Reference has already been made to the fact that excretory functions are ritualized, routinized, and relegated to secrecy. Natural reproductive functions are similarly distorted. Intercourse is taboo as a topic and scheduled as an act. Efforts are made to avoid pregnancy by the use of magical materials or by limiting intercourse to certain phases of the moon. Conception is actually very infrequent. When pregnant, women dress so as to hide their condition. Parturition takes place in secret, without friends or relatives to assist, and the majority of women do not nurse their infants.

•    •    •

## REFERENCES

Linton, Ralph, 1936, *The Study of Man*. New York, D. Appleton-Century Co.

Malinowski, Bronislaw, 1948, *Magic, Science, and Religion*. Glencoe, The Free Press.

Murdock, George P., 1949, *Social Structure*. New York, The Macmillan Co.

# Review Questions

1. Using Miner's style of analysis, describe dating and courtship among the Nacirema.

2. Miner's article on the Nacirema was intended to point out the ethnocentrism of American anthropologists and sociologists. How does it do this?

3. Give examples of the sociological concepts *values*, *beliefs*, and *norms* from Miner's article.

# CULTURAL COMPONENTS IN RESPONSES TO PAIN

Mark Zborowski

THIS PAPER REPORTS ON ONE ASPECT OF A LARGER STUDY: THAT CONCERNED with discovering the role of cultural patterns in attitudes toward and reactions to pain which is caused by disease and injury—in other words, responses to spontaneous pain.

## SOME BASIC DISTINCTIONS

In human societies biological processes vital for man's survival acquire social and cultural significance. Intake of food, sexual intercourse or elimination—physiological phenomena which are universal for the entire living world—become institutions regulated by cultural and social norms, thus fulfilling not only biological functions but social and cultural ones as well. Metabolic and endocrinal changes in the human organism may provoke hunger and sexual desire, but culture and society dictate to man the kind of food he may eat, the social setting for eating or the adequate partner for mating.

Moreover, the role of cultural and social patterns in human physiological activities is so great that they may in specific situations act against the direct biological needs of the individual, even to the point of endangering his survival. Only a human being may prefer starvation to the breaking of a religious dietary law or may abstain from sexual intercourse because of specific incest regulations. Voluntary fasting and celibacy exist only where food and sex fulfill more than strictly physiological functions.

Thus, the understanding of the significance and role of social and cultural patterns in human physiology is necessary to clarify those aspects of human experience which remain puzzling if studied only within the physiological frame of reference.

Pain is basically a physiological phenomenon and as such has been studied by physiologists and neurologists such as Harold Wolff, James Hardy, Helen Goodell, C. S. Lewis, W. K. Livingston and others. By using the most ingenious methods of investigation they have succeeded in

Mark Zborowski, "Cultural Components in Responses to Pain," *Journal of Social Issues*, 8 (1953): 16–31.

clarifying complex problems of the physiology of pain. Many aspects of perception and reaction to pain were studied in experimental situations involving most careful preparation and complicated equipment. These investigators have come to the conclusion that "from the physiological point of view pain qualifies as a sensation of importance to the self-preservation of the individual."[1] The biological function of pain is to provoke special reactive patterns directed toward avoidance of the noxious stimulus which presents a threat to the individual. In this respect the function of pain is basically the same for man as for the rest of the animal world.

However, the physiology of pain and the understanding of the biological function of pain do not explain other aspects of what Wolff, Hardy and Goodell call the *pain experience*, which includes not only the pain sensation and certain automatic reactive responses but also certain "associated feeling states."[2] It would not explain, for example, the acceptance of intense pain in torture which is part of the initiation rites of many primitive societies, nor will it explain the strong emotional reactions of certain individuals to the slight sting of the hypodermic needle.

In human society pain, like so many other physiological phenomena, acquires specific social and cultural significance, and, accordingly, certain reactions to pain can be understood in the light of this significance. As Drs. Hardy, Wolff and Goodell state in their . . . book, ". . . the culture in which a man finds himself becomes the conditioning influence in the formation of the individual reaction patterns to pain . . . A knowledge of group attitudes toward pain is extremely important to an understanding of the individual reaction."[3]

In analyzing pain it is useful to distinguish between *self-inflicted, other-inflicted* and *spontaneous* pain. Self-inflicted pain is defined as deliberately self-inflicted. It is experienced as a result of injuries performed voluntarily upon oneself, e.g., self-mutilation. Usually these injuries have a culturally defined purpose, such as achieving a special status in the society. It can be observed not only in primitive cultures but also in contemporary societies on a higher level of civilization. In Germany, for instance, members of certain student or military organizations would cut their faces with a razor in order to acquire scars which would identify them as members of a distinctive social group. By other-inflicted pain is meant pain inflicted upon the individual in the process of culturally accepted and expected activities (regardless of whether approved or disapproved), such as sports, fights, war, etc. To this category belongs also pain inflicted by the physician in the process of medical treatment. Spontaneous pain usually denotes the pain sensation which results from disease or injury. This term also covers pains of psychogenic nature.

Members of different cultures may assume differing attitudes toward these various types of pain. Two of these attitudes may be described as pain expectancy and pain acceptance. Pain expectancy is anticipation of pain as being unavoidable in a given situation, for instance, in childbirth, in sports activities or in battle. Pain acceptance is characterized by a willingness to experience pain. This attitude is manifested mostly as an inevitable component of culturally accepted experiences, for instance, as part of initiation rites or part of medical treatment. The following example will help to clarify the differences between pain expectancy and pain acceptance: Labor pain is expected as part of childbirth, but while in one culture, such as in the United States, it is not accepted and therefore various means are used to alleviate it, in some other cultures, for instance in Poland, it is not only expected but also accepted, and consequently nothing or little is done to relieve it. Similarly, cultures which emphasize military achievements expect and accept battle wounds, while cultures which emphasize pacificistic values may expect them but will not accept them.

In the process of investigating cultural attitudes toward pain it is also important to distinguish between *pain apprehension* and *pain anxiety*. Pain apprehension reflects the tendency to avoid the pain sensation as such, regardless of whether the pain is spontaneous or inflicted, whether it is accepted or not. Pain anxiety, on the other hand, is a state of anxiety provoked by the pain experience, focused upon various aspects of the causes of pain, the meaning of pain or its significance for the welfare of the individual.

Moreover, members of various cultures may react differently in terms of their manifest behavior toward various pain experiences, and this behavior is often dictated by the culture which provides specific norms according to the age, sex and social position of the individual.

The fact that other elements as well as cultural factors are involved in the response to a spontaneous pain should be taken into consideration. These other factors are the pathological aspect of pain, the specific physiological characteristics of the pain experience, such as the intensity, the duration and the quality of the pain sensation, and, finally, the personality of the individual. Nevertheless, it was felt that in the process of a careful investigation it would be possible to detect the role of the cultural components in the pain experience.

## THE RESEARCH SETTING

In setting up the research we were interested not only in the purely theoretical aspects of the findings in terms of possible contribution to the understanding of the pain experience in general; we also had in mind the practical goal of a contribution to the field of medicine. In the relationship between the doctor and his [or her] patient the respective attitudes toward pain may play a crucial role, especially when the doctor feels that the patient exaggerates his pain while the patient feels that the doctor minimizes his suffering. The same may be true, for instance, in a hospital where the members of the medical and nursing staff may have attitudes toward pain different from those held by the patient, or when they expect a certain pattern of behavior according to their cultural background while the patient may manifest a behavior pattern which is acceptable in his culture. These differences may play an important part in the evaluation of the individual pain experience, in dealing with pain at home and in the hospital, in administration of analgesics, etc. Moreover, we expected that this study of pain would offer opportunities to gain insight into related attitudes toward health, disease, medication, hospitalization, medicine in general, etc.

With these aims in mind the project was set up at the Kingsbridge Veterans Hospital, Bronx, New York,[4] where three ethnocultural groups were selected for an intensive study. These groups included patients of Jewish, Italian, . . . and "Old American" stock. [Two] groups—Jews [and] Italians . . .—were selected because they were described by medical people as manifesting striking differences in their reaction to pain. Italians and Jews were described as tending to "exaggerate" their pain. . . . [T]he "Old Americans" were chosen because the values and attitudes of this group dominate in the country and are held by many members of the medical profession and by many descendants of the immigrants who, in the process of Americanization, tend to adopt American patterns of behavior. The members of this group can be defined as white, native-born individuals, usually Protestant, whose grandparents, at least, were born in the United States and who do not identify themselves with any foreign group, either nationally, socially or culturally.

The Kingsbridge Veterans Hospital was chosen because its population represents roughly the ethnic composition of New York City, thus offering access to a fair sample of the [three] selected groups, and also because various age groups were represented among the hospitalized veterans of World War I, World War II and the Korean War. In one major respect this hospital was not adequate, namely, in not offering the opportunity to investigate sex differences in attitude toward pain. This aspect of research will be carried out in a hospital with a large female population.

In setting up this project we were mainly interested in discovering certain regularities in reactions and attitudes toward pain characteristic of the [three] groups. Therefore, the study has a qualitative character, and the efforts of the researchers were not directed toward a collection of material suitable for quantitative analysis. The main techniques used in the collection of the material were interviews with patients in the selected groups, observation of their behavior when in pain and discussion of the individual cases with doctors, nurses and other people directly or indirectly involved in the pain experience of the individual. In addition to the interviews with patients, "healthy" members of the respective groups were interviewed on their attitudes toward pain, because in terms of the original hypothesis those attitudes and reactions which are displayed by the patients of the given cultural groups are held by all members of the group regardless of whether or not they are in pain although [when] in pain these attitudes may come more sharply into focus. In certain cases the researchers have interviewed a member of the patient's immediate family in order to check the report of the patient on his pain experience and in order to find out what are the attitudes and reactions of the family toward the patient's experience.

These interviews, based on a series of open-ended questions, were focused upon the past and present pain experiences of the interviewee. However, many other areas were considered important for the understanding of this experience. For instance, it was felt that complaints of pain may play an important role in manipulating relationships in the family and the larger social environment. It was also felt that in order to understand the specific reactive patterns in controlling pain it is important to know certain aspects of child-rearing in the culture, relationships between parents and children, the role of infliction of pain in punishment, the attitudes of various members of the family toward specific expected, accepted pain experiences, and so on. The interviews were recorded on wire and transcribed verbatim for an ultimate detailed analysis. The interviews usually lasted for approximately two hours, the time being limited by the condition of the interviewee and by the amount and quality of his answers. When it was considered necessary an interview was repeated. In most of the cases the study of the interviewee was followed by informal conversations and by observation of his behavior in the hospital.

The information gathered from the interviews was discussed with members of the medical staff, especially in the areas related to the medical aspects of the problem, in order to get their evaluation of the pain experience of the patient. Information as to the personality of the patient was checked against results of psychological testing by members of the psychological staff of the hospital when these were available.

The discussion of the material presented in this paper is based on interviews with 103 respondents, including 87 hospital patients in pain and 16 healthy subjects. According to their ethnocultural background the respondents are distributed as follows: "Old Americans," 26; Italians, 24; Jews, 31; and others, 22.[5] In addition there were the collateral interviews and conversations noted above with family members, doctors, nurses and other members of the hospital staff.

With regard to the pathological causes of pain the majority of the interviewees fall into the group of patients suffering from neurological diseases, mainly herniated discs and spinal lesions. The focusing upon a group of patients suffering from a similar pathology offered the opportunity to investigate reactions and attitudes toward spontaneous pain which is symptomatic of one group of diseases. Nevertheless, a number of patients suffering from other diseases were also interviewed.

This paper is based upon the material collected during the first stage of study. The generalizations are to a great extent tentative formulations on a descriptive level. There has been no attempt as yet to integrate the results with the value system and the cultural pattern of the group, though here and there there will be indications to the effect that they are part of the culture pattern. The discussions will be limited to main regularities within three groups, namely, the Italians, the Jews and the "Old Americans." Factors related to variations within each group will be discussed after the main prevailing patterns have been presented.

## PAIN AMONG PATIENTS OF JEWISH AND ITALIAN ORIGIN

As already mentioned, the Jews and Italians were selected mainly because interviews with medical experts suggested that they display similar reactions to pain. The investigation of this similarity provided the opportunity to check a rather popular assumption that similar reactions reflect similar attitudes. The differences between the Italian and Jewish culture are great enough to suggest that if the attitudes are related to cultural pattern they will also be different despite the apparent similarity in manifest behavior.

Members of both groups were described as being very emotional in their responses to pain. They were described as tending to exaggerate their pain experience and being very sensitive to pain. Some of the doctors stated that in their opinion Jews and Italians have a lower threshold of pain than members of other ethnic groups, especially members of the so-called Nordic group. This statement seems to indicate a certain conclusion as to the concept of the threshold of pain. According to people who have studied the problem of the threshold of pain, for instance Harold Wolff and his associates, the threshold of pain is more or less the same for all human beings regardless of nationality, sex or age.

In the course of the investigation the general impressions of doctors were confirmed to a great extent by the interview material and by the observation of the patients' behavior. However, even a superficial study of the interviews has revealed that though reactions to pain appear to be similar the underlying attitudes toward pain are different in the two groups. While the Italian patients seemed to be mainly concerned with the immediacy of the pain experience and were disturbed by the actual pain sensation which they experienced in a given situation, the concern of patients of Jewish origin was focused mainly upon the symptomatic meaning of pain and upon the significance of pain in relation to their health, welfare and, eventually, for the welfare of the families. The Italian patient expressed in his behavior and in his complaints the discomfort caused by pain as such, and he manifested his emotions with regard to the effects of this pain experience upon his immediate situations in terms of occupation, economic situation and so on; the Jewish patient expressed primarily his worries and anxieties as to the extent to which the pain indicated a threat to his health. In this connection it is worth mentioning that one of the Jewish words to describe strong pain is *yessurim*, a word which is also used to describe worries and anxieties.

Attitudes of Italian and Jewish patients toward pain-relieving drugs can serve as an indication of their attitude toward pain. When in pain the Italian calls for pain relief and is mainly concerned with the analgesic effects of the drugs which are administered to him. Once the pain is relieved the Italian patient easily forgets his sufferings and manifests a happy and joyful disposition. The Jewish patient, however, often is reluctant to accept the drug, and he explains this reluctance in terms of concern about the effects of the drug upon his health in general. He is apprehensive about the habit-forming aspects of the analgesic. Moreover, he feels that the drug relieves his pain only temporarily and does not cure him of the disease which may cause the pain. Nurses and doctors have reported cases in which patients would hide the pill which was given to them to relieve their pain and would prefer to suffer. These reports were confirmed in the interviews with patients. It was also observed that many Jewish patients after being relieved from pain often continued to display the same depressed and worried behavior because they felt that though the pain was currently absent it may recur as long as the disease was not cured completely. From these observations it appears that when one deals with a Jewish and an Italian patient in pain, in the first case it is more important to relieve the anxieties with regard to the sources of pain, while in the second it is more important to relieve the actual pain.

Another indication as to the significance of pain for Jewish and Italian patients is their respective attitudes toward the doctor. The Italian patient seems to display a most confident attitude toward the doctor which is usually reinforced after the doctor has succeeded in relieving pain, whereas the Jewish patient manifests a skeptical attitude, feeling that the fact that the doctor has relieved his pain by some drug does not mean at all that he is skillful enough to take care of the basic illness. Consequently, even when the pain is relieved, he tends to check the diagnosis and the treatment of one doctor against the opinions of other specialists in the field. Summarizing the difference between the Italian and Jewish attitudes, one can say that the Italian attitude is characterized by a present-oriented apprehension with regard to the actual sensation of pain, and the Jew tends to manifest a future-oriented anxiety as to the symptomatic and general meaning of the pain experience.

It has been stated that the Italians and Jews tend to manifest similar behavior in terms of their reactions to pain. As both cultures allow for free expression of feelings and emotions by words, sounds and gestures, both the Italians and Jews feel free to talk about their pain, complain about it and manifest their sufferings by groaning, moaning, crying, etc. They are not ashamed of this expression. They admit willingly that when they are in pain they do complain a great deal, call for help and expect sympathy and assistance from other members of their immediate social environment, especially from members of their family. When in pain they are reluctant to be alone and prefer the presence and attention of other people. This behavior, which is expected, accepted and approved by the Italian and Jewish cultures often conflicts with the patterns of behavior expected from a patient by American or Americanized medical people. Thus they tend to describe the behavior of the Italian and Jewish patients as exaggerated and overemotional. The material suggests that they do tend to minimize the actual pain experiences of the Italian and Jewish patient regardless of whether they have the objective criteria for evaluating the actual amount of pain which the patient experiences. It seems that the uninhibited display of reaction to pain as manifested by the Jewish and Italian patient provokes distrust in American culture instead of provoking sympathy.

Despite the close similarity between the manifest reactions among Jews and Italians, there seem to be differences in emphasis especially with regard to what the patient achieves by these reactions and as to the specific manifestations of these reactions in the various social settings. For instance, they differ in their behavior at home and in the hospital. The Italian husband, who is aware of his role as an adult male, tends to avoid verbal complaining at home, leaving this type of behavior to the women. In the hospital, where he is less concerned with his role as a male, he tends to [be] more verbal and more emotional. The Jewish patient, on the contrary, seems to be more calm in the hospital than at home. Traditionally the Jewish male does not emphasize his masculinity through such traits as stoicism, and he does not equate verbal complaints with weakness. Moreover, the Jewish culture allows the patient to be demanding and complaining. Therefore, he tends more to use his pain in order to control interpersonal relationships within the family. Though similar use of pain to manipulate the relationships between members of the family may be present also in some other cultures it seems that in the Jewish culture this is not disapproved, while in others it is. In the hospital one can also distinguish variations in the reactive patterns among Jews and Italians. Upon his admission to the hospital and in the presence of the doctor the Jewish patient tends to complain, ask for help, be emotional even to the point of crying. However, as soon as he feels that adequate care is given to him he becomes more restrained. This suggests that the display of pain reaction serves less as an indication of the amount of pain experienced than as a means to create an atmosphere and setting in which the pathological causes of pain will be best taken care of. The Italian patient, on the other hand, seems to be less concerned with setting up a favorable situation for treatment. He takes for granted that adequate care will be given to him, and in the presence of the doctor he seems to be somewhat calmer than the Jewish patient. The mere presence of the doctor reassures the Italian patient, while the skepticism of the Jewish patient limits the reassuring role of the physician.

To summarize the description of the reactive patterns of the Jewish and Italian patients, the material suggests that on a semiconscious level the Jewish patient tends to provoke worry and concern in his social environment as to the state of his health and the symptomatic character of his pain, while the Italian tends to provoke sympathy toward his suffering. In one case the function of the pain reaction will be the mobilization of the efforts of the family and the doctors toward a complete cure, while in the second case the function of the reaction will be focused upon the mobilization of effort toward relieving the pain sensation.

On the basis of the discussion of the Jewish and Italian material two generalizations can be made: (1) *Similar reactions to pain manifested by members of different ethno-cultural groups do not necessarily reflect similar attitudes to pain.* (2) *Reactive patterns similar in terms of their manifestations may have different functions and serve different purposes in various cultures.*

## PAIN AMONG PATIENTS OF "OLD AMERICAN" ORIGIN

There is little emphasis on emotional complaining about pain among "Old American" patients. Their complaints about pain can best be described as reporting on pain. In describing his pain, the "Old American" patient tries to find the most appropriate ways of defining the quality of pain, its localization, duration, etc. When examined by the doctor he gives the impression of trying to assume the detached role of an unemotional observer who gives the most efficient description of his state for a correct diagnosis and treatment. The interviewees repeatedly state that there is no point in complaining and groaning and moaning, etc., because "it won't help anybody." However, they readily admit that when pain is unbearable they may react strongly, even to the point of crying, but they tend to do it when they are alone. Withdrawal from society seems to be a frequent reaction to strong pain.

There seem to be different patterns in reacting to pain depending on the situation. One pattern, manifested in the presence of members of the family, friends, etc., consists of attempts to minimize pain, to avoid complaining and provoking pity; when pain becomes too strong there is a tendency to withdraw and express freely such reactions as groaning, moaning, etc. A different pattern is manifested in the presence of people who, on account of their profession, should know the character of the pain experience because they are expected to make the appropriate diagnosis, advise the proper cure and give the adequate help. The tendency to avoid deviation from certain expected patterns of behavior plays an important role in the reaction to pain. This is also controlled by the desire to seek approval on the part of the social environment, especially in the hospital, where the "Old American" patient tries to avoid being a "nuisance" in the ward. He seems to be, more than any other patient, aware of an ideal pattern of behavior which is identified as "American," and he tends to conform to it. This was characteristically expressed by a patient who answered the question how he reacts to pain by saying, "I react like a good American."

An important element in controlling the pain reaction is the wish of the patient to cooperate with those who are expected to take care of him. The situation is often viewed as a team composed of the patient, the doctor, the nurse, the attendant, etc., and in this team everybody has a function and is supposed to do his [or her] share in order to achieve the most successful result. Emotionality is seen as a purposeless and hindering factor in a situation which calls for knowledge, skill, training and efficiency. It is important to note that this behavior is also expected by American or Americanized members of the medical or nursing staff, and the patients who do not fall into this pattern are viewed as deviants, hypochondriacs and neurotics.

As in the case of the Jewish patients, the American attitude toward pain can be best defined as a future-oriented anxiety. The "Old American" patient is also concerned with the symptomatic significance of pain which is correlated with a pronounced health consciousness. It seems that the "Old American" is conscious of various threats to his health which are present in his environment and therefore feels vulnerable and is prone to interpret his pain sensation as a warning signal indicating that something is wrong with his health and therefore must be reported to the physician. With some exceptions, pain is considered bad and unnecessary and therefore must be immediately taken care of. In those situations where pain is expected and accepted, such as in the process of medical treatment or as a result of sports activities, there is less concern with the pain sensation. In general, however, there is a feeling that suffering pain is unnecessary when there are means of relieving it.

Though the attitudes of the Jewish and "Old American" patients can be defined as pain anxiety they differ greatly. The future-oriented anxiety of the Jewish interviewee is characterized by pessimism or, at best, by skepticism, while the "Old American" patient is rather optimistic in his future orientation. This attitude is fostered by the mechanistic approach to the body and its functions and by the confidence in the skill of the expert which are so frequent in the American culture. The body is often viewed as a machine which has to be well taken care of, be periodically checked for dysfunctioning and eventually, when out of order, be taken to an expert who will "fix" the defect. In the case of pain the expert is the medical expert who has the "know-how" because of training and experience and therefore is entitled to full confidence. An important element in the optimistic outlook is faith in the progress of science. Patients with intractable pain often stated that though at the present moment the doctors do not have the "drug" they will eventually discover it, and they will give the examples of sulfa, penicillin, etc.

The anxieties of a pain-experiencing "Old American" patient are greatly relieved when he feels that something is being done about it in terms of specific activities involved in the treatment. It seems that his security and confidence increases in direct proportion to the number of tests, X-rays, examinations, injections, etc. that are given to him. Accordingly, "Old American" patients seem to have a positive attitude toward hospitalization, because the hospital is the adequate institution which is equipped for the necessary treatment. While a Jewish and an Italian patient seem to be disturbed by the impersonal character of the hospital and by the necessity of being treated there instead of at home, the "Old American" patient, on the contrary, prefers the hospital treatment to the home treatment, and neither he nor his family seems to be disturbed by hospitalization.

To summarize the attitude of the "Old American" toward pain, he is disturbed by the symptomatic aspect of pain and is concerned with its incapacitating aspects, but he tends to view the future in rather optimistic colors, having confidence in the science and skill of the professional people who treat his condition.

## SOME SOURCES OF INTRA-GROUP VARIATION

In the description of the reactive patterns and attitudes toward pain among patients of Jewish and "Old American" origin certain regularities have been observed for each particular group regardless of individual differences and variations. This does not mean that each individual in each group manifests the same reactions and attitudes. Individual variations are often due to specific aspects of pain experience, to the character of the disease which causes the pain or to elements in the personality of the patient. However, there are also other factors that are instrumental in provoking these differences and which can still be traced back to the cultural backgrounds of the individual patients. Such variables as the degree of Americanization of the patient, his socio-economic background, education and religiosity may play an important role in shaping individual variations in the reactive patterns. For instance, it was found that the patterns described are manifested most consistently among immigrants, while their descendants tend to differ in terms of adopting American forms of behavior and American attitudes toward the role of the medical expert, medical institutions and equipment in controlling pain. It is safe to say that the further the individual is from the immigrant generation the more American is his behavior. This is less true for the attitudes toward pain which seem to persist to a great extent even among members of the third generation and even though the reactive patterns are radically changed. A Jewish or Italian patient born in this country of American-born parents tend to *behave* like an "Old American" but often expresses *attitudes* similar to those which are expressed by the Jewish or Italian people. They try to appear unemotional and efficient in situations where the immigrant would be excited and disturbed. However, in the process of the interview, if a patient is of Jewish origin he is likely to express attitudes of anxiety as to the meaning of his pain, and if he is Italian he is likely to be rather unconcerned about the significance of his pain for his future.

The occupational factor plays an important role when pain affects a specific area of the body. For instance, manual workers with herniated discs are more disturbed by their pain than are professional or business people with a similar disease because of the immediate significance of this particular pain for their respective abilities to earn a living. It was also observed that headaches cause more concern among intellectuals than among manual workers.

The educational background of the patient also plays an important role in his attitude with regard to the symptomatic meaning of a pain sensation. The more educated patients are more health-conscious and more aware of pain as a possible symptom of a dangerous disease. However, this factor plays a less important role than might be expected. The less educated "Old American" or Jewish patient is still more health-conscious than the more educated Italian. On the other hand, the less educated Jew is as much worried about the significance of pain as the more educated one. The education of the patient seems to be an important factor in fostering specific reactive patterns. The more educated patient, who may have more anxiety with regard to illness, may be more reserved in specific reactions to pain than an unsophisticated individual, who feels free to express his feelings and emotions.

## THE TRANSMISSION OF CULTURAL ATTITUDES TOWARD PAIN

In interpreting the differences which may be attributed to different socioeconomic and educational backgrounds there is enough evidence to conclude that these differences appear mainly on the manifest and behavioral level, whereas attitudinal patterns toward pain tend to be more

uniform and to be common to most of the members of the group regardless of their specific backgrounds.

These attitudes toward pain and the expected reactive patterns are acquired by the individual members of the society from the earliest childhood along with other cultural attitudes and values which are learned
from the parents, parent-substitutes, siblings, peer groups, etc. Each
culture offers to its members an ideal pattern of attitudes and reactions,
which may differ for various sub-cultures in a given society, and each individual is expected to conform to this ideal pattern. Here, the role of the
family seems to be of primary importance. Directly and indirectly the
family environment affects the individuals' ultimate response to pain. In
each culture the parents teach the child how to react to pain, and by approval or disapproval they promote specific forms of behavior. This conclusion is amply supported by the interviews. Thus, the Jewish and Italian respondents are unanimous in relating how their parents, especially
mothers, manifested overprotective and overconcerned attitudes toward
the child's health, participation in sports, games, fights, etc. In these
families the child is constantly reminded of the advisability of avoiding
colds, injuries, fights and other threatening situations. Crying in complaint is responded to by the parents with sympathy, concern and help.
By their overprotective and worried attitude they foster complaining and
tears. The child learns to pay attention to each painful experience and to
look for help and sympathy which are readily given to him. In Jewish
families, where not only a slight sensation of pain but also each deviation from the child's normal behavior is looked upon as a sign of illness,
the child is prone to acquire anxieties with regard to the meaning and
significance of these manifestations. The Italian parents do not seem to
be concerned with the symptomatic meaning of the child's pains and
aches, but instead there is a great deal of verbal expression of emotions
and feelings of sympathy toward the "poor child" who happens to be in
discomfort because of illness or because of an injury in play. In these
families a child is praised when he avoids physical injuries and is
scolded when he does not pay enough attention to bad weather, to drafts
or when he takes part in rough games and fights. The injury and pain
are often interpreted to the child as punishment for the wrong behavior,
and physical punishment is the usual consequence of misbehavior.

In the "Old American" family the parental attitude is quite different.
The child is told not to "run to mother with every little thing." He is told
to take pain "like a man," not to be a "sissy," not to cry. The child's participation in physical sports and games is not only approved but is also
strongly stimulated. Moreover, the child is taught to expect to be hurt in
sports and games and is taught to fight back if he happens to be attacked
by other boys. However, it seems that the American parents are conscious of the threats to the child's health, and they teach the child to take
immediate care of any injury. When hurt the right thing to do is not to

cry and get emotional but to avoid unnecessary pain and prevent unpleasant consequences by applying the proper first aid medicine and by calling a doctor.

Often attitudes and behavior fostered in a family conflict with those patterns which are accepted by the larger social environment. This is especially true in the case of children of immigrants. The Italian or Jewish immigrant parents promote patterns which they consider correct, while the peer groups in the street and in the school criticize this behavior and foster a different one. In consequence, the child may acquire the attitudes which are part of his home life but may also adopt behavior patterns which conform to those of his friends.

The direct promotion of certain behavior described as part of the child-rearing explains only in part the influence of the general family environment and the specific role of the parents in shaping responses to pain. They are also formed indirectly by observing the behavior of other members of the family and by imitating their responses to pain. Moreover, attitudes toward pain are also influenced by various aspects of parent-child relationship in a culture. The material suggests that differences in attitudes toward pain in Jewish, Italian and "Old American" families are closely related to the role and image of the father in the respective cultures in terms of his authority and masculinity. Often the father and mother assume different roles in promoting specific patterns of behavior and specific attitudes. For example, it seems that in the "Old American" family it is chiefly the mother who stimulates the child's ability to resist pain thus emphasizing his masculinity. In the Italian family it seems that the mother is the one who inspires the child's emotionality, while in the Jewish family both parents express attitudes of worry and concern which are transmitted to the children.

Specific deviations from expected reactive and attitudinal patterns can often be understood in terms of a particular structure of the family. This became especially clear from the interviews of two Italian patients and one Jewish patient. All three subjects revealed reactions and attitudes diametrically opposite to those which the investigator would expect on the basis of his experience. In the process of the interview, however, it appeared that one of the Italian patients was adopted into an Italian family, found out about his adoption at the age of fourteen, created a phantasy of being of Anglo-Saxon origin because of his physical appearance and accordingly began to eradicate everything "Italian" in his personality and behavior. For instance, he denied knowledge of the Italian language despite the fact that he always spoke Italian in the family and even learned to abstain from smiling, because he felt that being happy and joyful is an indication of Italian origin. The other Italian patient lost his family at a very early age because of family disorganization and was brought up in an Irish foster home. The Jewish patient consciously adopted a "non-Jewish" pattern of behavior and attitude because of strong sibling rivalry. According to the respondent, his brother, a favored son in the immigrant Jewish family, always manifested "typical" Jewish reactions toward disease, and the patient who strongly disliked the brother and was jealous of him, decided to be "completely different."

## NOTES

1. James D. Hardy, Harold G. Wolff, and Helen Goodell, *Pain Sensations and Reactions*, (Baltimore: Williams and Wilkins Company, 1952), p. 23.

2. *Ibid.*, p. 204.

3. *Ibid.*, p. 262.

4. I should like to take the opportunity to express my appreciation to Dr. Harold G. Wolff, Professor of Neurology, Cornell University Medical College, Dr. Hiland Flowers, Chief of Neuropsychiatric Service, Dr. Robert Morrow, Chief of Clinical Psychology Section, Dr. Louis Berlin, Chief of Neurology Section, and the Management of the hospital for their cooperation in the setting up of the research at the Kingsbridge Veterans Hospital.

5. Italian respondents are mainly of South Italian origin; the Jewish respondents, with one exception, are all of East European origin. Whenever the Jews are mentioned they are spoken of in terms of the culture they represent and not in terms of their religion.

# Review Questions

1. Explain the difference between *reactions to pain* and *attitudes toward pain*. Give examples from Zborowski's study to illustrate the differing reactions and attitudes among the members of the various subsocieties.

2. Distinguish between pain as a biological experience and pain as a culturally shaped experience. Give examples from Zborowski's study to illustrate your points.

3. If the physician understands differences in patients' cultural background, will he or she be better able to understand the individual's response to pain? Explain your answer.

# THE ROLE OF BELIEFS AND CUSTOMS IN SANITATION PROGRAMS

Benjamin D. Paul

Humans are biological and social animals; they are also cultural animals. They are cultural in that their lives run and regulate society not by blind instincts or detached reason alone, but rather by a set of ideas and skills transmitted socially from one generation to the next and held in common by the members of their particular social group. Culture is a blueprint for social living. Humans reside in a double environment—an outer layer of climate, terrain and resources, and an inner layer of culture that mediates between humans and the world around them. By applying knowledge which comes to them as part of their cultural heritage, people transform their physical environment to enhance comfort and improve health. They also interpret the environment, assigning significance and value to its various features in accordance with the dictates of their particular culture. Among other things, culture acts as a selective device for perceiving and understanding the outer world. Since cultures vary from group to group, interpretations of the physical environment vary correspondingly.

Ordinarily people are unaware that culture influences their thoughts and acts. They assume their way is *the* way or the "natural" way. Interacting with others in their own society who share their cultural assumptions, they can ignore culture as a determinant of behavior; as a common denominator, it seems to cancel out. Engineers can construct health facilities in their home areas without worrying too much about the cultural characteristics of the people who will use the facilities. Sharing their habits and beliefs, they are in effect taking them into account. But in another country with another culture, their assumptions and those of the residents may not match so well. In parts of Latin America maternity patients of moderate means expect a private hospital room with an adjoining alcove to accommodate a servant or kinswoman who comes along to attend the patient around the clock. In parts of rural India the hospital should be built with a series of separate cooking stalls where the patient's family can prepare the meals, in view of cultural prohibitions against the handling of food by members of other castes. And of course the effect of cultural differences looms even larger where sanitation has

Benjamin D. Paul, "The Role of Beliefs and Customs in Sanitation Programs," *American Journal of Public Health* 48 (1958): 1502–1506.

to be built directly into the habit systems of people, rather than into structures and plants that serve the people.

## THREE MISINTERPRETATIONS OF CULTURAL DIFFERENCES

Anyone familiar with the operation of technical assistance programs knows about the kind of behavioral differences I have mentioned. Unfortunately, however, it is easy to misconstrue these observed differences. Three kinds of misinterpretation are common. The first is to suppose that "they" have more odd beliefs and habits, while we have less of them. We tend to see them as captives of blind custom and ourselves as relatively free from cultural peculiarities. The fact is that all people are creatures of their culture with its inevitable admixture of rational and nonrational elements. Cultures differ and rates of cultural change differ, but peoples do not differ appreciably in the degree to which their actions are influenced by their respective cultures. We are quick to apply the term "superstition" or the epithet "uncouth custom" to the other fellow's manner of thinking or behaving. We may be repelled by the custom of eating domesticated dogs and yet impatient with people who would rather go hungry than eat their cattle. Americans take offense at the odor of night soil in the settlements of Korea and other parts of eastern Asia; a Korean gentleman on his first visit to New York was asked by a friend how he liked the great city, whereupon he replied: "Oh, very well, but the smells are so bad!"[1] Measured by the standards of one culture the manifestations of another are bound to appear more or less arbitrary or bizarre. We need to realize that we have culture, too, and that our ways can seem as peculiar to others as theirs do to us.

Even allowing that our behavior as well as theirs bears the stamp of cultural conditioning, a second facile assumption is that our ways and ideas are more advanced than theirs, that they have yet to catch up with us. The trouble with this assumption is that it represents a partial truth: Some aspects of culture, notably scientific knowledge and technical skills, are indeed subject to measurement and relative ranking. But knowledge is not wisdom, and many aspects of culture, including language, esthetics, moral codes, and religious values, lie beyond objective rating for want of a culture-free standard of measurement. It is a mistake and an insult to imply, as we inadvertently do at times, that because some areas of the world are technically underdeveloped their people or their cultures are in general underdeveloped.

A third and particularly common shortcoming in our understanding of cultural differences is a tendency to view customs and beliefs as isolated elements rather than as parts of a system or pattern. The linkages between the parts of culture may be loose or tight and the connections are not always apparent upon first inspection, but it frequently turns out that people cling to a particular practice or belief not merely because it is familiar and traditional but because it is linked to other elements of the culture. Conversely, a change effected in one area of the culture may bring with it unexpected changes in other areas or may result in awkward dislocations, as the following illustrations will indicate.

## PALAUAN VISITING CUSTOMS

On the island of Palau in the western Pacific the pattern of living calls for frequent and large gatherings of people to celebrate or solemnize certain social events. In the old days, Palauan houses were large enough to hold many people. There were no partitions, and it was possible for each man attending a feast to receive his food in the order of rank and to sit in such a way as not to cause offense by turning his back on anyone. Since the last war, most Palauans live in small two- or three-room houses built in the Japanese or American style. They try to maintain the old customs but they have their troubles. Visitors overcrowd the small house and sit packed together on the floor. They must suffer the insult of having to look at a neighbor's back and must take their food in any order they can. The Palauans are incessant betel chewers—and spitters. The old houses had several doors and numerous floor cracks to accommodate this habit. The new buildings, especially the Quonset huts now being created for the chiefs' dwellings and council chambers, have caused a minor crisis. The two Quonset doors are premium locations: knotholes in the plywood floors are too scarce to provide relief for the majority of chewers. Tin cans are coming in as spittoons, but these are in scarce supply.[2]

Housing customs and hospitality customs, once closely linked in Palau, are now in strained relationship. It should be stated parenthetically that social or cultural strains are not necessarily good or bad in themselves; depending on the case, they can lead to increased cultural disorganization or to an eventual reorganization of the sociocultural system on a new basis.

## SOCIABILITY IN RURAL INDIA

In some instances people strive to prevent cultural strain by resisting environmental and sanitary improvements. In rural India, fecal contamination of food and water by direct contact or contact through flies and rodents constitutes a difficult problem. The source of the trouble is the custom of defecating in the open fields. Use of latrines would go far toward solving the problem. Public health engineers and others working in India have devised special types of latrine adapted to the local squat-

ting posture and designed to meet varied soil, climatic, and water supply conditions. Numerous latrines have in fact been installed, but fol-
low-up studies reveal that only a small proportion are used regularly.
Women in particular tend to avoid the latrines. Every morning and afternoon women go in groups to the field, not only to relieve themselves but
also to take time off from busy domestic routines, to gossip and exchange advice about husbands and mothers-in-law, and to bathe with
water from tanks located in the field. The linked habits of going to the
fields for social gatherings and for toilet and bathing activities meet a
strongly felt need for community living and relaxation from daily toil. In
the women's view, defecation customs are usefully linked to other customs. In the view of sanitation specialists these customs are harmfully
linked to a cycle of contamination and intestinal disease. To disrupt the
contamination cycle the women are urged to use the new latrines. They
shy away from following this advice, partly because doing so would disrupt an ensemble of customs they prefer to keep intact, and partly because their culture has given them little basis for comprehending the
connection between feces and enteric diseases.[3]

## THE "HOT-COLD" IDEA SYSTEM IN LATIN AMERICA

I began by saying that culture mediates between people and their material environment. In an article analyzing the outcome of a rural sanitation program in a small Peruvian town, the author explains how perceptions of so common an environmental element as water are culturally
screened:

> A trained health worker can perceive "contamination" in water because his
> perceptions are linked to certain scientific understandings which permit him
> to view water in a specially conditioned way. The Peruvian townsman also
> views water in a specially conditioned way. Between him and the water he ob-
> serves, his culture "filters out" bacteria and "filters in" cold, hot or other
> qualities that are as meaningful to him as they are meaningless to the outsider.

An important part of the local culture is a complex system of hot and
cold distinctions. Many things in nature, including foods, liquids, medi-
cines, body states, and illnesses, are classified as essentially "hot" or
"cold" or something in between, irrespective of actual temperature.
Sick people should avoid foods that are very cold, such as pork. "Raw"
water is cold and fit for well persons; "cooked" water is hot and fit for
the sick. The times of day when water can be boiled are hedged in by
limitations of time and fuel and further restricted by "hot" and "cold"
considerations. Water is consumed mainly around noon. Water boiled
later in the day and standing overnight becomes dangerously "cold"
and must be reboiled in the morning. So it is useless to boil it at any time

other than the morning in the first place. The patient efforts of a local hygiene worker to persuade housewives to decontaminate their drinking water by boiling it met with only limited success in the face of these cultural convictions.[4]

It is interesting to note that the hot-cold idea system now widely current in Latin American apparently goes back many centuries to the humoral theory of disease expounded by Hippocrates and Galen and transmitted by Arabs to Spain and by Spaniards to the New World, where it retained a place in formal medical teaching until the eighteenth century.[5] Folk theories of medicine in contemporary rural India and in other parts of Asia indicate that the humoral theory spread in that direction, too, if indeed it did not have its origin somewhere in Asia. In the course of its travels the humoral theory underwent modification, so that its present form in Asia is not identical to the one in Latin America. It is remarkable that cultural complexes such as the hot-cold idea system should persist, however altered, through such long periods of time.

Objectively viewed, the cosmos and all its contents are morally neutral; nothing is good or bad in itself; it simply is. But humans clothe their cosmos in a moral cloak. They evaluate it, holding some things to be good and others evil. Values, the fundamental bases for choosing between alternative courses of actions, are a central part of any group's culture. Values differ, but these differences are less apparent than differences in language, dress, posture, rules of etiquette, or other overt features of the culture. Because values usually remain below the level of awareness, we are particularly apt to impose our own values upon others on the innocent assumption that we are merely helping them achieve better health.

## CLEANLINESS IN WESTERN CULTURES

Members of our own middle class tend to make a virtue of tidiness, apart from possible bearing on sanitation. Cleanliness is both a health measure and a cultural value. This distinction can be appreciated if we glance back through history to see the shifting value assigned to bathing and cleanliness from the time of the ancient Greeks. Such a review also illustrates the connectedness of the parts of culture.[6]

Although they built no great baths, the Greeks valued athletic sports and despised the Persians for their false modesty in keeping the body covered. The Romans, taking over much of the Greek cult of the body, constructed enormous public baths where men of leisure spent hours daily. The early Christians set themselves against the established pagan religion and also against many of the attitudes and amenities inherent in Roman culture. Baths were construed as instruments of paganism and vice, as devices for softening the body rather than saving the soul. Before long, even minimum cleanliness by current standards was seen as the road to ruin. The ascetic saint was indifferent to filth; attention to personal cleanliness, especially on the part of a man, incurred the suspicion that one might not be too good a Christian.

Bathing occupied an important place, however, in the lives of Europeans during medieval times. As the vessel of the soul, the body needed to be preserved. The monastery of the early Middle Ages had its bathroom for friars and pilgrims. By the thirteenth century, public bathhouses had come into use in the cities, providing both steam and water baths along with haircuts and minor surgery. But the presence of food and drink, young women and music increasingly coverted the bathhouses into places of amusement and eventually earned the opposition of the clergy. Moreover, the bathhouses became centers of infection when syphilis began to plague Europe at the end of the fifteenth century. Municipal bathing disappeared from the urban scene, private houses lacked baths, and the entire custom of bathing was condemned for reasons of morality and health.

Interest in bodily cleanliness was revived in the eighteenth century with the growth of enlightenment, the increase in comforts, the refinement of social manners, and the rise of the bourgeoisie. The lead in this direction was taken in countries where the new wealthy middle class became especially influential; hence the scrubbing of Dutch doorsteps and the proverbial Englishman with his portable bath. Today, in the United States, prosperity, democracy, and frequency of bathing have become linked values. Americans say that cleanliness is next to godliness, an indication that bathing and cleanliness are affect-laden values in contemporary middle-class culture as well as a means to better health. Yet even in the United States bathing is neither as old nor as general as people now assume. Ackerknecht reminds us that President Fillmore was as much attacked for buying a bathtub for the White House in 1851 as was Harry Truman . . . for his balcony.[7]

We might have more success in exporting our technical means for improving the world's health if we could manage to divest these means of the values and other cultural trappings that accompany their use in the American scene. It might then be easier to fit our technical means into foreign cultural contexts. To do this we need to become skilled in perceiving our own cultural contours and those of the country we strive to help. . . .

## NOTES

1. J. Robert Moose, *Village Life in Korea, 1911.*

2. H.G. Barnett, *Innovation: The Basis of Cultural Change* (New York: McGraw-Hill, 1953,) p. 91.

3. Mimeographed material distributed by the Research-cum-Action Project in Environmental Sanitation, Government of India Ministry of Health.

4. Edward Wellin, "Water Boiling in a Peruvian Town." In *Health, Culture and Community: Public Reactions to Health Programs* (Benjamin D. Paul, Ed.) (New York: Russel Sage Foundation, 1955).

5. George M. Foster, *Use of Anthropological Methods and Data in Planning and Operation*. Pub. Health Rep., 68:848, 1953.

6. The following résumé is based on these sources: A.L. Kroeber, *Anthropology* (New York: Harcourt, Brace, 1948), pp. 600–602; H.E. Sigerist, *Medicine and Human Welfare* (New Haven, Conn.: Yale University Press, 1941), pp. 69–72; A.G. Varron, *Medieval Hygiene*, Ciba Symposia, vol. 1, 1939–1940, pp. 213–214.

7. Erwin H. Ackerknecht, Personal communication.

# REVIEW QUESTIONS

1. How are/were the following cultural elements linked to sanitation?
   a. smaller houses in Palau
   b. daily visits to the fields in rural India
   c. the "hot-cold" belief system in Latin America
   d. Western ideas about bathing
2. Why should we see the following statements as misinterpretations?
   a. "They" have more odd beliefs and habits than we do.
   b. Our ways and ideas are more advanced than "theirs."
   c. Customs and beliefs are isolated cultural elements.
3. Why is ethnocentrism a hindrance to understanding or working in another culture? Why is it a hindrance to understanding our own culture?
4. What specific steps could you take to decrease your own ethnocentric tendencies?

## Suggested Readings: Culture

Berger, Peter L., and Thomas Luckmann. *The Social Construction of Reality: A Trestise in the Sociology of Knowledge*. Garden City, N.Y.: Anchor Books, 1967.

Greenblat, Cathy Stein, and John H. Gagnon. "Temporary Strangers: Travel and Tourism from a Sociological Perspective," *Sociological Perspectives* 26 (Jan. 1983): 89–110.

Hall, Edward T. *The Silent Language*. Garden City, N.Y.: Anchor Books, 1959.

Horowitz, Ruth. *Honor and the American Dream: Culture and Identity in a Chicano Community.* New Brunswick, N.J.: Rutgers University Press, 1983.

Kephart, William. *Extraordinary Groups.* 2nd ed. New York: St. Martin's Press, 1982.

Largey, Gale Peter, and David Rodney Watson. "Sociology of Odors," *American Journal of Sociology* 77 (May 1972): 1021–1034.

# Part III. Transmission of Culture: Socialization

T HE HUMAN INFANT IS NOT BORN KNOWING WHAT TO EAT, WHAT TO VALUE, how to communicate, or what to believe about the social world or its own self. It is born with curiosity and, according to developmental psychologists, a need to "make sense" out of the events and objects it encounters. The infant interacts with others in its social milieu, searching for category systems, meanings, and rules. At the same time, other members of the child's social world attempt to mold, to instruct, to reward and punish, to explain the culture's symbols and ways of classifying experience. This two-way process of learning and teaching culture by and to new members, called *socialization*, enables the child to become a part of its society, to interact relatively smoothly with others, to share in the culture's common stock of symbols, norms, and knowledge.

Moreover, through the socialization process, the child develops a *self concept*. By this term we mean the sum of all cognitions or thoughts one holds about oneself. The self concept is comprised of what are sometimes called "identity elements" that are more or less organized into "subidentities" corresponding to societal statuses or categories. The child must learn the *categories* in which to think about itself—e.g., son, friend, female, driver, consumer, farmer, and so on—as well as learning *how to evaluate* its performance, relative to others, in these roles. Our self concepts are, then, learned by observing others and their reactions to us, as Charles Horton Cooley's term, "looking-glass self," implies.

In turn, our behavior is affected by our self concepts; we often act in ways that are consistent with the images of ourselves which we developed through interaction in our society. Sociologists say that the individual has *internalized* the culture once the societal categories and standards for evaluation are learned and applied to oneself. In other words, the individual comes to rely less on the input of others and to reward and punish him- or herself—by feeling guilt, pride, or shame—for behaving according to the rules of the culture.

The articles in this section illustrate a number of aspects of the socialization process. One of the most far-reaching categorizations in American culture is the one based on sex. No other social statuses have such an impact on the behavior of societal members. Children are socialized from infancy onward to the *social roles*, or scripts, attached to the statuses "male" and "female." Sandra and Daryl Bem's article, "Training the

Woman to Know Her Place: The Power of the Nonconscious Ideology,"
shows us how thoroughly most of us have internalized our culture's sex-
role scripts and how important are our gender subidentities. Although
some of our beliefs have changed in recent years, even the most "liberated" among us are still apt to see child care and housework as "wom-
en's work" and economic activity as largely "men's work." Furthermore, we often feel that we have chosen these roles from "free will,"
when in fact they have been learned. Bem and Bem argue that sex roles
have come to be problematic in today's society because it has become increasingly clear that they are inconsistent with other important values,
such as equality and freedom of choice. If we did not hold these latter
values, considerable confusion and tension would be avoided.

The next article, by Janet Lever, looks in depth at one of the subjects
introduced by Bem and Bem. Lever spent hundreds of hours observing
children at play. In "Sex Differences in the Games Children Play," she
shows us that boys' play activities are organized and structured differently from the activities that occupy girls. Furthermore, the structure of
play sends important messages to the players. "Boys' games" teach
players to be assertive, to compete, to be good team members, and to
protect their own rights. "Girls' play" teaches nurturance, role playing,
getting along with others, and protecting others' rights. The formal and
informal rules of boys' and girls' games and play activities, according to
Lever, have effects that may last long beyond childhood.

Sex roles are expectations that are important in almost all aspects of
one's life. Of course, there are many other roles that must be learned,
some of which are quite specific, like occupational roles. In advanced
technological societies, socialization to occupational roles most often begins in schools. But—as graduates of medical schools, truck-driving
schools, and police academies can all attest—conditions on the job and
expectations of co-workers play a major part in socialization to an occupation. Schools teach ideal norms, while the physician in the emergency
room, the driver on the interstate highway, and police on the street must
learn the "ropes," or the actual norms, to survive. We thus speak of socialization as occurring both formally and informally. In "New Cops on
the Street: Learning Normal Force," the final article in this section, Jennifer Hunt describes how rookie police officers are socialized, both formally (in the academy) and informally (on the streets), as to when and
how to use force on suspects.

As police academy graduates move along in their career, they will be
socialized to the new roles of perhaps rookie, sergeant, lieutenant, captain, and police chief. Likewise, all of us moving through occupational
and life-cycle stages will be socialized repeatedly to the new roles we are
to enact. Consider in your own case the process of learning the ins and
outs of the role of the "high school student" and then the "college student." Indeed, according to evidence collected by sociologists, as we
age, we are socialized to the role of "the dying."

# TRAINING THE WOMAN TO KNOW HER PLACE: THE POWER OF A NONCONSCIOUS IDEOLOGY

## Sandra L. Bem and Daryl J. Bem

IN THE BEGINNING GOD CREATED THE HEAVEN AND THE EARTH. . . . AND GOD said, let us make man in our image, after our likeness; and let them have dominion over the fish of the sea, and over the fowl of the air, and over the cattle, and over all the earth. . . . And the rib, which the Lord God had taken from man, made he a woman and brought her unto the man. . . . And the Lord God said unto the woman, What is this that thou has done? And the woman said, The serpent beguiled me, and I did eat. . . . Unto the woman He said, I will greatly multiply thy sorrow and thy conception; in sorrow, thou shalt bring forth children; and thy desire shall be to thy husband, and he shall rule over thee. (Gen. 1, 2, 3)

And lest anyone fail to grasp the moral of this story, Saint Paul provides further clarification:

For a man . . . is the image and glory of God; but the woman is the glory of man. For the man is not of the woman, but the woman of the man. Neither was the man created for the woman, but the woman for the man. (1 Cor. 11)

Let the woman learn in silence with all subjection. But I suffer not a woman to teach, nor to usurp authority over the man, but to be in silence. For Adam was first formed, then Eve. And Adam was not deceived, but the woman, being deceived, was in the transgression. Notwithstanding she shall be saved in childbearing, if they continue in faith and charity and holiness with sobriety. (1 Tim. 2)

And lest it be thought that only Christians have this rich heritage of ideology about women, consider the morning prayer of the Orthodox Jew:

Blessed art Thou, oh Lord our God, King of the Universe, that I was not born a gentile.

Blessed art Thou, oh Lord our God, King of the Universe, that I was not born a slave.

Blessed art Thou, oh Lord our God, King of the Universe, that I was not born a woman.

Or the Koran, the sacred text of Islam:

Men are superior to women on account of the qualities in which God has given them pre-eminence.

Sandra L. Bem and Daryl J. Bem, ''Training the Woman to Know Her Place: The Power of a Nonconscious Ideology,'' in Michele Hoffnung Garskof, ed., *Roles Women Play: Readings Toward Women's Liberation* (Belmont, Calif.: Brooks/Cole, 1971), pp. 84–96.

Because they think they sense a decline in feminine "faith, charity, and holiness with sobriety," many people today jump to the conclusion that the ideology expressed in these passages is a relic of the past. Not so. It has simply been obscured by an equalitarian veneer, and the ideology has now become nonconscious. That is, we remain unaware of it because alternative beliefs and attitudes about women go unimagined. We are like the fish who is unaware that his environment is wet. After all, what else could it be? Such is the nature of all nonconscious ideologies. Such is the nature of America's ideology about women. For even those Americans who agree that a black skin should not uniquely qualify its owner for janitorial or domestic service continue to act as if the possession of a uterus uniquely qualifies *its* owner for precisely that.

Consider, for example, the 1968 student rebellion at Columbia University. Students from the radical left took over some administration buildings in the name of equalitarian principles which they accused the university of flouting. Here were the most militant spokesmen one could hope to find in the cause of equalitarian ideals. But no sooner had they occupied the buildings than the male militants blandly turned to their sisters-in-arms and assigned them the task of preparing the food, while they—the menfolk—would presumably plan further strategy. The reply these males received was the reply they deserved, and the fact that domestic tasks behind the barricades were desegregated across the sex line that day is an everlasting tribute to the class consciousness of the ladies of the left.

But these conscious coeds are not typical, for the nonconscious assumptions about a woman's "natural" talents (or lack of them) are at least as prevalent among women as they are among men. A psychologist named Philip Goldberg (1968) demonstrated this by asking female college students to rate a number of professional articles from each of six fields. The articles were collated into two equal sets of booklets, and the names of the authors were changed so that the identical article was attributed to the male author (e.g., John T. McKay) in one set of booklets and to a female author (e.g., Joan T. McKay) in the other set. Each student was asked to read the articles in her booklet and to rate them for value, competence, persuasiveness, writing style, and so forth.

As he had anticipated, Goldberg found that the identical article received significantly lower ratings when it was attributed to a female author than when it was attributed to a male author. He had predicted this result for articles from professional fields generally considered the province of men, like law and city planning, but to his surprise, these coeds also downgraded articles from the fields of dietetics and elementary school education when they were attributed to female authors. In other words, these students rated the male authors as better at everything, agreeing with Aristotle that "we should regard the female nature as afflicted with a natural defectiveness." We repeated this experiment informally in our own classrooms and discovered that male students show the same implicit prejudice against female authors that Goldberg's female students showed. Such is the nature of a nonconscious ideology!

•   •   •

## INDIVIDUALITY AND SELF-FULFILLMENT

The dominant values of today's students concern personal growth on the one hand, and interpersonal relationships on the other. The first of these emphasizes individuality and self-fulfillment; the second stresses openness, honesty, and equality in all human relationships.

The values of individuality and self-fulfillment imply that each human being, male or female, is to be encouraged to "do his own thing." Men and women are no longer to be stereotyped by society's definitions. If sensitivity, emotionality, and warmth are desirable human characteristics, then they are desirable for men as well as for women. (John Wayne is no longer an idol of the young, but their pop-art satire.) If independence, assertiveness, and serious intellectual commitment are desirable human characteristics, then they are desirable for women as well as for men. The major prescription of this college generation is that each individual should be encouraged to discover and fulfill his own unique potential and identity, unfettered by society's presumptions.

But society's presumptions enter the scene much earlier than most people suspect, for parents begin to raise their children in accord with the popular stereotypes from the very first. Boys are encouraged to be aggressive, competitive, and independent, whereas girls are rewarded for being passive and dependent (Barry, Bacon, & Child, 1957; Sears, Maccoby, & Levin, 1957). In one study, six-month-old infant girls were already being touched and spoken to more by their mothers while they were playing than were infant boys. When they were thirteen months old, these same girls were more reluctant than the boys to leave their mothers; they returned more quickly and more frequently to them; and they remained closer to them throughout the entire play period. When a physical barrier was placed between mother and child, the girls tended to cry and motion for help; the boys made more active attempts to get around the barrier (Goldberg & Lewis, 1969). No one knows to what extent these sex differences at the age of thirteen months can be attributed to the mothers' behavior at the age of six months, but it is hard to believe that the two are unconnected.

As children grow older, more explicit sex-role training is introduced. Boys are encouraged to take more of an interest in mathematics and science. Boys, not girls, are given chemistry sets and microscopes for Christmas. Moreover, all children quickly learn that mommy is proud to be a moron when it comes to mathematics and science, whereas daddy knows all about these things. When a young boy returns from school all excited about biology, he is almost certain to be encouraged to think of becoming a physician. A girl with similar enthusiasm is told that she might want to consider nurse's training later so she can have ''an interesting job to fall back upon in case—God forbid—she ever needs to support herself.'' A very different kind of encouragement. And any girl who doggedly persists in her enthusiasm for science is likely to find her parents as horrified by the prospect of a permanent love affair with physics as they would be by the prospect of an interracial marriage.

These socialization practices quickly take their toll. By nursery school age, for example, boys are already asking more questions about how and why things work (Smith, 1933). In first and second grade, when asked to suggest ways of improving various toys, boys do better on the fire truck and girls do better on the nurse's kit, but by the third grade, boys do better regardless of the toy presented (Torrance, 1962). By the ninth grade, 25% of the boys, but only 3% of the girls, are considering careers in science or engineering (Flanagan, unpublished, cited by Kagan, 1964). When they apply for college, boys and girls are about equal on verbal aptitude tests, but boys score significantly higher on mathematical aptitude tests—about 60 points higher on the College Board examinations, for example (Brown, 1965, p. 162). Moreover, girls improve their mathematical performance if problems are reworded so that they deal with cooking and gardening, even though the abstract reasoning required for their solutions remains the same (Milton, 1958). Clearly, not just ability, but motivation too, has been affected.

But these effects in mathematics and science are only part of the story. A girl's long training in passivity and dependence appears to exact an even higher toll from her overall motivation to achieve, to search for new and independent ways of doing things, and to welcome the challenge of new and unsolved problems. In one study, for example, elementary school girls were more likely to try solving a puzzle by imitating an adult, whereas the boys were more likely to search for a novel solution not provided by the adult (McDavid, 1959). In another puzzle-solving study, young girls asked for help and approval from adults more frequently than the boys; and, when given the opportunity to return to the puzzles a second time, the girls were more likely to rework those they had already solved, whereas the boys were more likely to try puzzles they had been unable to solve previously (Crandall & Rabson, 1960). A girl's sigh of relief is almost audible when she marries and retires from the outside world of novel and unsolved problems. This, of course, is the most conspicuous outcome of all: the majority of American women become full-time homemakers [for some portion of their lives. Even women employed outside the home on a full-time basis continue to do the vast majority of child care and housework]. Such are the consequences of a nonconscious ideology.

But why does this process violate the values of individuality and self-fulfillment? It is *not* because some people may regard the role of homemakers as inferior to other roles. That is not the point. Rather, the point is that our society is managing to consign a large segment of its population to the role of homemaker solely on the basis of sex just as inexorably as it has in the past consigned the individual with a black skin to the role of janitor or domestic. It is not the quality of the role itself which is at issue here, but the fact that in spite of their unique identities, the majority of America's women end up in the *same* role.

Even so, however, several arguments are typically advanced to counter the claim that America's homogenization of its women subverts individuality and self-fulfillment. The three most common arguments invoke, respectively, (1) free will, (2) biology, and (3) complementarity.

1. The free will argument proposes that a 21-year-old woman is perfectly free to choose some other role if she cares to do so; no one is standing in her way. But this argument conveniently overlooks the fact that the society which has spent twenty years carefully marking the woman's ballot for her has nothing to lose in that twenty-first year by pretending to let her cast it for the alternative of her choice. Society has controlled not her alternatives, but her motivation to choose any but one of those alternatives. The so-called freedom to choose is illusory and cannot be invoked to justify the society which controls the motivation to choose.

2. The biological argument suggests that there may really be inborn differences between men and women in, say, independence or mathematical ability. Or that there may be biological factors beyond the fact that women can become pregnant and nurse children which uniquely dictate that they, but not men, should stay home all day and shun serious outside commitment. Maybe female hormones really are responsible somehow. One difficulty with this argument, of course, is that female hormones would have to be different in the Soviet Union where one-third of the engineers and 75% of the physicians are women. In America, women constitute less than 1% of the engineers and only 7% of the physicians (Dodge, 1966). Female physiology *is* different, and it may account for some of the psychological differences between the sexes, but America's sex-role ideology still seems primarily responsible for the fact that so few women emerge from childhood with the motivation to seek out any role beyond the one that our society dictates.

But even if there really were biological differences between the sexes along these lines, the biological argument would still be irrelevant. The reason can best be illustrated with an analogy.

Suppose that every black American boy were to be socialized to become a jazz musician on the assumption that he has a "natural" talent in that direction, or suppose that his parents should subtly discourage him from other pursuits because it is considered "inappropriate" for black men to become physicians or physicists. Most liberal Americans, we submit, would disapprove. But suppose that it *could* be demonstrated that black Americans, *on the average,* did possess an inborn better sense of rhythm than white Americans. Would *that* justify ignoring the unique characteristics of a *particular* black youngster from the very beginning and specifically socializing him to become a musician? We don't think so. Similarly, as long as a woman's socialization does not nurture her uniqueness, but treats her only as a member of a group on the basis of some assumed *average* characteristic, she will not be prepared to realize her own potential in the way that the values of individuality and self-fulfillment imply she should.

The irony of the biological argument is that it does not take biological differences seriously enough. That is, it fails to recognize the range of biological differences between individuals within the same sex. Thus, recent research has revealed that biological factors help determine many personality traits. Dominance and submissiveness, for example, have been found to have large inheritable components; in other words, biological factors *do* have the potential for partially determining how dominant or submissive an individual, male or female, will turn out to be. But the effects of this biological potential could be detected only in males (Gottesman, 1963). This implies that only the males in our culture are raised with sufficient flexibility, with sufficient latitude given to their biological differences, for their ''natural'' or biologically determined potential to shine through. Females, on the other hand, are subjected to a socialization which so ignores their unique attributes that even the effects of biology seem to be swamped. In sum, the biological argument for continuing America's homogenization of its women gets hoisted with its own petard.

3. Many people recognize that most women do [spend some or most of their lives as] full-time homemakers because of their socialization and that these women do exemplify the failure of our society to raise girls as unique individuals. But, they point out, the role of the homemaker is not inferior to the role of the professional man: it is complementary but equal.

This argument is usually bolstered by pointing to the joys and importance of taking care of small children. Indeed, mothers *and* fathers find child rearing rewarding, and it is certainly important. But this argument becomes insufficient when one considers that the average American woman now lives to age 74 and has her *last* child at about age 26; thus, by the time the woman is 33 or so, her children all have more important things to do with their daytime hours than to spend them entertaining an adult woman who has nothing to do during the second half of her life span. As for the other ''joys'' of homemaking, many writers (e.g., Friedan, 1963) have persuasively argued that the role of the homemaker has been glamorized far beyond its intrinsic worth. This charge becomes plausible when one considers that the average American homemaker spends the equivalent of a man's working day, 7.1 hours, in preparing meals, cleaning house, laundering, mending, shopping, and doing other household tasks. In other words, 43% of her waking time is spent in activity that would command an hourly wage on the open market well below the federally-set minimum for menial industrial work.

The point is not how little she would earn if she did these things in someone else's home, but that this use of time is virtually the same for homemakers with college degrees and for those with less than a grade school education, for women married to professional men and for women married to blue-collar workers. Talent, education, ability, interests, motivations: all are irrelevant. In our society, being female uniquely qualifies an individual for domestic work.

It is true, of course, that the American homemaker has, on the average, 5.1 hours of leisure time per day, and it is here, we are told, that each woman can express her unique identity. Thus, politically interested women can join the League of Women Voters; women with humane interests can become part-time Gray Ladies; women who love music can raise money for the symphony. Protestant women play Canasta; Jewish women play Mah-Jongg; brighter women of all denominations and faculty wives play bridge; and so forth.

But politically interested *men* serve in legislatures; *men* with humane interests become physicians or clinical psychologists; *men* who love music play in the symphony; and so forth. In other words, why should a woman's unique identity determine only the periphery of her life rather than its central core?

Again, the important point is not that the role of homemaker is necessarily inferior, but that the woman's unique identity has been rendered irrelevant. Consider the following "predictability test." When a boy is born, it is difficult to predict what he will be doing 25 years later. We cannot say whether he will be an artist, a doctor, or a college professor because he will be permitted to develop and to fulfill his own unique potential, particularly if he is white and middle class. But if the newborn child is a girl, we can usually predict with confidence how she will be spending her time 25 years later. Her individuality doesn't have to be considered; it is irrelevant.

The socialization of the American male has closed off certain options for him too. Men are discouraged from developing certain desirable traits such as tenderness and sensitivity just as surely as women are discouraged from being assertive and, alas, "too bright." Young boys are encouraged to be incompetent at cooking and child care just as surely as young girls are urged to be incompetent at mathematics and science.

Indeed, one of the errors of the early feminist movement in this country was that it assumed that men had all the goodies and that women could attain self-fulfillment merely by being like men. But that is hardly the utopia implied by the values of individuality and self-fulfillment. Rather, these values would require society to raise its children so flexibly and with sufficient respect for the integrity of individual uniqueness that some men might emerge with the motivation, the ability, and the opportunity to stay home and raise children without bearing the stigma of being peculiar. If homemaking is as glamorous as the women's magazines and television commercials portray it, then men, too, should have that option. Even if homemaking isn't all that glamorous, it would probably still be more fulfilling for some men than the jobs in which they now find themselves.

And if biological differences really do exist between men and women in "nurturance," in their inborn motivations to care for children, then this will show up automatically in the final distribution of men and women across the various roles: relatively fewer men will choose to stay at home. The values of individuality and self-fulfillment do not imply that there must be equality of outcome, an equal number of men and women in each role, but that there should be the widest possible variation in outcome consistent with the range of individual differences among people regardless of sex. At the very least, these values imply that society should raise its males so that they could freely engage in activities that might pay less than those being pursued by their wives without feeling that they were "living off their wives." One rarely hears it said of a woman that she is "living off her husband."

Thus, it is true that a man's options are limited by our society's sex-role ideology, but as the "predictability test" reveals, it is still the woman in our society whose identity is rendered irrelevant by America's socialization practices. In 1954, the United States Supreme Court declared that a fraud and hoax lay behind the slogan "separate but equal." It is unlikely that any court will ever do the same for the more subtle motto that successfully keeps the woman in her place: "complementary but equal."

## INTERPERSONAL EQUALITY

> Wives, submit yourselves unto your own husbands, as unto the Lord. For the husband is the head of the wife, even as Christ is the head of the church; and he is the savior of the body. Therefore, as the church is subject unto Christ, so let the wives be to their own husbands in everything. (Eph. 5)

As this passage reveals, the ideological rationalization that men and women hold complementary but equal positions is a recent invention of our modern "liberal" society, part of the equalitarian veneer which helps to keep today's version of the ideology nonconscious. Certainly those Americans who value open, honest, and equalitarian relationships generally are quick to reject this traditional view of the male-female relationship; and, an increasing number of young people even plan to enter "utopian" marriages very much like the following hypothetical example:

> Both my wife and I earned Ph.D. degrees in our respective disciplines. I turned down a superior academic post in Oregon and accepted a slightly less desirable position in New York where my wife could obtain a part-time teaching job and do research at one of the several other colleges in the area. Although I would have preferred to live in a suburb, we purchased a home near my wife's college so that she could have an office at home where she would be when the children returned from school. Because my wife earns a good salary, she can easily afford to pay a maid to do her major household chores. My wife and I share all other tasks around the house equally. For example, she cooks the meals, but I do the laundry for her and help her with many of her other household tasks.

Without questioning the basic happiness of such a marriage or its appropriateness for many couples, we can legitimately ask if such a marriage is, in fact, an instance of interpersonal equality. Have all the hidden assumptions about the woman's "natural" role really been eliminated? Has the traditional ideology really been exorcised? There is a very simple test. If the marriage is truly equalitarian, then its description should retain the same flavor and tone even if the roles of the husband and wife were to be reversed:

> Both my husband and I earned Ph.D. degrees in our respective disciplines. I turned down a superior academic post in Oregon and accepted a slightly less desirable position in New York where my husband could obtain a part-time teaching job and do research at one of the several other colleges in the area. Although I would have preferred to live in a suburb, we purchased a home near my husband's college so that he could have an office at home where he would be when the children returned from school. Because my husband earns a good salary, he can easily afford to pay a maid to do his major household chores. My husband and I share all other tasks around the house equally. For example, he cooks the meals, but I do the laundry for him and help him with many of his other household tasks.

It seems unlikely that many men or women in our society would mistake the marriage *just* described as either equalitarian or desirable, and thus it becomes apparent that the ideology about the woman's "natural" role nonconsciously permeates the entire fabric of such "utopian" marriages. It is true that the wife gains some measure of equality when her career can influence the final place of residence, but why is it the unquestioned assumption that the husband's career solely determines the initial set of alternatives that are to be considered? Why is it the wife who automatically seeks the part-time position? Why is it *her* maid instead of *their* maid? Why *her* laundry? Why *her* household tasks? And so forth throughout the entire relationship.

The important point here is not that such marriages are bad or that their basic assumptions of inequality produce unhappy, frustrated women. Quite the contrary. *It is the very happiness of the wives in such marriages that reveals society's smashing success in socializing its women.* It is a measure of the distance our society must yet traverse toward the goals of self-fulfillment and interpersonal equality that such marriages are widely characterized as utopian and fully equalitarian. It is a mark of how well the woman has been kept in her place that the husband in such a marriage is often idolized by women, including his wife, for "permitting" her to squeeze a career into the interstices of their marriage as long as his own career is not unduly inconvenienced. Thus is the white man blessed for exercising his power benignly while his "natural" right to that power forever remains unquestioned.

Such is the subtlety of a nonconscious ideology!

A truly equalitarian marriage would permit both partners to pursue careers or outside commitments which carry equal weight when all important decisions are to be made. It is here, of course, that the "problem" of children arises. People often assume that the woman who seeks a role beyond home and family would not care to have children. They assume that if she wants a career or serious outside commitment, then children must be unimportant to her. But of course no one makes this assumption about her husband. No one assumes that a father's interest in his career necessarily precludes a deep and abiding affection for his children or a vital interest in their development. Once again America applies a double standard of judgment. Suppose that a father of small children suddenly lost his wife. No matter how much he loved his children, no one would expect him to sacrifice his career in order to stay home with them on a full-time basis—*even if he had an independent source of income*. No one would charge him with selfishness or lack of parental feeling if he sought professional care for his children during the day. An equalitarian marriage simply abolishes this double standard and extends the same freedom to the mother, while also providing the framework for the father to enter more fully into the pleasures and responsibilities of child rearing. In fact, it is the equalitarian marriage which has the most potential for giving children the love and concern of two parents rather than one.

But few women are prepared to make use of this freedom. Even those women who have managed to finesse society's attempt to rob them of their career motivations are likely to find themselves blocked by society's trump card: the feeling that the raising of the children is their unique responsibility and—in time of crisis—ultimately theirs alone. Such is the emotional power of a nonconscious ideology.

In addition to providing this potential for equalized child care, a truly equalitarian marriage embraces a more general division of labor which satisfies what might be called "the roommate test." That is, the labor is divided just as it is when two men or two women room together in college or set up a bachelor apartment together. Errands and domestic chores are assigned by preference, agreement, flipping a coin, given to hired help, or—as is sometimes the case—left undone.

It is significant that today's young people, many of whom live this way prior to marriage, find this kind of arrangement within marriage so foreign to their thinking. Consider an analogy. Suppose that a white male college student decided to room or set up a bachelor apartment with a black male friend. Surely the typical white student would not blithely assume that his black roommate was to handle all the domestic chores. Nor would his conscience allow him to do so even in the unlikely event that his roommate would say: "No, that's okay. I like doing housework. I'd be happy to do it." We suspect that the typical white student would still not be comfortable if he took advantage of this offer, if he took advantage of the fact that his roommate had been socialized to be "happy" with such an arrangement. But change this hypothetical black roommate to a female marriage partner, and somehow the student's conscience goes to sleep. At most it is quickly tranquilized by the thought that "she is happiest when she is ironing for her loved one." Such is the power of a nonconscious ideology.

Of course, it may well be that she *is* happiest when she is ironing for her loved one.

Such, indeed, is the power of a nonconscious ideology!

## REFERENCES

Barry, H., III, Bacon, M. K., & Child, I. L. A cross-cultural survey of some sex differences in socialization, *Journal of Abnormal and Social Psychology*, 1957, 55, 327–332.

Brown, R. *Social psychology*. New York: Free Press, 1965.

Crandall, V. J. & Rabson, A. Children's repetition choices in an intellectual achievement situation following success and failure. *Journal of Genetic Psychology*, 1960, 97, 161–168.

Dodge, N. D. *Women in the Soviet economy*. Baltimore: The Johns Hopkins Press, 1966.

Flanagan, J. C. Project talent. Unpublished manuscript.

Friedan, B. *The feminine mystique*. New York: Norton, 1963.

Goldberg, P. Are women prejudiced against women? *Transaction*, April 1968, 5, 28–30.

Goldberg, S. & Lewis, M. Play behavior in the year-old infant: Early sex differences. *Child Development*, 1969, 40, 21–31.

Gottesman, I. I. Heritability of personality: A demonstration. *Psychological Monographs*, 1963, 77 (Whole No. 572).

Kagan, J. Acquisition and significance of sex typing and sex role identity. In M. L. Hoffman & L. W. Hoffman (Eds.), *Review of child development research, Vol. 1*. New York: Russell Sage Foundation, 1964. Pp. 137–167.

McDavid, J. W. Imitative behavior in preschool children. *Psychological Monographs*, 1959, 73 (Whole No. 486).

Milton, G. A. Five studies of the relation between sex role identification and achievement in problem solving. Technical Report No. 3, Department of Industrial Administration, Department of Psychology, Yale University, December, 1958.

Sears, R. R., Maccoby, E. E., & Levin, H. *Patterns of child rearing*. Evanston, Ill.: Row, Peterson, 1957.

Smith, M. E. The influences of age, sex, and situation on the frequency of form and functions of questions asked by preschool children. *Child Development*, 1933, 3, 201–213.

Torrance, E. P. *Guiding creative talent*. Englewood Cliffs, N.J.: Prentice-Hall, 1962.

# Review Questions

1. Bem and Bem state that, just as fish are not conscious of the water around them, so too may humans be unaware of the value systems, or ideologies, regarding inequality based on gender. Explain this statement, giving examples. What other value systems do we ignore?

2. What *agents* of socialization are involved in transmitting sex-role ideology in our culture?

3. Discuss the arguments based on (1) free will, (2) biology, and (3) complementarity, which are used in our society to justify the current distribution of the sexes in the occupational world. Then describe Bem and Bem's counterarguments.

4. The woman is effectively "trained to know her place" when she comes to accept traditional gender roles for herself. Explain how this process of *internalization* of norms occurs.

# SEX DIFFERENCES IN THE GAMES CHILDREN PLAY

Janet Lever

CHILDREN'S SOCIALIZATION IS ASSUMED TO HAVE CONSEQUENCES FOR their adult lives. When sex differences in socialization are considered, a chief concern is the extent to which one group (men) is advantaged over another (women). Assuming that girls' socialization equips them less well for occupational careers than boys', the question becomes, "what is it about socialization that has this effect?" Typically, the answers have focused on institutional agents, primarily the family but also the school, and on the values, attitudes, and bodies of knowledge imparted by them.

In this [article][1], I take a different tack. I examine the peer group as the *agent* of socialization, children's play as the *activity* of socialization, and role-skills as the *product* of socialization. Despite the importance attributed to peers during adolescence, the peer group and playtime have been relatively neglected in the study of child development. Perhaps social scientists have ignored the subject because they feel that sex differences in the preferred activities of children are obvious. Or maybe no one pauses to reflect upon the consequences of children's leisure activities because of the general tendency to view play as trivial. Yet it is during play that we have an opportunity to observe the development of precisely those role skills that are crucial for success in modern society.

Mead and Piaget are the foremost authorities who have recognized the social value of play and game participation. Mead (1934) suggests that the game experience is important as a situation in which the child can develop a sense of "self as object" and learn the complex role-playing skills relevant to later life. Mead illustrates his point by referring to the boys' games of baseball, but he does not tell us how girls, who are less familiar with team play, learn these critical lessons. Piaget (1965), through a close study of the game of marbles, meticulously explains how children develop moral values while they play rule-bounded games.[2]

He mentions almost as an afterthought that he did not find a single girls' game that has as elaborate an organization of rules as the boys' game of marbles. If we believe that games can be rich learning environments, then we must give serious attention to the differential exposure

Janet Lever, "Sex Differences in the Games Children Play," *Social Problems* 23, No. 4 (April 1976): 478–487.

of boys and girls to certain types of play.[3] The research question then becomes: Are there sex differences in the organization of children's playtime activities?

## METHODOLOGY

I used a variety of methods to gather as much data as possible in one year, 1972. Some 181 fifth-grade children, aged 10 and 11, were studied. Half were from a suburban school and the other half from two city schools in Connecticut. The entire fifth grade of each school was included in the study. I selected three schools whose student populations were predominantly white and middle-class—a choice made deliberately because I believe that race and class distinctions would only confound the picture at this stage of exploratory research.

Four techniques of data collection were employed: observation of schoolyards, semi-structured interviews, written questionnaires, and a diary record of playtime activities. The diary was a simple instrument used to document where the children had actually spent their time for the period of one week. Each morning I entered the classrooms and had the children fill out a short form on which they described *what* they had done the previous day after school, *whom* they did it with, *where* the activity took place, and *how long* it had lasted. Half the diaries were collected in the winter and half in the spring. Over two thousand diary entries were recorded. The questionnaire, designed to elicit how children spend their time away from school, was also administered by me inside the classroom. I conducted semi-structured interviews with one-third of the sample. Some were done in order to help me design the questionnaire and diary; others were done later to help me interpret the results. I gathered the observational data while watching children's play activity during recess, physical education classes, and after school.[4]

## THE DISTRIBUTION OF PLAY IN SPACE AND TIME

Children spend an extraordinary proportion of their day at play. For this reason alone the subject is worthy of serious investigation. Boys and girls alike spent only 24% of their free time (i.e., outside school) activities engaged in *non-play*. The activities most frequently mentioned were household chores, doing homework, and going to religious services.[5]

Another 24% of the activities listed in the diaries were neither "play" nor "non-play," but rather *vicarious pastimes*. The most important pastime, by far, was watching TV. Again, virtually no sex differences were found; both boys and girls watched TV from 15 to 20 hours per week. However, there were strong differences in the types of shows preferred by each sex. Generally speaking, girls preferred family-oriented situation comedies and boys preferred adventure shows.

Looking now at the 52% of the activities representing *real play*, we see that the differences between boys and girls become clear and strong. Following are six differences I observed:

*First, boys play outdoors far more than girls.* Many of the preferred activities of girls—like playing with Barbie dolls or board games—are best played indoors. Many of the boys' preferred activities—like team sports or fantasy games like "War"—have to be played outdoors. According to the diaries, 40% of the girls compared with 15% of the boys spent less than one-quarter of their playtime outdoors. This sex difference has several important implications. Girls, playing indoors, are necessarily restricted in body movement and vocal expressions. Boys, playing outdoors, move in larger, more open spaces and go farther away from the home, which, undoubtedly, is part of their greater independence training. We can think of girls' indoor games (usually played behind closed doors) as *private* affairs whereas boys' outdoor games are *public* and open to surveillance.

*Second*, even though boys and girls spent the same amount of their playtime alone (approximately 20%), when they were involved in social play, *boys more often played in larger groups*. This second sex difference is related to the first, for indoor environments place structural limitations on the maximum number of participants that can join in play. But this finding is also independent of the first point, for, according to the diary data, girls played in smaller groups even when they were outdoors. The nature of boys' games is such that a larger number of participants is required for proper play. For example, team sports require a larger number of players than activities like tag, hopscotch, or jumprope. On the questionnaire, 72% of the boys compared with 52% of the girls reported that their neighborhood games usually include four or more persons. Diary and observational data ran in the same direction, although the sex differences reflected were slightly weaker.[6]

*Third, boys' play occurs in more age-heterogeneous groups.* Children between ages 8 and 12 prefer to play in sex-segregated and age-homogeneous groups. But if boys' games require a larger number of participants, the limited availability of their age-peers necessitates allowing some younger children to join the game. The implicit understanding is that "you're better off with a little kid in the outfield than no one at all."

For example, I witnessed numerous ice hockey games where ages ranged from 9 to 15 or 16. The youngest children tried their best to keep up with the older ones or dropped out. They learned to accept their bruises, stifle their frustrations, or not be invited to play again. The very few times I observed girls in age-mixed play was at summer camp when the 10–12-year-olds used much younger children of 5 and 6 as "live dolls," leading them in circle songs like "ring around the rosy" or versions of tag like "duck, duck, goose." Here the oldest girls had to play on the level of the youngest instead of vice versa. The implications of this female play pattern for learning child care/nurturance skills are so obvious as to require little comment.[7]

*Fourth, girls more often play in predominantly male games than boys play in girls' games.* We would expect more girls to be included in boys' games in accordance with the same principle: "you're better off with even a girl in the outfield than no one at all." Besides, there are theoretical reasons to make this prediction. It is believed that girls are punished neither as early nor as severely for sex-inappropriate behavior (Lynn, 1966).

The evidence for this proposition is mixed. In each of the three schools, there were one or two girls who were skilled enough to be included as regular members of the boys' basketball or baseball teams. On the other hand, there were many occasions when boys were seen playing girls' games like hopscotch or jumprope too. They did this without being censured, for they entered the game in the role of "buffoon" or "tease"—there to interrupt and annoy the girls and not be taken as serious participants. This is a clear example of what Goffman (1961) calls "role distance." The point to be made here is that girls playing boys' games had to do so as serious participants and suffered the consequence of being labelled a "tomboy," whereas the boys had a convenient protective device available to soften the consequences of sex-inappropriate play behavior.

*Fifth, boys play competitive games more often than girls.* For the purposes of analysis, a distinction was made between play and games.[8] *Play* was defined as a *cooperative* interaction that has no explicit goal, no end point, and no winners. To the contrary, formal *games* are *competitive* interactions, governed by a set body of rules, and aimed at achieving an explicit, known goal (e.g., baskets, touchdowns). Formal games have a predetermined end point (e.g., when one opponent reaches so-many points, or at the end of the ninth inning) that is simultaneous with the declaration of a winner. Some activities may be organized as either play or game. For instance, just riding bikes is play whereas racing bikes is a game. Sixty-five percent of the play activities boys reported in their diaries were formal games, compared with 35% of the girls' activities.

In other words, *girls played more* than boys and *boys gamed more* than girls. Boys' greater involvement in team sports accounts for much of the strength of this sex difference in competitiveness, as well as the other sex differences described. But team sports constituted only 30% of the boys' play activities; if they were excluded from the analysis, the sex differences reported above would be weakened but by no means would they disappear. For example, eliminating team sports for both sexes, 54% of the boys' activities and 30% of the girls' activities are competitively structured. That is to say, if there were no team sports, we would still find important differences in the nature of the games boys and girls play.

*Sixth, boys' games last longer than girls' games.* According to the diary data, it was found that 72% of all boys' activities lasted longer than 60 minutes while only 43% of the girls' play activities did so. This finding was supported by recess observations. Boys' games lasting the entire period of 25 minutes were common, but in a whole year in the field, I did not observe a single girls' activity that lasted longer than 15 minutes.

There are several possible explanations for this sex difference. The most obvious is that the *ceiling of skill*[9] is higher in boys' games. A group of eight-year-olds find the game of baseball fun and challenging, and those same boys at twelve years of age can play the game and enjoy it just as much because the requisite skills have been developing all along; thus, the element of challenge remains. By contrast, girls who could play the games of jumprope and tag in the first grade are still playing them in the fifth grade but find them ''boring'' now. To be sure, they are better jumpers and runners, but the ceiling of skill was reached long ago. Moreover, girls' games have less structured potential for surprise, such as stealing bases or bunting as in the game of baseball. In short, it is likely that boys find their games more challenging and, therefore, have a longer span of attention.

Even when girls play games with a high ceiling of skill, the games often end shortly after they begin because the players have not developed the motor skills necessary to keep the action exciting. Some girls I watched could not catch or throw a volleyball. The one spontaneous girls' sports game I observed—a game of kickball—ended after fifteen minutes because the fielders had not succeeded in getting a single player out, and they were both frustrated and bored.

Another reason that boys' games continued for a longer period of time than girls' games is because boys could resolve their disputes more effectively. During the course of this study, boys were seen quarreling all the time, but not once was a game terminated because of a quarrel, and no game was interrupted for more than seven minutes. In the gravest debates, the final word was always to ''repeat the play,'' generally followed by a chorus of ''cheaters proof.'' The P.E. teacher in one school noted that his boys seemed to enjoy the legal debates every bit as much as the game itself. Even players who were marginal because of lesser skills or size took equal part in these recurring squabbles. Learning to deal with disputes may have been facilitated by the model set by the older boys during the age-mixed play referred to earlier.[10] Piaget argues that children learn respect for rules by playing rule-bounded games; Kohlberg (1964) adds that these lessons are greatest where there are areas of ambiguity and the players experience dissonance.

If Kohlberg is right, the moral lessons inherent in girls' play are fewer since there are almost no areas of ambiguity comparable to a player sliding into first base. Traditional girls' games like jumprope and hopscotch are *turn-taking* games where the nature of the competition is *indirect* (that is, there is preordained action: first my turn, then your turn, finally we compare achievements). "Hogging" is impossible when participation is determined by turn-taking; nor can personal fouls occur when competition is indirect. These turn-taking games do not contain contingent rules of strategy as in sports games; rather they are regulated by invariable rules of procedure. Given the structure of girls' games, disputes are not likely to occur. Thus, girls gain little experience in the judicial process. This lack of experience shows dramatically when they do play games where rule interpretation and adjudication are important. Most girls interviewed claimed that when a quarrel begins, the game breaks up, and little effort is made to resolve the problem. As I observed almost no examples of self-organized sports games, let me quote one interviewee, the captain of the girls' after-school soccer team, for a description of what occurs:

> Girls' soccer is pretty bad because most of the girls don't show up every time. We have to keep changing our teams to make them even. Then pretty soon we start arguing over whether something was fair or not. And then some girls quit and go home if they don't get their way. Sometimes calling them "babies" helps to get them to stay and play a while longer.

Other girls concurred, and some complained that their friends could not resolve the basic issues of choosing up sides, deciding who is to be captain, which team will start, and sometimes not even what game to play!

The most striking example of boys' greater consciousness and experience with rules was witnessed in a gym class when the teacher introduced a game called "newcombe," a variation on volleyball. The principle rule was that the ball had to be passed three times before it could be returned to the other side of the net. Although this game was new to both the boys and the girls, the boys did not once forget the "3-pass" rule, yet the girls forgot it on over half the volleys that first day.

## DISCUSSION

Even though barriers still exist, many forms of discrimination against women are beginning to be eliminated. Some social scientists have oriented their research to answer the question: If we succeed in ending all forms of discrimination on the basis of sex, is there anything about the way we raise our daughters that will present obstacles to their pursuance of any occupational choice, including the professions and higher levels of business administration? The answers have been in the affirmative; the focus has been on personality and motivation. Some have examined aspects of childhood socialization that produce dependent, passive, obedient personalities in girls (Bronfenbrenner, 1961; Kagan, 1964). Others have stressed aspects of training that limit girls' motivation for success in the occupational world (Horner, 1972).

My own observations, however, lead me to stress a rather different theme, namely, that the differences in leisure patterns of boys and girls lead to the development of particular *social skills* and capacities. These skills, in turn, are important for the performance of different adult roles. Specifically, I suggest that boys' games may help prepare their players for successful performance in a wide range of work settings in modern society. In contrast, girls' games may help prepare their players for the private sphere of the home and their future roles as wives and mothers.

Boys' games provide many valuable lessons. The evidence presented here suggests that boys' games further independence training, encourage the development of organizational skills necessary to coordinate the activities of a numerous and diverse group of persons, and offer experience in rule-bounded events and the adjudication of disputes. Mead offered us the insight that team sports teach young children to play a role at the same time as they take into account the roles of other players.

Furthermore, boys' experience in controlled and socially approved competitive situations may improve their ability to deal with interpersonal competition in a forthright manner. And experience in situations demanding interdependence between teammates should help boys incorporate more general cooperative skills, as well as giving some team members (especially the older boys during age-mixed play) very specific training in leadership skills. The social and organizational skills learned in large play groups may generalize to non-play situations.

On the other hand, girls' games may provide a training ground for the development of delicate socio-emotional skills. We have seen that girls' play occurs in small, intimate groups, most often the dyad. It occurs in private places and often involves mimicking primary human relationships instead of playing formal games. Their age-mixed play is the type that helps girls to develop nurturance skills. Finally, girls' play, to a large extent, is spontaneous and free of structure and rules; its organization is cooperative more often than competitive.

The qualitative data collected through interviews and observation present a more convincing picture of girls' early friendships as a training ground for their later heterosexual courtship relations. The girls in this study claimed to feel more comfortable in pairs, less so in a triad, and least comfortable in groups of four or more. Most girls interviewed said they had a single "best" friend with whom they played nearly every day. They learn to know that person and her moods so well that through non-verbal cues alone, a girl understands whether her playmate is hurt, sad, happy, bored, and so on. There is usually an open show of affection between these little girls—both physically in the form of hand-holding and verbally through "love notes" that reaffirm how special each is to the other. Sharing secrets binds the union together, and "telling" the secrets to outsiders is symbolic of the "break-up." Such friendships may vary from two weeks to two years or more in duration. These girls experience the heartbreak of serial monogamy long before heterosexual dating begins some three to six years later.

Simmel's (1950:123) reflections on the dyad explain the precarious nature of these special relationships and why the larger play groups of boys are more stable:

> The dyad has a different relation to each of its two elements than have larger groups to their members. . . . The social structure here rests immediately on the other of the two, and the secession of either would destroy the whole. The dyad, therefore, does not attain that super-personal life which the individual feels to be independent of himself.

There can be no shift from the person to the role, let alone from the role to the collectivity, for the dyadic relationship is characterized by the *unique* interaction between two individuals. A girl engaged in pastimes with one of a series of "best friends" may be gaining training appropriate for the later dating experiences where sensitivity skills are called for, but she is less likely than her sports-oriented brother to learn organizationally relevant skills. Returning to Meadian terms, boys develop the abillity to take the role of the *generalized other,* whereas girls develop empathy to take the role of the *particular other.*

To be sure, boys also have strong friendships, and the interpersonal skills they learn through their games are many. But these interpersonal skills are more instrumental than expressive. A boy and his best friend often find themselves on opposing teams. They must learn ways to resolve disputes so that the quarrels do not become so heated that they rupture friendships. Boys must learn to "depersonalize the attack." Not only do they learn to compete against friends, they also learn to cooperate with teammates whom they may or may not like personally. Such interpersonal skills have obvious value in an organizational milieu. Boys learn to share the limelight, for they are told that team goals must be put ahead of opportunities for self-glorification. The lessons in emotional discipline are repeated daily: boys must restrain their energy, temper, and frustration for the cohesiveness of the group. Self-control, rather than self-expression, is valued highly. Good-natured participation in any activity the majority elects to pursue is expected from all. In other words, boys must develop the social skills of "gregariousness" and "amiability"—social skills which Riesman (1961) claims are more closely linked to modern organizational life than are technical skills. . . .[10]

[T]he world of play and game activity may be a major force in the development and perpetuation of differential abilities between the sexes— differences that reinforce the preparation of girls for traditional socioemotional roles. It might be wise to review educational policy with these thoughts in mind. Perhaps we should support a broadening of physical education programs for girls to include learning opportunities now found primarily in boys' play activities. Since deeply ingrained patterns are slow to change, alternate opportunities might be developed in non-play situations—for example, encouraging teachers to design group projects in which girls can gain experience in specialization of labor, coordination of roles, and interdependence of effort. At the same time, males have roles as husbands and fathers as well as occupational roles. A fully considered social policy will have to assess the extent to which emphasis on large-scale, organized sports for boys means systematic underexposure to activities in which delicate socio-emotional skills are learned.

Children's play patterns are part of that vast behavioral repertoire passed on from generation to generation. American parents have always encouraged their boys to play contact team sports because they believe the "male nature" requires rough and tumble action, and organized competition is the best outlet for this surplus energy. Parents believe their girls are frail and less aggressive, and therefore do not enjoy serious competition; rather, they believe girls feel their maternal instincts early and prefer playing with dolls and reconstructing scenarios of the home. But parents give little thought to the structural components of those games and to the lessons inherent in each type of play. Yet it is perfectly clear that if the very different organization of children's play has *any* impact on the performance of adult roles, that influence must be a conservative one, serving to protect the traditional sex-role divisions within our society.

## NOTES

1. This paper is drawn from my Ph.D. dissertation (Lever, 1974). The research was supported by an N. I. M. H. Fellowship. I would like to thank Stanton Wheeler, Louis W. Goodman, and R. Stephen Warner for their advice and encouragement throughout this project.

2. Sometimes the word "rule" is used to refer to game norms or customs. Here the term "rule-bounded" is used in the narrower sense and refers to games in which the rules are known to all players before the game begins and remain reasonably constant from one game situation to the next and in which the infraction of those rules carries penalties (Eifermann, 1972).

3. Among others who have recognized the importance of play are Huizinga, 1955; Moore and Anderson, 1969; and Stone, 1965.

4. Further details on data collection can be found in Lever, 1974. As a contribution to the folklore of strategies of field research, I should mention that I sat in my car near a schoolyard every lunch hour for a month before formally beginning this study. I doubt a male researcher could have lasted three days before being questioned.

5. It should be said that the distinction between play and work for children is even fuzzier than it is for adults. A child walking to school appears to us only to be walking, but she may be involved in a private game like avoiding stepping on cracks; or, the newspaper boy making his deliveries appears to be working,

which he is, yet simultaneously he may be immersed in a game of target practice with each shot at our doors. Some things we adults consider work—like cooking and baking—the children clearly defined as play, and were so categorized in my study, while there was no doubt that boys and girls alike saw making beds and washing dishes as work.

6. One of the important features of using different measures is that one gets a feel for what different measures produce. In this study, the children's statements of what they *usually* do and what they *prefer* to do (i.e., the questionnaire and interview data) showed the strongest sex differences. My own observation of what children did in the arena of the public schoolyard reflected differences of intermediate strength. The diary data—i.e., what children *actually* do when away from the eyes of parents, teachers and peers of the opposite sex—showed the weakest differences. In other words, the diary data were furthest from the cultural stereotypes of what boys and girls *ought to be doing*. Nevertheless, sex differences reported in the diaries are often strong.

7. The opportunity for age-mixed play is different for fifth-grade boys and girls. While boys' sports continue to be of interest through the teens and beyond, girls have already dropped out of the game culture by the time they reach age 13 or 14. Psychologists who have noted an earlier decline in girls' participation in schoolyard play believe it is due to girls' earlier maturation rate and superior verbal skills. The accepted argument is that girls are able to exchange games for conversation earlier and with more satisfaction (Eifermann, 1968:76). Leaving aside the empirical question of differential skills, I suggest a reversal in the casual model. Based on evidence presented in this paper, we can conclude that our culture is deficient in non-sports games that are sufficiently sophisticated and challenging for older girls, thereby forcing them to drop out of playground activity. Development of verbal skills may be seen as a consequence, rather than a cause, of this pattern.

8. This distinction is consistent with that made by G. H. Mead (1934), as well as the classificatory schemes of contemporary observers of play and games (Sutton-Smith *et al.*, 1963).

9. Csikszentmihalyi and Bennett (1971) coined this term.

10. Wheeler (1966:60) points out the advantages of being part of a system with *serial* rather than disjunctive socialization. In this case, it means that when older boys permit younger ones to join them in their games, they in effect teach their juniors a great deal about the setting, not only in terms of the requisite physical skills but the social ones as well. In this context, such lessons are more often due to sheer exposure than to self-conscious instruction.

## REFERENCES

Brofenbrenner, Urie
    1961 "The changing American child: a speculative analysis." *Merrill-Palmer Quarterly* 7:73–83, 89.

Csikszentmihalyi, M. and S. Bennett
    1971 "An exploratory model of play." *American Anthropologist*, 73:45–58.

Eifermann, Rivka
  1968 "School children's games." U.S. Office of Education, Bureau of Research. (Mimeographed Report.)

  1972 "Free social play: a guide to directed playing." Unpublished paper.

Goffman, Erving
  1961 *Encounters.* Indianapolis: Bobbs-Merrill Co.

Horner, Matina
  1972 "Toward an understanding of achievement-related conflicts in women." *Journal of Social Issues,* 28:157–175.

Huizinga, Johan
  1955 *Homo Ludens: A Study of the Play-Element in Culture.* Boston: Beacon Press.

Kagan, Jerome
  1964 "Acquisition and significance of sex typing and sex-role identification." Pp. 137–167 in M. L. Hoffmann and L. W. Hoffmann (eds.), *Review of Child Development Research,* Vol. I, New York: Russell Sage Foundation.

Kohlberg, Lawrence
  1964 "Development of moral character and moral ideology." Pp. 383–431 in M. L. Hoffmann and L. W. Hoffmann (eds.), *Review of Child Development Research,* Vol. I. New York: Russell Sage Foundation.

Lever, Janet
  1974 *Games Children Play: Sex Differences and the Development of Role Skills.* Unpublished Ph.D. dissertation. Department of Sociology. Yale University.

Lynn, David B.
  1966 "The process of learning parental and sex-role identification." *Journal of Marriage and the Family,* 28:466–470.

Mead, George Herbert
  1934 "Play, the game and the generalized other." Pp. 152–164 in *Mind, Self and Society.* Chicago: University of Chicago Press.

Moore, O. K. and A. R. Anderson
  1969 "Some principles for the design of clarifying educational environments." Pp. 571–613 in David A. Goslin (ed.) *Handbook of Socialization Theory and Research.* Chicago: Rand McNally.

Piaget, Jean
  1965 *The Moral Judgment of the Child.* New York: Free Press.

Riesman, David
  1961 *The Lonely Crowd.* New Haven: Yale University Press.

Simmel, Georg
  1950 *The Sociology of Georg Simmel.* Trans. and ed. by Kurt H. Wolff, New York: Free Press.

Stone, Gregory P.
  1965 "The play of little children," *Quest* 4:23–31.

Sutton-Smith, B., B. G. Rosenberg, and E. F. Morgan, Jr.
   1963 "Development of sex differences in play choices during pre-adoles-
      cence." *Child Development* 34:119–126.

Wheeler, Stanton
   1966 "The structure of formally organized socialization settings." Pp. 53–116
      in Orville G. Brim, Jr., and Stanton Wheeler (eds.) *Socialization After
      Childhood.* New York: John Wiley and Sons.

# REVIEW QUESTIONS

1. In what ways are the play activities of the boys and girls in this study alike?

2. What are the six differences between boys' and girls' activities that Lever found?

3. What kinds of roles and skills do boys' activities ignore or discourage?

4. What kinds of roles and skills do girls' activities ignore or discourage?

# NEW COPS ON THE STREET: LEARNING NORMAL FORCE

Jennifer Hunt

THE POLICE ARE REQUIRED TO HANDLE A VARIETY OF PEACE-KEEPING AND law enforcement tasks including settling disputes, removing drunks from the street, aiding the sick, controlling crowds, and pursuing criminals. What unifies these diverse activities is the possibility that their resolution might require the use of force. Indeed, the capacity to use force stands at the core of the police mandate (Bittner, 1980).

• • •

The following research[1] . . . explores how police themselves classify and evaluate acts of force as either legal, normal, or excessive. Legal force is that coercion necessary to subdue, control, and restrain suspects in order to take them into custody. Although force not accountable in legal terms is technically labelled excessive by the courts and the public, the police perceive many forms of illegal force as normal. Normal force involves coercive acts that specific "cops" on specific occasions formulate as necessary, appropriate, reasonable, or understandable, although not always legitimated or admired. . . .

Most officers are expected to use both legal and normal force as a matter of course in policing the streets. In contrast, excessive force or brutality exceeds even working police notions of normal force. These are acts of coercion that cannot be explained by the routine police accounting practices ordinarily used to justify or excuse force. Brutality is viewed as illegal, illegitimate, and often immoral violence, but the police draw the lines in extremely different ways and at different points than do either the court system or the public.

These processes of assessing and accounting for the use of force, with special reference to the critical distinction between normal and excessive force as drawn by the police, will be explored [here]. The study begins by examining how rookie police learn on the street to use and account for force in a manner that contradicts what they were taught at the academy. It . . . is based on approximately eighteen months of participant observation in a major urban police department referred to as the Metro City

Excerpted from Jennifer Hunt, "Police Accounts of Normal Force," *URBAN LIFE* 13, No. 4 (January 1985): 315–341. The larger article contains an analysis of how police learn to justify and excuse the levels of force they employ.

P.D. I attended the police academy with male and female recruits and later rode with individual officers in one-person cars on evening and night shifts in high crime districts. . . . [2]

## LEARNING TO USE NORMAL FORCE

• • •

In the formal world of the police academy, the recruit learns to account for force by reference to legality. He or she is issued the regulation instruments and trained to use them to subdue, control, and restrain a suspect. If threatened with great bodily harm, the officer learns that he can justifiably use deadly force and fire his revolver. Yet the recruit is taught that he cannot use baton, jack, or gun unnecessarily to torture, maim, or kill a suspect.

When recruits leave the formal world of the academy and are assigned to patrol a district, they are introduced to an informal world in which police recognize normal as well as legal and brutal force. Through observation and instruction, rookies gradually learn to apply force and account for its use in terms familiar to the street cop. First, rookies learn to adjust their arsenals to conform to street standards. They are encouraged to buy the more powerful weapons worn by veteran colleagues as these colleagues point out the inadequacy of a wooden baton or compare their convoy jacks to vibrators. They quickly discover that their department-issued equipment marks them as new recruits. At any rate, within a few weeks, most rookies have dispensed with the wooden baton and convoy jack and substituted them with the more powerful plastic nightstick and flat headed slapjack.[3]

Through experience and informal instruction, the rookie also learns the street use of these weapons. In school, for example, recruits are taught to avoid hitting a person on the head or neck because it could cause lethal damage. On the street, in contrast, police conclude that they must hit wherever it causes the most damage in order to incapacitate the suspect before they themselves are harmed. New officers also learn that they will earn the respect of their veteran co-workers not by observing legal niceties in using force, but by being "aggressive" and using whatever force is necessary in a given situation.

Peer approval helps neutralize the guilt and confusion that rookies often experience when they begin to use force to assert their authority. One female officer, for example, learned she was the object of a brutality suit while listening to the news on television. At first, she felt so mortified that she hestitated to go to work and face her peers. In fact, male colleagues greeted her with a standing ovation and commented, "You can use our urinal now." In their view, any aggressive police officer regularly using normal force might eventually face a brutality suit or civilian complaint. Such accusations confirm the officer's status as a "street cop" rather than an "inside man" who doesn't engage in "real police work."[4]

Whereas male rookies are assumed to be competent dispensers of force unless proven otherwise, women are believed to be physically weak, naturally passive, and emotionally vulnerable.[5] Women officers are assumed to be reluctant to use physical force and are viewed as incompetent "street cops" until they prove otherwise. As a result, women rookies encounter special problems in learning to use normal force in the process of becoming recognized as "real street cops." It becomes crucial for women officers to create or exploit opportunities to display their physical abilities in order to overcome sexual bias and obtain full acceptance from co-workers. As a result, women rookies are encouraged informally to act more aggressively and to display more machismo than male rookies. Consider the following incident where a young female officer reflects upon her use of force during a domestic disturbance:

And when I get there, if goddamn, there isn't a disturbance going on. So Tom comes, the guy that I went to back up. The male talks to him. I take the female and talk to her. And the drunk (cop) comes and the sergeant comes and another guy comes. So while we think we have everything settled, and we have the guy calmed down, he turns around and says to his sister, no less, that's who it is, "Give me the keys to my car!" And with that, she rips them out of her pocket and throws them at him. Now, he goes nuts. He goes into a Kung fu stance and says he's gonna kill her. The drunk cop says, "Yo, knock it off!" and goes to grab him and the guy punches him. So Mike (the drunk cop) goes down. Tommy goes to grab him and is wrestling with him. And all the cops are trying to get in there. So I ran in with my stick and I stick the guy in the head. But I just missed Tommy's face and opened him (the suspect) up. So all of a sudden everybody's grabbin' him and I'm realizing that if we get him down, he won't hurt anybody. So I pushed the sergeant out of the way and I got my stick under the guy's legs and I pulled his legs out from under him and I yelled, "Tommy, take him down." I pulled his legs and he went down and I sat on him . . . .

So, when I [finally] get my cuffs, we cuff him. And we're sitting there talking. And Tommy, he has no regard for me whatsoever. . . . The guy's opened up and he bled all over Tommy's shirt. And I turned around and said, "Tommy, look at your shirt. There's blood all over your shirt." He said, "Who the hell almost clobbered me?" I said, "I'm sorry Tom, that was me." He said, "You're the one that opened him up?" And I said, "Yeh. I'm sorry, I didn't mean to get so close to you." . . .

So when the sergeant came out he said, "And you, what do you mean telling me to get outta the way." . . . And I said, "I didn't want you to get hurt . . . and I was afraid he was gonna kick one of you." And he says, "I still can't believe you pushed me outta your way. You were like a little dynamo." And I found after that I got respect from the sergeant. He doesn't realize it but he treated me differently after that.

Her colleagues' reactions provided informal instruction in the use of normal force, confirming that her actions under these circumstances were reasonable and even praiseworthy.

For a street cop, it is often a graver error to use too little force and develop a "shaky" reputation than it is to use too much force and be told to calm down. Thus officers, particularly rookies, who do not back up their partners in appropriate ways or who hesitate to use force in circumstances where it is deemed necessary are informally instructed regarding their aberrant ways. If the problematic incident is relatively insignificant and his general reputation is good, a rookie who "freezes" one time is given a second chance before becoming generally known as an untrustworthy partner. However, such incidents become the subject of degrading gossip, gossip that pressures the officer either to use force as expected or risk isolation. Such talk also informs rookies about the general boundaries of legal and normal force.

For example, a female rookie was accused of "freezing" in an incident that came to be referred to as a "Mexican standoff." A pedestrian had complained that "something funny is going on in the drugstore." The officer walked into the pharmacy where she found an armed man committing a robbery. Although he turned his weapon on her when she entered the premises, she still pulled out her gun and pointed it at him. When he ordered her to drop it, claiming that his partner was behind her with a revolver at her head, she refused and told him to drop his.[6] He refused, and the stalemate continued until a sergeant entered the drugstore and ordered the suspect to drop his gun.

Initially, the female officer thought she had acted appropriately and even heroically. She soon discovered, however, that her hesitation to shoot had brought into question her competence with some of her fellow officers. Although many veterans claimed that "she had a lotta balls" to take her gun out at all when the suspect already had a gun on her, most contended "she shoulda shot him." Other policemen confirmed that she committed a "rookie mistake"; she had failed to notice a "lookout" standing outside the store and hence had been unprepared for an armed confrontation. Her sergeant and lieutenant, moreover, even insisted that she had acted in a cowardly manner, despite her reputation as a "gung-ho cop," and cited the incident as evidence of the general inadequacy of policewomen.

In the weeks that followed, this officer became increasingly depressed and angry. She was particularly outraged when she learned that she would not receive a commendation, although such awards were commonly made for "gun pinches" of this nature. Several months later, the officer vehemently expressed the wish that she had killed the suspect and vowed that next time she would "shoot first and ask questions later." The negative sanctions of supervisors and colleagues clearly en-

couraged her to adopt an attitude favorable to using force with less restraint in future situations.

Reprimand, gossip, and avoidance constitute the primary means by
which police try to change or control the behavior of co-workers perceived as unreliable or cowardly. Formal accusations, however, are discouraged regardless of the seriousness of the misconduct. One male
rookie, for example, earned a reputation for cowardice after he allegedly
had to be "dragged" out of the car during an "assist officer." Even then,
he apparently refused to help the officers in trouble. Although no formal
charges were filed, everyone in the district was warned to avoid working
with this officer.

Indeed, to initiate formal charges against a co-worker may discredit
the accuser. In one incident a male rookie, although discouraged by veteran officers and even his district captain, filed charges of cowardice
against a female rookie. The rookie gained the support of two supervisors and succeeded in having the case heard before the Board of Inquiry.
During the trial he claimed the woman officer failed to aid him in arrest-
ing a man who presented physical resistance and had a knife on his person. In rebuttal, the woman testified that she perceived no need to participate in a physical confrontation because she saw no knife and the
policeman was hitting the suspect. In spite of conflicting testimony, she
was found guilty of "Neglect of Duty." Although most veterans thought
the woman was "flaky" and doubted her competence, they also felt the
male rookie had exaggerated his story. Moreover, they were outraged
that he filed formal charges, and he quickly found himself obstracized.

At the same time that male and female rookies are commended for using force under appropriate circumstances, they are reprimanded if their
participation in force is viewed as excessive or inappropriate. In this way,
rookies are instructed that although many acts of coercion are accepted
and even demanded, not everything goes. They thereby learn to distinguish between normal and brutal force. In the following incident, for example, a policewoman describes how she instructed a less experienced
officer that her behavior was unreasonable and should be checked. Here,
the new officer is chastised for misreading interactional cues and overre-
acting to minor affronts when treating a "crazy person" involved in a
minor dispute as if he were a serious felon.[7]

> . . . [W]hen I first heard about it (another fight) I'd wondered if Mary had pro-
> voked it any because we'd gone on a disturbance and it was a drunk black guy
> who called to complain that the kid who lived upstairs keeps walking through
> his apartment. The kid to me looks wacky. He's talking crazy. He's saying they
> shoulda sent men. What are you women going to do. Going on and on. And to
> me it was a bullshit job. But Mary turns around and says, "We don't have to
> take that from him. Let's lock him up." I said, "Mary forget it." And the kid
> has numchuck sticks on him and when he turned his back . . . he had them in

his back pocket. So, as he's pulling away saying you're scared, like a little kid, I turned around and said, "I've got your sticks." And I go away. Mary . . . was so disappointed in me . . . like I'd turned chicken on her. So I tried to explain to her, I said, "Mary, all we have is disorderly conduct. That's a summary offense. That's bullshit." I said, "Did you want to get hurt for a summary offense?" I said, "The guy was drunk who called to complain. It wasn't even a legit complaint." I said, "It's just . . . You've got to use discretion. If you think I'm chicken think of the times when a 'man with a gun' comes over the air and I'm the first car there." I said, "When it's worth it, I'll do anything. When it's not worth it, I'll back off." And I think she tries to temper herself some because Collette and her, they finally had a talk about why they hated each other. And Collette said to her, "I think you're too physical. I think you look for fights." And I think maybe Mary hearing it twice, once from me and once from Collette, might start to think that maybe she does provoke. . . .

In summary, when rookies leave the academy, they begin to familiarize themselves with street weapons and to gain some sense of what kinds of behavior constitute too little or too much force. They also begin to develop an understanding of street standards for using and judging appropriate and necessary force. By listening to and observing colleagues at work and by experiencing a variety of problematic interactions with the public, newcomers become cognizant of the occasions and circumstances in which to use various degrees and kinds of force. But at the same time, they are learning not only when and how to use force, but also a series of accounting practices to justify and to legitimate as "normal" (and sometimes to condemn) these acts of coercion. Normal force is thus the product of the police officers' accounting practices for describing what happened in ways that prefigure or anticipate the conclusion that it was in some sense justified or excusable and hence "normal."

•  •  •

## EXCESSIVE FORCE AND PEER RESPONSES

Although police routinely excuse and justify many incidents where they or their co-workers have used extreme force against a citizen or suspect, this does not mean that on any and every occasion the officer using such force is exonerated. Indeed, the concept of normal force is useful because it suggests that there are specific circumstances under which  police officers will not condone the use of force by themselves or colleagues as reasonable and acceptable. Thus, officer-recognized conceptions of normal force are subject to restrictions of the following kinds:

(1) Police recognize and honor some rough equation between the behavior of the suspect and the harmfulness of the force to which it is subject. There are limits, therefore, to the degree of force that is acceptable in particular circumstances. In [one] incident, for example, an officer re-

marked on his fear when a [rude drunk], a "symbolic assailant" (Skolnick, 1975: 45), was mistakenly subject to more force that he "deserved" and almost killed.

•   •   •

(2) Although it is considered normal and natural to become emotional and angry in highly charged, taut encounters, officers nonetheless prefer to minimize the harmful consequences of the use of force. As a result, officers usually acknowledge that emotional reactions that might lead to extreme force should be controlled and limited by co-workers if at all possible. In [one case involving a male officer and a female suspect], for example, [the] officer justified the use of force as a legitimate means to regain situational control when physically challenged. Nonetheless, he expressed gratitude to his partner for stopping him from doing serious harm when he "snapped out" and lost control.

•   •   •

(3) Similarly, even in cases where suspects are seen as deserving some violent punishment, this force should not be used randomly and without control. Thus, . . . an officer who "snapped out" and began to beat a child abuser clearly regarded his partner's attempt to stop the beating as reasonable.

•   •   •

Learning . . . restrictions on the use of normal force and . . . informal practices of peer control are important processes in the socialization of newcomers. This socialization proceeds both through ongoing observation and experience and, on occasion, through explicit instruction. For example, one veteran officer advised a rookie, "The only reason to go in on a pursuit is not to get the perpetrator but to pull the cop who gets there first offa the guy before he kills him."

It is against this background that patrol officers identify excessive force and the existence of violence-prone peers. Some officers become known for recurrently committing acts of coercion that exceed working notions of normal force and that cannot be excused or justified with routine accounting practices. In contrast to the officer who makes a "rookie mistake" and uses excessive force from inexperience, the brutal cop does not honor the practices of normal force. Such an officer is also not effectively held in check by routine means of peer control. As a result, more drastic measures must be taken to prevent him from endangering the public and his colleagues.

One rookie gained a reputation for brutality from frequent involvement in "unnecessary" fights. One such incident was particularly noteworthy: Answering a call on a demented male with a weapon, he came upon a large man pacing the sidewalk carrying a lead pipe. The officer got out of the patrol car and yelled in a belligerent tone of voice, "What the fuck are you doing, creep?" At this point "the creep" attacked the officer and tried to take away his gun. A policewoman arrived on the scene, joined the fight, called an assist, and rescued the patrolman. Although no one was hurt, colleagues felt the incident was provoked by the officer who aggressively approached a known crazy person who should have been assumed to be unpredictable and nonresponsible.

When colleagues first began to doubt this officer's competence, he was informally instructed to moderate his behavior by veteran and even rookie partners. When his behavior persisted, confrontations with fellow officers became explosive. When peers were unable to check his behavior, complaints were made to superiors. Officially, colleagues indicated they did not want to work with him because of "personality problems." Informally, however, supervisors were informed of the nature of his provocative and dangerous behavior. The sergeant responded by putting the rookie in a wagon with a responsible partner whom he thought might succeed in controlling him. When this strategy proved unsuccessful, he was eventually transferred to the subway unit. Such transfers to "punishment districts," isolated posts, "inside units," or the subway are typical means of handling police officers deemed dangerous and out of control.

As this discussion indicates, the internal control of an exceptionally or inappropriately violent police officer is largely informal. With the exception of civilian complaints and brutality suits, the behavior of such officers rarely becomes the subject of formal police documents. However, their reputations are often well-known throughout the department and the rumors about their indiscretions educate rookies about how the line between normal force and brutality is drawn among working police officers.

It takes more than one incident of excessively violent behavior for a police officer to attain a brutal reputation. The violent officer is usually involved in numerous acts of aggressive behavior that are not accountable as normal force either because of their frequency or because of their substance. However, once identified as "brutal," a "head beater," and so on, an officer's use of force will be condemned by peers in circumstances in which competent officers would be given the benefit of the doubt. For example, one officer gained national notoriety during a federal investigation into a suspicious shooting. Allegedly, a local resident had thrown an axe at the patrol wagon. According to available accounts, the police pursued the suspect inside a house, and the officer in question shot him in the head. Although witnesses claimed the victim was unarmed, the officer stated that he fired in self-defense. The suspect reportedly attacked him with a metal pipe. This policeman had an established reputation for being "good with his hands," and many colleagues assumed he had brutally shot an unarmed man in the aftermath of a pursuit.[8]

## CONCLUSION

The organization of policework reflects a poignant moral dilemma: for a variety of reasons, society mandates to the police the right to use force but provides little direction as to its proper use in specific, "real life" situations. Thus, the police, as officers of the law, must be prepared to use force under circumstances in which its rationale is often morally, legally, and practically ambiguous. This fact explains some otherwise puzzling aspects of police training and socialization.

The police academy provides a semblance of socialization for its recruits by teaching formal rules for using force. It is a semblance of socialization because it treats the use of force as capable of rationalization within the moral and legal conventions of the civilian world. The academy also, paradoxically, trains recruits in the use of tools of violence with potential for going far beyond the limitations of action imposed by those conventions. Consequently, the full socialization of a police officer takes place outside the academy as the officer moves from its idealizations to the practicalities of the street. This movement involves several phases: (1) a decisive, practical separation from the formal world established within the academy; (2) the cultivation of a working distinction between what is formally permissible and what is practically and informally required of the "street cop"; and (3) the demonstration of competence in using and accounting for routine street practices that are morally and legally problematic for those not working the street.

The original dilemma surrounding the use of force persists throughout the socialization process, but is increasingly dealt with by employing accounts provided by the police community that reduce and neutralize the moral tension. The experienced "street cop" becomes an expert at using techniques of neutralization (Sykes and Matza, 1957) to characterize the use of force on the streets, at judging its use by others and at evaluating the necessity for using force by standards those techniques provide. Use of these techniques also reinforces the radical separation of the formal and informal worlds of policework, duplicating within the context of the organization itself the distinction between members and outsiders. This ["second training"] guarantees that members will be able to distinguish between those who can and cannot be trusted to use force and to understand the conditions under which its use is "reasonable."

## NOTES

1. I am deeply indebted for both substansive and editorial assistance to Michael Brown and Robert M. Emerson. I would also like to thank Peter Manning, Bill DiFazio, Jim Birch, and Marie DeMay Della Guardia for their comments on an earlier draft of this article.

2. The female officers described in this research were among the first 100 women assigned to the ranks of uniformed patrol as a result of a discrimination

suit filed by the Justice Department and a policewoman plaintiff. Nonetheless masculine pronouns are generally used to refer to the police in this article, because the Metro P.D. remained dominated by men numerically, in style and in tone.

My fieldwork experience is discussed in detail in Hunt, 1984.

3. Some officers also substitute a large heavy duty flashlight for the nightstick. If used correctly, the flashlight can inflict more damage than the baton and is less likely to break when applied to the head or other parts of the body.

4. For a discussion of the cultural distinction between "inside men" who handle desk and administrative tasks and "real cops" who work outside on the street, see Hunt (1984).

5. As the Metro City Police Commissioner commented in an interview: "In general, they (women) are physically weaker than males. . . . I believe they would be inclined to let their emotions all to too frequently overrule their good judgment . . . there are periods in their life when they are psychologically unbalanced because of physical problems that are occurring within them."

6. The woman officer later explained that she did not obey the suspect's command because she saw no reflection of the partner in the suspect's glasses and therefore assumed he was lying.

7. Patrol officers do not view demented people as responsible for their acts and therefore do not hold them strictly culpable when they challenge an officer's authority (see Van Maanen, 1978: 231). In dealing with such persons, coercion other than that narrowly required for control and self-protection tends to be viewed as inappropriate and unjustifiable.

8. The suspect was known to other officers from prior encounters as a slightly demented cop antagonizer. Consequently, the officer's actions appeared completely unnecessary because he was not dealing with an unpredictable stranger. The suspect's neighbors depicted him as a mentally disturbed person who was deathly afraid of the police because he had been a frequent target of harrassment.

## REFERENCES

Bittner, E.
  (1980) *The Functions of the Police in Modern Society.* Cambridge, MA: Oelgeschlager, Gunn & Hain.

Hunt, J.
  (1984) "The development of rapport throughout the negotiation of gender in field work among police." *Human Organization* 43:283–96.

Skolnick, J.
  (1975) *Justice Without Trial.* New York: John Wiley.

Sykes, G. M. and D. Matza
  (1957) "Techniques of neutralization: A theory of delinquency." *Amer. Soc. Rev.* 22:664–70.

Van Maanen, J.
  (1978) "The asshole," in P. K. Manning and J. Van Maanen (eds.) *Policing: A View From the Street.* Santa Monica, CA: Goodyear.

## REVIEW QUESTIONS

1. In the police academy studied by Hunt, rookies learned both how to use tools of force and rules for when to use them. Describe these tools and rules.

2. Which of the rules taught in the academy turned out not to be followed on the street?

3. How did the rookies get their "second training" in how much force to use? What kinds of sanctions were used?

4. What were the consequences for the officers of using too little force?

5. What were the consequences for the officers of using too much force?

## Suggested Readings: Transmission of Culture: Socialization

Becker, Howard S. "Becoming a Marijuana User," *American Journal of Sociology,* vol. 59 (November 1953), 235–242.

Clausen, John A. *Socialization and Society.* Boston: Little, Brown, 1968.

Denzin, Norman K. "Play, Games and Interaction: The Contexts of Childhood Socialization." *Sociological Quarterly,* 16 (Autumn 1975), 458–478.

Dornbush, Sanford M. "The Military Academy as an Assimilating Institution," *Social Forces,* vol. 33 (May 1955), 316–321.

Goldstein, Bernard, and Jack Oldham. *Children and Work: A Study of Socialization.* New Brunswick, N.J.: Transaction Books, 1979.

Nelsen, Hart M. and Alice Kroliczak. "Parental Use of the Threat 'God Will Punish': Replication and Extension," *Journal of the Scientific Study of Religion* 23 (Sept. 1984): 267–277.

Nemerowicz, Gloria Morris. *Children's Perceptions of Gender and Work Roles.* New York: Praeger, 1979.

Spiro, Melford. *Children of the Kibbutz,* rev. ed. Cambridge, Mass.: Harvard University Press, 1975.

# Part IV. Interaction in Everyday Life

THE STUDY OF SOCIAL LIFE TAKES US INTO ALL KINDS OF ACTIVITIES AND settings. Even in situations where one might think that "nothing is happening here," sociologists see important elements and processes of social interaction. For one thing, social interaction is much more complicated than simply learning, through socialization, a set of cultural norms and roles and applying them in all situations with all people. Norms and roles are very often situationally tied, and we must try to determine the nature of the situation we are in, in order to behave more or less appropriately.

People are always, therefore, both *reading* and *giving off* cues from and to each other, communicating symbolically even though they may be unaware that they are doing so. When you walk through a lobby or enter a classroom before the class begins, it may seem that nothing is happening. But the others in that setting will begin to "define" who you are by assessing your clothing, appearance, gestures, props, tone of voice, facial expressions, and so on within the framework of meanings already learned from our culture. You will also pay attention to *their* clothing, appearance, etc. The ways in which they act toward you (even if they decide to ignore you) depend on their perceptions of you, and your actions depend on your perceptions of them. None of us acts or reacts in the same way in all settings or situations; we try to figure out what the nature of the situation is and what behavior it calls for. We can rarely say, therefore, that nothing is happening, because we would be ignoring a great deal of mental work involved in social perception and evaluation, as well as various forms of behavior actually taking place.

Consider how differently you would act if a person with gray hair, carrying a briefcase, and speaking forcefully entered your classroom on the first day of the term than if a younger person in informal attire carrying notebooks and texts entered the same room. In the first instance, you would probably decide that the person was the professor; in the second case, you would think you were in the presence of another student. (You may learn through further interaction that you were wrong, but your initial impression is all you have to guide you for the moment.) How might your own tone of voice, facial expressions, language, and behavior differ?

The process we are describing here is an important one for understanding interaction in everyday life. It was termed the "definition of the situation" by an early influential sociologist, W. I. Thomas. In 1923, Thomas outlined this process, contending that each of the participants in any social interaction must define for him or herself what kind of situation exists and what types of others are present, in order to call forth the culturally appropriate behaviors necessary to mesh with the other "actors" who are present. A situation is defined (as, say, a pleasant, informal encounter; a formal dance; or a no-nonsense workplace) by reading *cues* from the environment, including the other actors. In addition, the individual emits cues as to his or her social statuses, expectations, attitudes, and the like which are read by the others involved. Thus, a process of give-and-take occurs in which a more or less agreed upon definition of the situation is negotiated. This process is critical if interaction is to proceed.

W. I. Thomas is probably best remembered for his idea that one's own perception or definition of the situation—whether it is "accurate" or "inaccurate," shared by others or not—is of prime importance in determining one's own behavior, or line of action, in that situation. Thus, "a situation defined as real, is real in its consequences." Returning to our example of the persons entering your classroom, you would probably act toward the gray-haired person with the briefcase *as if* this person were the professor, even if your definition of the situation were inaccurate.

In this section of the book, we have collected four pieces which bear on one aspect or another of the process of defining situations as it affects ensuing interactions. First is an excerpt from *The Presentation of Self in Everyday Life*, a classic book by Erving Goffman. Goffman analyzes everyday interaction using what he terms the *dramaturgical approach*. This approach focuses on those aspects of the lives of everyday people that are similar to the behavior of stage actors and other dramatic performers. Thus, Goffman views *every* encounter between two or more people as an event that calls for each "actor" to present one or more of his or her social roles to the other(s), much as in a stage performance. Individuals are motivated to present (selected) information about themselves to others, a process called impression management by Goffman, in order to have some impact on the common definition of the situation. Sometimes we give honest and *sincere* performances, trying to convey accurate information about ourselves. At other times, we give *cynical* performances which we know to be false. Regardless of whether a performance is cynical or sincere, we may use a number of nonverbal means of communicating information about ourselves, including props (e.g., the physician's white coat), settings (furniture arrangements and the like), gestures (such as a shrug of the shoulders), tone of voice, and so on, in addition to strictly verbal cues. Goffman categorizes and describes these elements of impression management as well as showing the ubiquitous presence of self presentation in everyday interaction.

Goffman's view might be disturbing to some of you. If we are all on stage, manipulating what others see and think about us, then we must wonder when we are our "real selves." Goffman does not answer this question directly but, rather, shows us how social actors may present different aspects of themselves to different groups of people. His point is that we have *many* "real selves." After all, don't you act differently with various groups of people? It is unlikely, for example, that you behave the same way in class as you do in the dorm or at your parents' home. (What would your family think if you raised your hand during dinner to ask a question?) Why does your behavior change as the people around you change? Try to list the numerous ways in which your behavior changes during an average week. The tone of your voice, your language, dress, and posture are only a few aspects of your presentation that vary as you present each of your numerous "selves." Think too of what would happen if you did *not* modify your behavior.

The concepts of the definition of the situation and impression management are also central to the work of Edward Gross and Gregory Stone on "Embarrassment and the Analysis of Role Requirements," the second selection in this section. In order to interact with others in everyday life, they contend, individuals must be able to behave in ways that explain to others which role or roles they expect to perform—that is, to establish an "identity" by "presenting themselves." An identity exists when the individual's claims about who and what he or she is are accepted by the others in the situation. At this point, the individual is "located," and a definition of the situation is possible. The parties to the interaction have a fairly good idea not only of who and what each individual is, but also of what each individual can be expected to do in the "future," that is, as the interaction progresses. To summarize, then, in order to give interactants an idea of what we will be doing in the (very near or not so near) future, we must establish identities. Gross and Stone go on to indicate that "poise," or the maintenance of a unified identity, is also required for interaction to begin and to continue.

The focus of this article is actually on the problems that arise when an individual cannot establish an identity that others agree to or when the individual fails to maintain poise. Various "slips," either within or beyond the control of the individual, may disrupt the definition of the situation and lead to embarrassment for that person and for the other interactants, causing interaction to cease. Indeed, the fact that embarrassment occurs was what led Gross and Stone to infer the necessity for establishing and maintaining identities and poise.

Many aspects of our interactions in everyday life, from our self-presentations to the amount of space we take up, are affected by where we are located in the class structure. Charles Derber and Yale Magrass, in "The Pursuit of Attention," focus on how much notice or attention people from different classes, sexes, occupations, and educational levels can expect to get in everyday encounters. People go to great lengths and pay good money to get the kind of attention they want when they want it. "Negative" attention—prying questions from a case worker, a "lecture" from the principal, a "dressing down" by the boss—is avoided when possible. The less power, prestige, and money someone has, the lower the chance of controlling other people's attention. After reading the article by Derber and Magrass, you will no longer be able to ignore paying attention.

Anselm Strauss, in "Turning Points in Identity," shifts our attention to the issue of change in people's identities, or self-concepts. He looks at why and how these changes occur. What events and experiences lead to the statement: "I'm not the same person I used to be"? Meeting a goal or being betrayed—either of these can cause a reassessment and redefinition of oneself.

This excerpt from Strauss's book, *Mirrors and Masks: The Search for Identity*, makes several contributions to our understanding of interaction in everyday life. First, it offers a typology of the events that force people to adopt new identities and shed old ones. Second, it gives concrete illustrations of redefinitions of situations, showing that our understandings of ourselves and our environments can and do alter radically at times. Third, it gives support to the important sociological insight that people in similar positions in the social structure are likely to undergo similar "personal" experiences and changes.

The four readings in this section should give you a good idea of how the sociological perspective can take us beyond our "common sense" interpretations of everyday encounters. The articles illustrate the complexities of seemingly simple and straightforward actions and interactions. Ordinarily people don't take the time to read and analyze the meanings that lie behind daily events, but these authors open our eyes to new ways of seeing and understanding them.

# THE PRESENTATION OF SELF IN EVERYDAY LIFE

## Erving Goffman

W~HEN AN INDIVIDUAL ENTERS THE PRESENCE OF OTHERS, THEY COMMONLY~
seek to acquire information about him or to bring into play information
about him already possessed. They will be interested in his general socioeconomic status, his conception of self, his attitude toward them, his
competence, his trustworthiness, etc. Although some of this information
seems to be sought almost as an end in itself, there are usually quite
practical reasons for acquiring it. Information about the individual helps
to define the situation, enabling others to know in advance what he will
expect of them and what they may expect of him. Informed in these
ways, the others will know how best to act in order to call forth a desired
response from him.

For those present, many sources of information become accessible and
many carriers (or "sign-vehicles") become available for conveying this
information. If unacquainted with the individual, observers can glean
clues from his conduct and appearance which allow them to apply their
previous experience with individuals roughly similar to the one before
them or, more important, to apply untested stereotypes to him. They
can also assume from past experience that only individuals of a particular kind are likely to be found in a given social setting. They can rely on
what the individual says about himself or on documentary evidence he
provides as to who and what he is. If they know, or know of, the individual by virtue of experience prior to the interaction, they can rely on assumptions as to the persistence and generality of psychological traits as
a means of predicting his present and future behavior.

However, during the period in which the individual is in the immediate presence of the others, few events may occur which directly provide
the others with the conclusive information they will need if they are to
direct wisely their own activity. Many crucial facts lie beyond the time
and place of interaction or lie concealed within it. For example, the
"true" or "real" attitudes, beliefs, and emotions of the individual can
be ascertained only indirectly, through his avowals or through what appears to be involuntary expressive behavior. Similarly, if the individual
offers the others a product or service, they will often find that during the
interaction there will be no time and place immediately available for eating the pudding that the proof can be found in. They will be forced to ac-

Erving Goffman, *The Presentation of Self in Everyday Life* (Garden City, N.Y.: Anchor Books, 1959), pp. 1–15.

cept some events as conventional or natural signs of something not directly available to the senses. In Ichheiser's terms,[1] the individual will have to act so that he intentionally or unintentionally *expresses* himself, and the others will in turn have to be *impressed* in some way by him.

The expressiveness of the individual (and therefore his capacity to give impressions) appears to involve two radically different kinds of sign activity: the expression that he *gives*, and the expression that he *gives off*. The first involves verbal symbols or their substitutes which he uses admittedly and solely to convey the information that he and the others are known to attach to these symbols. This is communication in the traditional and narrow sense. The second involves a wide range of action that others can treat as symptomatic of the actor, the expectation being that the action was performed for reasons other than the information conveyed in this way. As we shall have to see, this distinction has an only initial validity. The individual does of course intentionally convey misinformation by means of both of these types of communication, the first involving deceit, the second feigning.

Taking communication in both its narrow and broad sense, one finds that when the individual is in the immediate presence of others, his activity will have a promissory character. The others are likely to find that they must accept the individual on faith, offering him a just return while he is present before them in exchange for something whose true value will not be established until after he has left their presence. (Of course, the others also live by inference in their dealings with the physical world, but it is only in the world of social interaction that the objects about which they make inferences will purposely facilitate and hinder this inferential process.) The security that they justifiably feel in making inferences about the individual will vary, of course, depending on such factors as the amount of information they already possess about him, but no amount of such past evidence can entirely obviate the necessity of acting on the basis of inferences. As William I. Thomas suggested:

> It is also highly important for us to realize that we do not as a matter of fact lead our lives, make our decisions, and reach our goals in everyday life either statistically or scientifically. We live by inference. I am, let us say, your guest. You do not know, you cannot determine scientifically, that I will not steal your money or your spoons. But inferentially I will not, and inferentially you have me as a guest.[2]

Let us now turn from the others to the point of view of the individual who presents himself before them. He may wish them to think highly of him, or to think that he thinks highly of them, or to perceive how in fact he feels toward them, or to obtain no clear-cut impression; he may wish to ensure sufficient harmony so that the interaction can be sustained, or to defraud, get rid of, confuse, mislead, antagonize, or insult them. Regardless of the particular objective which the individual has in mind and of his motive for having this objective, it will be in his interests to control the conduct of the others, especially their responsive treatment of him.[3] This control is achieved largely by influencing the definition of the situation which the others come to formulate, and he can influence this definition by expressing himself in such a way as to give them the kind of impression that will lead them to act voluntarily in accordance with his own plan. Thus, when an individual appears in the presence of others, there will usually be some reason for him to mobilize his activity so that it will convey an impression to others which it is in his interests to convey. Since a girl's dormitory mates will glean evidence of her popularity from the calls she receives on the phone, we can suspect that some girls will arrange for calls to be made, and Willard Waller's finding can be anticipated:

> It has been reported by many observers that a girl who is called to the telephone in the dormitories will often allow herself to be called several times, in order to give all the other girls ample opportunity to hear her paged.[4]

Of the two kinds of communication—expressions given and expressions given off—this report will be primarily concerned with the latter, with the more theatrical and contextual kind, the nonverbal, presumably unintentional kind, whether this communication be purposely engineered or not. As an example of what we must try to examine, I would like to cite at length a novelistic incident in which Preedy, a vacationing Englishman, makes his first appearance on the beach of his summer hotel in Spain:

> But in any case he took care to avoid catching anyone's eye. First of all, he had to make it clear to those potential companions of his holiday that they were of no concern to him whatsoever. He stared through them, round them, over them—eyes lost in space. The beach might have been empty. If by chance a ball was thrown his way, he looked surprised; then let a smile of amusement lighten his face (Kindly Preedy), looked around dazed to see that there *were* people on the beach, tossed it back with a smile to himself and not a smile *at* the people, and then resumed carelessly his nonchalant survey of space.
>
> But it was time to institute a little parade, the parade of the Ideal Preedy. By devious handlings he gave any who wanted to look a chance to see the title of his book—a Spanish translation of Homer, classic thus, but not daring, cosmopolitan too—and then gathered together his beachwrap and bag into a neat sand-resistant pile (Methodical and Sensible Preedy), rose slowly to stretch at ease his huge frame (Big-Cat Preedy), and tossed aside his sandals (Carefree Preedy, after all).
>
> The marriage of Preedy and the sea! There were alternate rituals. The first involved the stroll that turns into a run and a dive straight into the water, thereafter smoothing into a strong splashless crawl towards the horizon. But of course not really to the horizon. Quite suddenly he would turn on to his back and thrash great white splashes with his legs, somehow thus showing that he could have swum further had he wanted to, and then would stand up a quarter out of water for all to see who it was.

The alternative course was simpler, it avoided the cold-water shock and it avoided the risk of appearing too high-spirited. The point was to appear to be so used to the sea, the Mediterranean, and this particular beach, that one might as well be in the sea as out of it. It involved a slow stroll down and into the edge of the water—not even noticing his toes were wet, land and water all the same to *him!*—with his eyes up at the sky gravely surveying portents, invisible to others, of the weather (Local Fisherman Preedy).[5]

The novelist means us to see that Preedy is improperly concerned with the extensive impressions he feels his sheer bodily action is giving off to those around him. We can malign Preedy further by assuming that he has acted merely in order to give a particular impression, that this is a false impression, and that the others present receive either no impression at all, or, worse still, the impression that Preedy is affectedly trying to cause them to receive this particular impression. But the important point for us here is that the kind of impression Preedy thinks he is making is in fact the kind of impression that others correctly and incorrectly glean from someone in their midst.

I have said that when an individual appears before others his actions will influence the definition of the situation which they come to have. Sometimes the individual will act in a thoroughly calculating manner, expressing himself in a given way solely in order to give the kind of impression to others that is likely to evoke from them a specific response he is concerned to obtain. Sometimes the individual will be calculating in his activity but be relatively unaware that this is the case. Sometimes he will intentionally and consciously express himself in a particular way, but chiefly because the tradition of his group or social status require this kind of expression and not because of any particular response (other than vague acceptance or approval) that is likely to be evoked from those impressed by the expression. Sometimes the traditions of an individual's role will lead him to give a well-designed impression of a particular kind and yet he may be neither consciously nor unconsciously disposed to create such an impression. The others, in their turn, may be suitably impressed by the individual's efforts to convey something, or may misunderstand the situation and come to conclusions that are warranted neither by the individual's intent nor by the facts. In any case, insofar as the others act *as if* the individual had conveyed a particular impression, we may take a functional or pragmatic view and say that the individual has "effectively" projected a given definition of the situation and "effectively" fostered the understanding that a given state of affairs obtains.

There is one aspect of the others' response that bears special comment here. Knowing that the individual is likely to present himself in a light that is favorable to him, the others may divide what they witness into two parts: a part that is relatively easy for the individual to manipulate at will, being chiefly his verbal assertions, and a part in regard to which he seems to have little concern or control, being chiefly derived from the expressions he gives off. The others may then use what are considered to be the ungovernable aspects of his expressive behavior as a check upon the validity of what is conveyed by the governable aspects. In this a fundamental asymmetry is demonstrated in the communication process, the individual presumably being aware of only one stream of his communication, the witnesses of this stream and one other. For example, in Shetland Isle one crofter's [or farmer's] wife, in serving native dishes to a visitor from the mainland of Britain, would listen with a polite smile to his polite claims of liking what he was eating; at the same time she would take note of the rapidity with which the visitor lifted his fork or spoon to his mouth, the eagerness with which he passed food into his mouth, and the gusto expressed in chewing the food, using these signs as a check on the stated feelings of the eater. The same woman, in order to discover what one acquaintance (A) "actually" thought of another acquaintance (B), would wait until B was in the presence of A but engaged in conversation with still another person (C). She would then covertly examine the facial expressions of A as he regarded B in conversation with C. Not being in conversation with B, and not being directly observed by him, A would sometimes relax usual constraints and tactful deceptions, and freely express what he was "actually" feeling about B. This Shetlander, in short, would observe the unobserved observer.

Now given the fact that others are likely to check up on the more controllable aspects of behavior by means of the less controllable, one can expect that sometimes the individual will try to exploit this very possibility, guiding the impression he makes through behavior felt to be reliably informing.[6] For example, in gaining admission to a tight social circle, the participant observer may not only wear an accepting look while listening to an informant, but may also be careful to wear the same look when observing the informant talking to others; observers of the observer will then not as easily discover where he actually stands. A specific illustration may be cited from Shetland Isle. When a neighbor dropped in to have a cup of tea, he would ordinarily wear at least a hint of an expectant warm smile as he passed through the door into the cottage. Since lack of physical obstructions outside the cottage and lack of light within it usually made it possible to observe the visitor unobserved as he approached the house, islanders sometimes took pleasure in watching the visitor drop whatever expression he was manifesting and replace it with a sociable one just before reaching the door. However, some visitors, in appreciating that this examination was occurring, would blindly adopt a social face a long distance from the house, thus ensuring the projection of a constant image.

This kind of control upon the part of the individual reinstates the symmetry of the communication process, and sets the stage for a kind of information game—a potentially infinite cycle of concealment, discovery, false revelation, and rediscovery. It should be added that since the others are likely to be relatively unsuspicious of the presumably unguided aspect of the individual's conduct, he can gain much by controlling it. The others of course may sense that the individual is manipulating the presumably spontaneous aspects of his behavior, and seek in this very act of manipulation some shading of conduct that the individual has not managed to control. This again provides a check upon the individual's behavior, this time his presumably uncalculated behavior, thus re-establishing the asymmetry of the communication process. Here I would like only to add the suggestion that the arts of piercing an individual's effort at calculated unintentionality seem better developed than our capacity to manipulate our own behavior, so that regardless of how many steps have occurred in the information game, the witness is likely to have the advantage over the actor, and the initial asymmetry of the communication process is likely to be retained.

When we allow that the individual projects a definition of the situation when he appears before others, we must also see that the others, however passive their role may seem to be, will themselves effectively project a definition of the situation by virtue of their response to the individual and by virtue of any lines of action they initiate to him. Ordinarily the definitions of the situation projected by the several different participants are sufficiently attuned to one another so that open contradiction will not occur. I do not mean that there will be the kind of consensus that arises when each individual present candidly expresses what he really feels and honestly agrees with the expressed feeling of the others present. This kind of harmony is an optimistic ideal and in any case not necessary for the smooth working of society. Rather, each participant is expected to suppress his immediate heartfelt feelings, conveying a view of the situation which he feels the others will be able to find at least temporarily acceptable. The maintenance of this surface of agreement, this veneer of consensus, is facilitated by each participant concealing [his] wants behind statements while asserting values to which everyone present feels obliged to give lip service. Further, there is usually a kind of division of definitional labor. Each participant is allowed to establish the tentative official ruling regarding matters which are vital to him but not immediately important to others, e.g., the rationalizations and justifications by which he accounts for his past activity. In exchange for this courtesy he remains silent or non-committal on matters important to others but not immediately important to him. We have then a kind of interactional *modus vivendi*. Together, the participants contribute to a single over-all definition of the situation which involves not so much a real argument as to what exists but rather a real agreement as to whose claims concerning what issues will be temporarily honored. Real agreement will also exist concerning the desirability of avoiding an open conflict of definitions of the situation.[7] I will refer to this level of agreement as a "working consensus." It is to be understood that the working consensus established in one interaction setting will be quite different in content from the working consensus established in a different type of setting. Thus, between two friends at lunch, a reciprocal show of affection, respect, and concern for the other is maintained. In service occupations, on the other hand, the specialist often maintains an image of disinterested involvement in the problem of the client, while the client responds with a show of respect for the competence and integrity of the specialist. Regardless of such differences in content, however, the general form of these working arrangements is the same.

In noting the tendency for a participant to accept the definitional claims made by the others present, we can appreciate the crucial importance of the information that the individual *initially* possesses or acquires concerning his fellow participants, for it is on the basis of this initial information that the individual starts to define the situation and starts to build up lines of responsive action. The individual's initial projection commits him to what he is proposing to be and requires him to drop all pretenses of being other things. As the interaction among the participants progresses, additions and modifications in this initial informational state will of course occur, but it is essential that these later developments be related without contradiction to, and even built up from, the initial positions taken by the several participants. It would seem that an individual can more easily make a choice as to what line of treatment to demand from and extend to the others present at the beginning of an encounter than he can alter the line of treatment that is being pursued once the interaction is underway.

In everyday life, of course, there is a clear understanding that first impressions are important. Thus, the work adjustment of those in service occupations will often hinge upon a capacity to seize and hold the initiative in the service relations, a capacity that will require subtle aggressiveness on the part of the server when he is of lower socioeconomic status than his client. W. F. Whyte suggests the waitress as an example:

> The first point that stands out is that the waitress who bears up under pressure does not simply respond to her customers. She acts with some skill to control her behavior. The first question to ask when we look at the customer relationship is, "Does the waitress get the jump on the customer, or does the customer get the jump on the waitress?" The skilled waitress realizes the crucial nature of this question. . . .
> The skilled waitress tackles the customer with confidence and without hesitation. For example, she may find that a new customer has seated himself before she could clear off the dirty dishes and change the cloth. He is now leaning on the table studying the menu. She greets him, says, "May I change the cover, please?" and, without waiting for an answer, takes his menu away from him so that he moves back from the table, and she goes about her work. The relationship is handled politely but firmly, and there is never any question as to who is in charge.[8]

When the interaction that is initiated by "first impressions" is itself merely the initial interaction in an extended series of interactions involving the same participants, we speak of "getting off on the right foot" and feel that it is crucial that we do so. Thus, one learns that some teachers take the following view:

> You can't ever let them get the upper hand on you or you're through. So I start out tough. The first day I get a new class in, I let them know who's boss. . . . You've got to start off tough, then you can ease up as you go along. If you start out easy-going, when you try to be tough, they'll just look at you and laugh.[9]

Similarly, attendants in mental institutions may feel that if the new patient is sharply put in his place the first day on the ward and made to see who is boss, much future difficulty will be prevented.[10]

Given the fact that the individual effectively projects a definition of the situation when he enters the presence of others, we can assume that events may occur within the interaction which contradict, discredit, or otherwise throw doubt upon this projection. When these disruptive events occur, the interaction itself may come to a confused and embarrassed halt. Some of the assumptions upon which the responses of the participants had been predicated become untenable, and the participants find themselves lodged in an interaction for which the situation has been wrongly defined and is now no longer defined. At such moments the individual whose presentation has been discredited may feel ashamed while the others present may feel hostile, and all the participants may come to feel ill at ease, nonplussed, out of countenance, embarrassed, experiencing the kind of anomy that is generated when the minute social system of face-to-face interaction breaks down.

In stressing the fact that the initial definition of the situation projected by an individual tends to provide a plan for the cooperative activity that follows—in stressing this action point of view—we must not overlook the crucial fact that any projected definition of the situation also has a distinctive moral character. It is this moral character of projections that will chiefly concern us in this report. Society is organized on the principle that any individual who possesses certain social characteristics has a moral right to expect that others will value and treat him in an appropriate way. Connected with this principle is a second, namely that an individual who implicitly or explicitly signifies that he has certain social characteristics ought in fact to be what he claims he is. In consequence, when an individual projects a definition of the situation and thereby makes an implicit or explicit claim to be a person of a particular kind, he automatically exerts a moral demand upon the others, obliging them to value and treat him in the manner that persons of his kind have a right to expect. He also implicitly forgoes all claims to be things he does not appear to be[11] and hence forgoes the treatment that would be appropriate for such individuals. The others find, then, that the individual has informed them as to what is and as to what they *ought* to see as the "is."

One cannot judge the importance of definitional disruptions by the frequency with which they occur, for apparently they would occur more frequently were not constant precautions taken. We find that preventive practices are constantly employed to avoid these embarrassments and that corrective practices are constantly employed to compensate for discrediting occurrences that have not been successfully avoided. When the individual employs these strategies and tactics to protect his own projections, we may refer to them as "defensive practices"; when a participant employs them to save the definition of the situation projected by another, we speak of "protective practices" or "tact." Together, defensive and protective practices comprise the techniques employed to safeguard the impression fostered by an individual during his presence before others. It should be added that while we may be ready to see that no fostered impression would survive if defensive practices were not employed, we are less ready perhaps to see that few impressions could survive if those who received the impression did not exert tact in their reception of it.

In addition to the fact that precautions are taken to prevent disruption of projected definitions, we may also note that an intense interest in these disruptions comes to play a significant role in the social life of the group. Practical jokes and social games are played in which embarrassments which are to be taken unseriously are purposely engineered.[12] Fantasies are created in which devastating exposures occur. Anecdotes from the past—real, embroidered, or fictitious—are told and retold, detailing disruptions which occurred, almost occurred, or occurred and were admirably resolved. There seems to be no grouping which does not have a ready supply of these games, reveries, and cautionary tales, to be used as a source of humor, a catharsis for anxieties, and a sanction for inducing individuals to be modest in their claims and reasonable in their projected expectations. The individual may tell himself through dreams of getting into impossible positions. Families tell of the time a guest got his dates mixed and arrived when neither the house nor anyone in it was ready for him. Journalists tell of times when an all-too-meaningful misprint occurred, and the paper's assumption of objectivity or decorum was humorously discredited. Public servants tell of times a client ridiculously misunderstood form instructions, giving answers which implied an unanticipated and bizarre definition of the situation.[13] Seamen, whose home away from home is rigorously he-man, tell stories of coming back home and inadvertently asking mother to "pass the fucking butter."[14] Diplomats tell of the time a near-sighted queen asked a republican ambassador about the health of his king.[15]

To summarize, then, I assume that when an individual appears before others he will have many motives for trying to control the impression they receive of the situation.

## NOTES

1. Gustav Ichheiser, "Misunderstandings in Human Relations," Supplement to *The American Journal of Sociology*, 55 (September 1949): 6–7.

2. Quoted in E. H. Volkart, editor, *Social Behavior and Personality*, Contributions of W. I. Thomas to Theory and Social Research (New York: Social Science Research Council, 1951), p. 5.

3. Here I owe much to an unpublished paper by Tom Burns of the University of Edinburgh. He presents the argument that in all interaction a basic underlying theme is the desire of each participant to guide and control the responses made by the others present. A similar argument has been advanced by Jay Haley in a recent unpublished paper, but in regard to a special kind of control, that having to do with the relationship of those involved in the interaction.

4. Willard Waller, "The Rating and Dating Complex," *American Sociological Review*, 2: 730.

5. William Sansom, *A Contest of Ladies* (London: Hogarth, 1956), pp. 230–32.

6. The widely read and rather sound writings of Stephen Potter are concerned in part with signs that can be engineered to give a shrewd observer the apparently incidental cues he needs to discover concealed virtues the gamesman does not in fact possess.

7. An interaction can be purposely set up as a time and place for voicing differences in opinion, but in such cases participants must be careful to agree not to disagree on the proper tone of voice, vocabulary, and degree of seriousness in which all arguments are to be phrased, and upon the mutual respect which disagreeing participants must carefully continue to express toward one another. This debaters' or academic definition of the situation may also be invoked suddenly and judiciously as a way of translating a serious conflict of views into one that can be handled within a framework acceptable to all present.

8. W. F. Whyte, "When Workers and Customers Meet," Chap. VII, *Industry and Society*, ed. W. F. Whyte (New York: McGraw-Hill, 1946), pp. 132–33.

9. Teacher interview quoted by Howard S. Becker, "Social Class Variations in the Teacher-Pupil Relationship," *Journal of Educational Sociology*, 25: 459.

10. Harold Taxel, "Authority Structure in a Mental Hospital Ward" (unpublished Master's thesis, Department of Sociology, University of Chicago, 1953).

11. This role of the witness in limiting what it is the individual can be has been stressed by Existentialists, who see it as a basic threat to individual freedom. See Jean-Paul Sartre, *Being and Nothingness*, trans. by Hazel E. Barnes (New York: Philosophical Library, 1956), p. 365 ff.

12. Goffman, *op. cit.*, pp. 319–27.

13. Peter Blau, *Dynamics of Bureaucracy; A Study of Interpersonal Relationships in Two Government Agencies*, 2nd ed. (Chicago: University of Chicago Press, 1963).

14. Walter M. Beattie, Jr., "The Merchant Seaman" (unpublished M.A. Report, Department of Sociology, University of Chicago, 1950), p. 35.

15. Sir Frederick Ponsonby, *Recollections of Three Reigns* (New York: Dutton, 1952), p. 46.

# Review Questions

1. Distinguish between the two types of sign activity discussed by Goffman: "expressions given" and "expressions given off."

2. Give examples of performances which are sincere and honest and performances which are cynical and dishonest. Do our norms require us to give cynical performances in some situations?

3. Using Goffman's dramaturgical approach, analyze the behavior of a person being interviewed for a job.

4. When disruptive events occur in interaction which cast doubt on one participant's definitions, how do other participants react?

# EMBARRASSMENT AND THE ANALYSIS OF ROLE REQUIREMENTS

## Edward Gross and Gregory P. Stone

. . . EMBARRASSMENT OCCURS WHENEVER SOME *CENTRAL* ASSUMPTION IN a transaction has been *unexpectedly* and unqualifiedly discredited for at least one participant. The result is that he is incapacitated for continued role performance.[1] Moreover, embarrassment is infectious. It may spread out, incapacitating others not previously incapacitated. It is destructive dis-ease. In the wreckage left by embarrassment lie the broken foundations of social transactions. By examining such ruins, the investigator can reconstruct the architecture they represent.

To explore this idea, recollections of embarrassment were expressly solicited from two groups of subjects: (1) approximately 800 students enrolled in introductory sociology courses; and (2) about 80 students enrolled in an evening extension class. Not solicited, but gratefully received, were many examples volunteered by colleagues and friends who had heard of our interest in the subject. Finally we drew upon many recollections of embarrassment we had experienced ourselves. Through these means at least one thousand specimens of embarrassment were secured.

We found that embarrassments frequently occurred in situations requiring continuous and coordinated role performance—speeches, ceremonies, processions, or working concerts. In such situations embarrassment is particularly noticeable because it is so devastating. Forgetting one's lines, forgetting the wedding ring, stumbling in a cafeteria line, or handing a colleague the wrong tool, when these things occur without qualification, bring the performance to an obviously premature and unexpected halt. At the same time, manifestations of the embarrassment— blushing, fumbling, stuttering, sweating[2]—coerce awareness of the social damage and the need for immediate repair. In some instances, the damage may be potentially so great that embarrassment cannot be allowed to spread among the role performers. The incapacity may be qualified, totally ignored, or pretended out of existence.[3] For example, a minister, noting the best man's frantic search for an absent wedding ring, whispers to him to ignore it, and all conspire to continue the drama with

Edward Gross and Gregory P. Stone, "Embarrassment and the Analysis of Role Requirements," *The American Journal of Sociology,* LXX (July 1964), pp. 1–15.

an imaginary ring. Such rescues are not always possible. Hence we suggest that every enduring social relation will provide means of preventing embarrassment, so that the entire transaction will not collapse when embarrassment occurs. A second general observation would take into account that some stages in the life cycle, for example, adolescence in our society, generate more frequent embarrassments than others. These are points to which we shall return.

To get at the content of embarrassment, we classified the instances in categories that remained as close to the specimens as possible. A total of seventy-four such categories were developed, some of which were forced choices between friends, public mistakes, exposure of false front, being caught in a cover story, misnaming, forgetting names, slips of the tongue, body exposure, invasions of others' back regions, uncontrollable laughter, drunkenness in the presence of sobriety (or vice versa), loss of visceral control, and the sudden recognition of wounds or other stigmata. Further inspection of these categories disclosed that most could be included in three general areas: (1) inappropriate identity; (2) loss of poise; (3) disturbance of the assumptions persons make about one another in social transactions.

Since embarrassment always incapacitates persons for role performance (to embarrass is, literally, to bar or stop), a close analysis of the conditions under which it occurs is especially fruitful in the revelation of the requirements *necessary* for role-playing, role-taking, role-making, and role performance in general. These role requirements are thus seen to include the establishment of identity, poise, and valid assumptions about one another among all the parties of a social transaction. We turn now to the analysis of those role requirements.

## IDENTITY AND POISE

In every social transaction, selves must be established, defined, and accepted by the parties. Every person in the company of others is, in a sense, obligated to bring his best self forward to meet the selves of others also presumably best fitted to the occasion. When one is "not himself" in the presence of others who expect him to be just that, as in cases where his mood carries him away either by spontaneous seizure (uncontrollable laughter or tears) or by induced seizure (drunkenness), embarrassment ensues. Similarly, when one is "shown up" to other parties to the transaction by the exposure of unacceptable moral qualifications or inappropriate motives, embarrassment sets in all around. However, the concept, self, is a rather gross concept, and we wish to single out two phases that frequently provided focal points for embarrassment—identity and poise.[4]

*Identity*. Identity is the substantive dimension of the self.[5]

Almost all writers using the term imply that identity establishes what and where the person is in social terms. It is not a substitute word for "self." Instead, when one has identity, he is *situated*—that is, cast in the shape of a social object by the acknowledgement of his participation or membership in social relations. One's identity is established when others *place* him as a social object by assigning the same words of identity that he appropriates for himself or *announces*. It is in the coincidence of placements and announcements that identity becomes a meaning of the self.

Moreover, . . . identity stands at the base of role. When inappropriate identities are established or appropriate identities are lost, role performance is impossible.

If identity *locates* the person in social terms, it follows that locations or spaces emerge as symbols of identity, since social relations are spatially distributed. Moreover, as Goffman has remarked,[6] there must be a certain coherence between one's personal appearance and the setting in which he appears. Otherwise embarrassment may ensue with the resulting incapacitation for role performance. Sexual identity is pervasively established by personal appearance, and a frequent source of embarrassment among our subjects was the presence of one sex in a setting reserved for the other. Both men and women reported inadvertent invasions of spaces set aside for the other sex with consequent embarrassment and humiliation. The implication of such inadvertent invasions is, of course, that one literally does not know where one is, that one literally has no identity in the situation, or that the identity one is putting forward is so absurd as to render the proposed role performance totally irrelevant. Everyone is embarrassed, and such manifestations as, for example, cries and screams, heighten the dis-ease. In such situations, laughter cannot be enjoined to reduce the seriousness of the unexpected collapse of the encounter, and only flight can insure that one will not be buried in the wreckage.

To establish *what* he is in social terms, each person assembles a set of apparent[7] symbols which he carries about as he moves from transaction to transaction. Such symbols include the shaping of the hair, painting of the face, clothing, cards of identity, other contents of wallets and purses, and sundry additional marks and ornaments. The items in the set must cohere, and the set must be complete. Taken together, these apparent symbols have been called *identity documents*,[8] in that they enable others to validate announced identities. Embarrassment often resulted when our subjects made personal appearances with either invalid or incomplete identity documents. It was embarrassing for many, for example, to announce their identities as customers at restaurants or stores, perform the customer role and then, when the crucial validation of this identity was requested—the payoff—to discover that the wallet had been left at home.

Because the social participation of men in American society is relatively more frequently caught up in the central structures, for example, the structure of work, than is the social participation of women who are relatively more immersed in interpersonal relations, the identities put forward by men are often *titles*; by women, often *names*. Except for very unusual titles,[9] such identities are shared, and their presentation has the consequence of bringing people together. Names, on the other hand, mark people off from one another. So it is that a frequent source of embarrassment for women in our society occurs when they appear together in precisely the same dress. Their identity documents are invalidated. The embarrassment may be minimized, however, if the space in which they make their personal appearance is large enough. In one instance, both women met the situation by spending an entire evening on different sides of the ballroom in which their embarrassing confrontation occurred, attempting to secure validation from social circles with minimal intersection, or, at least, where intersection was temporally attenuated. Men, on the other hand, will be embarrassed if their clothing does not resemble the dress of the other men present in public and official encounters. Except for "the old school tie" their neckties seem to serve as numbers on a uniform, marking each man off from every other. Out of uniform, their structural membership cannot be visibly established, and role performance is rendered extremely difficult, if not impossible.[10]

Not only are identities undocumented, they are also misplaced, as in misnaming or forgetting, or other incomplete placements. One relatively frequent source of embarrassment we categorized as "damaging someone's personal representation." This included cases of ethnically colored sneers in the presence of one who, in fact, belonged to the deprecated ethnic group but did not put that identity forward, or behind-the-back slurs about a woman who turned out to be the listener's wife. The victim of such misplacement, however inadvertent, will find it difficult to continue the transaction or to present the relevant identity to the perpetrators of the embarrassment in the future. The awkwardness is reflexive. Those who are responsible for the misplacement will experience the same difficulties and dis-ease.

Other sources of embarrassment anchored in identity suggest a basic characteristic of all human transactions, which, as Strauss puts it, are "carried on in thickly peopled and complexly imaged contexts."[11] One always brings to transactions more identities than are necessary for his role performance. As a consequence, two or more roles are usually performed at once by each participant.[12]

If we designate the relevant roles in transactions as *dominant roles*[13] then we may note that *adjunct roles*—a type of side involvement, as Goffman would have it,[14] or better, a type of side *activity*—are usually performed in parallel with dominant role performance. Specifically, a lecturer may smoke cigarettes or a pipe while carrying out the dominant performance, or one may carry on a heated conversation with a passenger while operating a motor vehicle. Moreover, symbols of *reserve identities* are often carried into social transactions. Ordinarily, they are concealed, as when a court judge wears his golfing clothes beneath his robes. Finally, symbols of abandoned or *relict identities* may persist in settings where they have no relevance for dominant role performances.[15] For example, photographs of the performer as an infant may be thrust into a transaction by a doting mother or wife, or one's newly constituted household may still contain the symbols of a previous marriage.

In these respects, the probability of avoiding embarrassment is a function of at least two factors: (1) the extent to which adjunct roles, reserve identities and relict identities are not incongruent with the dominant role performance;[16] and (2) the allocation of prime attention to the dominant role performance so that less attention is directed toward adjunct role performance, reserve identities, and relict identities. Thus the professor risks embarrassment should the performance of his sex role appear to be the main activity in transactions with female students where the professorial role is dominant—for example, if the student pulls her skirt over her knees with clearly more force than necessary. The judge may not enter the courtroom in a golf cap, nor may the husband dwell on the symbols of a past marriage in the presence of a new wife while entertaining guests in his home. Similarly, should adjunct role performance prove inept, as when the smoking lecturer ignites the contents of a wastebasket or the argumentative driver fails to observe the car in front in time to avert a collision, attention is diverted from the dominant role performance. Even without the golf cap, should the judge's robe be caught so that his golfing attire is suddenly revealed in the courtroom, the transactions of the court will be disturbed. Fetishistic devotion to the symbols of relict identities by bereaved persons is embarrassing even to well-meaning visitors.

However, the matter of avoiding incongruence and allocating attention appropriately among the several identities a performer brings to a transaction verges very closely on matters of poise, as we shall see. Matters of poise converge on the necessity of controlling representations of the self, and identity-symbols are important self-representations.

*Personal poise.* Presentation of the self in social transactions extends considerably beyond making the appropriate personal appearance. It includes the presentation of an entire situation. Components of situations, however, are often representations of self, and in this sense self and situation are two sides of the same coin. Personal poise refers to the performer's control over self and situation, and whatever disturbs that control, depriving the transaction, as we have said before, of any relevant future, is incapacitating and consequently embarrassing. . . .

First, *spaces* must be so arranged and maintained that they are role-enabling. This is sometimes difficult to control, since people appear in spaces that belong to others, over which they exercise no authority and for which they are not responsible. Students, invited to faculty parties where faculty members behave like faculty members, will "tighten up" to the extent that the students' role performance is seriously impeded. To avoid embarrassment, people will go to great lengths to insure their appearance in appropriate places, and to some to be deprived of access to a particular setting is to limit performance drastically. . . .

We have already touched upon problems presented by invasions of spaces, and little more need be said. Persons lose poise when they discover they are in places forbidden to them, for the proscription itself means they have no identity there and hence cannot act. They can do little except withdraw quickly. It is interesting that children are continually invading the territories of others—who can control the course of a sharply hit baseball?—and part of the process of socialization consists of indications of the importance of boundaries. . . .

Such considerations raise questions concerning both how boundaries are defined and how boundary violations may be prevented. Walls provide physical limits, but do not necessarily prevent communications from passing through.[17] Hence walls work best when there is also tacit agreement to ignore audible communication on the other side of the wall. Embarrassment frequently occurs when persons on one side of the wall learn that intimate matters have been communicated to persons on the other side. A common protective device is for the captive listeners to become very quiet so that their receipt of the communication will not be discovered by the unsuspecting intimates. When no physical boundaries are present, a group gathered in one section of a room may have developed a common mood which is bounded by a certain space that defines the limits of their engagement to one another. The entry of someone new may be followed by an embarrassed hush. It is not necessary that the group should have been talking about that person. Rather, since moods take time to build up, it will take time for the newcomer to "get with it" and it may not be worth the group's trouble to "fill him in." However unintentionally, he has destroyed a mood that took some effort to build up and he will suffer for it, if only by being stared at or by an obvious change of subject. In some cases, when the mood is partially sustained by alcohol, one can prepare the newcomer immediately for the mood by loud shouts that the group is "three drinks ahead" of him and by thrusting a drink into his hand without delay. So, too, a function of foyers, halls, anterooms, and other buffer zones or decompression chambers around settings is to prepare such newcomers and hence reduce the likelihood of their embarrassing both themselves and those inside. . . .

Next, every social transaction requires the manipulation of *equipment*.

If props are ordinarily stationary during encounters, equipment is typically moved about, handled, or touched.[18] Equipment can range from *words* to *physical objects*, and a loss of control over such equipment is a frequent source of embarrassment. Here are included slips of the tongue, sudden dumbness when speech is called for, stalling cars in traffic, dropping bowling balls, spilling food, and tool failures. Equipment appearances that cast doubt on the adequacy of control are illustrated by the clanking motor, the match burning down to the fingers, tarnished silverware, or rusty work tools. Equipment sometimes extends beyond what is actually handled in the transaction to include the stage props. Indeed, items of equipment in disuse, reserve equipment, often become props—the Cadillac in the driveway or the silver service on the shelf—and there is a point at which the objects used or scheduled for use in a situation are both equipment and props. At one instant, the items of a table setting lie immobile as props; at the next, they are taken up and transformed into equipment. The close linkage of equipment and props may be responsible for the fact that *embarrassment* at times not only *infects* the participants in the transaction but the *objects* as well. For example, at a formal dinner, a speaker was discovered with his fly zipper undone. On being informed of this embarrassing oversight after he was reseated, he proceeded to make the requisite adjustment, unknowingly catching the table cloth in his trousers. When obliged to rise again at the close of the proceedings, he took the stage props with him and of course scattered the dinner tools about the setting in such a way that others were forced to doubt his control. His poise was lost in the situation. . . .

[C]*lothing* must also be maintained, controlled, and coherently arranged. Its very appearance must communicate this. Torn clothing, frayed cuffs, stained neckties, and unpolished shoes are felt as embarrassing in situations where they are expected to be untorn, neat, clean, and polished. Clothing is of special importance since, as William James observed,[19] it is as much a part of the self as the body—a part of what he called the "material me." Moreover, since it is so close to the body, it conveys the impression of body maintenance, paradoxically, by concealing body-maintenance activities.[20] Hence, the double wrap—outer clothes and underclothes. Underclothes bear the marks of body maintenance and tonic state, and their unexpected exposure is a frequent source of embarrassment. The broken brassière strap sometimes produces a shift in appearance that few women (or men, for that matter) will fail to perceive as embarrassing.

[T]he *body* must always be in a state of readiness to act, and its appearance must make this clear. Hence any evidence of unreadiness or clumsiness is embarrassing. Examples include loss of whole body control (stumbling, trembling, or fainting), loss of visceral control (flatulence, involuntary urination, or drooling), and the communication of other "signs of the animal." The actress who is photographed from her "bad side'' loses poise, for it shakes the foundation on which her fame rests. So does the person who is embarrassed about pimples, warts, or missing limbs, as well as those embarrassed in his presence.

Ordinarily, persons will avoid recognizing such stigmata, turn their eyes away, and pretend them out of existence, but on occasion stigmata will obtrude upon the situation causing embarrassment all around. A case in point was a minor flirtation reported by one of our students. Seated in a library a short distance from a beautiful girl, the student began the requisite gestural invitation to a more intimate conversation. The girl turned, smiling, to acknowledge the bid, revealing an amputated left arm. Our student's gestural line was brought to a crashing halt. Embarrassed, he abandoned the role he was building even before the foundation was laid, pretending that his inviting gestures were directed toward some imaginary audience suggested by his reading. Such stigmata publicize body-maintenance activities, and, when they are established in social transactions, interfere with role performances. The pimples on the face of the job applicant cast doubt on his maturity, and, consequently, on his qualifications for any job requiring such maturity. . . .

## MAINTENANCE OF CONFIDENCE

When identities have been validated and persons poised, interaction may begin. Its continuation, however, requires that a scaffolding be erected and that attention be given to preventing this scaffolding from collapsing. The scaffold develops as the relationship becomes stabilized. In time persons come to expect that the way they place the other is the way the other announces himself, and that poise will continue to be maintained. Persons now begin to count on these expectations and to have confidence in them. But at any time they may be violated. It was such violations of confidence that made up the greatest single source of embarrassment in our examples. Perhaps this is only an acknowledgment that the parties to every transaction must always maintain themselves *in role* to permit the requisite role-taking, or that identity-switching ought not be accomplished so abruptly that others are left floundering in the encounter as they grope for the new futures that the new identity implies.

This is all the more important in situations where roles are tightly linked together as in situations involving a division of labor. In one instance, a group of social scientists was presenting a progress report of research to a representative of the client subsidizing the research. The principal investigator's presentation was filled out by comments from the other researchers, his professional peers. Negatively critical comments were held to a bare minimum. Suddenly the principal investigator overstepped the bounds. He made a claim that they were well on the road to confirming a hypothesis which, if confirmed, would represent a major contribution. Actually, his colleagues (our informant was one of them) knew that they were very far indeed from confirming the hypothesis. They first sought to catch the leader's eye to look for a hidden message. Receiving none, they lowered their eyes to the table, bit their lips, and fell silent. In the presence of the client's representative, they felt they could not "call" their leader for that would be embarrassing, but they did seek him out immediately afterward for an explanation. The leader agreed that they were right, but said his claim was politic, that new data might well turn up, and that it was clearly too late to remedy the situation.

Careful examination of this case reveals a more basic reason for the researchers' hesitance to embarrass the leader before the client's representative. If their leader were revealed to be the kind of person who goes beyond the data (or to be a plain liar), serious questions could have been raised about the kind of men who willingly work with such a person. Thus they found themselves coerced into unwilling collusion. It was not simply that their jobs depended on continued satisfaction of the client. Rather they were unwilling to say to themselves and to the client's representative that they were the kind of researchers who would be party to a fraud. To embarrass the leader, then, would have meant embarrassing themselves by casting serious question upon their identities as researchers. Indeed, it was their desire to cling to their identities that led, not long afterward (and after several other similar experiences), to the breakup of the research team.

Just as, in time, an identity may be discredited, so too may poise be upset. Should this occur, each must be able to assume that the other will render assistance if he gets into such control trouble, and each must be secure in the knowledge that the assumption is tenable. Persons will be alert for incipient signs of such trouble—irrelevant attitudes—and attempt to avert the consequences. Goffman has provided many examples in his discussion of dramaturgical loyalty, discipline, and circumspection in the presentation of the self, pointing out protective practices that are employed, such as clearing one's throat before interrupting a conversation, knocking on doors before entering an occupied room, or begging the other's pardon before an intrusion.[21]

The danger that one's confidence in the other's continued identity or his ability to maintain his poise may be destroyed leads to the generation of a set of *performance norms*. These are social protections against embarrassment.[22] If persons adhere to them, the probability of embarrassment is reduced. We discovered two major performance norms.

First, *standards of role performance almost always allow for flexibility and tolerance*. One is rarely, if ever, totally in role (an exception might be highly ritualized performances where to acknowledge breaches of expectation is devastatingly embarrassing).[23] To illustrate, we expect one another to give attention to what is going on in our transactions, but the attention we anticipate is always *optimal*, never total. To lock the other person completely in one's glance and refuse to let go is very embarrassing. A rigid attention is coerced eventuating in a loss of poise. . . . Similarly, never to give one's attention to the other is role-incapacitating. If one focuses his gaze not on the other's eyes, but on his forehead, let us say, the encounter is visibly disturbed.[24] Norms allowing for flexibility and tolerance permit the parties to social transactions ordinarily to assume that they will not be held to rigid standards of conduct and that temporary lapses will be overlooked. . . .

The second performance norm was that of *giving the other fellow the benefit of the doubt.* For the transaction to go on at all, one has at least to give the other fellow a *chance* to play the role he seeks to play. Clearly, if everyone went around watching for chances to embarrass others, so many would be incapacitated for role performance that society would collapse. Such considerate behavior is probably characteristic of all human society, because of the dependence of social relations on role performance. A part of socialization, therefore, must deal with the prevention of embarrassment by the teaching of tact. People must learn not only not to embarrass others, but to ignore the lapses that can be embarrassing whenever they occur. In addition, people must learn to *cope* with embarrassment. Consequently, embarrassment will occasionally be deliberately perpetrated to ready people for role incapacitation when it occurs.

•   •   •

## CONCLUSION

In this paper, we have inquired into the conditions necessary for role performance. Embarrassment has been employed as a sensitive indicator of those conditions, for that which embarrasses incapacitates role performance. Our data have led us to describe the conditions for role performance in terms of identity, poise, and sustained confidence in one another. When these become disturbed and discredited, role performance cannot continue. Consequently, provisions for the avoidance or prevention of embarrassment, or quick recovery from embarrassment when it does occur, are of key importance to any society or social transaction, and devices to insure the avoidance and minimization of embarrassment will be part of every persisting social relationship. . . .

### NOTES

1. Not all incapacitated persons are always embarrassed or embarrassing, because others have come to expect their *incapacities* and are consequently prepared for them.

2. Erving Goffman, in "Embarrassment and Social Organization," *American Journal of Sociology*, LXII (November 1956), 264–71, describes these manifestations vividly.

3. A more general discussion of this phenomenon, under the rubric civil inattention, is provided in Erving Goffman, *Behavior in Public Places* (New York: Free Press of Glencoe, 1963), pp. 83–88 and *passim*.

4. Other dimensions of the self—value and mood—will be taken up in subsequent publications.

5. Gregory P. Stone, "Appearance and the Self," in Arnold Rose (ed.), *Human Behavior and Social Processes* (Boston: Houghton Mifflin, 1962), p. 93.

6. Erving Goffman, *The Presentation of Self in Everyday Life* (New York: Doubleday Anchor Books, 1959), p. 25.

7. We use the term "appearance" to designate that dimension of a social transaction given over to identifications of the participants. Apparent symbols are those symbols used to communicate such identifications. They are often nonverbal. Appearance seems, to us, a more useful term than Goffman's "front" (*ibid.*), which in everyday speech connotes misrepresentation.

8. Erving Goffman, *Stigma* (Englewood Cliffs, N.J.: Prentice-Hall, 1963), pp. 59–62. Goffman confines the concept to personal identity, but his own discussion extends it to include matters of social identity.

9. For example, the title, "honorary citizen of the United States," which was conferred on Winston Churchill, served the function of a name, since Churchill was the only living recipient of the title. Compare the titles, "professor," "manager," "punch-press operator," and the like.

10. The implication of the discussion is that structured activities are uniformed, while interpersonal activities emphasize individuation in dress. Erving Goffman suggests, in correspondence, that what may be reflected here is the company people keep in their transactions. The work of men in our society is ordinarily teamwork, and teams are uniformed, but housework performed by a wife is solitary work and does not require a uniformed appearance, though the "housedress" might be so regarded.

11. Anselm L. Strauss, *Mirrors and Masks* (Glencoe, Ill.: Free Press, 1959), p. 57.

12. This observation and the ensuing discussion constitute a contribution to and extension of present perspectives on role conflict. Most discussions conceive of such conflict as internalized contradictory obligations. They do not consider simultaneous multiple-role performances. An exception is Everett C. Hughes' discussion of the Negro physician innocently summoned to attend a prejudiced emergency case in "Dilemmas and Contradictions in Status," *American Journal of Sociology*, L (March 1945), pp. 353–59.

13. We have rewritten this discussion to relate to Goffman's classification which came to our attention after we had prepared an earlier version of this article. Goffman distinguishes between what people do in transactions and what the situation calls for. He recognizes that people do many things at once in their encounters and distinguishes those activities that command most of their attention and energies from those which are less demanding of energy and time. Here, the distinction is made between *main* and *side involvements*. On the other hand, situations often call for multiple activities. Those which are central to the situation,

Goffman speaks of as *dominant involvements*; others are called *subordinate involvements*. Dominant roles, therefore, are those that are central to the transactional situation—what the participants have come together to do (see Goffman, *Behavior in Public Places*, pp. 43–59).

14. Adjunct roles are one type of side involvement or activity. We focus on them because we are concerned here with identity difficulties. There are other side *activities* which are *not* necessarily adjunct *roles*, namely, sporadic nosepicking, scratching, coughing, sneezing, or stomach growling, which are relevant to matters of embarrassment, but not to the conceptualization of the problem in these terms. Of course, such activities, insofar as they are consistently proposed and anticipated, may become incorporated in the *personal role* (always an adjunct in official transactions), as in the case of Billy Gilbert, the fabulous sneezer.

15. This phenomenon provides the main theme and source of horror and mystery in Daphne du Maurier's now classic *Rebecca*.

16. Adjunct roles, reserve identities, and relict identities need not cohere with the dominant role; they simply must not clash so that the attention of participants in a transaction is not completely diverted from the dominant role performance.

17. See Erving Goffman, *Behavior in Public Places*, pp. 151–52.

18. Whether objects in a situation are meant to be moved, manipulated, or taken up provides an important differentiating dimension between equipment on the one hand and props (as well as clothing, to be discussed shortly) on the other. Equipment is meant to be moved, manipulated, or taken up *during* a social transaction whereas clothing and props are expected to remain unchanged during a social transaction but will be moved, manipulated, or taken up *between* social transactions. To change props, as in burning the portrait of an old girl friend (or to change clothes, as in taking off a necktie), signals a change in the situation. The special case of the strip-tease dancer is no exception, for her act transforms clothes into equipment. The reference above to the "stickiness" of props may now be seen as another way of describing the fact that they are not moved, manipulated, or taken up during transactions, but remain unchanged for the course of the transaction. Clothing is equally sticky but the object to which it sticks differs. Clothing sticks to the body; props stick to the settings.

19. William James, *Psychology* (New York: Henry Holt & Co., 1892), pp. 177–78.

20. A complete exposition of the body-maintenance function of clothing is set forth in an advertisement for Jockey briefs, entitled: "A Frank Discussion: What Wives Should Know about Male Support," *Good Housekeeping*, May, 1963, p. 237.

21. Goffman, *The Presentation of Self in Everyday Life*, pp. 212–33.

22. Implicit in Georg Simmel, *The Sociology of Georg Simmel*, trans. Kurt H. Wolff (Glencoe, Ill.: Free Press, 1950), p. 308.

23. See the discussion of "role distance" in Erving Goffman, *Encounters* (Indianapolis, Ind.: Bobbs-Merrill Co., 1961), pp. 105–52.

24. Here we are speaking of what Edward T. Hall calls the "gaze line." He points out there are cultural variations in this phenomenon. See his "A System for the Notation of Proxemic Behavior," *American Anthropologist*, LXV (October 1963), 1012–14.

# Review Questions

1. Define the terms *identity* and *poise*. How do threats to identity and poise disrupt interaction?

2. How are spaces, props, equipment, and clothing used to validate identities and to maintain poise?

3. Distinguish between dominant roles, adjunct roles, reverse identities, and relict identities. How are these related to embarrassment?

4. Discuss the two "performance norms" described by Gross and Stone which protect against embarrassment. Give examples of these norms from your own experiences.

# THE PURSUIT OF ATTENTION

## Charles Derber and Yale Magrass

. . . In America, wealth, occupation, and education all signifi-cantly affect who gets attention in everyday interactions, with members of privileged groups receiving the most and those in subordinate groups experiencing a certain daily invisibility. Inequalities of attention grow out of the most fundamental forms of social inequality and must be under-stood partly as a feature of a society divided into classes.

• • •

In America, the dominant classes are those which come to control eco-nomic, political, and cultural life. They include the monied class that owns economic resources and the emerging class of managers and pro-fessionals that exercises economic and cultural authority over the rest of the population. The subordinate classes include a marginal underclass comprising the poor, unemployed, and peripherally employed, and the working class, whose members are employed but do not own capital or exercise authority.[1] Members of dominant classes have advantages in gaining attention in . . . "formal" interactions principally because of their power and official status. They monopolize the commanding atten-tion-getting roles in cultural and political life and in workplaces. In addi-tion, they are advantaged in informal interactions because wealth, occu-pation, and education create added claims to attention in ordinary conversations. . . .

## ATTENTION AS A COMMODITY: WEALTH AND THE PURCHASE OF ATTENTION

In modern industrial societies, a growing percentage of the individual's social life occurs in "secondary" relationships mediated by money and commercial interests. People must seek to satisfy their basic needs—in-cluding attention—in interactions governed directly or indirectly by the market. Attention has become increasingly available as a commodity to be purchased from people who give attention in the course of their work

Excerpted from Charles Derber, *The Pursuit of Attention: Power and Individualism in Everyday Life* (New York: Oxford University Press, 1983), pp. 64–86.

and expect to be paid for their services. Members of the dominant classes are best able to afford atention of this kind and consume the greatest amount.

Consider, for example, the purchase of attention in psychotherapy. Therapy is a market-based formal interaction explicitly structured to assure the client-purchaser most of the attention. In exchange for a fee, the client is assured that the only legitimate focus or ''subject'' of the interaction is [him or] herself. . . . The therapist is the quintessential professional attention-giver, for the focus of his [or her] training is the development of attention-giving skills, and it is these skills for which [she or] he is paid.

In the therapeutic setting, unlike many other market settings, there is no subtlety cloaking the exchange of attention for money, as the therapist publicly offers . . . attention and the client openly purchases it. In the therapeutic process itself, however, the therapist must convince [the] client that [she or] he is giving . . . attention out of genuine concern and sympathy rather than for purely pecuniary ends or the therapeutic endeavor is likely to fail. This reflects the fact that people are most gratified by attention they believe others spontaneously choose to give. Thus, even people purchasing attention want to believe that the other is giving . . . attention freely rather than because [their] purchase requires it.

●   ●   ●

The purchase of attention in restaurants, a very different kind of market setting, illustrates [the] point [that the privileged can get more attention than the subordinate classes]. Getting attention is part of the pleasure of ''eating out,'' even in a modest restaurant where the amount of attention the customer can normally expect is limited to the simple serving of a meal.

But the attention purchased in the *expensive* restaurant is distinct. The reputation of an exclusive restaurant rests not only in the quality of its food, but its capacity to deliver in delicately structured interactions the extra attention for which its affluent clientele is presumably deserving and able to pay for. . . . Here, the role of customer is a source of exceptional attention. Patrons purchase the services of a variety of attention-givers, as well as the rights to a carefully cultivated face-to-face deference. [They] can immediately engage those serving [them][2] and, in face-to-face interaction, can expect unhurried and uninterrupted attention. These waiters[3] are trained to give undivided visual attention, to listen solicitously, and to refrain from making themselves the focus of the interaction. . . .

The waiter-patron interchange in the expensive restaurant reflects the way attention is typically allocated in formal interactions, with people in the dominant classes gaining the attention and members of the subordinate classes giving it. Since attention-giving is related to offering deference and respect, the transaction not only reflects the economic power of those in the giving and getting roles, but symbolically affirms their relative social worth.[4]

The privileged classes purchase attention not only in restaurants, shops, and other public settings, but also in formal interactions in private life, by employing attention-givers in the home. As depicted in chronicles of upper-class life, . . . members of the dominant classes have historically surrounded themselves with servants recruited from the subordinate classes who must routinely give attention to whoever pays for their services. Even in the contemporary affluent household, cooks, cleaning ladies, governesses, and other domestic help are employed in attention-giving roles and are judged partly by the quality of the attention they give.[5] In many upper-class homes, liveried servants continue to serve dinner, [and] valets and chauffeurs attend to the adults. The privileged classes are also able to purchase "overseers" (nannies, governesses, etc.) for their children, thus relieving parents of many attention-giving responsibilities.

## WEALTH AND INFORMAL INTERACTIONS: ATTENTION AND CONSUMPTION DISPLAYS

Attention is "purchased" in a different way in the informal interactions of everyday life. By displaying symbols of material success, an individual can increase his sense of his own worth and his rights to attention, while at the same time predisposing others to give the attention expected. Ostentatious or subtle exhibits of property can be used both to attract attention in public places and to help a person maintain the focus of attention in everyday conversations.

Displays of clothing are the most important evidences of property in ordinary interaction. Dressing fashionably is an extremely common means by which people seek to gain attention. Here, members of the dominant classes are especially advantaged. . . .

•   •   •

The automobile is another possession that symbolizes social worth and is "displayed" to bring attention to the self. By driving such luxury cars as Cadillacs, Continentals, Mercedes, and Rolls Royces, wealthy individuals attract attention in the streets and in public places.[6] . . . Nowadays, the acquisition of expensive but less blatantly garish vehicles, including sports cars, antique automobiles, and chauffeured limousines, remains a means by which dominant groups indirectly "purchase" attention.

There are many other areas in which dominant groups set standards of taste and draw attention by displays of consumer sophistication.

Tasteful displays of furniture, artwork, glassware, china and cutlery, stereophonic equipment, and other household items are used by members of affluent groups as subtle ways of establishing their worth and rights to special attention in everyday interactions. . . .

Subordinate groups also buy goods to attract desirable attention. A given toothpaste will buy a winning smile with sparkling white teeth; a given perfume will attract and hold the attention of that glamorous man in the office. People in the subordinate classes, without access to institutional attention-getting roles, may come to depend especially on the acquisition of goods to compensate. The worker in the factory or the clerk in the office who get little or no attention in their work roles may be able to afford the flashy car, clothes, and other goods that bring some attention in personal interaction. While for many consumption is one of the few avenues for gaining attention, it is part of a system that best serves the privileged classes, as they can purchase the commodities which most symbolize worth.

•    •    •

[T]he poor are a relatively small sector of the subordinate classes and face the greatest problems of visibility in formal interactions. [T]he attention-getting role is normally the powerful one, but there are exceptions affecting mainly the poor. A number of institutions, including welfare agencies, social work offices, and employment services, offer poor people roles in which they receive face-to-face attention. However, power in these interactions rests in the hands of those giving attention. Welfare client, as an example, is a role of weakness and helplessness, bringing attention at the cost of respect and requiring that the individual acknowledge personal incapacity, failure, or dependency.

Under these conditions, the attention-getting role is one the individual would ordinarily avoid. Those receiving such attention are less likely to feel supported or nurtured [than] intruded upon, violated, or humiliated. They have little control over the nature of the interaction and the attention given, or over how the parts of their personalities and life histories are examined and revealed. While attention is always potentially controlling or victimizing, this is especially true when the attention-giver represents social control agencies. Giving attention becomes part of the exercise of power and the attention itself a threat or weapon.[7]

## ATTENTION AND WORK

In addition to being a commodity that can be purchased, attention is a reward of authority and prestige in work. People in the dominant occupations[8] gain special attention in the formal interactions in their work life and also in their informal interactions in personal life. This is related both to the structure of work roles and to the growing importance of work as the governing symbol of social worth.

The claim to expertise is a primary source of power for those in dominant occupations and a formidable way of gaining attention. People approach most professionals for what they believe is valuable information, and not only pay generously for it, but give in return an uncommonly close form of attention. The worried patient will hang on every word of his doctor, the legal client will listen keenly to the advice of his lawyer, the avid student will give undivided attention to the professor who knows what the student wants to know.

•  •  •

A professional is normally granted attention automatically on the basis of assumed expertise and knowledge. A resort to conscious "displays," even of the subtle kind illustrated here, is thus likely to happen only under those circumstances—which occur frequently in the classroom—where the professional is uncertain that those required by their role to listen to him are actually doing so.[9]

The control of rewards and punishments also assures professionals and managers attention in formal interactions. In a courtroom, all parties extend respectful attention to the judge, not only because of the ritual formalities but because of the inordinate power he wields over the fate of the petitioners. Similarly, at the workplace, because the employer hires and fires, and controls conditions of work, employees focus on him. In face-to-face interactions with [one's] boss, a subordinate must give respectful attention even if [one] feels resentment or bitterness. This is a part of deference in formal interactions: the role of the subordinate is not only to listen and respond to instructions or commands, but also to show respect by being especially attentive and taking care not to draw undue attention to [oneself].

Professional services have traditionally required attention-giving to clients in face-to-face interactions. More recently, however, changes in professional work roles have shifted attention-giving responsibility from professionals to less skilled subordinates; the professional spends less of his time in interactions with clients and, during the time he does so, often gains attention as the "expert" rather than giving it as a helper. . . .

•  •  •

The difference in the two interactions is striking. With [a] nurse [helper], the focus of attention remains on the patient and the nurse exhibits a "bedside manner" traditionally associated with family doctors. The doctor, on the other hand, interacts with the patient less as a caretaker than as expert consultant. In the "expert" role he becomes the focus of attention himself and offers relatively little attention to the patient.

The same dynamics are evident in higher education. Professors are "experts" who meet with students in large classes to impart knowledge. To the extent that students receive any attention, they are less likely to receive it from their professors in the classroom than from teaching assistants or graduate students who lead discussion groups, read papers, and meet with students in individual consultations. Like nurses and medical paraprofessionals, teaching assistants are part of an emerging stratum of subordinates who buffer professionals from demands of clients and take over the routine burden of attention-giving.

In the business world, executives and bosses also delegate much of the responsibility of attention-giving to subordinates. The secretary-receptionist, for example, not only gives attention to clients, but must do so in a way conducive to her boss's interests. Secretaries give attention to their bosses as well as to clients, nurses to doctors as well as patients, and teaching assistants to professors as well as to students. These attention-givers thus benefit those in dominant occupations doubly, not only by lightening their attention-giving responsibilities but reinforcing their attention-getting status.[10]

## INVISIBILITY AT WORK: SUBORDINATE OCCUPATIONS

The work roles of those not in dominant occupations are rarely attention-getting ones. Most sales and service workers, clerical workers, and industrial workers do not have subordinates expected to give them attention. The only attention that these workers can typically expect in their formal interactions is from supervisors who regulate their behavior.[11]

It is useful to distinguish subordinate workers who remain visible and others who become invisible. Invisibility, as R. D. Laing has pointed out, is the most drastic form of attention-deprivation, ultimately more painful and dehumanizing than hostile or other "negative" attention. Anyone can become temporarily invisible in meetings, groups, and other kinds of everyday situations. But for those whose job is regarded as dirty, unpleasant, or unsightly, and are therefore required to work in hidden places such as kitchens or basements, it is routine to their daily experience. Other workers of very low status, such as the cleaning lady or the busboy, while they may work in the purview of other people, remain invisible because others feel no need to acknowledge their presence.

Erving Goffman's [1959] distinction between "front" and "back" regions of the workplace provides a basis for looking more closely at the difference between visible and invisible work roles. Goffman points out that work space can be divided into that accessible to the public or other outsiders (the "front" space) and those accessible only to the employees themselves (the "back" region). In a restaurant, the kitchen and stockroom are the back regions, while the dining room is the front region. There are normally physical barriers between front and back regions, designed to prevent those in the front regions from seeing what takes place in the back regions. Certain workers, such as waitresses, have access to both regions while others, such as dishwashers, are confined to the back region.

•    •    •

Workers restricted to the back regions become invisible to the public. The kitchen help, for example, remain completely unseen by the clientele of the restaurant. Similarly, stockboys, packers, inventory clerks, and many clerical workers, who are normally restricted to back regions of department stores, grocery stores, and other service or retail establishments, also work unnoticed.

Being in an invisible work role does not imply that the worker gets no attention at all in his job. The dishwasher may seek and get attention in informal interactions with fellow workers in his back region. Moreover, he is freed from having to give attention to the clientele. Nonetheless, his invisibility to the public is symbolic of his low worth and disadvantages him in gaining attention. Symbolically, it suggests that he is not entitled to acknowledgment or recognition from the clientele.

Workers confined to the back regions are not the only ones in invisible work roles. A more extreme form of dehumanization is experienced by those who work in front regions, but whose presence commands no attention whatsoever. The sweeper in the restaurant, for example, carries out his work in full view without anyone else noticing him and remains unseen unless he commits an offense which violates his role. . . . Similarly, transportation workers and the janitors and groundskeepers in many establishments carry out their work in view of others and yet receive minimal recognition. . . .

On the other hand, there are many work settings where the lower-status employees occupy the front regions while those with the greatest power are sheltered in exclusive back regions. In a bank, for example, the tellers are visible, while the executives are hidden within imposing offices. Similarly, in many bureaucracies, clerks and other low-status office workers can normally be seen within a large office space while the more powerful employees gradually disappear into asylums as they move up the ranks. In these circumstances, "invisibility" is actually a symbol of status. The executive suite is, however, a very different kind of back region from, say, the restaurant kitchen, and the "invisibility" of the high official radically distinct from that of the dishwasher. The executive office is designed to serve the interest of the one who occupies it, functioning in many ways as a sanctuary from the demands of others. . . .

Workers available to the public, moreover, such as bank tellers and receptionists, are normally in attention-giving roles. They typically receive from the public only the minimal acknowledgment of their presence that is required to conduct business. Their visibility merely reflects the obligation of giving attention to customers—a duty delegated to those in the front region—and not the privilege of receiving it, which is reserved for those in the back region.

. . . [A]ll lower-status workers are assured, however, of getting the one kind of attention that all work establishments direct toward their employees, even the least favored in formal interactions: *supervisory attention*. Employers extend the attention required to insure that they are doing their job, maintaining discipline, and working at the rhythm and efficiency expected of them. On the assembly line, the foreman focuses his attention on the workers to regulate their behavior and prevent interruptions of the production process. The gaze of the foreman is the immediate expression, face-to-face, of a larger system of social control that institutionalizes the power of the employer over the worker; it is the most important and least desired of the forms of attention that workers receive.

## WORK IDENTITY AND INFORMAL INTERACTION

We have seen that the competition for attention in ordinary informal interaction involves a struggle by each individual to establish his or her relative worth. High occupational status has become one of the most important symbols defining personal worth in ordinary social relations. As a result, professionals, executives, and others in dominant occupations enjoy a significant advantage in seeking and winning attention in ordinary conversation. . . .

To exploit occupational status as a means of getting attention, the individual must successfully display or communicate it to others. . . . Unlike a property display, disclosures of occupational identity are not usually communicated visually (although a doctor, for example, can give visual cues by wearing a "beeper" or white coat when off the job). Such information normally surfaces in conversation either by being openly discussed or by being subtly communicated through use of technical language or knowledge. . . . At the beginning of conversations between strangers or new acquaintances, people normally break the ice with the familiar question "What do you do?" . . .

In most social relations, those in dominant occupations need not disclose this information, as it is already known to family, friends, and others with whom they regularly interact. . . . Those . . . whose occupational status is clearly inferior will find their worth constantly in question. In order to win attention, they must struggle to establish it in other ways. This is reflected in subtle dynamics in conversations among people of different occupational statuses. People of low status may feel the pressure to talk constantly simply to prevent others from withdrawing their attention altogether. This is reflected in the stereotypical "talkativeness" of housewives, who cannot draw on occupational status to secure attention in ordinary situations. An analysis of the talk of working-class housewives indicates that their lack of occupational status forces them to seek alternative strategies (obsessive talking is one possibility) to mitigate the fear that they might be completely disregarded.[12]

## ATTENTION AND EDUCATION

An individual's education also has a major effect on the attention he or she receives in everyday interactions. Since access to higher education depends on one's class position[13] and is instrumental in one's gaining entry to dominant occupations, it becomes an indirect basis for access to the attention-getting roles already considered. In addition, independently of one's occupation and income, one's education can be a powerful claim on attention. In everyday conversation, people with college or advanced education have a number of advantages in gaining attention, stemming from the importance of schooling as a unique symbol of worth that entitles the individual to special forms of recognition.

This is partly due to the widespread tendency to equate schooling with intelligence. Intelligence is regarded as a fundamental kind of ability which commands enormous respect in contemporary culture, and its appearance or apparent absence has a major effect on the kinds of attention any individual receives. While there is no compelling evidence that those given special access to higher education are more intelligent than others, they are normally regarded as such, in part because education provides resources (mainly verbal skills and specialized information) for appearing so. Those without advanced education are widely considered deficient both in ability and intelligence, and thus lacking a claim to the interest and attention of others. . . .

Revelations about educational status are enormously important in shaping others' assessments of one's worth and regulating the flow of attention. . . . One does not ordinarily make explicit reference to educational accomplishments, although an individual who offhandedly mentions his undergraduate experience at Princeton or the fact that he has a Ph.D. will enhance his status. Usually, the display is more subtle and indirect, involving either the use of sophisticated vocabulary and manner of speaking or the display of specialized knowledge.

Speech is enormously important as an education display and attention-getting cue. Sociolinguists have accumulated considerable evidence that people can be identified in terms of class, subculture, and education on the basis of how they talk.[14] Such matters as vocabulary, grammar, intonation, and diction significantly affect how people respond to one another. Members of dominant classes uses an expanded vocabulary (including more technical, literary, or simply ''big'' words) as well as the ''proper'' or ''standard'' grammar and diction that others recognize as evidence of advanced schooling. . . . Studies in such diverse contexts as jury rooms, parent-teacher meetings, and community gatherings indicate that those who talk the most frequently and whose ideas are given the greatest attention are invariably individuals with high educational status and class background, and that those less educated normally speak less often and receive less attention.[15]

Members of subordinate classes who do not exhibit the "standard" vocabulary, grammar, and diction are handicapped as soon as they begin to speak. These handicaps begin early in life, since the working- or lower-class child is less likely to get attention from teachers in school because of the way he talks.[16] This is one of the most subtle forms of discrimination by class, reproduced in the everyday interactions within all our institutions.

## NOTES

1. The working class, as understood here, includes blue-collar and many white-collar and service workers who are often characterized as "middle class" in popular discourse. The characterization of "middle class" obscures the fact that these workers, many of whom are moderately well paid, do not exercise control over their work or cultural institutions and are subject to the authority of capital and the professional-managerial class. The dominant classes, as understood here, refer to those popularly referred to as the "upper class" and the "upper-middle" class and comprise at most between twenty and thirty percent of the population.

2. An important "privilege" of attention involves the conditions under which the customer can signal those serving him that he wants attention (that is, signal him to engage in direct "focused" interaction). In the ordinary restaurant, . . . the waiter, rushed by demands from a number of tables, can pretend not to see the signal of a customer at a given table and thus give himself more time to finish what he is in the process of doing. In the expensive restaurant, where a waiter is assigned to wait on only one party at a time, the patron is freed from the annoyance of these delays and can expect immediate response to signals for attention.

3. We refer to waiters rather than waitresses here because exclusive restaurants typically employ males to serve and attend to their clientele. This suggests that male attention is deemed more valuable. While attention-giving is expected more regularly of women, the dominant classes have the resources to purchase male attention as a scarce and more prized commodity.

4. An interesting analogy is suggested between the selling of labor power and the selling of attention. In the capitalist market system, both labor and attention are transformed into commodities, with purchase reserved for the dominant classes. The analogy is imperfect in certain ways, as members of the dominant classes, for example, therapists, doctors, lawyers, also sell their attention on the market. They market it, however, for a much higher price and command a much higher return.

5. . . . Richard Parker indicates that the employment of "domestic help" has declined considerably in the upper class since World War II, with only one in five

households employing regular help. Nonetheless, Gabriel Kolko has pointed out that 2.5 million butlers, maids, chauffeurs, and cooks are still employed in private households, predominantly from the upper class. See Richard Parker, *The Myth of the Middle Class*, p. 125, and Gabriel Kolko, *Wealth and Power in America*.

6. This is the "unfocused" attention that people receive from strangers with whom they are not directly interacting. Most displays of conspicuous consumption are useful in attracting such "unfocused" attention as well as "focused" attention in conversation. . . .

7. Studies of the interactional process in welfare offices and in public hospitals serving the poor make this abundantly clear. Frederick Wiseman's film *Welfare* is an especially powerful document in this regard. See also Erving Goffman, *Asylums*.

8. By dominant occupations, we mean those in the professional-managerial class vested with economic, political, and cultural authority. These fall primarily under the Department of Labor's occupational titles of "proprietary" or "professional and managerial."

9. It should be noted that teachers are given direct formal control over the allocation of attention in the classroom. This is institutionalized in the mechanism of hand-raising, which allows the teacher to determine who is the focus of attention at any given moment. In most work settings, those in authority are given the formal power of the chairperson over attention in office meetings and other structured interactions at the workplace.

10. In this way, secretaries and other subordinate attention-givers in the work world play an analogous role to dominant groups as domestic servants who, as we have already seen, are hired as attention-givers in the private sphere. In her analysis of the role of the secretary, Mary Benet indicates that her duties approximate those of a wife and servant combined: "She makes his plane reservations, protects him from subordinates, does his expense accounts, sends Christmas cards and listens to his domestic problems." Benet goes on to indicate that in face-to-face interactions with the boss, the secretary takes on a certain kind of invisibility and cannot expect any attention except a flirtatious or sexual kind that she may not desire. The delegation of the attention-giving role thus follows sex-role prescriptions, as secretaries, nurses, and receptionists are typically female while their bosses are characteristically male. See Mary Benet, *The Secretarial Ghetto*, pp. 72ff.

11. In informal interactions, as Robert Schrank has recently stressed, workers do give and get face-to-face attention from other workers in the "schmoozing" or sociability that is one of the most important and gratifying aspects of work life. Schrank shows, however, that the right to socialize is enjoyed most fully by professionals and others in dominant occupations, as rules, regimentation, and the noise of machines restrict informal interactions among most industrial and clerical workers. See Robert Schrank, *Ten Thousand Working Days*.

12. See Peter Trudgill, "Sex, Covert Prestige and Linguistic Change in the Urban British English of Norwich," in Thorne and Henley (eds.), *Language and Society*, pp. 88–104.

13. Members of dominant classes have the greatest resources to pursue higher education and are most likely to do so. Extensive research in the United States has demonstrated this empirical relation between education and class. See espe-

cially Jerome Karabel, "Community Colleges and Social Stratification," *Harvard Educational Review*.

14. See William Labov, *Sociolinguistic Patterns; The Social Stratification of English in New York City* (Washington D.C.: Center for Applied Linguistics, 1966); Roger W. Shuy, Walter A. Wolfram, and William K. Riley, *Linguistic Correlates of Social Stratification in Detroit Speech*.

15. See studies summarized in A. Paul Hare (ed.), *Handbook of Small Group Research* pp. 212ff.

16. See, for example, P.W. Jackson, *Life in Classrooms*, and Robert Rosenthal and Lenore Jacobson, *Pygmalion in the Classroom*.

## REFERENCES

Benet, Mary. *The Secretarial Ghetto*. New York: McGraw-Hill, 1972.

Goffman, Erving. *Asylums*. New York: Anchor, 1961.

_____. *The Presentation of Self in Everyday Life*. New York: Anchor, 1959.

Hare, A. Paul (ed.). *Handbook of Small Group Research*. Glencoe: Free Press, 1962.

Jackson, P.W. *Life in Classrooms*. New York: Holt, Rinehart and Winston, 1968.

Karabel, Jerome. "Community Colleges and Social Stratification." *Harvard Educational Review* 42 (November 1972).

Kolko, Gabriel. *Wealth and Power in America*. New York: Praeger, 1962.

Labov, William. *Sociolinguistic Patterns*. Philadelphia: University of Pennsylvania, 1972.

Parker, Richard. *The Myth of the Middle Class*. New York: Harper & Row, 1972.

Rosenthal, Robert, and Lenore Jacobson. *Pygmalion in the Classroom*. New York: Holt, Rinehart and Winston, 1968.

Schrank, Robert. *Ten-Thousand Working Days*. Cambridge, Mass.: MIT Press, 1978.

Shuy, Roger, Walter A. Wolfram, and William K. Riley, *Linguistic Correlates of Social Stratification in Detroit Speech*. Final Report, Project 6–1347. Washington, D.C.: U.S. Office of Education, 1967.

Trudgill, Peter. "Sex, Covert Prestige and Linguistic Change in the Urban British English of Norwich." In *Language and Society*. Cambridge: Cambridge University Press, 1972, pp. 179–195.

# Review Questions

1. Derber and Magrass note that upper- and upper-middle-class people can control the amount and kinds of attention they receive in everyday life. How do they command "positive" attention? How do they avoid "negative" attention?

2. Among people in working-class occupations, "backstage" workers often receive less attention than "front stage" workers. What are three backstage jobs with low visibility? What are three front stage jobs that also have low visibility?

3. How does one's work identity carry over to affect how much attention one can get in informal settings? Give examples.

4. Describe at least two ways in which education changes people, thereby affecting how much attention they are paid.

# TURNING POINTS IN IDENTITY

## Anselm Strauss

[IN TRANSFORMATIONS OF IDENTITIES, OR] COMING TO NEW TERMS, A PER-
son becomes something other than [she or] he once was. [Such] shifts
necessitate [and point up] new evaluations: of self and others, of events,
acts, and objects. . . . [T]ransformation of perception is irreversible; once
having changed, there is no going back. One can look back, but can evaluate only from the new status.

Some transformations of identity and perspective are planned, or at
least fostered, by institutional representatives; others happen despite,
rather than because of, such regulated anticipation; and yet other transformations take place outside the orbits of the more visible social structure. . . . As a way of introducing these several dimensions of personal
change, I shall discuss . . . certain critical incidents that occur to force a
person to recognize that "I am not the same as I was, as I used to be."
. . . These critical incidents constitute turning points in the onward
movement of personal careers.

## TURNING POINTS

. . . [W]hat takes place at . . . turning points [is often] misalignment—
surprise, shock, chagrin, anxiety, tension, bafflement, self-question-
ing—and also the need to try out the new self, to explore and validate the
new and often exciting or fearful conceptions. Rather than discussing
critical junctures in general, let us consider their typology. The list will
not be a long one, but long enough to suggest the value both of its extension and of relating turning points to changes of identity.

A change in your relations with others is often so mundane, so gradual that it passes virtually unnoticed. Some incident is needed to bring
home to you the extent of the shift. A *marker of progression, or retrogres-
sion,* is needed. When the incident occurs it is likely to strike with great
impact, for it tells you: "Look! you have come way out to here! This is a
milestone!" Recognition then necessitates new stances, new align-

Excerpted from Anselm Strauss, *Mirrors and Masks: Transformations of Identity* (San Francisco: Sociology Press, 1969), pp. 93–100.

ments. A striking example of the "milestone" is found in the autobiographies of many immigrants to America who later visited their native lands, only then realizing how little affinity they had retained, how identified they had become with America and Americans. Any return home, insofar as you have really left it, will signalize some sort of movement in identity. Some people literally go back home in an effort both to deny how far they have strayed and to prevent further defection.

Sometimes the path of development is foretold but is not believed, either because the one who forecasts is distrusted or because the prophecy cannot be understood. *Prophets* not only *point out new directions:* they *give you measuring rods* for calculating movement if you happen to traverse the paths prophesied. This is certainly one of the critical experiences in the psychology of conversion. For instance, a recruit to a religious sect, only partly convinced, is told what will happen when he [or she] tries to explain the new position to his [or her] old minister, attempts to sell pamphlets to the heathen, and so on, and lo! events turn out as predicted. The prediction will be in terms of a new vocabulary, hence when the vocabulary is shown to be workable the recruit is well on the road toward adopting it in part or *in toto*. The point holds for any kind of conversion—occupational, political, or what not. A novice is told by the old-timer, "Your clients will be of such and such sorts and you'll have such and such experiences with them." When the graph of experience is thus plotted and confirmed, then the person can recognize his [or her] own transformation.

Forecasting is often institutionalized in such a fashion that *public proclamation* is made: "Said candidate has followed the predicted and prescribed path of experience and has gotten to the desired point. Kneel, knight, and receive knighthood. Come to the platform and receive your diploma." When paths are institutionalized, candidates can easily mark their progress, note how far they have come, and how far they have yet to go. If there are the usual institutionalized acknowledgments of partial steps toward the goal, then these may constitute turning points in self-conception also. If the institutionalized steps are purely formalized, are no longer invested with meaning by the institution, or if the candidate believes them of no real significance, they will not, of course, be turning points for him [or her].

*Private proclamation to a public audience* is quite another matter. Having announced or avowed your position, it is not easy to beat a retreat. Often you find yourself in interpersonal situations climbing out on a limb, announcing a position, and then having to live up to it. In a more subtle sense, one often marks a recognition of self-change by announcement, but this announcement itself forces a stance facing forward since the way back, however tempting it may still look, is now blocked.

A related turning point—since ceremonial announcement often follows it—is *the meeting of a challenge*, either self-imposed or imposed by others. Any institution . . . possesses regularized means for testing and challenging its members. If you are closely identified with the institution, some tests will be crucial for your self-regard. If you pass them, everyone recognizes that you have met the challenge. However, some challenges, although they occur in institutional settings, are not themselves institutionalized. For instance every student nurse early in her training must face the situation of having a patient die in her arms. For some nurses this appears to be a turning point for self-conception: the test is passed and she—in her own eyes at least—has new status; she can now think of herself as more of a professional. Crucial tests are imposed by individuals on themselves; if they pass they have been psychologically baptized, so to speak, but if they fail then a new path must be taken, a new set of plans drawn up. Naturally, failure does not always result in immediate self-transformation, but may lead to more complete preparation until the test is definitely failed or passed.

One potent form of self-test is the deliberate *courting of temptation*. Failure to resist it is usually followed by new tests or by yielding altogether. The fuller meaning of temptation is this: you are withdrawing from an old psychological status and coming into a new, and in doing so something akin to the "withdrawal symptoms" of drug addiction occurs. When you are able to resist temptation then an advance is signalized; but when no longer even tempted, you are well aware of having progressed still further. Institutions find it easier to check upon the overt resistance of their members than upon their covert desires. Genuine conversion means the death of old desires. "Backsliding" signifies a failure to resist temptation; frequent backsliding results in a return to previous status or change to yet another.

A rather subtle type of transforming incident occurs when you have *played a strange but important role and unexpectedly handled it well*. Whether you had considered this an admirable or a despicable role does not matter. The point is that you never thought you could play it, never thought this potential "me" was in yourself. Unless you can discount your acts as "not me" or as motivated by something not under your control, you bear the responsibility or the credit for the performance. Cowardly and heroic roles are both likely to bring unexpected realignment in self-regard. But more usual, and more subtle, are those instances where you find yourself miraculously able to enact roles that you believed—at least as yet—beyond you. [All people] new to a job find [themselves], through no fault of [their] own, at some point taken by clients or fellow workers as of more advanced status than [they are]. . . . Once having carried off the disguise, you realize something new about yourself. The net result is likely to be that you wish to experiment with this new aspect of yourself. Conversely, there are roles previously viewed with suspicion, even despised, that you now find yourself enacting with unexpected success and

pleasure. You must either wash your hands of it, actually or symbolically—as in *Macbeth*—or come to grips with this new aspect of yourself.

It is probable that some of the effect of experimental role-dramas is
that the drama allows and forces [people] to play a range of roles [they]
did not believe [themselves] capable of playing, or never conceived of
playing; it brings [them] face to face with [their] potential as well as . . .
actual selves. Sociable parties . . . by their very episodic and expressive
nature, allow and further such exploration of roles. Similarly, some of
the effect of psychiatric therapy seems to rest upon the skill of the psychiatrist in making patients face up to the full range of [their] acts, rather
than repress awareness of them or blame them upon outside forces.

A critical experience with built-in ambivalence occurs when someone
*surpasses the performance of* [*a role model*], as when a student overtakes [a]
beloved teacher, or a son exceeds his father's social position. When allegiance is very strong this awareness of overtaking the model may be crip-
pling, and refuge is sought by drawing back from the abyss of departure.
To be a success, one must surpass . . . models and depart from them.
Departures are institutionalized in America by such mechanisms as
myths of success, by the easy accessiblility of higher social positions,
and by the blessings of parents who in turn experience vicarious success
through the performances of their offspring. Despite the institutionalized devices for reducing the strain of upward departure, ambivalence
and stress undoubtedly persist even for many of our most successful
climbers.

Another kind of transforming experience, one with shattering or sap-
ping impact, is *betrayal*—by your heroes, in fact by anybody with whom
you are closely "identified." Betrayal implicates you as well as [the
other], in exceedingly subtle ways. Consider three varieties. When you
have closely patterned yourself after a model, you have in effect "internalized" what you suppose are the model's values and motives. If the
model abandons these, it leaves you with a grievous dilemma. Has the
model gone over to the enemy?—then you may with wry smile redouble
your efforts along the path [originally] laid out. . . . Or did the model lead
you up an illusory path of values?—then with cynicism and self-hate you
had better abandon your former self too. A different species of betrayal,
involving search for atonement, is illustrated by the stunned . . . mother
whose [child . . . becomes converted to another religious or political phi-
losophy]. The cry here is always: "Where did I go wrong that my child,
an extension of me, should go wrong?" A third variety of betrayal often
goes by the name of "rejection"; that is, rejection of you after you had
closely identified with the model. Here the beloved has symbolically announced that you and your values are not right, or at least are not wholly
satisfying. [Children who] reject and drift away from immigrant parents
illustrate this. Betrayal of this type consists, usually, of a series of inci-

dents, rather than of a single traumatic event. During the course of day-to-day living, decisions are made whose full implications are not immediately apparent. People can go on deceiving themselves about paths that actually have been closed by those decisions. At the point when it becomes apparent that former possibilities are dead issues, the person stands at the crossroads. A severe instance of such a turning point occurs when one traps oneself into an occupation—much as a house painter might paint himself unthinkingly into a corner of the room—believing that he can always get out when he wants to. Jazz musicians who go commercial "just for a while" to make money may find eventually that the commercial style has caught them, that they can no longer play real jazz as it should be played. This kind of crossroad may not be traumatic, but nostalgically reminiscent, signifying then that the gratifications arising from past decisions are quite sufficient to make past possibilities only pleasantly lingering "maybes." Final recognition that they are really dead issues is then more of a ritualistic burial and is often manifested by a revisiting of old haunts—actually or symbolically.

A final type of critical experience that I shall discuss is akin to betrayal, but the agent of destruction is less personal. A [person] may realize that he [or she] has been *deceived*, not by any specific person but *by events in general*. If the deception strikes home severely, [one] may respond with self-hate. "Why did I not discover this before?"; with personalized resentment against someone, "Why did they not tell me?"; or with diffuse resentment against the world in general. An essential aspect of this critical experience is that a [person's] naming of self is disoriented. [One] is not what [one] thought [one] was. Self-classificatory disorientation, of course, can be mild. For instance, a Jewish boy, brought up in a moderately Orthodox home, discovered later that all Jews were not Orthodox, but that there were Reformed Jews (who made him feel not at all Jewish) and very Orthodox Jews (who made him feel not at all Jewish). Such discoveries come as shocks, but not necessarily as traumas. There is more anguish involved when a [person] finds that although he believed he possessed a comfortable dual indentity, [black] and American, significant others are now challenging one of those identities. This is, or at least was, an unnerving experience for many Northern [blacks] who visited in the South, however much they may have read or been warned. This negation of a portion of identity may not provide much of a crisis if the person withdraws from his attackers, but if [one] stays, as some [blacks] have stayed in the South, [one] must make [. . .] peace with the challenging audience. A more crucial juncture in the maintenance of identity occurs when a person discovers that [a] chief self-referential term is completely erroneous. Cases in point are adopted children who do not discover until later years the fact of their adoption, and those occasional tragic cases of children who are raised as members of the opposite sex and eventually discover the mis-naming. Imagine also the destructive effects, compounded with guilt and self-hate, of discovering an actual identity with a group formerly reviled and despised, as for instance an anti-Semite discovering that he [or she] is partly Jewish.

Enough has been said about various types of turning points to suggest that these are points in development when an individual has to take stock, to reevaluate, revise, resee, and rejudge. Although stock-taking goes on within the single individual, it is obviously both a socialized and a socializing process. Moreover, the same kinds of incidents that precipitate the revision of identity are extremely likely to befall and to be equally significant to other persons of the same generation, occupation, and social class. This is equivalent to saying that insofar as experiences and interpretations are socially patterned, so also will be the development of personal indentities. . . .

## Review Questions

1. Strauss presents ten kinds of turning points in this article. Give examples from your own experience of each of them.

2. Strauss maintains that people in a similar social status, or social location, may face similar turning points. Discuss two such statuses and the turning points their occupants are likely to face.

3. Discuss the implications for people's self-concepts of living through turning points.

## Suggested Readings: Interaction in Everyday Life

Becker, Ernest. *The Birth and Death of Meaning.* 2nd ed. New York: Free Press, 1971.

Clark, Candace. "Sympathy Biography and Sympathy Margin," *American Journal of Sociology*, 93 (September 1987).

Cooley, Charles Horton. *Human Nature and the Social Order.* New York: Schocken Books, 1964.

Festinger, Leon, Henry W. Riecken, and Stanley Schacter. *When Prophecy Fails.* Minneapolis: University of Minnesota Press, 1956.

Goffman, Erving. *The Presentation of Self in Everyday Life.* Garden City, N.Y.: Anchor Books, 1959.

_____. *Behavior in Public Places.* New York: Free Press, 1963.

Lemert, Edwin. "Paranoia and the Dynamics of Exclusion," *Sociometry* 25 (1962), 2–20.

Lyman, Stanford M., and Marvin B. Scott. *The Sociology of the Absurd.* New York: Appleton-Century-Crofts, 1970.

Mead, George Herbert, in Charles W. Morris, ed., *Mind, Self and Society: From the Standpoint of a Social Behaviorist.* Chicago: University of Chicago Press, 1934.

Perinbanayagam, Robert S. *Signifying Acts.* Carbondale, Ill.: Southern Illinois University Press, 1985.

Sherif, Muzafer. "Experiments in Group Conflict," *Scientific American* 195 (1956), 54–58.

Stone, Gregory P. "Appearance and the Self," in Arnold Rose, ed., *Human Behavior and Social Processes.* Boston: Houghton Mifflin, 1962, pp. 86–118.

_____, and Harvey A. Farberman, eds., *Social Psychology Through Symbolic Interaction.* 2nd ed. New York: Wiley, 1980.

# Part V. Social Organization: Life in Groups

ALTHOUGH A GREATER PROPORTION OF OUR INTERACTIONS OCCURS WITH strangers than was the case in agricultural societies of the past, still most occur within groups. All of the groups of which we are members—from the level of the primary group, to the secondary group, to the formal organization, to the society—are organized. What we mean by this is that each of these types of groups—even the small friendship group—develops a system of beliefs and norms, a division of labor, a method of ranking members, and a system of social-control techniques to ensure conformity to the group's goals and rules. Sociologists have paid attention to a number of elements of group organization: group size (primary groups usually being small, societies large), the ways in which norms are created (informally within primary groups, formally in secondary groups or large-scale organizations), the degree of intimacy among members (greater within the primary group than the secondary group), the method of determining leadership and power positions (informally in the primary group, usually formally in secondary groups and societies), and so on. They have also focused on the internal processes of both small and large groups such as communication, development of group cohesion, boundary maintenance, and facilitation of smooth interaction.

Of course, we are all members of many groups, of all types, simultaneously; and within large groups, smaller ones may be found. The expectations and demands of these groups may conflict at times, causing problems for the individual torn between competing claims. As societies themselves have become larger, more complex, more industrialized, and more interdependent, the number of claims on the individual have increased and, as a result, the very character of everyday life has changed.

The articles and excerpts presented in this part of our reader are intended to illustrate the patterning and constraining aspects of various levels of social organization, as well as the differences between types of groups in the kinds of behavior they call for. The *organization* of the small, intimate groups into which we are born (families); of the associations we join; of the formal organizations in which we work, study, and even play; and of the larger society has important implications for our daily lives.

First, Lyn Lofland asks, What is the nature of human bonds in primary groups? What do people "do" for each other as they interact? She approaches this question from an ingenious angle: she looks at what is *missing* from the lives of people who have lost family members and friends through death. In "Loss and Human Connection," Lofland spells out the important aspects of relationships as seen through the eyes of those whose relationships have just ended. She discovers that people experiencing the loss of a significant other miss not only the other person but also one or more of the following: a role partner, help with everyday chores, linkages to the wider community, support for their self-concepts, support for comforting myths, confirmation of their views of reality, and possible futures.

Furthermore, Lofland discusses cultural and historical differences in *patterns* of connectedness. Here she points out that the way in which a society is organized influences the number and types of others to whom people are connected. In some societies, for instance, people tend to count on one type of person for, say, help with everyday chores and another type of person for confirmation of their views of reality. In contemporary American society, we tend to put our eggs in fewer baskets—to count on a smaller number of significant others to provide all the functions listed above—than is the case in many societies.

In the next selection, "Corner Boys," William Foote Whyte directs our attention to interaction in one type of primary group: the peer group. Whyte moved into a neighborhood where groups of young men spent much of their free time hanging around on the street. He spent more than three years as a participant observer studying these peer groups, and his research resulted in one of the best known and frequently cited works in sociology, *Street Corner Society*.

In this article by Whyte, he explains his research methods and a few of the research findings pertaining to group processes. He demonstrates, for example, the determinants of leadership among the corner boys. We are also shown how an individual's status within the group affects with whom he or she is likely to spend time. Further, there is the issue of who initiates and who receives more interaction. At the most general level, Whyte's research shows the powerful influence of the group upon individual behavior.

As you read this article, think of similar examples of group processes in your own social groups. To take one example, have you noticed that followers often must convince more powerful group members to introduce or implement their ideas rather than voicing them directly? Also, are you aware of the altruistic behavior of leaders? Do the leaders of your groups spend more time and money on followers than the reverse? That is, do leaders do favors for followers so they can call in their markers later? You should be able to illustrate from your own experience these and many other general principles of peer group behavior that Whyte sets forth.

The college classroom, a setting familiar to us all, is the situation which David Karp and William Yoels have chosen for study. The members of a classroom form a collectivity which is much less intimate and more formal than a primary group (although, to be sure, primary groups may exist *within* the classroom). Role relationships, as in other *secondary groups*, are segmental, which means that teacher and students interact within (usually) fairly narrow boundaries rather than becoming involved with each other in a more total way. The occupants of each of these reciprocal positions have expectations both for their own behavior and for the behavior of those in the reciprocal role. When these expectations differ, a kind of *role strain* may develop. Whose definition of the situation will win out? Can social processes arise to alleviate the strain?

The professor expects the students to be prepared for class—to have read and carefully considered the assigned material and, in class, to ask questions or make comments based on their reading. Ideally, much of the class period will be spent in a stimulating discussion that will involve most of the students.

Many of the students, on the other hand, prefer to take a passive role. They view their professor as an expert who will ''feed'' them his or her views on the subject at hand. Because they know that the professor expects them to have read the material thoroughly, perhaps with a greater commitment than they actually care to generate, they enter the classroom with a ''presentation of self'' that indicates a solid knowledge of the material. As long as they are not asked to discuss anything, an uneasy silence is maintained.

How is the issue of participation actually resolved? Fortunately, each class contains a few talkers. These individuals assume the responsibility of carrying on class discussion and thus take the pressure off both the ''silent majority'' and the professor. When the professor asks a question, it is almost always one of the group of ''regulars'' who responds. Although a regular talker in one class may not fulfill that role in another, someone will probably do so, easing the strain so that the class may proceed. Rarely will the teacher or the students place one another under such stress that their behavior will deviate from the relatively distant, formal attitude appropriate in secondary groups.

Formality and politeness may be top priority in the college classroom, but in the type of organization we call the *total institution*, they are not. A total institution is an organization with highly rigid rules and roles; one of its key features is that the lives of the clients or inmates are restricted and regimented 24 hours a day. Prisons, boarding schools, monasteries, hospitals, military bases, and nursing homes are all examples of the total institution, the type of group setting we will analyze in the final article in this section.

In order to study nursing home life, Andrea Fontana joined the janitorial staff of Sunny Hill convalescent center. He documents, in ''Growing Old Between Walls,'' that client care took a backseat to the profit motive.

The lowest level of staff—who maintained the highest levels of contact with the patients—did the least desirable, physically draining tasks and were paid poorly. Their work goals quickly came to be getting through the day, not meeting the needs and demands of the clients. Growing old in the care of workers like these is, for most people, dismal.

Membership in any group involves a certain loss of freedom, but being a member of the Sunny Hill community affords the client no autonomy at all over the basic activities that make up the day. It is ironic that those who directly control the timing and tenor of everyday activities are *not* the top administrators and medical professionals, but the people who do the "dirty work" for the management. In this case, the clients themselves *are* the dirty work.

# LOSS AND HUMAN CONNECTION

## Lyn H. Lofland

. . . THE ENDING—THROUGH DEATH, DESERTION, OR GEOGRAPHICAL SEP-
aration, for example—of a relationship defined by an actor as "significant" or "meaningful" is generally conceived of as a "loss" experience.
In this essay,[1] I want to pursue the question: What is lost? Stated more
positively, I want to ask what it is that humans *do* for one another? What
links self to other, what is the nature of the social bond?

•   •   •

## ATTACHMENT, GRIEF, AND LOSS

Humans are social animals. This rather simple, even simplistic, statement covers a multitude of complexities. Lift it up and we see such matters as these: that the human animal is slow to mature and thus stands in
a relationship of need to older members of the species for a considerable
period of time; that "humanness"—the capacities and characteristics of
the species—is a social creation, forged from the biological clay by the
group; that all human behavior is necessarily social; and that attachments—emotional linkages—to other humans occur. It is this latter
"fact," as part of the complex of "socialness," that is of concern here.
Humans do not simply live in proximity to one another. They link themselves to one another. They tie. They bond. They bind.

•   •   •

Attachment behavior . . . most certainly is a contributor to human
pain. For the dark side of attachment is grief. . . .
[W]hen some modern Westerners undergo the rupturing of a relationship they define as significant, they report experiencing a discomforting
combination of physical and psychic symptoms, typically labeled, grief.[2]
I want to ask: For these persons, what is the cause of the pain? The simple answer, the breaking of an attachment, is satisfactory at one level.

This selection comes from Lyn H. Lofland, "Loss and Human Connection." In W. Ickes
and E. S. Knowles, eds., *Personality, Roles and Social Behavior*, 1982, pp. 219–242.

But I wish to delve more deeply. I wish to inquire into the nature of the attachment itself. I want to ask, with *what* do we attach ourselves to others? What, more specifically, are the ties that bind?

•    •    •

## THREADS OF HUMAN CONNECTEDNESS

In this section, I will propose seven "threads of connectedness": seven kinds of ways that humans bond themselves to one another. The materials from which this formulation emerges are of four types: (1) intensive interviews with persons who had experienced an involuntary[3] relational loss; (2) published first-person accounts of a grief experience; (3) published case and interview data from scholarly investigations of the grief experience; and (4) unpublished letters of condolence, funeral memorializations, and personal anecdotes. Of these diverse materials, I continually asked the questions: What are these people saying about what it is that is missed? What do they say the "lost" person did for them? What is it they think they have lost?

Although the formulation that follows cannot be said to be built upon prior efforts to categorize types of relationships or types of interpersonal loss, it is nonetheless thoroughly informed by them. In 1967, for example, Warren Breed, noting that "loss" is a recurrent notion in the psychological and psychoanalytic literature on suicide causation, asks (as I do) "What is lost?" and answers: position, person, mutuality (Breed, 1967). Robert Weiss (1969) has proposed five categories of relational functions, each of which, he postulated, was for the most part provided by a different relationship: intimacy, social integration, opportunity for nurturant behavior, reassurance of worth, and assistance—with guidance added as a possible sixth function (see also Lopata, 1969).

But it is Samuel Wallace's (1973) ruminations about the meanings of his interview data on the bereavement experience of widows of suicides which most clearly herald the route taken herein:

> The loss . . . is not simply the loss of an *object*; a *relationship*, a *status*, a *way of being* are also lost when someone goes out of our lives. The "object" or person lost also takes with him or her that part of our self that they alone maintained—our self which was a son, our self which was a mother, our self which was a spouse. The loss of object and relationship also loses us a status, a position in the social universe. No longer are we married, have children, or are known as the lost one's friends. And within whatever status is lost lies an equally lost way of being.
>
> Bereavement, then, is social loss, of person, relationship, status, and way of being. The experience may be said to *vary* with our life's involvement with the person, relationship, status and way of being which is lost. (p. 231 [italics added])

Let us now examine each of the seven "connections" in turn. They are, as will be clear, both logically and empirically interrelated. But that interrelationship is not invariant. . . .

## ROLE PARTNER

Much of the descriptive and analytic literature on loss and grief seems to touch on the role partner "thread of connectedness"—unsurprisingly, since it is one of the easiest to see and conceptualize, both for the actor and observer. Clearly, certain roles—certain organized and recurrent ways of being and acting—require for their realization, an "other." If the other is lost, so is the opportunity for playing the role. One cannot "be" daughter without mother, father without child, lover without lover, helper without helped, employee without employer, even enemy without enemy (see Lifton, 1973, pp. 45–46). It is primarily to this kind of loss that widows in Helena Lopata's study refer when they report that they are "lonely for the husband as [among other things] . . . a partner or companion in activities; an escort in couple-companionate interaction; 'someone' with whom to talk; 'someone' around whom work and time are organized . . ." (Lopata, 1973, p. 68; see also 1979, pp. 117–118). Similarly, a young male informant speaks of missing his deceased grandmother as a "playmate" and a young widow writes, in her diary, a letter to her dead husband about what their sons are missing.

> At times Keith is so frustrated; he misses you, Dwight, and needs you. He needs you as only an eight-year-old boy can need a father. I love him and try to show my love but that doesn't take your place. He needs that father and son shoulder-to-shoulder companionship and approval of work well done. But you knew he would need you! And Gary needs you; he needs you to help with all of his many building projects. He wants to build and create rockets, boats, hot rods.[4] (Beck, 1965, pp. 53–54)

Of course, most role partners, *qua* partners, are replaceable. The line of activity can be reactivated as part of one's continuing repertoire, although the speed or ease of replacement will vary according to the role itself and across time and space. And, when a single other serves as a partner in multiple roles, as in C. S. Lewis's (1961) description of his dead wife,

> She was my daughter and my mother, my pupil and my teacher, my subject and my sovereign; and always, holding all these in solution, my trusty comrade, friend, shipmate, fellow-soldier. (p. 39)

replacement, even substituting multiple others for the one, may become highly problematic. But until replacement occurs, the individual is in a condition of loss.

## MUNDANE ASSISTANCE

People help one another. When the help is desired (it may not be, of course), the absence of the helper engenders a loss. The death of a neighbor may mean that one now has no one to look after pets and plants when one is away. The death of a work acquaintance may mean that one no longer has a ready source of job advice. . . . The death of a teenaged son may leave many household tasks undone, as this extract from the summary of an interview with a bereaved mother makes clear.

> She says that the entire family did not fully appreciate just how much he did in the way of helping tasks until he died. He was the kind of boy, she says, who did things without being asked—cleaning his room, emptying the trash, pruning the roses, mowing the lawn. On this past Christmas day, her two other children got up about 6 A.M. She asked them why, since they hadn't gotten up that early the year before. "Oh, yes, we did," they said, "but [the teenaged son] wouldn't let us come downstairs until 7:30."[5]

Or the death of a husband may eliminate a buffer in one's relations with others.

> Anytime the children do something wrong that goes against me, I start to think about him. They fly up against me, they never did when their father was here. They say things to hurt me, you know, and that's when I think about him. He would never have allowed them to talk to me that way. . . . (Wallace, 1973, p. 166)

It is important to recognize that removal of a helper may necessitate more than simply "picking up the slack" or finding substitute sources of aid. It may, as often in the illness or death of a spouse, necessitate learning a whole new set of skills, and as such, require the jettisoning of old "selves" or aspects of selves—yet another loss.

> A year ago, he was the boss, he managed this house completely, even the kids he controlled with the strictest discipline. I had to learn how to pay bills, I had never even written a check and I had to balance the checkbook, and oh, that was so hard to learn, everything that he used to do. Everything I did I used to ask him about first. I needed his advice, I depended on him so. He always knew the answers to everything. Then when he got sick, I had nobody, no one to take his place. *I had to learn how to live all over, to be a different person.* (Wallace, 1973, p. 39 [italics added]; see also Lopata, 1969, p. 253; Weiss, 1975, p. 97)

In fact, the literature on the experience of widowhood—as well as what little is available on widowers—suggests that a large element of the trauma engendered by the loss of a spouse in contemporary Western societies has to do with the loss of mundane assistance. People find themselves burdened with other aspects of the loss at the same time that they have to cope with such new matters as earning a living, balancing a checkbook, cooking, driving a car, making household repairs, cleaning house, and washing clothes. This has led some observers—quite independent of any feminist inclinations—to call for a reduction in sex-role specialization in the marital relationship (see, for example, Caine, 1974; Wedemyer, 1974).

## LINKAGES TO OTHERS

The considerable social isolation of men and women following the deaths of their spouses or the breakup of their marriages is reported frequently in the literature on "loneliness." As Lopata notes,

> Many wives enjoy company parties, golf, couple-companionate dinners, and such events, and will not engage in them after the husband dies or have them no longer available *since it was his presence which formed the connecting link in the first place.* (Lopata, 1969, p. 253 [italics added]; see also Lopata, 1979, p. 118; Weiss, 1975, pp. 52, 58)

But it is clearly not only in the multiple bondedness of a marital relationship that persons can serve this linking function for one another. Friends and acquaintances often involve one another in their larger individual friendship and acquaintance networks—person A meets and relates to persons C, D, and E primarily through the arrangements of person B. One informant told me of feeling absolutely devastated when a close friend moved to another city, importantly because, rather to her surprise, she discovered that she had "no friends of my own"—only acquaintances through the now absent friend. Of course, the secondary linkage that B has provided between A and C, D, and E may eventually become primary. But when it does not, then loss of B occasions the simultaneous loss of C, D, and E, as well.

## THE CREATION AND MAINTENANCE OF SELF

. . . [I]n the loss of a single other, part or all of self is lost as well.

> When the loss has been sudden, large, and forced upon the attention, words implying mutilation and outrage tend to be used. One widow described her feelings on viewing the corpse of her husband: "It's as if my inside had been torn out and left a horrible wound there." A comparison is sometimes made to amputation: widows say that their husband has been "cut off," "as if half of myself was missing." In less violent terms, the loss of self is often referred to as a "gap"—"it's a great emptiness," "an unhappy void." (Parkes, 1972, p. 97)

. . . [S]ocial psychology . . . understands the self and its components importantly as the ongoing creation of the significant others who surround the actor.[6] . . . [R]eports of self loss are not viewed merely as description through analogy but as literal depiction. That aspect of self (or those multiple aspects) that was significantly and uniquely generated and/or sustained in interaction with the other is, quite literally, lost when the other is lost.

If one's desirability, for example, is proffered and affirmed only in interaction with a single other human, the death of that human is the death of that part of self. A widow remembers:

> Here I am so big and fat and sometimes I'd be reading and would look up and he'd be sitting there looking at me—and I'd say, "What are you thinking about?" And he would say, "Oh, I was just thinking how pretty you are." (Lopata, 1969, p. 252)

Another widow reports,

> I think he found me as a very strong person. And being able to handle almost anything. And I think I probably saw in him someone who needed me very much. Which my first husband obviously did not. . . . When someone needs you, you . . . just automatically respond to them. . . . And I needed to be needed. (Wallace, 1973, p. 27; see also Thomas, 1957, Chap. 4; McCabe, 1970)

Similarly, a woman writes of a recently deceased friend:

> But the main thing that welded me to her so strongly was that she thought so much of me. She didn't flatter; she just never seemed to suspect that I wasn't as witty or wise or talented or nice as she thought I was, so I tried never to let on. In our 13 years of friendship, there was nothing she thought I couldn't do, and there was, in turn, nothing I wouldn't have done for her. (Barthel, 1972, p. 56)

Even when there are multiple others in the actor's milieu who help to maintain some aspect of self, a particular individual may be viewed as pivotal, as especially crucial to the actor's conception of self. Speaking of a man, now deceased, who had been important to him in his boyhood, a male informant muses over what this person had meant to him.

> He believed in me. He gave of his self to me, in the sense that he gave me responsibility, trusted me with responsibility for his very body [during epileptic seizures], his very physical existence which I was very honored to have someone trust me that way. That was probably the most responsibility I'd ever been given. Let's say the most meaningful responsibility.

•   •   •

It might be argued, of course, that self-maintenance is not threatened by the death or other loss of a significant other because memory allows continued—if entirely internal—interaction. To some degree, and for some period of time, this may be true. But the author, C. S. Lewis, writing about his "grief" over the death of his wife, suggests that the continued evocation of the other through memory has serious limitations.

Slowly, quietly, like snow-flakes—like the small flakes that come when it is going to snow all night—little flakes of me, my impressions, my selections, are settling down on the image of her. The real shape will be quite hidden in the end. Ten minutes—ten seconds—of the real H. would correct all of this. And yet, even if those ten seconds were allowed me, one second later the little flakes would begin to fall again. The rough, sharp, cleaning tang of her otherness is gone. (Lewis, 1961, p. 19)

## SUPPORT FOR COMFORTING MYTHS

For many humans, living comfortably in a world beset by the possibility of sudden death, catastrophic illness, unforeseen financial difficulties—all the hazards of existence—would seem to be made possible by the embrace of myth, of comforting stories about possibilities, situations, eventualities, self, others. These are stories that the individual knows, quite rationally, to be impossible, but which are clung to nonetheless. Like aspects of self, the reality of which seem to reside in the eyes of others, some of these myths appear to depend for their continued viability on the presence, or at least existence, of other persons. If these persons disappear, so do the myths and all the comfort and protection they afford. A particularly articulate informant, who shared with me some entries in her private journal, writes of just such a loss.

> Bob, like Ann, was so intertwined with so many memories of Rocklane [her home town] and my growing up there, that he and the town are, in some sense, synonymous. Not that he was always there while I was growing up. I was 10 to 11 or 12 before I ever met him, and he was gone for a period between about 8th grade and second year high school. But the time he was there, he was so crucial, that especially during my adolescent years, I cannot think of Rocklane without a memory of him crowding in. When my folks moved, I felt a tie to the home town cut, but it was not until Bob's death that I felt the real sense of the break. He was dead. The years of my adolescence were really gone. The hometown of my childhood was passed and could never be regained, because the person who had been so much a part of that time and that town was dead. *For the first time, really for the first time, I understood that I was growing older and that what was passed was forever, irremediably passed. It could never come again.* Of course, we always know this in our heads. I mean, one can't be alive without knowing it. But only with Bob's death did the full realization of this "fact of life" hit me with full force. I would never be 16 again, Rocklane would never again be for me the place it had been at 16. The people who peopled my memories of those years were gone; their older versions might still be around, but they were gone. The past was passed. It could not be reclaimed. [italics added]

The comfort from the myths seems not to reside in their sharpness or detail. Rather, they sit in the mind, shadowy, rather unsubstantial, off to the side, obliquely and intermittently viewed. Only when the myth is destroyed must its content be fully recognized.

• • •

It should be noted that the keystone of the myth may reside less in the person than in the relationship itself, as in the following interview extract in which a woman informant speaks of her separation from her husband.

> I had an almost mystical sense that no matter what I did, no matter how I behaved, no matter what, he'd be there, sticking to me, my assurance not only that I could "hold a man," but that somebody cared for me. Rather like a child feels with very loving parents. We'd had a lot of fights and threatened each other with divorce many times, but it was all unreal. He was my secure future, my "Linus blanket," which told me that the things that happened to other people, the terrible painful things, couldn't happen to me. (see also, Caine, 1974, p. 135; Weiss, 1975, p. 49)

## REALITY MAINTENANCE

Peter Berger and Hansfried Kellner in "Marriage and the Construction of Reality" [see Part VIII A of this volume] have written persuasively of the reality-validating character of marital and other intimate relationships.

> Every individual requires the ongoing validation of his world, including crucially the validation of his identity and place in this world, by those few who are his truly significant others. . . . Again, in the broad sense, all the actions of the significant others and even their simple presence serve this sustaining function. In everyday life, however, the principal method employed is speech. In this sense, it is proper to view the individual's relationship with his significant others as on ongoing conversation. As the latter occurs, it validates over and over again the fundamental definitions of reality once entered into, not, of course, so much by explicit articulation, but precisely by taking the definitions silently for granted and conversing about all conceivable matters on this taken-for-granted basis. (1964, pp. 4–5)

Certainly, the scholarly and popular literature on grief would appear to confirm these observations. . . . Colin Parkes has noted, for example, how the death of a husband alters the character of the world inhabited by the wife. "Even when words remain appropriate, their meaning changes—'the family' is no longer the same object it was, neither is 'home' or 'marriage'; even 'old age' now has a new meaning" (1972, p. 93). First-person accounts of the grief experience, as another example, typically contain references to feeling "odd," "strange," "peculiar," "out of touch with reality," "weird"—in fact, an "altered sensorium" is considered part of the normal symptomatology of grief (see references cited in Footnote 2).

But reality maintenance would appear to connect more than just intimates. As Berger and Kellner argue,

> This validation [of common-sense reality] . . . requires ongoing interaction with others who co-inhabit this same socially constructed world. In a broad sense, all the other co-inhabitants of the world serve a validating function. Every morning the newspaper boy validates the widest co-ordinates of my world and the mailman bears tangible validation of my own location within these co-ordinates. (1964, p. 4)

In this sense, the death or other loss of any noticed other in one's world threatens, however mildly, the validity of common-sense reality, and mass death may, as Robert Lifton (1967) has argued, destroy the survivor's very faith in the "connectedness of the world". . . .

## THE MAINTENANCE OF POSSIBLE FUTURES

Finally, the materials here under analysis suggest that persons are connected to one another through the parts they play in one another's futures. To "lose" certain persons is to lose certain futures, certain quite realistic possibilities for action, the very possibility of which provides comfort and/or pleasure to the actor. C. S. Lewis, for example, found pain in the realization that

> Never, in any place or time, will she [his deceased wife] have her son on her knees, or bathe him, or tell him a story, or plan for his future, or see her grandchild. (1961, p. 24)

A widow spoke of watching

> this older couple—I think this gets to me quicker than anything—is to see an older couple walking along the street, you know, and I say to myself, "I'll never be there." (Wallace, 1973, p. 114)

And a woman whose son had been killed in an accident told me that her sense of loss seemed to revolve primarily around a sense of potential not realized. She felt that her son was on his way to manhood, that he was in the process of becoming an interesting person, not just a son, but someone of whom she could feel proud, whom she could enjoy, with whom she could be friends. It was this potential that had been stripped away. She had been cheated—deprived—of the person her son was in the process of becoming.

The future that is destroyed by the loss of the other may be broadly and generally conceived, as the foregoing interview extracts suggest. But very circumscribed and/or detailed scenarios may also be cherished and relinquished with pain—a "scene" that will bring a relationship right again, for example.

> When I heard, in a letter when I was in college, that he had died, I was very angry that no one had told me because I had felt this strong need to put things right between us. To come to an understanding. I don't know what kind of understanding. To have corrected any misunderstanding that might have been there. To tell him how much I appreciated all that he had cared for me. Which I never got to tell him. . . .

Or, a "place" in which a relationship is to be played out. A woman, separated from her husband, describes one such, now forfeited, location.

> Do you know what [the southern part of a state] is like? Well, up towards . . . we wanted to buy some land and build an A-frame and it's, like, really hilly and forested and we had an area picked out where we wanted to buy some land there and we drew up this house that we wanted to build and there was room in it for two kids. . . . We called it the gingerbread house.

In sum, then, I am postulating that the "ties that bind," the "threads of connectedness" are of seven sorts. We are linked to others by the *roles* we play, by the *help* we receive, by the wider *network* of others made available to us, by the *selves* others create and sustain, by the comforting *myths* they allow us, by the *reality* they validate for us and by the *futures* they make possible. I make no claim that this listing is exhaustive, nor even that it is the most felicitous that could be conceived. I have, however, found it useful in thinking about varying patterns of connectedness and the possible relationship between such patterns and the grief experience. To those matters, let us now turn.

## PATTERNS OF CONNECTEDNESS

• • •

Table 1 illustrates four different ways that a person (A) might distribute his or her "connections"—each of the seven variations in linking symbols between Person A and Person B, Person A and Person C, and so forth, standing for one of the seven links. Thus, in the first pattern, we conceive of a person who, in a network of others, manages to encompass all seven ties, but with a minimum of multiple bonding to any one person. That is, Person A in this pattern is tied to Person B as role partner and for mundane assistance, to Person C as a link to others, to Person D through reality and future maintenance and to Person E as a creator and maintainer of self and as a supporter of comforting myths. Pattern 2 imagines a person, also with a minimum of multiple bonding, but in this

## Table 1. Patterns of Connectedness[a]

1. Full range of connections, spread among multiple others

```
       -----------                    =============
A ++++++++++++ B      A : : : : : : : : : : : C     A . . . . . . . . . . . D
                      #############
                      ★ ★ ★ ★ ★ ★ ★ ★ ★ ★ ★
```

2. Limited connections, spread among multiple others

```
A ----------- B      A : : : : : : : : : : : C     A . . . . . . . . . . . D
                   A ############# E
```

3. All connections to a single other, multipes of such others

```
★ ★ ★ ★ ★ ★ ★ ★ ★ ★ ★      ★ ★ ★ ★ ★ ★ ★ ★ ★ ★ ★      ★ ★ ★ ★ ★ ★ ★ ★ ★ ★ ★
-----------                -----------                -----------
: : : : : : : : : : :      : : : : : : : : : : :      : : : : : : : : : : :
A ++++++++++++ B           A ++++++++++++ C           A ++++++++++++ D
=============              =============              =============
. . . . . . . . . . .      . . . . . . . . . . .      . . . . . . . . . . .
#############              #############              #############
```

4. All connections linked to a single other

```
              ★ ★ ★ ★ ★ ★ ★ ★ ★ ★ ★
              -----------
              : : : : : : : : : : :
          A ++++++++++++ B
              =============
              . . . . . . . . . . .
              #############
```

-----, role partner; +++++, mundane assistance; :::::, linkages to others; #####, creation and maintenance of self; ★ ★ ★ ★ ★, support for comforting myths, =====, reality maintenance; . . . . ., maintenance of possible futures.

instance, lacking the full range of possible linkages. Here Person A is tied to B as a role partner, to C as a link to others, and as a creator and maintainer of self and to D through future maintenance; the other possible connections are simply missing. Pattern 3 postulates someone who is maximally multiply bonded to multiple others, while Pattern 4 illustrates maximal multiple bonding, but to a single other. The reader can imagine many other possible patterns and can complicate the picture enormously simply by varying, more than has been done here, the number of others to whom any given actor is linked.

There are additional "complications" which, in this brief essay, I will not address. For example, some linkages can themselves be compounded or intensified in a single relationship, as in many intimacies involving multiple role partnerships. Or, as another matter, I have throughout assumed the status of adult among relational participants. When it is a child, especially a very young child, who is at the receiving end of a set of connections, one would expect the "power" of any single tie to be intensified.

. . . We might ask, as one line of inquiry, whether there is *historical and cultural variation* in the *range, dominance and idealization* of [these] patterns. And, assuming such variation to be discovered, we might ask further whether or in what way it relates to possible differences in the emotional experience of grief, to observed differences in mourning practices and to other social psychological and/or structural diversities among human groups.

For example, might it be that "death demographics" are importantly linked to the dominant pattern or patterns or even range of patterns to be found in a given social order during a given period? That is, might it be that what appears to be, by modern standards, relative emotional coolness in the face of the death of presumed intimates among historic Westerners is best understood as a quite reasonable "spread" or connections (e.g., a preponderance of Patterns 1 and 2 over 3 and 4) under conditions of high mortality rates? When the demographer E. A. Wrigley reports that

> It was entirely in accord with the usage of that time [early 1600's in England], that the children's father, William, should have remarried so soon after the death of his first wife. Remarriages within a period of weeks rather than months were not uncommon. (1969, p. 83)

are we observing not an historically different social psychology, nor even a greater . . . acceptance of death, but a different structural patterning of *connectedness?*

As another example, might observed cultural differences in mourning practices be linked to a group's typical patterning of linkages? Edmund Volkart postulated exactly such a connection nearly 25 years ago . . .

> In his study of the Ifaluk people, [M. E.] Spiro was puzzled by some features of bereavement behavior there. When a family member died, the immediate survivors displayed considerable pain and distress . . . in accordance with local custom. However, as soon as the funeral was over, the bereaved were able to laugh, smile and behave in general as if they had suffered no loss or injury at all. Their "grief" seemed to disappear as if by magic, and this too was approved by custom. . . . In terms of the thesis being developed here, the bereavement behavior of the Ifaluk suggests that their family system is such as to develop selves that are initially less vulnerable in bereavement than are the selves we are accustomed to. . . . Another way of stating this is that in self-

other relations among the Ifaluk, the other is not valued by the self as a unique and necessary personality. . . . [T]he roles of others [are] dispersed. . . . Multiple and interchangeable personnel performing the same functions for the individual provides the individual with many psychological anchors in his social environment; the death of any one person leaves the others and thus diminishes the loss. (1976, pp. 247–249; for further discussions on cultural variation, see Anderson, 1965; Devereux, 1942; Levy, 1973; Lutz, 1986; Plath, 1968; Yamamoto, 1970. On historical variation, see L. H. Lofland, 1985; Rosenblatt, 1983; Stearns, 1986).

Taking the lead from Volkart, is it possible that there exists a dominance of and/or preference for some variant on Pattern 3 (which might be termed "the multiple intimates pattern") among contemporary Americans? . . . That is, might it be that Americans cannot substitute one "relational provision for another" because they believe that the only meaningful relationships—the only relationships that provide "emotional attachment"—are intimate ones? . . .

I have suggested that inquiry into historical and cultural variation in patterns of connectedness might be fruitful. Let me suggest further that inquiries into *experiential variation* might prove equally so. . . .

One such variant in the experience of death provides the focus of a goodly portion of the scholarly and first-person literature on grief—what might be called *devastating loss*. It is in reference to devastating loss that the literature, quite properly, speaks of survivors, for the language of its accompanying grief is the language of personal disaster.

Devasting loss may occur when there is a death involving a *solitary multibonded relationship*. If we imagine a continuum of connectedness based on numbers of persons involved, we can visualize at one end an actor who is linked in diverse ways (some multiple bonding, some single bonding, etc.) to a very large number of others. At the other end is a person who has literally placed all his or her eggs in one basket—all the linkages are to a single other person (Pattern 4, above). Now, this latter situation is probably empirically very infrequent, possibly nonexistent. Even if others are linked to us in no other ways, they are, as Berger and Kellner (1964) have pointed out, at least contributing to the validation of our commonsense reality. Nonetheless, close approximations of this extreme situation are anything but rare.

> Everything I did revolved around him. He was my whole world. [When he died] my heart was gone. My reason to live, everything.

And death involving such a relationship (or its approximation) is devasting because in one fell swoop all (or almost all) of the actor's "connections" are severed.

As numerous commentators have suggested, it may be that the very intense grief experience reported so frequently by widows and widowers in the contemporary United States and Britain . . . has importantly to do with a tendency for marital relationships to become solitary and multi-bonded. *A* significant other becomes *the most* significant other—permeating every corner of our lives.

•  •  •

Another sort of devasting loss results not from the removal of a single person in whom all connections are encompassed but from the simultaneous removal of all connections, that is, in circumstances of *mass death*. Of course, once again, we are dealing with a continuum. The extreme case where every single known other in the actor's world is removed, is empiraclly rare. But, tragically, close approximations are less so. Robert Lifton's studies of the survivors of Hiroshima provides one of the most detailed records of this particular death experience (1967, 1976)—an experience that in its intensity and profundity seems almost to defy our capacity to understand it. . . .

I suggested at the beginning of this essay that my intent was to make a modest foray into that area of inquiry which sociologists would identify as involving the nature of the social bond. . . . I happen to believe, and I think others working in the areas of attachment, connection, grief, and loss would concur, that these areas provide one plausible route to the achievement of that goal (see also Lofland, 1982). Certainly we have a long way to go. As the reader has discovered, we are far from understanding even experiential variations in patterns of connection and loss, much less the historical and cultural structuring of connection and loss, and even less the relation between such patterning and structuring and the organization of social orders. To strive for such an understanding, however, as I hope I have made clear, is well worth the effort. Such an understanding should bring us closer to grasping that very social and socially connected animal that is ourself and that matrix of connectedness that is our social order and our home.

## NOTES

1. I owe a great debt of gratitude to many informants, friends, and colleagues—all of whom must remain anonymous—who have shared so freely of personal mementos, anecdotes, memories, and musings about matters that for many of them are still sources of pain. I am grateful as well for the generosity of colleagues who read earlier drafts of this paper and who provided support and comments and/or criticisms. I wish to thank Kathy Charmaz, Candace Clark, Gary Hamilton, John Lofland, Victor Marshall, and Howard Robboy. I must admit, however, to having resisted dealing with a number of their more telling and well-taken criticisms. I trust this resistance will in no way threaten any of our "threads of connection."

2. Enumerations of the diverse but consistently reported "symptoms" of grief may be found in Charmaz, 1980; Clayton et al., 1968; Glick, Weiss, and Parkes, 1974; Hoyt, 1980–1981; Lindemann, 1944; Marris, 1958; Parkes, 1970, 1972; Stern, 1965.

3. I here emphasize *involuntary* severance on the presumption that situations of *voluntary* severance are likely to tell us more about frustrated expectations than about relational components. However, in his study of broken marriages, Robert Weiss (1975) found considerable evidence of "grieving" among the *instigators* of the separation/divorce. Clearly, a relationship, however unsatisfactory, is still a relationship, involving "connections," and is thus relevant to the matters under consideration here. Nonetheless, I shall restrict my inquiry to instances of involuntary severance on the strategic grounds of "cleanliness."

4. One sees here a first example of the frequent empirical compounding of "ties"—in this instance, the tie of "role partner" between son and father is compounded by "mundane assistance" (see below).

5. Quotations not otherwise referenced are from my interviews.

6. I am here separating out "role" from self. . . . In my reading of the data, people are simply not talking about the same things when they speak of the loss of someone as role partner and when they speak of loss of self through loss of other. . . .

## REFERENCES

Anderson, B. G. Bereavement as a subject of cross-cultural inquiry: An American sample. *Anthropological Quarterly*, 1965, *38*, 181–200.

Barthel, J. I promise you, it will be all right. The dilemma of a friend's dying. *Life*, March 17, 1972.

Beck, F. *The diary of a widow*. Boston: Beacon Press, 1965.

Berger, P., and Kellner, H. Marriage and the construction of reality. *Diogenes*, 1964, *46*, 1–24.

Breed, W. Suicide and loss in social interaction. In E. S. Shneidman (Ed.), *Essays in self-destruction*. New York: Science House, 1967.

Caine, L. *Widow*. New York: William Morrow, 1974.

Charmaz, K. C. *The social reality of death*. Reading, Mass.: Addison-Wesley, 1980.

Clayton, P., Desmarais, L., & Winokur, G. A study of normal bereavement. *American Journal of Psychiatry*, 1968, *125*, 64–74.

Devereux, G. Social structure and the economy of affective bonds. *The Psychoanalytic Review*, 1942, *29*, 303–314.

Glick, I. O., Weiss, R. S., and Parkes, C. M. *The first year of bereavement*. New York: Wiley, 1974.

Hoyt, M. F. Clinical notes regarding the experiences of "presences" in mourning. *Omega*, 1980–1981, 11, 105–111.

Levy, R. I. *Tahitians: Mind and experience in the Society Islands*. Chicago: University of Chicago Press, 1973.

Lewis, C. S. *A grief observed*. New York: Seabury Press, 1961.

Lifton, R. J. *Death in life; Survivors of Hiroshima*. New York: Vintage, 1967.

Lifton, R. J. *Home from the war*. New York: Simon & Schuster, 1973.

Lifton, R. J. Psychological effects of the atomic bomb in Hiroshima: The theme of death. In R. Fulton (Ed.), *Death and Identity* (rev. ed.). Bowie, Md.: Charles Press Publishers, 1976. (Originally published, 1963)

Lindemann, E. Symptomatology and Management of Acute Grief. *American Journal of Psychiatry*, 1944, 101, 141–148.

Lofland, L. H. The Social Shaping of Emotion: The Case of Grief. *Symbolic Interaction*, 1985, *8*, 171–190.

Lopata, H. Z. Loneliness: Forms and components. *Social Problems*, 1969, *17*, 248–261.

Lopata, H. Z. *Widowhood in an American city*. Cambridge, Mass.: Schenkman, 1973.

Lopata, H. Z. *Women as widows: Support systems*. New York: Elsevier, 1979.

Lutz, C. Depression and the Translation of Emotional Worlds. In A. Kleinman and B. Good (Eds.), *Culture and Depression*. Berkeley: University of California Press, 1986.

McCabe, C. A sprig of rosemary. *San Francisco Chronicle*, May 5, 1970.

Marris, P. *Widows and their families*. London: Routledge & Kegan Paul, 1958.

Parkes, C. M. "Seeking" and "finding" a lost object: Evidence from recent studies of the reaction to bereavement. *Social Science and Medicine*, 1970, *4*, 187–201.

Parkes, C. M. *Bereavement: Studies of grief in adult life*. New York: International Universities Press, 1972.

Plath, D. W. Maintaining relations with kin: Social ties after death in Japan. In H. K. Geiger (Ed.), *Comparative perspectives on marriage and the family*. Boston: Little, Brown, 1968.

Rosenblatt, P. C. *Bitter, Bitter Tears: 19th Century Diarists and the 20th Century Grief Theories*. Minneapolis: University of Minnesota Press, 1983.

Stearns, P. N. The Problems of Change in Emotions Research. Paper presented at the meetings of the American Sociological Association, New York, New York, 1986.

Stern, K., Williams, G., and Prados, M. Grief reactions in later life. In R. Fulton (Ed.), *Death and identity*. New York: Wiley, 1965.

Thomas, C. *Leftover life to kill*. Boston: Little, Brown, 1957.

Volkart, E. H. (with collaboration of S. T. Michael). Bereavement and mental health. In R. Fulton (Ed.), *Death and identity* (rev. ed.). Bowie, Md.: Charles Press, 1976. (Originally published, 1957.)

Wallace, S. E. *After Suicide*. New York: Wiley, 1973.

Wedemeyer, D. "Widowers: They Face Unique Problems Which Widows Do Not." *Sacramento Bee*, November 16, 1974.

Weiss, R. S. The fund of sociability. *Trans-action* (now, Society), July/August, 1969, 36–43.

Weiss, R. S. *Marital separation*. New York: Basic Books, 1975.

Wrigley, E. A. *Population and history*. New York: McGraw-Hill, 1969.

Yamamoto, J. Cultural factors in loneliness, death and separation. *Medical Times*, 1970, *98*, 177–183.

# Review Questions

1. Provide examples from your own circle of family, friends, and acquaintances of the seven threads of connectedness that Lofland describes:
   a. role partner
   b. mundane assistance
   c. linkages to others
   d. creation and maintenance of self
   e. support for comforting myths
   f. reality maintenance
   g. maintenance of possible futures

2. How have you "distributed your connections"? That is, how many other people in your social world do you count on to provide you with roles, mundane assistance, and the like? Which (if any) of the four patterns of connectedness best describes you?

3. Which of the four patterns of connectedness best characterizes American society today? Explain your answer.

4. In which of the four patterns of connectedness is devastating loss most likely to occur? Explain your answer.

# CORNER BOYS: A STUDY OF CLIQUE BEHAVIOR

## William Foote Whyte

This paper presents some of the results of a study of leadership in informal groupings or gangs of corner boys in "Cornerville," a slum area of a large eastern city. The aim of the research was to develop methods whereby the position (rank or status) of the individual in his clique might be empirically determined; to study the bases of group cohesion and of the subordination and superordination of its members; and, finally, to work out means for determining the position of corner gangs in the social structure of the community.

● ● ●

While my subjects called themselves corner boys, they were all grown men, most of them in their twenties, and some in their thirties. . . . While some of the men I observed were engaged in illegal activities, I was not interested in crime as such; instead, I was interested in studying the nature of clique behavior, regardless of whether or not the clique was connected with criminal activity. . . . I made an intensive and detailed study of 5 gangs on the basis of personal observation, intimate acquaintance, and participation in their activities for an extended period of time. Throughout three-and-a-half years of research, I lived in Cornerville, not in a settlement house, but in tenements such as are inhabited by Cornerville people.

The population of the district is almost entirely of Italian extraction. Most of the corner boys belong to the second generation of immigrants. In general, they are men who have had little education beyond grammar school and who are unemployed, irregularly employed, or working steadily for small wages.

Their name arises from the nature of their social life. For them "the corner" is not necessarily at a street intersection. It is any part of the sidewalk which they take for their social headquarters, and it often includes a poolroom, barroom, funeral parlor, barbershop, or clubroom. Here they may be found almost any afternoon or evening, talking and joking about sex, sports, personal relations, or politics in season. Other social activities either take place "on the corner" or are planned there.

William Foote Whyte, "Corner Boys: A Study of Clique Behavior," *American Journal of Sociology* 46 (March 1941): 647–664.

## HIERARCHY OF PERSONAL RELATIONS

The existence of a hierarchy of personal relations in these cliques is seldom explicitly recognized by the corner boys. Asked if they have a leader or boss, they invariably reply, ''No, we're all equal.'' It is only through the observation of actions that the group structure becomes apparent. My problem was to apply methods which would produce an objective and reasonably exact picture of such structures.

In any group containing more than two people there are subdivisions to be observed. No member is equally friendly with all other members. In order to understand the behavior of the individual member it is necessary to place him not only in his group but also in his particular position in the subgroup.

My most complete study of groupings was made from observations in the rooms of the Cornerville Social and Athletic Club. This was a club of corner boys, which had a membership of about fifty and was divided primarily into two cliques, which had been relatively independent of each other before the formation of the club. There were, of course, subdivisions in each clique.

I sought to make a record of the groupings in which I found the members whenever I went into the club. While the men were moving around, I would be unable to retain their movements for my record, but on most occasions they would settle down in certain spatial arrangements. In the accompanying example (Figure 1) two were at a table playing checkers with one watching, four at another table playing whist and three more watching the game, and six talking together toward the back of the room. As I looked around the room, I would count the number of men present so that I should know later how many I should have to account for. Then I would say over to myself the names of the men in each grouping and try to fix in my mind their positions in relation to one another. In the course of an evening there might be a general reshuffling of positions. I would not be able to remember every movement, but I would try to observe with which members the movements began; and, when another spatial arrangement had developed, I would go through the same mental process as I had with the first. As soon as I got home from the club, I would draw a map or maps of the spatial positions I had observed and add any movements between positions which I recalled. The map (Figure 1) indicates the sort of data that came out of these observations.

In this case I have the following notes on movements of the members:

> Eleven walked over to One and pinched his cheek hard, went out of the club rooms, returned and pinched cheek again. One pretended to threaten Eleven with an ash tray. Eleven laughed and returned to seat on couch. I [the observer] asked Eleven about the purpose of the club meeting. He asked Ten and Ten explained. Eleven laughed and shrugged his shoulders. Sixteen, the janitor, served beer for the card players.

**Figure 1. The Cornerville S & A Club, February 29, 1940, 8–8:15 P.M.**

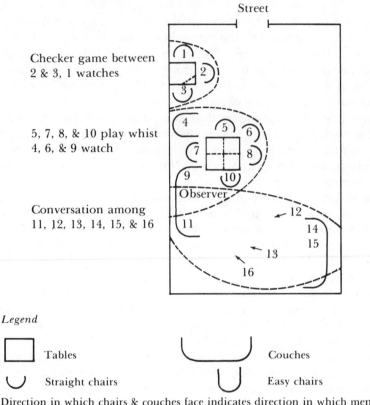

Checker game between
2 & 3, 1 watches

5, 7, 8, & 10 play whist
4, 6, & 9 watch

Conversation among
11, 12, 13, 14, 15, & 16

*Legend*

☐ Tables

⊔ Couches

⊔ Straight chairs

⊔ Easy chairs

Direction in which chairs & couches face indicates direction in which men face.
Arrows indicate direction in which standing men face.
Dotted lines enclose those interacting.

On the basis of a number of maps such as this it is not difficult to place most of the men in the clique and grouping within the clique to which they belong. I did not attempt to place all the men, because the club had a fluctuating membership and some of the men were available for observation for only a short time. There were, throughout the ten months of my observation, some thirty-odd members who were active most of the time. Events in the club could be explained largely in terms of the actions of these men; and, therefore, when I had placed them in relation to one another, I did not need to press further in this direction.

Positional map-making is simply an extension of the techniques of observation and recording which have been used in the past by social anthropologists and sociologists. All these techniques require practice before they can be effectively applied. While my first maps left out a number of men, later I was able to record accurately enough so that on most occasions I could account for every man present at a particular time; and on several occasions I was able to work out two maps giving different positional arrangements during the course of the same period of observation. Beyond two I did not attempt to go, and it was not necessary to do so because there would rarely be more than two positional arrangements in the course of an evening sufficiently different from one another to require additional maps.

While the data from such maps enable one to determine groupings, they do not reveal the position or rank of the men in the groupings. For this purpose other data are needed. In practice they may be gathered at the same time as the positional arrangements are observed.

As I conceive it, position in the informal group means power to influence the actions of the group. I concentrated my attention upon the origination of action, to observe who proposed an action, to whom he made the proposal, and the steps that followed up to the completion of the action. I was dealing with "pair events" and "set events," to use the terminology of Arensberg and Chapple.[1] A "pair event" is an event between two people. A "set event" is an event in which one person originates action for two or more others at the same time. In working out the relations between men in an informal group, this is an important distinction to bear in mind. I found that observations of pair events did not provide a safe guide for the ranking of the members of the pair. At times A would originate action for B, at other times B would originate action for A. In some cases there would be a predominance of originations in one direction; but on the whole the data did not support rankings based upon quantitative comparisons of the rates of origination of action in pair events. Qualitatively one could say that when A originated action for B he used a tone of voice and words which indicated that he held a superior position. To take the extreme case, it is not difficult to tell the difference between an order and a request, although both may originate action. It is not safe, however, to rely upon such qualitative differences. The observer may read into the situation his own impression of the relative positions of the men and thus lose the objective basis for his conclusions.

It is observation of set events which reveals the hierarchical basis of informal group organization. As defined by Arensberg and Chapple,

> a *set* is an aggregate of relations such that every individual related in the set is a member either (*a*) of a class of individuals who only originate action, or (*b*) of an intermediate class of individuals who at some time originate action and at another time terminate action, or (*c*) of a class of individuals who only terminate action.[2]

Study of corner-boy groups reveals that the members may, indeed, be divided and ranked upon this basis. Several examples will illustrate.

At the top of the Cornerville S. and A. Club (see Figure 2), we have Tony, Carlo, and Dom. They were the only ones who could originate action for the entire club. At the bottom were Dodo, Gus, Pop, Babe, Marco, and Bob, who never originated action in a set event involving anyone above their positions. Most of the members fell into the intermediate class. They terminated action on the part of the top men and originated action for the bottom men. Observations of the actions of the men of the intermediate class when neither top nor bottom men were present revealed that there were subdivisions or rankings within that class. This does not mean that the intermediate or bottom men never have any ideas as to what the club should do. It means that their ideas must go through the proper channels if they are to go into effect.

In one meeting of the Cornerville S. and A. Club, Dodo proposed that he be allowed to handle the sale of beer in the clubrooms in return for 75 percent of the profits. Tony spoke in favor of Dodo's suggestion but proposed giving him a somewhat smaller percentage. Dodo agreed. Then Carlo proposed to have Dodo handle the beer in quite a different way, and Tony agreed. Tony made the motion, and it was carried unanimously. In this case Dodo's proposal was carried through, after substantial modifications, upon the actions of Tony and Carlo.

In another meeting Dodo said that he had two motions to make: that the club's funds be deposited in a bank and that no officer be allowed to serve two consecutive terms. Tony was not present at this time. Dom, the president, said that only one motion should be made at a time and that, furthermore, Dodo should not make any motions until there had been opportunity for discussion. Dodo agreed. Dom then commented that it would be foolish to deposit the funds when the club had so little to deposit. Carlo expressed his agreement. The meeting passed on to other things without action upon the first motion and without even a word of discussion on the second one. In the same meeting Chris moved that a member must be in the club for a year before being allowed to hold office. Carlo said that it was a good idea, he seconded the motion, and it carried unanimously.

All my observations indicate that the idea for group action which is carried out must originate with the top man or be accepted by him so that he acts upon the group. A follower may originate action for a leader in a pair event, but he does not originate action for the leader and other followers at the same time—that is, he does not originate action in a set event which includes the leader.

One may also observe that, when the leader originates action for the group, he does not act as if his followers were all of equal rank. Implicitly he takes the structure of the group into account. An example taken from the corner gang known as the "Millers" will illustrate this point. The Millers were a group of twenty corner boys, who were divided into two subgroups. Members of both subgroups frequently acted together; but, when two activities occupied the men at the same time, the division generally fell between the subgroups. Sam was the leader of the Millers. Joe

**Figure 2. Informal Organization of the Cornerville S & A Club, February 1940**

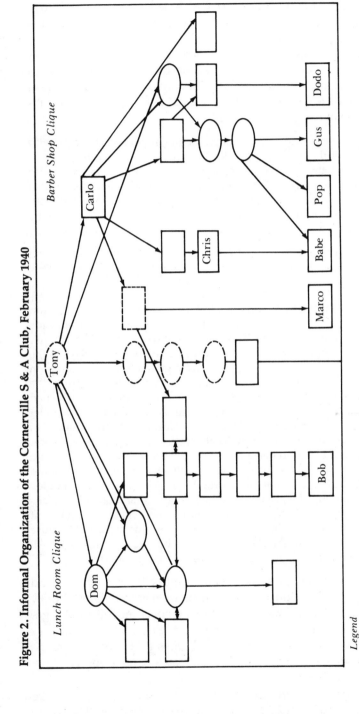

Legend

⬭ Members employed in the policy racket organization.

▭ Members not employed in the policy racket organization.

------ Those infrequently present.
Level of boxes indicates relative status.
Arrows indicate chief lines of influence.
For purposes of simplification, names of members not mentioned in text are omitted.

177

was directly below him in one subgroup. Chichi led the other subgroup. Joe as well as Sam was in a position to originate action for Chichi and his subgroup.

It was customary for the Millers to go bowling every Saturday night. On this particular Saturday night Sam had no money, so he set out to persuade the boys to do something else. They followed his suggestion. Later Sam explained to me how he had been able to change the established social routine of the group. He said:

> I had to show the boys that it would be in their own interests to come with me—that each one of them would benefit. But I knew I only had to convince two of the fellows. If they start to do something, the other boys will say to themselves, "If Joe does it—or if Chichi does it—it must be a good thing for us too." I told Joe and Chichi what the idea was, and I got them to come with me. I didn't pay no attention to the others. When Joe and Chichi came, all the other boys came along too.

Another example from the Millers indicates what happens when the leader and the man next to him in rank disagree upon group policy. This is Sam talking again:

> One time we had a raffle to raise money to build a camp on Lake _____ [on property lent them by a local business man]. We had collected $54, and Joe and I were holding the money. . . . That week I knew Joe was playing pool, and he lost three or four dollars gambling. When Saturday came, I says to the boys, "Come on, we go out to Lake _____. We're gonna build that camp on the hill. . . ." Right away Joe said, "If yuz are gonna build the camp on the hill, I don't come. I want it on the other side. . . ." All the time I knew he had lost the money, and he was only making up excuses so he wouldn't have to let anybody know. . . . Now the hill was really the place to build that camp. On the other side, the ground was swampy. That would have been a stupid place. . . . But I knew that if I tried to make them go through with it now, the group would split up into two cliques. Some would come with me, and some would go with Joe. . . . So I let the whole thing drop for a while. . . . After, I got Joe alone, and I says to him, "Joe, I know you lost some of that money, but that's all right. You can pay up when you have it and nobody will say nothin'. But Joe, you know we shouldn't have the camp on the other side of the hill because the land is no good there. We should build it on the hill. . . ." So he said, "All right," and we got all the boys together, and we went out to build the camp.

Under ordinary circumstances the leader implicitly recognizes and helps to maintain the position of the man or men immediately below him, and the group functions smoothly. In this respect the informal organization is similar to the formal organization. If the executive in a factory attempts to pass over his immediate subordinates and gives orders directly to the men on the assembly line, he creates confusion. The customary channels must be used.

The social structures vary from group to group, but each one may be represented in some form of hierarchy. The members have clearly defined relations of subordination and superordination, and each group has a leader. Since we are concerned with informal organization, the Cornerville S. and A. members must be considered as two groups, with Carlo leading the barbershop boys, and Dom leading the lunchroom boys. Since Tony's position requires special consideration, he will be discussed later.

## BASES OF GROUP STRUCTURE

Observation not only serves to provide a description of the group structure. It also reveals information upon the bases of structure and the factors differentiating between the positions of members. The clique structure arises out of the habitual association of the members over a long period of time. The nuclei of most gangs can be traced back to early boyhood years when living close together provided the first opportunities for social contacts. School years modified the original pattern somewhat, but I know of no corner gangs which arose through classroom or school-playground association. The gangs grew up "on the corner" and have remained there with remarkable persistence. In the course of years some groups have been broken up by the movement of families away from Cornerville, and the remaining members have merged with gangs on nearby corners; but frequently movement out of the district does not take the corner boy away from his corner. On any evening in Cornerville on almost any corner one finds corner boys who have come in from other parts of the city or from suburbs to be with their old friends. The residence of the corner boy may also change within the district, but nearly always he retains his allegiance to his original corner.

The leader of one group spoke to me in this way about corner boys:

> Fellows around here don't know what to do except within a radius of about 300 yards. That's the truth, Bill. . . . They come home from work, hang on the corner, go up to eat, back on the corner, up (to) a show, and they come back to hang on the corner. If they're not on the corner, it's likely the boys there will know where you can find them. . . . Most of them stick to one corner. It's only rarely that a fellow will change his corner.

The stable composition of the group over a long period and the lack of social assurance felt by most of the members contribute toward producing a very high rate of social interaction within the group. *The structure to be observed is a product of past interactions.*

Out of these interactions there arises a system of mutual obligations which is fundamental to group cohesion. If the men are to carry on their activities as a unit, there are many occasions when they must do favors for one another. Frequently, one member must spend money to help another who does not have the money to participate in some of the group activities. This creates an obligation. If the situation is later reversed, the recipient is expected to help the man who gave him aid. The code of the corner boy requires him to help his friends when he can and to refrain from doing anything to harm them. When life in the group runs smoothly, the mutual obligations binding members to one another are not explicitly recognized. A corner boy, asked if he helped a fellow-member because of a sense of obligation, will reply, "No, I didn't have to do it. He's my friend. That's all." It is only when the relationship breaks down that the underlying obligations are brought to light. When two members of the group have a falling-out, their actions form a familiar pattern. One tells a story something like this: "What a heel Blank turned out to be. After all I've done for him, the first time I ask him to do something for me, he won't do it." The other may say: "What does he want from me? I've done plenty for him, but he wants you to do everything." In other words, the actions which were performed explicitly for the sake of friendship are now revealed as being part of a system of mutual obligations.

## THE SOCIAL ROLE OF LEADER

Not all the corner boys live up to their obligations equally well, and this factor partly accounts for the differentiation in status among the men. The man with a low status may violate his obligations without much change in his position. His fellows know that he has failed to discharge certain obligations in the past, and his position reflects his past performances. On the other hand, the leader is depended upon by all the members to meet his personal obligations. He cannot often fail to do so without causing confusion and losing his position. The relationship of status to the system of mutual obligations is most clearly revealed when we consider the use of money. While all the men are expected to be generous, the flow of money between members can be explained only in terms of the group structure.

The Millers provide an illustration of this point. During the time that I knew them, Sam, the leader, was out of work except for an occasional odd job; yet, whenever he had a little money, he spent it on Joe and Chichi, his closest friends, who were next to him in the structure of the group. When Joe or Chichi had money, which was less frequent, they reciprocated. Sam frequently paid for two members who stood close to the bottom of the structure and occasionally for others. The two men who held positions immediately below Joe and Chichi in the subgroups were considered very well off according to Cornerville standards. Sam said that he occasionally borrowed money from them, but never more than fifty cents at a time. Such loans he tried to repay at the earliest possible moment. There were four other members, with positions ranging from intermediate to the bottom, who nearly always had more money than Sam. He did not recall ever having borrowed from them. He said that the only time he had obtained a substantial sum from anyone around his corner was when he borrowed eleven dollars from a friend who was the *leader* of another corner-boy group.

The system is substantially the same for all the groups on which I have information. The leader spends more money on his followers than they on him. The farther down in the structure one looks, the fewer are the financial relations which tend to obligate the leader to a follower. This does not mean that the leader has more money than others or even that he necessarily spends more—though he must always be a free spender. It means that the financial relations must be explained in social terms. Unconsciously, and in some cases consciously, the leader refrains from putting himself under obligations to those with low status in the group.

Relations of rivalry or outright hostility with other groups are an important factor in promoting in-group solidarity, as has been well recognized. . . . Present-day corner gangs grew up in an atmosphere of street fighting against gangs of Irish or of fellow-Italians. While actual fights are now infrequent, the spirit of gang loyalty is maintained in part through athletic contests and political rivalries.

As the structures indicate, members have higher rates of interaction with men close to their own positions in their subgroups than with men who rank much higher or much lower or belong to a different subgroup. That is a significant fact for the explanation of group cohesion.

In the case of the Millers, Sam's best friends were Joe and Chichi. As his remarks have indicated, Sam realized that the solidarity of the Millers depended in the first instance upon the existence of friendly and cooperative relations between himself, Joe, and Chichi. A Cornerville friend, who was aware of the nature of my observations, commented in this manner:

> On any corner, you would find not only a leader but probably a couple of lieutenants. They could be leaders themselves, but they let the man lead them. You would say, they let him lead because they like the way he does things. Sure, but he leans upon them for his authority. . . . Many times you find fellows on a corner that stay in the background until some situation comes up, and then they will take over and call the shots. Things like that can change fast sometimes.

Such changes are the result not of an uprising of the bottom men but of a shift in the relations between men at the top of the structure. When a gang breaks into two parts, the explanation is to be found in a conflict between the leader and one who ranked close to him in the structure of the original gang.

The distinctive functions of the top men in promoting social cohesion are readily observable in the field. Frequently, in the absence of their leader the members of a gang are divided into a number of small groups. There is no common activity or general conversation. When the leader appears, the situation changes strikingly. The small units form into one large group. The conversation becomes general, and unified action frequently follows. The leader becomes the focal point in discussion. One observes a follower start to say something, pause when he notices that the leader is not listening, and begin again when he has the leader's attention. When the leader leaves the group, unity gives way to the divisions that existed before his appearance. To a certain extent the lieutenants can perform this unifying function; but their scope is more limited because they are more closely identified with one particular subgroup than is the leader.

The same Cornerville friend summed up the point in this way:

> If we leave the followers, they'll go find some other leader. They won't know what they're doing, but that's what they'll do, because by themselves they won't know what to do. They gather around the leader, and it is the leader that keeps them together.

The leader is the man who knows what to do. He is more resourceful than his followers. Past events have shown that his ideas were right. In this sense "right" simply means satisfactory to the members. He is the most independent in judgment. While his followers are undecided as to a course of action or upon the character of a newcomer, the leader makes up his mind. When he gives his word to one of "his boys," he keeps it. The followers look to him for advice and encouragement, and he receives more of the confidences of the members than any other man. Consequently, he knows more about what is going on in the group than anyone else. Whenever there is a quarrel among the boys, he will hear of it almost as soon as it happens. Each party to the quarrel may appeal to him to work out a solution; and, even when the men do not want to compose their differences, each one will take his side of the story to the leader at the first opportunity. A man's standing depends partly upon the leader's belief that he has been conducting himself as he should.

The leader is respected for his fair-mindedness. Whereas there may be hard feelings among some of the followers, the leader cannot bear a grudge against any man in the group. He has close friends (men who stand next to him in position), and he is indifferent to some of the members; but if he is to retain his reputation for impartiality, he cannot allow personal animus to override his judgment.

The leader need not be the best baseball player, bowler, or fighter, but he must have some skill in whatever pursuits are of particular interest to the group. It is natural for him to promote activities in which he excels and to discourage those in which he is not skillful; and, insofar as he is thus able to influence the group, his competent performance is a natural consequence of his position. At the same time his performance supports his position.

It is significant to note that the leader is better known and more respected outside of his group than is any of his followers. His social mobility is greater. One of the most important functions he performs is that of relating his group to other groups in the district. His reputation outside the group tends to support his standing within the group, and his position in the group supports his reputation among outsiders.

It should not be assumed from this discussion that the corner boys compete with one another for the purpose of gaining leadership. Leadership is a product of social interaction. The men who reach the top in informal groups are those who can perform skillfully the actions required by the situation. Most such skills are performed without long premeditation.

What the leader is has been discussed in terms of what he does. I doubt whether an analysis in terms of personality traits will add anything to such an explanation of behavior. One can find a great variety of personality traits among corner-boy leaders, just as one can among business or political leaders. Some are aggressive in social contacts, and others appear almost retiring. Some are talkative, and others have little to say. Few uniformities of this nature are to be found. On the other hand, there are marked uniformities to be observed in the functions performed by men who hold similar positions in society, and the study of them promises to provide the best clues for the understanding of social behavior.

## THE GANGS AND THE WIDER COMMUNITY

For a community study, data upon five corner gangs are hardly more than a beginning. Two problems were involved in extending the research. First, I had to discover whether I could safely generalize my conclusions to apply them to all corner gangs in Cornerville. Second, I had to fit the corner gangs into the fabric of Cornerville society.

To accomplish the first end I solicited the aid of a number of corner-boy leaders, who made for me more or less systematic observations of their own groups and of groups about them. The generalizations, presented earlier, upon the functions of leaders, indicate why I found them the best sources of information upon their groups. This procedure could not be relied upon as a substitute for observation, for it is only through observation that the student can discover what his informants are talking about and understand their remarks in terms of group structure. Observation suggests a framework of significant behavior patterns and indicates subjects that are relevant for discussion with informants.

The student should realize that this procedure changes the attitude of the corner boy toward himself and his group. The quotations from Cornerville men presented here all show the effects of prior discussion with me. However, the effort of informants to make explicit statements upon unreflective behavior does not distort the factual picture as long as they are required to tell their stories in terms of observed interactions.

The most thorough study of this kind was made for me by Sam of the Millers upon his own group. The structure of the Millers was worked out by Sam over a period of months on the basis of such material as I have quoted. My function was to discuss Sam's observations with him, to point out gaps in his data, and to check them with some independent observations.

All the generalizations presented here have been checked against the experience and observations of four such informants. In this way I have been able to expand my study far beyond what I should have been able to cover alone.

Accomplishment of the second purpose—fitting corner gangs into the fabric of society—required study of the relations which linked group to group and the group to persons who held superior positions in Cornerville—politicians and racketeers, for example.

The observation that the leader is the person to relate his group to other people provides the most important lead for such a study. We see that the social behavior of groups pivots around the actions of certain men who hold strategic positions in them. This does not mean that the leader can make his followers do anything he desires. It does mean that he customarily leads the group activity and that outsiders, in order to influence the members, must deal with the group through him. This is to be observed particularly at the time of a political campaign when politicians seek to mobilize group support. Similar observations may be made in order to explain the position and influence of the racketeer in relation to corner-boy groups.

Brief reference to the Cornerville S. and A. study will indicate the nature of the results that may be obtained. Tony, the top man in the chart, was a prominent policy racketeer. The chart indicates that certain members were agents who turned their policy slips in to him. While Tony belonged to the club, his interests were so widespread that he had little time to spend with the members. It was recognized that he held a higher status, that he was not a corner boy.

At the time of the formation of the club, Tony knew Dom, his agent, and recognized Dom's position among the lunchroom boys. He knew Carlo only casually and was not aware of his position as leader of the barbershop clique. In the course of a political campaign (November 1939) a conflict arose over the endorsement of a candidate for alderman. By playing off one clique against the other, Tony was able to secure the adoption of his policy, but Carlo opposed him vigorously and lost out in a close vote. Carlo's position was strengthened when his candidate defeated the man supported by Tony. Following the election, there was a marked change in Tony's actions. He began to attend every meeting and to spend more time with the members. For his purposes Carlo was the most important man in the club, and he made every effort to cement his social relations with Carlo and to place Carlo under obligations to him. During this period a basis for co-operation between the two men was established. When Tony turned his attention to other activities, he was able to deal with the club through Carlo as well as through Dom.

This story illustrates a method of study, not a set of conclusions. Through observing the interactions between Tony and Dom, Tony and Carlo, Dom and the members of his clique, and Carlo and the members of his clique, one can establish the position and influence of the racketeer in relation to this particular organization of corner boys. Other observations establish Tony's position in the racket organization, which extends throughout the district and far beyond it. They also point out Tony's relations with certain politicians. Only in the study of such specific situations can one arrive at reliable generalizations upon the positions and influence of men in the community.

## CONCLUSION

The methods I have used call for precise and detailed observation of spatial positions and of the origination of action in pair and set events between members of informal groups. Such observations provide data by means of which one may chart structures of social relations and determine the basis of the structures—a system of mutual obligations growing out of the interactions of the members over a long period of time. Observations also point out the distinctive functions of the leader, who serves as chief representative of his group and director and co-ordinator of group activity. A knowledge of the structure and of the social processes carried on through it serves to explain the behavior of individual members in a manner which could not be accomplished if one considered the men as an unstructured aggregation.

Such an understanding of clique behavior seems a necessary first step in the development of knowledge of the nature of the larger social organization into which the cliques fit. Instead of seeking to place each clique member in relation to the total social organization, the investigator may concentrate his attention upon the actions of the leader, who relates his corner boys to other groups and to persons holding superior positions. By discovering these strategic points for social integration and by extending the network of social relations through them, the investigator can place a large number of the inhabitants of his community in their social positions.

This is a painstaking and time-consuming method. While it does not produce statistics which count all the inhabitants in terms of certain characteristics, it does provide the investigator with a close-up view of the social organization in action.

## NOTES

1. *Measuring Human Relations: An Introduction to the Study of the Interaction of Individuals* ("Genetic Psychology Monographs" [Provincetown, Mass.: Journal Press, 1940]).

2. *Op. cit.*, p. 54. To terminate an action is to follow the initiative of another person.

## Review Questions

1. How are various aspects of the groups studied by Whyte *similar to* and *different from* formal organizations?

2. According to Whyte, how do clique structures arise? How did his methods of research allow him to discover the answer to this question?

3. Explain Whyte's statement, "Leadership is a product of social interaction." Give examples from the groups he discussed as well as from your own experience.

4. Explain how providing aid to friends built up a network of obligations among the corner boys. Were they aware that they expected reciprocity from the friends they aided?

# THE COLLEGE CLASSROOM: SOME OBSERVATIONS ON THE MEANINGS OF STUDENT PARTICIPATION

## David A. Karp and William C. Yoels

A RECENT REPORT ON THE EMPLOYMENT OF SOCIOLOGISTS AND ANTHROPOL-ogists indicated that 97 percent of the sociologists in the United States were teaching either full-time or part-time in an institution of higher education (NIMH: 1969). While sociologists earn their "daily bread" by teaching, they earn their scholarly reputations by engaging in research studies of almost every conceivable kind of social setting except, it seems, that of the college classroom. The failure to explore the "routine grounds" of our everyday lives as teachers is testimony to the existence of the college classroom as part of what Alfred Schutz (1962) referred to as "the world as taken-for-granted."

•   •   •

Rarely have researchers attempted to consider the processes through which students and teachers formulate definitions of the classroom as a social setting. The problem of how students and teachers assign "meaning" to the classroom situation has been largely neglected in the various studies mentioned. Although writing about primary and secondary school classrooms, we would suggest that the following statement from Jackson's (1968:vii) *Life in Classrooms* holds true for college classrooms as well. He writes that:

> Classroom life . . . is too complex an affair to be viewed or talked about from any single perspective. Accordingly, as we try to grasp the meaning of what school is like for students and teachers, we must not hesitate to use all the ways of knowing at our disposal. This means we must read and look and listen and count things, and talk to people, and even muse introspectively.

The present study focuses on the meanings of student participation in the college classroom. Our examination of this problem will center on the way in which definitions of classrooms held by students and teachers relate to their actual behavior in the classroom.

David A. Karp and William C. Yoels, "The College Classroom: Some Observations on the Meanings of Student Participation," *Sociology and Social Research* 60, 421–439.

## METHODS OF STUDY

In an attempt to investigate the issues mentioned above we initiated an exploratory study of classroom behavior in several classes of a private university located in a large city in the northeastern United States. Our familiarity with the literature on the "words-deeds" problem (Deutcher, 1973; Phillips, 1971) led us to employ a two-fold process of data collection—namely, systematic observation of classroom behavior in selected classes, accompanied by questionnaires administered at the end of the semester in the classes under observation. None of the previously reviewed studies employed this type of research strategy, and it was hoped that such an approach would yield insights not attainable from reliance on a single data gathering procedure. In addition to the foregoing procedures we also drew upon our numerous years of experience as both students and teachers in college classrooms.

Ten classes were selected for observation. The observers were undergraduate and graduate sociology students who were doing the research as part of a Readings and Research arrangement. The classes were not randomly selected but were chosen in terms of observers' time schedules and the possibility of their observing behavior in the classrooms on a regular basis throughout the semester. The observed classes were located in the following departments: sociology, philosophy, English, psychology, economics, theology. While the classes are certainly not a representative sample of all classes taught in this university, questionnaire responses from an additional sample of students in classes selected at random at the end of the semester indicate a remarkable similarity to the questionnaire responses of the students in the ten classes under observation.[1]

At the end of the semester a questionnaire was distributed in class to the students in the ten classes which had been under prior observation. A shortened version of this questionnaire was also given to the teachers of these classes. Questionnaire items centered on factors deemed important in influencing students' decisions on whether to talk or not in class.[2]

## FINDINGS

Table 1 presents a summary of selected observational items by class size. Classes with less than 40 students have a higher average number of interactions per session than those with more than 40 students. More important, however, is the fact that in both categories of class size the *average number* of students participating is almost identical. Moreover, a handful of students account for more than 50 percent of the total interactions in both under 40 and over 40 classes. In classes with less than 40 students, between 4 and 5 students account for 75 percent of the total in-

## Table 1. Summary Table by Class Size of Selected Observational Items(a)

| CLASS SIZE | AVERAGE NUMBER OF INTERACTIONS PER CLASS | AVERAGE NUMBER OF STUDENTS PAR-TICIPATING | AVERAGE % OF STUDENTS PRESENT PAR-TICIPATING | AVERAGE NUMBER OF STUDENTS MAKING TWO OR MORE COMMENTS | % OF THOSE PRESENT MAKING TWO OR MORE COMMENTS | % OF TOTAL INTERACTIONS ACCOUNTED FOR BY THOSE MAKING TWO OR MORE COMMENTS |
|---|---|---|---|---|---|---|
| Under 40 | 25.96 | 9.83 | 47.84 | 4.64 | 25.06 | 75.61 |
| 40+ | 19.40 | 9.88 | 23.98 | 2.70 | 5.74 | 51.00 |

(a)THE SMALLEST CLASS CONTAINED 12 STUDENTS; THE LARGEST CLASS CONTAINED 65 STUDENTS.

teractions per session; in classes of more than 40 students, between 2 and 3 students account for 51 percent of the total interactions per session. From the limited data presented here it would appear that class size has relatively little effect on the average number of students participating in class. Such a finding is particularly interesting in view of the fact, as indicated in Table 5, that more than 65 percent of both male and female students indicated that the large size of the class was an important factor in why students would choose not to talk in class.

Data also indicate that students have a conception of classroom participation as being concentrated in the hands of a few students. Ninety-three percent of the males and 94 percent of the females strongly agreed or agreed with the item "In most of my classes there are a small number of students who do most of the talking." Such a conception is in congruence with the observations of actual classroom behavior noted inTable 1.

The students' conception that a handful of students do most of the talking is also coupled with annoyance on the part of many students at those who "talk too much." Responses to a questionnaire item indicated that 62 percent of the males and 61 percent of the females strongly agreed or agreed with the item "I sometimes find myself getting annoyed with students who talk too much in class."

Students also believe it possible to make a decision very early in the semester as to whether professors really want class discussion. Ninety-four percent of the males and 96 percent of the females strongly agreed or agreed with the item "students can tell pretty quickly whether a professor really wants discussion in his/her class."

Students were also asked whether the teacher's sex is likely to influence their participation in class. The overwhelming response of both male and female students to this question is that the professor's sex makes *no difference* in their likelihood of participating in class. Over 93 percent of the males and 91 percent of the female students answered "No Difference" to this question. In effect, then, both male and female students tend to define the classroom as a situation in which the sexual component of the professor's identity is completely irrelevant.

The contrast between what students say about the previous item and what they actually do in classroom is highlighted in Table 2. The data indicate a very clearcut relationship between the sex of the teacher and the likelihood of male or female participation in class. In male taught classes men account for 75.4 percent of the interactions, three times the percentage for women—24.6 percent. In female taught classes, men still account for more of the interactions than women—57.8 percent to 42.2 percent— but the percentage of female participation increases almost 75 percent from 24.7 percent in male taught classes to 42.2 percent in female taught classes. Female student participation is maximized under the influence of female professors.

Since the participation of men and women may be a function of their proportion in class, the right-hand side of Table 2 presents data on the composition of the male and female taught classes. In both male and female taught classes the percentage of male and female students is almost equal, therefore eliminating the possibility that the rate of male-female participation is a function of male student overrepresentation in these classes.

Table 3 presents observational data regarding what the students were responding to when they participated in classroom interactions. There was very little student-to-student interaction occurring in the ten classes under observation. Ten percent of the total number of classroom interactions involved cases in which students responded to the questions or comments of other students. Table 3 indicates quite dramatically that the actions of the teacher are indeed most crucial in promoting classroom interaction. Questions posed by the teacher and teacher comments accounted for 88 percent of the classroom interactions. Especially signifi-

**Table 2. Observed Classroom Interaction by Sex of Student and Sex of Teacher**

| SEX OF TEACHER | % OF OBSERVED INTERACTIONS | | | | % OF STUDENTS IN CLASSES(a) | | | |
|---|---|---|---|---|---|---|---|---|
| | Male | Female | Total | N | Male | Female | Total | N |
| Male | 75.4 | 24.6 | 100.0 | 565 | 52.0 | 48.0 | 100.0 | 152 |
| Female | 57.8 | 42.2 | 100.0 | 774 | 51.5 | 48.5 | 100.0 | 163 |
| Total | 65.3 | 34.7 | 100.0 | 1339 | 51.7 | 48.3 | 100.0 | 315 |

Note: $X^2 = 44.05$, df = 1, p < .001

(a)REFERS TO THE NUMBER OF STUDENTS ANSWERING THE QUESTIONNAIRE IN CLASS.

## Table 3. Source of Interaction by Sex of Student

|  | SOURCE OF "STIMULUS" | | | | | | | |
|---|---|---|---|---|---|---|---|---|
| Sex of Student | Teacher Question Direct | Teacher Question Indirect | Teacher Comment | Student Question | Student Comment | Source Not Specified | Total | N |
| Male | 10.0% | 46.5% | 31.9% | 3.6% | 6.3% | 1.5% | 99.8% | 840 |
| Female | 9.8% | 45.9% | 31.3% | 1.6% | 8.9% | 2.2% | 99.7% | 437 |
| Total | 9.9% | 46.3% | 31.7% | 2.9% | 7.2% | 1.8% | 99.8% | 1,277(a) |

(a) 62 CASES WERE EXCLUDED BECAUSE OF INSUFFICIENT INFORMATION.

cant is the fact that very few cases occur in which the teacher directly calls on a particular student to answer a question (category labelled "Direct" under TQ). The percentage for the Direct Question category is 9.9 percent, compared to 46.3 percent for the Indirect Question in which the teacher poses a question to the class in general. Indeed, it might be argued that the current norm in college classrooms is for both students and teachers to avoid any type of direct *personal confrontation* with one another. It might be that "amicability" in the classroom is part of the larger process, described by Riesman (1950) in *The Lonely Crowd*, in which the desire to "get ahead" is subordinated to the desire to "get along." In the college classroom "getting along" means students and teachers avoiding any situation that might be potentially embarrassing to one or the other.

Table 4 indicates that in male-taught classes male students are more likely than female students to be directly questioned by the instructor (7.1 percent to 3.1 percent). In addition, men are twice as likely as female students (30.3 percent to 15.0 percent) to respond to a comment made by a male teacher. In female-taught classes the percentage of male and female responses are almost identical in each category under observation. Of interest here is the fact that female teachers are equally likely to directly question male and female students (12.8 percent versus 12.5 percent).

Table 5 presents the student responses to a series of items concerning why students would choose not to talk in class. The items are ranked in terms of the percentage of students who indicated that the particular item was important in keeping them from talking. As the rankings indicate, male and female students are virtually identical in their conceptions of what factors inhibit or promote their classroom participation. The items accorded the most importance—not doing the assigned reading, ignorance of the subject matter, etc.—are in the highest ranks. The lowest ranking items are those dealing with students and teachers not respecting the student's point of view, the grade being negatively affected by classroom participation, etc.

**Table 4. Source of Interaction by Sex of Student, Controlling for Sex of Teacher**

| Sex of Student | Teacher Question Direct | Teacher Question Indirect | Teacher Comment | Student Question | Student Comment | Source Not Specified | Total | N |
|---|---|---|---|---|---|---|---|---|
| | | | | SOURCE OF "STIMULUS" | | | | |
| | | | Male-Taught Classes | | | | | |
| Male | 7.1% | 55.3% | 30.3% | 1.9% | 2.6% | 2.6% | 99.8% | 419 |
| Female | 3.1% | 67.4% | 15.0% | 3.9% | 3.9% | 6.3% | 99.6% | 126 |
| Total | 6.2% | 58.1% | 26.7% | 2.3% | 2.9% | 3.4% | 99.6% | 545 |
| | | | Female-Taught Classes | | | | | |
| Male | 12.8% | 37.7% | 33.4% | 5.4% | 9.9% | .4% | 99.6% | 421 |
| Female | 12.5% | 37.2% | 37.9% | .6% | 10.9% | .6% | 99.7% | 311 |
| Total | 12.7% | 37.5% | 35.3% | 3.4% | 10.3% | .5% | 99.7% | 732 |

In comparing the teachers' rankings of these same items with that of the students, it appears that, with one important exception, the rankings are very similar. About 42 percent of both male and female students ranked as important the item concerning the possibility that other students would find them unintelligent. Eighty percent of the teachers, on the other hand, indicated that this was likely an important factor in keeping students from talking.

## DISCUSSION

Although we did not begin this study with any explicit hypotheses to be tested, we did begin with some general guiding questions. Most comprehensive among these, and of necessary importance from a symbolic interactionist perspective, was the question, "What is a college classroom?" We wanted to know how both students and teachers were defining the social setting, and how these definitions manifested themselves in the activity that goes on in the college classrooms. More specifically, we wanted to understand what it was about the definition of the situation held by students and teachers that led to, in most instances, rather little classroom interaction.

What knowledge, we might now ask, do students have of college classrooms that makes the decision not to talk a "realistic" decision? There would seem to be two factors of considerable importance as indicated by our data.

First, students believe that they can tell very early in the semester whether or not a professor really wants class discussion. Students are

**Table 5. Percentage of Students Who Indicated That an Item Was an Important Factor in Why Students Would Choose Not to Talk in Class, by Sex of Student (in Rank Order)**

| | MALE | | | | FEMALE | |
|---|---|---|---|---|---|---|
| Rank | Item | % | | Rank | Item | % |
| 1. | I had not done the assigned reading | 80.9 | | 1. | The feeling that I don't know enough about the subject matter | 84.8 |
| 2. | The feeling that I don't know enough about the subject matter | 79.6 | | 2. | I had not done the assigned reading | 76.3 |
| 3. | The large size of the class | 70.4 | | 3. | The feeling that my ideas are not well enough formulated | 71.1 |
| 4. | The feeling that my ideas are not well enough formulated | 69.8 | | 4. | The large size of the class | 68.9 |
| 5. | The course simply isn't meaningful to me | 67.3 | | 5. | The course simply isn't meaningful to me | 65.1 |
| 6. | The chance that I would appear unintelligent in the eyes of the teacher | 43.2 | | 6. | The chance that I would appear unintelligent in the eyes of other students | 45.4 |
| 7. | The chance that I would appear unintelligent in the eyes of other students | 42.9 | | 7. | The chance that I would appear unintelligent in the eyes of the teacher | 41.4 |
| 8. | The small size of the class | 31.0 | | 8. | The small size of the class | 33.6 |
| 9. | The possibility that my comments might negatively affect my grade | 29.6 | | 9. | The possibility that my comments might negatively affect my grade | 24.3 |
| 10. | The possibility that other students in the class would not respect my point of view | 16.7 | | 10. | The possibility that the teacher would not respect my point of view | 21.1 |
| 11. | The possibility that the teacher would not respect my point of view | 12.3 | | 11. | The possibility that other students in the class would not respect my point of view | 12.5 |

also well aware that there exists in college classrooms a rather distinctive "consolidation of responsibility." In any classroom there seems almost inevitably to be a small group of students who can be counted on to respond to questions asked by the professor or to generally have comments on virtually any issue raised in class. Our observational data (Table 1) indicated that on the average a very small number of students are responsible for the majority of all talk that occurs in class on any given day. The fact that this "consolidation of responsibility" looms large in students' consciousness is indicated by the fact, reported earlier, that more than 90 percent of the students strongly agreed or agreed with the statement "In most of my classes there are a small number of students who do most of the talking."

Once the group of "talkers" gets established and identified in a college classroom the remaining students develop a strong expectation that these "talkers" can be relied upon to answer questions and make comments. In fact, we have often noticed in our own classes that when a question is asked or an issue raised the "silent" students will even begin to orient their bodies towards and look at this coterie of talkers with the expectation, presumably, that they will shortly be speaking.

Our concept of the "consolidation of responsibility" is a modification of the idea put forth by Latane and Darley (1970) in *The Unresponsive Bystander*. In this volume Latane and Darley developed the concept of "the diffusion of responsibility" to explain why strangers are often reluctant to "get involved" in activities where they assist other strangers who may need help. They argue that the delegation of responsibility in such situations is quite unclear and, as a result, responsibility tends to get assigned to no one in particular—the end result being that no assistance at all is forthcoming. In the case of the classroom interaction, however, we are dealing with a situation in which the responsibility for talking gets assigned to a few who can be relied upon to carry the "verbal load"— thus the *consolidation of responsibility*. As a result, the majority of students play a relatively passive role in the classroom and see themselves as recorders of the teacher's information. This expectation is mutually supported by the professor's reluctance to directly call on *specific* students, as indicated in Table 3.

While students expect that only a few students will do most of the talking, and while these talkers are relied upon to respond in class, the situation is a bit more complicated than we have indicated to this point. It would appear that while these talkers are "doing their job" by carrying the discussion for the class as a whole, there is still a strong feeling on the part of many students that they ought not to talk *too much*. As noted earlier, more than 60 percent of the students responding to our questionnaire expressed annoyance with students who "talk too much in class." This is interesting to the extent that even those who talk very regularly in class still account for a very small percentage of total class time. While we have no systematic data on time spent talking in class, the comments of the observers indicate that generally a total of less than five minutes of class time (in a fifty-minute period) is accounted for by student talk in class.

A fine balance must be maintained in college classes. Some students are expected to do most of the talking, thus relieving the remainder of the students from the burdens of having to talk in class. At the same time, these talkers must not be "rate-busters." We are suggesting here that students see "intellectual work" in much the same way that factory workers define "piecework." Talking too much in class, or what might be called "linguistic rate-busting," upsets the normative arrangement of the classroom and, in the students' eyes, increases the probability of raising the professor's expectations vis-a-vis the participation of other students. It may be said, then, that a type of "restriction of verbal output" norm operates in college classrooms, in which those who engage in linguistic rate-busting or exhibit "overinvolvement" in the classroom get defined by other students as "brown-noses" and "apostates" from the student "team." Other students often indicate their annoyance with these "rate-busters" by smiling wryly at their efforts, audibly sighing, rattling their notebooks and, on occasion, openly snickering.

A second factor that insures in students' minds that it will be safe to refrain from talking is their knowledge that only in rare instances will they be directly called upon by teachers in a college classroom. Our data (Table 3) indicate that of all the interaction occurring in the classes under observation only about 10 percent were due to teachers calling directly upon a specific student. The unwillingness of teachers to call upon students would seem to stem from teachers' beliefs that the classroom situation is fraught with anxiety for students. It is important to note that teachers, unlike students themselves, viewed the possibility that "students might appear unintelligent in the eyes of other students" as a very important factor in keeping students from talking (Table 6). Unwilling to exacerbate the sense of risk which teachers believe is a part of student consciousness, they refrain from directly calling upon specific students.

The direct result of these two factors is that students feel no obligation or particular necessity for keeping up with reading assignments so as to

**Table 6. Percentage of Teachers Who Indicated That an Item Was an Important Factor in Why Students Would Choose Not to Talk in Class (in Rank Order)**

| RANK | ITEM | % |
|---|---|---|
| 1.5 | The large size of the class | 80 |
| 1.5 | The chance that I would appear unintelligent in the eyes of other students | 80 |
| 4.0 | The feeling that I don't know enough about the subject matter | 70 |
| 4.0 | The feeling that my ideas are not well enough formulated | 70 |
| 4.0 | The possibility that my comments might negatively affect my grade | 70 |
| 6.0 | The course simply isn't meaningful to me | 50 |
| 7.5 | I had not done the assigned reading | 40 |
| 7.5 | The chance that I would appear unintelligent in the eyes of the teacher | 40 |
| 9.5 | The possibility that the teacher would not respect my point of view | 30 |
| 9.5 | The possibility that other students in the class would not respect my point of view | 30 |
| 11.0 | The small size of the class | 10 |

be able to participate in class. Such a choice is made easier still by the fact that college students are generally tested infrequently. Unlike high school, where homework is the teacher's "daily insurance" that students are prepared for classroom participation, college is a situation in which the student feels quite safe in coming to class without having done the assigned reading and, not having done it, safe in the secure knowledge that one won't be called upon.[3] It is understandable, then, why such items as "not having done the assigned reading" and "the feeling that one does not know enough about the subject matter" would rank so high (Table 5) in students' minds as factors keeping them from talking in class.

In sum, we have isolated two factors relative to the way that classrooms actually operate that make it "practically" possible for students not to talk in class. These factors make it possible for the student to pragmatically abide by an early decision to be silent in class. We must now broach the somewhat more complicated question: what are the elements of students' definitions of the college classroom situation that prompt them to be silent in class? To answer this question we must examine how students perceive the teacher as well as their conceptions of what constitutes "intellectual work."

By the time that students have finished high school they have been imbued with the enormously strong belief that teachers are "experts" who possess the "truth." They have adopted, as Freire (1970) has noted, a "banking" model of education. The teacher represents the bank, the huge "fund" of "true" knowledge. As a student it is one's job to make weekly "withdrawals" from the fund, never any "deposits." His teachers, one is led to believe, and often led to believe it by the teachers themselves, are possessors of the truth. Teachers are in the classroom to *teach*, not to *learn*.

If the above contains anything like a reasonable description of the way that students are socialized in secondary school, we should not find it strange or shocking that our students find our requests for criticism of ideas a bit alien. College students still cling to the idea that they are knowledge seekers and that faculty members are knowledge dispensers. Their view of intellectual work leaves little room for the notion that ideas themselves are open to negotiation. It is simply not part of their view of the classroom that ideas are generated out of dialogue, out of persons questioning and taking issue with one another, out of persons being *critical* of each other.

It comes as something of a shock to many of our students when we are willing to give them, at best, a "B" on a paper or exam that is "technically" proficient. When they inquire about their grade (and they do this rarely, believing strongly that our judgment is unquestionable), they want to know what they did "wrong." Intellectual work is for them dichotomous. It is either good or bad, correct or incorrect. They are genuinely surprised when we tell them that nothing is wrong, that they simply have not been critical enough and have not shown enough reflection on the ideas. Some even see such an evaluation as unfair. They claim a kind of incompetence at criticism. They often claim that it would be illegitimate for them to disagree with an author.

Students in class respond as uncritically to the thoughts of their professors as they do to the thoughts of those whom they read. Given this general attitude toward intellectual work, based in large part on students' socialization, and hence their definition of what should go on in classrooms, the notion of using the classroom as a place for generating ideas is a foreign one.

Part of students' conceptions of what they can and ought to do in classrooms is, then, a function of their understanding of how ideas are to be communicated. Students have expressed the idea that if they are to speak in class they ought to be able to articulate their point logically, systematically, and above all completely. The importance of this factor in keeping students from talking is borne out by the very high ranking given to the item (Table 5) "the feeling that my ideas are not well enough formulated."

In their view, if their ideas have not been fully formulated in advance, then the idea is not worth relating. They are simply unwilling to talk "off the top of their heads." They feel, particularly in an academic setting such as the college classroom, that there is a high premium placed on being articulate. This feeling is to a large degree prompted by the relative articulateness of the teacher. Students do not, it seems, take into account the fact that the teacher's coherent presentation is typically a function of the time spent preparing his/her ideas. The relative preparedness of the teacher leads to something of paradox vis-à-vis classroom discussion.

We have had students tell us that one of the reasons they find it difficult to respond in class involves the professor's preparedness; that is, students have told us that because the professor's ideas as presented in lectures are (in their view) so well formulated they could not add anything to those ideas. Herein lies something of a paradox. One might suggest that, to some degree at least, the better prepared a professor is for his/her class, the less likely are students to respond to the elements of his lecture.

We have both found that some of our liveliest classes have centered around those occasions when we have talked about research presently in progress. When it is clear to the student that we are ourselves struggling with a particular problem, that we cannot fully make sense of a phenomenon, the greater is the class participation. In most classroom instances, students read the teacher as the "expert,"[4] and once having cast the professor into that role it becomes extremely difficult for students to take issue with or amend his/her ideas.

It must also be noted that students' perceptions about their incapacity to be critical of their own and others' ideas leads to an important source of misunderstanding between college students and their teachers. In an open-ended question we asked students what characteristics they thought made for an "ideal" teacher. An impressionistic reading of these responses indicated that students were overwhelmingly uniform in their answers. They consensually found it important that a teacher "not put them down" and that a teacher "not flaunt his/her superior knowledge." In this regard the college classroom is a setting pregnant with possibilities for mutual misunderstanding. Teachers are working under one set of assumptions about "intellectual work" while students proceed under another. Our experiences as college teachers lead us to believe that teachers tend to value *critical* responses by students and tend to respond critically themselves to the comments and questions of college students. Students tend to perceive these critical comments as in some way an assault on their "selves" and find it difficult to separate a critique of their thoughts from a critique of themselves. Teachers are for the most part unaware of the way in which students interpret their comments.

The result is that when college teachers begin to critically question a student's statement, trying to get the student to be more critical and analytical about his/her assertions, this gets interpreted by students as a "put-down." The overall result is the beginning of a "vicious circle" of sorts. The more that teachers try to instill in students a critical attitude toward one's own ideas, the more students come to see faculty members as condescending, and the greater still becomes their reluctance to make known their "ill formulated" ideas in class. Like any other social situation where persons are defining the situation differently, there is bound to develop a host of interactional misunderstandings.

Before concluding this section, let us turn to a discussion of the differences in classroom participation rates of male versus female students. Given the fact that men and women students responded quite similarly to the *questionnaire items* reported here, much of our previous discussion holds for both male and female students. There are some important differences, however, in their *actual behavior* in the college classroom (as revealed by our observational data) that ought to be considered. Foremost among these differences is the fact that the sex of the teacher affects the likelihood of whether male or female teachers in these classes are "giving off expressions" that are being interpreted very differently by male and female students. Male students play a more active role in all observed classes regardless of the teacher's sex, but with female instructors the percentage of female participation sharply increases. Also of interest, as indicated in Table 4, is the fact that the male instructors are more likely to directly call on male students than on female students (7.1 percent to 3.1 percent), whereas female instructors are just as likely to call on female students as on male students (12.5 percent to 12.8 percent). Possibly female students in female-taught classes interpret the instructor's responses as being more egalitarian than those of male professors and thus more sympathetic to the views of female students. With the growing [awareness] of women faculty and students [of women's issues] it may not be unreasonable to assume that female instructors are more sensitive to the problem of female students both inside and outside the college classroom.

With the small percentage of women faculty currently teaching in American universities it may well be that the college classroom is still defined by both male and female students as a setting "naturally" dominated by men. The presence of female professors, however, as our limited data suggest, may bring about some changes in these definitions of "natural" classroom behavior.

## IMPLICATIONS

For the reasons suggested in the last few pages, it may be argued that most students opt for noninvolvement in their college classroom. This being the case, and because organizational features of the college classroom allow for noninvolvement (the consolidation of responsibility, the unwillingness of professors to directly call on specific students, the infrequency of testing), the situation allows for a low commitment on the part of students. The college classroom, then, rather than being a situation where persons must be deeply involved, more closely approximates a situation of "anonymity" where persons' obligations are few.

We can now perceive more clearly the source of the dilemma for college instructors who wish to have extensive classroom dialogues with students. To use the terminology generated by Goffman (1963) in *Behavior in Public Places*, we can suggest that instructors are treating the classroom as an instance of "focused" interaction while students define the classroom more as an "unfocused" gathering. Focused gatherings are those where persons come into one another's audial and visual presence and see it as their obligation to interact. These are to be distinguished from unfocused gatherings where persons are also in a face-to-face situation but either feel that they are not privileged to interact or have no obligation to do so.[5]

It may very well be that students more correctly "read" how professors interpret the situation than vice versa.[6] Knowing that the teacher expects involvement, and having made the decision not to be deeply involved, students reach a compromise. Aware that it would be an impropriety to be on a total "away" from the social situation, students engage in what might be called "civil *attention*." They must *appear* committed enough to not alienate the teacher without at the same time showing so much involvement that the situation becomes risky for them. Students must carefully create a show of interest while maintaining noninvolvement. A show of too great interest might find them more deeply committed to the encounter than they wish to be.

So, students are willing to attend class regularly, and they do not hold private conversations while the teacher is talking; they nod their heads intermittently, and maintain enough attention to laugh at the appropriate junctures during a lecture, and so on. Students have become very adept at maintaining the social situation without becoming too involved in it. Teachers interpret these "shows" of attention as indicative of a real involvement (the students' performances have proved highly successful) and are, therefore, at a loss to explain why their involvement is not even greater—why they don't talk very much in class.

## NOTES

1. Some relevant demographic characteristics of the students in the ten classes under observation are as follows: sex: males—52 percent, females—48 percent; year in college: freshmen and sophomores—60 percent, juniors and seniors—40 percent; father's occupation: proprietor—7 percent, management or executive—21 percent, professional—34 percent, clerical and sales—15 percent, skilled worker—16 percent, unskilled worker—7 percent; religious affiliation: Catholic—79 percent, Protestant—7 percent, Other—14 percent. In comparing the students in the observed classes to those students in unobserved classes which were selected at random at the end of the semester, the following differences should be noted: the observed classes contain more women (48 percent) than the unobserved classes (33 percent); there were twice as many freshmen in the observed classes (31 percent) than in the unobserved classes (14 percent); there were twice as many students whose fathers were in clerical and sales occupations in the observed classes (15 percent) than in the unobserved classes (8 percent).

The questionnaire responses of the students in the unobserved classes are not reported here since these were selected only to check on the representativeness of the students in the original ten classes under observation.

2. Spatial limitations preclude a full treatment of the methodology and findings. More complete details are available from the authors.

3. We have no "hard" data concerning student failure to do the assigned reading other than our own observations of countless instances where we posed questions that went unanswered, when the slightest familiarity with the material would have been sufficient to answer them. We have also employed "pop" quizzes and the student performance on these tests indicated a woefully inadequate acquaintance with the readings assigned for that session. The reader may evaluate our claim by reflecting upon his/her own experience in the college classroom.

4. This attribution of power and authority to the teacher may be particularly exaggerated in the present study due to its setting in a Catholic university with a large number of students entering from Catholic high schools. Whether college students with different religious and socioeconomic characteristics attribute similar degrees of power and authority to professors is a subject worthy of future comparative empirical investigation.

5. If we think of communication patterns in college classrooms as ranging along a continuum from open-discussion formats to lecture arrangements, the

classes studied here all fall toward the traditional lecture end of the continuum. Thus, generalizations to other formats, such as the open discussion ones, may not be warranted by the present data.

6. Of interest here is the recent study by Thomas *et al.* (1972) in which support was found for the "theoretical proposition that role-taking ability varies inversely with the degree of power ascribed to social positions" (1972:612).

## REFERENCES

Deutscher, I.
   1973 *What We Say/What We Do.* Glenview, Ill.: Scott, Foresman and Company.

Freire, P.
   1970 *Pedagogy of the Oppressed.* New York: Seabury Press.

Goffman, E.
   1963 *Behavior in Public Places.* New York: Free Press.

Jackson, P.
   1968 *Life in Classrooms.* New York: Holt, Rinehart and Winston.

Latane, B. and J. Darley
   1970 *The Unresponsive Bystander: Why Doesn't He Help?* New York: Appleton-Century-Crofts.

National Institute of Mental Health
   1969 *Sociologists and Anthropologists: Supply and Demand in Educational Institutions and Other Settings.* Chevy Chase, Md: U.S. Government Printing Office.

Phillips, D.
   1971 *Knowledge From What?* Chicago: Rand McNally and Co.

Riesman, D.
   1950 *The Lonely Crowd.* New Haven: Yale University Press.

Schutz, A.
   1962 *Collected Papers: I. The Problem of Social Reality.* Edited by Maurice Natanson, The Hague: Martinus Nijhoff.

Thomas, D.L., D. D. Franks, and J.M. Calonico
   1972 "Role-Taking and Power in Social Psychology," *American Sociological Review* 37: 605–614.

# Review Questions

1. What is Karp and Yoels's "banking" model of education? What factors cause students to adopt this model? What are some sociological consequences of the model?

2. Summarize Karp and Yoels's findings regarding the number of students who participate in class and the frequency of participation. What factors affected the rate of participation and what factors didn't?

3. What differences exist in the expectations of students and teachers for their own role and for the reciprocal role?

4. What were students' attitudes toward those who participated in class? Why is it ironic that these attitudes were held? Incorporate the concept of "consolidation of responsibility" in your answer.

5. How did teachers and students differ in terms of why they thought students didn't participate in class?

# GROWING OLD BETWEEN WALLS

## Andrea Fontana

I HAD TAKEN A SUMMER JOB AT THE [SUNNY HILL] CONVALESCENT CENTER AS a janitor (actually, housekeeper was the definition given to my job) with the intention of studying the setting, and coming back later as a researcher, which I did the following summer. This [article] is based on the data gathered in these periods.

Having worked at the center proved very helpful to my research in three ways. First, I was part of the staff, thus being able to partake in "backstage" interaction.[1] By this I mean that I took part in "gripe sessions"; I listened to the aides' accounts, not in an official form or through formal work relations, but relaxedly over a cup of coffee, from one "low-rank" employee to another. In this fashion I learned how Joe did not have a bowel movement in two days, why Bill was so confused after the new medication, or why that "old bitch" down the hall wouldn't eat unless you pinched her nose closed; things one would not find in records or would not be told to an "outsider." This gave me an understanding of how the aides felt and allowed me to sit right in with them during breaks or to walk around with them while they worked in the center.

Second, I was able to spend time with the patients while cleaning their rooms, and I came to know some of them well. While this does not matter with some patients, who would talk to anybody willing to listen, it is important with others, who become suspicious and taciturn.

Third, I viewed the patients as a staff member, thus coming to see the patients in terms of my job. That summer I had a lot of patients classified:

> This one spits on the floor all the time; I'll have to give him a butt can. That one throws his food all over the floor; it'll be hard to mop. Old Anne always had a puddle of urine under her wheelchair. Sarah will walk away with the mop and the bucket if I don't watch her; Dan will talk my leg off so I'll skip his room today.[2]

I came to see the patients as "work objects" rather than as human beings. But I also slowly became aware of other important concerns which made me realize the meaning of growing old between the walls of the

Excerpted from Andrea Fontana, *The Last Frontier* (Beverly Hills, Calif.: Sage Library of Social Research, vol 4, 1977), pp. 143–145, 147–167.

convalescent center for the patients. This [article] is not an ethnography of the operations of a convalescent center[3]; it is not a collection of survey data on convalescent centers[4]; it is not a critical indictment of convalescent centers[5]; this [article] intends to explore what happens to the meaning of the "golden years," to the "consummatory period of life" for that handful of elderly[6]; who come to "convalesce" in the waning years of their lives.

• • •

## THE STAGE

The proscenium upon which this drama of life is played serves an important function as the setting for the interaction between the staff and the patients. Thus, before being introduced to the actors, as the curtain pulls back, the reader will be presented with a vision of the center itself. The brochure advertising the center reads:

> At the Sunny Hill Convalescent Center the guest wants for nothing . . . screened sunbathing and patio areas, television, telephone facilities, planned recreational activities and beautiful six-acre site are at the disposal of the guests . . . especially noted for the delicious food prepared in the spotless, modern kitchen.

However, as one looks closely around the center, the picture which emerges is quite different. The convalescent center is located in the middle of the small town of Verde, which is about twenty miles away from the nearest city. Although centrally located, the center is isolated from the town because it is situated atop a steep hill, which is accessible only by a road leading to the center; no other building is located on the hill.

The center comprises two wards, situated one below the other on the slope of the hill. The lower ward is a long one-story construction, while the upper one is a two-story building; both appear fairly new from the outside. The "six-acre" site is indeed there, but the "sunbathing and patio areas" are small and enclosed by a high chain-linked fence.

The inside is almost identical in both wards. It consists of a long corridor running the length of the slightly V-shaped buildings. Rooms with two beds in each are located at both sides of the corridor, with adjoining toilets between two rooms; the same toilet is at times shared by two men in one room and by two women in the next. Both wards have a large recreational lounge, with a view overlooking the town through a large, dark blue-tinted picture window. The recreation lounge is furnished with sofas, armchairs, chairs, and a television set.

Both wards have a kitchen right across from the recreation room. The upstairs kitchen is used only for warming up food, since all the cooking is done in the downstairs kitchen. Small dining rooms are adjacent to the kitchens. The kitchens contain some old, greasy-looking gas stoves, a large sink, a hot-water sterilizing unit (for dishes), refrigerators, and other assorted equipment. Both wards have a nursing station, which is a smallish place located behind a long counter. At the end of each corridor is a large bathroom containing a tub and a shower in which the aides wash the patients (four bathrooms in all). The lower ward has a small waiting hall for incoming visitors. This room can be separated from the rest of the ward by a heavily blue-tinted glass sliding door.

The only telephones available are in the offices and nursing station and are to be used only by the staff on official business. I only witnessed a couple of "emergency" personal calls by employees and none whatsoever by patients. All doors are locked at all times, and the staff are forever unlocking and locking doors and closets in their daily rounds. A couple of times the outside door was accidentally left unlocked, and a patient managed to "escape" but was soon found wandering in downtown Verde. One time I saw Wilma, a sixty-year-old ex-ballerina (she had a tracheotomy operation so she cannot speak and has a small hole at the base of her neck), gingerly vault over the high chain fence, and I had to unlock the gate and guide her back inside. One final point: One of my duties was to wash breakfast dishes in the "spotless kitchen," and the only spotless thing about the kitchen were my hands after I had summarily rinsed off a pile of muck-covered plates.

## THE ACTORS

Having described the setting, it is time to introduce the cast. The staff consists of an administrator, who manages the facility, a bookkeeper, two janitors, a laundry person, the kitchen staff (a cook, two second-cooks, and part-time helpers), and the nursing staff.

The director of nurses is a registered nurse who is in charge of another nurse and the aides. The other nurse is a licensed vocational nurse managing the lower ward when the registered nurse is in the upper one, which is most of the time. The remainder of the staff is composed of nurse's aides.

The aides are either white women from nearby towns or Indian women from the reservation three miles away. The turnover is great due to the harshness of the job, the extremely low pay, and the nature of the place. I witnessed quite a few cases of aides who left aghast after their first day and never came back. Actually, that almost happened to me, as I was not yet trained in the arts of doing field research while cleaning toilets. There are two kinds of aides: the old "battle axes" who have seen it all, have been there forever, and are not shaken by anything that happens; the others are much younger women, usually fresh out of high school, often on their first job, who live in the town of Verde, where no other jobs are available, or are just filling a gap while waiting for a better job to materialize.

The other people on the payroll as staff members do not work in the center but make periodic visits. There are three doctors, each caring for a certain number of patients, who come by to visit the patients every other week. . . . There are others: a hairdresser, who comes over from the reservation once a week; a social worker, who comes every other week; a handyman, who is on call; and a dietician, who is consulted by telephone.

The rest of the cast is made up of the patients. The patients are not identified in any visible way and are not divided in the wards in any fashion. The only rule is to have two individuals of the same sex in a room, but if one is senile and incontinent and the other is not, it is of no concern to the staff; contingencies such as availability of rooms are much more pressing. Usually the center is filled to capacity; even the room supposed to be used as an emergency room has a patient in it, an old blind wrestler, who must at one time have been a giant, but now has stumps where legs used to be and has lost most of his cognitive ability on various rings across the country years ago.

Not being able to identify the patients at sight[7] was a problem for me, but it was not a problem for the staff, who classified the patients in terms of physical attributes related to their daily work routine. There are the "up and about," those patients who can walk and get in and out of bed by themselves, walk to the dining room for meals, go to the toilet, etc. The others are called "in chair," meaning that they are confined to a wheelchair and that they must be helped in and out of bed; they need containers to urinate in while sitting in their chair, etc. Another classification is that of "feeders" and "nonfeeders." "Nonfeeders" are those patients (whether "in chair" or "up and about") who are capable of eating in the dining room by themselves, whereas "feeders" need to be hand-fed by an aide. With this system of classification, the nurses and aides can categorize patients in terms of "work time." An "up-and-about nonfeeder" will require little of their time, while an "in-chair feeder" will take a lot more time: he will have to be fed, have his diapers changed, and his bed sores medicated. Most "in-chair" patients spend a lot of time in bed, hence developing bed sores. At one time I wondered out loud why they bothered getting them out of bed at all, and the licensed vocational nurse said that it was required by [the state] that all patients be up and out of bed for at least two hours daily. The classification system is an effective tool in planning one's daily work schedule. This is no different from my classification of patients while I was a janitor (spitter, wet-the-floor type, mess-up-the-toilet type, and so on).

•   •   •

The behavior of the patients was markedly different outside of the categories of "work time" invoked by the staff. By this it is meant that categorizing patients in classes based upon the care they require does not account for those periods which place no (or minimal) demands upon the staff. These periods comprise a large part of the day of the patients, and are spend in different ways by them.

Many elderly patients no longer have to worry about the problem of how to occupy their time in meaningful ways because their selves have escaped long ago, leaving behind babbling biological husks which are carted about by unkind hands and spend their time strapped to beds or wheelchairs. But there are others. And it is to these and to their attempts to keep their selves from escaping their weakened frames that attention shall now be paid.

## THE INTERACTION

• • •

There are three kinds of interaction which are relevant to the understanding that shapes the everyday lives of the patients: staff-to-patient interaction, patient-to-staff interaction, and patient-to-patient interaction. It must be mentioned that Sunny Hill has a mental health license, hence mental patients can be found mixing freely with those whose only fault is to be old.[8]

## STAFF TO PATIENT

Staff-to-patient interaction is characterized by what Strauss and Glaser call "work-time."[9] The same problem noticed by the two sociologists in their study of a hospital ward is found at the Sunny Hill center: The patients and the staff's conceptions of time are very often at variance. There are not enough nurse's aides, and they consequently have a very busy work schedule and minimal time to give the patients any attention as human beings; the patients are work objects, as is exemplified by their categorization in terms of work (feeders, etc.).

Given that the staff-to-patient interaction takes place in terms of work, a typical daily work routine will be described. The aides begin getting the patients out of bed and into their wheelchairs at about 6:30 a.m. At 7:00 the day-shift aides come in and finish preparing the patients for breakfast. The aides distribute trays to the patients who sit in their rooms in their wheelchairs, while the ambulatory cases walk to the dining room. Next, the aides feed the "feeders":

> I was going around with Mary and Glenda feeding the patients. Mary was literally stuffing food in a woman's mouth, and the semi-liquid yellowish substance was dribbling down the woman's chin onto her nightgown, which had been washed so many times that it was now an amorphous gray sack.

Louise was feeding lunch to an old patient, and she explained to me that he always refused his water and that was bad for his kidneys. After having finished feeding him, she held a glass of water to his mouth, which he shut tightly. So Louise turned to me and said, ''See, I told you so'' and left, making no further effort to give the man a drink.[10]

During breakfast the licensed vocational nurse goes around with a medicine cart slipping pills in bowls of cornflakes or oatmeal, while the janitor mops up the floor between the chairs, cleaning spilled oatmeal, wheelchair scuffs, and small puddles of urine underneath some of the chairs because the patients' requests to go to the toilet are being ignored by the aides. The aides are still feeding ''feeders'' down the wing somewhere (some patients do not ask for help to go to the toilet anymore, they just urinate in their wheelchairs).

After the chaos of breakfast, with things and people running around, everything calms down. The patients are dressed (or they dress themselves, or are put. back in bed) and either sit in their rooms or are wheeled into the lounge room where the television is broadcasting its usual variety of morning quiz shows. The patients look at the television, but most of them are just staring at a box with light and colors. . . .

The 9:00 aide is here now[11] and she begins to make beds on her assigned wing. Some days I go around with her:

> Today the 9:00 aide is Louise and I join her. She is making beds in and around patients. As I talk to her, she is going right on making beds and talking to me. Some of the patients are up and in the wheelchairs, but others are in bed. Louise picks them up and sits them in a chair, then proceeds to make the beds. After having changed the linen and the plastic sheet, Louise puts the patients back to bed, either saying nothing to them or things like—here you go—that's good—while carrying on a conversation with me or with another aide if there is one nearby.

After the morning activities, the mealtime bedlam of rushing food trays, cleaning up floors, and pushing around patients begins all over. After lunch it is quiet again as some patients are wheeled into the lounge room to watch some soap operas while others are put to bed to take a nap.

At 3:00 P.M. the evening shift comes in while the day shift retires to the dining room to fill in their daily reports on the patients. These reports summarize the activities of the patients in terms of physical and mental functions. Emphasis is given by the aides to things such as b.m.'s (bowel movements) and unusual behavior; since each aide fills only some charts, there is a continuous negotiation on whether Billy had a bowel movement today or whether Elma had a quiet day or was restless. The reports are jotted down in about twenty minutes and the charts returned to the nursing station.

These reports are very important for the patients since the nurse in charge compiles her monthly reports by summarizing the aides' reports.

The social worker also uses the aides' reports to give her account of the patients, and the various reports are used by the doctors to determine the status of the patients. A doctor comes in, sits behind the nurses' station, and inquires about his breakfast, which is promptly served. Having thumbed through the charts for a while, he walks quickly up and down the corridors, asking from time to time, "How are you today, Mr. Smith, and you, Mrs. Jones?" Without waiting for an answer, he keeps on walking. At times he visits one or two patients who may be experiencing serious problems, and then he is gone, not to be seen for another two weeks.

The following is an example of how the information in the reports is acquired in many cases. Mr. Anderson's medical records stated that he had been committed to the convalescent center as a manic-depressive case. The records made mention of the fact that he had been a former patient and had left to go to a boarding house. However, Dr. Bell (his doctor throughout this whole period) brought him back to the center, since Mr. Anderson was in a severe state of depression (listed as spitting and cursing at doctors and nurses).

I thumbed through the reports of the aides and found that Mr. Anderson was often reported as "depressed" (aides have five choices in their chart: satisfactory, confused, depressed, irritable, noisy). On the back of the report, under "nurses' progress notes," it was often generally stated that Mr. Anderson had shown signs of depression, and occasionally he was reported as having said things such as, "If I had a gun I would shoot myself."

I happened to be present during one of Mr. Anderson's "depressive" conditions.

> Mr. Anderson said that he could not understand why they locked the windows, that all it would take to get out would be a kitchen knife used as a screwdriver. The aide wrote down in her report that he was very agitated and talked about escaping from the center.

My impression of the "incident" was entirely different. I had heard Mr. Anderson make the comment about the windows to an aide.[12] The incident assumed new meaning in the aide's account of it. Dramatic overtones kept piling on until what had seemed to me a frustrated remark about the futility of certain security measures became a dramatic plan to escape from the center. The incident shows that the interpretation of Mr. Anderson's behavior as deviant was taken by an aide who had a preconceived notion of his depression and was in a hurry to finish her report. Her account became of extreme importance since the other members of the staff rely solely upon such reports to pass judgment on the patients.

After this example of "form filling," it is time to return to the daily scheduled events. The daily work routine is now in the hands of the evening shift. The circle starts all over again—getting patients up from their naps, making beds, getting patients ready for dinner. It is 5:00 p.m., the last meal of the day, the last moment of a kaleidoscope of colors, odors, noises. Food is served, forced into mouths, spat out, cleaned up, dropped on the floor, aides yell at patients, and patients scream in the hall, in their rooms, in their chairs, and then, silence again. Some patients, a few, walk back to the lounge room, the others are put to bed, the day at the center is over.

The rush imposed by a heavy work load leads the aides to treat the patients in the same fashion. It becomes legitimate to stuff food down their throats because the goal has become serving the meal, not nourishing the patient; or to lift them in and out of bed as if they were inanimate dummies because the goal is bed making not making the patient comfortable. The patients thus end up suffering from "organization contingencies" similar to those found by many sociologists in other settings.[13] But what is suffering here from problems stemming from work-flow contingencies is not a car malfunctioning from shoddy workmanship, but human beings who by being treated as inanimate objects end up becoming inanimate objects.

## PATIENT TO STAFF

Patients find themselves competing for the staff's attention. The patients are not rushed by a busy work schedule, on the contrary they have nothing but time on their hands. Apart from the scheduled rounds of activities such as meals, baths, haircuts, etc., there are scarcely any other goings-on available to the patients. The patients who still have the physical and mental capabilities to do so return to their rooms after the scheduled activities are over; others never leave their rooms; the rest, who fall somewhere in between, are carted to the recreation room to watch television.

Confined to a restricted setting beyond their control, the patients attempt to break the monotony of the empty periods of waiting for the next scheduled activity. The patients employ various strategies to attract the attention of the aides. . . . "Bob waves his hand at the aide who is passing by and mumbles—toilet—she looks at him and says—oh you don't have to go—and goes on." When they attract someone's attention, usually a new aide or me, they smile and ask for a glass of water (or milk) or for a dime to buy a Coke. Five minutes later, up goes the same hand, and the same person asks for another glass of water. Doing beds or cleaning rooms is also a good time to attempt to engage the aide in conversation because she cannot just turn around and leave. These attempts to create diversions in the period between meals, or between a meal and a bath, are treated by the staff unanimously in the same fashion—they are ignored unless they become a problem which will disrupt the daily schedule: things such as a patient defacating in the hallway or pulling another patient's hair can no longer be ignored as they would soon attract the attention of the licensed vocational nurse or the administrator.

## PATIENT TO PATIENT

• • •

The interaction among patients is mainly characterized by its absence. Patients do not have anything to do with each other. To fraternize with other patients would mean to place oneself at their level, to admit that one indeed belongs here.

Thus the others are ignored. Once I asked Al, who was a great sports fan, why he did not watch the ball games on television. He replied that he would not go into the recreation room during the day because he did not like to see and smell the result of other incontinent patients, and the aides would not let him watch the night games.

• • •

At Christmas I had sent Mr. Adams a set of checkers, and when I returned to the center the next summer, he invited me to play with him. The checker set had not been opened yet, and Mr. Adams said that there was nobody to play with at the center. Later I discovered that this was not true since I played with other patients. When I mentioned this to Mr. Adams, he claimed that they were not good enough players to play with him. But neither was I, because after an initial doubt as to whether I should let "poor old Mr. Adams" beat me at checkers, I realized that I had as much of a chance of beating him at checkers as I would have had of spotting Bobby Fischer a rook and then beating him at chess.

When interaction between patients does take place, it is not of a desirable kind. The following examples illustrate this point. The administrator decided to put Mr. Adams and Mr. Ritter, two of the "better" patients, in the same room. This arrangement did not last long. Both fellows liked their privacy and the freedom of doing what they liked in their rooms. . . . They tolerated each other for a while but began complaining about each other's quirks privately (often to me). . . . This eventually led to open confrontation, which occurred when they were both listening to their favorite program on their transistor radios and tried to outdo each other by a battle of volumes. The nurse rushed in to see what was going on, and as a result Mr. Adams went back upstairs to a new room.

• • •

At times, the interaction between patients became violent as when somebody grabbled hold of a hank of hair and pulled as hard as he or she could. A couple of times punches were thrown by some patients, but these flare-ups were rare. What caused most of the problems was the mixing of mental cases with normal patients. . . .

• • •

The patients respond in different ways to their confinement in the center. Those who manage to survive the heavy odds against them and retain a lucid mind are few indeed. They may or may not have reconciled themselves with spending the remainder of their days at the center, but they all agree that their stay is against their will, that they are for all practical purposes being kept prisoners in the center.

Mr. Anderson is a tall, thin man in his early eighties; his vivid, alert eyes peer at you from his hollow cheeks, and his long, bony hands are tightly held in his lap. He walks slowly, slightly hunched, but he walks.

Mr. Anderson used to live in a boarding house. One day the people who managed the house told him that he had to go to the doctor for a check-up. He was taken to the center and has been there ever since. He feels that this is illegal, and that the doctor signed his release to the center because he is a good patient, ambulatory and quiet, and they wanted his money. He has written to his daughter about it but has received no reply.

Mr. Anderson told me his story in a calm, resigned manner. He feels as if he were in a prison. He spends his days voraciously reading old novels and magazines. Mr. Anderson said that when he reads he loses track of time, and before he knows it, it is time for lunch or dinner. At times, however, he feels very depressed about being in the convalescent center; then he closes the door and stares out of the window since he doesn't feel like reading.

Mr. Ritter, a tall, heavy-set fellow in his late fifties, is another case. He used to be a minor-league pitcher, and he went on to become a professional heavy-weight fighter. . . . He was placed in custody in 1971 as decreed by court order after psychiatric examination. . . . He had trouble subtracting numbers from 100 in descending order, seven at a time (he became confused at 93). He also forgot to mention Kennedy when listing our presidents backward. . . . He has to be reexamined every year to determine whether his mental state warrants commitment. While no cure or therapy is prescribed for Mr. Ritter, his is being administered quite a few phenobarbital drugs as sedatives on an "as-needed" basis. . . . Mr. Ritter feels that he is being kept at the center as a captive, but he is resigned and he will not attempt to escape. He spends his days mending old trousers or sewing buttons on shirts and listens to the radio from time to time.

•    •    •

The regularity with which the "better" patients view themselves as prisoners seems to indicate that believing that they are being held by some conspiracy in a place in which they do not belong allows these individuals to reconcile themselves with their being at the center. . . . But as long as the "better" patients view themselves as prisoners, they can survive in the center: The other people here are not their equals, and the staff's treatment is a part of the conspiracy to keep them here.

•    •    •

## THE OTHERS

There are other patients at the center who hang on to a remainder of self. It is often impossible to know how much lucidity they retain because it is hard to crack the solid wall that these patients have erected between themselves and the institution. At times, only at times, a crack appears, and one can catch a glimpse of life beneath the dull outside.

. . . Mrs. Leister had come to the center willingly because she had a heart condition and felt that she would want medical care nearby all the time. When she came in, she was an active and talkative lady. She walked up and down the corridors, talked to people, smiled a lot, and chirpily moved about. One day she was very excited because her daughter was coming to visit her from back East. She showed me a picture of her daughter and told me all about her daughter's husband and children. That very day I witnessed the kind of interaction that was to force Mrs. Leister behind her wall.

The aide came into the room without knocking and left the door opened behind her. Mrs. Leister was fully dressed, but she was lying on the bed awaiting her doctor's visit. The aide, taking no notice of either of us, began making the bed around Mrs. Leister. The doctor walked in and nodded good morning to the aide. He had no way of knowing who I was since he had never met me before, thus I was a stranger of the opposite sex of the patient he was examining; nevertheless, he casually unbuttoned Mrs. Leister's blouse while asking her about her health and began listening with a stethoscope to her heart. He left after a few minutes, and the nurse resumed making the bed while telling me what a terrible doctor that was.

That day Mrs. Leister had her first taste of what it is like to be treated as an object. When she attempted to be a human being, she was met by the unyielding iron hand of regulations. No, she could not go outside the center and take walks, that was against regulations; no, she could not watch television in the evenings, that would disturb the other patients, and it was not allowed; no, there was no portion of the six acres around the center that was set aside for gardening by the patients. Other patients spoke curtly to Mrs. Leister or returned her conversation with an idiotic grin. Old Maria, in her ramblings, once more reverted to the language of her youth when she was a prostitute in the streets of New York, and invested Mrs. Leister with a barrage of profanities, which brought laughter and a thorazine shot from the ''battle axe'' on duty.

Four months later, Mrs. Leister was spending all of her time on her bed. She no longer walked up and down the corridors. ''I can look at the sky from here,'' she told me, perhaps in her last attempt to have something of her own.

Others who have been at the center longer have finished their wall and devised small ways to show that the center is an abhorrent entity outside of themselves. This enables them to keep a distance between themselves and the center.

And the rest of the patients? They are shadows who no longer possess a cognitive self. They wander aimlessly through the corridors or sit whimpering in a wheelchair, or groan as their bed sores grow redder. When one displays a spark and begins to rage against a ghost from the past which torments him, another pill is popped in his mouth. Slowly, the eyes turn glassy again and, as order and discipline are restored, the patient, a babbling idiot once more, slowly shuffles away.

●   ●   ●

In attempting to understand why patients present such a hostile front to others rather than unite and share the burden of their destiny, an analogy must be drawn. Seymour Martin Lipset and his associates,[14] in studying the typesetters union, discovered that typesetters fraternized with other typesetters in their off-duty activities. Lipset and the others attributed this to a problem of perceived status versus accorded status.

A group feels that it belongs to a certain status category and, therefore, believes that it should be its right to interact with groups in the same status bracket. However, the rest of society accords the group a status inferior to that which it itself perceives. The group is, in other words, rejected by others who feel superior to it and, in turn, rejects groups which it perceives as inferior.

In the center, a single patient can be considered the equivalent of the whole group of typesetters. The patient feels that he belongs to a certain status—being sane—and attempts to interact with individuals whom he considers sane: doctors, nurses, aides, janitors, etc. But they perceive the patient as belonging to an inferior status—work-object, insane, senile, etc.—and refuse to interact with him. On the other hand, the patient perceives the other patients as inferior because he assumes them to be bona fide patients deserving of being in the center and thus refuses to interact with them. The patient has only one group left with which to interact: himself.

## NOTES

1. Erving Goffman, *The Presentation of the Self in Everyday Life* (Garden City, N.Y.: Anchor, 1959).

2. For a detailed account of patients in hospitals in terms of time and work, see Barney Glaser and Anselm Strauss, *Awareness of Dying*. Chicago: Aldine, 1965; *Time for Dying*. Chicago: Aldine, 1968; and *Anguish*. Mill Valley, Ca.: Sociology Press, 1970.

3. For a detailed ethnography of a convalescent center, see Jaber F. Gubrium, *Living and Dying at Murray Manor*. New York: St. Martin's Press, 1975.

4. Matilda W. Riley and Anne Foner, *Aging and Society* (New York: Russell Sage, 1968) Vol. 1, Chapter 25.

5. Claire Townsend, *Old Age: The Last Segregation* (New York: Grossman, 1971); Mary Adelaide Mendelson, *Tender Loving Greed.* New York: Alfred A. Knopf, 1974.

6. Less than 5 percent of the people over sixty-five years of age in the United States are institutionalized. See *Social and Economic Characteristics of the Older Populations 1974*, U.S. Department of Commerce, Bureau of the Census. Washington, D.C.: U.S. Government Printing Office, 1975.

7. However, I had access to all the medical records of the patients.

8. In the latter part of my research an increasing number of young mental patients began replacing the old ones in the upper ward. At times I was mistaken by a new aide or a delivery man for a patient because I did not wear a white coat and wandered around the facilities.

9. Barney Glaser and Anselm Strauss, *Anguish*, op. cit.

10. This quote and the remainder . . . , unless otherwise noted, are from my field notes taken in the summer of 1974.

11. There are four aides on day shift (7:00 to 3:30), two per wing on each ward, plus two 9:00 aides (9:00 to 5:00).

12. The aide is an older lady in her sixties; she has been at the center for many years and somehow feels responsible for all that goes on in there. This leads her to become easily excitable, as I had the opportunity to witness many times.

13. See, for instance, Abraham Blumberg, *Criminal Justice.* Chicago: Quadrangle, 1967.

14. S. M. Lipset, Martin Trow, and James Coleman, *Union Democracy* (Garden City, N.Y.: Anchor, 1956).

# Review Questions

1. Of all the types of actors on the "stage" at Sunny Hill, which ones had the most prestige and income? Which ones had the most contact with the patients?

2. What factors determined how the aides interacted with the patients? Are these the same factors that determine how teachers interact with students, how friends interact with each other, how guards interact with prisoners? Explain.

3. How did the "better" patients and those confined to beds and chairs develop responses to their treatment?

4. To what degree were there true groups among the patients? Why?

5. Overall, how much was the patient's life at Sunny Hill shaped by the staff and how much by the patients themselves?

# Suggested Readings: Social Organization: Life in Groups

Adler, Patricia A. *Wheeling and Dealing: An Ethnography of an Upper-Level Drug Dealing and Smuggling Community*. New York: Columbia University Press, 1985.

Denzin, Norman K. "Notes on the Criminogenic Hypothesis: A Case Study of the American Liquor Industry," *American Sociological Review* 42, 6 (December 1977): 905–920.

Farberman, Harvey A. "A Criminogenic Market Structure: The Automobile Industry," *Sociological Quarterly* 16 (Autumn 1975): 438–457.

Friedson, Eliot. *Profession of Medicine: A Study of the Sociology of Applied Knowledge*. New York: Harper & Row, 1970.

Glaser, Barney G., and Anselm M. Strauss. *Time for Dying*. Chicago: Aldine, 1968.

Goffman, Erving. *Asylums: Essays on the Social Situation of Mental Patients and Other Inmates*. Chicago: Aldine, 1961.

Roy, Donald F. "Quota Restriction and Goldbricking in a Machine Shop," *American Journal of Sociology* 57 (March 1952): 427–442.

Schwartz, Barry. "Notes on the Sociology of Sleep," *Sociological Quarterly* 11 (Fall 1970): 485–499.

Sudnow, David. *Passing On: The Social Organization of Dying*. Englewood Cliffs, N.J.: Prentice-Hall, 1967.

Tonnies, Ferdinand. *Community and Society*. East Lansing, Mich.: Michigan State University Press, 1957.

Whyte, William Foote. *Street Corner Society: The Social Structure of an Italian Slum*. Chicago: University of Chicago Press, 1943.

Zimbardo, Phillip. "Pathology of Imprisonment," *Society*, 9, 6, 1976.

# Part VI. Inequalities: Class, Race, and Gender

IN NEARLY EVERY KNOWN SOCIETY, LIMITED SOCIAL AND MATERIAL REWARDS are distributed unevenly. Prestige, esteem, honor, and social power as well as wealth are granted to societal members unequally. Instead, social groupings develop ranking, or *stratification*, systems in which various "ascribed" (determined at birth) and "achieved" (acquired) attributes— which may include gender, age, race or ethnicity, family name, occupation, and even sometimes physique—are weighted. One's attributes, once ranked in the stratification system, determine those societal rewards which one can claim and which others are willing to bestow.

The rewards and resources one is able to claim determine to a large extent one's *life chances*. By life chances we do not mean merely the opportunities to make a million dollars or to become president of the United States, but rather the chances of surviving infancy, avoiding malnutrition, obtaining education, securing a decent-paying and satisfying job, and living in good health to an advanced age. These life chances are *not* distributed equally in the United States or in any other modern nation.

Large categories of people who receive similar societal resources—and who have similar life chances—are termed *social classes*. Social-class ranking is usually applied to families, so that children inherit their parents' positions in the stratification hierarchy. Their inherited positions may adhere to them long after they have become independent from their parents, since *social mobility*, even in relatively "open" modern industrial societies, is not as common as we like to think. That is, individuals' rankings in the stratification system tend to be perpetuated.

The coherence and stability of stratification systems is maintained in part through social interaction. Interaction with people from other classes often involves "reminders" of one's own class position and actual barriers to upward movement. Interaction with those at one's own class level is, first of all, much more frequent, since many aspects of our lives, from residence to religious services, are somewhat segregated on the basis of social class and even sex, age, race, and the like. It is also more comfortable, because class members share similar life experiences and develop similar interpretations of those experiences. Those of you who have grown up in middle-class families may recall uncomfortable instances when you have crossed class boundaries. Have you ever been invited to a formal affair at an exclusive restaurant and wondered which of the three spoons to use first, what to do with the four forks? Have you come in contact with a prestigious personage who interrupted your conversation in order to talk to someone "more important"? Have you felt, or been made to feel, "out of place" because of your clothing, income, manners, or ignorance of upper-class customs? Have you been passed over for a job or promotion for these reasons? Have you judged people from a lower social class than your own on similar grounds?

The purpose of this section of our reader is to help you to become aware of the interactional bases of stratification and of the inequalities which result. Our selections place the dynamics of social inequality in an everyday context and illustrate how stratification can be viewed as a *social process* which begins in social interaction and which affects individuals' opportunities, self-conceptions, and even their survival. The "system" of distributing social power, prestige, and wealth is not some far-removed, non-human force. It is comprised of the everyday behavior of us all, as we socialize each other to accept both the cultural rationales for stratification and our own particular positions in the ranking system.

We begin by looking at elites in American society. The writings of G. William Domhoff are part of a tradition or school of thought in sociology called "conflict theory," which stems most directly from the work of C. Wright Mills in the 1950s and 1960s on the U.S. "power elite." Mills argued (along with former Republican President Dwight D. Eisenhower) that major decisions affecting the course of our society and the everyday lives of Americans are *not* made solely by our elected representatives as our traditions tell us they are. Rather, a small cluster of *military*, *industrial*, and *political* leaders exercise a great deal of both official and behind-the-scenes power.

According to Mills's research, the powerful in these three arenas are likely to come from *privileged backgrounds* and/or to have amassed great wealth in their adult lives. Furthermore, they are likely to *know each other* from prep school, college, and professional contacts; to *circulate* among top positions in the three crucial arenas; and to *overlap* with each other on boards of directors in industry, education, and community organizations.

Eisenhower himself, who actually warned Americans of the increasing power of what he called the "military-industrial complex," was a general and a military hero in World War II, president of the Ivy League's Columbia University, and eventually President of the United States. A close look at the members of President Reagan's Cabinet (or the Cabinet of any President, for that matter) will reveal a number of millionaires with previous corporate leadership positions, former military "top brass," and the like. Military and political leaders often move into private industry after their "public" service. Those who run large (often multinational) corporations are less visible to the public, but their decisions to manufacture and market their products affect employment rates and patterns, as well as how we eat, dress, drive, keep warm or cool, and entertain ourselves. They are also able to affect lawmakers and laws and questions of peace and war.

Most sociologists agree with the general picture described above: some Americans are simply more powerful than others. They disagree, however, as to how cohesive or competitive the top leaders of our country are. Some sociologists, termed "pluralists," argue that there is a great deal of *diversity*, competition, argument, and divisiveness among those leaders. Decisions made in one issue area, they claim, may be affected by a different set of actors than decisions on other issues. Another group, which includes Domhoff and Mills, contend that the men comprising the "higher circles" of power share a *consensus* over the *major questions* of how the society should operate, only disagreeing over minor issues of how best to implement policies that will achieve their valued goals. They argue further that the interests of the powerful coincide, since the same policies, laws, and customs benefit corporate *and* military *and* political elites.

In the selection from Domhoff's writings presented here, we are offered a glimpse of some of America's major decision makers as they interact, not in the boardroom or the halls of Congress or the White House, but as participants in adult "summer camps" for wealthy and powerful men (no women allowed)—at "The Bohemian Grove and Other Retreats." Sipping martinis under redwood trees or engaging in various forms of "horseplay" on the California ranch lands, the men form and renew bonds of friendship.

As Domhoff notes, his data do not offer conclusive proof that a cohesive national upper-class subculture exists. But, by focusing on the patterns and processes of recreational interaction, he shows us how it could be possible. In this excerpt from his book, we are led to put aside some of our stereotypes of the serious and staid executive or general or statesman, smiling only for press photographers between one high-level meeting and another. We see that the top power- and wealth-holders are not an abstract category of anonymous and isolated individuals, but real human beings whose friendships, networks, contacts, and interactions shape their lives—and ours.

Next we see that judgments about people's class affiliations can have a profound effect on their life chances. In "The Saints and the Roughnecks," William Chambliss traces the interaction between authoritative agents of the community and two white, adolescent youth gangs—the upper-middle-class Saints and the lower-class Roughnecks. His study reveals a pattern of discrimination based on class.

The Saints and the Roughnecks differed little from each other aside from the crucial factors of class background; the visibility of their activities to others; and the biased perceptions of their activities on the part of schoolteachers and officials, the police, and the townspeople. Coming from wealthy families and having the mobility that wealth can buy, the Saints were able to carry out what the community, in ignorance, regarded as "pranks" in places beyond the townspeople's visibility. The Saints' low visibility, their polite demeanor before school and police authorities, and the community's bias in their favor combined to keep the gang free of any taint of delinquency. The way remained clear for the Saints to pursue the adult careers to which, in the community's eyes, their class status, school grades, and behavior entitled them.

The Roughnecks, by contrast, had no barriers to the visibility of their behavior to protect them. Both their defiant demeanor and the bias against them assured that their activities would be stamped with a criminal label. (For a discussion of labeling, see the section entitled *Deviance, Conformity, and Social Control.*) The attitudes of the community that produced the label affected the Roughnecks' expectations of their own futures. Thus, when the Roughnecks turned to adult criminal careers, the community's prophecy was fulfilled. Chambliss's study shows us how class labels, imposed in the course of interaction between groups, have an enormous effect on life chances.

Many observers of American society have seen the great differences in the distribution of wealth as resulting from the values and attitudes that prevail in the different social classes. According to this view, middle-class values are different from lower-class values, the latter forming a pattern that has come to be known as the "culture of poverty." The culture-of-poverty theory holds that lower-class values and attitudes form a way of life that keeps poor people from attaining job security and upward mobility. Where middle-class people are seen as future-oriented, lower-class people are seen as present-oriented. The middle class is said to defer its gratifications (they wait to have their desires fulfilled), an attitude favorable to saving; the lower class is said to seek immediate gratification of its needs, an attitude favorable to immediate consumption. The middle class is described as optimistic, and the lower class as fatalistic. These supposed differences between the cultures of the lower class and the middle class are assumed to explain poverty among the lower classes.

Elliot Liebow *challenges* the culture-of-poverty theory in the selection "Men and Jobs on Tally's Corner." He provides us with a detailed account of his observations of the attitudes and values that lower-class, black, streetcorner men hold toward their jobs, the attitudes that middle-class employers have with respect to those same jobs, and the objective conditions that surround the jobs available to men on the streetcorner.

From a superficial point of view, the men on Tally's Corner might seem to embody every value imparted to them by the culture-of-poverty theory. They appear to be irresponsible and indolent. But, as Liebow points out, most of the men on the corner have jobs—the least prestigious, lowest-paying jobs society has to offer. Both the middle-class employer and the lower-class employee consider the jobs contemptible. Indeed, they are boring, dirty, and monotonous. The wages are insufficient to support a family, and the jobs provide no chance for advancement. Better-paying jobs are usually either physically debilitating, out of reach of the corner men, seasonal, weather-bound, machine-paced, or beyond the training of the corner men.

The system of paying wages for the retail and service jobs available to the streetcorner men provides an excellent illustration of how middle-class employers express their contempt for jobs that lower-class men perform. We see how the power of the employer can be used not only to demean the job but also to threaten whatever marginal security the job might provide.

The men on Tally's corner hold jobs that "are not much to talk about." They are convinced of their own incompetence. They cannot save, and they are reluctant to assume responsibility when responsible jobs are offered. Furthermore, these attitudes and experiences are likely to have been those of their fathers and their fathers' fathers. What is important, indeed critical, to note is that the attitudes that the streetcorner men express are not produced by a culture of poverty but, rather, are the results of objective, valid experience. The culture-of-poverty theory fails to explain why poverty and inequality exist, because it locates the faults in the victims instead of in the system. Liebow's essay demonstrates that the attitudes and values that support inequality are formed not in an isolated subculture but by a process of "self-fulfilling prophecy" in which the beliefs of the more powerful are translated into reality in the course of interaction between groups.

Lenore Weitzman sensitizes us to another way in which the social structure produces inequality in contemporary society. One of the most alarming trends in income stratification in recent years has been the increasing number of women and children in poverty. The U.S. Bureau of the Census estimates that, for the first time in history, *almost all* of the more than 30 million Americans who will live in povetry are *women and children*. Several factors are responsible for this phenomenal social transformation. One of them is the introduction of "no-fault" divorce laws. Weitzman's research and analysis of California's divorce laws are presented in "The Divorce Revolution and the Feminization of Poverty." She shows how and why these laws, in conjunction with more favorable treatment of men in the workplace, have had such dire unanticipated consequences. Her findings send a warning to today's woman: your past social statuses, ascribed or achieved, are no guarantee of a comfortable future.

We turn our attention next to the ways in which *status reminders* are manifested in everyday interactions involving waiting. Time is, as we know, an important, scarce resource, and the use or waste of it can gain or deny us access to other valued resources. Since time can be socially used or abused, it entails social costs. And the ability to affect how other people use their time is an indicator of power. In his essay, "Waiting, Exchange, and Power," Barry Schwartz examines the social costs, uses, and abuses of time as a medium of exchange in the interactional relationship of waiting. Waiting, as Schwartz points out, affects the value of the goods, services, and persons one waits for. The social costs that whole categories of people bear in order to obtain some valued thing may be very high.

Waiting is closely related to power, because those who have power can impose waiting upon those who don't. The phrase, "being forced to wait," expresses the coercive power of waiting used as a policy. The power to make others wait is often held by those who have a monopoly on valued things. Our decision to wait expresses "status deference," the willingness to defer to others higher on the pecking order than we are. Yet it is not always the powerful for whom we wait. People low in power may impose waiting upon us because of their access to the powerful.

Schwartz examines the dynamics of waiting in terms of the value we give the objects for which we wait and the distribution of power between servers and their clients. Waiting is thus demonstrated to be not merely an annoyance, as it is often seen, but an indication and a reminder of inequality.

# THE BOHEMIAN GROVE AND OTHER RETREATS

## G. William Domhoff

## THE BOHEMIAN GROVE

Picture yourself comfortably seated in a beautiful open-air dining hall in the midst of twenty-seven hundred acres of giant California redwoods. It is early evening and the clear July air is still pleasantly warm. Dusk has descended, you have finished a sumptuous dinner, and you are sitting quietly with your drink and your cigar, listening to nostalgic welcoming speeches and enjoying the gentle light and the eerie shadows that are cast by the two-stemmed gaslights flickering softly at each of the several hundred outdoor banquet tables.

You are part of an assemblage that has been meeting in this redwood grove sixty-five miles north of San Francisco for nearly a hundred years. It is not just any assemblage, for you are a captain of industry, a well-known television star, a banker, a famous artist, or maybe a member of the President's Cabinet. You are one of fifteen hundred men gathered together from all over the country for the annual encampment of the rich and the famous at the Bohemian Grove.

•   •   •

["Bohemians" of the 1970s and 1980s include such personages as President Ronald Reagan; Vice President George Bush; former Attorney General William French Smith; Secretary of State George P. Shultz; former President Richard Nixon; former President Gerald Ford; Supreme Court Justice Potter Stewart; Herbert Hoover, Jr.; Herbert Hoover III; newspaperman William R. Hearst, Jr.; five members of the Dean Witter family of investment bankers; entertainers Art Linkletter and Edgar Bergen; presidents and chairmen of several oil companies such as Marathon Oil and Standard Oil; the president of Rockefeller University; officers of Anheuser-Busch breweries; the president of Kaiser Industries; bank presidents from California to New York; the president and chairman of Hewlett-Packard Co.; and many other representatives of American industry, finance, government, and entertainment. When these participants arrive for the annual "campout," an elaborate ritual called the

Excerpted from G. William Domhoff, *The Bohemian Grove and Other Retreats* (New York: Harper & Row, 1974), pp. 1; 7–8; 11; 14–15; 17; 19–21; 31; 72–74; 79–83; 86–96.

Cremation of Care welcomes them and instructs them to leave all cares behind while they join together for two weeks of lavish entertainment, fellowship, and "communion with nature."]

The Cremation of Care is the most spectacular event of the midsummer retreat that members and guests of San Francisco's Bohemian Club have taken every year since 1878. However, there are several other entertainments in store. Before the Bohemians return to the everyday world, they will be treated to plays, variety shows, song fests, shooting contests, art exhibits, swimming, boating, and nature rides.

•    •    •

A cast for a typical Grove play easily runs to seventy-five or one hundred people. Add in the orchestra, the stagehands, the carpenters who make the sets, and other supporting personnel, and over three hundred people are involved in creating the High Jinks each year. Preparations begin a year in advance, with rehearsals occurring two or three times a week in the month before the encampment, and nightly in the week before the play.

Costs are on the order of $20,000 to $30,000 per High Jinks, a large amount of money for a one-night production which does not have to pay a penny for salaries (the highest cost in any commercial production). "And the costs are talked about, too," reports my . . . informant. "'Hey, did you hear the High Jinks will cost $25,000 this year?' one of them will say to another. The expense of the play is one way they can relate to its worth."

•    •    •

Entertainment is not the only activity at the Bohemian Grove. For a little change of pace, there is intellectual stimulation and political enlightenment every day at 12:30 P.M. Since 1932 the meadow from which people view the Cremation of Care also has been the setting for informal talks and briefings by people as varied as Dwight David Eisenhower (before he was President), Herman Wouk (author of The Caine Mutiny), Bobby Kennedy (while he was Attorney General), and Neil Armstrong (after he returned from the moon).

Cabinet officers, politicans, generals, and governmental advisers are the rule rather than the exception for Lakeside Talks, especially on weekends. Equally prominent figures from the worlds of art, literature and science are more likely to make their appearance during the weekdays of the encampment, when Grove attendance may drop to four or five hundred (many of the members only come up for one week or for the weekends because they cannot stay away from their corporations and law firms for the full two weeks).

•    •    •

[T]he Grove is an ideal off-the-record atmosphere for sizing up politicians. "Well, of course when a politician comes here, we all get to see him, and his stock in trade is his personality and his ideas," a prominent Bohemian told a *New York Times* reporter who was trying to cover Nelson Rockefeller's 1963 visit to the Grove for a Lakeside Talk. The journalist went on to note that the midsummer encampments "have long been a major showcase where leaders of business, industry, education, the arts, and politics can come to examine each other."[1]

• • •

For 1971, [then-] President Nixon was to be the featured Lakeside speaker. However, when newspaper reporters learned that the President planned to disappear into a redwood grove for an off-the-record speech to some of the most powerful men in America, they objected loudly and vowed to make every effort to cover the event. The flap caused the club considerable embarrassment, and after much hemming and hawing back and forth, the club leaders asked the President to cancel his scheduled appearance. A White House press secretary then announced that the President had decided not to appear at the Grove rather than risk the tradition that speeches there are strictly off the public record.[2]

However, the President was not left without a final word to his fellow Bohemians. In a telegram to the president of the club, which now hangs at the entrance to the reading room in the San Francisco clubhouse, he expressed his regrets at not being able to attend. He asked the club president to continue to lead people into the woods, adding that he in turn would redouble his efforts to lead people out of the woods. He also noted that, while anyone could aspire to be President of the United States, only a few could aspire to be president of the Bohemian Club.

• • •

Not all the entertainment at the Bohemian Grove takes place under the auspices of the committee in charge of special events. The Bohemians and their guests are divided into camps which evolved slowly over the years as the number of people on the retreat grew into the hundreds and then the thousands. These camps have become a significant center of enjoyment during the encampment.

At first the camps were merely a place in the woods where a half-dozen to a dozen friends would pitch their tents. Soon they added little amenities like their own special stove or a small permanent structure. Then there developed little camp "traditions" and endearing camp names like Cliff Dwellers, Moonshiners, Silverado Squatters, Woof, Zaca, Toyland, Sundodgers, and Land of Happiness. The next steps were special emblems, a handsome little lodge or specially constructed tepees, a permanent bar, and maybe a grand piano.[3] Today there are 129 camps of varying sizes, structures, and statuses. Most have between 10 and 30 members, but there are one or two with about 125 members and several with less than 10. A majority of the camps are strewn along what is called the River Road, but some are huddled in other areas within five or ten minutes of the center of the Grove.

The entertainment at the camps is mostly informal and impromptu. Someone will decide to bring together all the jazz musicians in the Grove for a special session. Or maybe all the artists or writers will be invited to a luncheon or a dinner at a camp. Many camps have their own amateur piano players and informal musical and singing groups which perform for the rest of the members.

But the joys of the camps are not primarily in watching or listening to performances. Other pleasures are created within them. Some camps become known for their gastronomical specialties, such as a particular drink or a particular meal. The Jungle Camp features mint juleps, Halcyon has a three-foot-high martini maker constructed out of chemical glassware. At the Owl's Nest [President Reagan's club] it's the gin-fizz breakfast—about a hundred people are invited over one morning during the encampment for eggs Benedict, gin fizzes, and all the trimmings.

•   •   •

The men of Bohemia are drawn in large measure from the corporate leadership of the United States. They include in their numbers directors from major corporations in every sector of the American economy. An indication of this fact is that one in every five resident members and one in every three nonresident members is found in Poor's *Register of Corporations, Executives, and Directors,* a huge volume which lists the leadership of tens of thousands of companies from every major business field except investment banking, real estate, and advertising.

Even better evidence for the economic prominence of the men under consideration is that at least one officer or director from 40 of the 50 largest industrial corporations in America was present, as a member or a guest, on the lists at our disposal. Only Ford Motor Company and Western Electric were missing among the top 25! Similarly, we found that officers and directors from 20 of the top 25 commercial banks (including all of the 15 largest) were on our lists. Men from 12 of the first 25 life-insurance companies were in attendance (8 of these 12 were from the top 10). Other business sectors were represented somewhat less: 10 of 25 in transportation, 8 of 25 in utilities, 7 of 25 in conglomerates, and only 5 of 25 in retailing. More generally, of the top-level businesses ranked by *Fortune* for 1969 (the top 500 industrials, the top 50 commercial banks, the top 50 life-insurance companies, the top 50 transportation companies, the top 50 utilities, the top 50 retailers, and the top 47 conglomerates), 29 *percent of these 797 corporations were "represented" by at least 1 officer or director.*

•   •   •

## OTHER WATERING HOLES

[Other camps and retreats were founded by wealthy and powerful men, based on the model provided by the Bohemian Grove. One example is the Rancheros Visitadores (Visiting Ranchers) who meet each May for horse-back rides through the California ranch land. These are accompanied by feasts, entertainment, and general merrymaking with a Spanish-ranch motif.]

[Among the Rancheros a] common interest in horses and horseplay provides a social setting in which men with different forms of wealth get to know each other better. *Sociologically speaking, the Rancheros Visitadores is an organization which serves the function (whether the originators planned it that way or not) of helping to integrate ranchers and businessmen from different parts of the country into a cohesive social class.*

•   •   •

[T]he Rancheros had to divide into camps because of a postwar increase in membership. There are seventeen camps, sporting such Spanish names as Los Amigos, Los Vigilantes, Los Tontos (bums), Los Bandidos, and Los Flojos (lazy ones). They range in size from fifteen to ninety-three, with the majority of them listing between twenty and sixty members. Most camps have members from a variety of geographical locations, although some are slightly specialized in that regard. Los Gringos, the largest camp, has the greatest number of members from out of state. Los Borrachos, Los Picadores, and Los Chingadores, the next largest camps, have a predominance of people from the Los Angeles area. Los Vigilantes, with twenty members, began as a San Francisco group, but now includes riders from Oregon, Washington, New York and southern California.

In 1928 the Bohemian Grove provided John J. Mitchell with the inspiration for his retreat on horseback, the Rancheros Visitadores. Since 1930 the RVs have grown to the point where they are an impressive second best to the Grove in size, entertainment, and stature. Their combination of businessmen and ranchers is as unique as the Bohemian's amalgamation of businessmen and artists. It is hardly surprising that wealthy men from Los Angeles, San Francisco, Honolulu, Spokane, and Chicago would join Mitchell in wanting to be members of both.

•   •   •

[Another club, the Colorado-based Roundup Riders of the Rockies, imitates the RVs in its emphasis on "roughing it" and socializing.]

The riders do not carry their fine camp with them. Instead, twenty camphands are employed to move the camp in trucks to the next campsite. Thus, when the Roundup Riders arrive at their destination each evening they find fourteen large sleeping tents complete with cots, air mattresses, portable toilets, and showers. Also up and ready for service are a large green dining tent and an entertainment stage. A diesel-powered generator provides the camp with electricity.

Food service is provided by Martin Jetton of Fort Worth, Texas, a caterer advertised in the southwest as "King of the Barbecue." Breakfasts and dinners are said to be veritable banquets. Lunch is not as elaborate, but it does arrive to the riders on the trail in a rather unusual fashion that only those of the higher circles could afford: "lunches in rugged country are often delivered by light plane or helicopter."[4] One year the men almost missed a meal because a wind came up and scattered the lunches which were being parachuted from two Cessna 170s.

In addition to the twenty hired hands who take care of the camp, there are twenty wranglers to look after the horses. The horses on the ride—predominantly such fine breeds as Arabian, Quarter Horse, and Morgan—are estimated to be worth more than $200,000. Horses and riders compete in various contests of skill and horsemanship on a layover day in the middle of the week. Skeet shooting, trap shooting, and horseshoes also are a part of this event.

• • •

The Roundup Riders, who hold their trek at the same time the Bohemians hold their encampment, must be reckoned as a more regional organization. Although there are numerous millionaires and executives among them, the members are not of the national stature of most Bohemians and many Rancheros. They can afford to invest thousands of dollars in their horses and tack, to pay a $300 yearly ride fee, and to have their lunch brought to them by helicopter, but they cannot compete in business connections and prestige with those who assemble at the Bohemian Grove. Building from the Denver branch of the upper class, the Roundup Riders reach out primarily to Nebraska (six), Texas (five), Illinois (five), Nevada (three), California (three), and Arizona (three). There are no members from New York, Boston, Philadelphia, or other large Eastern cities.

Several other regional rides have been inspired by the Rancheros, rides such as the Desert Caballeros in Wickenburg, Arizona, and the Verde Vaqueros in Scottsdale, Arizona. These groups are similar in size and membership to the Roundup Riders of the Rockies. Like the Roundup Riders, they have a few overlapping members with the Rancheros. But none are of the status of the Rancheros Visitadores. They are minor legacies of the Bohemian Grove, unlikely even to be aware of their kinship ties to the retreat in the redwoods.

## DO BOHEMIANS, RANCHEROS, AND ROUNDUP RIDERS RULE AMERICA?

The foregoing material on upper-class retreats, which I have presented in as breezy a manner as possible, is relevant to highly emotional questions concerning the distribution of power in modern America. In this final [section] I will switch styles somewhat and discuss these charged questions in a sober, simple, and straightforward way. . . .

It is my hypothesis that there is a ruling social class in the United States. This class is made up of the owners and managers of large corporations, which means the members have many economic and political interests in common, and many conflicts with ordinary working people. Comprising at most 1 percent of the total population, members of this class own 25 to 30 percent of all privately held wealth in America, own 60 to 70 percent of the privately held corporate wealth, receive 20 to 25 percent of the yearly income, direct the large corporations and foundations, and dominate the federal government in Washington.

Most social scientists disagree with this view. Some dismiss it out of hand, others become quite vehement in disputing it. The overwhelming majority of them believe that the United States has a "pluralistic" power structure, in which a wide variety of "veto groups" (e.g., businessmen, farmers, unions, consumers) and "voluntary associations" (e.g., National Association of Manufacturers, Americans for Democratic Action, Common Cause) form shifting coalitions to influence decisions on different issues. These groups and associations are said to have differing amounts of interest and influence on various questions. Contrary to my view, pluralists assert that no one group, not even the owners and managers of large corporations, has the cohesiveness and ability to determine the outcome of a large variety of social, economic, and political issues.

•   •   •

As noted, I believe there is a national upper class in the United States. . . . [T]his means that wealthy families from all over the country, and particularly from major cities like New York, San Francisco, Chicago, and Houston, are part of interlocking social circles which perceive each other as equals, belong to the same clubs, interact frequently, and freely intermarry.

Whether we call it a "social class" or a "status group," many pluralistic social scientists would deny that such a social group exists. They assert that there is no social "cohesiveness" among the various rich in different parts of the country. For them, social registers, blue books, and club membership lists are merely collections of names which imply nothing about group interaction.

There is a wealth of journalistic evidence which suggests the existence of a national upper class. It ranges from Cleveland Amory's *The Proper Bostonians* and *Who Killed Society?* to Lucy Kavaler's *The Private World of High Society* and Stephen Birmingham's *The Right People.* But what is the systematic evidence which I can present for my thesis? There is first of all the evidence that has been developed from the study of attendance at private schools. It has been shown that a few dozen prep schools bring together children of the upper class from all over the country. From this evidence it can be argued that young members of the upper class develop lifetime friendship ties with like-status age-mates in every section of the country.[5]

There is second the systematic evidence which comes from studying high-status summer resorts. Two such studies show that these resorts bring together upper-class families from several different large cities.[6] Third, there is the evidence of business interconnections. Several . . . studies have demonstrated that interlocking directorships bring wealthy men from all over the country into face-to-face relationships at the board meetings of banks, insurance companies, and other corporations.[7]

And finally, there is the evidence developed from studying exclusive social clubs. Such studies have been made in the past, but the present investigation of the Bohemian Club, the Rancheros Visitadores, and the Roundup Riders of the Rockies is a more comprehensive effort. *In short, I believe the present [study] to be significant evidence for the existence of a cohesive American upper class.*

The Bohemian Grove, as well as other watering holes and social clubs, are relevant to the problem of class cohesiveness in two ways. First, the very fact that rich men from all over the country gather in such close circumstances as the Bohemian Grove is evidence for the existence of a socially cohesive upper class. It demonstrates that many of these men do know each other, that they have face-to-face communications, and that they are a social network. In this sense, we are looking at the Bohemian Grove and other social retreats as a *result* of social processes that lead to class cohesion. But such institutions also can be viewed as *facilitators* of social ties. Once formed, these groups become another avenue by which the cohesiveness of the upper class is maintained.

In claiming that clubs and retreats like the Bohemians and the Rancheros are evidence for my thesis of a national upper class, I am assuming that cohesion develops within the settings they provide. Perhaps some readers will find that assumption questionable. So let us pause to ask: Are there reasons to believe that the Bohemian Grove and its imitators lead to greater cohesion within the upper class?

For one thing, we have the testimony of members themselves. There are several accounts by leading members of these groups, past and present, which attest to the intimacy that develops among members. John J. Mitchell, El Presidente of Los Rancheros Visitadores from 1930 to 1955, wrote as follows on the twenty-fifth anniversary of the group:

> All the pledges and secret oaths in the universe cannot tie men, our kind of men, together like the mutual appreciation of a beautiful horse, the moon behind a cloud, a song around the campfire or a ride down the Santa Ynez Valley. These are experiences common on our ride, but unknown to most of our daily lives. Our organization, to all appearances, is the most informal imaginable. Yet there are men here who see one another once a year, yet feel a bond closer than between those they have known all their lives.[8]

F. Burr Betts, chairman of the board of Security Life of Denver, says the following about the Roundup Riders:

> I think you find out about the Roundup Riders when you go to a Rider's funeral. Because there you'll find, no matter how many organizations the man belonged to, almost every pallbearer is a Roundup Rider. I always think of the Roundup Riders as the first affiliation. We have the closest knit fraternity in the world.[9]

* * *

A second reason for stressing the importance of retreats and clubs like the Bohemian Grove is a body of research within social psychology which deals with group cohesion. "Group dynamics" suggests the following about cohesiveness. (1) *Physical proximity is likely to lead to group solidarity.* Thus, the mere fact that these men gather together in such intimate physical settings implies that cohesiveness develops. (The same point can be made, of course, about exclusive neighborhoods, private schools, and expensive summer resorts.) (2) *The more people interact, the more they will like each other.* This is hardly a profound discovery, but we can note that the Bohemian Grove and other watering holes maximize personal interactions. (3) *Groups seen as high in status are more cohesive.* The Bohemian Club fits the category of a high-status group. Further, its stringent membership requirements, long waiting lists, and high dues also serve to heighten its valuation in the eyes of its members. Members are likely to think of themselves as "special" people, which would heighten their attractiveness to each other, and increase the likelihood of interaction and cohesiveness. (4) *The best atmosphere for increasing group cohesiveness is one that is relaxed and cooperative.* Again the Bohemian Grove, the Rancheros, and the Roundup Riders are ideal examples of this kind of climate. From a group-dynamics point of view, then, we could argue that one of the reasons for upper-class cohesiveness is the fact that the class is organized into a wide variety of small groups which encourage face-to-face interaction and ensure status and security for members.[10]

In summary, if we take these several common settings together— schools, resorts, corporation directorships, and social clubs—and assume on the basis of members' testimony and the evidence of small-group research that interaction in such settings leads to group cohesiveness, then I think we are justified in saying that wealthy families from all over the United States are linked together in a variety of ways into a national upper class.

Even if the evidence and arguments for the existence of a socially cohesive national upper class are accepted, there is still the question of whether or not this class has the means by which its members can reach policy consensus on issues of importance to them.

A five-year study based upon information obtained from confidential informants, interviews, and questionnaires has shown that social clubs such as the Bohemian Club are an important consensus-forming aspect of the upper class and big-business environment. According to sociologist Reed Powell, "the clubs are a repository of the values held by the upper-level prestige groups in the community and are a means by which these values are transferred to the business environment." Moreover, the clubs are places where problems are discussed:

> On the other hand, the clubs are places in which the beliefs, problems, and values of the industrial organization are discussed and related to other elements in the larger community. Clubs, therefore, are not only effective vehicles of informal communication, but also valuable centers where views are presented, ideas are modified, and new ideas emerge. Those in the interview sample were appreciative of this asset; in addition, they considered the club as a valuable place to combine social and business contacts.[11]

The revealing interview work of Floyd Hunter, an outstanding pioneer researcher on the American power structure, also provides evidence for the importance of social clubs as informal centers of policy making. Particularly striking for our purposes is a conversation he had with one of the several hundred top leaders that he identified in the 1950s. The person in question was a conservative industrialist who was ranked as a top-level leader by his peers:

> Hall [a pseudonym] spoke very favorably of the Bohemian Grove group that met in California every year. He said that although over the entrance to the Bohemian Club there was a quotation, "Weaving spiders come not here," there was a good deal of informal policy made in this association. He said that he got to know Herbert Hoover in this connection and that he started work with Hoover in the food administration of World War I.[12]

Despite the evidence presented by Powell and Hunter that clubs are a setting for the development of policy consensus, I do not believe that such settings are the only, or even the primary, locus for developing policy on class-related issues. For policy questions, other organizations are far more important, organizations like the Council on Foreign Relations, the Committee for Economic Development, the Business Council, and the National Municipal League. These organizations, along with many others, are the "consensus-seeking" and "policy-planning" organizations of the upper class. Directed by the same men who manage the major corporations, and financed by corporation and foundation monies, these groups sponsor meetings and discussions wherein wealthy men from all over the country gather to iron out differences and formulate policies on pressing problems.

No one discussion group is *the* leadership council within the upper class. While some of the groups tend to specialize in certain issue areas, they overlap and interact to a great extent. Consensus slowly emerges from the interplay of people and ideas within and among the groups.[13] This diversity of groups is made very clear in the following comments by Frazar B. Wilde, chairman emeritus of Connecticut General Life Insurance Company and a member of the Council on Foreign Relations and the Committee for Economic Development. Mr. Wilde was responding to a question about the Bilderbergers, a big-business meeting group which includes Western European leaders as well as American corporation and foundation directors:

> Business has had over the years many different seminars and discussion meetings. They run all the way from large public gatherings like NAM [National Association of Manufacturers] to special sessions such as those held frequently at Arden House. Bilderberg is in many respects one of the most important, if not the most important, but this is not to deny that other strictly off-the-record meetings and discussion groups such as those held by the Council on Foreign Relations are not in the front rank.[14]

Generally speaking, then, it is in these organizations that leaders within the upper class discuss the means by which to deal with problems of major concern. Here, in off-the-record settings, these leaders try to reach consensus on general issues that have been talked about more casually in corporate boardrooms and social clubs. These organizations, aided by funds from corporations and foundations, also serve several other functions:

1. They are a training ground for new leadership within the class. It is in these organizations, and through the publications of these organizations, that younger lawyers, bankers, and businessmen become acquainted with general issues in the areas of foreign, domestic, and municipal policy.

2. They are the place where leaders within the upper class hear the ideas and findings of their hired experts.

3. They are the setting wherein upper-class leaders "look over" young experts for possible service as corporation or governmental advisers.

4. They provide the framework for expert studies on important issues. Thus, the Council on Foreign Relations undertook a $1 million study of the "China question" in the first half of the 1960s. The Committee for

Economic Development created a major study of money and credit about the same time. Most of the money for these studies was provided by the Ford, Rockefeller, and Carnegie foundations.[15]

5. Through such avenues as books, journals, policy statements, discussion groups, press releases, and speakers, the policy-planning organizations greatly influence the "climate of opinion" within which major issues are considered. For example, *Foreign Affairs,* the journal of the Council on Foreign Relations, is considered the most influential journal in its field, and the periodic policy statements of the Committee for Economic Development are carefully attended to by major newspapers and local opinion leaders.

It is my belief, then, that the policy-planning groups are essential in developing policy positions which are satisfactory to the upper class as a whole. As such, I think they are a good part of the answer to any social scientist who denies that members of the upper class have institutions by which they deal with economic and political challenges.

However, the policy-planning groups could not function if there were not some common interests within the upper class in the first place. The most obvious, and most important, of these common interests have to do with the shared desire of the members to maintain the present monopolized and subsidized business system which so generously overrewards them and makes their jet setting, fox hunting, art collecting, and other extravagances possible. But it is not only shared economic and political concerns which make consensus possible. The Bohemian Grove and other upper-class social institutions also contribute to this process: *Group-dynamics research suggests that members of socially cohesive groups are more open to the opinions of other members, and more likely to change their views to those of fellow members.*[16] Social cohesion is a factor in policy consensus because it creates a desire on the part of group members to reconcile differences with other members of the group. It is not enough to say that members of the upper class are bankers, businessmen, and lawyers with a common interest in profit maximization and tax avoidance who meet together at the Council on Foreign Relations, the Committee for Economic Development, and other policy-planning organizations. We must add that they are Bohemians, Rancheros, and Roundup Riders.

## NOTES

1. Wallace Turner, "Rockefeller Faces Scrutiny of Top Californians: Governor to Spend Weekend at Bohemian Grove among State's Establishment" (*New York Times,* July 26, 1963), p. 30. In 1964 Senator Barry Goldwater appeared at the Grove as a guest of retired General Albert C. Wedemeyer and Herbert Hoover, Jr. For that story see Wallace Turner, "Goldwater Spending Weekend in Camp at Bohemian Grove" (*New York Times,* July 31, 1964), p. 10.

2. James M. Naughton, "Nixon Drops Plan for Coast Speech" (*New York Times,* July 31, 1971), p. 11.

3. There is a special moisture-proof building at the Grove to hold the dozens of expensive Steinway pianos belonging to the club and various camps.

4. Robert Pattridge, "Closer to Heaven on Horseback" (*Empire Magazine, Denver Post*, July 9, 1972), p. 12. I am grateful to sociologist Ford Cleere for bringing this article to my attention.

5. E. Digby Baltzell, *Philadelphia Gentlemen* (New York: Free Press, 1958), chapter 12. G. William Domhoff, *The Higher Circles* (New York: Random House, 1970), p. 78.

6. Baltzell, *Philadelphia Gentlemen*, pp. 248–51. Domhoff, *The Higher Circles*, pp. 79–82. For recent anecdotal evidence on this point, see Stephen Birmingham, *The Right People* (Boston: Little, Brown, 1968), Part 3.

7. *Interlocks in Corporate Management* (Washington: U.S. Government Printing Office, 1965) summarizes much of this information and presents new evidence as well. See also Peter Dooley, "The Interlocking Directorate" (*American Economic Review*, December, 1969).

8. Neill C. Wilson, *Los Rancheros Visitadores: Twenty-Fifth Anniversary* (Rancheros Visitadores, 1955), p. 2.

9. Robert Pattridge, "Closer to Heaven on Horseback," p. 11.

10. Dorwin Cartwright and Alvin Zander, *Group Dynamics* (New York: Harper & Row, 1960), pp. 74–82; Albert J. Lott and Bernice E. Lott, "Group Cohesiveness as Interpersonal Attraction" (*Psychological Bulletin*, 64, 1965), pp. 259–309; Michael Argyle, *Social Interaction* (Chicago: Aldine Publishing Company, 1969), pp. 220–23. I am grateful to sociologist John Sonquist of the University of California, Santa Barbara, for making me aware of how important the small-groups literature might be for studies of the upper class. Findings on influence processes, communication patterns, and the development of informal leadership also might be applicable to problems in the area of upper-class research.

11. Reed M. Powell, *Race, Religion, and the Promotion of the American Executive* (College of Administrative Science Monograph No. AA-3, Ohio State University, 1969), p. 50.

12. Floyd Hunter, *Top Leadership, U.S.A.* (Chapel Hill: University of North Carolina Press, 1959), p. 109. Hunter also reported (p. 199) that the most favored clubs of his top leaders were the Metropolitan, Links, Century, University (New York), Bohemian, and Pacific Union. He notes (p. 223 n.) that he found clubs to be less important in policy formation on the national level than they are in communities.

13. For a detailed case study of how the process works, see David Eakins, "Business Planners and America's Postwar Expansion," in David Horowitz, editor, *Corporations and the Cold War* (New York: Monthly Review Press, 1969). For other examples and references, see Domhoff, *The Higher Circles*, chapters 5 and 6.

14. Carl Gilbert, personal communication, June 30, 1972. Mr. Gilbert has done extensive research on the Bilderberg group, and I am grateful to him for sharing his detailed information with me. For an excellent discussion of this group, whose role has been greatly distorted and exaggerated by ultra-conservatives, see Eugene Pasymowski and Carl Gilbert, "Bilderberg, Rockefeller, and the CIA" (*Temple Free Press*, No. 6, September 16, 1968). The article is most conveniently located in a slightly revised form in the *Congressional Record*, September 15, 1971, E9615, under the title "Bilderberg: The Cold War Internationale."

15. The recent work of arch-pluralist Nelson Polsby is bringing him danger-

ously close to this formulation. Through studies of the initiation of a number of new policies, Polsby and his students have tentatively concluded that "innovators are typically professors or interest group experts." Where Polsby goes wrong is in failing to note that the professors are working on Ford Foundation grants and/or Council on Foreign Relations fellowships. If he would put his work in a sociological framework, people would not gain the false impression that professors are independent experts sitting in their ivory towers thinking up innovations for the greater good of humanity. See Nelson Polsby, "Policy Initiation in the American Political System,"in Irving Louis Horowitz, editor, *The Use and Abuse of Social Science* (New Brunswick, N.J.: TransAction Books, 1971), p. 303.

16. Cartwright and Zander, *Group Dynamics*, p. 89; Lott and Lott, "Group Cohesiveness as Interpersonal Attraction," pp. 291–96.

# Review Questions

1. The theoretical position on the U.S. class structure taken by Domhoff is called a "conflict" or "elitist" approach. How does this perspective contrast with the "pluralist" approach?

2. *Compare* and *contrast* the Bohemian Club with a club of which you are a member.

3. What does Domhoff argue is the importance of recreational social interaction for the formation of a cohesive national upper class?

4. The members of the Bohemian Club, the Rancheros Visitadores, and to a lesser extent the Roundup Riders of the Rockies include top officials of both the Democratic and Republican Parties. Why does this mixing occur? What are its consequences?

5. What is the significance of the fact that many members of the clubs described by Domhoff are industrialists and businessmen?

# THE SAINTS AND THE ROUGHNECKS

## William J. Chambliss

EIGHT PROMISING YOUNG MEN—CHILDREN OF GOOD, STABLE, WHITE UPPER-middle-class families, active in school affairs, good pre-college students—were some of the most delinquent boys at Hanibal High School. While community residents knew that these boys occasionally sowed a few wild oats, they were totally unaware that sowing wild oats completely occupied the daily routine of these young men. The Saints were constantly occupied with truancy, drinking, wild driving, petty theft and vandalism. Yet no one was officially arrested for any misdeed during the two years I observed them.

This record was particularly surprising in light of my observations during the same two years of another gang of Hanibal High School students, six lower-class white boys known as the Roughnecks. The Roughnecks were constantly in trouble with police and community even though their rate of delinquency was about equal with that of the Saints. What was the cause of this disparity? the result? The following consideration of the activities, social class and community perceptions of both gangs may provide some answers.

## THE SAINTS FROM MONDAY TO FRIDAY

The Saints' principal daily concern was with getting out of school as early as possible. The boys managed to get out of school with minimum danger that they would be accused of playing hookey through an elaborate procedure for obtaining "legitimate" release from class. The most common procedure was for one boy to obtain the release of another by fabricating a meeting of some committee, program or recognized club. Charles might raise his hand in his 9:00 chemistry class and ask to be excused—a euphemism for going to the bathroom. Charles would go to Ed's math class and inform the teacher that Ed was needed for a 9:30 rehearsal of the drama club play. The math teacher would recognize Ed and Charles as "good students" involved in numerous school activities and would permit Ed to leave at 9:30. Charles would return to his class,

William J. Chambliss, "The Saints and the Roughnecks," *Society* 11 (November–December 1973): 24–31.

and Ed would go to Tom's English class to obtain his release. Tom would engineer Charles' escape. The strategy would continue until as many of the Saints as possible were freed. After a stealthy trip to the car (which had been parked in a strategic spot), the boys were off for a day of fun.

Over the two years I observed the Saints, this pattern was repeated nearly every day. There were variations on the theme, but in one form or another, the boys used this procedure for getting out of class and then off the school grounds. Rarely did all eight of the Saints manage to leave school at the same time. The average number avoiding school on the days I observed them was five.

Having escaped from the concrete corridors the boys usually went either to a pool hall on the other (lower-class) side of town or to a cafe in the suburbs. Both places were out of the way of people the boys were likely to know (family or school officials), and both provided a source of entertainment. The pool hall entertainment was the generally rough atmosphere, the occasional hustler, the sometimes drunk proprietor and, of course, the game of pool. The cafe's entertainment was provided by the owner. The boys would "accidentally" knock a glass on the floor or spill cola on the counter—not all the time, but enough to be sporting. They would also bend spoons, put salt in sugar bowls and generally tease whoever was working in the cafe. The owner had opened the cafe recently and was dependent on the boys' business which was, in fact, substantial since between the horsing around and the teasing they bought food and drinks.

## THE SAINTS ON WEEKENDS

On weekends the automobile was even more critical than during the week, for on weekends the Saints went to Big Town—a large city with a population of over a million 25 miles from Hanibal. Every Friday and Saturday night most of the Saints would meet between 8:00 and 8:30 and would go into Big Town. Big Town activities included drinking heavily in taverns or nightclubs, driving drunkenly through the streets, and committing acts of vandalism and playing pranks.

By midnight on Fridays and Saturdays the Saints were usually thoroughly high, and one or two of them were often so drunk they had to be carried to the cars. Then the boys drove around town, calling obscenities to women and girls; occasionally trying (unsuccessfully so far as I could tell) to pick girls up; and driving recklessly through red lights and at high speeds with their lights out. Occasionally they played "chicken." One boy would climb out the back window of the car and across the roof to the driver's side of the car while the car was moving at high speed (between 40 and 50 miles an hour); then the driver would move over and the boy who had just crawled across the car roof would take the driver's seat.

Searching for "fair game" for a prank was the boys' principal activity after they left the tavern. The boys would drive alongside a foot patrolman and ask directions to some street. If the policeman leaned on the car in the course of answering the question, the driver would speed away, causing him to lose his balance. The Saints were careful to play this prank only in an area where they were not going to spend much time and where they could quickly disappear around a corner to avoid having their license plate number taken.

Construction sites and road repair areas were the special province of the Saints' mischief. A soon-to-be-repaired hole in the road inevitably invited the Saints to remove lanterns and wooden barricades and put them in the car, leaving the hole unprotected. The boys would find a safe vantage point and wait for an unsuspecting motorist to drive into the hole. Often, though not always, the boys would go up to the motorist and commiserate with him about the dreadful way the city protected its citizenry.

Leaving the scene of the open hole and the motorist, the boys would then go searching for an appropriate place to erect the stolen barricade. An "appropriate place" was often a spot on a highway near a curve in the road where the barricade would not be seen by an on-coming motorist. The boys would wait to watch an unsuspecting motorist attempt to stop and (usually) crash into the wooden barricade. With saintly bearing the boys might offer help and understanding.

A stolen lantern might well find its way onto the back of a police car or hang from a street lamp. Once a lantern served as a prop for a reenactment of the "midnight ride of Paul Revere" until the "play," which was taking place at 2:00 A.M. in the center of a main street of Big Town, was interrupted by a police car several blocks away. The boys ran, leaving the lanterns on the street, and managed to avoid being apprehended.

Abandoned houses, especially if they were located in out-of-the-way places, were fair game for destruction and spontaneous vandalism. The boys would break windows, remove furniture to the yard and tear it apart, urinate on the walls and scrawl obscenities inside.

Through all the pranks, drinking and reckless driving the boys managed miraculously to avoid being stopped by police. Only twice in two years was I aware that they had been stopped by a Big City policeman. Once was for speeding (which they did every time they drove whether they were drunk or sober), and the driver managed to convince the policeman that it was simply an error. The second time they were stopped they had just left a nightclub and were walking through an alley. Aaron stopped to urinate and the boys began making obscene remarks. A foot patrolman came into the alley, lectured the boys and sent them home. Before the boys got to the car one began talking in a loud voice again. The policeman, who had followed them down the alley, arrested this boy for disturbing the peace and took him to the police station where the other Saints gathered. After paying a $5 fine, and with the assurance that there would be no permanent record of the arrest, the boy was released.

The boys had a spirit of frivolity and fun about their escapades. They did not view what they were engaged in as "delinquency," though it surely was by any reasonable definition of that word. They simply viewed themselves as having a little fun and who, they would ask, was really hurt by it? The answer had to be no one, although this fact remains one of the most difficult things to explain about the gang's behavior. Unlikely though it seems, in two years of drinking, driving, carousing and vandalism no one was seriously injured as a result of the Saints' activities.

## THE SAINTS IN SCHOOL

The Saints were highly successful in school. The average grade for the group was "B" with two of the boys having close to a straight "A" average. Almost all of the boys were popular and many of them held offices in the school. One of the boys was vice president of the student body one year. Six of the boys played on athletic teams.

At the end of their senior year, the student body selected ten seniors for special recognition as the "school wheels"; four of the ten were Saints. Teachers and school officials saw no problem with any of these boys and anticipated that they would all "make something of themselves."

How the boys managed to maintain this impression is surprising in view of their actual behavior while in school. Their technique for covering truancy was so successful that teachers did not even realize that the boys were absent from school much of the time. Occasionally, of course, the system would backfire and then the boy was on his own. A boy who was caught would be most contrite, would plead guilty and ask for mercy. He inevitably got the mercy he sought.

Cheating on examinations was rampant, even to the point of orally communicating answers to exams as well as looking at one another's papers. Since none of the group studied, and since they were primarily dependent on one another for help, it is surprising that grades were so high. Teachers contributed to the deception in their admitted inclination to give these boys (and presumably others like them) the benefit of the doubt. When asked how the boys did in school, and when pressed on specific examinations, teachers might admit that they were disappointed in John's performance, but would quickly add that they "knew that he was capable of doing better," so John was given a higher grade than he had actually earned. How often this happened is impossible to know. During the time that I observed the group, I never saw any of the boys take homework home. Teachers may have been "understanding" very regularly.

One exception to the gang's generally good performance was Jerry, who had a "C" average in his junior year, experienced disaster the next year and failed to graduate. Jerry had always been a little more nonchalant than the others about the liberties he took in school. Rather than wait for someone to come get him from class, he would offer his own excuse and leave. Although he probably did not miss any more class than most of the others in the group, he did not take the requisite pains to cover his absences. Jerry was the only Saint whom I ever heard talk back to a teacher. Although teachers often called him a "cut up" or a "smart kid," they never referred to him as a troublemaker or as a kid headed for trouble. It seems likely, then, that Jerry's failure his senior year and his mediocre performance his junior year were consequences of his not playing the game the proper way (possibly because he was disturbed by his parents' divorce). His teachers regarded him as "immature" and not quite ready to get out of high school.

## THE POLICE AND THE SAINTS

The local police saw the Saints as good boys who were among the leaders of the youth in the community. Rarely, the boys might be stopped in town for speeding or for running a stop sign. When this happened the boys were always polite, contrite and pled for mercy. As in school, they received the mercy they asked for. None ever received a ticket or was taken into the precinct by the local police.

The situation in Big City, where the boys engaged in most of their delinquency, was only slightly different. The police there did not know the boys at all, although occasionally the boys were stopped by a patrolman. Once they were caught taking a lantern from a construction site. Another time they were stopped for running a stop sign, and on several occasions they were stopped for speeding. Their behavior was as before: contrite, polite and penitent. The urban police, like the local police, accepted their demeanor as sincere. More important, the urban police were convinced that these were good boys just out for a lark.

## THE ROUGHNECKS

Hanibal townspeople never perceived the Saints' high level of delinquency. The Saints were good boys who just went in for an occasional prank. After all, they were well dressed, well mannered and had nice cars. The Roughnecks were a different story. Although the two gangs of boys were the same age, and both groups engaged in an equal amount of wild-oat sowing, everyone agreed that the not-so-well-dressed, not-so-well-mannered, not-so-rich boys were heading for trouble. Townspeople would say, "You can see the gang members at the drugstore, night after night, leaning against the storefront (sometimes drunk) or slouching around inside buying Cokes, reading magazines, and probably stealing old Mr. Wall blind. When they are outside and girls walk by, even respectable girls, these boys make suggestive remarks. Sometimes their remarks are downright lewd."

From the community's viewpoint, the real indication that these kids were in trouble was that they were constantly involved with the police. Some of them had been picked up for stealing, mostly small stuff, of course, "but still it's stealing small stuff that leads to big time crimes." "Too bad," people said. "Too bad that these boys couldn't behave like the other kids in town; stay out of trouble, be polite to adults, and look to their future."

The community's impression of the degrees to which this group of six boys (ranging in age from 16 to 19) engaged in delinquency was somewhat distorted. In some ways the gang was more delinquent than the community thought; in other ways they were less.

The fighting activities of the group were fairly readily and accurately perceived by almost everyone. At least once a month, the boys would get into some sort of fight, although most fights were scraps between members of the group or involved only one member of the group and some peripheral hanger-on. Only three times in the period of observation did the group fight together: once against a gang from across town, once against two blacks and once against a group of boys from another school. For the first two fights the group went out "looking for trouble"—and they found it both times. The third fight followed a football game and began spontaneously with an argument on the football field between one of the Roughnecks and a member of the opposition's football team.

Jack had a particular propensity for fighting and was involved in most of the brawls. He was a prime mover of the escalation of arguments into fights.

More serious than fighting, had the community been aware of it, was theft. Although almost everyone was aware that the boys occasionally stole things, they did not realize the extent of the activity. Petty stealing was a frequent event for the Roughnecks. Sometimes they stole as a group and coordinated their efforts; other times they stole in pairs. Rarely did they steal alone.

The thefts ranged from very small things like paperback books, comics and ballpoint pens to expensive items like watches. The nature of the thefts varied from time to time. The gangs would go through a period of systematically shoplifting items from automobiles or school lockers. Types of thievery varied with the whim of the gang. Some forms of thievery were more profitable than others, but all thefts were for profit, not just thrills.

Roughnecks siphoned gasoline from cars as often as they had access to an automobile, which was not very often. Unlike the Saints, who owned their own cars, the Roughnecks would have to borrow their parents' cars, an event which occurred only eight or nine times a year. The boys claimed to have stolen cars for joy rides from time to time.

Ron committed the most serious of the group's offenses. With an unidentified associate the boy attempted to burglarize a gasoline station. Although this station had been robbed twice previously in the same month, Ron denied any involvement in either of the other thefts. When Ron and his accomplice approached the station, the owner was hiding in the bushes beside the station. He fired both barrels of a double-barreled shotgun at the boys. Ron was severely injured; the other boy ran away and was never caught. Though he remained in critical condition for several months, Ron finally recovered and served six months of the following year in reform school. Upon release from reform school, Ron was put back a grade in school, and began running around with a different gang of boys. The Roughnecks considered the new gang less delinquent than themselves, and during the following year Ron had no more trouble with the police.

The Roughnecks, then, engaged mainly in three types of delinquency: theft, drinking and fighting. Although community members perceived that this gang of kids was delinquent, they mistakenly believed that their illegal activities were primarily drinking, fighting and being a nuisance to passersby. Drinking was limited among the gang members, although it did occur, and theft was much more prevalent than anyone realized.

Drinking would doubtless have been more prevalent had the boys had ready access to liquor. Since they rarely had automobiles at their disposal, they could not travel very far, and the bars in town would not serve them. Most of the boys had little money, and this, too, inhibited their purchase of alcohol. Their major source of liquor was a local drunk who would buy them a fifth if they would give him enough to buy himself a pint of whiskey or a bottle of wine.

The community's perception of drinking as prevalent stemmed from the fact that it was the most obvious delinquency the boys engaged in. When one of the boys had been drinking, even a casual observer seeing him on the corner would suspect that he was high.

There was a high level of mutual distrust and dislike between the Roughnecks and the police. The boys felt very strongly that the police were unfair and corrupt. Some evidence existed that the boys were correct in their perception.

The main source of the boys' dislike for the police undoubtedly stemmed from the fact that the police would sporadically harass the group. From the standpoint of the boys, these acts of occasional enforcement of the law were whimsical and uncalled for. It made no sense to them, for example, that the police would come to the corner occasionally and threaten them with arrest for loitering when the night before the boys had been out siphoning gasoline from cars and the police had been nowhere in sight. To the boys, the police were stupid on the one hand, for not being where they should have been and catching the boys in a serious offense, and unfair on the other hand, for trumping up "loitering" charges against them.

From the viewpoint of the police, the situation was quite different. They knew, with all the confidence necessary to be a policeman, that these boys were engaged in criminal activities. They knew this partly from occasionally catching them, mostly from circumstantial evidence ("the boys were around when those tires were slashed"), and partly because the police shared the view of the community in general that this was a bad bunch of boys. The best the police could hope to do was to be sensitive to the fact that these boys were engaged in illegal acts and arrest them whenever there was some evidence that they had been involved. Whether or not the boys had in fact committed a particular act in a particular way was not especially important. The police had a broader view; their job was to stamp out these kids' crimes; the tactics were not as important as the end result.

Over the period that the group was under observation, each member was arrested at least once. Several of the boys were arrested a number of times and spent at least one night in jail. While most were never taken to court, two of the boys were sentenced to six months' incarceration in boys' schools.

## THE ROUGHNECKS IN SCHOOL

The Roughnecks' behavior in school was not particularly disruptive. During school hours they did not all hang around together, but tended instead to spend most of their time with one or two other members of the gang who were their special buddies. Although every member of the gang attempted to avoid school as much as possible, they were not particularly successful and most of them attended school with surprising regularity. They considered school a burden—something to be gotten through with a minimum of conflict. If they were "bugged" by a particular teacher, it could lead to trouble. One of the boys, Al, once threatened to beat up a teacher and, according to the other boys, the teacher hid under a desk to escape him.

Teachers saw the boys the way the general community did, as heading for trouble, as being uninterested in making something of themselves. Some were also seen as being incapable of meeting the academic standards of the school. Most of the teachers expressed concern for this group of boys and were willing to pass them despite poor performance, in the belief that failing them would only aggravate the problem.

The group of boys had a grade point average just slightly above "C."

No one in the group failed either grade, and no one had better than a ''C'' average. They were very consistent in their perception of the boys' achievement.

Two of the boys were good football players. Herb was acknowledged to be the best player in the school and Jack was almost as good. Both boys were criticized for their failure to abide by training rules, for refusing to come to practice as often as they should, and for not playing their best during practice. What they lacked in sportsmanship they made up for in skill, apparently, and played every game no matter how poorly they had performed in practice or how many practice sessions they had missed.

## TWO QUESTIONS

Why did the community, the school and the police react to the Saints as though they were good, upstanding, nondelinquent youths with bright futures but to the Roughnecks as though they were tough, young criminals who were headed for trouble? Why did the Roughnecks and the Saints in fact have quite different careers after high school—careers which, by and large, lived up to the expectations of the community?

The most obvious explanation for the differences in the community's and law enforcement agencies' reactions to the two gangs is that one group of boys was ''more delinquent'' than the other. Which group *was* more delinquent? The answer to this question will determine in part how we explain the differential responses to these groups by the members of the community and, particularly, by law enforcement and school officials.

In sheer number of illegal acts, the Saints were the more delinquent. They were truant from school for at least part of the day almost every day of the week. In addition, their drinking and vandalism occurred with surprising regularity. The Roughnecks, in contrast, engaged sporadically in delinquent episodes. While these episodes were frequent, they certainly did not occur on a daily or even a weekly basis.

The difference in frequency of offenses was probably caused by the Roughnecks' inability to obtain liquor and to manipulate legitimate excuses from school. Since the Roughnecks had less money than the Saints, and teachers carefully supervised their school activities, the Roughnecks' hearts may have been as black as the Saints', but their misdeeds were not nearly as frequent.

There are really no clear-cut criteria by which to measure qualitative differences in antisocial behavior. The most important dimension is generally referred to as the ''seriousness'' of the offenses.

If seriousness encompasses the relative economic costs of delinquent acts, then some assessment can be made. The Roughnecks probably stole an average of about $5 worth of goods a week. Some weeks the figure was considerably higher, but these times must be balanced against long periods when almost nothing was stolen.

The Saints were more continuously engaged in delinquency but their acts were not for the most part costly to property. Only their vandalism and occasional theft of gasoline would so qualify. Perhaps once or twice a month they would siphon a tankful of gas. The other costly items were street signs, construction lanterns and the like. All of these acts combined probably did not quite average $5 a week, partly because much of the stolen equipment was abandoned and presumably could be recovered. The difference in cost of stolen property between the two groups was trivial, but the Roughnecks probably had a slightly more expensive set of activities than did the Saints.

Another meaning of seriousness is the potential threat of physical harm to members of the community and to the boys themselves. The Roughnecks were more prone to physical violence; they not only welcomed an opportunity to fight; they went seeking it. In addition, they fought among themselves frequently. Although the fighting never included deadly weapons, it was still a menace, however minor, to the physical safety of those involved.

The Saints never fought. They avoided physical conflict both inside and outside the group. At the same time, though, the Saints frequently endangered their own and other people's lives. They did so almost every time they drove a car, especially if they had been drinking. Sober, their driving was risky; under the influence of alcohol it was horrendous. In addition, the Saints endangered the lives of others with their pranks. Street excavations left unmarked were a very serious hazard.

Evaluating the relative seriousness of the two gangs' activities is difficult. The community reacted as though the behavior of the Roughnecks was a problem, and they reacted as though the behavior of the Saints was not. But the members of the community were ignorant of the array of delinquent acts that characterized the Saints' behavior. Although concerned citizens were unaware of much of the Roughnecks' behavior as well, they were much better informed about the Roughnecks' involvement in delinquency than they were about the Saints'.

## VISIBILITY

Differential treatment of the two gangs resulted in part because one gang was infinitely more visible than the other. This differential visibility was a direct function of the economic standing of the families. The Saints had access to automobiles and were able to remove themselves from the sight of the community. In as routine a decision as to where to go to have a milkshake after school, the Saints stayed away from the mainstream of community life. Lacking transportation, the Roughnecks could not make it to the edge of town. The center of town was the only practical place for them to meet since their homes were scattered throughout the town and any noncentral meeting place put an undue hardship on some members. Through necessity the Roughnecks congregated in a crowded area where everyone in the community passed frequently, including teachers and law enforcement officers. They could easily see the Roughnecks hanging around the drugstore.

The Roughnecks, of course, made themselves even more visible by making remarks to passersby and by occasionally getting into fights on the corner. Meanwhile, just as regularly, the Saints were either at the cafe on one edge of town or in the pool hall at the other edge of town. Without any particular realization that they were making themselves inconspicuous, the Saints were able to hide their time-wasting. Not only were they removed from the mainstream of traffic, but they were almost always inside a building.

On their escapades the Saints were also relatively invisible, since they left Hanibal and traveled to Big City. Here, too, they were mobile, roaming the city, rarely going to the same area twice.

## DEMEANOR

To the notion of visibility must be added the difference in the responses of group members to outside intervention with their activities. If one of the Saints was confronted with an accusing policeman, even if he felt he was truly innocent of a wrongdoing, his demeanor was apologetic and penitent. A Roughnecks' attitude was almost the polar opposite. When confronted with a threatening adult authority, even one who tried to be pleasant, the Roughneck's hostility and disdain were clearly observable. Sometimes he might attempt to put up a veneer of respect, but it was thin and was not accepted as sincere by the authority.

School was no different from the community at large. The Saints could manipulate the system by feigning compliance with the school norms. The availability of cars at school meant that once free from the immediate sight of the teacher, the boys could disappear rapidly. And this escape was well enough planned that no administrator or teacher was nearby when the boys left. A Roughneck who wished to escape for a few hours was in a bind. If it were possible to get free from class, downtown was still a mile away, and even if he arrived there, he was still very visible. Truancy for the Roughnecks meant almost certain detection, while the Saints enjoyed almost complete immunity from sanctions.

## BIAS

Community members were not aware of the transgressions of the Saints. Even if the Saints had been less discreet, their favorite delinquencies would have been perceived as less serious than those of the Roughnecks.

In the eyes of the police and school officials, a boy who drinks in an alley and stands intoxicated on the street corner is committing a more serious offense than is a boy who drinks to inebriation in a nightclub or a tavern and drives around afterwards in a car. Similarly, a boy who steals a wallet from a store will be viewed as having committed a more serious offense than a boy who steals a lantern from a construction site.

Perceptual bias also operates with respect to the demeanor of the boys in the two groups when they are confronted by adults. It is not simply that adults dislike the posture affected by boys of the Roughneck ilk; more important is the conviction that the posture adopted by the Roughnecks is an indication of their devotion and commitment to deviance as a way of life. The posture becomes a cue, just as the type of the offense is a cue, to the degree to which the known transgressions are indicators of the youths' potential for other problems.

Visibility, demeanor and bias are surface variables which explain the day-to-day operations of the police. Why do these surface variables operate as they do? Why did the police choose to disregard the Saints' delinquencies while breathing down the backs of the Roughnecks?

The answer lies in the class structure of American society and the control of legal institutions by those at the top of the class structure. Obviously, no representative of the upper class drew up the operational chart for the police which led them to look in the ghettoes and on street corners—which led them to see the demeanor of lower-class youth as troublesome and that of upper-middle-class youth as tolerable. Rather, the procedures simply developed from experience—experience with irate and influential upper-middle-class parents insisting that their son's vandalism was simply a prank and his drunkenness only a momentary "sowing of wild oats"—experience with cooperative or indifferent, powerless, lower-class parents who acquiesced to the laws' definition of their son's behavior.

## ADULT CAREERS OF THE SAINTS AND THE ROUGHNECKS

The community's confidence in the potential of the Saints and the Roughnecks apparently was justified. If anything, the community members underestimated the degree to which these youngsters would turn out "good" or "bad."

Seven of the eight members of the Saints went on to college immediately after high school. Five of the boys graduated from college in four years. The sixth one finished college after two years in the army, and the seventh spent four years in the air force before returning to college and receiving a B.A. degree. Of these seven college graduates, three went on for advanced degrees. One finished law school and is now active in state politics, one finished medical school and is practicing near Hanibal, and one boy is now working for a Ph.D. The other four college graduates entered submanagerial, managerial or executive training positions with large firms.

The only Saint who did not complete college was Jerry. Jerry had failed to graduate from high school with the other Saints. During his second senior year, after the other Saints had gone on to college, Jerry began to hang around with what several teachers described as a "rough crowd"— the gang that was heir apparent to the Roughnecks. At the end of his second senior year, when he did graduate from high school, Jerry took a job as a used-car salesman, got married and quickly had a child. Although he made several abortive attempts to go to college by attending night school, when I last saw him (ten years after high school) Jerry was unemployed and had been living on unemployment for almost a year. His wife worked as a waitress.

Some of the Roughnecks have lived up to community expectations. A number of them were headed for trouble. A few were not.

Jack and Herb were the athletes among the Roughnecks and their athletic prowess paid off handsomely. Both boys received unsolicited athletic scholarships to college. After Herb received his scholarship (near the end of his senior year), he apparently did an about-face. His demeanor became very similar to that of the Saints. Although he remained a member in good standing of the Roughnecks, he stopped participating in most activities and did not hang around on the corner as often.

Jack did not change. If anything, he became more prone to fighting. He even made excuses for accepting the scholarship. He told the other gang members that the school had guaranteed him a "C" average if he would come to play football—an idea that seems far-fetched, even in this day of highly competitive recruiting.

During the summer after graduation from high school, Jack attempted suicide by jumping from a tall building. The jump would certainly have killed most people trying it, but Jack survived. He entered college in the fall and played four years of football. He and Herb graduated in four years, and both are teaching and coaching in high schools. They are married and have stable families. If anything, Jack appears to have a more prestigious position in the community than does Herb, though both are well respected and secure in their positions.

Two of the boys never finished high school. Tommy left at the end of his junior year and went to another state. That summer he was arrested and placed on probation on a manslaughter charge. Three years later he was arrested for murder; he pleaded guilty to second degree murder and is serving a 30-year sentence in the state penitentiary.

Al, the other boy who did not finish high school, also left the state in his senior year. He is serving a life sentence in a state penitentiary for first degree murder.

Wes is a small-time gambler. He finished high school and "bummed around." After several years he made contact with a bookmaker who employed him as a runner. Later he acquired his own area and has been working it ever since. His position among the bookmakers is almost identical to the position he had in the gang; he is always around but no one is really aware of him. He makes no trouble and he does not get into any. Steady, reliable, capable of keeping his mouth closed, he plays the game by the rules, even though the game is an illegal one.

That leaves only Ron. Some of his former friends reported that they had heard he was "driving a truck up north," but no one could provide any concrete information.

## REINFORCEMENT

The community responded to the Roughnecks as boys in trouble, and the boys agreed with that perception. Their pattern of deviancy was reinforced, and breaking away from it became increasingly unlikely. Once the boys acquired an image of themselves as deviants, they selected new friends who affirmed that self-image. As that self-conception became more firmly entrenched, they also became willing to try new and more extreme deviances. With their growing alienation came freer expression of disrespect and hostility for representatives of the legitimate society. This disrespect increased the community's negativism, perpetuating the entire process of commitment to deviance. Lack of a commitment to deviance works the same way. In either case, the process will perpetuate itself unless some event (like a scholarship to college or a sudden failure) external to the established relationship intervenes. For two of the Roughnecks (Herb and Jack), receiving college athletic scholarships created new relations and culminated in a break with the established pattern of deviance. In the case of one of the Saints (Jerry), his parents' divorce and his failing to graduate from high school changed some of his other relations. Being held back in school for a year and losing his place among the Saints had sufficient impact on Jerry to alter his self-image and virtually to assure that he would not go on to college as his peers did. Although the experiments of life can rarely be reversed, it seems likely in view of the behavior of the other boys who did not enjoy this special treatment by the school that Jerry, too, would have "become something" had he graduated as anticipated. For Herb and Jack outside intervention worked to their advantage, for Jerry it was his undoing.

Selective perception and labeling—finding, processing and punishing some kinds of criminality and not others—means that visible, poor, non-mobile, outspoken, undiplomatic "tough" kids will be noticed, whether their actions are seriously delinquent or not. Other kids, who have established a reputation for being bright (even though underachieving), disciplined and involved in respectable activities, who are mobile and monied, will be invisible when they deviate from sanctioned activities. They'll sow their wild oats—perhaps even wider and thicker than their lower-class cohorts—but they won't be noticed. When it's time to leave adolescence most will follow the expected path, settling into the ways of the middle class, remembering fondly the delinquent but unnoticed fling of their youth. The Roughnecks and others like them may turn around, too. It is more likely that their noticeable deviance will have been so reinforced by police and community that their lives will be effectively channeled into careers consistent with their adolescent background.

# Review Questions

1. What were the typical activities of the Saints? The Roughnecks? Which group committed more illegal acts?

2. Were the community's perceptions of the Saints accurate? Were the community's perceptions of the Roughnecks accurate? What role did the *visibility* of the two groups play in the community's perceptions of them?

3. How did the social-class backgrounds of the Saints and the Roughnecks affect their visibility to adult members of the community?

4. Why is it important to understand "surface variables"—visibility, demeanor, and bias—to explain the actions of the police?

5. How does Chambliss's research demonstrate the usefulness of looking beyond commonly accepted explanations of social life?

# MEN AND JOBS
# ON TALLY'S CORNER

## Elliot Liebow

IN SUMMARY OF OBJECTIVE JOB CONSIDERATIONS [OF STREETCORNER MEN], the most important fact is that a man who is able and willing to work cannot earn enough money to support himself, his wife, and one or more children. A man's chances for working regularly are good only if he is willing to work for less than he can live on, and sometimes not even then. On some jobs, the wage rate is deceptively higher than on others, but the higher the wage rate, the more difficult it is to get the job, and the less the job security. Higher-paying construction work tends to be seasonal and, during the season, the amount of work available is highly sensitive to business and weather conditions and to the changing requirements of individual projects.[1] Moreover, high-paying construction jobs are frequently beyond the physical capacity of some of the men, and some of the low-paying jobs are scaled down even lower in accordance with the self-fulfilling assumption that the man will steal part of his wages on the job.[2]

Bernard assesses the objective job situation dispassionately over a cup of coffee, sometimes poking at the coffee with his spoon, sometimes staring at it as if, like a crystal ball, it holds tomorrow's secrets. He is twenty-seven years old. He and the woman with whom he lives have a baby son, and she has another child by another man. Bernard does odd jobs—mostly painting—but here it is the end of January, and his last job was with the Post Office during the Christmas mail rush. It pays well (about $2 an hour) but he has twice failed the Post Office examination (he graduated from a Washington high school) and has given up the idea as an impractical one. He is supposed to see a man tonight about a job as a parking attendant for a large apartment house. The man told him to bring his birth certificate and driver's license, but his license was suspended because of a backlog of unpaid traffic fines. A friend promised to lend him some money this evening. If he gets it, he will pay the fines tomorrow morning and have his license reinstated. He hopes the man with the job will wait till tomorrow night.

Elliot Liebow, "Men and Jobs," in Elliot Liebow, *Tally's Corner: A Study of Negro Streetcorner Men* (Boston: Little, Brown, 1967), pp. 50–71.

A "security job" is what he really wants, he said. He would like to save up money for a taxicab. (But having twice failed the postal examination and having a bad driving record as well, it is highly doubtful that he could meet the qualifications or pass the written test.) That would be "a good life." He can always get a job in a restaurant or as a clerk in a drugstore but they don't pay enough, he said. He needs to take home at least $50 to $55 a week. He thinks he can get that much driving a truck somewhere. . . . Sometimes he wishes he had stayed in the army. . . . A security job, that's what he wants most of all, a real security job. . . .

When we look at what the men bring to the job rather than at what the job offers the men, it is essential to keep in mind that we are not looking at men who come to the job fresh, just out of school perhaps, and newly prepared to undertake the task of making a living, or from another job where they earned a living and are prepared to do the same on this job. Each man comes to the job with a long job history characterized by his not being able to support himself and his family. Each man carries this knowledge, born of his experience, with him. He comes to the job flat and stale, wearied by the sameness of it all, convinced of his own incompetence, terrified of responsibility—of being tested still again and found wanting. Possible exceptions are the younger men not yet, or just, married. They suspect all this but have yet to have it confirmed by repeated personal experience over time. But those who are or have been married know it well. It is the experience of the individual and the group; of their fathers and probably their sons. Convinced of their inadequacies, not only do they not seek out those few better-paying jobs which test their resources, but they actively avoid them, gravitating in a mass to the menial, routine jobs which offer no challenge—and therefore pose no threat—to the already diminished images they have of themselves.

Thus Richard does not follow through on [a] real estate agent's offer. He is afraid to do on his own—minor plastering, replacing broken windows, other minor repairs and painting—exactly what he had been doing for months on a piece-work basis under someone else (and which provided him with a solid base from which to derive a cost estimate).

Richard once offered an important clue to what may have gone on in his mind when the job offer was made. We were in the Carry-out, at a time when he was looking for work. He was talking about the kind of jobs available to him.

> I graduated from high school [Baltimore] but I don't know anything. I'm dumb. Most of the time I don't even say I graduated, 'cause then somebody asks me a question and I can't answer it, and they think I was lying about graduating. . . .They graduated me but I didn't know anything. I had lousy grades but I guess they wanted to get rid of me.
>
> I was at Margaret's house the other night and her little sister asked me to help her with her homework. She showed me some fractions and I knew right

away I couldn't do them. I was ashamed so I told her I had to go to the bathroom.

And so it must have been, surely, with the real estate agent's offer. Convinced that "I'm dumb. . . I don't know anything," he "knew right away" he couldn't do it, despite the fact that he had been doing just this sort of work all along.

Thus, the man's low self-esteem generates a fear of being tested and prevents him from accepting a job with responsibilities or, once on a job, from staying with it if responsibilities are thrust on him, even if the wages are commensurately higher. Richard refuses such a job, Leroy leaves one, and another man, given more responsibility and more pay, knows he will fail and proceeds to do so, proving he was right about himself all along. The self-fulfilling prophecy is everywhere at work. In a hallway, Stanton, Tonk and Boley are passing a bottle around. Stanton recalls the time he was in the service. Everything was fine until he attained the rank of corporal. He worried about everything he did then. Was he doing the right thing? Was he doing it well? When would they discover their mistake and take his stripes (and extra pay) away? When he finally lost his stripes, everything was all right again.

Lethargy, disinterest and general apathy on the job, so often reported by employers, has its streetcorner counterpart. The men do not ordinarily talk about their jobs or ask one another about them.[3] Although most of the men know who is or is not working at any given time, they may or may not know what particular job an individual man has. There is no overt interest in job specifics as they relate to this or that person, in large part perhaps because the specifics are not especially relevant. To know that a man is working is to know approximately how much he makes and to know as much as one needs or wants to know about how he makes it. After all, how much difference does it make to know whether a man is pushing a mop and pulling trash in an apartment house, a restaurant, or an office building, or delivering groceries, drugs, or liquor, or, if he's a laborer, whether he's pushing a wheelbarrow, mixing mortar, or digging a hole. So much does one job look like every other that there is little to choose between them. In large part, the job market consists of a narrow range of nondescript chores calling for nondistinctive, undifferentiated, unskilled labor. "A job is a job."

A crucial factor in the streetcorner man's lack of job commitment is the overall value he places on the job. *For his part, the streetcorner man puts no lower value on the job than does the larger society around him.* He knows the social value of the job by the amount of money the employer is willing to pay him for doing it. In a real sense, every pay day, he counts in dollars and cents the value placed on the job by society at large. He is no more (and frequently less) ready to quit and look for another job than his employer is ready to fire him and look for another man. Neither the streetcorner man who performs these jobs nor the society which requires him to perform them assesses the job as one "worth doing and worth doing well." Both employee and employer are contemptuous of the job. The employee shows his contempt by his reluctance to accept it or keep it, the employer by paying less than is required to support a family.[4] Nor does the low-wage job offer prestige, respect, interesting work, opportunity for learning or advancement, or any other compensation. With few exceptions, jobs filled by the streetcorner men are at the bottom of the employment ladder in every respect, from wage level to prestige. Typically, they are hard, dirty, uninteresting and underpaid. The rest of society (whatever its ideal values regarding the dignity of labor) holds the job of the dishwasher or janitor or unskilled laborer in low esteem if not outright contempt.[5] So does the streetcorner man. He cannot do otherwise. He cannot draw from a job those social values which other people do not put into it.[6]

Only occasionally does spontaneous conversation touch on these matters directly. Talk about jobs is usually limited to isolated statements of intention, such as "I think I'll get me another gig [job]," "I'm going to look for a construction job when the weather breaks," or "I'm going to quit. I can't take no more of this shit." Job assessments typically consist of nothing more than a noncommittal shrug and "It's O.K." or "It's a job."

One reason for the relative absence of talk about one's job is, as suggested earlier, that the sameness of job experiences does not bear reiteration. Another and more important reason is the emptiness of the job experience itself. The man sees middle-class occupations as a primary source of prestige, pride and self-respect; his own job affords him none of these. To think about his job is to see himself as others see him, to remind him of just where he stands in this society.[7] And because society's criteria for placement are generally the same as his own, to talk about his job can trigger a flush of shame and a deep, almost physical ache to change places with someone, almost anyone, else.[8] The desire to be a person in his own right, to be noticed by the world he lives in, is shared by each of the men on the streetcorner. Whether they articulate this desire (as Tally does below) or not, one can see them position themselves to catch the attention of their fellows in much the same way as plants bend or stretch to catch the sunlight.[9]

Tally and I were in the Carry-out. It was summer, Tally's peak earning season as a cement finisher, a semiskilled job a cut or so above that of the unskilled laborer. His take-home pay during these weeks was well over a hundred dollars—"a lot of bread." But for Tally, who no longer had a family to support, bread was not enough.

> "You know that boy came in last night? That Black Moozlem? That's what I ought to be doing. I ought to be in his place."

"What do you mean?"

"Dressed nice, going to [night] school, got a good job."

"He's no better than you, Tally. You make more than he does."

"It's not the money. [Pause] It's position, I guess. He's got position. When he finish school he gonna be a supervisor. People respect him. . . . Thinking about people with position and education gives me a feeling right here [pressing his fingers into the pit of his stomach]."

"You're educated, too. You have a skill, a trade. You're a cement finisher. You can make a building, pour a sidewalk."

"That's different. Look, can anybody do what you're doing? Can anybody just come up and do your job? Well, in one week I can teach you cement finishing. You won't be as good as me 'cause you won't have the experience but you'll be a cement finisher. That's what I mean. Anybody can do what I'm doing and that's what gives me this feeling. [Long pause] Suppose I like this girl. I go over to her house and I meet her father. He starts talking about what he done today. He talks about operating on somebody and sewing them up and about surgery. I knows he's a doctor 'cause of the way he talks. Then she starts talking about what she did. Maybe she's a boss or a supervisor. Maybe she's a lawyer and her father says to me, 'And what do you do, Mr. Jackson?'' [Pause] You remember at the courthouse, Lonny's trial? You and the lawyer was talking in the hall? You remember? I just stood there listening. I didn't say a word. You know why? 'Cause I didn't even know what you was talking about. That's happened to me a lot."

"Hell, you're nothing special. That happens to everybody. Nobody knows everything. One man is a doctor, so he talks about surgery. Another man is a teacher, so he talks about books. But doctors and teachers don't know anything about concrete. You're a cement finisher and that's your specialty."

"Maybe so, but when was the last time you saw anybody standing around talking about concrete?"

The streetcorner man wants to be a person in his own right, to be noticed, to be taken account of, but in this respect, as well as in meeting his money needs, his job fails him. The job and the man are even. The job fails the man and the man fails the job.

Furthermore, the man does not have any reasonable expectation that, however bad it is, his job will lead to better things. Menial jobs are not, by and large, the starting point of a track system which leads to even better jobs for those who are able and willing to do them. The busboy or dishwasher in a restaurant is not on a job track which, if negotiated skillfully, leads to chef or manager of the restaurant. The busboy or dishwasher who works hard becomes, simply, a hard-working busboy or dishwasher. Neither hard work nor perseverance can conceivably carry the janitor to a sit-down job in the office building he cleans up. And it is the apprentice who becomes the journeyman electrician, plumber, steam fitter or bricklayer, not the common unskilled Negro laborer.

Thus, the job is not a stepping-stone to something better. It is a dead end. It promises to deliver no more tomorrow, next month or next year than it does today.

Delivering little, and promising no more, the job is "no big thing." The man appears to treat the job in a cavalier fashion, working and not working as the spirit moves him, as if all that matters is the immediate satisfaction of his present appetites, the surrender to present moods, and the indulgence of whims with no thought for the cost, the consequences, the future. To the middle-class observer, this behavior reflects a "present-time orientation"—an "inability to defer gratification." It is this "present-time" orientation—as against the "future orientation" of the middle-class person—that "explains" to the outsider why Leroy chooses to spend the day at the Carry-out rather than report to work; why Richard, who was paid Friday, was drunk Saturday and Sunday and penniless Monday; why Sweets quit his job today because the boss looked at him "funny" yesterday.

But from the inside looking out, what appears as a "present-time" orientation to the outside observer is, to the man experiencing it, as much a future orientation as that of his middle-class counterpart.[10] The difference between the two men lies not so much in their different orientations to time as in their different orientations to future time or, more specifically, to their different futures.[11]

The future orientation of the middle-class person presumes, among other things, a surplus of resources to be invested in the future and a belief that the future will be sufficiently stable both to justify his investment (money in a bank, time and effort in a job, investment of himself in marriage and family, etc.) and to permit the consumption of his investment at a time, place and manner of his own choosing and to his greater satisfaction. But the streetcorner man lives in a sea of want. He does not, as a rule, have a surplus of resources, either economic or psychological. Gratification of hunger and the desire for simple creature comforts cannot be long deferred. Neither can support for one's flagging self-esteem. Living on the edge of both economic and psychological subsistence, the streetcorner man is obliged to expend all his resources on maintaining himself from moment to moment.[12]

As for the future, the young streetcorner man has a fairly good picture of it. In Richard or Sea Cat or Arthur he can see himself in his middle twenties; he can look at Tally to see himself at thirty, at Wee Tom to see himself in his middle thirties, and at Budder and Stanton to see himself in his forties. It is a future in which everything is uncertain except the ultimate destruction of his hopes and the eventual realization of his fears. The most he can reasonably look forward to is that these things do not come too soon. Thus, when Richard squanders a week's pay in two days it is not because, like an animal or a child, he is "present-time oriented," unaware of or unconcerned with his future. He does so precisely because he is aware of the future and the hopelessness of it all.

Sometimes this kind of response appears as a conscious, explicit choice. Richard had had a violent argument with his wife. He said he was going to leave her and the children, that he had had enough of everything and could not take any more, and he chased her out of the house. His chest still heaving, he leaned back against the wall in the hallway of his basement apartment.

> "I've been scuffling for five years," he said. "I've been scuffling for five years from morning till night. And my kids still don't have anything, my wife don't have anything, and I don't have anything.
>
> "There," he said, gesturing down the hall to a bed, a sofa, a couple of chairs and a television set, all shabby, some broken. "There's everything I have and I'm having trouble holding onto that."
>
> Leroy came in, presumably to petition Richard on behalf of Richard's wife, who was sitting outside on the steps, afraid to come in. Leroy started to say something but Richard cut him short.
>
> "Look, Leroy, don't give me any of that action. You and me are entirely different people. Maybe I look like a boy and maybe I act like a boy sometimes but I got a man's mind. You and me don't want the same things out of life. Maybe some of the same, but you don't care how long you have to wait for yours and I—want—mine—right—now."[13]

Thus, apparent present-time concerns with consumption and indulgences—material and emotional—reflect a future-time orientation. "I want mine right now" is ultimately a cry of despair, a direct response to the future as he sees it.[14]

In many instances, it is precisely the streetcorner man's orientation to the future—but to a future loaded with "trouble"—which not only leads to a greater emphasis on present concerns ("I want mine right now") but also contributes importantly to the instability of employment, family and friend relationships, and to the general transient quality of daily life.

Let me give some concrete examples. One day, after Tally had gotten paid, he gave me four twenty-dollar bills and asked me to keep them for him. Three days later he asked me for the money. I returned it and asked why he did not put his money in a bank. He said that the banks close at two o'clock. I argued that there were four or more banks within a two-block radius of where he was working at the time and that he could easily get to any one of them on his lunch hour. "No, man," he said, "you don't understand. They close at two o'clock and they closed Saturday and Sunday. Suppose I get into trouble and I got to make it [leave]. Me get out of town, and everything I got in the world layin' up in that bank? No good! No good!"

In another instance, Leroy and his girl friend were discussing "trouble." Leroy was trying to decide how best to go about getting his hands on some "long green" (a lot of money), and his girl friend cautioned him about "trouble." Leroy sneered at this, saying he had had "trouble" all his life and wasn't afraid of a little more. "Anyway," he said, "I'm famous for leaving town."[15]

Thus, the constant awareness of a future loaded with "trouble" results in a constant readiness to leave, to "make it," to "get out of town," and discourages the man from sinking roots into the world he lives in.[16] Just as it discourages him from putting money in the bank, so it discourages him from committing himself to a job, especially one whose payoff lies in the promise of future rewards rather than in the present. In the same way, it discourages him from deep and lasting commitments to family and friends or to any other persons, places or things, since such commitments could hold him hostage, limiting his freedom of movement and thereby compromising his security which lies in that freedom.

. . . The streetcorner man is under continuous assault by his job experiences and job fears. His experiences and fears feed on one another. The kind of job he can get—and frequently only after fighting for it, if then— steadily confirms his fears, depresses his self-confidence and self-esteem until finally, terrified of an opportunity even if one presents itself, he stands defeated by his experiences, his belief in his own self-worth destroyed and his fears a confirmed reality.

## NOTES

1. The overall result is that, in the long run, a Negro laborer's earnings are not substantially greater—and may be less—than those of the busboy, janitor, or stock clerk. Herman P. Miller, for example, reports that in 1960, 40 percent of all jobs held by Negro men were as laborers or in the service trades. The average annual wage for nonwhite nonfarm laborers was $2,400. The average earning of nonwhite service workers was $2,500 (*Rich Man, Poor Man*, p. 90). Francis Greenfield estimates that in the Washington vicinity, the 1965 earnings of the union laborer who works whenever work is available will be about $3,200. Even this figure is high for the man on the streetcorner. Union men in heavy construction are the aristocrats of the laborers. Casual day labor and jobs with small firms in the building and construction trades, or with firms in other industries, pay considerably less.

2. For an excellent discussion of the self-fulfilling assumption (or prophecy) as a social force, see "The Self-Fulfilling Prophecy," Ch. XI, in Robert K. Merton's *Social Theory and Social Structure* (Glencoe, Ill.: Free Press, 1957).

3. This stands in dramatic contrast to the leisure-time conversation of stable, working-class men. For the coal miners (of Ashton, England), for example, "the topic [of conversation] which surpasses all others in frequency is work—the difficulties which have been encountered in the day's shift, the way in which a particular task was accomplished, and so on." Josephine Klein, *Samples from English Cultures*, Vol. 1 (London: Routledge and Kegan Paul, 1956), p. 88.

4. It is important to remember that the employer is not entirely a free agent. Subject to the constraints of the larger society, he acts for the larger society as well as for himself. Child labor laws, safety and sanitation regulations, minimum wage scales in some employment areas, and other constraints, are already on the books; other control mechanisms, such as a guaranteed annual wage, are to be had for the voting.

5. See, for example, the U.S. Bureau of the Census, *Methodology and Scores of Socioeconomic Status.* The assignment of the lowest SES ratings to men who hold such jobs is not peculiar to our own society. A low SES rating for "the shoeshine boy or garbage man . . . seems to be true for all [industrial] countries." Alex Inkeles, "Industrial Man," *American Journal of Sociology* 66 (July 1960), p. 8.

6. That the streetcorner man downgrades manual labor should occasion no surprise. Merton points out that "the American stigmatization of manual labor . . . *has been found to hold rather uniformly in all social classes*" (emphasis in original; *Social Theory and Social Structure*, p. 145). That he finds no satisfaction in such work should also occasion no surprise: "[There is] a clear positive correlation between the overall status of occupations and the experience of satisfaction in them." Inkeles, "Industrial Man," *American Journal of Sociology* 66 (July 1960), p. 12.

7. "[In our society] a man's work is one of the things by which he is judged, and certainly one of the more significant things by which he judges himself. . . . A man's work is one of the more important parts of his social identity, of his self; indeed, of his fate in the one life he has to live." Everett C. Hughes, *Men and Their Work* (Glencoe, Ill.: Free Press, 1958), pp. 42–43.

8. Noting that lower-class persons "are constantly exposed to evidence of their own irrelevance," Lee Rainwater spells out still another way in which the poor are poor: "The identity problems of lower-class persons make the soul-searching of middle-class adolescents and adults seem rather like a kind of conspicuous consumption of psychic riches," "Work and Identity in the Lower Class," in Sam Bass Warner, Jr., *Planning for a Nation of Cities* (Cambridge: Cambridge Univ. Press, forthcoming), p. 3.

9. Sea Cat cuts his pants legs off at the calf and puts a fringe on the raggedy edges. Tonk breaks his "shades" and continues to wear the horn-rimmed frames minus the lenses. Richard cultivates a distinctive manner of speech. Lonny gives himself a birthday party. And so on.

10. Taking a somewhat different point of view, S. M. Miller and Frank Riessman suggest that "the entire concept of deferred gratification may be inappropriate to understanding the essence of workers' lives," "The Working Class Subculture: A New View," *Social Problems* 9 (1961), p. 87.

11. This sentence is a paraphrase of a statement made by Marvin Cline at a 1965 colloquium at the Mental Health Study Center, National Institute of Mental Health.

12. And if, for the moment, he does sometimes have more money than he chooses to spend or more food than he wants to eat, he is pressed to spend the money and eat the food anyway since his friends, neighbors, kinsmen, or acquaintances will beg or borrow whatever surplus he has or, failing this, they may steal it. In one extreme case, one of the men admitted taking the last of a woman's surplus food allotment after she had explained that, with four children, she could not spare any food. The prospect that consumer soft goods not consumed by oneself will be consumed by someone else may be related to the way in which portable consumer durable goods, such as watches, radios, television sets or phonographs, are sometimes looked at as a form of savings. When Shirley was on welfare, she regularly took her television set out of pawn when she got her monthly check. Not so much to watch it, she explained, as to have something to fall back on when her money runs out toward the end of the month. For her and

others, the television set or phonograph is her savings, the pawnshop is where she banks her savings, and the pawn ticket is her bankbook.

13. This was no simple rationalization for irresponsibility. Richard had indeed "been scuffling for five years" trying to keep his family going. Until shortly after this episode, Richard was known and respected as one of the hardest-working men on the street. Richard had said, only a couple of months earlier, "I figure you got to get out there and try. You got to try before you can get anything." His wife Shirley confirmed that he had always tried. "If things get tough, with me I'll get all worried. But Richard get worried, he don't want to see me worried. . . . He *will* get out there. He's shoveled snow, picked beans, and he's done some of everything. . . . He's not ashamed to get out there and get us something to eat." At the time of the episode reported above, Leroy was just starting marriage and raising a family. He and Richard were not, as Richard thought, "entirely different people." Leroy had just not learned, by personal experience over time, what Richard had learned. But within two years Leroy's marriage had broken up and he was talking and acting like Richard. "He just let go completely," said one of the men on the street.

14. There is no mystically intrinsic connection between "present-time" orientation and lower-class persons. Whenever people of whatever class have been uncertain, skeptical or downright pessimistic about the future, "I want mine right now" has been one of the characteristic responses, although it is usually couched in more delicate terms: e.g., Omar Khayyam's "Take the cash and let the credit go," or Horace's "*Carpe diem.*" In wartime, especially, all classes tend to slough off conventional restraints on sexual and other behavior (i.e., become less able or less willing to defer gratification). And when inflation threatens, darkening the fiscal future, persons who formerly husbanded their resources with commendable restraint almost stampede one another rushing to spend their money. Similarly, it seems that future-time orientation tends to collapse toward the present when persons are in pain or under stress. The point here is that, the label notwithstanding, (what passes for) present-time orientation appears to be a situation-specific phenomenon rather than a part of the standard psychic equipment of Cognitive Lower Class Man.

15. And proceeded to do just that the following year when "trouble"—in this case, a grand jury indictment, a pile of debts, and a violent separation from his wife and children—appeared again.

16. For a discussion of "trouble" as a focal concern of lower-class culture, see Walter Miller, "Lower Class Culture as a Generating Milieu of Gang Delinquency," *Journal of Social Issues* 14 (1958), pp. 7, 8.

# Review Questions

1. According to Liebow, for the streetcorner man, the job fails the man, and the man fails the job. Discuss this statement and give specific examples that support or refute it.

2. Describe Liebow's assessment of the present-time and future-time

orientations of streetcorner men. Are there any indications that middle-class people are not always future-time oriented?

3. How do our society's sex roles contribute to the streetcorner men's feelings of failure?

4. Describe the sociological concept of self-fulfilling prophecy and give examples from Liebow's study of streetcorner men.

# THE DIVORCE REVOLUTION
# THE FEMINIZATION OF POVERTY

## Lenore J. Weitzman

## INTRODUCTION

[STATES HAVE VARIED GREATLY THROUGH OUR COUNTRY'S HISTORY IN BOTH the types of divorce laws they have and how the laws are interpreted by judges. California pioneered in introducing a "no-fault" divorce law in 1970. The law is based on the modern idea that spouses can agree to divorce rather than fighting an adversarial battle in a court. In interpreting the new law, judges are not so quick to protect women as they once were. They award women alimony even more rarely than in the past. At the same time, the courts continue to give mothers primary responsibility for rearing children. Thus, the new law and its interpretation have contributed to a widening gender gap in income.]

Divorce has radically different economic consequences for men and women. While most divorced men find that their standard of living improves after divorce, most divorced women and the minor children in their households find that their standard of living plummets. This [article] shows that when income is compared to needs, divorced men experience an average 42 percent rise in their standard of living in the first year after the divorce, while divorced women (and their children) experience a 73 percent decline.

These apparently simple statistics have far-reaching social and economic consequences. For most women and children, divorce means precipitous downward mobility—both economically and socially. The reduction in income brings residential moves and inferior housing, drastically diminished or nonexistent funds for recreation and leisure, and intense pressures due to inadequate time and money. Financial hardships in turn cause social dislocation and a loss of familiar networks for emotional support and social services, and intensify the psychological stress for women and children alike. On a societal level, divorce increases female and child poverty and creates an ever-widening gap between the economic well-being of divorced men, on the one hand, and their children and former wives on the other.

Excerpted from chapter 10 of Lenore J. Weitzman, *The Divorce Revolution: The Unexpected Consequences for Women and Children in America*. (New York: Free Press, 1985), pp. 323–324, 330–332, 337–343, 350–356.

The data reviewed in this [article] indict the present legal system of divorce: it provides neither economic justice nor economic equality.

The economic consequences of the current system of divorce emerge from two different types of analysis. In the first analysis we focus on income. Here we compare men's and women's *incomes* before and after divorce. The second analysis focuses on *standards of living*. Here we ask how the husbands' postdivorce standards of living compare with that of their former wives. Since it is reasonable to expect postdivorce incomes and standards of living to vary with the length of marriage and the family income level before divorce, these two factors are controlled in the following analyses. . . .

## LONG-MARRIED COUPLES AND DISPLACED HOMEMAKERS

Economically, older and longer-married women suffer the most after divorce. Their situation is much more drastic—and tragic—than that of their younger counterparts because the discrepancy between men's and women's standards of living after divorce is much greater than for younger couples, and few of these women can ever hope to recapture their loss.

Once again, among this group the discrepancy between former husbands and wives is evident at all income levels, and most pronounced—and severe—for those with predivorce family incomes of $40,000 or more a year.

When the courts project the postdivorce prospects for women after shorter marriages, they assume that most of these women will be able to build new lives for themselves.[1] They reason that a woman in her twenties or early thirties is young enough to acquire education or training and thus has the potential to find a satisfying and well-paid job. To be sure, such women will probably have a hard time catching up with their former husbands, but most of them will be able to enter or re-enter the labor force. In setting support for these younger women, the underlying assumption is that they will become self-sufficient. (I am not questioning that assumption. What has been questioned is the court's optimism about the ease and speed of the transition. Younger divorced women need more generous support awards for training and education to maximize their long-run job prospects.[2] But their potential for some level of "self-sufficiency" is not questioned.)

But what about the woman in her forties or fifties—or even sixties at the point of divorce? What are her prospects? Is it reasonable for judges to expect her to become self-sufficient? This woman's problems of job placement, retraining, and self-esteem are likely to be much more severe.[3] Her divorce award is likely to establish her standard of living for the rest of her life.

The hardest case is that of the long-married woman who has devoted her life to raising children who are now grown. Consider, for example, the hypothetical Ann Thompson, age fifty-three, who was formerly married to a wealthy corporate executive. She is much better off after divorce than the vast majority of divorced women her age because her former husband earns $6,000 a month net. The average Los Angeles judge would award Ann Thompson $2,000 a month in spousal support, giving her a total income of $24,000 a year in contrast to her former husband's $48,000 a year (after alimony payments are deducted from his income). Her former husband will be able to maintain his comfortable standard of living on his $48,000 income (which is likely to rise) and the tax benefits he gets from paying alimony. But Ann, with her house sold, no employment prospects, and the loss of her social status and social networks, will not be able to sustain anything near her former standard of living.

Since Ann Thompson's three children are over eighteen, she is not legally entitled to any child support for them.[4] She is likely, however, to be contributing to their college expenses. In addition, one or more of them is likely to still be living with her, and all probably return from time to time for extended visits. Thus she may well be providing as much if not more for their support than their well-to-do father.*

The combined effects of a less than equal income and a greater than equal share of the children's expenses invariably result in extreme downward mobility for long-married divorced women in California. They are both absolutely and relatively worse off than their former husbands. Although the courts are supposed to aim at balancing the resources of the two postdivorce households, the data reveal that they do not come near this goal. . . .

The data indicate that men married more than eighteen years have a much higher *per capita* income—that is, they have much more money to spend on themselves—than their former wives at every level of (predivorce family) income. Even where the discrepancy is smallest, in lower-income families, the husband and every member of this postdivorce family have *twice* as much money as his former wife and his children. In higher-income families, the discrepancy is enormous. The husband and each person in his postdivorce household—his new wife, cohabitor, or child—have three times as much disposable income as his former wife and the members of her postdivorce household. When we realize that the "other members" of the wife's postdivorce household are almost al-

---

*When Stanford University students from divorced families were interviewed for a class research project most reported that they first asked their mother for money, even though they knew she had less than their father, because they found her more sympathetic and willing to support to them.

ways the husband's children, the discrepancy between the two standards of living seems especially unjust. . . .

## POSTDIVORCE STANDARDS OF LIVING: IMPOVERISHMENT OF WOMEN AND CHILDREN

The income disparity between men and women after divorce profoundly affects their relative standards of living.

To examine this effect we rely on an index of economic well-being developed by the U.S. government. The model for our analysis was constructed by Michigan researchers who followed a sample of 5,000 American families, weighted to be representative of the U.S. population. Economists Saul Hoffman and John Holmes compared the incomes of men and women who stayed in intact families with the incomes of divorced men and divorced women over a seven-year period.*

A comparison of the married and divorced couples yielded two major findings. First, as might be expected, the dollar income of both divorced men and divorced women declined, while the income of married couples rose. Divorced men lost 19 percent in income while divorced women lost 29 percent.[5] In contrast, married men and women experienced a 22 percent rise in income.[6] These data confirm our commonsense belief that both parties suffer after a divorce. They also confirm that women experience a greater loss than their former husbands.

The second finding of the Michigan research is surprising. To see what the income loss meant in terms of family purchasing power, Hoffman and Holmes constructed an index of family income in relation to family needs.[7] Since this income/need comparison is adjusted for family size, as well as for the each member's age and sex, it provides an individually tailored measure of a family's economic well-being in the context of marital status changes.

The Michigan researchers found that the experiences of divorced men and women were strikingly different when this measure was used. Over the seven-year period, the economic position of divorced men actually improved by 17 percent.[8] In contrast, over the same period divorced women experienced a 29 percent decline in terms of what their income could provide in relation to their needs.[9]

To compare the experiences of divorced men and women in California to those in Michigan, we devised a similar procedure to calculate the ba-

---

*Detailed information from the interviews provided the researchers with precise income data, including income from employment, intra-family transfers, welfare, and other government programs. Alimony and/or child support paid by the husband was subtracted from his income and added to the wife's postdivorce income. Finally, to facilitate direct comparisons, all income was calculated in constant 1968 dollars so that changes in real income could be examined without the compounding effect of inflation.

sic needs of each of the families in our interview sample. This procedure used the living standards for urban families constructed by the Bureau of Labor Statistics of the U.S. Department of Labor.[10] First, the standard budget level for each family in the interview sample was calculated in three different ways: once for the predivorce family, once for the wife's postdivorce family, and once for the husband's postdivorce family. Then the income in relation to needs was computed for each family. (Membership in postdivorce families of husbands and wives included any new spouse or cohabitor and any children whose custody was assigned to that spouse.) These data are presented in Figure 1.

Figure 1 reveals the radical change in the standards of living to which we alluded earlier. Just one year after legal divorce, *Men experience a 42 percent improvement in their postdivorce standard of living, while women experience a 73 percent decline.*

**FIGURE 1. Change in Standards of Living\* of Divorced Men and Women (Approximately one year after divorce)**

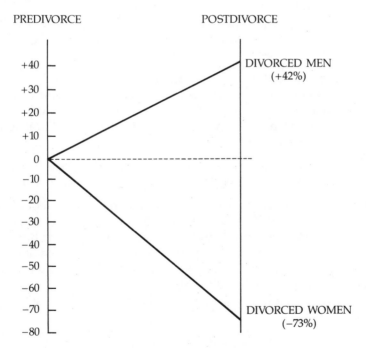

\*Income in relation to needs with needs based on U.S. Department of Agriculture's low standard budget.

Based on weighted sample of interviews with divorced persons, Los Angeles County, California, 1978.

These data indicate that *divorce is a financial catastrophe for most women:* in just one year they experience a dramatic decline in income and a calamitous drop in their standard of living. It is hard to imagine how they deal with such severe deprivation: every single expenditure that one takes for granted—clothing, food, housing, heat—must be cut to one-half or one-third of what one is accustomed to.

It is difficult to absorb the full implications of these statistics. What does it mean to have a 73 percent decline in one's standard of living? When asked how they coped with this drastic decline in income, many of the divorced women said that they themselves were not sure. It meant "living on the edge" and "living without." As some of them described it:

> We ate macaroni and cheese five nights a week. There was a Safeway special for 39 cents a box. We could eat seven dinners for $3.00 a week. . . . I think that's all we ate for months.

> I applied for welfare. . . . It was the worst experience of my life. . . . I never dreamed that I, a middle class housewife, would ever be in a position like that. It was humiliating . . . they make your feel it. . . . But we were desperate, and I *had* to feed my kids.

> You name it, I tried it—food stamps, soup kitchens, shelters. It just about killed me to have the kids live like that. . . . I finally called my parents and said we were coming . . . we couldn't have survived without them.

Even those who had relatively affluent life-styles before the divorce experienced a sharp reduction in their standard of living and faced hardships they had not anticipated. For example, the wife of a dentist sold her car "because I had no cash at all, and we lived on that money—barely—for close to a year." And an engineer's wife:

> I didn't buy my daughter any clothes for a year—even when she graduated from high school we sewed together two old dresses to make an outfit.

The wife of a policeman told an especially poignant story about "not being able to buy my twelve-year-old son Addidas sneakers." The boy's father had been ordered to pay $100 a month child support but had not been paying. To make up that gap in her already bare-bone budget, she had been using credit cards to buy food and other household necessities. She had exceeded all her credit limits and felt the family just could not afford to pay $25 for a new pair of Addidas sneakers. But, as she said a year later,

> Sometimes when you are so tense about money you go crazy . . . and you forget what it's like to be twelve years old and to think you can't live without Adidas sneakers . . . and to feel the whole world has deserted you along with your father.

Others spoke of cutting out all the nonessentials. For one woman it meant "no movies, no ice cream cones for the kids." For another it meant not replacing tires on her son's bike "because there just wasn't the money." For another woman it meant not using her car—a real handicap in Los Angeles—and waiting for two buses in order to save the money she would have had to spend for gas. In addition to scaled-down budgets for food ("We learned to love chicken backs") and clothing ("At Christmas I splurged at the Salvation Army—the only "new" clothes they got all year"), many spoke of cutting down on their children's school lunches ("I used to plan a nourishing lunch with fruit and juice; now she's lucky if we have a slice of ham for a sandwich") and school supplies and after-school activities ("he had to quit the Little League and get a job as a delivery boy").

Still, some of the women were not able to "make it." Fourteen percent of them moved onto the welfare rolls during the first year after the divorce, and a number of others moved back into their parents' homes when they had "no money left and nowhere to go and three children to feed."

## EXPLAINING THE DISPARITY BETWEEN HUSBANDS' AND WIVES' STANDARDS OF LIVING

How can we explain the strikingly different economic consequences of divorce for men and women? How could a law that aimed at fairness create such disparities between divorced men and their former wives and children?

The explanation lies first in the inadequacy of the court's awards, second in the expanded demands on the wife's resources after divorce, and third in the husband's greater earning capacity and ability to supplement his income.

Consider first the court awards for child support (and in rarer cases, alimony). Since judges do not require men to support either their children or their former wives as they did during marriage, they allow the husband to keep most of his income for himself. Since only a few wives are awarded alimony, the only supplementary income they are awarded is child support and the average child support award covers less than half of the cost of raising a child. Thus, the average support award is simply inadequate: even if the husband pays it, it often leaves the wife and children in relative poverty. The custodial mother is expected to somehow make up the deficit alone even though she typically earns much less than her former husband.

In this regard, it is also important to note the role that property awards play in contributing to—rather than alleviating—the financial disparities between divorced women and men. Under the old law, when the wife with minor children was typically awarded the family home, she started her postdivorce life on a more equal footing because the home provided some stability and security and reduced the impact of the income loss suffered at divorce. Today, when the family home is more commonly sold to allow an "equal" division of property, there is no cushion to soften the financial devastations that low support awards create for women and children. Rather, the disruptive costs of moving and establishing a new household further strain their limited income—often to the breaking point.

The second explanation for the disparity between former husbands and wives lies in the greater demands on the wife's household after divorce, and the diminished demands on the husband's. Since the wife typically assumes the responsibility for raising the couple's children, her need for help and services increases as a direct result of her becoming a single parent. Yet at the very time that her need for more income and more financial support is greatest, the courts have drastically reduced her income. Thus the gap between her income and her needs is wider after divorce.

In contrast, the gap between the husband's income and needs narrows. Although he now has fewer absolute dollars, the demands on his income have diminished: he often lives alone and he is no longer financially responsible for the needs of his ex-wife and children. While he loses the benefits of economies of scale, and while he may have to purchase some services (such as laundry and cooking) that he did not have to buy during marriage, he is nevertheless much better off because he has so much more money to spend on himself. Since he has been allowed to retain most of his income for himself, he can afford these extra expenses and still have more surplus income than he enjoyed during marriage.

The final explanation for the large income discrepancy between former husbands and wives lies in the different earning capacities and starting points of the two adults at the time of the divorce. Not only do men in our society command higher salaries to begin with, they also benefit from the common marital pattern that gives priority to their careers. Marriage gives men the opportunity, support, and time to invest in their own careers. Thus marriage itself builds and enhances the husband's earning capacity. For women, in contrast, marriage is more likely to act as a career liability. Even though family roles are changing, and even though married women are increasingly working for pay during marriage, most of them nevertheless subordinate their careers to their husbands' and to their family responsibilities. This is especially true if they have children. Thus women are often doubly disadvantaged at the point of divorce. Not only do they face the "normal" 60 percent male/female income gap that affects all working women, they also suffer from the toll the marital years have taken on their earning capacity.

Thus marriage—and then divorce—impose a differential disadvantage on women's employment prospects, and this is especially severe for women who have custody of minor children. The responsibility for children inevitably restricts the mother's job opportunities by limiting her work schedule and location, her availability for overtime, and her freedom to take advantage of special training, travel assignments, and other opportunities for career advancement.

Although the combined income of the former spouses typically increases after divorce, most of the rise is a result of the husband's increased income. Even though women who have not been employed during marriage seek jobs after divorce, and part-time workers take full-time jobs, neither of these factors accounts for as much as the rise in male wages in the first year after divorce.

It is, in fact, surprising to see how many divorced men receive salary increases (and bonuses) immediately after divorce. While some of these are probably routine raises, and others may be the result of more intense work efforts or overtime work, it is also evident that some men manage to delay a bonus or commission or raise until after the divorce is final. This allows them to minimize the income they have to report to the court when child support (or alimony) awards are being made. . . .

During the same period, the obligations that these men have for alimony and child support typically remain fixed or diminish: some support obligations have been reduced or terminated by terms of the divorce settlement (and others have been reduced or stopped without the courts' permission). The result, once again, is that divorced men have more "surplus income" for themselves.

The discrepancy between divorced men and women has been corroborated by other research. Sociologist Robert Weiss and economist Thomas Espenshade . . . and Census Bureau data also document the disparities in both income and standards of living of men and women after divorce. In 1979, the median per capita income of divorced women who had not remarried was $4,152, just over half of the $7,886 income of divorced men who had not remarried.[11]

The situation of divorced women with young children is even more grim. The median income in families headed by women with children under six years of age was only 30 percent of the median income for all families whose children were under six.[12] Thus, for the United States as a whole, the "income of families headed by women is at best half that of other families; the income of families headed by women with young children is even less, one-third of that of other families."[13] . . .

## SOCIETAL CONSEQUENCES

The rise in divorce has been the major cause of the increase in female-headed families,[14] and that increase has been the major cause of the feminization of poverty. Sociologist Diana Pearce, who coined the phrase "feminization of poverty," was one of the first to point to the critical link between poverty and divorce for women.[15] It was, she said, the mother's burden for the economic and emotional responsibility for child-rearing that often improverished her family.

Contrary to popular perception, most female-headed single parent families in the United States are *not* the result of unwed parenthood: they are the result of marital dissolution.[16] Only 18 percent of the nearly ten million female-headed families in the United States are headed by an unwed mother: over 50 percent are headed by divorced mothers and the remaining 31 percent by separated mothers.[17]

*When a couple with children divorces, it is probable that the man will become single but the woman will become a single parent. And poverty, for many women, begins with single parenthood.* More than half of the poor families in the United States are headed by a single mother.[18]

The National Advisory Council on Economic Opportunity estimates that if current trends continue, the poverty population of the United States will be composed solely of women and children by the year 2000.[19] The Council declares that the "feminization of poverty has become one of the most compelling social facts of the decade."[20]

## THE RISE IN FEMALE POVERTY

The well-known growth in the number of single-parent, female-headed households has been amply documented elsewhere. (The 8 percent of all children who lived in mother-child families in 1960, rose to 12 percent by 1970,[21] and to 20 percent by 1981.[22]) Also well-documented is the fact that these mother-headed families are the fastest growing segment of the American poor.[23]

What has not been well documented, and what appears to be relatively unknown—or unacknowledged—is the direct link between divorce, the economic consequences of divorce, and the rise in female poverty. The high divorce rate has vastly multiplied the numbers of women who are left alone to support themselves and their minor children. When the courts deny divorced women the support and property they need to maintain their families, they are relying, they say, on the woman's ability to get a job and support herself. But with women's current disadvantages in the labor market, getting a job cannot be the only answer—because it does not guarantee a woman a way out of poverty.[24] Even with full-time employment, one-third of the women cannot earn enough to enable them and their children to live above the poverty level.[25] The structure of the job market is such that *only half* of all full-time female workers are able to support two children without supplemental income from either the children's fathers or the government.[26]

In recent years there have been many suggestions for combating the feminization of poverty. Most of these have focused on changes in the labor market[27] (such as altering the sex segregation in jobs and professions, eliminating the dual labor market and the disparity between jobs in the primary and secondary sectors, eradicating the discriminatory structure of wages, and providing additional services, such as child care,[28] for working mothers) and on expanding social welfare programs (such as increasing AFDC benefits to levels above the poverty line, augmenting Medicaid, food stamp, and school lunch programs, and making housewives eligible for Social Security and unemployment compensation).[29]

A third possibility, which has not received widespread attention, is to change the way that courts allocate property and income at divorce. If, for example, custodial mothers and their children were allowed to remain in the family home, and if the financial responsibility for children were apportioned according to the means of the two parents, and if court orders for support were enforced, a significant segment of the population of divorced women and their children would not be improverished by divorce.

## THE RISE IN CHILD POVERTY AND ECONOMIC HARDSHIPS FOR MIDDLE-CLASS CHILDREN OF DIVORCE

Beyond question, the present system of divorce is increasing child poverty in America. From 1970 to 1982, the percentage of American children living in poverty rose from 14.9 percent to 21.3 percent.[30] According to demographer Samuel Preston, most of the growth in the number of children in poverty occurred in the category of female-headed families.[31]

While the vast majority (82 percent) of all children born in the United States today are born into two-parent families, more than half of these children are likely to experience the disruption of their parents' marriage before they reach age eighteen. As noted above, U.S. Census Bureau data show that close to 60 percent of the children born in 1983 *would not* spend their entire childhood living with both natural parents,[32] while Sandra Hofferth of the National Institute of Child Health and Human Development, projected that two-thirds of the children born in wedlock in 1980 would experience a parental divorce before they reach age seventeen.[33]

*Whichever figures we use, the statistics suggest that we are sentencing a significant proportion of the current generation of American children to lives of financial impoverishment.*

Clearly, living in a single-parent family does not have to mean financial hardship. The economic well-being of many of these children is in jeopardy only because their mothers bear the whole responsibility for their support. That jeopardy would end if courts awarded more alimony, higher amounts of child support, and a division of property that considered the interests of minor children. It would also be greatly reduced if the child support awards that the courts have already made were systematically enforced. Under the present legal system, however, the financial arrangements of divorce foster the financial deprivation of millions of children.

Although the deprivation is most severe below the poverty level, it affects children at every income level. In fact, middle-class children, like their mothers, experience the greatest relative deprivation. The economic dislocations of divorce bring about many changes which are particularly difficult for children: moving to new and less secure neighborhoods, changing schools, losing friends, being excluded from activities that have become too expensive for the family's budget, and having to work after school or help care for younger siblings.

Not surprisingly, the children of divorce often express anger and resentment when their standard of living is significantly less than that in their father's household.[34] They realize that their lives have been profoundly altered by the loss of "their home" and school and neighborhood and friends, and by the new expectations their mother's reduced income creates for them. . . .

The middle-class children of divorce may also feel betrayed by their disenfranchisement in their parents' property settlement. Since the law divides family property between the husband and wife and makes no provision for a child's share of the marital assets, many children feel they have been unfairly deprived of "their" home, "their" piano, "their" stereo set, and their college education. . . . The U.S. Census Bureau data on child support which indicated that even though child support awards are quite modest, less than half of all fathers comply fully with court orders for child support. Another quarter make some payment, and close to 30 percent do not pay anything at all.[35]

Inasmuch as about 1.2 million children's parents divorce each year, the 30 percent who receive no support from their fathers adds up to 360,000 new children each year. Over a ten-year period, this amounts to 4 million children. If we add to these the approximately 3 million over the years who receive only part of their child support (or receive it only some of the time), we find a ten-year total of 7 million children deprived of the support to which they are entitled. Remembering that fewer than 4 million children are born each year helps to put all these figures in perspective.[36]

The failure of absent parents to provide child support has taken an especially severe toll in recent years because of sharp cutbacks in public programs benefiting children since 1979. The Children's Defense Fund shows that children's share of Medicaid payments dropped from 14.9

percent in 1979, to 11.9 percent in 1982, despite a rise in the child proportion among the eligible.[37] The Aid to Families with Dependent Children
(AFDC) program has also been sharply cut back. In 1979, there were 72
children in AFDC for every 100 children in poverty, but only 52 per 100 in
1982.[38]

It is not surprising to find a strong relationship between the economic
and psychological effects of divorce on children. Economic deprivation
following divorce has been linked to increased anxiety and stress among
American children.[39] Mounting evidence also shows that children of divorce who experience the most psychological stress are those whose
postdivorce lives have been impaired by inadequate income. For example, Hodges, Tierney, and Bushbaum find "income inadequacy" the
most important factor in accounting for anxiety and depression among
preschool children in divorced families.[40] When family income is adequate, there are no differences in anxiety-depression levels between children in divorced families and those in intact families. However, "children of divorced families with inadequate income had substantially
higher levels of anxiety-depression."[41] Hodges, Wechsler, and Ballan-
tine also find significant correlations between income and adjustment
for preschool children of divorce (but not, interestingly, for preschool
children of intact families).[42]

In summary, the accumulating evidence shows that children in divorced families are likely to suffer a variety of adjustment problems if
they experience greater geographic mobility, lower income, and poorer
adequacy of income. Unfortunately, these experiences are common to
most children of divorce.

## CONCLUSION: THE TWO-TIER SOCIETY

The economic consequences of the present system of divorce reverberate
throughout our society. Divorce awards not only contribute heavily to the
well-documented income disparity between men and women, they also
lead to the widespread impoverishment of children and enlarge the ever-
widening gap between the economic well-being of men and women in
the larger society. Indeed, if current conditions continue unabated we
may well arrive at a two-tier society with an underclass of women and
children.

Thrust into a spiral of downward mobility by the present system of divorce, a multitude of middle-class women and the children in their
charge are increasingly cut off from sharing the income and wealth of
former husbands and fathers. Hampered by restricted employment opportunities and sharply diminished income, these divorced women are
increasingly expected to shoulder alone the burden of providing for both
themselves and their children.

Most of the children of divorce share their mother's financial hardships. Their presence in her household increases the strains on her meager income at the same time that they add to her expenses and restrict her opportunities for economic betterment.

Meanwhile, divorced men increasingly are freed of the major financial responsibility for supporting their children and former wives. Moreover, these men retain more than higher incomes. They experience less day-to-day stress than their ex-wives, they enjoy relatively greater mental, physical, and emotional well-being, and have greater freedom to build new lives and new families after divorce.

The economic disparities between men and women after divorce illuminate the long-standing economic disparities between the incomes of men and women during marriage. In theory, those differences did not matter in marriage, since they were partners in the enterprise and shared the husband's income. As Christopher Jencks observes, "As long as most American men and women married and pooled their economic resources, as they traditionally did, the fact the men received 70 percent of the nation's income had little effect on women's material well being."[43] But with today's high divorce rate, the ranks of unmarried women are vastly increased, and the relative numbers of women who share a man's income are greatly diminished.

The result is that the economic gulf between the sexes in the larger society is increasing. Some of this would have occurred even if the traditional divorce law remained everywhere in force. But the new divorce laws—and the way these laws are being applied—have exacerbated the effects of the high divorce rate by assuring that ever greater numbers of women and children are being shunted out of the economic mainstream.

The data on the increase in female poverty, child poverty, and the comparative deprivation of middle-class women and children suggest that we are moving toward a two-tier society in which the upper economic tier is dominated by men (and the women and children who live with them). The former wives of many of these men, the mothers of their children, and the children themselves are increasingly found in the lower economic tier. Those in the first tier enjoy a comfortable standard of living; those in the lower tier are confined to lives of economic deprivation and hardship.

Obviously the two tiers are not totally segregated by sex: professional women for example, whether married or divorced, are more likely to be found in the first tier, and members of many minority groups, both men and women, are more likely to fall into the second. Yet among these groups, and among all families at the lower income levels, divorce brings a better economic future for men than for their former wives. . . .

Obviously, membership in the second tier is not necessarily permanent. Some women will find jobs or return to school or obtain training that will enable them to improve their status. Many of those who are under thirty and some of those who are under forty will accomplish the same result by remarrying. But even those women who manage eventually to improve their financial situation will typically spend their early postdivorce years in acute economic hardship. The fact that they are poor only temporarily does not mean that they and their children suffer any the less[44] or that they can ever recapture the losses of those wasted years.

## NOTES

1. These assumptions are discussed in Chapters 6 and 7 of *The Divorce Revolution*, on alimony awards, pp. 157–158, 165–166, 176–177 in Chapter 6, and pp. 184–187, 197, 204–206, in Chapter 7.

2. See Chapter 7 of *The Divorce Revolution*, pp. 206, 209, and Chapter 6, 165–169.

3. The special problems that older women face at divorce are discussed in Chapter 7 of *The Divorce Revolution*, pp. 187–194, 198–201, 209–212.

4. The issue of support for dependent children over eighteen is discussed in Chapter 9 of *The Divorce Revolution*, pp. 278–281.

5. Ibid., p. 27 (Table 2.1), p. 31 (Table 2.2). Hoffman and Holmes are frequently cited as showing that divorced men have only a 10 percent decline in real money income. While this figure is shown in Table 2.1, it is based on the husband's total postdivorce income before alimony and/or child support is paid. Once these support payments are deducted from the husband's income, husbands experience a 19 percent decline in real income.

6. Ibid., p. 27 (Table 2.1).

7. This index, which is based on the Department of Agriculture's "Low-Cost Food Budget," adjusted for the size, age, and sex composition of the family, is described in note 10, below.

8. Saul Hoffman and John Holmes, "Husbands, Wives, and Divorce," in *Five Thousand Families—Patterns of Economic Progress* [Ann Arbor, MI.: Institute for Social Research, 1976], p. 27 (Table 2.1). This is closer to the rate of improvement of married couples who improved their standard of living by 21 percent. (Note that their income rose 22 percent, but their income in relation to needs rose 21 percent.)

9. Ibid., p. 31 (Table 2.2).

10. We assumed that the basic needs level for each family was the Lower Standard Budget devised by the Bureau of Labor Statistics, U.S. Department of Labor, *Three Standards of Living for an Urban Family of Four Persons* (1967). This budget is computed for a four-person urban family (husband and wife and two children) and kept current by frequent adjustments. See, e.g., McCraw, "Medical Care Costs Lead Rise in 1976–77 Family Budgets," *Monthly Labor Review*, Nov. 1978, p. 33. A Labor Department report devised a method for adjusting this standard budget to other types of families, depending on family size, age of oldest child, and age of head of household. Bureau of Labor Statistics, U.S. Department of Labor, *Revised Equivalence Scale for Estimating Equivalent Incomes or Budget Costs by Family Type*, Bulletin No. 1570–2 (1968). For example, the needs of a family of two

persons (husband and wife) with the head of household of age thirty-five was calculated at 60 percent of the base figure for a Lower Standard Budget.

A Lower Standard Budget was calculated for each family in our interview sample three different ways: once for the predivorce family, once for the wife's post-divorce family, and once for the the husband's postdivorce family. The income over needs for each family was then computed. Membership in postdivorce families of husbands and wives included a new spouse or cohabitor (where applicable), and any children whose custody was assigned to that spouse. I am indebted to my research assistant, David Lineweber, for programming this analysis.

11. Bureau of the Census, U.S. Dept. of Commerce, "Money Income of Families and Persons in the United States: 1979," *Current Population Reports* Series P-60, No. 129, 1981, p. 23.

12. Bureau of the Census, U.S. Dept. of Commerce, "Families Maintained by Female Householders 1970–79," *Current Population Reports* Series P-23, No. 107, 1980, p. 36.

13. National Center on Women and Family Law, "Sex and Economic Discrimination in Child Custody Awards," *Clearinghouse Review* Vol. 16, no. 11, April 1983, p. 1132.

14. Jane R. Chapman and Gordon Chapman, "Poverty Viewed as a Woman's Problem—the U.S. Case," in *Women and the World of Work*, Anne Hoiberg, ed. (New York: Plenum, 1982).

15. Diana Pearce, "The Feminization of Poverty: Women, Work and Welfare," *Urban and Social Change Review*, Feb. 1978; and Diana Pearce and Harriette McAdoo, "Women and Children: Alone and in Poverty" (Washington, D.C.: National Advisory Council on Economic Opportunity, September 1981), p. 1 (hereafter cited as Pearce and McAdoo, "Women and Children in Poverty").

16. House Hearings on Child Support Enforcement legislation before the subcommittee on Public Assistance and Unemployment Compensation of the Committee on Ways and Means of the U.S. House of Representatives on July 14, 1983, p. 13 (Washington, D.C.: U.S. Government Printing Office, 1984) (hereafter cited as House Hearings 1983).

17. Ibid.

18. Barbara Ehrenreich and Francis Fox Piven, "The Feminization of Poverty: When the Family Wage System Breaks Down," *Dissent*, 1984, p. 162 (hereafter cited as Ehrenreich and Piven, "Feminization of Poverty").

19. National Advisory Council on Economic Opportunity, *Critical Choices for the '80s*, August 1980, p. 1 (Washington, D.C.: National Advisory Council, 1980).

20. Ibid.

21. Christopher Jencks, "Divorced Mothers, Unite," *Psychology Today*, November 1982, pp. 73–75 (hereafter cited as Jencks, "Divorced Mothers").

22. Ehrenreich and Piven, "Feminization of Poverty," p. 163.

23. Ibid., p. 162; Pearce and McAdoo, "Women and Children in Poverty"; Heather L. Ross and Isabel V. Sawhill, *Time of Transition: The Growth of Families Headed by Women* (Washington, D.C.: The Urban Institute Press, 1975).

24. Pearce and McAdoo, "Women and Children in Poverty," pp. 6, 18.

25. Briefing paper prepared for California Assemblyman Thomas H. Bates for hearings on "The Feminization of Poverty," San Francisco, Calif., April 8, 1983, mimeo, p. 6 (hereafter cited as Bates brief).

26. Ibid. Pearce and McAdoo, "Women and Children in Poverty."

27. See generally, Pearce and McAdoo, "Women and Children in Poverty," and Ehrenreich and Piven, "Feminization of Poverty."

28. Child care is clearly one of the most fundamental needs of single mothers, and yet, in 1983, fully 84 percent of the working mothers were *not* able to obtain government-licensed child care for their children. California Commission on the Status of Women, Briefing Paper for hearings on the Feminization of Poverty conducted by California Assemblyman Thomas H. Bates, April 8, 1983.

29. Ehrenreich and Piven, "Feminization of Poverty."

30. Samuel H. Preston, "Children and the Elderly: Divergent Paths for Americans' Dependents," Presidential address to the Population Association to be published in *Demography* Vol. 21, no. 4, forthcoming, citing Bureau of the Census, U.S. Dept. of Commerce, "Money Income and Poverty Status 1982," *Current Population Reports* Series P-60, No. 140, 1983. Citations that follow are to pages in the Preston manuscript.

31. Ibid., p. 15.

32. Interview with Dr. Arthur Norton, March, 1984.

33. Sandra Hofferth, "Updating Children's Life Course," Center for Population Research, National Institute for Child Health and Development, 1983.

34. Judith Wallerstein and Joan Kelly, *Surviving The Breakup: How Parents and Children Cope with Divorce* [New York: Basic Books, 1980], p. 231.

35. See Chapter 9, pp. 283–284, citing Bureau of the Census, "Child Support and Alimony, 1981," *Current Population Reports*, Series P-23, No. 124.

36. House Hearings 1983, p. 27.

37. Children's Defense Fund, *American Children in Poverty* (Washington, D.C.: Children's Defense Fund, 1984).

38. Ibid.

39. Ann Goetting, "Divorce Outcome Research: Issues and Perspectives," in *The Family in Transition*, Fourth Edition, Arlene S. Stolnick, eds. [Boston: Little Brown & Co., 1983]; and Nicholas Zil and James Peterson, "Trends in the Behavior and Emotional Well-Being of U.S. Children," Paper given at the 1982 Annual Meeting of the Association for the Advancement of Science, Washington, D.C., 1982.

40. William F. Hodges, Carol W. Tierney, and Helen K. Bushbaum, "The Cumulative Effect of Stress on Preschool Children of Divorced and Intact Families," *Journal of Marriage and the Family* Vol. 46, no. 3, August 1984, pp. 611–629, 614.

41. Ibid.

42. Ibid., citing their earlier work.

43. Jencks, "Divorced Mothers."

44. Ibid.

# Review Questions

1. Based on the research findings cited by Weitzman, does the financial situation after a divorce improve or decline, on the average, for children? for women? for men? Explain why.

2. What are the three reasons that Weitzman gives for the differences in per capita income between divorced men's families and divorced women's families?

3. What does the phrase *ferminization of poverty* mean? Why has poverty become feminized?

4. By the twenty-first century, what percentage of people living in poverty in the United States are women and children expected to make up? How does this fact relate to the "two-tier society" that social scientists predict?

5. What part does "no-fault" divorce legislation play in creating the two-tiered society?

# WAITING, EXCHANGE, AND POWER: THE DISTRIBUTION OF TIME IN SOCIAL SYSTEMS[1]

## Barry Schwartz

So FAR AS IT LIMITS PRODUCTIVE USES OF TIME, WAITING GENERATES DIS-tinct social and personal costs. The purpose of this paper is to explore the way these costs are distributed throughout a social structure and to identify the principles to which this allocation gives expression. The main proposition of our analysis is that the distribution of waiting time coincides with the distribution of power. . . .The broader implications of this correlation allow us to characterize stratification systems in terms of the apportionment of time as well as the distribution of other kinds of resources.

Delay and congestion are relevant to the analysis of social systems be-cause they undermine the efficiency with which these systems conduct their business. Indeed, one Russian economist (Liberman 1968–69) re-cently observed that because of its enormous cost in terms of more pro-ductive activities foregone, delay in waiting rooms and queues merit the status of a social problem (pp. 12–16). A gross estimate of the dimen-sions of this problem is furnished by Orlov, who reports that the Soviet population wastes about 30 billion hours a year waiting during their shopping tours alone. This is the equivalent of a year's work for no less than 15 million men (*New York Times*, May 13, 1969, p. 17). Another study shows that monthly queuing for the payment of rent and utilities wastes at least 20 million man-hours a year in Moscow alone (*New York Times*, June 25, 1972, p. 23). If figures like these were aggregated for the entire service sector of the labor force, social inefficiency occasioned by clients waiting would stand out even more dramatically.

The problem of delay may be more acute in some societies than in oth-ers; however, no modern society can claim immunity in this respect. Every social system must "decide" not only how much different mem-bers are to be given from a collective supply of goods and services; there must also be a decision as to the priority in which their needs are to be satisfied. Queuing for resources is in this sense a fundamental process of social organization, regardless of the specific level of its affluence. In-deed, though the amount of waiting time per unit consumption may be

Barry Schwartz, "Waiting, Exchange, and Power: The Distribution of Time in Social Sys-tems," *American Journal of Sociology* 79 (1973): 841–870.

minimal in the richer, consumer-oriented societies, a higher volume of consumption leaves open the possibility that more time is lost in waiting under conditions of affluence than under conditions of scarcity.

On the other hand, it may be said that the social costs of waiting, no matter where they are incurred or what their absolute level may be, merely derive from the summation over an entire population of rather negligible individual losses. But this does not seem to be the case. As one American commentator (Bradford 1971) puts it: "None of us would think of throwing away the nickels and quarters and dimes that accumulate in our pockets. But almost all of us do throw away the small-change time—five minutes here, a quarter hour there—that accumulates in any ordinary day. I figure I probably threw away a full working day in the dentist's office this past year, flicking sightlessly through old magazines" (p. 82). Even in the more opulent of modern societies, then, waiting time creates significant deficits for the individual as well as the system. At issue, however, is (1) the way such cost is distributed throughout a social structure and (2) the principles which govern this distribution. These questions are the subject of the present inquiry.

We begin with the assumption that delay is immediately caused by the relations of supply and demand: when the number of arrivals in some time unit is less than the number an organization can accommodate, waiting time will be relatively brief; but if the arrival rate exceeds the service rate, a "bottleneck" is created and a longer waiting period results. Delay is in this sense occasioned by limitations of access to goods and services. However, this model does not explain socially patterned variations in waiting time. We must therefore explore the institutional constraints which sustain observable levels of scarcity and which organize the priorities granted to different groups of clients. These constraints are shown to be the expressions of existing power relations.

• • •

## WAITING, SCARCITY, AND POWER

• • •

### Stratification of Waiting

Typical relationships obtain between the individual's position within a social system and the extent to which he waits for and is waited for by other members of the system. In general, the more powerful and important a person is, the more others' access to him must be regulated. Thus, the least powerful may almost always be approached at will; the most powerful are seen only "by appointment." Moreover, because of heavy demands on their time, important people are most likely to violate the terms of appointments and keep their clients waiting. It is also true that the powerful tend not to ask for appointments with their own subordinates; rather, the lowly are summoned—which is grounds for them to cancel their own arrangements so as not to "keep the boss waiting."

The lowly must not only wait for their appointments with superiors; they may also be called upon to wait during the appointment itself. This may be confirmed in innumerable ways. For one, consider everyday life in bureaucracies. When, in their offices, superordinates find themselves in the company of a subordinate, they may interrupt the business at hand to, say, take a phone call, causing the inferior to wait until the conversation is finished. Such interruption may be extremely discomforting for the latter, who may wish not to be privy to the content of the conversation but, having no materials with which to express alternative involvement, must wait in this exposed state until his superior is ready to reengage him. The event becomes doubly disturbing when the superior is unable to recover from the distraction, loses his train of thought, and is unable to properly devote himself to the moment's business. Of course, the subordinate is demeaned not only by the objective features of this scene but also by his realization that for more important clients the superior would have placed an embargo on all incoming calls or visitors. He would have made others wait. The assumption that the client correctly makes is that his own worth is not sufficient to permit the superior to renounce other engagements; being unworthy of full engagement, he is seen, so to speak, between the superior's other appointments. In this way, the client is compelled to bear witness to the mortification of his own worthiness for proper social interaction.

While the derogatory implications for self are clear when the person must repeatedly step aside and wait until the superordinate decides that the granting of his time will not be excessively costly, debasement of self may be attenuated by the client's own consideration that his superior is, after all, in a position of responsibility and assailed by demands over which he may not exercise as much control as he would like. But even this comforting account may be unavailable when the server himself initiates the interruption. It is possible for him to make a call, for example, or to continue his work after the client enters, perhaps with the announcement that he will "be through in a minute."

It is especially mortifying when the superior initiates a wait when an engagement is in progress. Thus, a subordinate, while strolling along a corridor in conversation with his superior may find himself utterly alone when the latter encounters a colleague and breaks off the ongoing relationship in his favor. The subordinate (who may not do the same when encountering one of his peers) is compelled to defer by standing aside and waiting until the unanticipated conversation is finished. Nothing less is expected by his superior, who, finding himself gaining less from the engagement than his inferior, assumes the right to delay or interrupt it at will if more profitable opportunities should arise.

THE IMMUNITY OF THE PRIVILEGED: The relationship between rank and accessibility implies that waiting is a process which mediates interchanges between those who stand on different sides of a social boundary. These divisions and the rules of access which correspond to them are found in organizations which are themselves bounded with respect to the outside world. This fact raises the problem of access when outsiders or clients (as well as insiders, that is, employees or co-workers) seek contact with persons situated at different points in a service hierarchy:

> Low down on the scale are the men you can walk right up to. They are usually behind a counter waiting to serve you on the main floor, or at least on the lower floors. As you go up the bureaucracy you find people on the higher floors and in offices: first bull pens, then private offices, then private offices with secretaries—increasing with each step in inaccessibility and therefore the necessity for appointments and the opportunity to keep people waiting. Recently, for example, I had an experience with a credit card company. First, I went to the first floor where I gave my complaint to the girl at the desk. She couldn't help me and sent me to the eighth floor to talk to someone in a bullpen. He came out, after a suitable waiting time, to discuss my problem in the reception room. I thought that if I were to straighten this matter out I was going to have to find a vice-president in charge of something, who would keep me waiting the rest of the day. I didn't have time to wait so I took my chances with said clerk, who, of course, didn't come through. I'm still waiting for the time when I have an afternoon to waste to go back and find that vice-president to get my account straightened out.[2]

The above statement suggests that delaying a typical client may be a prerogative of important servers. However, we must also recognize that powerful clients are relatively immune from waiting. This remark accords with Tawney's (1931) emphasis on the asymmetry of power relations. "Power," he writes, "may be defined as the capacity of an individual, or group of individuals, to modify the conduct of other individuals or groups in the manner which he desires, *and to prevent his own conduct being modified in the manner in which he does not*" (p. 229; emphasis added).

The relative immunity from waiting which the powerful enjoy is guaranteed because they have the resources to refuse to wait; that is, because they can often afford to go elsewhere for faster service or cause others, such as servants or employees, to wait in their places. Thus, while the relationship between privilege and the necessity of waiting cannot be generalized in any deterministic way, there appears nevertheless to be a relationship between the two, with the least-privileged clients compelled to do the most waiting. This general statement is consistent with Mann's

(1969) more specific observations regarding the stratification of waiting in lined queues:

> The relationship between cultural equality and public orderliness is attenu-ated in the area of queuing because waiting in line is not a habit of all social classes in Western society. It is reasonable to suppose that if Mrs. Gottrocks joined a theater or a football line in the United States, Australia, or England, she would not be treated differently than anyone else, but it would be a rare event for someone of Mrs. Gottrock's status to use a line. Ordinarily, in both class-conscious and relatively class-free societies, the privileged class circum-vent the line altogether and get their tickets through agents or other contacts.[3] Our point, then, is that queuing is confined largely to the less-privileged groups in society. [p.353]

The privileged also wait less because they are least likely to tolerate its costs; they are more inclined to renege* from as well as balk† at entering congested waiting channels. On the other hand, the less advantaged may wait longer not only because of their lack of resources but also be-cause their willingness to wait exceeds the readiness of those in higher strata. While they might have something else to do besides sitting and waiting, they might not have anything better to do. As a result, the least advantaged may pay less in profitable alternatives foregone and there-fore suffer less than even those whose objective wait is shorter.

This relationship may be informed by another consideration, for which health-care delivery systems provide an example. Because of their scarcity, those who are able to pay for medical services are often forced to wait well beyond the time a server agreed to provide them. Yet there is some limit to the server's inconsiderateness, for, in principle at least, the client may decide that he has waited long enough and go elsewhere. On the other hand, those who are unable to pay for medical care may spend the better part of the day in outpatient waiting rooms, for consideration of the value of clients' time is far less imperative when these clients can-not take their business to someone else. In Britain's government-run ma-ternity hospitals, for example, "a major complaint was that women de-pendent on the health service are treated offhandedly in hospitals and frequently have to wait more than an hour for checkups at antenatal clin-ics. Women who paid up to $700 for private treatment were dealt with speedily and efficiently" (*Chicago Tribune,* June 12, 1971, p. 10). Thus, while long, agonizing waiting periods may be avoided only if one is will-ing to settle for more expensive service, the poor may avoid waiting only if they are willing to settle for no service at all. (The frequency with

---

*"Reneging" refers to giving up waiting after initially committing oneself to a line or wait-ing room.

†"Balking" means refusal to wait at all.

which they do select this option is, of course, unknown—as is the consequence of the selection.)

The above principle may be further illustrated in other, altogether different connections. It is noticeable, for one example, that in the "best" of urban department stores a customer is met by a salesperson as soon as he enters; the customer makes a selection under his guidance and makes payment to him. In establishments which are a grade below the best, customers may have difficulty finding someone to serve them during busy periods but, when they do, are accompanied by him, that is, "waited on," until the transaction is consummated by payment. The lowest-grade stores, however, provide few servers; as a result, customers must for the most part wait on themselves, then line up behind others at a cashier counter in order to make payment.

The above patterns are to be observed within as well as among organizations. In the typical department store, customers surveying high-priced goods like furniture and appliances will typically be approached immediately by a salesperson. Those in the process of selecting a handkerchief or pair of socks will not be so quickly attended and, when they finally are, will be dealt with more quickly. Likewise, clients who show interest in very expensive jewelry will be served at once and at length; those who are fascinated with costume jewelry will wait.

In general, it may be said that establishments which cater to a relatively wealthy clientele must serve them quickly (if the clients desire) not only because of the objective or assumed value of clients' time but also because they have the means to take their business elsewhere if it is not respected. Commercial places which service the less wealthy are less constrained in this respect because they tend to deal with a larger and/or less independent clientele. Within organizations, clients who promise to bring the most profit to a server enjoy a competitive advantage; they wait the least, to the disadvantage of their lesser endowed brethren who can find no one to honor the value of their time.[4]

## Waiting and the Monopolization of Services

The above rule, however, rests on the assumption that faster alternative services are available to those who want and can pay for them. In fact, the availability of such alternatives is itself variable. Waiting is therefore affected not only by clients' resources and consequent ability to go elsewhere for service but also by the opportunity to do so.

It follows that establishments with many competitors are most likely to be concerned about the amount of time they keep clients waiting. Chicago Loop banks are among such organizations. In the words of one banking consultant, "The industry is too competitive to allow a dozen people waiting in line when they could just as easily take their business across the street where there is a teller at every window, a customer at every teller and waiting time is less than one minute" (*Chicago Tribune*, September 28, 1971, p. 7). However, organizations with few or no competitors are less obliged to reduce the waiting time of clients. (This condition makes waiting a national pastime in the Soviet Union, where most services are rendered by government-run establishments that are not subject to market forces.)

The enormous amounts of waiting time expended in dealings with public people-serving bureaucracies is directly related to monopolization of the various services which they offer or impose. Monopolization accords governmental units the power to maximize their efficiency of operation by minimizing service costs and, in so doing, maximizing client waiting. This "optimum solution" is exemplified by bureaus which distribute welfare benefits to long lines of disadvantaged people:

> The number of Medicaid and public assistance applicants and recipients has become so great that [New York's] Department of Social Services is literally shutting its doors in their faces.
>
> Many of the 45 social service centers close their doors early—12, 1 or 2 o'clock—rather than admit persons the workers realistically know cannot be seen that particular day.
>
> The Medicaid office advises applicants to line up outside the doors before dawn. "You'd better get down here around 6:30 or 7 o'clock," said a person answering the telephone at the Medicaid office. . . . "We can only see 200 persons a day. If you want to be in the first 200 you better get here then—with your application filled out." The Medicaid office does not open until 8:30 A.M. . . .
>
> Last week the department announced it had saved $39 million by employing fewer case workers. [*New York Times*, November 21, 1971, p. 58]

However, the relatively wealthy as well as the poor are put to inconvenience by having to wait in person for licenses, permits, visas, tickets, information and the like. Dealings with government-sponsored transportation facilities can also be cited as an example:

> Before Amtrak took over, I would have had to call the Illinois Central to go to Miami. If I wanted to go to New York, I'd call the Penn Central. To go west, the Santa Fe. But now, under the streamlined, tax-supported Amtrak, one number, one central office, makes the reservations. They have computers and other modern devices the old system didn't have.
>
> At 10 minutes after noon, I dialed the new Amtrak reservation number. The line was busy, so I hung up and waited a few minutes and dialed again. It was still busy. Five minutes later, I tried again. It was busy. By 1 o'clock I had tried 10 times, and had heard only busy signals.
>
> Enough was enough. I phoned the Amtrak executive office, to ask what was wrong with their reservation number. A woman there put me on hold. I was on hold for seven minutes. Then when she finally took me off hold, she switched me to somebody's office, and a secretary laughed and said: "Oh, yes, our lines are very busy."
>
> At 2 P.M. it finally happened. Instead of getting a busy signal, it rang. It actually rang. . . . It rang. And it rang. And it rang. For eight minutes it rang.

. . . So I hung up, got another cup of coffee and tried again. That was a mistake, because I heard another busy signal.

Then at 2:47 it happened. It rang. And somebody answered. I listened closely to make sure it wasn't a recorded message. No, it was really somebody alive. After that it was easy. In about eight or nine minutes the reservations were made.

The clock said 3 P.M. So I have to congratulate Amtrak. It took me only two hours and 50 minutes to complete a telephone call and make reservations. It would have probably taken me at least 10 minutes more than that to take a cab to O'Hare, board a plane, fly to Miami, and get off the plane. [*Chicago Daily News*, June 9, 1972, p. 3]

This instance is an especially informative one, for it demonstrates that the amount of time clients of an organization are called upon to wait is in large measure determined by the broader competitive structure in which the organization is situated. Longitudinal and cross-sectional means are brought to bear in this assessment. By reference to the temporal barrier to access to rail service after centralization and monopolization, relative ease of access before the transformation is implicitly affirmed. And after documenting the lengthy waiting time required in a noncompetitive service market, we find explicit reference to the ready availability of service offered in highly competitive ones (airlines, in this case). In this double sense, the institutional grounding of waiting time is a conclusion warranted by the facts.

We now turn to public services which by their very nature admit of no alternatives and which at the same time are so organized as to constitute the most radical instance of the principle we are now discussing.

A DAY IN COURT: Discrepancy between demand for and supply of "authoritative judgment" is perhaps the most notorious source of waiting for both rich and poor. In fact, those who look forward to their "day in court," whether civil, criminal, or juvenile, very often find themselves spending their day in the courthouse corridor (many courts do not provide waiting rooms). In some courts, in fact, all parties whose cases are scheduled to be heard on a particular day are instructed to be present at its beginning when the judge arrives.[5] This is a most pronounced manifestation of what we earlier referred to as "overscheduling," which in this case ensures that the judge (whose bench is separated from his office or working area) will not be left with idle time that cannot be put to productive use—a consideration which may help us understand the seemingly irrational practice of assembling together at the beginning of the day those who are to be served during its course. While this tactic guarantees that the judge's valuable time will not be wasted, it also ensures that most parties will be kept waiting for a substantial period of time; some, all day long. Indeed, because they have no means to retaliate against the judge's own tardiness or excessive lunch breaks, some individuals may not be served at all and must return on the next day to wait further. Clients' attorneys, incidentally, keep them company during much of this time—a service for which the former pay dearly.

All of this is not to say that the organization of justice profits. It must, on the contrary, pay a very high price for support of its prima donnas. As one juvenile-court officer puts it: "[W]aiting to be called into court . . . is the most serious problem. Just from an internal point of view this means that a probation counselor usually accomplishes nothing in the hour or more he often has to wait to get his case into court. Usually during this waiting period he sees no people, does no counselling, can't do dictation or other 'desk-work'—his wait is complete, unproductive waste. These same problems apply to other professional people: caseworkers from the Department of Social Services, school principals, lawyers, etc." (Fairfax County [Virginia] Juvenile and Domestic Relations Court, Memorandum, 1971, p.1). While attorneys[6] and other professionals are fortunate enough to claim a fee for doing nothing in a professional way, others are often denied this luxury. Authorities who are mindful of civil security, for example, wisely find it more expedient to dismiss cases (particularly such misdemeanants as traffic violators) for lack of witnesses and evidence than to tie up a large sector of the police force for the better part of the day in a crowded corridor. In this particular sense, the police are too important—their time too valuable—to be kept waiting. On the other hand, it may be claimed that by tying up defendants all day long in these same corridors justice may be served—provided, of course, that the defendants are in fact guilty as charged. However, the situation is quite different in felony cases, where casual dismissals are less probable. Under these circumstances police wait as long as defendants. In the Chicago Gun Court, for example, "40 or 45 police are waiting to testify at 9:30 A.M., when court begins. Cases are not scheduled for specific times, so most of them wait and wait. One recent day 31 were still waiting around at 1 P.M. The next day 20 were there at 1 P.M. And 23 the following day." The same conditions prevail at the Narcotics Court where police waiting time "translates on an annual basis to 13,000 police days lost and $700,000 in expenses" (*Chicago Daily News*, August 21, 1973, p. 14).

Two observations emerge from and transcend the particular content of what has just been said. First, the assertion that clients may pay a high price, in terms of time, in their dealings with public bureaucracies means that a societal cost, expressed in terms of aggregate client time diverted from more productive activities, must be written into the usually implicit but sometimes explicit "optimum solution formulae" by which particular "public service" organizations maximize their own efficiency. Because of this factor, the real cost of governmental services is not to be obviated by budgetary considerations alone.

Second, minimization of a powerful server's idle time may subtract from the productivity of the organization as well as its clients. This observation, which is merely grotesquely evident in court settings, reflects the general principle that increments in efficiency in one part of a social organization often entail malfunction in other sectors. Accordingly, just as high concentration of power in an organization may lend itself to societal inefficiency, indexed by more productive client-time foregone, so concentration of power and honor in an elevated server may render organizations ineffective by maximizing idle time of subordinated servers. The more general import of this statement is that it amends the overly simplistic scarcity theory of waiting, which fixates our attention upon server shortage as a condition of client delay. The present statement shows that the organization of services, as well as their volume, provides occasion for waiting.

An additional point is that some persons and groups are relatively exempt from waiting. If we turn our attention once more to the courtroom, we find that the powerful are most likely to enjoy such advantage. In making up the docket, for example, resources are taken into account. Defendants who are represented by an attorney are very often scheduled before those who are not (in Chicago traffic courts, at least). And cases involving important and powerful contestants, witnesses, and/or lawyers may be scheduled at their convenience and not be delayed for long periods of time. Similarly, attorneys who enjoy favor with the court clerk are also able to avoid long waits because they are allowed to schedule their case early.[7] Thus, while waiting time may be maximized by persons or in organizations which enjoy full or near monopoly on the services they offer, the relationship between the power and waiting time of their clients is probably attenuated rather than negated. For, while the powerful may lack the opportunity to take their business elsewhere, they nevertheless possess the resources to ensure that their needs will be accommodated before the needs of those with fewer means.

•   •   •

## SOCIAL PSYCHOLOGICAL ASPECTS OF DELAY

### Making Others Wait

•   •   •

Because the worth of a person is not independent of the amount of time others must wait for him, that person can maintain and dramatize his worth by purposely causing another to wait.

Of course, the imposition of a waiting period does not in itself make a person or his services valuable; it can only magnify existing positive evaluations or transform neutral feelings into positive ones. If these initial feelings are not favorable, or at least neutral, the waiting caused by a server may lower clients' estimations of his worth. Instead of a sought-after and important man, the server becomes an incompetent who cannot perform his job properly; thus is his initial inferiority confirmed. (This is why subordinates who know where they stand do not like to keep their superiors waiting.) Generally, the dramatization of ascendency by keeping another waiting will do a server the most good when his social rank exceeds that of his client or when the difference between their ranks is ambiguous. In the latter case, ascendency accrues to him who can best dramatize it; in the former, ascendency may be dramatized by him to whom it already accrues.

Thus, just as authority is affirmed by the placement of social distance between super and subordinate, so temporal distance subserves the ascendency of the person who imposes it. More precisely, the restriction of access to oneself by forcing another to "cool his heels" is instrumental to the cultivation of social distance.

•   •   •

## The Imposition of Waiting as an Aggressive Act

If the temporal aspect of relationships between those occupying different social positions may be stated in terms of who waits for whom, then we would expect to find a reversal of the waiting-delaying pattern when persons "switch" positions. Furthermore, this reversal may be accentuated through retaliation by the one who suffered under the initial arrangement. A former president furnishes us with an example:

> Ken Hechler, who was director of research at the White House from 1948 to 1952, recalled the day Mr. Truman kept Winthrop Aldrich, president of the Chase Manhattan Bank, waiting outside the White House office for 30 minutes. Hechler quoted Mr. Truman as saying:
> "When I was a United States senator and headed the war investigation committee, I had to go to New York to see this fella Aldrich. Even though I had an appointment he had me cool my heels for an hour and a half. So just relax. He's got a little while to go yet." [*Chicago Daily News*, December 27, 1972, p. 4]

Punitive sanctioning through the imposition of waiting is met in its most extreme forms when a person is not only kept waiting but is also kept ignorant as to how long he must wait, or even of what he is waiting for. One manifestation of the latter form is depicted by Solzhenitsyn (1968a):

> Having met the man (or telephoned him or even specially summoned him), he might say: "Please step into my office tomorrow morning at ten." "Can't I drop in now?" the individual would be sure to ask, since he would be eager to know what he was being summoned for and get it over with. "No, not now," Rusanov would gently, but strictly admonish. He would not say that he was

busy at the moment or had to go to a conference. He would on no account offer a clear, simple reason, something that could reassure the man being summoned (for that was the crux of this device). He would pronounce the words "not now" in a tone allowing many interpretations—not all of them favorable. "About what?" the employee might ask, out of boldness or inexperience. "You'll find out tomorrow," Pavel Nikolaevich would answer in a velvet voice, bypassing the tactless question. But what a long time it is until tomorrow. [p. 222]

The underlying technique for the aggressive use of delay involves the withdrawal or withholding of one's presence with a view to forcing another into an interactionally precarious state wherein he might confront, recognize, and flounder in his own vulnerability or unworthiness.[8] By such means, the superordinate not only affirms his ascendency but does so at the direct expense of his inferior's dignity. Russian bureaucrats are masters at invoking this routine in their dealings with waiting clients:

Casting a disapproving eye at the janitor's wet overshoes, and looking at him severely, Shikin let him stand there while he sat down in an armchair and silently looked over various papers. From time to time, as if he was astonished by what he was reading . . . , he looked up at him in amazement, as one might look at a maneating beast that has finally been caged. All this was done according to the system and was meant to have an annihilating effect on the prisoner's psyche. A half-hour passed in the locked office in inviolate silence. The lunch bell rang out clearly. Spiridon hoped to receive his letter from home, but Shikin did not even hear the bell; he rifled silently through thick files, he took something out of a box and put it in another box, he leafed, frowning, through various papers and again glanced up briefly in surprise at the dispirited, guilty Spiridon.

All the water from Spiridon's overshoes had dripped on the rubber runner, and they had dried when Shikin finally spoke: "All right, move closer!" [Solzhenitsyn 1968b, pp. 482–83]

This kind of strategy can only be employed by superordinates who have power over a client in the first place. The effect on the client is to further subordinate him, regardless of a server's initial attractiveness or a client's realization that the delay has been deliberately imposed. Furthermore, this practice leaves the client in a psychologically as well as a ritually unsatisfactory state. The two presumably act back on each other in a mutually subversive way, for by causing his client to become tense or nervous the server undermines the self-confidence necessary for him to maintain proper composure. This tendency, incidentally, is routinely applied by skillful police interrogators who deliberately ignore a suspect waiting to be questioned, assuming that a long, uncertain wait will "rattle him" sufficiently to disorganize the kinds of defenses he could use to protect himself (Arthur and Caputo 1959, p. 31).

## Ritual Waiting and Autonomy

We have tried to show that while servers may cause others to wait in order to devote their attention to other necessary matters, they may also make people wait for the pure joy of dramatizing their capacity to do so. Such elation, we saw, is understandable, for by effecting a wait the server demonstrates that his presence is not subject to the disposition or whim of another and that access to him is a privilege not to be taken lightly. And, if access is a privilege, then one may sanction another by deliberately holding oneself apart from him. But we must now make explicit a point that was only implied in our previous discussions: that the imposition of waiting expresses and sustains the autonomy as well as the superiority of the self.

While the imposition of delay allows a superordinate to give expression to his authority, waiting may also be imposed in protest against that authority. The latter achievement is valued, naturally, among those of despised status and low rank. Because they lack the wherewithal to do so in most of their other relations, the powerless, in their capacity as servers, delight in keeping their superiors waiting. The deliberately sluggish movements of many store clerks, telephone operators, cashiers, toll collectors, and the like, testify to the ability of the lowly as well as the lofty to dramatize their autonomy. This accords with Meerloo's (1966) assertion that "the strategy of delay is an ambivalent attack on those who command us" (p. 249). This kind of aggression is perhaps most pronounced under sociologically ambivalent conditions: as the legitimacy of the existing distribution of status honor ceases to be taken for granted, prescribed deference patterns give way to institutionalized rudeness, which may be expressed by appearing late for appointments with a superordinate as well as by dillydallying while he waits for his needs to be serviced.

•  •  •

## SUMMARY

[V]alue foregone through idleness is an extrinsic disadvantage. On the other hand, the degradational implications of being kept idle are intrinsic to waiting and can arise in no way other than through involuntary delay. The purpose of this paper was to explore the way these costs are distributed throughout the social structure and to identify the principles to which this allocation gives expression.

We have introduced the category of power . . . as the ultimate determinant of delay, the main assertion being that the distribution of waiting time coincides with the distribution of power . . . [R]esourceful persons wait less within both competitive and monopolistic markets, while delay will be more pronounced in the latter regardless of personal power.

If waiting is related to a person's position in a power network, then a server may confirm or enhance his status by deliberately making another wait for him. In a more general sense, this is to say that the management of availability itself, regardless of the purpose for which an individual makes himself available, carries with it distinct psychological implications. Because a person's access to others indexes his scarcity as a social object, that person's social worth may only be realized by demonstrated inaccessibility. Openness to social relations may therefore be restricted not only to regulate interactional demands but also to enhance the self that one brings to an interaction. . . . The initial relationship between waiting and power thus gives rise to processes which strengthen it. . . .

The broader implication of this essay is that it finds . . . time itself a generalized resource whose distribution affects life chances with regard to the attainment of other, more specific kinds of rewards. This is true in a number of respects. Time, like money, is valuable because it is necessary for the achievement of productive purposes; ends cannot be reached unless an appropriate amount of it is "spent" or "invested" on their behalf. On the other hand, the power that a time surplus makes possible may be protected and/or expanded by depriving others of their time. By creating queues to reduce idle periods, for example, a server exploits clients by converting their time to his own use. A server does the same by "overcharging" in the sense of deliberately causing a particular client to wait longer than necessary.

The monetary analogies we have used are not without some justification. Just as money possesses no substantive value independent of its use as a means of exchange, time can only be of value if put to substantive use in an exchange relationship. Both time and money may be regarded as generalized means because of the infinity of possibilities for their utilization: both are possessed in finite quantities; both may be counted, saved, spent, lost, wasted, or invested. . . . Accordingly, while the powerful can allocate monetary means to their own desired ends by controlling the *budget*, they also regulate the distribution of time—rewarding themselves, depriving others—through their control of the *schedule*. What is at stake in the first instance is the *amount* of resources to which different parts of a system are entitled; in the second, it is the *priority* of their entitlements. Far from being a coincidental by-product of power, then, control of time comes into view as one of its essential properties.

## NOTES

1. This paper was supported by grant 1–5690–00–4335 from the Ford Foundation and by the Center for Health Administration Studies, University of Chicago.

The writer wishes to acknowledge the very useful comments made on this paper by Peter Blau and Morris Janowitz.

2. Personal communication from Florence Levinsohn.

3. Other "contacts" include the radio, over which Saturday and Sunday morning waiting times at many metropolitan golf courses are broadcast. This service, which saves many players many long delays, is performed almost exclusively for the middle and upper-middle classes.

4. Even when circumstances make it necessary for the resourceful to wait, they suffer less than their inferiors. As a general rule, the wealthier the clientele, the more adequate the waiting accommodations. Thus, persons who can afford bail can await their trial (or, far more frequently, attorneys' bargaining on their behalf) in the free community. The poor must wait in jail. The same is true of facilities. In airports, for example, those who can afford it may simultaneously avoid contamination by the masses and engross themselves in a variety of activities, including fabulous eating and drinking, in "VIP lounges." The term "lounge" instead of the vulgar "waiting area" or "gate" is also applied to facilities set aside for those who travel a specified number of miles with (and pay a substantial sum of money to) a particular airline. In this as in many other settings, waiting locales for the poor and less rich lack the elaborate involvement supplies, pleasant decor, and other physical and psychological comforts that diminish the pain of waiting among those who are better off.

5. A functional equivalent is found in the Soviet Union. "Aleksandr Y. Kabalkin and Vadim M. Khinchuk . . . describe what they termed 'classic cases' in everyday life in the Soviet Union, in which customers wait for the television repairman or for a messenger delivering a train or plane ticket that had been ordered by phone. To the question 'About what time can I expect you?' the stereotyped reply is, 'It can be any time during the day.' And people have to excuse themselves from work and wait—there is no other way out" (*New York Times,* November 7, 1971, p. 5).

6. It may not be assumed that all lawyers earn while they wait. For example, the *New York Times* (August 25, 1971, p. 24) recently reported: "A lawyer who specializes in prosecuting landlords' claims against tenants asked permission in Bronx Supreme Court yesterday to bring his cases there rather than in Civil Court because . . . he spent much time 'just sitting and waiting.' And consequently, he said, he was suffering 'financial loss' and felt he could not continue working in Civil Court."

7. This is to say that, as a scarce commodity, time or priority of service routinely becomes the object of struggle. Recognizing this, a court intake officer writes in a memo to his supervisor: "Intake counselors should assume more control over the setting of cases on the docket, with a proportionate decrease in the control now exercised by clerks" (Fairfax County [Virginia] Juvenile and Domestic Relations Court, Memorandum, 1971, p. 1).

8. Of course, the impulse of stationary servers to make others wait for reasons that are independent of the scarcity of time is paralleled by the tactic used by mobile servers, of keeping them waiting for these same reasons. Thus, a person may simultaneously exhibit contempt for a gathering and underscore his own presence (Parkinson 1962, pp. 73–74) by purposely arriving late. This measure is particularly effective when the proceedings require his presence.

## REFERENCES

Arthur, R., and R. Caputo
  1959  *Interrogation for Investigators.* New York: Copp.

Bradford, Jean
  1971  "Getting the Most out of Odd Moments." *Reader's Digest* (June), pp. 82–84.

Liberman, E. G.
  1968–69  "The Queue: Anamnesis, Diagnosis, Therapy." *Soviet Review* 9 (Winter): 12–16.

Mann, Leon
  1969  "Queue Culture: The Waiting Line as a Social System." *American Journal of Sociology* 75 (November): 340–54.

Meerloo, Joost
  1966  "The Time Sense in Psychiatry." In *The Voices of Time,* edited by J. T. Fraser. New York: Braziller.

Parkinson, C., Northcote
  1962  *Parkinson's Law.* Boston: Houghton-Mifflin.

Solzhenitsyn, Aleksandr
  1968a  *The Cancer Ward.* New York: Dial.
  1968b  *The First Circle.* New York: Harper & Row.

Tawney, R. H.
  1931  *Equality.* London: Allen & Unwin.

# Review Questions

1. Compare and contrast the positions in the hierarchy of a formal organization such as a factory or school in terms of control over one's own and others' time.

2. Explain how waiting may differ in monopolistic as opposed to competitive types of organizations. In which type of organization will the most waiting on the part of the clients occur? Will powerful clients have an advantage over the lowly in both types of organizations? Explain.

3. Discuss the practice of consciously *forcing* others to wait as it is engaged in by (1) the powerful, and (2) the lowly.

4. When are "reneging" and "balking" likely to occur? Are powerful people or subordinates more likely to renege and balk? Explain your answer.

5. Schwartz contends that waiting is structured (that is, occupants of some positions will usually spend more time waiting than occupants of

other positions). Furthermore, waiting entails costs which are both material and psychological. Discuss these contentions, giving evidence from your own experiences.


# Suggested Readings: Inequalities: Class, Race, and Gender

Blau, Peter. *Exchange and Power in Social Life*. New York: Wiley, 1964.

Coser, Lewis A., and Rose Laub Coser. "The Housewife and Her 'Greedy Family,'" pp. 89–100 in Coser and Coser, *Greedy Insitutions: Patterns of Undivided Commitment*. New York: Free Press, 1974.

Gold, Ray. "Janitors Versus Tenants: A Status Income Dilemma," *American Journal of Sociology* 57 (1962): 486–493.

Henley, Nancy M. *Body Politics: Power, Sex and Nonverbal Communication*. Englewood Cliffs, N. J.: Prentice-Hall, 1977.

Hoiberg, Anne, ed. *Women and the World of Work*. New York: Plenum, 1982.

Hughes, Langston. "That Powerful Drop," p. 93, in Gregory P. Stone and Harvey A. Farberman, eds., *Social Psychology Through Symbolic Interaction*. Waltham, Mass.: Ginn-Blaisdell, 1970.

Jencks, Christopher. *Who Gets Ahead?* New York: Basic Books, 1979.

Liebow, Elliot. *Tally's Corner: A Study of Negro Streetcorner Men*. Boston: Little, Brown, 1967.

Mills, C. Wright. *The Power Elite*. New York: Oxford University Press, 1956.

Pearce, Diana. "The Feminization of Poverty: Women, Work and Welfare," *Urban and Social Change Review* (Feb. 1978).

Ross, Catherine E., and John Mirowsky. "Worst Place and Best Face," *Social Forces* 62 (Dec. 1983): 529–536.

Rubin, Lillian. *World of Pain*. New York. Basic Books, 1976.

Schwartz, Barry. *Queuing and Waiting: Studies in the Social Organization of Access and Delay*. Chicago: University of Chicago Press, 1975.

Sennett, Richard, and Jonathan Cobb. *The Hidden Injuries of Class*. New York: Vintage, 1973.

Stone, Gregory P. "The Circumstance and Situation of Social Status," in Gregory P. Stone and Harvey A. Farberman, eds., *Social Psychology Through Symbolic Interaction*. Waltham, Mass.: Ginn-Blaisdell, 1970.

Zetterberg, Hans. "The Secret Ranking," *Journal of Marriage and the Family* (1966): 134–142.

# Part VII. Deviance, Conformity, and Social Control

FOR MANY YEARS, MOST SOCIOLOGISTS VIEWED DEVIANCE AND CONFORMITY as states that could be easily distinguished on the basis of whether a norm had been violated or not. A deviant was defined as a person who violated a custom, rule, or law; conformists were those who did not violate norms. In reality, there is often no way to determine validly who has or has not actually violated a norm, and researchers using this approach usually had to rely on the definitions of the courts, the schools, and other authorities to classify criminals and juvenile delinquents. (Such a procedure is of questionable usefulness, of course, since not everyone who violates rules gets caught, and not everyone who is "caught" has violated rules.) What these sociologists then attempted to do was to understand *why some individuals broke the rules and others did not.* They searched for social forces such as poverty, social disruption of neighborhoods, broken homes, or improper socialization which might be associated with rule violation.

More recently, there has emerged widespread recognition of the limitations of the early approach. It was, in a word, too simple to reflect the complexities of deviance and conformity. By asking a limited set of questions, it paid too little attention to the social forces that *produce deviant labels* and *attach them* to some people and not others. A newer approach, called labeling theory or societal-reaction theory, focuses our attention on *social-control agents*—lawmakers, prison guards, parents, the local gossip, and the like—who have varying amounts of power to decide what conditions and behaviors will be considered deviant and/or to decide who should receive negative societal sanctions for alleged deviance. As Edwin Schur explained, in every society labeling processes occur on the levels of (1) *collective rule making,* as when legislatures enact a law or members of a peer group informally arrive at a norm to guide the members' behavior; (2) *interpersonal reactions* such as stares, gossip, "dirty looks," and rule-enforcement techniques including whistle-blowing by sports officials; and (3) *organizational processing,* from detention after school to incarceration in a prison or mental hospital. These are the rule-enforcement processes that students of deviance and conformity are now addressing.

One of the most important assumptions of labeling theory is that almost no behaviors have been automatically considered deviant across all societies. What is "right" and what is "wrong" are decided upon by societal members within their own cultural, or even subcultural, frameworks. The cannibalism of certain native American groups would be considered deviant in our own society, and the relatively free interaction between girls and boys in American society today would be viewed as sinful in many Latin American societies and even by our own ancestors. Walking about a college campus with a brick tied to one's ankle may appear foolish to many, but the individual who engages in this act may be conforming to the norms of the fraternity. What is to be deemed deviant, then, is *relative* to a given culture's or subculture's normative framework. If we accept that behavior is not automatically deviant, it follows that the *creation of rules* for behavior *creates deviants*. Society, not individuals, makes deviance.

Furthermore, as we noted briefly, not everyone who engages in a culturally disapproved behavior is reacted to as a deviant. And, equally important, not all people who conform to the norms are seen as conformists. Almost anyone who has grown up with brothers and sisters can remember cases in which two children engaged in exactly the same behavior, yet one was punished and the other was not. Not uncommon also are cases in which a child who is conforming is blamed for deviant acts which she or he did not commit. In the larger society as well, "mistakes" such as these are commonplace. Referring to the table below, we can find many instances which could be classified into cells b and c. What's more, *it may be more important in the long run if a person has been labeled than if a person has actually deviated from a norm*. That is, the consequences of labels for the individual's life chances and future interactions may be of greater weight than the individual's own conforming or deviating behavior. In fact, many sociologists argue that one is not deviant unless defined as deviant by other members of society. Deviance is, thus, a social label.

Finally, any given act is usually sufficiently *ambiguous* that it (and its perpetrator) could be interpreted in a number of ways. Norms are often situationally tied, which means that the context of one's behavior must also be evaluated. Killing someone in an officially declared war is not considered murder, for instance, while killing an adulterous spouse may or may not be so viewed. Contracting arthritis may be considered devi-

|  |  | ENGAGED IN A DEVIANT ACT? | |
|  |  | Yes | No |
|---|---|---|---|
| RECEIVED A DEVIANT LABEL? | Yes | a | b |
|  | No | c | d |

ant among the young, but not among the elderly. Just how a condition or act comes to receive meaning within a society of interacting individuals is an important issue for labeling theory.

What factors determine if someone will be labeled as a conformist or a deviant? We know that some types of individuals are more likely to be labeled than others, regardless of their actions. The wealthy person who has several martinis and a bottle of wine with dinner each night is called a "social drinker," while the poor person imbibing an equal amount of (less expensive) liquor is deemed a "drunk" or an "alcoholic." It may be easier for a middle-class person who has political influence or access to lawyers than for a poor person with no "contacts" to escape labeling from police officers, judges, and other agents of the criminal-justice system. Minority-group members may commit no more serious offenses than the WASP, yet because of stereotyping be more readily perceived as deviants (or less readily perceived as conformists). In our society, the poor are often considered less "worthy" in general than are those of greater means. Moreover, once an individual has been successfully labeled by public opinion, by the courts, by parents, or by teachers, other labels may be attached more easily—as with the child who was once caught breaking a family heirloom and who continues to get blamed for all manner of breakage that occurs thereafter, or with the teenager who has a police record and elicits a greater negative reaction from the police officer than the "nice kid." We have seen examples of the latter in Chambliss's article, "The Saints and the Roughnecks," in Part VI.

Another important question is whose interests are served by the laws and rules of society and on whose behalf the agents of social control act when they administer sanctions. The issue of power comes into play here, and there is much evidence to suggest that, in most societies, the rules and rule enforcers function to maintain existing power relations. In the U.S., for instance, the legal system provides more serious punishments for offenses such as burglary and theft committed by individuals than for corporate crimes, from price fixing to the marketing of dangerous products. Deaths resulting from unnecessary surgery are rarely punished as severely as deaths resulting from a barroom brawl. In other words, those with prestige and power may engage in behavior with consequences as serious as those ensuing from the actions of the less powerful and prestigious, but the societal reactions to the former are less severe than reactions to the latter.

Thus, the labeling perspective on deviance and conformity directs our attention *away from* those who have been labeled *toward* those who do the labeling. The questions which researchers are led to ask include: What are the characteristics of the social-control agents who are empowered to make and enforce rules? What systems are developed to define deviance and label deviants? What are the consequences of the labeling process for the individual and for society? Who benefits from the labels and designations of deviance that gain acceptance in a society? How do societal members cope with or attempt to avoid labels?

The articles gathered in this section address a number of these questions. Psychologist D. L. Rosenhan asks how people come to be labeled as mentally ill, how they are controlled in mental hospitals, and what the consequences of psychiatric labels might be for those who receive them. By having a number of normal, "sane" people approach mental hospitals for help with a (false) complaint, he discovered that the psychiatric branch of medicine was quick to attribute mental illness to his pseudo-patients. Furthermore, once an individual received a psychiatric label, the hospital staff reinforced the label by interpreting much of the "normal" behavior that occurred as evidence of insanity. Rosenhan's study shows us how ambiguous conditions and behavior can easily come to be viewed from a deviance perspective. It also shows the constraints of the institutional environment, and especially, of drug treatment, on the behavior of the inmates. We see many ways in which social control creates deviance.

Next, in Marcia Millman's article, "Kids at Fat Camp," we find a poignant example of how social control can have lasting effects on people's self-concepts, thereby creating a self-fulfilling prophecy. It is common knowledge that definitions of fatness and attitudes toward weight vary dramatically from one society to another and from one time period to another. In some societies, thin people are the deviants. In our own society today, however, thinness is the ideal. As one consequence, obese and even plump adolescents are candidates for weight-loss camps.

Parents and camp personnel are the agents of social control who restrict, cajole, and humiliate in order to produce thin children. Whether these agents of social control are successful or not depends on the time frame we adopt: in the short run, pounds come off; in the long run, they return. Millman gives us first-hand data that show that the social-control processes themselves serve to perpetuate the problem, in part by creating "fat" self-concepts. The children internalize the society's labeling scheme and become their own agents of humiliation.

The final article in this section introduces a new perspective in the study of deviance, the perspective of the sociology of emotions. In the past decade more and more sociologists have begun to study the social sides of emotions, sentiments, and feeling states. That is, they are asking how social norms and situations cause or influence the emotions people feel and how they display them. Furthermore, they are studying the consequences of emotions for people's behavior.

The study carried out by Charles Frazier and Thomas Meisenhelder is pathbreaking because it is one of the first to focus on how criminals *feel* before, during, and after their crimes. It seems obvious now that such research could bring us a long way toward an understanding of the interplay of norms and crime, but it took these two sociologists to start. Their article, "Exploratory Notes on Criminality and Emotional Ambivalence," documents the excitement and sense of challenge, as well as the shame and guilt, felt by property offenders. The person who feels shame and guilt has necessarily internalized the norms and labels of the larger society. Again we see examples of self-labeling, the ultimate effect of social control.

# ON BEING SANE IN INSANE PLACES

## D. L. Rosenhan

If SANITY AND INSANITY EXIST, HOW SHALL WE KNOW THEM?

The question is neither capricious nor itself insane. However much we may be personally convinced that we can tell the normal from the abnormal, the evidence is simply not compelling. It is commonplace, for example, to read about murder trials wherein eminent psychiatrists for the defense are contradicted by equally eminent psychiatrists for the prosecution on the matter of the defendant's sanity. More generally, there are a great deal of conflicting data on the reliability, utility, and meaning of such terms as "sanity," "insanity," "mental illness," and "schizophrenia."[1] Finally, as early as 1934, Benedict suggested that normality and abnormality are not universal.[2] What is viewed as normal in one culture may be seen as quite aberrant in another. Thus, notions of normality and abnormality may not be quite as accurate as people believe they are.

To raise questions regarding normality and abnormality is in no way to question the fact that some behaviors are deviant or odd. Murder is deviant. So, too, are hallucinations. Nor does raising such questions deny the existence of the personal anguish that is often associated with "mental illness." Anxiety and depression exist. Psychological suffering exists. But normality and abnormality, sanity and insanity, and the diagnoses that flow from them may be less substantive than many believe them to be.

At its heart, the question of whether the sane can be distinguished from the insane (and whether degrees of insanity can be distinguished from each other) is a simple matter: do the salient characteristics that lead to diagnoses reside in the patients themselves or in the environments and contexts in which observers find them? From Bleuler, through Kretchmer, through the formulators of the recently revised *Diagnostic and Statistical Manual* of the American Psychiatric Association, the belief has been strong that patients present symptoms, that those symptoms can be categorized, and, implicitly, that the sane are distinguishable from the insane. More recently, however, this belief has been questioned. Based in part on theoretical and anthropological considerations, but also on philosophical, legal, and therapeutic ones, the view has grown that psychological categorization of mental illness is useless at

D. L. Rosenhan, "On Being Sane in Insane Places," *Science* 179 (Jan. 1973): 250–258.

best and downright harmful, misleading, and pejorative at worst. Psychiatric diagnoses, in this view, are in the minds of the observers and are not valid summaries of characteristics displayed by the observed.[3-5]

Gains can be made in deciding which of these is more nearly accurate by getting normal people (that is, people who do not have, and have never suffered, symptoms of serious psychiatric disorders) admitted to psychiatric hospitals and then determining whether they were discovered to be sane and, if so, how. If the sanity of such pseudopatients were always detected, there would be prima facie evidence that a sane individual can be distinguished from the insane context in which he is found. Normality (and presumably abnormality) is distinct enough that it can be recognized wherever it occurs, for it is carried within the person. If, on the other hand, the sanity of the pseudopatients were never discovered, serious difficulties would arise for those who support traditional modes of psychiatric diagnosis. Given that the hospital staff was not incompetent, that the pseudopatient had been behaving as sanely as he had been outside of the hospital, and that it had never been previously suggested that he belonged in a psychiatric hospital, such an unlikely outcome would support the view that psychiatric diagnosis betrays little about the patient but much about the environment in which an observer finds him.

This article describes such an experiment. Eight sane people gained secret admission to 12 different hospitals.[6] Their diagnostic experiences constitute the data of the first part of this article; the remainder is devoted to a description of their experiences in psychiatric institutions. Too few psychiatrists and psychologists, even those who have worked in such hospitals, know what the experience is like. They rarely talk about it with former patients, perhaps because they distrust information coming from the previously insane. Those who have worked in psychiatric hospitals are likely to have adapted so thoroughly to the settings that they are insensitive to the impact of that experience. And while there have been occasional reports of researchers who submitted themselves to psychiatric hospitalization,[7] these researchers have commonly remained in the hospitals for short periods of time, often with the knowledge of the hospital staff. It is difficult to know the extent to which they were treated like patients or like research colleagues. Nevertheless, their reports about the inside of the psychiatric hospital have been valuable. This article extends those efforts.

## PSEUDOPATIENTS AND THEIR SETTINGS

The eight pseudopatients were a varied group. One was a psychology graduate student in his 20's. The remaining seven were older and ''established.'' Among them were three psychologists, a pediatrician, a psychiatrist, a painter, and a housewife. Three pseudopatients were women, five were men. All of them employed pseudonyms, lest their alleged diagnoses embarrass them later. Those who were in mental health professions alleged another occupation in order to avoid the special attentions that might be accorded by staff, as a matter of courtesy or caution, to ailing colleagues.[8] With the exception of myself (I was the first pseudopatient and my presence was known to the hospital administrator and chief psychologist and, so far as I can tell, to them alone), the presence of pseudopatients and the nature of the research program w[ere] not known to the hospital staffs.[9]

The settings were similarly varied. In order to generalize the findings, admission into a variety of hospitals was sought. The 12 hospitals in the sample were located in five different states on the East and West coasts. Some were old and shabby, some were quite new. Some were research-oriented, others not. Some had good staff-patient ratios, others were quite understaffed. Only one was a strictly private hospital. All of the others were supported by state or federal funds or, in one instance, by university funds.

After calling the hospital for an appointment, the pseudopatient arrived at the admissions office complaining that he had been hearing voices. Asked what the voices said, he replied that they were often unclear, but as far as he could tell they said "empty," "hollow," and "thud." The voices were unfamiliar and were of the same sex as the pseudopatient. The choice of these symptoms was occasioned by their apparent similarity to existential symptoms. Such symptoms are alleged to arise from painful concerns about the perceived meaninglessness of one's life. It is as if the hallucinating person were saying, "My life is empty and hollow." The choice of these symptoms was also determined by the *absence* of a single report of existential psychoses in the literature.

Beyond alleging the symptoms and falsifying name, vocation, and employment, no further alterations of person, history, or circumstances were made. The significant events of the pseudopatient's life history were presented as they had actually occurred. Relationships with parents and siblings, with spouse and children, with people at work and in school, consistent with the aforementioned exceptions, were described as they were or had been. Frustrations and upsets were described along with joys and satisfactions. These facts are important to remember. If anything, they strongly biased the subsequent results in favor of detecting sanity, since none of their histories or current behaviors were seriously pathological in any way.

Immediately upon admission to the psychiatric ward, the pseudopatient ceased simulating *any* symptoms of abnormality. In some cases, there was a brief period of mild nervousness and anxiety, since none of the pseudopatients really believed that they would be admitted so easily. Indeed, their shared fear was that they would be immediately exposed as frauds and greatly embarrassed. Moreover, many of them had never visited a psychiatric ward; even those who had, nevertheless had some genuine fears about what might happen to them. Their nervousness, then, was quite appropriate to the novelty of the hospital setting, and it abated rapidly.

Apart from that short-lived nervousness, the pseudopatient behaved on the ward as he "normally" behaved. The pseudopatient spoke to patients and staff as he might ordinarily. Because there is uncommonly little to do on a psychiatric ward, he attempted to engage others in conversation. When asked by staff how he was feeling, he indicated that he was fine, that he no longer experienced symptoms. He responded to instructions from attendants, to calls for medication (which was not swallowed), and to dining-hall instructions. Beyond such activities as were available to him on the admissions ward, he spent his time writing down his observations about the ward, its patients, and the staff. Initially these notes were written "secretly," but as it soon became clear that no one much cared, they were subsequently written on standard tablets of paper in such public places as the dayroom. No secret was made of these activities.

The pseudopatient, very much as a true psychiatric patient, entered a hospital with no foreknowledge of when he would be discharged. Each was told that he would have to get out by his own devices, essentially by convincing the staff that he was sane. The psychological stresses associated with hospitalization were considerable, and all but one of the pseudopatients desired to be discharged almost immediately after being admitted. They were, therefore, motivated not only to behave sanely, but to be paragons of cooperation. That their behavior was in no way disruptive is confirmed by nursing reports, which have been obtained on most of the patients. These reports uniformly indicate that the patients were "friendly," "cooperative," and "exhibited no abnormal indications."

## THE NORMAL ARE NOT DETECTABLY SANE

Despite their public "show" of sanity, the pseudopatients were never detected. Admitted, except in one case, with a diagnosis of schizophrenia,[10] each was discharged with a diagnosis of schizophrenia "in remission." The label "in remission" should in no way be dismissed as a formality, for at no time during any hospitalization had any question been raised about any pseudopatient's simulation. Nor are there any indications in the hospital records that the pseudopatient's status was suspect. Rather, the evidence is strong that, once labeled schizophrenic, the pseudopatient was stuck with that label. If the pseudopatient was to be discharged, he must naturally be "in remission"; but he was not sane, nor, in the institution's view, had he ever been sane.

The uniform failure to recognize sanity cannot be attributed to the quality of the hospitals, for, although there were considerable variations among them, several are considered excellent. Nor can it be alleged that there was simply not enough time to observe the pseudopatients. Length of hospitalization ranged from 7 to 52 days, with an average of 19 days. The pseudopatients were not, in fact, carefully observed, but this failure clearly speaks more to traditions within psychiatric hospitals than to lack of opportunity.

Finally, it cannot be said that the failure to recognize the pseudopatients' sanity was due to the fact that they were not behaving sanely. While there was clearly some tension present in all of them, their daily visitors could detect no serious behavioral consequences—nor, indeed, could other patients. It was quite common for the patients to "detect" the pseudopatients' sanity. During the first three hospitalizations, when accurate counts were kept, 35 of a total of 118 patients on the admissions ward voiced their suspicions, some vigorously. "You're not crazy. You're a journalist, or a professor [referring to the continual note-taking]. You're checking up on the hospital." While most of the patients were reassured by the pseudopatient's insistence that he had been sick before he came in but was fine now, some continued to believe that the pseudopatient was sane throughout his hospitalization.[11] The fact that the patients often recognized normality when staff did not raises important questions.

Failure to detect sanity during the course of hospitalization may be due to the fact that physicians operate with a strong bias toward what statisticians call the type 2 error. This is to say that physicians are more inclined to call a healthy person sick (a false positive, type 2) than a sick person healthy (a false negative, type 1). The reasons for this are not hard to find: it is clearly more dangerous to misdiagnose illness than health. Better to err on the side of caution, to suspect illness even among the healthy.

But what holds for medicine does not hold equally well for psychiatry. Medical illnesses, while unfortunate, are not commonly pejorative. Psychiatric diagnoses, on the contrary, carry with them personal, legal, and social stigmas.[12] It was therefore important to see whether the tendency toward diagnosing the sane insane could be reversed. The following experiment was arranged at a research and teaching hospital whose staff had heard these findings but doubted that such an error could occur in their hospital. The staff was informed that at some time during the following 3 months, one or more pseudopatients would attempt to be admitted into the psychiatric hospital. Each staff member was asked to rate each patient who presented himself at admissions or on the ward according to the likelihood that the patient was a pseudopatient. A 10-point scale was used, with a 1 and 2 reflecting high confidence that the patient was a pseudopatient.

Judgments were obtained on 193 patients who were admitted for psychiatric treatment. All staff who had had sustained contact with or primary responsibility for the patient—attendants, nurses, psychiatrists, physicians, and psychologists—were asked to make judgments. Forty-one patients were alleged, with high confidence, to be pseudopatients by at least one member of the staff. Twenty-three were considered suspect by at least one psychiatrist. Nineteen were suspected by one psychiatrist *and* one other staff member. Actually, no genuine pseudopatient (at least from my group) presented himself during this period.

The experiment is instructive. It indicates that the tendency to designate sane people as insane can be reversed when the stakes (in this case, prestige and diagnostic acumen) are high. But what can be said of the 19 people who were suspected of being "sane" by one psychiatrist and another staff member? Were these people truly "sane," or was it rather the case that in the course of avoiding the type 2 error the staff tended to make more errors of the first sort—calling the crazy "sane"? There is no way of knowing. But one thing is certain: any diagnostic process that lends itself so readily to massive errors of this sort cannot be a very reliable one.

## THE STICKINESS OF PSYCHODIAGNOSTIC LABELS

Beyond the tendency to call the healthy sick—a tendency that accounts better for diagnostic behavior on admission than it does for such behavior after a lengthy period of exposure—the data speak to the massive role of labeling in psychiatric assessment. Having once been labeled schizophrenic, there is nothing the pseudopatient can do to overcome the tag. The tag profoundly colors others' perceptions of him and his behavior.

From one viewpoint, these data are hardly surprising, for it has long been known that elements are given meaning by the context in which they occur. Gestalt psychology made this point vigorously, and Asch[13] demonstrated that there are "central" personality traits (such as "warm" versus "cold") which are so powerful that they markedly color the meaning of other information in forming an impression of a given personality.[14] "Insane," "schizophrenic," "manic-depressive," and "crazy" are probably among the most powerful of such central traits. Once a person is designated abnormal, all of his other behaviors and characteristics are colored by that label. Indeed, that label is so powerful that many of the pseudopatients' normal behaviors were overlooked entirely or profoundly misinterpreted. Some examples may clarify this issue.

Earlier I indicated that there were no changes in the pseudopatient's personal history and current status beyond those of name, employment, and where necessary, vocation. Otherwise, a[n accurate] description of personal history and circumstances was offered. Those circumstances were not psychotic. How were they made consonant with the diagnosis of psychosis? Or were those diagnoses modified in such a way as to bring them into accord with the circumstances of the pseudopatient's life, as described by him?

As far as I can determine, diagnoses were in no way affected by the relative health of the circumstances of a pseudopatient's life. Rather, the reverse occurred: the perception of his circumstances was shaped entirely by the diagnosis. A clear example of such translation is found in the case of a pseudopatient who had had a close relationship with his mother but was rather remote from his father during his early childhood. During adolescence and beyond, however, his father became a close friend, while his relationship with his mother cooled. His present relationship with his wife was characteristically close and warm. Apart from occasional angry exchanges, friction was minimal. The children had rarely been spanked. Surely there is nothing especially pathological about such a history. Indeed, many readers may see a similar pattern in their own experiences, with no markedly deleterious consequences. Observe, however, how such a history was translated in the psychopathological context, this from the case summary prepared after the patient was discharged.

> This white 39-year-old male . . . manifests a long history of considerable ambivalence in close relationships, which begins in early childhood. A warm relationship with his mother cools during his adolescence. A distant relationship to his father is described as becoming very intense. Affective stability is absent. His attempts to control emotionality with his wife and children are punctuated by angry outbursts and, in the case of the children, spankings. And while he says that he has several good friends, one senses considerable ambivalence embedded in those relationships also. . . .

The facts of the case were unintentionally distorted by the staff to achieve consistency with a popular theory of the dynamics of a schizophrenic reaction.[15] Nothing of an ambivalent nature had been described in relations with parents, spouse, or friends. To the extent that ambivalence could be inferred, it was probably not greater than is found in all human relationships. It is true the pseudopatient's relationships with his parents changed over time, but in the ordinary context that would hardly be remarkable—indeed, it might very well be expected. Clearly, the meaning ascribed to his verbalizations (that is, ambivalence, affective instability) was determined by the diagnosis: schizophrenia. An entirely different meaning would have been ascribed if it were known that the man was "normal."

All pseudopatients took extensive notes publicly. Under ordinary circumstances, such behavior would have raised questions in the minds of observers, as, in fact, it did among patients. Indeed, it seemed so certain that the notes would elicit suspicion that elaborate precautions were taken to remove them from the ward each day. But the precautions proved needless. The closest any staff member came to questioning these notes occurred when one pseudopatient asked his physician what kind of medication he was receiving and began to write down the response. "You needn't write it," he was told gently. "If you have trouble remembering, just ask me again."

If no questions were asked of the pseudopatients, how was their writing interpreted? Nursing records for three patients indicate that the writing was seen as an aspect of their pathological behavior. "Patient engages in writing behavior" was the daily nursing comment on one of the pseudopatients who was never questioned about his writing. Given that the patient is in the hospital, he must be psychologically disturbed. And given that he is disturbed, continuous writing must be a behavioral manifestation of that disturbance, perhaps a subset of the compulsive behaviors that are sometimes correlated with schizophrenia.

One tacit characteristic of psychiatric diagnosis is that it locates the sources of aberration within the individual and only rarely within the complex of stimuli that surrounds him. Consequently, behaviors that are stimulated by the environment are commonly misattributed to the patient's disorder. For example, one kindly nurse found a pseudopatient pacing the long hospital corridors. "Nervous, Mr. X?" she asked. "No, bored," he said.

The notes kept by pseudopatients are full of patient behaviors that were misinterpreted by well-intentioned staff. Often enough, a patient would go "berserk" because he had, wittingly or unwittingly, been mistreated by, say, an attendant. A nurse coming upon the scene would rarely inquire even cursorily into the environmental stimuli of the patient's behavior. Rather, she assumed that his upset derived from his pathology, not from his present interactions with other staff members. Occasionally, the staff might assume that the patient's family (especially when they had recently visited) or other patients had stimulated the outburst. But never were the staff found to assume that one of themselves or the structure of the hospital had anything to do with a patient's behavior. One psychiatrist pointed to a group of patients who were sitting outside the cafeteria entrance half an hour before lunchtime. To a group of young residents he indicated that such behavior was characteristic of the oral-acquisitive nature of the syndrome. It seemed not to occur to him that there were very few things to anticipate in a psychiatric hospital besides eating.

A psychiatric label has a life and an influence of its own. Once the impression has been formed that the patient is schizophrenic, the expectation is that he will continue to be schizophrenic. When a sufficient amount of time has passed, during which the patient has done nothing bizarre, he is considered to be in remission and available for discharge. But the label endures beyond discharge, with the unconfirmed expectation that he will behave as a schizophrenic again. Such labels, conferred by mental health professionals, are as influential on the patient as they are on his relatives and friends, and it should not surprise anyone that the diagnosis acts on all of them as a self-fulfilling prophecy. Eventually, the patient himself accepts the diagnosis, with all of its surplus meanings and expectations, and behaves accordingly.

The inferences to be made from these matters are quite simple. Much as Zigler and Phillips have demonstrated that there is enormous overlap in the symptoms presented by patients who have been variously diagnosed,[16] so there is enormous overlap in the behaviors of the sane and the insane. The sane are not "sane" all of the time. We lose our tempers "for no good reason." We are occasionally depressed or anxious, again for no good reason. And we may find it difficult to get along with one or another person—again for no reason that we can specify. Similarly, the insane are not always insane. Indeed, it was the impression of the pseudopatients while living with them that they were sane for long periods of time—that the bizarre behaviors upon which their diagnoses were allegedly predicated constituted only a small fraction of their total behavior. If it makes no sense to label ourselves permanently depressed on the basis of an occasional depression, then it takes better evidence than is presently available to label all patients insane or schizophrenic on the basis of bizarre behaviors or cognitions.

•  •  •

## THE EXPERIENCE OF PSYCHIATRIC HOSPITALIZATION

The term "mental illness" is of recent origin. It was coined by people who were humane in their inclinations and who wanted very much to raise the station of (and the public's sympathies toward) the psychologically disturbed from that of witches and "crazies" to one that was akin to the physically ill. And they were at least partially successful, for the treatment of the mentally ill *has* improved considerably over the years. But while treatment has improved, it is doubtful that people really regard the mentally ill in the same way that they view the physically ill. A broken leg is something one recovers from, but mental illness allegedly endures forever.[17] A broken leg does not threaten the observer, but a crazy schizophrenic? There is by now a host of evidence that attitudes toward the mentally ill are characterized by fear, hostility, aloofness, suspicion, and dread.[18] The mentally ill are society's lepers.

That such attitudes infect the general population is perhaps not surprising, only upsetting. But that they affect the professionals—attendants, nurses, physicians, psychologists, and social workers—who treat and deal with the mentally ill is more disconcerting, both because such attitudes are self-evidently pernicious and because they are unwitting. Most mental health professionals would insist that they are sympathetic toward the mentally ill, that they are neither avoidant nor hostile. But it is more likely that an exquisite ambivalence characterizes their relations with psychiatric patients, such that their avowed impulses are only part of their entire attitude. Negative attitudes are there too and can easily be detected. Such attitudes should not surprise us. They are the natural offspring of the labels patients wear and the places in which they are found.

Consider the structure of the typical psychiatric hospital. Staff and patients are strictly segregated. Staff have their own living space, including their dining facilities, bathrooms, and assembly places. The glassed quarters that contain the professional staff, which the pseudopatients came to call "the cage," sit out on every dayroom. The staff emerge primarily for caretaking purposes—to give medication, to conduct a therapy or group meeting, to instruct or reprimand a patient. Otherwise, staff keep to themselves, almost as if the disorder that afflicts their charges is somehow catching.

So much is patient-staff segregation the rule that, for four public hospitals in which an attempt was made to measure the degree to which staff and patients mingle, it was necessary to use "time out of the staff cage" as the operational measure. While it was not the case that all time spent out of the cage was spent mingling with patients (attendants, for example, would occasionally emerge to watch television in the dayroom), it was the only way in which one could gather reliable data on time for measuring.

The average amount of time spent by attendants outside of the cage was 11.3 percent (range, 3 to 52 percent). This figure does not represent only time spent mingling with patients, but also includes time spent on such chores as folding laundry, supervising patients while they shave, directing ward clean-up, and sending patients to off-ward activities. It was the relatively rare attendant who spent time talking with patients or playing games with them. It proved impossible to obtain a "percent mingling time" for nurses, since the amount of time they spent out of the cage was too brief. Rather, we counted instances of emergence from the cage. On the average, daytime nurses emerged from the cage 11.5 times per shift, including instances when they left the ward entirely (range, 4 to 39 times). Late afternoon and night nurses were even less available, emerging on the average 9.4 times per shift (range, 4 to 41 times). Data on early morning nurses, who arrived usually after midnight and departed at 8 A.M., are not available because patients were asleep during most of this period.

Physicians, especially psychiatrists, were even less available. They were rarely seen on the wards. Quite commonly, they would be seen only when they arrived and departed, with the remaining time being spent in their offices or in the cage. On the average, physicians emerged on the ward 6.7 times per day (range, 1 to 17 times). It proved difficult to make an accurate estimate in this regard, since physicians often maintained hours that allowed them to come and go at different times.

The hierarchical organization of the psychiatric hospital has been commented on before,[19] but the latent meaning of that kind of organization is worth noting again. Those with the most power have least to do with patients, and those with the least power are most involved with them. Recall, however, that the acquisition of role-appropriate behaviors occurs mainly through the observation of others, with the most powerful having the most influence. Consequently, it is understandable that attendants not only spend more time with patients than do any other members of the staff—that is required by their station in the hierarchy—but also, insofar as they learn from their superiors' behavior, spend as little time with patients as they can. Attendants are seen mainly in the cage, which is where the models, the action, and the power are.

I turn now to a different set of studies, these dealing with staff response to patient-initiated contact. It has long been known that the amount of time a person spends with you can be an index of your significance to him. If he initiates and maintains eye contact, there is reason to believe that he is considering your requests and needs. If he pauses to chat or actually stops and talks, there is added reason to infer that he is individuating you. In four hospitals, the pseudopatient approached the staff member with a request which took the following form: "Pardon me, Mr. [or Dr. or Mrs.] X, could you tell me when I will be eligible for grounds privileges?" (or " . . . when I will be presented at the staff meeting?" or ". . . when I am likely to be discharged?"). While the content of the question varied according to the appropriateness of the target and the pseudopatient's (apparent) current needs the form was always a courteous and relevant request for information. Care was taken never to approach a particular member of the staff more than once a day, lest the staff member become suspicious or irritated. In examining these data, remember that the behavior of the pseudopatients was neither bizarre nor disruptive. One could indeed engage in good conversation with them.

The data for these experiments are shown in Table 1, separately for physicians (column 1) and for nurses and attendants (column 2). Minor differences between these four institutions were overwhelmed by the degree to which staff avoided continuing contacts that patients had initiated. By far, their most common response consisted of either a brief response to the question, offered while they were "on the move" and with head averted, or no response at all.

The encounter frequently took the following bizarre form: (pseudopatient) "Pardon me, Dr. X. Could you tell me when I am eligible for

**Table 1. Self-initiated Contact by Pseudopatients with Psychiatrists and Nurses and Attendants, Compared to Contact with Other Groups**

| CONTACT | PSYCHIATRIC HOSPITALS | | UNIVERSITY CAMPUS (NONMEDICAL) | UNIVERSITY MEDICAL CENTER PHYSICIANS | | |
| --- | --- | --- | --- | --- | --- | --- |
| | *(1)* Psychiatrists | *(2)* Nurses and attendants | *(3)* Faculty | *(4)* "Looking for a psychiatrist" | *(5)* "Looking for an internist" | *(6)* No additional comment |
| **Responses** | | | | | | |
| Moves on, head averted (%) | 71 | 88 | 0 | 0 | 0 | 0 |
| Makes eye contact (%) | 23 | 10 | 0 | 11 | 0 | 0 |
| Pauses and chats (%) | 2 | 2 | 0 | 11 | 0 | 10 |
| Stops and talks (%) | 4 | 0.5 | 100 | 78 | 100 | 90 |
| Mean number of questions answered (out of 6) | * | * | 6 | 3.8 | 4.8 | 4.5 |
| Respondents (No.) | 13 | 47 | 14 | 18 | 15 | 10 |
| Attempts (No.) | 185 | 1283 | 14 | 18 | 15 | 10 |

*NOT APPLICABLE.

grounds privileges?'' (physician) ''Good morning, Dave. How are you today?'' (Moves off without waiting for a response.)

It is instructive to compare these data with data recently obtained at Stanford University. It has been alleged that large and eminent universities are characterized by faculty who are so busy that they have no time for students. For this comparison, a young lady approached individual faculty members who seemed to be walking purposefully to some meeting or teaching engagement and asked them the following six questions.

1. ''Pardon me, could you direct me to Encina Hall?'' (at the medical school: ''. . . to the Clinical Research Center?'').
2. ''Do you know where Fish Annex is?'' (there is no Fish Annex at Stanford).
3. ''Do you teach here?''
4. ''How does one apply for admission to the college?'' (at the medical school: ''. . . to the medical school?'').
5. ''Is it difficult to get in?''
6. ''Is there financial aid?''

Without exception, as can be seen in Table 1 (column 3), all of the questions were answered. No matter how rushed they were, all respondents not only maintained eye contact, but stopped to talk. Indeed, many of the respondents went out of their way to direct or take the questioner to the office she was seeking, to try to locate ''Fish Annex,'' or to discuss with her the possibilities of being admitted to the university.

Similar data, also shown in Table 1 (columns 4, 5, and 6), were obtained in the hospital. Here too, the young lady came prepared with six questions. After the first question, however, she remarked to 18 of her respondents (column 4), ''I'm looking for a psychiatrist,'' and to 15 others (column 5), ''I'm looking for an internist.'' Ten other respondents received no inserted comment (column 6). The general degree of cooperative responses is considerably higher for these university groups than it was for pseudopatients in psychiatric hospitals. Even so, differences are apparent within the medical school setting. Once having indicated that she was looking for a psychiatrist, the degree of cooperation elicited was less than when she sought an internist.

## POWERLESSNESS AND DEPERSONALIZATION

Eye contact and verbal contact reflect concern and individuation; their absence, avoidance and depersonalization. The data I have presented do not do justice to the rich daily encounters that grew up around matters of depersonalization and avoidance. I have records of patients who were beaten by staff for the sin of having initiated verbal contact. During my own experience, for example, one patient was beaten in the presence of other patients for having approached an attendant and told him, "I like you." Occasionally, punishment meted out to patients for misdemeanors seemed so excessive that it could not be justified by the most radical interpretations of psychiatric canon. Nevertheless, they appeared to go unquestioned. Tempers were often short. A patient who had not heard a call for medication would be roundly excoriated, and the morning attendants would often wake patients with, "Come on, you m——f——s, out of bed!"

Neither anecdotal nor "hard" data can convey the overwhelming sense of powerlessness which invades the individual as he is continually exposed to the depersonalization of the psychiatric hospital. It hardly matters *which* psychiatric hospital—the excellent public ones and the very plush private hospital were better than the rural and shabby ones in this regard, but, again, the features that psychiatric hospitals had in common overwhelmed by far their apparent differences.

Powerlessness was evident everywhere. The patient is deprived of many of his legal rights by dint of his psychiatric commitment.[20] He is shorn of credibility by virtue of his psychiatric label. His freedom of movement is restricted. He cannot initiate contact with the staff, but may only respond to such overtures as they make. Personal privacy is minimal. Patient quarters and possessions can be entered and examined by any staff member, for whatever reason. His personal history and anguish is available to any staff member (often including the "grey lady" and "candy striper" volunteer) who chooses to read his folder, regardless of their therapeutic relationship to him. His personal hygiene and waste evacuation are often monitored. The water closets may have no doors.

At times, depersonalization reached such proportions that pseudopatients had the sense that they were invisible, or at least unworthy of account. Upon being admitted, I and other pseudopatients took the initial physical examinations in a semipublic room, where staff members went about their own business as if we were not there.

On the ward, attendants delivered verbal and occasionally serious physical abuse to patients in the presence of other observing patients, some of whom (the pseudopatients) were writing it all down. Abusive behavior, on the other hand, terminated quite abruptly when other staff members were known to be coming. Staff are credible witnesses. Patients are not.

A nurse unbuttoned her uniform to adjust her brassiere in the presence of an entire ward of viewing men. One did not have the sense that she was being seductive. Rather, she didn't notice us. A group of staff persons might point to a patient in the dayroom and discuss him animatedly, as if he were not there.

One illuminating instance of depersonalization and invisibility occurred with regard to medications. All told, the pseudopatients were administered nearly 2100 pills, including Elavil, Stelazine, Compazine, and Thorazine, to name but a few. (That such a variety of medications should have been administered to patients presenting identical symptoms is itself worthy of note.) Only two were swallowed. The rest were either pocketed or deposited in the toilet. The pseudopatients were not alone in this. Although I have no precise records on how many patients rejected their medications, the pseudopatients frequently found the medications of other patients in the toilet before they deposited their own. As long as they were cooperative, their behavior and the pseudopatients' own in this matter, as in other important matters, went unnoticed throughout.

Reactions to such depersonalization among pseudopatients were intense. Although they had come to the hospital as participant observers and were fully aware that they did not "belong," they nevertheless found themselves caught up in and fighting the process of depersonalization. Some examples: a graduate student in psychology asked his wife to bring his textbooks to the hospital so he could "catch up on his homework"—this despite the elaborate precautions taken to conceal his professional association. The same student, who had trained for quite some time to get into the hospital, and who had looked forward to the experience, "remembered" some drag races that he had wanted to see on the weekend and insisted that he be discharged by that time. Another pseudopatient attempted a romance with a nurse. Subsequently, he informed the staff that he was applying for admission to graduate school in psychology and was very likely to be admitted, since a graduate professor was one of his regular hospital visitors. The same person began to engage in psychotherapy with other patients—all of this as a way of becoming a person in an impersonal environment.

## THE SOURCES OF DEPERSONALIZATION

What are the origins of depersonalization? I have already mentioned two. First are attitudes held by all of us toward the mentally ill—including those who treat them—attitudes characterized by fear, distrust, and horrible expectations on the one hand, and benevolent intentions on the other. Our ambivalence leads, in this instance as in others, to avoidance.

Second, and not entirely separate, the hierarchical structure of the psychiatric hospital facilitates depersonalization. Those who are at the top have least to do with patients, and their behavior inspires the rest of the staff. Average daily contact with psychiatrists, psychologists, residents, and physicians combined ranged from 3.9 to 25.1 minutes, with an overall mean of 6.8 (six pseudopatients over a total of 129 days of hospitalization). Included in this average are time spent in the admissions interview, ward meetings in the presence of a senior staff member, group and individual psychotherapy contacts, case presentation conferences, and discharge meetings. Clearly, patients do not spend much time in interpersonal contact with doctoral staff. And doctoral staff serve as models for nurses and attendants.

There are probably other sources. Psychiatric installations are presently in serious financial straits. Staff shortages are pervasive, staff time at a premium. Something has to give, and that something is patient contact. Yet, while financial stresses are realities, too much can be made of them. I have the impression that the psychological forces that result in depersonalization are much stronger than the fiscal ones and that the addition of more staff would not correspondingly improve patient care in this regard. The incidence of staff meetings and the enormous amount of recordkeeping on patients, for example, have not been as substantially reduced as has patient contact. Priorities exist, even during hard times. Patient contact is not a significant priority in the traditional psychiatric hospital, and fiscal pressures do not account for this. Avoidance and depersonalization may.

Heavy reliance upon psychotropic medication tacitly contributes to depersonalization by convincing staff that treatment is indeed being conducted and that further patient contact may not be necessary. Even here, however, caution needs to be exercised in understanding the role of psychotropic drugs. If patients were powerful rather than powerless, if they were viewed as interesting individuals rather than diagnostic entities, if they were socially significant rather than social lepers, if their anguish truly and wholly compelled our sympathies and concerns, would we not *seek* contact with them, despite the availability of medications? Perhaps for the pleasure of it all?

## THE CONSEQUENCES OF LABELING AND DEPERSONALIZATION

Whenever the ratio of what is known to what needs to be known approaches zero, we tend to invent "knowledge" and assume that we understand more than we actually do. We seem unable to acknowledge that we simply don't know. The needs for diagnosis and remediation of behavioral and emotional problems are enormous. But rather than acknowledge that we are just embarking on understanding, we continue to label patients "schizophrenic," "manic-depressive," and "insane," as if in those words we had captured the essence of understanding. The facts of the matter are that we have known for a long time that diagnoses are often not useful or reliable, but we have nevertheless continued to use them. We now know that we cannot distinguish insanity from sanity. It is depressing to consider how that information will be used.

Not merely depressing, but frightening. How many people, one wonders, are sane but not recognized as such in our psychiatric institutions? How many have been needlessly stripped of their privileges of citizenship, from the right to vote and drive to that of handling their own accounts? How many have feigned insanity in order to avoid the criminal consequences of their behavior, and, conversely, how many would rather stand trial than live interminably in a psychiatric hospital—but are wrongly thought to be mentally ill? How many have been stigmatized by well-intentioned, but nevertheless erroneous, diagnoses? On the last point, recall again that a "type 2 error" in psychiatric diagnosis does not have the same consequences it does in medical diagnosis. A diagnosis of cancer that has been found to be in error is cause for celebration. But psychiatric diagnoses are rarely found to be in error. The label sticks, a mark of inadequacy forever.

Finally, how many patients might be "sane" outside the psychiatric hospital but seem insane in it—not because craziness resides in them, as it were, but because they are responding to a bizarre setting, one that may be unique to institutions which harbor nether people? Goffman calls the process of socialization to such institutions "mortification"—an apt metaphor that includes the processes of depersonalization that have been described here. And while it is impossible to know whether the pseudopatients' responses to these processes are characteristic of all inmates—they were, after all, not real patients—it is difficult to believe that these processes of socialization to a psychiatric hospital provide useful attitudes or habits of response for living in the "real world." . . .[21]

## REFERENCES AND NOTES

1. P. Ash, *J. Abnorm. Soc. Psychol.* 44, 272 (1949); A. T. Beck, *Amer. J. Psychiat.* 119, 210 (1962); A. T. Boisen, *Psychiatry* 2, 233 (1938); N. Kreitman, *J. Ment. Sci.* 107, 876 (1961); N. Kreitman, P. Sainsbury, J. Morrisey, J. Towers, J. Scrivener, *ibid.*, p. 887; H. O. Schmitt and C. P. Fonda, *J. Abnorm. Soc. Psychol.* 52, 262 (1956); W. Seeman, *J. Nerv. Ment. Dis.* 118, 541 (1953). For an analysis of these artifacts and summaries of the disputes, see J. Zubin, *Annu. Rev. Psychol.* 18, 373 (1967); L. Phillips and J. G. Draguns, *ibid.* 22, 447 (1971).

2. R. Benedict, *J. Gen. Psychol.* 10, 59 (1934).

3. See in this regard H. Becker, *Outsiders: Studies in the Sociology of Deviance* (Free Press, New York, 1963); B. M. Braginsky, D. D. Braginsky, K. Ring, *Methods of Madness: The Mental Hospital as a Last Resort* (Holt, Rinehart & Winston, New York, 1969); G. M. Crocetti and P. V. Lemkau, *Amer. Sociol. Rev.* 30, 577 (1965); E. Goffman, *Behavior in Public Places* (Free Press, New York, 1964); R. D. Laing, *The Divided Self: A Study of Sanity and Madness* (Quadrangle, Chicago, 1960); D. L. Phillips, *Amer. Sociol. Rev.* 28, 963 (1963); T. R. Sarbin, *Psychol. Today* 6, 18 (1972); E. Schur, *Amer. J. Sociol.* 75, 309 (1969); T. Szasz, *Law, Liberty and Psychiatry* (Macmillan, New York, 1963); *The Myth of Mental Illness: Foundations of a Theory of Mental Illness* (Hoeber-Harper, New York, 1963). For a critique of some of these views, see W. R. Gove, *Amer. Sociol. Rev.* 35, 873 (1970).

4. E. Goffman, *Asylums* (Doubleday, Garden City, N.Y., 1961).

5. T. J. Scheff, *Being Mentally Ill: A Sociological Theory* (Aldine, Chicago, 1966).

6. Data from a ninth pseudopatient are not incorporated in this report be-

cause, although his sanity went undetected, he falsified aspects of his personal history, including his marital status and parental relationships. His experimental behaviors therefore were not identical to those of the other pseudopatients.

7. A. Barry, *Bellevue Is a State of Mind* (Harcourt Brace Jovanovich, New York, 1971); I. Belknap, *Human Problems of a State Mental Hospital* (McGraw-Hill, New York, 1956); W. Caudill, F. C. Redlich, H. R. Gilmore, E. B. Brody, *Amer. J. Orthopsychiat.* 22, 314 (1952); A. R. Goldman, R. H. Bohr, T. A. Steinberg, *Prof. Psychol.* 1, 427 (1970); unauthored, *Roche Report* 1 (No. 13), 8 (1971).

8. Beyond the personal difficulties that the pseudopatient is likely to experience in the hospital, there are legal and social ones that, combined, require considerable attention before entry. For example, once admitted to a psychiatric institution, it is difficult, if not impossible, to be discharged on short notice, state law to the contrary notwithstanding. I was not sensitive to these difficulties at the outset of the project, nor to the personal and situational emergencies that can arise, but later a writ of habeas corpus was prepared for each of the entering pseudopatients and an attorney was kept "on call" during every hospitalization. I am grateful to John Kaplan and Robert Bartels for legal advice and assistance in these matters.

9. However distasteful such concealment is, it was a necessary first step to examining these questions. Without concealment, there would have been no way to know how valid these experiences were; nor was there any way of knowing whether whatever detections occurred were a tribute to the diagnostic acumen of the staff or to the hospital's rumor network. Obviously, since my concerns are general ones that cut across individual hospitals and staffs, I have respected their anonymity and have eliminated clues that might lead to their identification.

10. Interestingly, of the 12 admissions, 11 were diagnosed as schizophrenic and one, with the identical symptomatology, as manic-depressive psychosis. This diagnosis has a more favorable prognosis, and it was given by the only private hospital in our sample. On the relations between social class and psychiatric diagnosis, see A. deB. Hollingshead and F. C. Redlich, *Social Class and Mental Illness: A Community Study* (Wiley, New York, 1958).

11. It is possible, of course, that patients have quite broad latitudes in diagnosis and therefore are inclined to call many people sane, even those whose behavior is patently aberrant. However, although we have no hard data on this matter, it was our distinct impression that this was not the case. In many instances, patients not only singled us out for attention, but came to imitate our behaviors and styles.

12. J. Cumming and E. Cumming, *Community Ment. Health* 1, 135 (1965); A. Farina and K. Ring, *J. Abnorm. Psychol.* 70, 47 (1965); H. E. Freeman and O. G. Simmons, *The Mental Patient Comes Home* (Wiley, New York, 1963); W. J. Johannsen, *Ment. Hygiene* 53, 218 (1969); A. S. Linsky, *Soc. Psychiat.* 5, 166 (1970).

13. S. E. Asch, *J. Abnorm. Soc. Psychol.* 41, 258 (1946); *Social Psychology* (Prentice-Hall, New York, 1952).

14. See also I. N. Mensh and J. Wishner, *J. Personality* 16, 188 (1947); J. Wishner, *Psychol. Rev.* 67, 96 (1960); J. S. Bruner and R. Tagiuri, in *Handbook of Social Psychology*, G. Lindzey, Ed. (Addison-Wesley, Cambridge, Mass., 1954), vol. 2, pp. 634–654; J. S. Bruner, D. Shapiro, R. Tagiuri, in *Person Perception and Interpersonal Behavior*, R. Tagiuri and L. Petrullo, Eds. (Stanford Univ. Press, Stanford, Calif., 1958), pp. 277–288.

322    D. L. Rosenhan

15. For an example of a similar self-fulfilling prophecy in this instance dealing with the "central" trait of intelligence, see R. Rosenthal and L. Jacobson, *Pygmalion in the Classroom* (Holt, Rinehart & Winston, New York, 1968).

16. E. Zigler and L. Phillips, *J. Abnorm. Soc. Psychol.* 63, 69 (1961). See also R. K. Freudenberg and J. P. Robertson, *A.M.A. Arch. Neurol. Psychiatr.* 76, 14 (1956).

17. The most recent and unfortunate instance of this tenet is that of Senator Thomas Eagleton.

18. T. R. Sarbin and J. C. Mancuso, *J. Clin. Consult. Psychol.* 35, 159 (1970); T. R. Sarbin, *ibid.* 31, 447 (1967); J. C. Nunnally, Jr., *Popular Conceptions of Mental Health* (Holt, Rinehart & Winston, New York, 1961).

19. A. H. Stanton and M. S. Schwartz, *The Mental Hospital: A Study of Institutional Participation in Psychiatric Illness and Treatment* (Basic, New York, 1954).

20. D. B. Wexler and S. E. Scoville, *Ariz. Law Rev.* 13, 1 (1971).

21. I thank W. Mischel, E. Orne, and M. S. Rosenhan for comments on an earlier draft of this manuscript.

# Review Questions

1. According to Rosenhan, how easy is it for mental-health workers to determine who is "really" sane and who is "really" insane?

2. How did the staff members of mental hospitals act to legitimate the labels that psychiatrists gave to the "mental patients"?

3. How does psychiatric labeling in general serve social-control functions for society? What particular social-control techniques were used in the hospitals studied here to make the everyday routine run smoothly?

4. Why did none of the "patients" in Rosenhan's study get turned away from the mental hospitals?

# KIDS AT FAT CAMP

## Marcia Millman

*Girl Camper:* Adele, is toothpaste fattening? Because some kids are eating it.

*Adele (Camp Owner and Director):* Very nice. Now what does that tell you?

*Second Girl Camper:* (Shouts out, laughing) It tells you that we're hungry.

*Adele:* No, it doesn't tell me you're hungry. It tells me that you are obsessed with eating and that's all you think about.

Camp Laurel, which used to be a motel, consists of two dozen bungalows arranged in a circle around a concrete driveway. In the middle of the circle is a dirt playground with swings, seesaws, and a turning platform.

For the hundreds of fat children who have been sent here for the summer to lose weight, the camp represents many contradictory things: a prison, a refuge, a place to be transformed.

Camp Laurel is attended by children and teenagers, both male and female, from ages seven to eighteen, and by older counselors who have also come to lose weight. Although some of the children are very heavy (100 pounds or more overweight) others are barely plump, and certainly not more than five or ten pounds overweight. Most are from Jewish middle-class families. The cost for each camper will come close to $1,800. Throughout the summer each will be restricted to a daily diet of under twelve hundred calories and forced to exercise as much as possible.

We can already see among these campers the early stages of life themes [that are recounted by adults as well]. It is well known that the great majority (80 to 90 percent) of fat children become fat adults. But as early as childhood we can also see the beginnings of experiences and world views that will probably follow the overweight person all through life: being excluded and separated from normal society because of their weight, believing that losing weight will solve all their problems, and experiencing dieting as unjust punishment imposed from the outside.

"Girls Bunks one through four, and Boys three through nine, get to the dining hall, *now!* Judy Cohen come to the office for a phone call. David Goodman report to your bunk."

This article is chapter 3 in Marcia Millman, *Such a Pretty Face* (New York: Berkley Books, 1980), pp. 49–64.

It is noontime, and the camp owner's voice booms over the loud-speaker, reaching every corner of the grounds. The voice comes often. There is rarely more than five minutes of respite from the loudspeaker.

The announcement that it is time to eat is hardly necessary, for as usual, lunch has been eagerly anticipated all morning, and speculations about what will be served have dominated talk around the camp for the past two hours. But as the children file through the food line, collect their portions, and take places with their bunk-mates at the long tables and benches, their fantasies dissolve before the paltry meal. Lunch today is a slice of bologna and a slice of American cheese on a single thin piece of white bread, a small portion of canned mandarin oranges, washed of their syrup, and served in a little accordion paper cup (the size used at lunch counters to serve mayonnaise), four ounces of reconstituted in-stant nonfat milk mixed with artificial sweetener, and a small serving of iceberg lettuce topped with a ring of green pepper. The meal is served on paper plates and eaten with plastic utensils.

While they silently eat, more information comes over the loudspeaker, and one girl is sent out of dining hall for talking to her neighbor before the announcements are completed. Although they have been instructed to eat slowly, lunch is finished in ten minutes and soon the campers con-gregate in small groups in the playground outside. Reminiscing about the foods they used to eat, their faces and voices becoming animated once again.

"My mother makes them with *both* chocolate chips and butterscotch bits," boasts one camper. "Does your mother make them with nuts?" counters another. Across the playground a camper recalls the "s'mores" they used to serve at the camp she went to the previous summer and still another proudly announces that the very block she lives on in Manhat-tan's Upper West Side has a Baskin-Robbins ice cream parlor and both a Barton's and Barricini's candy store.

What makes diet camp seem so much like prison is that, by being sent there, the child is implicitly told that he or she is not fit to be with normal children. And although some eventually come to believe (or partly be-lieve) that they are being sent for their own good, few are happy about it at first. Not only does the experience segregate fat children from the world of normals, but it also takes a happy time—summer—and turns it into a season of deprivation and labor. It denies these children what they most enjoy doing—eating—and substitutes what they hate most: strenu-ous exercise. Several campers lie to their winter friends about where they are going for the summer, because they are ashamed and feel that being sent to a special camp will further mark them as fat and different in the eyes of their peers.

Some of the younger children are first-timers to the camp and are es-pecially upset at the news of being sent there. Several are hardly over-weight but have parents who are fat and want to make sure their children won't be. Indeed, one slightly overweight ten-year-old recalls that her mother forced her to come. The girl had no part in the decision, even though when the camp brochures arrived in the mail, she ripped them up and ran to her room, threatening to leave home.

Not only do the children feel constantly starved for food (and indeed, one might well ask whether young children should be on such a restricted diet) but to some extent they also regard the staff as jailers. The presumption is made by the staff that without constant surveillance many of the children will be importing forbidden food into the camp, cheating on their diets, and avoiding exercise. The enforcement of diets and exercise is both a cause and outcome of the children's noncompliance.

Feeling pushed around, the children do rebel wherever they can. Complaining of how the camp is "killing them," many approach exercises and sports that children usually enjoy with a lethargy and disdain that is remarkable. And excuses for sitting out activities are made so frequently that the counselors quite rightly argue, "Girls, you can't be having your period for a month at a time." The counselors also calculate that if all the complained-of ailments were legitimate, roughly a quarter of the camp children might be considered badly injured at any given time. This is difficult to believe, considering the care with which the children move themselves.

But most rebellious of all are the food smugglers. Dreaming up ways to cheat on the diet is a continuous project among campers, pursued with far more interest and enthusiasm than the exercises. The camp has a fairly tight food control system. For example, all packages arriving in the mail must be opened in a counselor's presence, and even money is forbidden to campers since it might be used to commission the purchase of candy when someone gets permission to go into town. The camp expects this mutiny from the diet. The older children know that all campers are sent to the movies the afternoons after parents' visiting days so their bunks and mattresses can be thoroughly searched by counselors for hidden food.

Finally, many campers are cynical about whose interests are served by camp policies. While they do not believe that they are really the victims of staff cruelty (most of the campers think the counselors, being fat themselves, are sympathetic), they do suspect that the profit motive rather than concern for their welfare is behind most of the policies. For example, when some campers petitioned for a higher ration of protein in their diet they were skeptical of the camp owner's explanations: that she served such foods as cereal for breakfast because the children would always be exposed to foods like these, and needed to learn how to eat them in modified portions.

The children's skepticism is logical. Many have attended the camp during previous summers and always regained the lost weight by New

Year's. And many admit that even though they want to lose weight, if left free of external control, they would be eating fattening foods.

What ultimately undermines their faith in the camp and makes it seem even more like a prison is the hypocrisy of the staff. The counselors are supposed to be role models for the campers in diet and exercise, but they frequently show the smallest weight losses. It it obvious why: they are allowed into town so they have more opportunities to cheat. Despite their presumed greater maturity the counselors illustrate the principle that once external control is removed, many will abandon the diet.

Furthermore, the camp owner herself is overweight, and though her lectures are wise and she is the object of some affection from the campers, she, too, is considered a hypocrite. Because she allowed some of the "homesick" campers to come to her house (on the camp grounds) and do chores like make her bed, they have had opportunities to observe her own eating habits. Word got around and now campers complain that "Adele doesn't practice what she preaches. She eats half a cherry pie and washes it down with nonfat milk." Other children gossip about how she has not one, but *two* refrigerators in her kitchen and how one is always filled with ice cream and cake.

If the children are cynical about the ultimate benefits of the diet camp, so are the staff and management. Asked whether the camp could be the subject of a story in the media, the top administrators considered among themselves whether they had anything to lose by this kind of coverage. One administrator speculated, "Well, they could say that 95 percent of diets fail and people gain the weight back, but even if they do say it, that can't hurt us. All the parents who send their children here think their kids will be one of the 5 percent."

One of the most significant dangers of sending children to a diet camp is that they learn to associate dieting with punishment or at least arbitrary external rule rather than as something voluntarily pursued as a way of being good to themselves. The source of control for what can or can't be eaten rests outside the child, and the child's sense of control can then come only from cheating or resisting. Thus begins a long career of associating dieting with oppressive restrictions imposed from the outside and to be resisted or abandoned. Thus the camp may be experienced as a prison in a fundamental way; put someone in prison and all they will think about is how to get out. Put people on a diet with external monitors and enforcement and all they will think about is how to cheat. What campers may be learning, like first-time offenders in jail, may be why they should resent the authorities and how to circumvent them rather than why and how they should "rehabilitate" themselves.

Of course, the children at Camp Laurel complain in the same ways that children always complain about camp: that the management is repressive, that there aren't enough good activities, that the food is terrible. Slender children at regular camps, too, often feel that camp is like a prison and fight with the staff about unfair rules. The difference between Camp Laurel and the others is that for the fat children struggles with authority are centered around food and dieting, just as fat adults often focus exclusively on weight as the cause of their troubles.

It would be very mistaken, however, to think that Camp Laurel represents merely a prison for its residents. It is also a refuge from a hostile world. Although children new to the camp may at first resent being sent, many come to like it. Some of the older children even come of their own choice. For them, Camp Laurel is a last resort, all other diets having failed. Some already feel excluded from the world of normal teenagers, so the camp represents a friendly, comfortable home rather than bitter exile.

Having acknowledged that they are indeed fat, many children find pleasure in being with others of their own kind. It is often said at Camp Laurel that the kids there are "nicer" than children at regular camps. Indeed, given the teasing and exclusion these children would probably experience among slim children, this is probably true. Many children also remark that only among other fat children could they feel comfortable enough to wear bathing suits, shorts, and halters and participate in sports and physical activities.

Many are relieved to learn that others use the very same lies and deceits they have used to obtain and eat forbidden foods. Others are comforted in discovering that others have suffered through the same fights with parents and humiliations in gym class or embarrassment from being unable to keep up with other children in physical activities. In the special world of the camp, their sensitivity about weight is even reduced enough for some to willingly adapt to fat-associated nicknames such as Blimp or Stubby—names they would never tolerate in the outside world.

Learning to be comfortable around other fat children is just one of the many identity experiences children have at camp. In some ways, being with other fat children minimizes the salience of their weight for their social identities. Since all the children are fat, they can see and relate to each other and themselves in terms of other characteristics. But in other ways being segregated from the normal world also underscores and enlarges the importance of their weight. In an ironic way the camp actually schools them in the ways of surviving as a fat person in a hostile, unsympathetic world and, indeed, teaches them to view the world from the perspective of a member of an oppressed minority group. Whether the camp is considered a refuge or a prison, one thing is certain: the outside world is a place to be dealt with guardedly. A much-talked-about camp episode . . . illustrates this point.

During an athletic meet between Camp Laurel and a neighboring (regular) boys' camp, the Laurel boys were successfully baited by their adversaries. While the counselors weren't around, the "normal" boys taunted the fat children with Oreo cookies. Dangling the cookies before

them, the thinner boys teased, "Here, doggie. Have a cookie, doggie."
Starved for long-missed sweets and not knowing when they would have
such an opportunity again, the Laurel boys gratefully grabbed the cookies and ate them.

In a camp meeting that followed this event, the camp owner lectured
about the disgrace the campers had brought on themselves by eating the
cookies. This was placed in the context of reminding the children that
they must always remember their disadvantaged position in the world:

*Adele:* They weren't being friendly when they offered you cookies.
They don't look at you the way we see ourselves. Thin people look at us
differently. They don't understand us. When they offered you food it
was like offering food to the animals at the zoo. They are offering you
food as a big joke and they are laughing *at* you, not with you.

Despite the lethargy and occasional cheating, and the doubtfulness of
the camp's programs as a long-term solution, most of the children do
lose a substantial amount of weight (over 20 pounds) during the summer. For the smaller ones, this amount of weight loss can transform a fat
child into a slim one. Moreover, since the children are separated from
their families and friends all summer, the change in appearance takes on
the dramatic character of a life transformation.

If food is one of the main topics of conversation among campers, losing weight is the other. Over the weeks as they lose weight they constantly ask one another, "If you saw me on the street and you didn't
know me, would you think I was fat?" Undaunted by their previous experiences of gaining back lost weight, they frequently vow that this will
be their last year at the camp and that they are confident of the future:
"When I lose weight, I'll be *perfect.*" Their exhilaration goes beyond the
certainty that they will be slim, for after all, they have been raised to believe that their weight is the cause of all their unhappiness. All kinds of
major benefits are expected to follow: "When I lose weight, I'll do better
in school and I'll be more entroverted." Faith in the millennium even
carries them through trying experiences. Said one camper, "When the
kids from the other camp tease me and call me a fat pig I say, 'I may be
fat, but I'm doing something about it. You're stupid; what can you do
about that?' If you're ugly or stupid, you're stuck with it, but fat you can
always lose."

"Half of you is missing when you go home," one camper explains. It
is an interesting way to describe the transformation, for it suggests the
feeling that part of their identities will be left behind with the weight that
is shed. When one considers what it must feel like to come from a family
where slimness is associated with upward social mobility and fatness
with one's ethnic origins (as it is among many Jewish and Italian Americans), this statement has special poignancy.

The contradictory meanings and nature of the camp are nowhere better expressed than in the weekly nutrition classes held for each division.

It is the time, once a week, when the campers are weighed and thus rewarded for their week's labors.

The owner of the camp starts each class by reading the "ideal" weights for every height represented in the group, and the children listen, transfixed, asking her to repeat the weights over and over again. A few argue with the "ideal" and point out that individual build should be taken into account, and to this point Adele always agrees. One boy can be heard complaining, "According to that chart I should lose 15 more pounds. If I lost another 15 pounds I'd be *dead*."

One nutrition class for the twelve-year-old girls got under way when Adele invited them to raise problems or questions:

*Adele:* While we're waiting for the counselors to set up the scales, let me take some questions.

*Girl:* Adele, will I ever be able to eat cake?

*Adele:* I wouldn't say you can never eat cake, but you have to remember we're different from other people. Thin people only eat when they're hungry. Do you ever turn down food? After dinner, when you have company and your mother serves cake do you ever say no? Skinny people only eat when they're hungry.

There were no other questions, so Adele decided to grill them. "Let me ask *you* a question. Who can tell us all a good reason for losing weight? Raise your hand."

One small girl raised her hand and answered, "I don't *like* being fat." Another volunteered, "You're fat and people laugh at you." A third added, "You can't go places."

By now the scales were set up on the auditorium stage and the children lined up. One came running down the steps screaming and crying. "Five pounds—I lost five pounds." Tears of joy rolled down her face. Others repeated the gesture, hugging their friends and wildly jumping up and down. They seemed to mimic contestants on a television game show. One girl called to her friends, "I can't believe it—I'm in my *teens*" (meaning she weighed under 120). More quietly, another told a friend that she weighed under 200 pounds for the first time since she was ten years old.

But there were also disappointments. Some had lost only a pound or two in the last week, or perhaps only 10 pounds since camp had started four weeks earlier, and they complained that the small losses didn't justify the costs and sacrifice. Adele had an answer ready.

*Adele:* This is a small town and I hear everything that goes on. If you belch at the other end of town, I can hear it here. Of those of you who lost less than two pounds, how many of you went horseback riding in town on Tuesday?

[Several raise hands]

*Adele:* Of you girls, is there anyone who has something to tell the group?

[Silence]

*Adele:* Doesn't anyone have anything they would like to share?

*Girl [near tears]:* I cheated.

*Adele:* You what? Say it louder.

*Girl:* I cheated.

*Adele:* O.K. I knew this happened. [To the girl] Would you tell me where you got the money to buy food?

*Girl:* I'm not telling.

*Adele:* You know it's against the rules for you to have money, so I'm asking you where you got it.

*Girl:* I'm not saying.

*Adele:* You don't have to tell me any names—just tell me whether it was a friend who gave you the money, or did you steal the candy?

*Girl:* No, it was a friend.

*Adele:* That was no friend. A friend wouldn't give you money to do something self-destructive. You might think she's a friend, but she's not. Girls, you're just going to have to ask yourselves what's more important to you—eating or your self-respect.

[Silence, then another girl raises her hand]

*2nd Girl:* Adele, what's for lunch?

*Adele:* I'm not going to answer that question.

The conversation now turned to the controversial question of chewing gum. All the campers had been asked to turn in their gum, but a few had hoarded their supply and gotten caught when they threw the wrappers on the lawn. Because of this, Adele had prohibited gum for another few weeks:

*Adele:* Because of Dana, no one in camp will be getting gum. Come up here, Dana. Where did you get that gum?

*Dana:* Somebody gave it to me.

*Adele:* Who?

*Dana:* Somebody.

*Adele:* I want you to learn how to live with one another. You were told that until everyone stops chewing, no one will. Now, Dana, you are personally responsible for stopping everyone from chewing. How do you feel about it?

*Dana:* [Shrugs her shoulders].

*Adele:* You don't care.

Because parents' visiting day was coming up soon, and the campers would be going out for the day, Adele handed out copies of sample menus from restaurants in order to drill them on what they could order.

"Okay, girls. What would be better, french fried potatoes or baked potatoes?"

In chorus, they answered back, "Baked potatoes," but a few giggled, "French fries!"

"What would be better, steak or fish?"

"Fish!"

Time was running out, but Adele had a moment for one more question. A slim girl raised her hand: "Adele, if you're on maintenance, are you allowed to eat french fries?" "Girls, I've answered that question a million times. I hate to cut this short, but the next class is waiting." As they started to file out of the room she called some final advice after them, "Girls, are you chewing your food well and eating slowly?"

Comparisons between the campers in nutrition class are inevitable. The fact that some have reached their goal and become slim and that for most this would have been impossible in one summer points out the wide range of sizes among the campers. And sadly, there are strains between the groups. For if the camp generally has the aura of a sanctuary, it is also true that some of the painful experiences the children encounter in the outside world are reproduced within the camp as well. As one of the larger fourteen-year-old girls explained, a small group of the thinnest girls in the camp formed an elite clique and made mean remarks to the fatter girls, gossiping behind their backs about what size pants the larger girls wore. According to this camper, these thin "beauties" of the camp would frequently admire themselves in the mirror while complaining, "Oh, I'm so fat," in front of the larger girls in a deliberate attempt to make them feel uncomfortable. In the view of the fatter campers, several girls of essentially normal weight had come to camp so they could feel "superior" to the others and have all the boys chasing after them.

There is some evidence to support these observations and interpretations. There are many fewer boys than girls attending Camp Laurel, and most of the boys are indeed interested in dating the slimmer girls. For example, one seventeen-year-old male counselor who was quite a bit overweight himself admitted that he preferred the thinner girls and would certainly never date a fat girl at home, because his parents had told him that he should have "the best." Fat girls, in his estimation, had no self-respect because they had to settle for what they could get. He also expressed concern about how fat girlfriends would reflect on him: "If I dated a fat girl and walked down the street, someone would say, 'Oh look at that fat couple. Aren't they cute.' But if I was with a thin girl, I wouldn't mind if someone said, 'How did that fat guy get that beautiful girl—he must be pretty good.' " Asked if he thought it was worse to be a fat woman than a fat man he replied, "A guy can be big, but a girl should be petite. Girl goes with petite like pie goes with coffee or bagels go with cream cheese."

The relationship between the slimmer and fatter girls is complicated. To the larger girls, the thin ones represent both their persecutors and also what they might become. For even though there is a division, all are on a continuum of suffering and triumph, symbolized by their ritual of trading clothes up the weight line as the campers get slimmer. As their clothes become too big, each passes the discarded items along to others who can just now fit into them. So, even if all cannot become thin over the summer, they all can experience some taste of transformation. If all do not go home transformed into "normal" children, each has had an opportunity to see herself in a different way. When their parents collect them at the end of the summer, most go home looking forward to a new life.

For many, this taste of transformation will not be enough to sustain their weight loss. Even on visiting day, it is already obvious that the transformation is only skin deep, and once free of external control they will revert to their old habits. Despite what they learned in nutrition class and even in the presence of their parents, many go on a binge, jamming so much eating into their day-long furlough that they actually make themselves sick with indigestion after weeks of dieting. And like paroled prisoners who go back to the old neighborhood, once on the loose at the end of summer many of the campers will reacquaint themselves with all their old friends: pizza, ice cream, candy, and french fries. Many will be back at Camp Laurel the next summer.

## Review Questions

1. Why do sociologists view the fat children at Camp Laurel as deviant?

2. What other types of deviants could the fat children be compared to? contrasted with? Why?

3. How did the treatment of the campers by the camp owner, the counselors, and the other children differ from how they were treated outside the camp?

4. What evidence does Millman present to demonstrate that the self-concepts of the fat children were affected by their treatment in the camp?

5. How did this treatment guarantee that any changes in the campers would be temporary? That is, what aspects of the treatment actually taught the children how to enact the "fat role" and remain fat?

# CRIMINALITY AND EMOTIONAL AMBIVALENCE

## Charles E. Frazier and Thomas Meisenhelder

AMERICAN CRIMINALS HAVE BEEN DEPICTED AS UNWITTING VICTIMS OF A subculture that . . . favor[s] deviance (Miller, 1958), as natural adapters who develop deviant subcultures in response to disjointed social systems (Merton, 1938[1]; Cohen, 1956; Cloward and Ohlin, 1960), or as prisoners of class or regional traditions where violence and crime are valued behaviors (Wolfgang and Ferracuti, 1967). . . . [M]ost major sociological theories of crime depict offenders as feeling comfortable (if not self-righteous) in their criminality (Becker, 1960; Glazer, 1964). Criminal offenders are said to be so thoroughly absorbed in a deviant subculture or in a deviant value system that they are unaffected by dominant culture standards. This image overlooks the possibility that criminal offenders may be motivated by transient emotions, that they either feel remorse for their acts, or even that they regard crime as wrong.

• • •

The picture of the criminal as committed to or encapsulated by deviant values and mental states is also apparent in psychoanalytic writing on criminality. Though some attention is given to the emotional life of the offender, it is generally considered only within Freudian theory. Freud (1948) believed that criminal behavior is best understood as a substitute for or symbolic release of repressed elements of the personality. Unconscious conflict causes feelings of guilt and anxiety which, in turn, result in a desire for punishment to remove the preexisting guilt. Criminals commit law-violating acts so they will be caught and punished [Freud thought].

• • •

## DATA AND METHODS

The purpose of this paper[2] is to explore the subjective world of criminal offenders and to compare the findings with established theories of criminality. . . . In order to examine the possibility of a relationship between emotions and criminality, we draw on case study data of 95 ordinary

Charles E. Frazier and Thomas Meisenhelder, "Exploratory Notes on Criminality and Emotional Ambivalence," *Qualitative Sociology* 8, 3 (fall 1985), 226–284.

property offenders. Ordinary property offenders are those adult offenders who commit offenses mainly against property and are nonprofessional in their orientation to crime (Shover, 1983). The criminals studied ranged in age from 18 to 55 years old, all were male, 70% were white, all had multiple arrests for property offenses, and all had at least one conviction resulting in a prison sentence. These individuals were incarcerated in prisons in Illinois, Florida, or California when they were interviewed. The sample was purposively selected to screen cases with a high likelihood of having been deeply (though not exclusively) involved in criminal offenses against property. Offense histories of potential sample cases were checked by examining official records (e.g., the FBI identification records or "rap sheets" and local arrest records recorded on presentence investigation forms) and by asking for self-reports from the subjects. Those individuals having records of crimes all of which were against persons or against the moral order (e.g., drug offenses) were not selected.

In broad terms, the sample is roughly representative of a class of criminal cases variously described as "semi-professional property criminals" (Gibbons, 1968) or "conventional property criminals" (Clinard and Quinney, 1973). As many as 75% of all offenders processed by and through the American criminal justice system are of this general type. We do not claim that ordinary property offenders are a clearly identifiable population or that our cases are fully representative. Generalizations from the present data must be drawn with caution considering first the degree of fit between our cases and one or more of the categories above and, second, the extent to which these categorizations are applicable to the thousands of property offenders each year who do not become involved in the official justice process.

The case data used in the present analysis were collected through intensive life-history style interviews. A life-history is a special type of personal document that may consist of a complete subjective reporting of a life or that may aim for a partial accounting emphasizing either a narrow aspect (education, family life, deviant behavior) or a special stage of life (early childhood, adolescence, post-retirement). The life-histories we collected are closest to what Denzin (1970) calls topical life-histories because our focus was upon the inception and subsequent development of criminal behavior. Our aim with the life-histories, like that of previous researchers (Angell, 1945:78) was to obtain detailed information about the way situations appeared to the persons interviewed. We sought to understand criminal behavior by studying the subjective meaning of perceptions and self-feelings of criminal offenders . . . as represented to us in interviews.

•   •   •

A unique feature of this study that may be a cause of concern for some readers is that our subjects were incarcerated at the time of their interviews. Because practitioners are frequently manipulated by inmates who lie to them about their crimes and their feelings, it is reasonable to wonder whether we were in the same position. . . . For this reason, we attempted partial protection against self-conscious manipulative attempts by not indicating our theoretical or philosophical leanings. Respondents were asked to report their life-histories as they lived them . . . stage by stage. We guided them only by asking for them to recall in chronological sequence the subjective perceptions of events remembered as important.

The life-history interviews were not originally directed toward the exploration of emotions as they relate to criminality. Instead, they were collected for use in analyses aimed at evaluations of theories of criminal behavior (Frazier, 1973, 1976; Meisenhelder, 1975). Respondents were not asked to delve into their emotions in the life-histories. Emotional statements and behavioral indications of emotion states either emerged naturally or were inadvertently evoked by requests from the researchers to the respondents to describe their reactions to specific events or situations. Another reason we are confident the emotions observed in the interview data are credible is that the respondents exhibited many nonverbal indications of emotion (see Goffman, 1979: 1–4), such as eyes moist with tears, cracking voices, facial expressions indicating excitement, joy, fear, anger, or exhilaration, and varying body postures. These physical indications of emotion are [often] less subject to voluntary control than is the content of speech. While the relationship between such physical signs and emotion is not uncomplicated, we believe the credibility of the reports was enhanced by these nonverbal displays.

## DOING WRONG: THE MEANING OF CRIME TO ORDINARY PROPERTY OFFENDERS

The topical life-histories of ordinary property offenders showed that frequent law violators do not think of crime as morally correct. They do not appear to be "programmed" with the wrong values, nor do they seem to be motivated by a sense of guilt or a desire for punishment. Most offenders frequently repeated their view that crime was not commendable and that the punishment associated with being incarcerated in prison was unwelcomed. That criminals do not hold that crime is acceptable behavior, however, does not mean crime for many does not afford certain gains or emotional rewards. In fact, our respondents used crime for monetary, material, style of life, or status gains and, as such, crime afforded emotional rewards for them.

Many respondents enjoyed the feelings of excitement and adventure while committing crimes. To say crime can be emotionally satisfying also opens the possibility that emotions may motivate crime (Douglas, 1970;

Douglas and Johnson, 1977). The following excerpts from the life-history documents are illustrative. A . . . check-forger (Lemert, 1951) reports:

> It [doing crime] was mainly for the excitement of it. Exciting part was going in and cashing the check.

A long time "sneak thief" and house burglar says:

> . . . it's hard to say. Sometimes I'd feel good about it. . . . I'd say to myself "Wow, I can do this and I am doing something somebody else can't."

Another man describes the heightened sense of excitement he felt as a youth knowing a county sheriff suspected him of wrong doing.

> That would be another reason I was kind of scared and maybe it even made it [theft] more exciting. . . . I never thought of punishment right then [pause] . . . just excitement. Excitement . . . and uh, we got the gas and took off. It was a big joke. It was one over on him [the sheriff]. We was laughing . . . laughing at the time. . . .

If crime is emotionally satisfying only *after* apprehension and punishment (as psychoanalysts and some psychologists argue), how could these positive feelings be present during, immediately following the act, and *before* apprehension? The same man who remained highly involved in criminal activity for several years reports how he felt before and during a house burglary in his career. While his first emotions were of fear and trepidation . . . the burglary was induced in part by the excitement of the act and anticipation of a sense of satisfaction that would result when the act was completed.

> And uh, we didn't have no money at all this night and we needed some booze. So we said well up here in this cabin they've been having some pretty good parties. Nobody up there tonight. So, we thought, we would split up there and check it out, you know. . . . We went around in back of the house and, uh, I was scared. Breaking in a house! Man! Bad! Is anyone in there? You know, I wasn't sure whether there was anyone in the house or not. . . . If we bust the door down and we're looking at a shotgun all of a sudden, and, uh, there was cars going by on and on, wondering if one of them could be the fuzz—whew! We sit up there on this bank for at least an hour thinking about it—just thinking whether to do it or not. Scared, you know. Exciting. Boy! My stomach was turning. So I thought "well, I am going to show off in front of Ray." I figured, "show off," you know, cause he's scared to do it. And I am scared to do it. One of us is going to show off, you know, and beat the other one to the gun. So, I jumps up and I say "well, I'll go do it, follow me." Three times I kicked it, you know, "bam, bam, bam and the third time. . . ." It had a padlock and one of those things that comes over to lock and that came right off the door. And I went in and I says "come in." Boy, I love it! Big shot now. After I look around and nobody in there that I could see, I am looking around for stuff I can pick up. Ray is rummaging through the drawers of the dresser and he's finding all kinds of goodies. Little things, like, you know, he found coins. . . . And, uh, lot of barbeque tools, pencils, stuff, just small stuff, things I can

remember we was rippin' off with. And, uh, I'm thirsty. So, I split to the ice-box and I open it up and, "Eureka," they got it. They had beer down one side and down at the bottom they had whiskey. And Boy! Boy! I almost fell over dead. It was just what I was looking for too. I think this really set me off in crime.

A major component of the motive to commit the crime described above is the pleasurable feelings that come with doing the act and being suc-cessful, "getting away with it." The thrill of crime also seems to include references to a "sporting" sense of fear that is produced by the risk of apprehension and punishment. The rewards of daring and excitement are increased when a fear-inspiring presence of a threatening opponent is present.[3]

Not all offenders we interviewed derived emotional satisfactions from crime in the form of excitement or adventure. Some found crime a way to release frustration or anger or a way to strike out at others who caused them emotional discomfort. The following excerpt is an example of one such case.

I would be playing with some kid my age or something, you know, and his mother or old man would come out and say "get the hell out of my yard, you little bastard." I mean things like this, you know. Just because Dad had been in trouble they took it out on me. So, that night I would get them. . . . I would sit there and wait for them to leave and I would get them. I would do some-thing, destroy something. It didn't matter what it was, just anything to get even with them. I broke in this one guy's house and stole some money.

It is common for offenders to discuss their crimes in terms of the emo-tional value they felt while committing the acts. In many cases, the crimi-nals appear to value crimes as ends in themselves rather than as particu-lar means to some valued ends. Despite the emotional satisfactions of crime, however, offenders also frequently experience . . . guilt or shame. These feelings suggest that offenders experience emotional ambivalence concerning their criminal behavior. On the one hand, it appears that crime is partially produced by and results in emotional satisfactions and, on the other hand, offenders often seem to be left with an enduring sense of guilt or shame.


## GUILT, SHAME, AND CRIME

Most offenders we interviewed expressed contrition concerning their crimes. Matza (1964:41) describes this feeling as "based on guilt, or more likely shame. . . ." Our findings suggest that both feelings are components of the moral ambivalence toward crime that seems charac-teristic of ordinary property offenders. That is, our respondents related *compound feelings* (Hochschild, 1983:224–226). . . .

Guilt and shame may indicate moral ambivalence. The guilty or shamed person feels bad due to having committed a behavior that he or she judges to be "wrong." Both emotions involve using cultural-moral standards, whether external (shame) or internalized (guilt), to judge oneself within some social situation. Each emotion, by definition, expresses moral ambivalence in the sense that one disapproves of an action in which one has engaged. As Hochschild (1983:224) suggested, such "compound" emotions often result from "serial perceptions." That is, driven by anger, frustration, or excitement, a person acts and then reacts with disapproval to that action. If the disapproving reaction is based on internal standards, the actor feels guilty; if the judgement is based on external comparisons, the person feels shame (Hochschild, 1983:227–233).

## Guilt

Guilt is based on a sense of "anxiety occasioned by our having violated our tribe's codes" (Nettler, 1978:308). It derives from the presence of internal principles and controls or one's "conscience. . . . "

Although guilt relies on a conscience for its existence, obviously a conscience does not always inhibit wrongful conduct (see Nettler, 1978:322). As Hirschi (1969:205) and others have demonstrated, some individuals who are "controlled," in the sense that they hold conventional beliefs, nevertheless commit crimes. While we cannot completely reconstruct the process through which guilt is produced, indications of guilt were apparent in the interviews of many of our respondents. For example, some of our respondents resorted to crime because they were low on money, they could not find work, and/or because they were able to rationalize their acts. Interestingly, rationalizing the crime, resolving never to do it again, and suffering punishment after being caught did not eliminate their sense of guilt. The following excerpt by a man who committed burglaries for only a short period illustrates the point:

> We said, "we'll do it now but when we get back we won't do it." When we got to Illinois, we swore to ourselves that we'd never do it [burglary] again—that we would, uh, go ahead and work and never do something like that again. I knew I had done wrong before prison. You know, they say they rehabilitate you. You know, uh, I knew I did wrong before.

Another man, in circumstances he perceived as desperate, summed up his thoughts with the following statements while displaying physical signs of emotion:

> I feel bad I take their stuff. People work hard for their stuff, work hard for it. You think about it, people work hard for their stuff then come home and it's gone. . . .

Even more clear is the case of the offender discussed earlier who described the excitement and the adventure of breaking into a cabin and stealing alcoholic beverages. He reports a keen sense of guilt after stealing from a person he knew well. In part, his guilt is caused by an identification with the feelings and moral codes of the victim.

> I think what really hurt me or made me feel so bad right there was that I didn't have to do it . . . but I went ahead and stole it off of him. I didn't have to. I wasn't hurting for money or anything but I went ahead and stole it off him and I suppose that is what made me feel so bad.

Another man put it this way:

> I often think of the past . . . the people I've hurt. It bothers me. Once I stole money from a collection for the blind. I just felt disgraced at myself. I mean I just felt like kicking myself in the ass for doing it. I didn't keep the money. I gived it back. I don't know why I took it out of there.

These excerpts indicate the ability of offenders to identify with or to share the moral codes of their victims and experience guilt as a result. Many offenders also believe that all crime is wrong and, despite their specific reasons for carrying out crimes (and whether positive or negative emotions such as excitement or anger are involved), they are unable to sustain a rationalization that relieves them of guilt. Because they lack the capacity to fully rationalize criminal acts, guilt results. . . .

> The more you be around me, you see I'm not that way. I mean people like me the more they be around me. The only thing is I played the tough role, you know what I mean. You know, ''I can scuffle, I can fight, . . . box. I'm not afraid, you know what I mean.'' *But, don't want to be this way.* But all the time I'm trying to impress the people I'm with and they get the impression that I really am a bad ass. The simple reason they think that is because the fear that I have in them from the impression I be puttin'. They have fear also, so, therefore they respect me as a bad ass. That's the way it was. I mean all the time. *Never no really good, like I say important thing, every really happened that made me feel happy.* It—almost everyday, the fightin' sort of thing. I mean fist fighting, stealing and running, throwing rocks at cars, it was always violent. *It was nothing, never was nothing really good in my life* [emphasis added].

We asked the respondent to tell us as best he could how he felt at the time of these acts, to give us an example of an event and tell what it meant to him at that time. The following was his answer:

> I, you know, I felt bad. I mean on the inside. That's something you can't see— what a person feels on the inside. But, of course, to other people I show to where I really didn't care, you know. But uh, I felt bad. Anything (mostly any crime), I ever done I felt bad about. But it was just something I just held, held it back, I never did show it, you know.

For this offender, crime was a way to get money and get some attention. His case makes it clear, however, that even if criminal behavior is induced and maintained by culture or by deviant subcultures, this does not remove the sense of guilt. This respondent, more than some of those quoted previously, became enmeshed in constant contact with other criminals. Yet he still related that he " . . . felt sorry for the people [he] . . . was doing it to."

•   •   •

Our respondents' apparent guilt may be related to their attachments to other people . . .

> I've got some people that has stood by me, and to me, it makes me feel bad that I let them people down. That hurt. You know, he didn't even suspect me the least bit. He knew everything I had done and it kinda—I don't know—it just made me feel real guilty.

Another respondent mentioned the guilt-inducing quality of his relationship with his wife:

> It's hard for her, she's on welfare trying to make ends meet . . . she's paying for my part in it all.

•   •   •

Guilt arises from these postive relationships via the respondents' interpretations of the effects of their own behavior on others. That is, others provide a psychological anchor for the processes of internal moral judgement that results in personal feelings of wrongdoing and guilt. Guilt does not derive from the actual experience of rejection or from the negative judgments of other people. When the sense of wrong-doing is based on external sources, it is better understood as shame (Nettler, 1978:308).

## Shame

The moral ambivalence of our respondents toward their crimes becomes even clearer when we examine their expressed feelings of shame. Unlike guilt, shame is based in "external controls" (Nettler, 1978:308). It results from the embarrassment of being observed as one behaves in a discreditable fashion. . . . Thus, as we shall see, offenders sometimes feel shamed by their crimes, not because of their internal moral codes . . . but . . . the stupidity of their crime and their resultant loss of self-esteem.

In one case, the offender recounted that his long history of committing burglaries and thefts made him ashamed in the company of conventional people.

> . . . I think, "well, how would they react if they knew what I really was and what I'd done?" How would they treat me then? What would they do, kick me out? . . . And so, I hate to go where there is, you know, people like in a home or something.

This respondent felt shamed because of his criminal and deviant acts, but he did not feel guilt. In fact, there is no indication in this life-history that this offender reacted to internalized standards relating to crime. His comments below are illustrative.

> I never did consider myself a burglar. I guess there is a technical name for a person who goes in homes and steals. Well, I just didn't think of myself as a thief. . . .

• • •

Shame is . . . also produced by the message concerning one's intelligence implicit in *arrests* and in the crimes themselves. Even if criminals are unattached to conventional others, and even if they do not empathize with their victims, they can still be embarrassed by the stupidity of their pasts. This embarrassment was the most common emotional response we found. As one man described it:

> I really can't say it's something to be proud of. . . . I wish I hadn't done it. I could kick myself for doing it.

Many respondents bemoaned the fact that they had wasted much of their lives and had now arrived at middle age with "nothing to show for my life except a lot of 'time.' "

• • •

## DISCUSSION

The case material and discussion presented here are designed to challenge the sociological image of ordinary criminals. Contrary to the guiltless, shameless offender implied by many sociological and criminological theories, our respondents made it evident that a complex sense of wrong was somehow related to their criminal acts. . . . Ordinary property offenders do not seem to be committed to crime as a value system. It seems more likely that crime is emphatically devalued by offenders.

There are, no doubt, offenders who feel little guilt, shame, or sense of wrong, but our life-histories suggest that these cases may be exceptions to the rule. Indeed, if our observations are accurate, it is possible that much criminological theory has reified a falsehood. The view that crime is a value to those who develop patterns of criminal behavior is not consistent with our data. . . . The results of our analysis also suggest that, at the very least, both sociological and psychological criminologists need to reconsider their theoretical portrait of the offender and allow for the existence of emotions . . . [and] moral ambivalence. . . . [C]rime may be, for large numbers of offenders, both an attempt to exercise some control over the forces that shape social identity and the cause of the emotions that assure that they never achieve personal satisfactions usually associated with money, status, and autonomy.

## NOTES

1. While Merton's innovator is sometimes regarded as a rational actor who reasons out the alternative courses of action and pursues crime or deviance as a calculated choice, this was not Merton's intended meaning. Instead, anomie was seen by Merton to generate a culture (an adaptive culture) which emphasized deviant modes of individual adaptation: "I assume that the structure constrains individuals variously situated within it to develop cultural emphases, social behavior patterns and psychological bents" (Merton, 1968:1977).

2. An earlier version of this paper was presented at the annual conference of Society for Life History Research in Psychopathology at Radcliffe College, Cambridge, Massachusetts, May 31–June 2, 1983. We are grateful to Donna Bishop, Pamela Richards, and three anonymous reviewers for *Qualitative Sociology* for helpful comments on earlier drafts of this paper.

3. Interestingly, some of our respondents seem to be saying that traditional deterrence theory has things backwards. That is, a high threat of or risk of arrest and the resultant fear may paradoxically increase, rather than decrease, the criminal's attraction to crime. This is not a new idea; Werthman (1967) noted that gang youth create "character games" in which the risk of apprehension may, for some, induce more criminal behavior.

## REFERENCES

Angell, Robert C.
    1945 "A critical review of the development of the personal document method in sociology 1920–1940." In Louis Gottschalk, C. Kluckhold, and Robert C. Angell (eds.), *The Use of Personal Documents in History, Anthropology, and Sociology.* Bulletin 53, New York: Social Science Research Council.

Becker, Howard
    1960 "Notes on the concept of commitment." *American Journal of Sociology* 64: 32–40.

Clinard, Marshall B. and Richard Quinney
    1973 *Criminal Behavior Systems: A Typology.* New York: Holt Rinehart and Winston.

Cloward, Richard and Lloyd Ohlin
    1960 *Delinquency and Opportunity.* New York: Free Press.

Cohen, Albert K.
    1955 *Delinquent Boys: The Subculture of the Gang.* New York: Free Press.

Denzin, Norman
    1970 *The Research Act.* Chicago: Aldine.

Douglas, Jack D.
1970 "Deviance and respectability: The social construction of moral meanings." Pp. 3–30 in Jack D. Douglas (ed.), *Deviance and Respectability.* New
York: Basic Books.

Douglas, Jack D. and John M. Johnson (eds.)
1977 *Existential Sociology.* New York: Cambridge University Press.

Frazier, Charles E.
1973 *Alternative Theories of Deviance.* Unpublished Ph.D. Dissertation, Southern Illinois University.
1976 *Theoretical Approaches to Deviance.* Columbus, Ohio: Charles Merrill.

Freud, Sigmund
1948 *The Ego and the Id.* In the *Complete Psychological Works of Sigmund Freud,*
Vol. 19. London: Hogarth.

Gibbons, Don C.
1968 *Changing the Lawbreaker: The Treatment of Delinquents and Criminals.* Englewood Cliffs, N.J.: Prentice-Hall.

Glazer, Daniel
1964 "Criminality theories and behavioral images." *American Journal of Sociology* 61: 441.

Goffman, Erving
1979 *Gender Advertisements.* Cambridge: Harvard University Press.

Hirschi, Travis
1969 *The Cause of Delinquency.* Berkeley: University of California Press.

Hochschild, Arlie Russell
1983 *The Managed Heart.* Berkeley: University of California Press.

Lemert, Edwin H.
1951 *Social Pathology.* New York: McGraw-Hill.

Matza, David
1964 *Delinquency and Drift.* New York: John Wiley.

Meisenhelder, Thomas
1975 *The Nonprofessional Property Offender.* Unpublished Ph.D. Dissertation,
University of Florida.

Merton, Robert
1938 "Social structure and anomie." *American Sociological Review* 3: 672–682.
1968 *Social Theory and Social Structure.* New York: Free Press.

Miller, Walter
1958 "Lower class culture as a generating milieu of gang delinquency." *Journal of Social Issues* 14: 5–19.

Nettler, Gwynn
1978 *Explaining Crime.* New York: McGraw-Hill.

Shover, Neal
   1983 "The later stages of ordinary property offender careers." *Social Problems*
        31 (December): 208–218.

Werthman, Carl
   1967 "The function of social definitions in the development of delinquency
        careers." Task Force Report: Juvenile Delinquency and Youth Crime.
        U.S. Government Printing Office, pp. 170.

Wolfgang, Marvin and F. Ferracuti
   1967 *The Subculture of Violence.* London: Tavistock.

# Review Questions

1. Previous theories of criminal behavior have tended to emphasize 1) cultural or subcultural values or 2) a need for punishment as causes of crime. Describe these sociological and psychological theories.

2. What evidence do Frazier and Meisenhelder present that argues against a "cultural" or "subcultural" theory of crime?

3. What evidence do Frazier and Meisenhelder present that argues against a "need-for-punishment" theory of crime?

4. What emotions did the burglar display before, during, and after their crimes?

# Suggested Readings: Deviance, Conformity, and Social Control

Becker, Howard S. *Outsiders.* New York: Free Press, 1963.

Campbell, Anne. *Girls in the Gang.* Oxford, England: Basil Blackwell Ltd., 1984.

Chambliss, William J. *On the Take.* Bloomington, Ind.: Indiana University Press, 1978.

Conrad, Peter and Joseph W. Schneider. *Deviance and Medicalization: From Badness to Sickness.* St. Louis: C.V. Mosby, 1980.

Erikson, Kai T. *Wayward Puritans.* New York: Wiley, 1966.

Goffman, Erving. *Stigma: Notes on the Management of Spoiled Identity.* Englewood Cliffs, N.J.: Prentice-Hall, 1963.

Molstad, Clark. "Choosing and Coping with Boring Work," *Urban Life* 15 (July 1986): 215–236.

Scheff, Thomas J. *Being Mentally Ill,* 2nd ed. New York: Aldine, 1984.

Schur, Edwin M. *Crimes Without Victims—Deviant Behavior and Public Policy.* Englewood Cliffs, N.J.: Prentice-Hall, 1965.

_____. *Labeling Women Deviant: Gender, Stigma, and Social Control.* New York: Random House, 1984.

Szasz, Thomas. *The Manufacture of Madness.* New York: Harper & Row, 1970.

Wiseman, Jacqueline P. *Stations of the Lost: The Treatment of Skid Row Alcoholics.* Chicago: University of Chicago Press, 1979.

# Part VIII. Interaction in Institutional Contexts

INDIVIDUALS FACE A HOST OF PROBLEMS AS THEY ATTEMPT TO SURVIVE IN their environments. Societies, too, must develop strategies, plans, or systems to deal with problems that occur *at the collective level*. That is, in order for the *group* to survive—regardless of what happens to any given individual—solutions to group problems must be worked out and agreed upon, formally or informally, by societal members. A complex system of attitudes, norms, beliefs, and roles outlining what *should* occur to solve a societal problem is called an *institution*.

Suppose your sociology class were stranded on a Caribbean island, with no prospect of contact with or aid from any other human society. A number of threats to the survival of your group will sooner or later arise, requiring the interdependent action of societal members. For instance, the society will no longer exist if all of its members die of starvation or exposure, so some coordinated system of producing and distributing food and shelter will have to be worked out. That system—a plan, or set of norms, governing the behavior of your societal members with regard to who engages in what productive functions and what will have to be done to acquire goods once they are produced—is called the *economic institution* of your society. Literally thousands of interrelated norms may be involved in the institution: One should begin work promptly at 7 A.M. and work for ten hours. One should take all goods produced to a central storehouse. All members who need or want any of the goods merely collect them from the storehouse. No private property will be permitted. People who work too hard or not hard enough will receive negative sanctions. Women should do one kind of work, while men do another. People must begin their work activities when they are eight years old. And so on. The specific rules will vary from one culture to another—your sociology class might not develop the same economic institution as ours— but some economic system is sure to emerge.

Your society will face other problems and develop other institutional solutions. Questions of how to create new members to replace those who eventually die will probably be answered with a *family institution* specifying who is allowed to marry whom (marriage seems to be a cultural universal), how the spouses will interact, who will be allowed to have how many children and at what times in their lives, how children are to be cared for and socialized, and so on. To keep your societal members from killing each other off or being killed by outsiders before they can reproduce enough people to take their places, you will develop a system to control and protect your members, or a *political institution*. Problems of *health and illness* will be met by an *institution* which includes rules for defining what should be seen as health and what as illness and how the latter should be treated. Transmitting your culture to new members may require the creation of an *institution* or system of rules and roles to provide *education*. Questions about aspects of your world which defy other culturally available explanations may be answered by a *religious institution*, a set of beliefs, rules for religious expression, and roles for religious leaders and followers.

There are several important points regarding social institutions which the articles in this section address. First, a *society's institutions are taught and learned in the process of socialization*, once they have been created. Although the general problems societies confront are similar, the emergent institutions which attempt to cope with these problems vary from one society to another and from one historical period to another. They are not fixed or immutable, nor are they automatically understood by the society's children. Institutions must be transmitted from one generation to the next, and of course they may be changed somewhat in the process.

Second, once these arrangements or systems are incorporated into the culture, *they constrain the behavior of individuals in many ways*. Institutions are not usually so rigid that people are allowed *no* choice in type of work, marriage partners, religious beliefs, and the like. At the same time, the individual does not have total freedom to work, marry, or believe as he or she chooses without running the risk of receiving negative sanctions from other societal members.

Moreover, institutions tend to structure one's time and activities. For instance, beliefs about how best to prepare children for adult life have resulted in the school—a social organization of rules and roles which requires some people to spend long periods of time sitting in small rooms at desks facing toward an older person who stands or sits in front of the room. The young people may be separated by age into classes. One result of this arrangement is that the population becomes "age-segregated." Old people have fewer and fewer structured opportunities to interact with children, and children themselves are not always allowed free interaction with other children of different ages. As one consequence, children (and all students) are much better able to distinguish small differences in age than are adults. The structural constraints produced by age-segregation and age-grading in schools may entail benefits *and/or* costs for individuals and for societies; the point here is that the educational institution channels and limits human activity and interaction.

As another example of the constraining effects of social institutions, consider the norms of the economic institution of the U.S. They specify that one must use money in order to obtain goods and services and, further, that this money may be gained by inheritance, by work, or by providing capital (factories, equipment, and the like) for the production process. Permitting money and other valuable assets to be passed from one generation to the next automatically insures that the children of poor parents will have fewer chances to acquire wealth than the children of affluent parents. In other words, the structural arrangement that allows for inheritance of money, wealth, and capital creates inequality as a feature of social life. Thus, while our society's myths tell us that poverty and wealth are the results of individual efforts, the sociological perspective allows us to see that the way a society is organized, including its institutional systems, actually produces its own effects on the individual's behavior and life chances.

A third important point regarding institutions is that *they tend to be interrelated* so that a change in one area—say a declaration of war to protect a society's interests—will have effects in other institutional areas—the rules about marriage and childbearing may change as young people are removed from their normal activities to perform military duties. Many sociologists contend that the one institution which is most likely to affect all the others is the economic system. The society's economic norms may have a powerful impact on the system of courtship and marriage; the system of educating the young for adult roles; the system of laws, law making, and law enforcement; and so on. The change from an agricultural economy to one based on industry, for example, upsets prior beliefs and norms concerning work itself as well as beliefs and norms about religious observance, family size, and what constitutes a proper education. Furthermore, the *structural changes* in the way society is organized which accompany industrialization have a limiting effect on other institutions, and on individuals as well. Consider the consequences of the change from working on one's own homesite to working in a factory or office.

Try to keep in mind these general characteristics of institutions—they are learned sets of norms which represent collective responses to collective problems, they constrain human activity and interaction, and they are interrelated—as we move to a discussion of the nature and consequences of several specific institutions in the United States.

# A. Family

THE FIRST INSTITUTIONAL CONTEXT FOR HUMAN INTERACTION THAT WE will examine here is the one that first affects our lives—the family system. Everyone knows a great deal about families. After all, most of us grew up in one and were probably socialized to want to form new families as adults. Our own personal family involvements, however, form a very *poor* base of knowledge about family norms and patterns of the larger society. We must step outside our own lives to gain a sociological perspective on the family.

Sociologically, a society's family institution serves several important functions. It provides societal members with ascribed statuses—a position in the social-class structure and racial, ethnic, and sexual identities. The family system also affects sexual behavior and reproduction. It further provides a plan for socializing infants and children and for providing emotional support and stability to family members. It is in interaction with family members that our self-concepts are initially developed.

Within the family circle—whatever members the society defines this as including—intensive interaction takes place. This interaction is not unstructured, however, since a division of labor is usually present, with parents and children, and perhaps men and women, performing different tasks to meet the needs of the group as a whole. Thus learned social roles generally guide our interaction here.

The first sociological question addressed in this section is, "What is a family?" To most Americans, the image conjured up by this question is a *nuclear* family with a mother, father, and their nonadult children. But this is not the only type of family possible. Nor is it even the most common form, since divorce, death, and children leaving the "nest" can truncate families, and more than two generations may live together in what we call *extended* families.

Sociologically speaking, a family is any group of people who interact with one another on the basis of familial roles—who act toward one another *as if* they were a family. Carol Stack's research clearly shows that the role obligations being fulfilled by a set of people are more important than the biological or legal ties between them. In "Sex Roles and Survival Strategies in an Urban Black Community," Stack reports on the flexible families formed by people living in The Flats, an extremely poor

351

area of a midwestern city that she calls "Jackson Harbor." In doing so, she also explains why these families have to be flexible: their economic situations are so tenuous and so variable that mutual support networks are essential to survival. The data she gathered from living in The Flats and becoming part of these families herself contradict many common American stereotypes about the families of poor people.

Families contain within them several types of relationships—such as those between parents and children, husbands and wives, in-laws, and others. One of the most important elements of a family is the relationship between husband and wife: marriage. The second selection in this section addresses the social processes produced by marriage.

The norms of our culture specify that a newly married couple should live in a private household, interacting frequently and intensely with each other. These norms create an isolated setting in which each couple is likely to develop a unique world view, or "nomic order." In "Marriage and the Construction of Reality," Peter Berger and Hansfried Kellner discuss why and how marriage in our society (as well as other long-term relationships) results in new "nomic (normative) orders." In essence, the partners alter their definitions of themselves, of their daily lives, of their past experiences, and of their futures. All of these come to be seen from a perspective different from the one either partner had before marriage.

In general, we arrive at constructions of what is going on in the world around us by using ready-made "typifications" and by "objectivating," or *validating*, these typifications through discussion and interaction with other people. From our culture's common stock of knowledge, we draw typifications, categories or meanings, which seem to be applicable to an event we are trying to "make sense of," thereby *typifying* (or classifying) that event. In other words, we match the event to what we think are the relevant cultural categories for describing it. Then, because most events are ambiguous and could be interpreted in a number of ways, we turn to others to validate our use of the culture's typifications. If those whose opinions are important to us do not seem to share our matching of the typification to the event, we may redefine the event, drawing on other categories or meanings (other typifications) from our culture to explain it. If others do seem to concur with our application of the typification, it becomes "objectivated," or turned into a validated, agreed-upon "fact." We need no longer wonder what the event means (unless we are philosophers or social scientists); our actions and sentiments toward the event will be aligned with the actions and sentiments of others, and further interaction can proceed smoothly. In this way, reality is constructed.

In marriage, the partners' former interpretations or constructions of reality are reexamined and redefined. The social processes that lead to the construction of a new "nomic order" are subtle, and few people are aware that they are occurring. The key mechanism by which the new "coupled" world view is constructed is *conversation*, itself a normatively encouraged activity for spouses. In discussions, chats, and quarrels, former friends of the husband and wife come to be redefined and reevaluated—reobjectivated. New comparisons are made of one's self with friends and family members, and new self-definitions are formed.

Marriage, then, is much more than an agreement to live with another person. Marriage has consequences for the individual in all spheres of public and private life—even to the extent of determining how one views the world.

The aptness of Berger and Kellner's description of the construction of a coupled identity is perhaps most apparent when we examine those who are *leaving* a marriage, and a "nomic order," because of the death of a spouse or divorce. The formerly married must adjust in a number of obvious ways to their change in marital status. One less obvious problem of adjustment involves creating a new "single" world view. Consider the husband who was uninterested in the theater before his marriage to a theater "buff." Over the years, he has heard his wife discussing the theater a great deal and has himself come to see himself as a "theatergoer," to pay attention to new performers, openings on Broadway, and such. After his divorce, he hears on the radio an announcement of a new play and automatically thinks, "We should get tickets to that." Then he realizes that "we" no longer exist, and he's really not very interested in sitting in some stuffy theater straining to understand the play's existential message anyway. In this hypothetical incident, we see in a small way that the former husband is caught between a coupled identity created in his marriage and a new single identity that reflects his own views (or the views of his new associates) more closely.

Diane Vaughan explores the theme of shifting identities corresponding to shifting marital statuses in "Uncoupling: The Social Construction of Divorce." Previously, "uncoupling" was thought to be a chaotic period in the lives of those involved, characterized by pain, guilt, and anxiety about their uncertain futures. Through intensive interviews with people who have undergone this experience, Vaughan uncovers the order that lies behind the apparent chaos. She finds that the individual usually goes through identifiable stages, gradually shedding his or her marital identity and gaining a new world view and a new self-concept as a single adult, possibly available for future "re-coupling."

Vaughan's work is indeed timely, since divorce has come to be a common and accepted feature of life in the United States over the past half-century. It is estimated that about half of the marriages formed in our society at this time will end in divorce. Of course, remarriage rates are also high, but many more people than ever before are finding that they must rely more on "single" identities—and "single" strategies for survival—for substantial portions of their adult lives.

Other changes in family form and functioning which have come about in recent decades reinforce this trend. The combination of increased divorce rates with postponement of marriage, decreased fertility rates, postponement of childbearing, and longer life expectancies have led to the current situation in which about a fifth to a fourth of all households in our country are comprised of a single individual *living alone* rather than in a family group. Many others find themselves living with their children as single parents. All of these changes, and more, bring about new interaction patterns and strategies and necessitate adaptations of the old institutional system.

In summary, we will be looking at how marriage norms set up a situation in which spouses construct a new, "coupled" world view and how that world view is affected if uncoupling occurs. We will also look at nontraditional responses to family needs emerging out of interaction among family members who find themselves, in circumstances which are not conducive to the older patterns of family organization. It is interesting to note that, even as institutional changes such as these come about, they do not represent radical departures from the previous values and norms, but rather adaptations that preserve a great deal from the past.

# SEX ROLES AND SURVIVAL STRATEGIES IN AN URBAN BLACK COMMUNITY

## Carol B. Stack

THE POWER AND AUTHORITY ASCRIBED TO WOMEN IN THE BLACK GHETTOS OF America, women whose families are locked into lifelong conditions of poverty and welfare, have their roots in the inexorable unemployment of Black males and the ensuing control of economic resources by females. These social-economic conditions have given rise to special features in the organization of family and kin networks in Black communities, features not unlike the patterns of domestic authority that emerge in matrilineal societies, or in cultures where men are away from home in wage labor (Gonzalez, 1969, 1970). The poor in Black urban communities have evolved, as the basic unit of their society, a core of kinsmen and non-kin who cooperate on a daily basis and who live near one another or coreside. This core, or nucleus, has been characterized as the basis of the consanguineal household (Gonzalez, 1965) and of matrifocality (Tanner, 1975; Abrahams, 1963; Moynihan, 1965; Rainwater, 1966).

The concept of "matrifocality," however, has been criticized as inaccurate and inadequate. Recent studies (Ladner, 1971; Smith, 1970; Stack, 1970; Valentine, 1970) show convincingly that many of the negative features attributed to matrifocal families—that they are fatherless, unstable, and produce offspring that are "illegitimate" in the eyes of the folk culture—are not general characteristics of low-income Black families in urban America. Rather than imposing widely accepted definitions of the family, the nuclear family, or the matrifocal family on the ways in which the urban poor describe and order their world, we must seek a more appropriate theoretical framework. Elsewhere I have proposed an analysis based on the notion of a domestic network (Stack, 1974). In this view, the basis of familial structure and cooperation is not the nuclear family of the middle class, but an extended cluster of kinsmen related chiefly through

Carol B. Stack, "Sex Roles and Survival Strategies in an Urban Black Community," in Michelle Zimbalist Rosaldo and Louise Lamphere, eds., *Women, Culture and Society*: Stanford, Calif.: Stanford University Press, 1975, pp. 113–128. This article is adapted for the most part from Chapter 7 of the book *All Our Kin: Strategies for Survival in a Black Community*, by Carol B. Stack (Harper & Row, 1974). I am grateful to Harper & Row for permission to use most of the material from that chapter. I should like to thank Professors Louise Lamphere, Michelle Rosaldo, Robert Weiss, Nancie Gonzalez, and Eva Hunt for helpful suggestions in the analysis and organization of this paper, and William W. Carver, of Stanford University Press, for his thoughtful editorial advice.

children but also through marriage and friendship, who align to provide domestic functions. This cluster, or domestic network, is diffused over several kin-based households, and fluctuations in individual household composition do not significantly affect cooperative arrangements.

In this paper I shall analyze the domestic network and the relationships within it from a woman's perspective—from the perspective that the women in this study provided and from my own interpretations of the domestic and social scene. Many previous studies of the Black family (e.g. Liebow, 1967 and Hannerz, 1969) have taken a male perspective, emphasizing the streetcorner life of Black men and viewing men as peripheral to familial concerns. Though correctly stressing the economic difficulties that Black males face in a racist society, these and other studies (Moynihan, 1965; Bernard, 1966) have fostered a stereotype of Black families as fatherless and subject to a domineering woman's matriarchal rule. From such simplistic accounts it is all too easy to come to blame juvenile delinquency, divorce, illegitimacy, and other social ills on the Black family, while ignoring the oppressive reality of our political and economic system and the adaptive resiliency and strength that Black families have shown.

My analysis will draw on life-history material as well as on personal comments from women in The Flats, the poorest section of a Black community in the Midwestern city of Jackson Harbor.[1] I shall view women as strategists—active agents who use resources to achieve goals and cope with the problems of everyday life. This framework has several advantages. First, because the focus is on women rather than men, women's views of family relations, often ignored or slighted, are given prominence. Second, since households form around women because of their role in child care, ties between women (including paternal aunts, cousins, etc.) often constitute the core of a network; data from women's lives, then, crucially illuminate the continuity in these networks. Finally, the life-history material, taken chiefly from women, also demonstrates the positive role that a man plays in Black family life, both as the father of a woman's children and as a contributor of valuable resources to her network and to the network of his own kin.

I shall begin by analyzing the history of residential arrangements during one woman's life, and the residential arrangements of this woman's kin network at two points in time, demonstrating that although household composition changes, members are selected or self-selected largely from a single network that has continuity over time. Women and men, in response to joblessness, the possibility of welfare payments, the breakup of relationships, or the whims of a landlord, may move often. But the very calamities and crises that contribute to the constant shifts in residence tend to bring men, women, and children back into the households of close kin. Newly formed households are successive recombinations of the same domestic network of adults and children, quite often in the same dwellings. Residence histories, then, are an important reflection of the strategy of relying on and strengthening the domestic kin network, and also reveal the adaptiveness of households with "elastic boundaries." (It may be worth noting that middle-class whites are beginning to perceive certain values, for their own lives, in such households.)

In the remainder of the paper, the importance of maximizing network strength will be reemphasized and additional strategies will be isolated by examining two sets of relationships within kin networks—those between mothers and fathers and those between fathers and children. Women's own accounts of their situations show how they have developed a strong sense of independence from men, evolved social controls against the formation of conjugal relationships, and limited the role of the husband-father within the mother's domestic group. All of these strategies serve to strengthen the domestic network, often at the expense of any particular male-female tie. Kin regard any marriage as a risk to the woman and her children, and the loss of either male or female kin as a threat to the durability of the kin network. These two factors continually augment each other and dictate, as well, the range of socially accepted relationships between fathers and children.

## RESIDENCE AND THE DOMESTIC NETWORK

In The Flats, the material and cultural support needed to sustain and socialize community members is provided by cooperating kinsmen. The individual can draw upon a broad domestic web of kin and friends— some who reside together, others who do not. Residents in The Flats characterize household composition according to where people sleep, eat, and spend their time. Those who eat together may be considered part of a domestic unit. But an individual may eat in one household, sleep in another, contribute resources and services to yet another, and consider himself or herself a member of all three households. Children may fall asleep and remain through the night wherever the late-evening visiting patterns of the adult females take them, and they may remain in these households and share meals perhaps a week at a time. As R. T. Smith suggests in an article on Afro-American kinship (1970), it is sometimes difficult "to determine just which household a given individual belongs to at any particular moment." These facts of ghetto life are, of course, often disguised in the statistical reports of census takers, who record simply sleeping arrangements.

Households in The Flats, then, have shifting memberships, but they maintain for the most part a steady state of three generations of kin: males and females beyond child bearing age; a middle generation of mothers raising their own children or children of close kin; and the children. This observation is supported in a recent study by Ladner (1971: 60), who writes, "Many children normally grow up in a three-genera- tion household and they absorb the influences of a grandmother and grandfather as well as a mother and father." A survey of eighty-three residence changes among welfare families, whereby adult females who are heads of their own households merged households with other kin, shows that the majority of moves created three-generation households. Consequently, it is difficult to pinpoint structural beginning or end to household cycles in poor Black urban communities (Buchler and Selby, 1968; Fortes, 1958; Otterbein, 1970). But it is clear that authority patterns within a kin network change with birth and death; with the death of the oldest member in a household, the next generation assumes authority.

Residence changes themselves are brought on by many factors, most related to the economic conditions in which poor families live. Women who have children have access to welfare, and thus more economic secu- rity than women who do not, and more than all men. Welfare regula- tions encourage mothers to set up separate households, and women ac- tively seek independence, privacy, and improvement in their lives. But these ventures do not last long. Life histories of adults show that the at- tempts by women to set up separate households with their children are short-lived: houses are condemned; landlords evict tenants; and needs for services among kin arise. Household composition also expands or contracts with the loss of a job, the death of a relative, the beginning or end of a sexual partnership, or the end of a friendship. But fluctuations in household composition rarely affect the exchanges and daily depen- dencies of participants. The chronology of residence changes made by Ruby Banks graphically illuminates these points (see Table 1).

Ruby's residential changes, and the residences of her own children and kin, reveal that the same factors contributing to the high frequency of moving also bring men, women, and children back into the household of close kin. That one can repeatedly do so is a great source of security and dependence for those living in poverty.

A look in detail at the domestic network of Ruby's parents, Magnolia and Calvin Waters, illustrates the complexity of the typical network and also shows kin constructs at work both in the recruitment of individuals to the network and in the changing composition of households within the network, over less than three months (see Table 2).

These examples do indeed indicate the important role of the Black woman in the domestic structure. But the cooperation between male and female siblings who share the same household or live near one another has been underestimated by those who have isolated the female-headed household as the most significant domestic unit among the urban Black poor. The close cooperation of adult siblings arises from the residential patterns typical of young adults (Stack, 1970). Owing to poverty, young women with or without children do not perceive any choice but to re-

**Table 1.**

| AGE | HOUSEHOLD COMPOSITION AND CONTEXT OF HOUSEHOLD FORMATION |
|---|---|
| Birth | Ruby lived with her mother, Magnolia, and her maternal grandparents. |
| 4 | To be eligible for welfare, Ruby and Magnolia were required to move out of Ruby's grandparents' house. They moved into a separate residence two houses away, but ate all meals at the grandparents' house. |
| 5 | Ruby and Magnolia returned to the grandparents' house and Magnolia gave birth to a son. Magnolia worked and the grandmother cared for her children. |
| 6 | Ruby's maternal grandparents separated. Magnolia remained living with her father and her (now) two sons. Ruby and her grandmother moved up the street and lived with her maternal aunt Augusta and maternal uncle. Ruby's grandmother took care of Ruby and her brothers, and Magnolia worked and cooked and cleaned for her father. |
| 7–16 | The household was now composed of Ruby, her grandmother's new husband, Augusta and her boyfriend, and Ruby's maternal uncle. At age sixteen Ruby gave birth to a daughter. |
| 17 | Ruby's grandmother died and Ruby had a second child, by Otis, the younger brother of Ruby's best friend, Willa Mae. Ruby remained living with Augusta, Augusta's boyfriend, Ruby's maternal uncle and her daughters. |
| 18 | Ruby fought with Augusta and she and Otis moved into an apartment with her two daughters. Ruby's first daughter's father died. Otis stayed with Ruby and her daughters in the apartment. |
| 19 | Ruby broke up with Otis. Ruby and her two daughters joined Magnolia, Magnolia's "husband," and her ten half-siblings. Ruby had a miscarriage. |
| 19½ | Ruby left town and moved out of state with her new boyfriend, Earl. She left her daughters with Magnolia and remained out of state for a year. Magnolia then insisted she return home and take care of her children. |
| 20½ | Ruby and her daughters moved into a large house rented by Augusta and her mother's brother. It was located next door to Magnolia's house, where Ruby and her children ate. Ruby cleaned for her aunt and uncle, and gave birth to another child, by Otis, who had returned to the household. |
| 21 | Ruby and Otis broke up once again. She found a house and moved there with her daughters, Augusta, and Augusta's boyfriend. Ruby did the cleaning, and Augusta cooked. Ruby and Magnolia, who now lived across town, shared child care, and Ruby's cousin's daughter stayed with Ruby. |
| 21½ | Augusta and her boyfriend have moved out because they were all fighting, and the two of them wanted to get away from the noise of the children. Ruby has a new boyfriend. |

**Table 2.**

| HOUSEHOLD | DOMESTIC ARRANGEMENTS, APRIL 1969 | DOMESTIC ARRANGEMENTS, JUNE 1969 |
|---|---|---|
| 1 | Magnolia, her husband Calvin, their eight children (4–18.) | Unchanged. |
| 2 | Magnolia's sister Augusta, Augusta's boyfriend, Ruby, Ruby's children, Ruby's boyfriend Otis. | Augusta and boyfriend have moved to #3 after a quarrel with Ruby. Ruby and Otis remain in #2. |
| 3 | Billy (Augusta's closest friend), Billy's children, Lazar (Magnolia's sister Carrie's husband, living in the basement), Carrie (from time to time—she is an alcoholic). | Augusta and boyfriend have moved to a small, one-room apartment upstairs from Billy. |
| 4 | Magnolia's sister Lydia, Lydia's daughters Georgia and Lottie, Lydia's boy-friend, Lottie's daughter. | Lottie and her daughter have moved to an apartment down the street, joining Lottie's girl friend and child. Georgia has moved in with her boyfriend. Lydia's son has moved back into Lydia's home #4. |
| 5 | Ruby's friend Willa Mae, her husband and son, her sister, and her brother James (father of Ruby's daughter). | James has moved in with his girl friend, who lives with her sister; James keeps most of his clothes in household #5. James's brother has returned from the army and moved into #5. |
| 6 | Eloise (Magnolia's first son's father's sister), her husband, their four young children, their daughter and her son, Eloise's friend Jessie's brother's daughter and her child. | Unchanged. |
| 7 | Violet (wife of Calvin's closest friend Cecil, now dead several years), her two sons, her daughter Odessa, and Odessa's four children. | Odessa's son Raymond has fathered Clover's baby. Clover and baby have joined household #7. |

main living at home with their mothers or other adult female relatives. Even when young women are collecting welfare for their children, they say that their resources go further when they share food and exchange goods and services daily. Likewise, the jobless man, or the man working at a part-time or seasonal job, often remains living at home with his mother—or, if she is dead, with his sisters and brothers. This pattern continues long after such a man becomes a father and establishes a series of sexual partnerships with women, who are in turn living with their own kin or friends or are alone with their children. A result of this pattern is the striking fact that households almost always have men around: male relatives, affines, and boyfriends. These men are often intermittent members of the households, boarders, or friends who come and go— men who usually eat, and sometimes sleep, in these households. Children have constant and close contact with these men, and especially in the case of male relatives, these relationships last over the years. The most predictable residential pattern in The Flats is that individuals reside in the households of their natal kin, or the households of those who raised them, long into their adult years.

Welfare workers, researchers, and landlords in Black ghetto communities have long known that the residence patterns of the poor change frequently and that females play a dominant domestic role. What is much less understood is the relationship between household composition and domestic organization in these communities. Household boundaries are elastic, and no one model of a household, such as the nuclear family, extended family, or matrifocal family, is the norm. What is crucial and enduring is the strength of ties within a kin network; the maintenance of a strong network in turn has consequences for the relationships between the members themselves, as demonstrated in the following discussion of relationships between mothers and fathers and between fathers and their children.

## MOTHERS AND FATHERS

Notwithstanding the emptiness and hopelessness of the job experience in the Black community, men and women fall in love and wager buoyant new relationships against the inexorable forces of poverty and racism. At the same time, in dealing with everyday life, Black women and men have developed a number of attitudes and strategies that appear to mitigate against the formation of long-term relationships. Even when a man and woman set up temporary housekeeping arrangements, they both maintain primary social ties with their kin. If other members of a kin network view a particular relationship as a drain on the network's resources, they will act in various and subtle ways to break up the relationship. This is what happened in the life of Julia Ambrose, another resident of The Flats.

When I first met Julia, she was living with her baby, her cousin Teresa, and Teresa's "old man." After several fierce battles with Teresa over the bills, and because of Teresa's hostility toward Julia's boyfriends, Julia decided to move out. She told me she was head over heels in love with Elliot, her child's father, and they had decided to live together.

For several months Julia and Elliot shared a small apartment, and their relationship was strong. Elliot was very proud of his baby. On weekends he would spend an entire day carrying the baby around to his sister's home, where he would show it to his friends on the street. Julia, exhilarated by her independence in having her own place, took great care of the house and her baby. She told me, "Before Elliot came home from work I would have his dinner fixed and the house and kid clean. When he came home he would take his shower and then I'd bring his food to the bed. I'd put the kid to sleep and then get into bed with him. It was fine. We would get in a little piece and then go to sleep. In the morning we'd do the same thing."

After five months, Elliot was laid off from his job at a factory that hires seasonal help. He couldn't find another job, except part-time work for a cab company. Elliot began spending more time away from the house with his friends at the local tavern, and less time with Julia and the baby. Julia finally had to get back "on aid" and Elliot put more of his things back in his sister's home so the social worker wouldn't know he was staying with Julia. Julia noticed changes in Elliot. "If you start necking and doing the same thing that you've been doing with your man, and he don't want it, you know for sure that he is messing with someone else, or don't want you anymore. Maybe Elliot didn't want me in the first place, but maybe he did 'cause he chased me a lot. He wanted me and he didn't want me. I really loved him, but I'm not in love with him now. My feelings just changed. I'm not in love with no man, really. Just out for what I can get from them."

Julia and Elliot stayed together, but she began to hear rumors about him. Her cousin, a woman who had often expressed jealousy toward Julia, followed Elliot in a car and told her that Elliot parked late at night outside the apartment house of his previous girl friend. Julia told me that her cousin was "nothing but a gossip, a newspaper who carried news back and forth," and that her cousin was envious of her having an "old man." Nevertheless, Julia believed the gossip.

After hearing other rumors and gossip about Elliot, Julia said, "I still really liked him, but I wasn't going to let him get the upper hand on me. After I found out that he was messing with someone else, I said to myself, I was doing it too, so what's the help in making a fuss. But after that, I made him pay for being with me!

"I was getting a check every month for rent from welfare and I would take the money and buy me clothes. I bought my own wardrobe and I gave my mother money for keeping the baby while I was working. I worked here and there while I was on aid and they were paying my rent.

I didn't really need Elliot, but that was extra money for me. When he asked me what happened to my check I told him I got off and couldn't get back on. My mother knew. She didn't care what I did so long as I didn't let Elliot make an ass out of me. The point is a woman has to have her own pride. She can't let a man rule her. You can't let a man kick you in the tail and tell you what to do. Anytime I can make an ass out of a man, I'm going to do it. If he's doing the same to me, then I'll quit him and leave him alone.''

After Elliot lost his job, and kin continued to bring gossip to Julia about how he was playing around with other women, Julia became embittered toward Elliot and was anxious to hurt him. There had been a young Black man making deliveries for a local store who would pass her house every day, and flirt with her. Charles would slow down his truck and honk for Julia when he passed the house. Soon she started running out to talk to him in his truck and decided to ''go'' with him. Charles liked Julia and brought nice things for her child.

''I put Elliot in a trick,'' Julia told me soon after she stopped going with Charles. ''I knew that Elliot didn't care nothing for me, so I made him jealous. He was nice to the kids, both of them, but he didn't do nothing to show me he was still in love with me. Me and Elliot fought a lot. One night Charles and me went to a motel room and stayed there all night. Mama had the babies. She got mad. But I was trying to hurt Elliot. When I got home, me and Elliot got into it. He called me all kinds of names. I said he might as well leave. But Elliot said he wasn't going nowhere. So he stayed and we'd sleep together, but we didn't do nothing. Then one night something happened. I got pregnant again by Elliot. After I got pregnant, me and Charles quit, and I moved in with a girl friend for a while. Elliot chased after me and we started going back together, but we stayed separate. In my sixth month I moved back in my mother's home with her husband and the kids.''

Many young women like Julia feel strongly that they cannot let a man make a fool out of them, and they react quickly and boldly to rumor, gossip, and talk that hurts them. The power that gossip and information have in constraining the duration of sexual relationships is an important cultural phenomenon. But the most important single factor affecting interpersonal relationships between men and women in The Flats is unemployment. The futility of the job experience for street-corner men in a Black community is sensitively portrayed by Elliot Liebow in *Tally's Corner*. As Liebow (1967: 63) writes, ''The job fails the man and the man fails the job.'' Liebow's discussion (p. 142) of men and jobs leads directly to his analysis of the streetcorner male's exploitive relationships with women: ''Men not only present themselves as economic exploiters of women but they expect other men to do the same.'' Ghetto-specific male roles that men try to live up to at home and on the street, and their alleged round-the-clock involvement in peer groups, are interpreted in *Soulside* (Hannerz, 1969) as a threat to marital stability.

Losing a job, then, or being unemployed month after month debili-
tates one's self-importance and independence and, for men, necessitates
sacrificing a role in the economic support of their families. Faced with
these familiar patterns in the behavior and status of men, women call
upon life experiences in The Flats to guide them. When a man loses his
job, that is the time he is most likely to begin "messing around."

And so that no man appears to have made a fool of them, women respond with vengeance, out of pride and self-defense. Another young
woman in The Flats, Ivy Rodgers, told me about the time she left her two
children in The Flats with her mother and took off for Indiana with
Jimmy River, a young man she had fallen in love with "the first sight I
seen." Jimmy asked Ivy to go to Gary, Indiana, where his family lived.
"I just left the kids with my mama. I didn't even tell her I was going. My
checks kept coming so she had food for the kids, but I didn't know he let
his people tell him what to do. While he was in Gary, Jimmy started
messing with another woman. He said he wasn't, but I caught him. I
quit him, but when he told me he wasn't messing, I loved him so much I
took him back. Then I got to thinking about it. I had slipped somewhere.
I had let myself go. Seems like I forgot that I wasn't going to let Jimmy or
any man make an ass out of me. But he sure was doing it. I told Jimmy
that if he loved me, he would go and see my people, take them things,
and tell them we were getting married. Jimmy didn't want to go back to
The Flats, but I tricked him and told him I really wanted to visit. I picked
out my ring and Jimmy paid thirty dollars on it and I had him buy my
outfit that we was getting married in. He went along with it. What's so
funny was when we come here and he said to me, 'You ready to
go back?' and I told him, 'No, I'm not going back. I never will marry
you.' "

Forms of social control in the larger society also work against successful marriages in The Flats. In fact, couples rarely chance marriage unless
a man has a job; often the job is temporary, low-paying, and insecure,
and the worker is arbitrarily laid off whenever he is not needed. Women
come to realize that welfare benefits and ties within kin networks provide greater security for them and their children. In addition, caretaker
agencies such as public welfare are insensitive to individual attempts for
social mobility. A woman may be immediately cut off the welfare rolls
when a husband returns home from prison or the army, or if she gets
married. Unless there is either a significant change in employment opportunities for the urban poor or a livable guaranteed minimum income,
it is unlikely that urban low-income Blacks will form lasting conjugal
units.

Marriage and its accompanying expectations of a home, a job, and a
family built around the husband and wife have come to stand for an individual's desire to break out of poverty. It implies the willingness of an individual to remove himself from the daily obligations of his kin network.

People in The Flats recognize that one cannot simultaneously meet kin expectations and the expectations of a spouse. Cooperating kinsmen continually attempt to draw new people into their personal network; but at the same time they fear the loss of a central, resourceful member in the network. The following passages are taken from the detailed residence life history of Ruby Banks. Details of her story were substantiated by discussions with her mother, her aunt, her daughter's father, and her sister.

"Me and Otis could be married, but they all ruined that. Aunt Augusta told Magnolia that he was no good. Magnolia was the fault of it, too. They don't want to see me married! Magnolia knows that it be money getting away from her. I couldn't spend the time with her and the kids and be giving her the money that I do now. I'd have my husband to look after. I couldn't go where she want me to go. I couldn't come every time she call me, like if Calvin took sick or the kids took sick, or if she took sick. That's all the running I do now. I couldn't do that. You think a man would put up with as many times as I go over her house in a cab, giving half my money to her all the time? That's the reason they don't want me married. You think a man would let Aunt Augusta come into the house and take food out of the icebox from his kids? They thought that way ever since I came up.

"They broke me and Otis up. They kept telling me that he didn't want me, and that he didn't want the responsibility. I put him out and I cried all night long. And I really did love him. But Aunt Augusta and others kept fussing and arguing so I went and quit him. I would have got married a long time ago to my first baby's daddy, but Aunt Augusta was the cause of that, telling Magnolia that he was too old for me. She's been jealous of me since the day I was born.

"Three years after Otis I met Earl. Earl said he was going to help pay for the utilities. He was going to get me some curtains and pay on my couch. While Earl was working he was so good to me and my children that Magnolia and them started worrying all over again. They sure don't want me married. The same thing that happened to Otis happened to many of my boyfriends. And I ain't had that many men. I'm tired of them bothering me with their problems when I'm trying to solve my own problems. They tell me that Earl's doing this and that, seeing some girl.

"They look for trouble to tell me every single day. If I ever marry, I ain't listening to what nobody say. I just listen to what he say. You have to get along the best way you know how, and forget about your people. If I got married they would talk, like they are doing now, saying, 'He ain't no good, he's been creeping on you. I told you once not to marry him. You'll end up right back on aid.' If I ever get married, I'm leaving town!"

Ruby's account reveals the strong conflict between kin-based domestic units and lasting ties between husbands and wives. When a mother in The Flats has a relationship with an economically nonproductive man, the relationship saps the resources of others in her domestic network.

Participants in the network act to break up such relationships, to maintain kin-based household groupings over the life cycle, in order to maximize potential resources and the services they hope to exchange. Similarly, a man's participation is expected in his kin network, and it is understood that he should not dissipate his services and finances to a sexual or marital relationship. These forms of social control made Ruby afraid to take the risks necessary to break out of the cycle of poverty. Instead, she chose the security and stability of her kin group. Ruby, recognizing that to make a marriage last she would have to move far away from her kin, exclaimed, "If I ever get married, I'm leaving town!" While this study was in progress, Ruby did get married, and she left the state with her husband and her youngest child that very evening.

## FATHERS AND CHILDREN

People in The Flats show pride in all their kin, and particularly new babies born into their kinship networks. Mothers encourage sons to have babies, and even more important, men coax their "old ladies" to have their babies. The value placed on children, the love, attention, and affection children receive from women and men, and the web of social relationships spun from the birth of a child are all basic to the high birthrate among the poor.

The pride that kinsmen take in the children of their sons and brothers is seen best in the pleasure that the mothers and sisters of these men express. Such pride was apparent during a visit I made to Alberta Cox's home. She introduced me to her nineteen-year-old son Nate and added immediately, "He's a daddy and his baby is four months old." Then she pointed to her twenty-two-year-old son Mac and said, "He's a daddy three times over." Mac smiled and said, "I'm no daddy," and his friend in the kitchen said, "Maybe going on four times, Mac." Alberta said, "Yes you are. Admit it, boy!" At that point Mac's grandmother rolled back in her rocker and said, "I'm a grandmother many times over, and it make me proud." A friend of Alberta's told me later that Alberta wants her sons to have babies because she thinks it will make them more responsible. Although she usually dislikes the women her sons go with, claiming they are "no-good trash," Alberta accepts the babies and asks to care for them whenever she has a chance.

Although Blacks, like most Americans, acquire kin through their mothers and fathers, the economic insecurity of the Black male and the availability of welfare to the mother-child unit make it very difficult for an unemployed Black husband-father to compete with a woman's kin for authority and control over her children. As we have seen, women seek to be independent, but also, in order to meet everyday needs, they act to strengthen their ties with their kin and within their domestic network.

Though these two strategies, especially in the context of male joblessness, may lead to the breakup of a young couple, a father will maintain
his ties with his children. The husband-father role may be limited, but,
contrary to the stereotype of Black family life, it is not only viable but culturally significant.

Very few young couples enter into a legal marriage in The Flats, but a
father and his kin can sustain a continuing relationship with the father's
children if the father has acknowledged paternity, if his kin have activated their claims on the child, and if the mother has drawn these people
into her personal network. Widely popularized and highly misleading
statistics on female-headed households have contributed to the assumption that Black children derive nothing of sociological importance from
their fathers. To the contrary, in my recent study of domestic life among
the poor in a Black community in the Midwest (Stack, 1972), I found that
70 percent of the fathers of 1,000 children on welfare recognized their
children and provided them with kinship affiliations. But because many
of these men have little or no access to steady and productive employment, out of the 699 who acknowledged paternity, only 84 (12 percent)
gave any substantial financial support to their children. People in The
Flats believe a father should help his child, but they know that the
mother cannot count on his help. Community expectations of fathers do
not generally include the father's *duties* in relation to a child; they do,
however, assume the responsibilities of the father's kin. Kinship through
males in The Flats is reckoned through a chain of acknowledged geni-
tors, but social fatherhood is shared by the genitor with his kin, and with
the mother's husband or with her boyfriends.

Although the authority of a father over his genealogical children or his
wife's other children is limited, neither the father's interest in his child
nor the desire of his kin to help raise the child strains the stability of the
domestic network. Otis's kin were drawn into Ruby's personal network
through his claims on her children, and through the long, close friendship between Ruby and Otis's sister, Willa Mae. Like many fathers in
The Flats, Otis maintained close contact with his children, and provided
goods and care for them even when he and Ruby were not on speaking
terms. One time when Otis and Ruby separated, Otis stayed in a room
in Ruby's uncle's house next door to Ruby's mother's house. At that time
Ruby's children were being kept by Magnolia each day while Ruby went
to school to finish working toward her high school diploma. Otis was out
of work, and he stayed with Ruby's uncle over six months helping Magnolia care for his children. Otis's kin were proud of the daddy he was,
and at times suggested they should take over the raising of Otis and Ruby's children. Ruby and other mothers know well that those people you
count on to share in the care and nurturing of your children are also
those who are rightfully in a position to judge and check upon how you
carry out the duties of a mother. Shared responsibilities of motherhood

in The Flats imply both a help and a check on how one assumes the parental role.

Fathers like Otis, dedicated to maintaining ties with their children, learn that the relationship they create with their child's mother largely determines the role they may assume in their child's life. Jealousy between men makes it extremely difficult for fathers to spend time with their children if the mother has a boyfriend, but as Otis said to me, "When Ruby doesn't have any old man then she starts calling on me, asking for help, and telling me to do something for my kids." Between such times, when a man or a woman does not have an ongoing sexual relationship, some mothers call upon the fathers of their children and temporarily "choke" these men with their personal needs and the needs of the children. At these times, men and women reinforce their fragile but continuing relationship, and find themselves empathetic friends who can be helpful to one another.

A mother generally regards her children's father as a friend of the family whom she can recruit for help, rather than as a father failing his parental duties. Although fathers voluntarily help out with their children, many fathers cannot be depended upon as a steady source of help. Claudia Williams talked to me about Harold, the father of her two children. "Some days he be coming over at night saying, 'I'll see to the babies and you can lay down and rest, honey,' treating me real nice. Then maybe I don't even see him for two or three months. There's no sense nagging Harold. I just treat him as some kind of friend even if he is the father of my babies." Since Claudia gave birth to Harold's children, both of them have been involved in other relationships. When either of them is involved with someone else, this effectively cuts Harold off from his children. Claudia says, "My kids don't need their daddy's help, but if he helps out then I help him out, too. My kids are well behaved, and I know they make Harold's kinfolk proud."

## CONCLUSIONS

The view of Black women as represented in their own words and life histories coincides with that presented by Joyce Ladner: "One of the chief characteristics defining the Black woman is her [realistic approach] to her [own] resources. Instead of becoming resigned to her fate, she has always sought creative solutions to her problems. The ability to utilize her existing resources and yet maintain a forthright determination to struggle against the racist society in whatever overt and subtle ways necessary is one of her major attributes" (Ladner, 1971: 276–77).

I have particularly emphasized those strategies that women can employ to maximize their independence, acquire and maintain domestic authority, limit (but positively evaluate) the role of husband and father, and strengthen ties with kin. The last of these—maximizing relationships in the domestic network—helps to account for patterns of Black family life among the urban poor more adequately than the concepts of nuclear or matrifocal family. When economic resources are greatly limited, people need help from as many others as possible. This requires expanding their kin networks—increasing the number of people they hope to be able to count on. On the one hand, female members of a network may act to break up a relationship that has become a drain on their resources. On the other, a man is expected to contribute to his own kin network, and it is assumed that he should not dissipate his services and finances to a marital relationship. At the same time, a woman will continue to seek aid from the man who has fathered her children, thus building up her own network's resources. She also expects something of his kin, especially his mother and sisters. Women continually activate these lines to bring kin and friends into the network of exchange and obligation. Most often, the biological father's female relatives are poor and also try to expand their network and increase the number of people they can depend on.

Clearly, economic pressures among cooperating kinsmen in the Black community work against the loss of either males or females—through marriage or other long-term relationships—from the kin network. The kin-based cooperative network represents the collective adaptations to poverty of the men, women, and children within the Black community. Loyalties and dependencies toward kinsmen offset the ordeal of unemployment and racism. To cope with the everyday demands of ghetto life, these networks have evolved patterns of co-residence; elastic household boundaries; lifelong, if intermittent, bonds to three-generation households; social constraints on the role of the husband-father within the mother's domestic group; and the domestic authority of women.

## NOTES

1. This work is based on a recent urban anthropological study of poverty and domestic life of urban-born Black Americans who were raised on public welfare and whose parents had migrated from the South to a single community in the Urban North (Stack, 1972). Now adults in their twenties to forties, they are raising their own children on welfare in The Flats. All personal and place names in this paper are fictitious.

# Review Questions

1. While place of residence and family may coincide for many people in our society, for the poor community described by Stack they do not. What can we say about the meaning of the term "family" in light of this fact?

2. What is the importance of economic factors in shaping both the residence patterns and family interactions of residents of The Flats?

3. What are the roles played by men in the family system of this poor neighborhood? What features of our society affect which family roles men occupy and how they are performed?

4. Despite the fact that the poor families described here have developed flexible household boundaries and extensive networks of kin support and obligations not characteristic of the nuclear family, family life in The Flats can be seen as embodying and responding to many of the central values and norms of the family institution of the larger culture. Give examples of conformity to cultural norms and values.

# MARRIAGE AND THE CONSTRUCTION OF REALITY

## Peter L. Berger and Hansfried Kellner

Ever since Durkheim it has been a commonplace of family sociology that marriage serves as a protection against anomie [normlessness] for the individual. Interesting and pragmatically useful though this insight is, it is but the negative side of a phenomenon of much broader significance. If one speaks of *anomic* states, then one ought properly to investigate also the *nomic* processes that, by their absence, lead to the aforementioned states. If, consequently, one finds a negative correlation between marriage and anomie, then one should be led to inquire into the character of marriage as a *nomos*-building instrumentality, that is, of marriage as a social arrangement that creates for the individual the sort of order in which he can experience his life as making sense. It is our intention here to discuss marriage in these terms. While this could evidently be done in a macrosociological perspective, dealing with marriage as a major social institution related to other broad structures of society, our focus will be microsociological, dealing primarily with the social processes affecting the individuals in any specific marriage, although, of course, the larger framework of these processes will have to be understood. In what sense this discussion can be described as microsociology of knowledge will hopefully become clearer in the course of it.[1]

Marriage is obviously only *one* social relationship in which this process of *nomos*-building takes place. It is, therefore, necessary to first look in more general terms at the character of this process. In doing so, we are influenced by three theoretical perspectives—the Weberian perspective on society as a network of meanings, the Meadian perspective on identity as a social phenomenon, and the phenomenological analysis of the social structuring of reality especially as given in the work of Schutz and Merleau-Ponty.[2] Not being convinced, however, that theoretical lucidity is necessarily enhanced by terminological ponderosity, we shall avoid as much as possible the use of the sort of jargon for which both sociologists and phenomenologists have acquired dubious notoriety.

The process that interests us here is the one that constructs, maintains and modifies a consistent reality that can be meaningfully experienced

Peter L. Berger and Hansfried Kellner, "Marriage and the Construction of Reality," *Diogenes* 45 (1964): 1–25.

by individuals. In its essential forms this process is determined by the society in which it occurs. Every society has its specific way of defining and perceiving reality—its world, its universe, its overarching organization of symbols. This is already given in the language that forms the symbolic base of the society. Erected over this base, and by means of it, is a system of ready-made *typifications* [stereotypical explanations of events in the world], through which the innumerable experiences of reality come to be ordered.[3] These typifications and their order are held in common by the members of society, thus acquiring not only the character of objectivity, but being taken for granted as *the* world *tout court*, the only world that normal men can conceive of.[4] The seemingly objective and taken-for-granted character of the social definitions of reality can be seen most clearly in the case of language itself, but it is important to keep in mind that the latter forms the base and instrumentality of a much larger world-erecting process.

The socially constructed world must be continually mediated to and actualized by the individual, so that it can become and remain indeed *his* world as well. The individual is given by his society certain decisive cornerstones for his everyday experience and conduct. Most importantly, the individual is supplied with specific sets of typifications and criteria of relevance, predefined for him by the society and made available to him for the ordering of his everyday life. This ordering or (in line with our opening considerations) nomic apparatus is biographically cumulative. It begins to be formed in the individual from the earliest stages of socialization on, then keeps on being enlarged and modified by himself throughout his biography.[5] While there are individual biographical differences making for differences in the constitution of this apparatus in specific individuals, there exists in the society an overall consensus on the range of differences deemed to be tolerable. Without such consensus, indeed, society would be impossible as a going concern, since it would then lack the ordering principles by which alone experience can be shared and conduct can be mutually intelligible. This order, by which the individual comes to perceive and define his world, is thus not chosen by him, except perhaps for very small modifications. Rather, it is discovered by him as an external datum, a ready-made world that simply is *there* for him to go ahead and live in, though he modifies it continually in the process of living in it. Nevertheless, this world is in need of *validation*, perhaps precisely because of an ever-present glimmer of suspicion as to its social manufacture and relativity. This validation, while it must be undertaken by the individual himself, requires ongoing interaction with others who co-inhabit this same socially constructed world. In a broad sense, *all* the other co-inhabitants of this world serve a validating function. Every morning the newspaper boy validates the widest coordinates of my world and the mailman bears tangible validation of my own location within these coordinates. However, some validations are more significant than others. Every individual requires the ongoing validation of his world, including crucially the validation of his identity and place in this world, by those few who are his truly significant others.[6] Just as the individual's deprivation of relationship with his significant others will plunge him into anomie, so their continued presence will sustain for him that *nomos* by which he can feel at home in the world at least most of the time. Again in a broad sense, all the actions of the significant others and even their simple presence serve this sustaining function. In everyday life, however, the principal method employed is speech. In this sense, it is proper to view the individual's relationship with his significant others as an ongoing conversation. As the latter occurs, it validates over and over again the fundamental definitions of reality once entered into, not, of course, so much by explicit articulation, but precisely by taking the definitions silently for granted and conversing about all conceivable matters on this taken-for-granted basis. Through the same conversation the individual is also made capable of adjusting to changing and new social contexts in his biography. In a very fundamental sense it can be said that one converses one's way through life.

If one concedes these points, one can now state a general sociological proposition: the plausibility and stability of the world, as socially defined, is dependent upon the strength and continuity of significant relationships in which conversation about this world can be continually carried on. Or, to put it a little differently: *the reality of the world is sustained through conversation with significant others.* This reality, of course, includes not only the imagery by which fellowmen are viewed, but also includes the way in which one views oneself. The reality-bestowing force of social relationships depends on the degree of their nearness,[7] that is, on the degree to which social relationships occur in face-to-face situations and to which they are credited with primary significance by the individual. In any empirical situation, there now emerge obvious sociological questions out of these considerations, namely, questions about the patterns of the world-building relationships, the social forms taken by the conversation with significant others. Sociologically, one must ask how these relationships are *objectively* structured and distributed, and one will also want to understand how they are *subjectively* perceived and experienced.

With these preliminary assumptions stated we can now arrive at our main thesis here. Namely, we would contend that marriage occupies a privileged status among the significant validating relationships for adults in our society. Put slightly differently: marriage is a crucial nomic instrumentality in our society. We would further argue that the essential social functionality of this institution cannot be fully understood if this fact is not perceived.

. . . Marriage in our society is a *dramatic* act in which two strangers come together and redefine themselves. The drama of the act is internally anticipated and socially legitimated long before it takes place in the individual's biography, and amplified by means of a pervasive ideology, the dominant themes of which (romantic love, sexual fulfillment, self-discovery and self-realization through love and sexuality, the nuclear family as the social site for these processes) can be found distributed through all strata of the society. The actualization of these ideologically predefined expectations in the life of the individual occurs to the accompaniment of one of the few traditional rites of passage that are still meaningful to almost all members of the society. It should be added that, in using the term "strangers," we do not mean, of course, that the candidates for the marriage come from widely discrepant social backgrounds—indeed, the data indicate that the contrary is the case. The strangeness rather lies in the fact that, unlike marriage candidates in many previous societies, those in ours typically come from different face-to-face contexts—in the terms used above, they come from different areas of conversation. They do not have a shared past, although their pasts have a similar structure. In other words, quite apart from prevailing patterns of ethnic, religious and class endogamy [or marriage within the same group], our society is typically exogamous [involving marriage between those who differ] in terms of nomic relationships. Put concretely, in our mobile society the significant conversation of the two partners previous to the marriage took place in social circles that did not overlap. With the dramatic redefinition of the situation brought about by the marriage, however, all significant conversation for the two new partners is now centered in their relationship with each other—and, in fact, it was precisely with this intention that they entered upon their relationship.

It goes without saying that this character of marriage has its root in much broader structural configurations of our society. The most important of these, for our purposes, is the crystallization of a so-called private sphere of existence, more and more segregated from the immediate controls of the public institutions (especially the economic and political ones), and yet defined and utilized as the main social area for the individual's self-realization.[8] It cannot be our purpose here to inquire into the historical forces that brought forth this phenomenon, beyond making the observation that these are closely connected with the industrial revolution and its institutional consequences. The public institutions now confront the individual as an immensely powerful and alien world, incomprehensible in its inner workings, anonymous in its human character. If only through his work in some nook of the economic machinery, the individual must find a way of living in this alien world, come to terms with its power over him, be satisfied with a few conceptual rules of thumb to guide him through a vast reality that otherwise remains opaque to his understanding, and modify its anonymity by whatever *human relations* he can work out in his involvement with it. It ought to be emphasized, against some critics of "mass society," that this does not inevitably leave the individual with a sense of profound unhappiness and lostness. It would rather seem that large numbers of people in our society are quite content with a situation in which their public involvements have little subjective importance, regarding work as a not too bad necessity and politics as at best a spectator sport. . . . The individual in this situation, no matter whether he is happy or not, will turn elsewhere for the experiences of self-realization that do have importance for him. The private sphere, this interstitial area created (we would think) more or less haphazardly as a by-product of the social metamorphosis [or unfolding] of industrialism, is mainly where he will turn. It is here that the individual will seek power, intelligibility and, quite literally, a name—the apparent power to fashion a world, however Lilliputian, that will reflect his own being: a world that, seemingly having been shaped by himself and thus unlike those other worlds that insist on shaping him, is translucently intelligible to him (or so he thinks); a world in which, consequently, he is *somebody*—perhaps even, within its charmed circle, a lord and master. What is more, to a considerable extent these expectations are not unrealistic. The public institutions have no need to control the individual's adventures in the private sphere, as long as they really stay within the latter's circumscribed limits. The private sphere is perceived, not without justification, as an area of individual choice and even autonomy. This fact has important consequences for the shaping of identity in modern society that cannot be pursued here. All that ought to be clear here is the peculiar location of the private sphere within and between the other social structures. In sum, it is above all and, as a rule, only in the private sphere that the individual can take a slice of reality and fashion it into his world.[9] . . .

The private sphere includes a variety of social relationships. Among these, however, the relationships of the family occupy a central position and, in fact, serve as a focus for most of the other relationships (such as those with friends, neighbors, fellow-members of religious and other voluntary associations). . . . [T]he central relationship in this whole area is the marital one. It is on the basis of marriage that, for most adults in our society, existence in the private sphere is built up. It will be clear that this is not at all a universal or even a cross culturally wide function of marriage. Rather . . . marriage in our society [has] taken on a very peculiar character and functionality. It has been pointed out that marriage in contemporary society has lost some of its older functions and taken on new ones instead.[10] This is certainly correct, but we would prefer to state the matter a little differently. Marriage and family used to be firmly embedded in a matrix of wider community relationships, serving as extensions and particularizations of the latter's social controls. There were few separating barriers between the world of the individual family and the wider community, a fact even to be seen in the physical conditions under which the family lived before the industrial revolution.[11] The same social life pulsated through the house, the street and the community. In our terms, the family and within it the marital relationship were part and parcel of a considerably larger area of conversation. In our contemporary society, by contrast, each family constitutes its own segregated sub-world, with its own controls and its own closed conversation.

This fact requires a much greater effort on the part of the marriage partners. Unlike an earlier situation in which the establishment of the new marriage simply added to the differentiation and complexity of an already existing social world, the marriage partners now are embarked on the often difficult task of constructing for themselves the little world in which they will live. To be sure, the larger society provides them with certain standard instructions as to how they should go about this task, but this does not change the fact that considerable effort of their own is required for its realization. The monogamous character of marriage enforces both the dramatic and the precarious nature of this undertaking. Success or failure hinges on the present idiosyncrasies and the fairly unpredictable future development of these idiosyncrasies of *only two individuals* (who, moreover, do not have a shared past)—as Simmel has shown, the most unstable of all possible social relationships.[12] Not surprisingly, the decision to embark on this undertaking has a critical, even cataclysmic connotation in the popular imagination, which is underlined as well as psychologically assuaged by the ceremonialism that surrounds the event.

Every social relationship requires *objectivation*, that is, requires *a process by which subjectively experienced meanings become objective to the individual and*, in interaction with others, *become common property* and thereby massively objective.[13] The degree of objectivation will depend on the number and the intensity of the social relationships that are its carriers. A relationship that consists of only two individuals called upon to sustain, by their own efforts, an ongoing social world will have to make up in intensity for the numerical poverty of the arrangement. This, in turn, accentuates the drama and the precariousness. The later addition of children will add to the . . . "density" of objectivation taking place within the nuclear family, thus rendering the latter a good deal less precarious. . . .

The attempt can now be made to outline the ideal-typical process that takes place as marriage functions as an instrumentality for the social construction of reality. The chief protagonists of the drama are two individuals, each with a biographically accumulated and available stock of experience.[14] As members of a highly mobile society, these individuals have already internalized a degree of readiness to redefine themselves and to modify their stock of experience, thus bringing with them considerable psychological capacity for entering new relationships with others.[15] Also, coming from broadly similar sectors of the larger society (in terms of region, class, ethnic and religious affiliations), the two individuals will have organized their stock of experience in similar fashion. In other words, *the two individuals have internalized the same overall world, including the general definitions and expectations of the marriage relationship itself.* Their society has provided them with a taken-for-granted image of marriage and has socialized them into an anticipation of stepping into the taken-for-granted roles of marriage. All the same, *these relatively empty projections now have to be actualized, lived through and filled with experiential content* by the protagonists. This will require a dramatic change in their definitions of reality and of themselves.

As of the marriage, most of each partner's actions must now be projected in conjunction with those of the other. Each partner's definitions of reality must be continually correlated with the definitions of the other. The other is present in nearly all horizons of everyday conduct. Furthermore, the identity of each now takes on a new character, having to be constantly matched with that of the other, indeed being typically perceived by the people at large as being symbiotically conjoined with the identity of the other. In each partner's psychological economy of significant others, the marriage partner becomes the other *par excellence*, the nearest and most decisive co-inhabitant of the world. Indeed, all other significant relationships have to be almost automatically reperceived and regrouped in accordance with this drastic shift.

In other words, from the beginning of the marriage each partner has new modes in his meaningful experience of the world in general, of other people and of himself. By definition, then, marriage constitutes a nomic rupture. In terms of each partner's biography, the event of marriage initiates a new nomic process. Now, the full implications of this fact are rarely apprehended by the protagonists with any degree of clarity. There rather is to be found the notion that one's world, one's other-relationships and, above all, oneself have remained what they were before—only, of course, that world, others and self will now be shared with the marriage partner. It should be clear by now that this notion is a grave misapprehension. Just because of this fact, marriage now propels the individual into an unintended and unarticulated development, in the course of which the nomic transformation takes place. What typically *is* apprehended are certain objective and concrete problems arising out of the marriage—such as tensions with in-laws, or with former friends, or religious differences between the partners, as well as immediate tensions between them. These are apprehended as external, situational and practical difficulties. What is *not* apprehended is the subjective side of these difficulties, namely, the transformation of *nomos* and identity that has occurred and that continues to go on, so that all problems and relationships are experienced in a quite new way, that is, experienced within a new and ever-changing reality.

Take a simple and frequent illustration—the male partner's relationships with male friends before and after the marriage. It is a common observation that such relationships, especially if the extramarital partners

are single, rarely survive the marriage, or, if they do, are drastically redefined after it. This is typically the result of neither a deliberate decision
by the husband nor deliberate sabotage by the wife. What rather happens, very simply, is a slow process in which the husband's image of his
friend is transformed as he keeps talking about this friend with his wife.
Even if no actual talking goes on, the mere presence of the wife forces
him to see his friend differently. This need not mean that he adopts a
negative image held by the wife. Regardless of what image she holds or
is believed by him to hold, it will be different from that held by the husband. This difference will enter into the joint image that now must needs
be fabricated in the course of the ongoing conversation between the marriage partners—and, in due course, must act powerfully on the image
previously held by the husband. Again, typically, this process is rarely
apprehended with any degree of lucidity. The old friend is more likely to
fade out of the picture by slow degrees, as new kinds of friends take his
place. The process, if commented upon at all within the marital conversation, can always be explained by socially available formulas about
"people changing," "friends disappearing" or oneself "having become
more mature." This process of conversational liquidation is especially
powerful because it is one-sided—the husband typically talks with his
wife about his friend, but *not* with his friend about his wife. Thus the
friend is deprived of the defense of, as it were, counterdefining the relationship. *This dominance of the marital conversation over all others is one of its
most important characteristics.* It may be mitigated by a certain amount of
protective segregation of some non-marital relationships (say "Tuesday
night out with the boys," or "Saturday lunch with mother"), but even
then there are powerful emotional barriers against the sort of conversation (conversation *about* the marital relationship, that is) that would serve
by way of counterdefinition.

Marriage thus posits a new reality. The individual's relationship with
this new reality, however, is a dialectical one—he acts upon it, in collusion with the marriage partner, and it acts back upon both him and the
partner, welding together their reality. Since, as we have argued before,
the objectivation that constitutes this reality is precarious, the groups
with which the couple associates are called upon to assist in co-defining
the new reality. The couple is pushed towards groups that strengthen
their new definition of themselves and the world, avoids those that
weaken this definition. This in turn releases the commonly known pressures of group association, again acting upon the marriage partners to
change their definitions of the world and of themselves. Thus the new
reality is not posited once and for all, but goes on being redefined not
only in the marital interaction itself but also in the various maritally
based group relationships into which the couple enters.

In the individual's biography marriage, then, brings about a decisive
phase of socialization that can be compared with the phases of child-

hood and adolescence. This phase has a rather different structure from the earlier ones. There the individual was in the main socialized into already existing patterns. Here he actively collaborates rather than passively accommodates himself. Also, in the previous phases of socialization, there was an apprehension of entering into a new world and being changed in the course of this. In marriage there is little apprehension of such a process, but rather the notion that the world has remained the same, with only its emotional and pragmatic connotations having changed. This notion, as we have tried to show, is illusionary.

The reconstruction of the world in marriage occurs principally in the course of conversation, as we have suggested. *The implicit problem of this conversation is how to match two individual definitions of reality.* By the very logic of the relationship, a common overall definition must be arrived at—otherwise the conversation will become impossible and, *ipso facto*, the relationship will be endangered. Now, this conversation may be understood as the working away of an ordering and typifying apparatus—if one prefers, an objectivating apparatus. Each partner ongoingly contributes his conceptions of reality, which are then "talked through," usually not once but many times, and in the process become objectivated by the conversational apparatus. The longer this conversation goes on, the more massively real do the objectivations become to the partners. In the marital conversation a world is not only built, but it is also kept in a state of repair and ongoingly refurnished. The subjective reality of this world for the two partners is sustained by the same conversation. The nomic instrumentality of marriage is concretized over and over again, from bed to breakfast table, as the partners carry on the endless conversation that feeds on nearly all they individually or jointly experience. Indeed, it may happen eventually that no experience is fully real unless and until it has been thus "talked through."

This process has a very important result—namely, *a hardening or stabilization of the common objectivated reality*. It should be easy to see now how this comes about. The objectivations ongoingly performed and internalized by the marriage partners become ever more massively real, as they are confirmed and reconfirmed in the marital conversation. The world that is made up of these objectivations at the same time gains in stability. For example, the images of other people, which before or in the earlier stages of the marital conversation may have been rather ambiguous and shifting in the minds of the two partners, now become hardened into definite and stable characterizations. A casual acquaintance, say, may sometimes have appeared as lots of fun and sometimes as quite a bore to the wife before her marriage. Under the influence of the marital conversation, in which this other person is frequently "discussed," she will now come down more firmly on one *or* the other of the two characterizations, or on a reasonable compromise between the two. In any of these three options, though, she will have concocted with her husband a much more stable image of the person in question than she is likely to have had before her marriage, when there may have been no conversational pressure to make a definite option at all. The same process of stabilization may be observed with regard to self-definitions as well. In this way, the wife in our example will not only be pressured to assign stable characterizations to others but also to herself. Previously uninterested politically, she now identifies herself as liberal. Previously alternating between dimly articulated religious positions, she now declares herself an agnostic. Previously confused and uncertain about her sexual emotions, she now understands herself as an unabashed hedonist in this area. And so on and so forth, with the same reality—and identity—stabilizing process at work on the husband. Both world and self thus take on a firmer, more reliable character for both partners.

Furthermore, it is not only the ongoing experience of the two partners that is constantly shared and passed through the conversational apparatus. The same *sharing extends into the past*. The two distinct biographies, as subjectively apprehended by two individuals who have lived through them, are overruled and reinterpreted in the course of their conversation. Sooner or later, they will "tell all"—or, more correctly, they will tell it in such a way that it fits into the self-definitions objectivated in the marital relationship. The couple thus construct not only present reality but reconstruct past reality as well, fabricating a common memory that integrates the recollections of the two individual pasts.[16] The comic fulfillment of this process may be seen in those cases when one partner "remembers" more clearly what happened in the other's past than the other does—and corrects him accordingly. Similarly, there occurs a *sharing of future horizons*, which leads not only to stabilization, but inevitably to a narrowing of the future projections of each partner. Before marriage the individual typically plays with quite discrepant daydreams in which his future self is projected.[17] Having now considerably stabilized his self-image, the married individual will have to project the future in accordance with this maritally defined identity. This narrowing of future horizons begins with the obvious external limitation that marriage entails, as, for example, with regard to vocational and career plans. However, it extends also to the more general possibilities of the individual's biography. To return to a previous illustration, the wife, having "found herself" as a liberal, an agnostic and a "sexually healthy" person, *ipso facto* liquidates the possibilities of becoming an anarchist, a Catholic or a Lesbian. At least until further notice she has decided upon who she is—and, by the same token, upon who she will be. The stabilization brought about by marriage thus affects that total reality in which the partners exist. In the most far-reaching sense of the word, the married individual "settles down"—and *must* do so, if the marriage is to be viable, in accordance with its contemporary institutional definition.

It cannot be sufficiently strongly emphasized that this process is typically unapprehended, almost automatic in character. The protagonists of the marriage drama do *not* set out deliberately to create their world. Each continues to live in a world that is taken for granted—and keeps its taken-for-granted character even as it is metamorphosed. The new world that the married partners, Prometheuslike, have called into being is perceived by them as the normal world in which they have lived before. Reconstructed present and reinterpreted past are perceived as a continuum, extending forward into a commonly projected future. *The dramatic change that has occurred remains in bulk, unapprehended and unarticulated.* And where it forces itself upon the individual's attention, it is retrojected into the past, explained as having always been there, though perhaps in a hidden way. Typically, the reality that has been "invented" within the marital conversation is subjectively perceived as a "discovery." Thus the partners "discover" themselves and the world, "who they really are," "what they really believe," "how they really feel, and always have felt, about so-and-so." This retrojection of the world being produced all the time by themselves serves to enhance the stability of this world and at the same time to assuage the "existential anxiety" that, probably inevitably, accompanies the perception that nothing but one's own narrow shoulders supports the universe in which one has chosen to live. . . .

The use of the term "stabilization" should not detract from the insight into the difficulty and precariousness of this world-building enterprise. Often enough, the new universe collapses *in statu nascendi*. Many more times it continues over a period, swaying perilously back and forth as the two partners try to hold it up, finally to be abandoned as an impossible undertaking. If one conceives of the marital conversation as the principal drama and the two partners as the principal protagonists of the drama, then one can look upon the other individuals involved as the supporting chorus for the central dramatic action. Children, friends, relatives and casual acquaintances all have their part in reinforcing the tenuous structure of the new reality. It goes without saying that the *children form the most important part of this supporting chorus*. Their very existence in predicated on the maritally established world. The marital partners themselves are in charge of their socialization *into* this world, which to them has a pre-existent and self-evident character. They are taught from the beginning to speak precisely those lines that lend themselves to a supporting chorus, from their first invocations of "Daddy" and "Mummy" on to their adoption of the parents' ordering and typifying apparatus that now defines *their* world as well. The marital conversation is now in the process of becoming a family symposium, with the necessary consequence that its objectivations rapidly gain in density, plausibility and durability.

In sum: the process that we have been inquiring into is, ideal-typically, one in which reality is crystallized, narrowed and stabilized. Ambivalences are converted into certainties. Typifications of self and of others become settled. Most generally, possibilities become facticities. What is more, this process of transformation remains, most of the time, unapprehended by those who are both its authors and its objects.[18]

•   •   •

## NOTES

1. The present article has come out of a larger project on which the authors have been engaged in collaboration with three colleagues in sociology and philosophy. The project is to produce a systematic treatise that will integrate a number of now separate theoretical strands in the sociology of knowledge.

2. Cf. especially Max Weber, *Wirtschaft und Gesellschaft* (Tuebingen: Mohr 1956), and *Gesammelte Aufsaetze zur Wissenschaftslehre* (Tuebingen: Mohr 1951); George H. Mead, *Mind, Self and Society* (University of Chicago Press 1934); Alfred Schutz, *Der sinnhafte Aufbau der sozialen Welt* (Vienna: Springer, 2nd ed. 1960) and *Collected Papers*, 1 (The Hague: Nijhoff 1962); Maurice Merleau-Ponty, *Phenomenologie de la perception* (Paris: Gallimard 1945) and *La Structure du comportement* (Paris: Presses universitaires de France 1953).

3. Cf. Schutz, *Aufbau*, 202-20 and *Collected Papers*, I, 3-27, 283-6.

4. Cf. Schutz, *Collected Papers*, I, 207-28.

5. Cf. especially Jean Piaget, *The Child's Construction of Reality* (Routledge & Kegan Paul 1955).

6. Cf. Mead, *op. cit.*, 135-226.

7. Cf. Schutz, *Aufbau*, 181-95.

8. Cf. Arnold Gehlen, *Die Seele im technischen Zeitalter* (Hamburg: Rowohlt 1957), 57-69 and *Anthropologische Forschung* (Hamburg: Rowohlt 1961), 69-77, 127-40; Helmut Schelsky, *Soziologie der Sexualitaet* (Hamburg: Rowohlt 1955), 102-33. Also cf. Thomas Luckmann, "On religion in modern society," *Journal for the Scientific Study of Religion* (Spring 1963), 147-62.

9. In these considerations we have been influenced by certain presuppositions of Marxian anthropology, as well as by the anthropological work of Max Scheler, Helmuth Plessner and Arnold Gehlen. We are indebted to Thomas Luckmann for the clarification of the social-psychological significance of the private sphere.

10. Cf. Talcott Parsons and Robert Bales, *Family: Socialization and Interaction Process* (London: Routledge & Kegan Paul 1956), 3-34, 353-96.

11. Cf. Philippe Aries, *Centuries of Childhood* (New York: Knopf 1962), 339-410.

12. Cf. Georg Simmel (Kurt Wolff ed.), *The Sociology of Georg Simmel* (New York: Collier-Macmillan 1950), 118-44.

13. Cf. Schutz, *Aufbau*, 29-36, 149-53.

14. Cf. Schutz, *Aufbau*, 186-92, 202-10.

15. David Riesman's well-known concept of "other-direction" would also be applicable here.

16. Cf. Maurice Halbwachs, *Les Cadres sociaux de la memoire* (Paris: Presses universitaires de France 1952), especially 146-77; also cf. Peter Berger, *Invitation to Sociology—A Humanistic Perspective* (Garden City, N.Y.: Doubleday-Anchor 1963), 54-65 (available in Penguin).

17. Cf. Schutz, *Collected Papers*, I, 72-3, 79-82.

18. The phenomena here discussed could also be formulated effectively in terms of the Marxian categories of reification and false consciousness. Jean-Paul Sartre's recent work, especially *Critique de la raison dialectique,* seeks to integrate these categories within a phenomenological analysis of human conduct. Also cf. Henri Lefebvre, *Critique de la vie quotidienne* (Paris: l'Arche 1958–61).

# Review Questions

1. Berger and Kellner explain that "reality is socially constructed." What do they mean?

2. The process of constructing social reality involves: (a) matching the "typifications," or taken-for-granted cultural explanations, to events or people in our worlds; and (b) "objectivating," or validating (and redefining if necessary), our typifications of reality through interaction with significant others. Discuss how husbands and wives in the contemporary world validate and redefine ("objectivate") each other's world views, thus engaging in "nomos-building." How do they develop a "common memory"? How do they stabilize their coupled world view?

3. Why do former friends and other family members exert little influence on the redefinition process experienced by the marital pair?

4. How and why do children strengthen the couple's world view?

# UNCOUPLING: THE SOCIAL CONSTRUCTION OF DIVORCE

## Diane Vaughan

B ERGER AND KELLNER (1964) DESCRIBE MARRIAGE AS A DEFINITIONAL PRO-
cess. two autonomous individuals come together with separate and distinct biographies and begin to construct for themselves a subworld in
which they will live as a couple. A redefinition of self occurs as the autonomous identity of the two individuals involved is reconstructed as a
mutual identity. This redefinition is externally anticipated and socially
legitimated before it actually occurs in the individual's biography.

Previously, significant conversation for each partner came from nonoverlapping circles, and self-realization came from other sources. Together, they begin to construct a private sphere where all significant
conversation centers in their relationship with each other. The coupled
identity becomes the main source of their self-realization. Their definitions of reality become correlated, for each partner's actions must be projected in conjunction with the other. As their worlds come to be defined
around a relationship with a significant other who becomes *the* significant other, all other significant relationships have to be reperceived, regrouped. The result is the construction of a joint biography and a mutually coordinated common memory.

Were this construction of a coupled identity left only to the two participants, the coupling would be precarious indeed. However, the new reality is reinforced through objectivation, that is, "a process by which subjectively experienced meanings become objective to the individual, and,
in interaction with others, become common property, and thereby massively objective" (Berger and Kellner, 1964:6). Hence, through the use of
language in conversation with significant others, the reality of the coupling is constantly validated.

Of perhaps greater significance is that this definition of coupledness
becomes taken for granted and is validated again and again, not by explicit articulation, but by conversing around the agreed [upon] definition
of reality that has been created. In this way a consistent reality is maintained, ordering the individual's world in such a way that it validates his

This paper was presented at the annual meetings of the American Sociological Association
in 1977 and first appeared in print in the first edition of this reader in 1979. Another version
was later published in *Alternative Life Styles*.

identity. Marriage, according to Berger and Kellner, is a constructed reality which is "nomosbuilding" (1964:1). That is, it is a social arrangement that contributes order to individual lives, and therefore should be considered as a significant validating relationship for adults in our society.

Social relationships, however, are seldom static. Not only do we move in and out of relationships, but the nature of a particular relationship, though enduring, varies over time. Given that the definitions we create become socially validated and hence constraining, *how do individuals move from a mutual identity, as in marriage, to assume separate, autonomous identities again?* What is the process by which new definitions are created and become validated?

The Berger and Kellner analysis describes a number of interrelated yet distinguishable stages that are involved in the social construction of a mutual identity; for example, the regrouping of all other significant relationships. In much the same way, the *demise* of a relationship should involve distinguishable social processes. Since redefinition of self is basic to both movement into and out of relationships, the social construction of a singular identity also should follow the patterns suggested by Berger and Kellner. This paper is a qualitative examination of this process. Hence, the description that follows bears an implicit test of Berger and Kellner's ideas.

The dimensions of sorrow, anger, personal disorganization, fear, loneliness, and ambiguity that intermingle every separation are well known.[1] Their familiarity does not diminish their importance. Though in real life these cannot be ignored, the researcher has the luxury of selectivity. Here, it is not the pain and disorganization that are to be explored, but the existence of an underlying orderliness.

Though the focus is on divorce, the process examined appears to apply to *any* heterosexual relationship in which the participants have come to define themselves and be defined by others as a couple. The work is exploratory and, as such, not concerned with generalizability. However, the process may apply to homosexual couples as well. Therefore, the term "uncoupling" will be used because it is a more general concept than divorce. Uncoupling applies to the redefinition of self that occurs as mutual identity unravels into singularity, regardless of marital status or sex of the participants.

The formal basis from which this paper developed was in-depth, exploratory interviews. The interviews, ranging from two to six hours, were taped and later analyzed. All of the interviewees were at different stages in the uncoupling process. Most were divorced, though some were still in stages of consideration of divorce. Two of the interviews were based on long-term relationships that never resulted in marriage. All of the relationships were heterosexual. The quality of these interviews has added much depth to the understanding of the separation process. The interviewees were of high intellectual and social level, and their sensitivity and insight have led to much valuable material, otherwise unavailable.

A more informal contribution to the paper comes from personal experiences and the experiences of close friends. Further corroboration has come from autobiographical accounts, newspapers, periodicals, and conversations, which have resulted in a large number of cases illustrating certain points. Additional support has come from individuals who have read or heard the paper with the intent of proving or disproving its contentions by reference to their own cases.

Since the declared purpose here is to abstract the essential features of the process of uncoupling, some simplification is necessary. The separation of a relationship can take several forms. To trace all of them is beyond the scope of this study. Therefore, to narrow the focus, we must first consider the possible variations.

Perhaps the coupled identity was not a major mechanism for self-validation from the outset of the union. Or the relationship may have at one time filled that function, but, as time passed, this coupled identity was insufficient to meet individual needs. Occasionally this fact has implications for both partners simultaneously, and the uncoupling process is initiated by both. More frequently, however, one partner still finds the marriage a major source of stability and identity, while the other finds it inadequate. In this form, one participant takes the role of initiator of the uncoupling process. However, this role may not consistently be held by one partner, but instead may alternate between them, due to the difficulty of uncoupling in the face of external constraints, social pressure not to be the one responsible for the demise of the marriage, and the variability in the self-validating function of the union over time. For the purpose of this study, the form of uncoupling under consideration is that which results when one partner, no longer finding the coupled identity self-validating, takes the role of initiator in the uncoupling process. The other partner, the significant other, still finds the marriage a major source of stability and identity.

## UNCOUPLING: THE INITIATION OF THE PROCESS

I was never psychologically married. I always felt strained by attempts that coupled me into a marital unit. I was just never comfortable as "Mrs." I never got used to my last name. I never wanted it. The day after my marriage was probably the most depressed day of my life, because I had lost my singularity. The difference between marriage and a deep relationship, living together, is that you have this ritual, and you achieve a very definite status, and it was *that* that produced my reactions—because I became in the eyes of the world a man's wife. And I was never comfortable and happy with it. It didn't make any difference who the man was.

An early phase in the uncoupling process occurs as one or the other of the partners begins to question the coupled identity. At first internal, the challenging of the created world remains for a time as a doubt within one of the partners in the coupling. Though there is a definition of coupledness, subjectively the coupledness may be experienced differently by each partner. Frequently, these subjective meanings remain internal and unarticulated. Thus, similarly, the initial recognition of the coupling as problematic may be internal and unarticulated, held as a secret. The subworld that has been constructed, for some reason, doesn't "fit."

A process of definition negotiation is begun, initiated by the one who finds the mutual identity an inadequate definition of self. Attempts to negotiate the definition of the coupledness are likely to result in the subjective meaning becoming articulated for the first time, thus moving the redefinition process toward objectivation. The secret, held by the initiator, is shared with the significant other. When this occurs, it allows both participants to engage in the definitional process.

Though the issue is made "public" in that private sphere shared by the two, the initiator frequently finds that a lack of shared definitions of the coupled identity stalemates the negotiations. While the initiator defines the marriage as a problem, the other does not. The renegotiation of the coupled identity cannot proceed unless both agree that the subworld they have constructed needs to be redefined. Perhaps for the significant other, the marriage as it is still provides important self-validation. If so, the initiator must bring the other to the point of sharing a common definition of the marriage as "troubled."

## ACCOMPANYING RECONSTRUCTIONS

Though this shared definition is being sought, the fact remains that, for the initiator, the coupled identity fails to provide self-validation. In order to meet this need, the initiator engages in other attempts at redefining the nature of the relationship. Called "accompanying reconstructions," these *may* or *may not* be shared with the significant other. They may begin long before the "secret" of the troubled marriage is shared with the other, in an effort to make an uncomfortable situation more comfortable without disrupting the relationship. Or they may occur subsequent to sharing the secret with the significant other, as a reaction to the failure to redefine the coupledness satisfactorily. Time order for their occurrence is not easily imposed—thus, "accompanying reconstructions."

The initiator's accompanying reconstructions may be directed toward the redefinition of (1) the coupledness itself, (2) the identity of the significant other, or (3) the identity of the initiator. A change in definition of either of the three implies a change in at least one of the others. Though they are presented here separately, they are interactive rather than mutually exclusive and are not easily separable in real life.

The first form of accompanying reconstruction to be considered is the initiator's redefinition of the coupledness itself. One way of redefining the coupledness is by an unarticulated conversion of the agreed-upon norms of the relationship.

> I had reconceptualized what marriage was. I decided sexual fidelity was not essential for marriage. I never told her that. And I didn't even have anyone I was interested in having that intimate a relationship with—I just did a philosophical thing. I just decided it was O.K. for me to have whatever of what quality of other relationship I needed to have. Something like that—of that caliber—was something I could never talk to her about. So I did it all by myself. I read things and decided it. I was at peace with me. I knew that we could stay married, whatever that meant. O.K., I can stay legally tied to you, and I can probably live in this house with you, and I can keep working the way I have been. I decided I can have my life and still be in this situation with you, but you need some resources, because I realize now I'm not going to be all for you. I don't want to be all for you, and I did tell her that. But I couldn't tell her this total head trip I'd been through because she wouldn't understand.

Or, the coupledness may be redefined by acceptance of the relationship with certain limitations. Boundaries can be imposed on the impact that the relationship will have on the total life space of the initiator.

> I finally came to the point where I realized I was never going to have the kind of marriage I had hoped for, the kind of relationship I had hoped for. I didn't want to end it, because of the children, but I wasn't going to let it hurt me any more. I wasn't going to depend on him any more. The children and I were going to be the main unit, and, if he occasionally wanted to participate, fine—and if not, we would go ahead without him. I was no longer willing to let being with him be the determining factor as to whether I was happy or not. I ceased planning our lives around his presence or absence and began looking out for myself.

A second form of accompanying reconstruction occurs when the initiator attempts to redefine the significant other in a way that is more compatible with his own self-validation needs. The initiator may direct efforts toward specific behaviors, such as drinking habits, temper, sexual incompatibilities, or finance management. Or, the redefinition attempt may be of a broader scope.

> I was aware of his dependence on the marriage to provide all his happiness, and it wasn't providing it. I wanted him to go to graduate school, but he postponed it, against my wishes. I wanted him to pursue his own life. I didn't want him to sacrifice for me. I wanted him to become more exciting to me in

the process. I was aware that I was trying to persuade him to be a different person.

Redefinition of the significant other may either be directed toward maintaining the coupledness, as above, or moving away from it, as is the case following.

> The way I defined being a good wife and the way John defined being a good wife were two different quantities. He wanted the house to look like a hotel and I didn't see it that way. He couldn't see why I couldn't meet his needs. . . . When he first asked for a divorce and I refused, he suggested I go back to school. I remembered a man who worked with John who had sent his wife back to school so she could support herself, so he could divorce her. I asked John if he was trying to get rid of me. He didn't answer that. He insisted I go, and I finally went.

A third form of accompanying reconstruction may be directed toward the redefinition of the initiator. Intermingled with attempts at redefinition of the significant other and redefinition of the coupledness itself is the seeking of self-validation outside the marriage by the initiator. A whole set of other behaviors may evolve that have the ultimate effect of moving the relationship away from the coupledness toward a separation of the joint biography.

## SELF-VALIDATION OUTSIDE THE MARRIAGE

What was at first internally experienced and recognized as self-minimizing takes a more concrete form and becomes externally expressed in a search for self-maximization. Through investment of self in career, in a cause requiring commitment, in a relationship with a new significant other, in family, in education, or in activities and hobbies, the initiator develops new sources of self-realization. These alternative sources of self-realization confirm not the coupled identity but the singularity of the initiator.

Furthermore, in the move toward a distinct biography, the initiator finds ideological support that reinforces the uncoupling process. Berger and Kellner (1964:3) note the existence of a supporting ideology which lends credence to marriage as a significant validating relationship in our society. That is, the nuclear family is seen as the site of love, sexual fulfillment, and self-realization. In the move toward uncoupling, the initiator finds confirmation for a belief in *self* as a first priority.

> I now see my break with religion as a part of my developing individuality. At the time I was close friends with priests and nuns, most of whom have since left the church. I felt a bitterness toward the church for its definition of marriage. I felt constrained toward a type of marriage that was not best for me.

Whether this ideology first begins within the individual, who then actively *seeks* sources of self-realization that are ideologically congruent, or whether the initiator's own needs come to be met by a serendipitous "elective affinity" of ideas (Weber:1930), is difficult to say. The interconnections are subtle. The supporting ideology may come from the family of orientation, the women's movement, the peer group, or a new significant other. It may grow directly, as through interaction, or indirectly, as through literature. No matter what the source, the point is that, in turning away from the marriage for self-validation, a separate distinct biography is constructed in interaction with others, and this beginning autonomy is strengthened by a supporting belief system.

The initiator moves toward construction of a separate subworld wherein significant conversation comes from circles which no longer overlap with those of the significant other. And, the significant other is excluded from that separate subworld.

> I shared important things with the children that I didn't share with him. It's almost as if I purposefully punished him by not telling him. Some good thing would happen and I'd come home and tell them and wouldn't tell him.

The initiator's autonomy is further reinforced as the secret of the troubled marriage is shared with others in the separate subworld the initiator is constructing. It may be directly expressed as a confidence exchanged with a close friend, family member, or children, or it may be that the sharing is indirect. Rather than being expressed in significant conversation, the definition of the marriage as troubled is created for others by a variety of mechanisms that relay the message that the initiator is not happily married. The definition of the marriage as problematic becomes further objectivated as the secret, once held only by the initiator, then shared with the significant other, moves to a sphere beyond the couple themselves.

Other moves away occur that deeply threaten the coupled identity for the significant other and at the same time validate the autonomy of the initiator.

> I remember going to a party by myself and feeling comfortable. She never forgot that. I never realized the gravity of that to her.

> Graduate school became a symbolic issue. I was going to be a separate entity. That's probably the one thing I wanted to do that got the biggest negative emotional response from him.

> All that time I was developing more of a sense of being away from her. I didn't depend on her for any emotional feedback, companionship. I went to plays and movies with friends.

The friendship group, rather than focusing on the coupledness, relies on splintered sources that support separate identities. Though this situation can exist in relationships in which the coupled identity is validating for both participants, the distinction is that, in the process of uncoupling, there may not be shared conversation to link the separate subworld of the initiator with that of the significant other.

These movements away by the initiator heighten a sense of exclusion for the significant other. Deep commitment to other than the coupled identity—to a career, to a cause, to education, to a hobby, to another person—reflects a lessened commitment to the marriage. The initiator's search for self-validation outside the marriage even may be demonstrated symbolically to the significant other by the removal of the wedding ring or by the desire, if the initiator is a woman, to revert to her maiden name. If the initiator's lessened commitment to the coupled identity is reflected in a lessened desire for sexual intimacy, the challenge to the identity of the significant other and the coupledness becomes undeniable. As the significant other recognizes the growing autonomy of the initiator, he, too, comes to accept the definition of the marriage as "troubled."

The roles assumed by each participant have implications for the impact of the uncoupling on each. Whereas the initiator has found other sources of self-realization outside the marriage, usually the significant other has not. The marriage still performs the major self-validating function. The significant other is committed to an ideology that supports the coupled identity. The secret of the "troubled" marriage has not been shared with others as it has by the initiator, meaning for the significant other the relationship in its changed construction remains unobjectivated. The challenge to the identity of the significant other and to the coupledness posed by the initiator may result in increased commitment to the coupled identity for the significant other. With the joint biography already separated in these ways, the couple enters into a period of "trying."

## TRYING

Trying is a stage of intense definition negotiation by the partners. Now both share a definition of the marriage as troubled. However, each partner may seek to construct a new reality that is in opposition to that of the other. The significant other tries to negotiate a shared definition of the marriage as savable, whereas the initiator negotiates toward a shared definition that marks the marriage as unsavable.[2]

For the initiator, the uncoupling process is well underway. At some point the partner who originally perceived the coupled identity to be problematic and sought self-validation outside the coupled identity has experienced "psychological divorce." Sociologically, this can be defined as the point at which the individual's newly constructed separate sub-world becomes the major nomos-building mechanism in his life space, replacing the nomos-building function of the coupled identity.

The initiator tries subtly to prepare the significant other to live alone. By encouraging the other to make new friends, find a job, get involved in outside activities, or seek additional education, the initiator hopes to decrease the other's commitment to and dependence upon the coupled identity for self-validation and move the other toward autonomy. This stage of preparation is not simply one of cold expediency for the benefit of the initiator, but is based on concern for the significant other and serves to mitigate the pain of the uncoupling process for both the initiator and the other.

For both, there is a hesitancy to sever the ties. In many cases, neither party is fully certain about the termination of the marriage. Mutual uncertainty may be more characteristic of the process. The relationship may weave back and forth between cycles of active trying and passive acceptance of the status quo due to the failure of each to pull the other to a common definition and the inability of either to make the break.

> I didn't want to hurt him. I didn't want to be responsible for the demise of a marriage I no longer wanted. I could have forced him into being the one to achieve the breach, for I realized it was never going to happen by itself.

> I didn't want to be the villain—the one to push her out into the big, bad world. I wanted to make sure she was at the same point I was.

> I kept hoping some alternative would occur so that he would be willing to break. I kept wishing it would happen.

Frequently, in the trying stage, the partners turn to outside help for formal negotiation of the coupled identity. Counseling, though entered into with apparent common purpose, becomes another arena in which the partners attempt to negotiate a shared definition from their separately held definitions of the marriage as savable or unsavable. For the initiator, the counseling may serve as a step in the preparation of the significant other to live alone. Not only does it serve to bring the other to the definition of the marriage as unsavable, but also the counseling provides a resource for the significant other, in the person of the counselor. Often it happens that the other has turned to no one for comfort about the problem marriage. The initiator, sensitive to this need and unable to fill it himself, hopes the counselor will fill this role. The counseling has yet another function. It further objectivates the notion of the coupled identity as problematic.

At some point during this period of trying, the initiator may suggest separation. Yet, separation is not suggested as a formal leave-taking but as a *temporary* separation meant to clarify the relationship for both partners. Again, the concern on the part of the initiator for the significant other appears. Not wanting to hurt, yet recognizing the coupled identity as no longer valid, the temporary separation is encouraged as a further means of bringing the other to accept a definition of the marriage as un-savable, to increase reliance of the other on outside resources of self-realization, and to initiate the physical breach gently.

> Even at that point, at initial separation, I wasn't being honest. I knew fairly certainly that when we separated, it was for good. I let her believe that it was a means for us first finding out what was happening and then eventually possibly getting back together.

Should the initiator be hesitant to suggest a separation, the significant other may finally tire of the ambiguity of the relationship. No longer finding the coupling as it exists self-validating, the significant other may be the one to suggest a separation. The decision to separate may be the result of discussion and planning, or it may occur spontaneously, in a moment of anger. It may be mutually agreed upon, but more often it is not. However it emerges, the decision to separate is a difficult one for both partners.

## OBJECTIVATION: RESTRUCTURING OF THE PRIVATE SPHERE

The separation is a transitional state in which everything needs definition, yet very little is capable of being defined. Economic status, friendship networks, personal habits, and sex life are all patterns of the past which need simultaneous reorganization. However, reorganization is hindered by the ambiguity of the relationship. The off-again, on-again wearing of the wedding rings is symbolic of the indecision in this stage. Each of the partners searches for new roles, without yet being free of the old.

For the initiator who has developed outside resources, the impact of this uncertainty is partially mitigated. For the significant other, who has not spent time in preparation for individual existence, the major self-validating function of the marriage is gone and nothing has emerged as a substitute.

> I had lost my identity somewhere along the way. And I kept losing my identity. I kept letting him make all the decisions. I couldn't work. I wasn't able to be myself. I was letting someone else take over. I didn't have any control over it. I didn't know how to stop it. I was unsure that if anything really happened I could actually make it on my own or not.

The separation precipitates a redefinition of self for the significant other. Without other resources for self-validation, and with the coupled identity now publicly challenged, the significant other begins a restructuring of the private sphere.

This restructuring occurs not only in the social realm but also entails a form of restructuring that is physical, tangible, and symbolic of the break in the coupled identity. For instance, if the initiator has been the one to leave, at some point the significant other begins reordering the residence they shared to suit the needs of one adult rather than two. Furniture is rearranged or thrown out. Closets and drawers are reorganized. A thorough house-cleaning may be undertaken. As the initiator has moved to a new location that reinforces his singularity, the significant other transforms the home that validated the coupling into one that likewise objectivates the new definition. Changes in the physical appearance of either or both partners may be a part of the symbolic restructuring of the private sphere. Weight losses, changes of hair style, or changes in clothing preferences further symbolize the yielding of the mutual identity and the move toward autonomy.

Should the significant other be the one to leave, the move into a new location aids in the redefinition of self as an autonomous individual. For example, the necessity of surviving in a new environment, the eventual emergence of a new set of friends that define and relate to the significant other as a separate being instead of as half of a couple, and the creation of a new residence without the other person are all mechanisms which reinforce autonomy and a definition of singularity.

Though the initiator has long been involved in objectivating a separate reality, frequently for the significant other this stage is just beginning. Seldom does the secret of the troubled marriage become shared with others by this partner until it can no longer be deferred. Although the initiator actively has sought objectivation, the significant other has avoided it. Confronted with actual separation, however, the significant other responds by taking the subjectively experienced meanings and moving them to the objective level—by confiding in others, perhaps in writing, in letters or in diaries—any means that helps the other deal with the new reality.

There are some who must be told of the separation—children, parents, best friends. Not only are the two partners reconstructing their own reality, but they now must reconstruct the reality for others. Conversation provides the mechanism for reconstruction, simultaneously creating common definitions and working as a major objectivating apparatus. The longer the conversation goes on, the more massively real do the objectivations become to the partners. The result is a stabilization of the objectivated reality, as the new definition of uncoupledness continues to move outward.

Uncoupling precipitates a reordering of all other significant relationships. As in coupling, where all other relationships are reperceived and regrouped to account for and support the emergence of *the* significant other, in uncoupling the reordering supports the singularity of each partner. Significant relationships are lost, as former friends of the couple now align with one or the other or refuse to choose between the two. Ties with families of orientation, formerly somewhat attenuated because of the coupling, are frequently renewed. For each of the partners, pressure exists to stabilize characterizations of others and of self so that the world and self are brought toward consistency. Each partner approaches groups that strengthen the new definition each has created, and avoids those that weaken it. The groups with which each partner associates help co-define the new reality.

## OBJECTIVATION: THE PUBLIC SPHERE

The uncoupling is further objectivated for the participants as the new definition is legitimized in the public sphere. Two separate households demand public identification as separate identities. New telephone listings, changes of mailing address, separate checking accounts, and charge accounts, for example, all are mechanisms by which the new reality becomes publicly reconstructed.

The decision to initiate legal proceedings confirms the uncoupling by the formal negotiation of a heretofore informally negotiated definition. The adversary process supporting separate identities, custody proceedings, the formal separation of the material base, the final removal of the rings all act as means of moving the new definition from the private to the public sphere. The uncoupling now becomes objectivated not only for the participants and their close intimates, but for casual acquaintances and strangers.

Objectivation acts as a constraint upon whatever social identity has been constructed. It can bind a couple together, or hinder their recoupling, once the uncoupling process has begun. Perhaps this can better be understood by considering the tenuous character of the extramarital affair. The very nature of the relationship is private. The coupling remains a secret shared by the two and seldom becomes objectivated in the public realm. Thus, the responsibility for the maintenance of that coupling usually rests solely with the two participants. When the relationship is no longer self-validating for one of the participants, the uncoupling does not involve a reconstruction of reality for others. The constraints imposed by the objectivation of a marital relationship which function to keep a couple in a marriage do not exist to the same extent in an affair. The fragility of the coupling is enhanced by its limited objectivation.

Berger and Kellner (1964:6) note that the "degree of objectivation will depend on the number and intensity of the social relationships that are its carriers." As the uncoupling process has moved from a nonshared secret held within the initiator to the realm of public knowledge, the degree of objectivation has increased. The result is a continuing decline in the precariousness of the newly constructed reality over time.

## DIVORCE: A STAGE IN THE PROCESS

Yet a decrease in precariousness is not synonymous with a completion of the uncoupling process. As marriage, or coupling, is a dramatic act of redefinition of self by two strangers as they move from autonomous identities to the construction of a joint biography, so uncoupling involves yet another redefinition of self as the participants move from mutual identity toward autonomy. It is this redefinition of self, for each participant, that completes the uncoupling. Divorce, then, may not be the final stage. In fact, divorce could be viewed as a nonstatus that is at some point on a continuum ranging from marriage (coupling) as an achieved status, to autonomy (uncoupling), likewise an achieved status. In other words, the uncoupling process might be viewed as a status transformation which is complete when the individual defines his salient status as "single" rather than "divorced." When the individual's newly constructed separate subworld becomes nomos-building—when it creates for the individual a sort of order in which he can experience his life as making sense— the uncoupling process is completed.

The completion of uncoupling does not occur at the same moment for each participant. For either or both of the participants, it may not occur until after the other has created a coupled identity with another person. With that step, the tentativeness is gone.

> When I learned of his intention to remarry, I did not realize how devastated I would be. It was just awful. I remember crying and crying. It was really a very bad thing that I did not know or expect. You really aren't divorced while that other person is still free. You still have a lot of your psychological marriage going—in fact, I'm still in that a little bit because I'm still single.

For some, the uncoupling may never be completed. One or both of the participants may never be able to construct a new and separate subworld that becomes self-validating. Witness, for example, the widow who continues to call herself "Mrs. John Doe," who associates with the same circle of friends, who continues to wear her wedding ring and observes wedding anniversaries. For her, the coupled identity is still a major mechanism for self-validation, even though the partner is gone.

In fact, death as a form of uncoupling may be easier for the significant other to handle than divorce. There exist ritual techniques for dealing with it, and there is no ambiguity. The relationship is gone. There will be no further interaction between the partners. With divorce, or any uncoupling that occurs through the volition of one or both of the partners, the interaction may continue long after the relationship has been formally terminated. For the significant other—the one left behind, without resources for self-validation—the continuing interaction between the partners presents obstacles to autonomy.

> There's a point at which it's over. If your wife dies, you're a lot luckier, I think, because it's over. You either live with it, you kill yourself, or you make your

own bed of misery. Unlike losing a wife through death, in divorce, she doesn't die. She keeps resurrecting it. I can't get over it, she won't die. I mean, she won't go away.

## CONTINUITIES

Continuities are linkages between the partners that exist despite the formal termination of the coupled identity. Most important of these is the existence of shared loved ones—children, in-laws, and so on. Though in-laws may of necessity be excluded from the separately constructed subworlds, children can rarely be and, in their very existence, present continued substantiation of the coupled identity.

In many cases continuities are actively constructed by one or both of the participants after the formal termination of the relationship. These manufactured linkages speak to the difficulty of totally separating that common biography, by providing a continued mechanism for interaction. They may be constructed as a temporary bridge between the separated subworlds, or they may come to be a permanent interaction pattern. Symbolically, they seem to indicate caring on the part of either or both of the participants.

> The wife moves out. The husband spends his weekend helping her get settled—hanging pictures, moving furniture.

> The husband moves out, leaving his set of tools behind. Several years later, even after his remarriage, the tools are still there, and he comes to borrow them one at a time. The former wife is planning to move within the same city. The tools are boxed up, ready to be taken with her.

> The wife has moved out, but is slow to change her mailing address. Rather than marking her forwarding address on the envelopes and returning them by mail, the husband either delivers them once a week or the wife picks them up.

> The wife moves out. The husband resists dividing property with her that is obviously hers. The conflict necessitates many phone calls and visits.

> The husband moves out. Once a week he comes to the house to visit with the children on an evening when the wife is away. When she gets home, the two of them occasionally go out to dinner.

> A nice part of the marriage was shared shopping trips on Sunday afternoons. After the divorce, they still occasionally go shopping together.

> The holidays during the first year of separation were celebrated as they always had been—with the whole family together.

> During a particularly difficult divorce, the husband noted that he had finally succeeded in finding his wife a decent lawyer.

Continuities present unmeasurable variables in the uncoupling process. In this paper, uncoupling is defined as a reality socially constructed by the participants. The stages that mark the movement from a coupled identity to separate autonomous identities are characterized, using divorce for an ideal-type analysis. Yet, there is no intent to portray uncoupling as a compelling linear process from which there is no turning back. Such conceptualization would deny the human factor inherent in reality construction. Granted, as the original secret is moved from private to public, becoming increasingly objectivated, reconstructing the coupled identity becomes more and more difficult.

Each stage of objectivation acts as the closing of a door. Yet at any stage the process may be interrupted. The initiator may not find mechanisms of self-validation outside the coupling that reinforce his autonomy. Or the self-validation found outside the coupling may be the very stuff that allows the initiator to stay *in* the relationship. Or continuities may intervene and reconstruction of the coupled identity may occur, despite the degree of objectivation, as in the following case.

> Ellen met Jack in college. They fell in love and married. Jack had been blind since birth. He had pursued a college career in education and was also a musician. Both admired the independence of the other. In the marriage, she subordinated her career to his and helped him pursue a masters degree, as well as his musical interests. Her time was consumed by his needs—for transportation and the taping and transcribing of music for the musicians in his group. He was teaching at a school for the blind by day and performing as a musician at night. They had a son, and her life, instead of turning outward, as his, revolved around family responsibilities. She gained weight. Jack, after twelve years of marriage, left Ellen for his high school sweetheart. Ellen grieved for a while, then began patching up her life. She got a job, established her own credit, went back to college, and lost weight. She saw a lawyer, filed for divorce, joined Parents Without Partners, and began searching out singles groups. She dated. Throughout, Jack and Ellen saw each other occasionally and maintained a sexual relationship. The night before the divorce was final, they reconciled.

The uncoupling never was completed, though all stages of the process occurred, including the public objectivation that results from the initiation of the legal process. Ellen, in constructing an autonomous identity, became again the independent person Jack had first loved.[3] This, together with the continuities that existed between the two, created the basis for a common definition of the coupling as savable.

## DISCUSSION

Berger and Kellner describe the process by which two individuals create a coupled identity for themselves. Here, we have started from the point of the coupled identity and examined the process by which people move out of such relationships. Using interview data, we have found that, although the renegotiation of separate realities is a complex web of subtle modifications, clear stages emerge which mark the uncoupling process. The emergent stages are like benchmarks which indicate the increasing objectivation of the changing definitions of reality, as these definitions move from the realm of the private to the public.

Beginning within the intimacy of the dyad, the initial objectivation occurs as the secret of the troubled marriage that the initiator has held is shared with the significant other. With this, the meaning has begun to move from the subjective to the objective. Definition negotiation begins. While attempting to negotiate a common definition, the initiator acts to increase the validation of his identity and place in the world by use of accompanying reconstructions of reality. The autonomy of the initiator increases as he finds self-validation outside the marriage and an ideology that supports the uncoupling. The increased autonomy of the initiator brings the significant other to accept a definition of the marriage as troubled, and they enter into the stage of "trying." The process continues, as counseling and separation further move the new definition into the public sphere.

The telling of others, the symbolic physical signs of the uncoupling, and the initiation of formal legal proceedings validate the increasing separation of the partners as they negotiate a new reality which is different from that constructed private sphere which validated their identity as a couple. Eventually, a redefinition of the mutual identity occurs in such a way that the joint biography is separated into two separate autonomous identities. As Berger and Kellner state that marriage is a dramatic act of redefinition of self by two individuals, so uncoupling is characterized by the same phenomenon. Self-realization, rather than coming from the coupledness, again comes from outside sources. Significant conversation again finds its source in nonoverlapping circles. The new definition of the relationship constructed by the participants has, in interaction with others, become common property.

Language is crucial to this process. Socially constructed worlds need validation. As conversation constantly reconfirms a coupled identity, so also does it act as the major validating mechanism for the move to singularity, not by specific articulation, but by the way in which it comes to revolve around the uncoupled identity as taken for granted.

The notion that the stages uncovered do broadly apply needs to be further confirmed. We need to know whether the process is invariant regardless of the heterosexuality, homosexuality, or social class of couples. Does it also apply for close friends? In what ways does the sex of the interviewer bias the data? Additionally, the stages in the process should be confirmed by interviews with both partners in a coupling. Due to the delicacy of the subject matter, this is difficult. In only one instance were both partners available to be interviewed for this study. Notwithstanding these limitations, the findings which emerge deserve consideration.

Most significant of these is the existence of an underlying order in a phenomenon generally regarded as a chaotic and disorderly process. Undoubtedly the discovery of order was encouraged by the methodology of the study. The information was gained by retrospective analysis on the part of the interviewees. Certainly the passage of time allowed events to be reconstructed in an orderly way that made sense. Nonetheless, as was previously noted, the interviewees were all at various stages in the uncoupling process—some at the "secret" stage and some five years hence. Yet, the stages which are discussed here appeared without fail in every case and have been confirmed repeatedly by the other means described earlier.

In addition to this orderliness, the examination of the process of uncoupling discloses two other little-considered aspects of the process that need to be brought forth and questioned.

One is the caring. Generally, uncoupling is thought of as a conflict-ridden experience that ends as a bitter battle between two adversaries intent on doing each other in. Frequently, this is the case. Yet, the interviews for this study showed that in all cases, even the most emotion generating, again and again the concern of each of the participants for the other revealed itself. Apparently, the patterns of caring and responsibility that emerge between the partners in a coupling are not easily dispelled and in many cases persist throughout the uncoupling process and after, as suggested by the concept of continuities.

A second question that emerges from this examination of uncoupling is related to Berger and Kellner's thesis. They state that, for adults in our society, marriage is a significant validating relationship, one that is nomos-building. Marriage is, in fact, described as "a crucial nomic instrumentality" (1964:4). Though Berger and Kellner at the outset do delimit the focus of their analysis to marriage as an ideal type, the question to be answered is, To what degree is this characterization of marriage appropriate today?

Recall, for example, the quote from one interviewee: "I was never psychologically married. I always felt strained by attempts that coupled me into a marital unit. I was just never comfortable as 'Mrs.' " The interviews for this study suggest that the nomos-building quality assumed to derive from marriage to the individual should be taken as problematic rather than as given. Gouldner (1959) suggests that the parts of a unit vary in the degree to which they are interdependent. His concept of functional autonomy may be extended to illuminate the variable forms that marriage, or coupling, may take and the accompanying degree of nomos. A relationship may exist in which the partners are highly interdependent, and the coupled identity does provide the major mechanism for self-validation, as Berger and Kellner suggest. Yet it is equally as likely that the participants are highly independent, or "loosely coupled" (Weick, 1976; Corwin, 1977), wherein mechanisms for self-validation originate *outside* the coupling rather than from the coupling itself. The connection between the form of the coupling, the degree to which it is or is not nomos-building, and the subsequent implications for uncoupling should be examined in future research.

## NOTES

1. For a sensitive and thought-provoking examination of these as integral components of divorce, see Willard Waller's beautiful qualitative study, *The Old Love and the New*.

2. This statement must be qualified. There are instances when the partners enter a stage of trying with shared definitions of the marriage as savable. The conditions under which the coupling can be preserved have to be negotiated. If they can arrive at a common definition of the coupling that is agreeable to both, the uncoupling process is terminated. But this analysis is of uncoupling, and there are two alternatives: (1) that they enter with common definitions of the marriage as savable but are not able to negotiate the conditions of the coupling so that the self-validation function is preserved or (2) that they enter the period of trying with opposing definitions, as stated here.

3. Waller interprets this phenomenon by using Jung's conceptualization of the container and the contained, analogous to the roles of initiator and significant other, respectively, in the present discussion. Notes Waller, ''Or the contained, complicated by the process of divorcing, may develop those qualities whose lack the container previously deplored'' (Waller:163–168).

## REFERENCES

Berger, Peter L. and Hansfried Kellner, 1964, ''Marriage and the Construction of Reality,'' *Diogenes*, 46:1–23.

Berger, Peter L. and Thomas Luckmann, 1966, *The Social Construction of Reality*. New York: Doubleday.

Bohanon, Paul, 1971, *Divorce and After*. Garden City, N.Y.: Anchor.

Corwin, Ronald G., 1976, ''Organizations as Loosely Coupled Systems: Evolution of a Perspective,'' Paper presented, Seminar on Educational Organizations as Loosely Coupled Systems. Palo Alto, Calif.

Davis, Murray S., 1973, *Intimate Relations*. New York: Free Press.

Epstein, Joseph E., 1975, *Divorce: The American Experience*. London: Jonathan Cape.

Goode, William J., 1956, *Women in Divorce*. New York: Free Press.

Gouldner, Alvin W., 1959, ''Organizational Analysis,'' in R. K. Merton, L. Bloom, and L. S. Cottrell, Jr., eds. *Sociology Today*. New York: Basic Books, pp. 400–428.

Krantzler, Mel, 1973, *Creative Divorce*. New York: New American Library.

Nichols, Jack, 1975, *Men's Liberation: A New Definition of Masculinity*. New York: Penguin.

Sullivan, Judy, 1974, *Mama Doesn't Live Here Anymore*. New York: Pyramid.

Waller, Willard, 1930, *The Old Love and the New*. Carbondale: Southern Illinois University Press.

Walum, Laurel Richardson, 1977, *The Dynamics of Sex and Gender: A Sociological Perspective*. Chicago: Rand McNally.

Weber, Max, 1930, *The Protestant Ethic and the Spirit of Capitalism*, translated by Talcott Parsons. New York: Charles Scribner's Sons.

Weick, Karl E., 1976, "Educational Organizations as Loosely Coupled Systems," *Administrative Science Quarterly*, 21:1–19.

Weiss, Robert, 1975, *Marital Separation*. New York: Basic Books.

# Review Questions

1. Briefly describe the following stages of "uncoupling": (1) initiation, (2) accompanying reconstructions and redefinitions, (3) self-validation outside marriage, (4) trying, (5) objectivation in the private sphere, (6) objectivation in the public sphere, (7) divorce, and (8) continuities.

2. Once a couple moves through several or all of these stages, is uncoupling inevitable? Why, or why not?

3. How do the "initiator" and the "significant other" each work to define the marital situation differently?

4. Vaughan's research shows that divorce is neither the beginning nor the end of the uncoupling process. Why? What part does the coupled world view play in the various stages of the process?

# Suggested Readings: Interaction in Institutional Contexts: Family

Goode, William. *After Divorce*. New York: Free Press, 1956.

_____, "The Theoretical Importance of Love," *American Sociological Review*, 24 (February 1959): 38–47.

Gutman, Herbert G. *The Black Family in Slavery and Freedom, 1750–1925*. New York: Pantheon, 1976.

Lopata, Helena Z. *Occupation Housewife*. New York: Oxford University Press, 1971.

Motz, Annabelle B. "The Family as a Company of Players," *Transaction*, 2 (March–April 1965): 27–30.

Rubin, Lillian Breslow. *Worlds of Pain: Life in the Working-Class Family*. New York: Basic Books, 1976.

_____. *Intimate Strangers*. New York: Harper & Row, 1983.

Rubin, Zick. *Liking and Loving: An Invitation to Social Psychology*. New York: Holt, Rinehart & Winston, 1973.

Scanzoni, John. *Sexual Bargaining: Power Politics in the American Marriage*, 2nd ed. Englewood Cliffs, N.J.: Prentice-Hall, 1982.

Stack, Carol B. *All Our Kin: Strategies for Survival in a Black Community*. New York: Harper & Row, 1974.

Staples, Robert, ed. *The Black Family: Essays and Studies*. Belmont, Calif.: Wadsworth, 1971.

Stein, Peter, ed. *Single Life: Unmarried Adults in Social Context*. New York: St. Martin's Press, 1981.

Waller, Willard, "The Rating and Dating Complex," *The American Sociological Review*, 2 (1937): 727–734.

Weitzman, Lenore J. *The Marriage Contract: Spouses, Lovers and the Law*. New York: Free Press, 1983.

# B. Education

THE CONCEPT OF EDUCATION AS A SET OF ACTIVITIES SEPARATE FROM WHAT transpires in the course of everyday interactions is relatively new. Although all societies throughout human history have developed family systems, it is only in the past two or three centuries that the roles of teacher and student have occupied more than a tiny fraction of the population. Schooling has become so widespread and highly valued today that we can scarcely imagine that it was not always so. We begin dividing our time and attention between the family and the school at about the same age that generation after generation of people living in pre-industrial societies were beginning to move directly into work and apprenticeship roles.

How did we come from the point where schooling was a luxury for those (of any age) who had sufficient money and leisure time to the point where schooling is compulsory for many years of one's life and intimately tied to other institutions of our culture? The most obvious answer is that the skills required of individuals by an industrial, technological society are more *diverse* and more *specialized* than the skills needed to survive in an agricultural age. Parents today simply cannot give their children enough information to carry them through their adult lives, while earlier generations of parents usually could. Furthermore, factories and corporations benefit from having skills taught in schools, rather than having to train and educate workers themselves. Thus, one explanation for the rise of a separate educational institution is that it is functional in economic terms, both for soon-to-be workers and for employers.

Other less obvious factors have also contributed to the growth and spread of schooling in the United States. Legislation removing children from factory work in the late 1800s, often seen as a humanitarian movement to protect children from dreadful working conditions, was actually passed in order to keep children from competing with adults for employment opportunities in the urban centers. Once large numbers of children were "freed" from employment by this legislation, the question became what to do with them. The answer was often schooling, and in time education came to be seen as a duty of the young.

But schooling was not made *compulsory* until the early 1900s, when vast waves of Southern- and Eastern-European immigrants arrived in our country. These groups were less likely to speak English or to have economically valued skills than previous immigrants, and "Americanizing" their children was attempted by enacting compulsory-education laws. Schooling thus came to be seen as a vehicle for socialization, and education as a prime factor in upward social mobility.

As a result of the growing number of students, more and more jobs were created in the educational field and in allied industries—from teacher to administrator, from text-book publisher to cap-and-gown manufacturer. It is, you will agree, unlikely that individuals who earn a living from these activities would favor decreasing the role of schooling in society. In fact, these categories of people have worked consistently throughout this century to protect their own employment by expanding the educational sector.

As for post-secondary education, many of the same forces (except for compulsory legislation) have been operating to increase its importance. In addition, the G.I. Bill (providing tuition and living expenses for former military personnel) and the availability of federally financed college loans led to a virtual explosion of college enrollments in the post-World War II period. That explosion continues to the present day in terms of the *proportion* of "college-age" people who are enrolled (rather than the actual number, which is declining because of lower birth rates after the post-war baby boom). Currently, over half of those graduating from high school are attending college. Only about half of these will complete a four-year course, but the trend is sufficient to lead many observers to speak of the United States as a mass-educated society, especially when we consider that many adults are entering or returning to college and that graduate education is also being pursued at unprecedented rates. The "pull" of the learning environment is only part of the story; a "push" is also provided by employers who rely on the college or graduate degree as a criterion for employment. The meaning and value of these degrees has changed substantially in recent decades, because of the increasing number of college graduates. A college diploma may be the required ticket to board the economic train, but it no longer guarantees one a seat.

The institutionalization of schooling has had a number of important consequences for the ways in which we form our self-concepts and interact with others. The reader will recall our earlier discussion of the effects of age-segregation and age-grading on social interaction among the old and the young. We can further note that the age-segregation associated with mass schooling has, in conjunction with other societal trends, shaped new social roles—childhood, adolescence, and youth. Childhood was little different from adulthood until industrialization, urbanization, schooling, and a new religious view of the very young as needing moral molding were underway. Adolescence was not seen as a stage of life until around 1900, when educators began arguing that teenagers (the age of high-school students) had special needs. Of course, teenagers probably did *not* have special needs before this time, since their lives were essentially indistinguishable from the lives of their elders. Since the Second World War, another stage of movement toward adulthood has been created—youth—corresponding to the ages of college (and perhaps graduate-school) attendance. Each of these stages now has a special role specifying rights and obligations of those occupying the age-status. In sum, as entry into work roles is postponed for longer and longer periods, and as new stages of schooling emerge to occupy the time and energy of the postponers, our conceptions of what it means to be a certain age have changed and new social roles have been added.

These processes have also meant that the young person today interacts with new types of significant others within new organizational arrangements. The *teacher* and the *peer group* of age-mates have become sources of socialization to be reckoned with. Both may have a significant impact on the values, self-concept, aspirations, and behavior of the young in their roles as student, child, adolescent, and youth, as well as in their future roles as adults. The *bureaucratic* style of organizing the activities of large numbers of students and educators is a rather rigid system for keeping order and processing people. Some of the key features of educational bureaucracies, such as the grading system of evaluating student performance, have often been cited as producing competition and frustration among students. The informal systems emerging to cope with bureaucratic rules and regulations—often termed the *student culture*—are also modern developments that could not have arisen without schools.

The articles in this section cannot, of course, detail all the consequences of the rise of schooling or of educational systems for social interaction. In the first selection, entitled "Skimming and Dumping at Penrose High: Career Mobility and the Perpetuation of Inequality," Demie Kurz takes a close look at the teachers, students, administrators, and parents associated with "Penrose High School." She approaches the school as an example of a bureaucratic organization with formal and informal rules and processes. What she documents is a fairly common practice of teachers trying to enhance their own prestige by attempting to select classes with prestigious students. The students they considered to be ideal were the high achievers. Low acheivers were often "dumped" into the classes of teachers with less power and seniority in the system. How does this practice come about? What do parents and administrators contribute to the dumping process? What are the consequences of dumping for public-school students? These are some of the important questions Kurz addresses.

The college campus was the focus of research by Howard Becker, Blanche Geer, and Everett C. Hughes. Over twenty years ago, they examined in detail the workings of a midwestern state university. What struck them most forcibly was the degree to which students' and professors' academic roles were structured around grades, as we see in "Making the Grade." Faculty members often deplored the students' emphasis on grades, and students themselves often felt that grades interfered with learning. Both groups, however, found that their actions and interactions centered on the giving and receiving of grades.

Dissension, upheaval, and even revolution have shaken college and university campuses in the decades since this piece of research was undertaken. As we noted previously, economic and social changes have also affected the importance and value of a college education. One enduring structural feature of most colleges, however, is the grading system. Although college students now face a different set of contingencies after college than the students whom Becker, Geer, and Hughes observed, we submit that much still hinges on grades and that, therefore, this research can tell us much about the formal and informal structuring of the school experience today, as it did in that earlier generation.

Both of the articles in this section present pictures that are at odds with the official version of what is, and what is supposed to be, taking place in the educational process. By looking behind the scenes at the lives of the actors involved in the school, and by listening to those who are actually "processing" or being "processed" by the bureaucracies, the authors are able to document some of the ways in which the educational institution can shape the lives of the young.

# SKIMMING AND DUMPING AT PENROSE HIGH: CAREER MOBILITY AND THE PERPETUATION OF INEQUALITY

Demie Kurz

## INTRODUCTION

SOCIOLOGISTS AND EDUCATIONAL RESEARCHERS HAVE LONG BEEN CON-cerned with what causes and perpetuates inequality in schools (Coleman et al., 1961, 1966; Coleman and Hoffer, 1986; Ryan, 1976; Jencks et al., 1972, 1979; Lightfoot, 1978, 1983; Bowles and Gintis, 1976). We still find today that many students labeled "low-achieving"—those most in need of positive educational experiences—are precisely the ones whom some, maybe most, teachers consider undesirable. Teachers who have the most power and seniority often manage to "skim" for their own classes the students who "achieve" in conventional terms and to "dump" undesirable students into the classes of the newest and least powerful teachers.

Why does this situation persist? Why do teachers skim and dump? What social processes foster an educational system that often labels as undesirable and fails to serve a segment of the school's clientele?

In this article, I look in depth at one school—and especially at its teachers—to suggest answers to these questions. We should keep in mind as we study teachers that this occupational group is not totally unique. It shares features with other occupations, especially those with clients to serve. Julius Roth (1973) has noted that many professionals (like physicians) and semiprofessionals (like nurses) attempt to control who their clients are. Everett Hughes (1956) was first to point out that as workers advance in their jobs, they try to delegate "dirty work," or un-rewarding, low-prestige work, to others. For workers who are client-servers, dirty work consists of work with undesirable clients (Walsh and Elling, 1968). As a consequence, undesirable clients are often delegated by the most senior and powerful to be served by workers who are less powerful and are said to be less qualified (Becker, 1955).

Demie Kurz, "Skimming and Dumping at Penrose High," is drawn from *Organizational and Teacher Strategies of Control*, unpublished doctoral dissertation, Department of Sociology, Northwestern University, 1976. The author wishes to thank the teachers and staff at Henry Penrose High School, a pseudonym for a large suburban high school located in the mid-west. Louise Haberman, Howard Robboy, and Candace Clark provided valuable comments and suggestions on various drafts of this article.

Psychiatrists, for example, tend to prefer young, intelligent clients of at least middle-class background. Such clients have a higher probability of achieving success as adults than working-class clients. Psychiatry, like teaching, is a field in which practitioners have little means of assessing the quality of their work. Therefore, when well-established psychiatrists in private practice choose clients who are likely to succeed in life, they can employ these successes as testaments to their professional effectiveness. In the same vein, by avoiding lower-status and/or severely ill clients, these psychiatrists can minimize doubting their own abilities. Undesirable patients, in turn, get dumped on younger, less established psychiatrists, clinical psychologists, psychiatric social workers, and paraprofessionals who are employed by public mental-health facilities (Lorber and Satow, 1977).

Like other client-serving professionals, teachers want "clean" clients to enhance their work experiences, their sense of accomplishment, and their status. Teachers, however, have special problems actually controlling their clientele. First, the fact that schooling is compulsory guarantees that *some* teachers will have to do dirty work. Second, teaching is a "horizontal" career (Becker, 1952). There is no formal career ladder for teachers, no set of distinctive ranks like, say, "junior teacher," "regular teacher," "super teacher." If teachers advance, they become administrators and no longer teach. Because of the lack of ranks, there are no formal mechanisms for passing *down* dirty clients. Finally, teachers have less power to resist dumping by administrators than do other professional groups (Bidwell, 1965; Corwin, 1965; Lortie, 1969).

Given these constraints, how do teachers manage to skim and dump particular clients? We turn now to the staff and students of Henry Penrose High School to see how one school—typical, I believe, of many suburban high schools—has systematized the processes of skimming and dumping.

## THE RESEARCH SITE AND METHOD

A decade ago, I undertook a year of fieldwork at Henry Penrose High School, a recently constructed, large, two-story brick building located in a middle-class suburb of 80,000 inhabitants. Penrose High enrolls some 5,000 students, of whom 80 percent are white, 19 percent are black, and 1 percent are other ethnic and foreign students. The teaching staff consists of slightly more than 200 faculty members, most of whom are well educated and hold at least a masters degree. Over 90 percent of the faculty are white. School officials claim that Penrose High has an outstanding academic record and even a national reputation for excellence.

In my year at Henry Penrose High School, I conducted interviews and conversations with representative samples of the school's staff: teachers, department heads, counselors, assistant principals, all four principals, and department supervisors. I observed classes and faculty meetings. I analyzed school documents and literature.

## CAREER ENHANCEMENT AND THE PERPETUATION OF INEQUALITY

In the following section I examine the origins and nature of "skimming" and "dumping." First I consider why the students who are below average in academic performance are shunned as undesirables by those who are hired to teach them. I then examine how teachers negotiate with their supervisors to skim and dump. Last, I discuss how these practices are tolerated in a community that is well aware of them.

Like many or most teachers, those at Penrose High prefer to teach students who perform well. They are rewarded by administrators and the school board for evidence of achievement—producing students who score high on standardized tests, win competitions and awards, and gain admission to prestigious colleges. Obviously, it is more difficult to produce the desired product if one begins with lower-achieving students. Furthermore, the self-images of many Penrose teachers militate against an interest in teaching such students. These teachers feel they were trained to teach their disciplines at higher levels than the abilities of their students permit. They report feeling bored by the elementary level of the material. Finally, teachers expect lower-track classes to present discipline problems that they are eager to avoid.

As a result, most teachers at Penrose High are in the business of negotiating with department heads and administrators to win as many high- or at least middle-track classes as possible and avoid low-track classes. Competition also exists for the senior students (thought to be most capable), while freshmen (thought to be least capable) are avoided. A few teachers are repeatedly more successful than others in these negotiations (in which seniority is important but not, by itself, sufficient). A small number of those most junior and least adept at negotiation habitually find themselves with large numbers of low-track students. The most and least desirable students having been accounted for, most of the faculty teach the majority of students in between. Teachers in each of these groups frequently negotiate to better or maintain their positions.

In their attempts to select their clientele, Penrose teachers face certain obstacles, as well as gaining a certain amount of support, from the community and from school administrators. For instance, upper-middle-class parents—whose children tend to do well in school—are active in promoting classes and programs for high-achieving students. Several nearby communities that are predominantly upper-middle class provide a point of reference for Penrose parents, who are able to say with conviction and credibility, "The moment they let the standards go down around here, that's the moment I move to _____." Because the prospect of mass migration of the socioeconomic cream of the community into a more attractive school district is a serious issue in any prosperous town, these parents exert considerable influence on policy and curriculum.

The option of moving into a more desirable school district is not open, by and large, to parents of lower-tracked students, who come disproportionately (but not solely) from less wealthy households and from minority backgrounds. These parents, who cannot use economic pressure or presume on social acquaintance to promote their wishes, must rely principally on verbal protest in public meetings and on the desire of district officials to avoid embarrassment and confrontation.

The parents of low-tracked students do succeed in extracting some concessions and improved services for their children; but Penrose's reputation for "academic excellence"—that is, for the production of nationally high-achieving students—remains the dominant concern and rule for action among administrators. So the influence of pressure groups poses only a *potential* threat to Penrose teachers' freedom to select their clientele. In practice the overall effect has been to promote, rather than constrain, the tendency of senior, more competent, and more favored teachers to dump unattractive clients on their less well-protected colleagues.

Administrators have the power and authority to pose more of a problem. In general, though, top-level administrators feel that their own careers are best served by protecting and nurturing Penrose's outstanding performance on such traditional indicators of academic success as test scores, college acceptance rates, and state and national student prizes. This usually means giving priority to educating those students most likely to pull off winning performances—those already performing at average or above average levels. Rarely did any school board members or superintendents suggest changing the indicators of success by, for example, trying to dramatically raise the showing of students beginning from a lower point on the ladder.

Lower-level administrators with different sorts of concerns can also constrain teachers' autonomy in selecting students. Department heads must somehow staff all classes. They are constantly in the business of negotiating with individual teachers to try to assign lower-track classes without creating morale problems among the faculty. Principals and assistant principals, whose job is to maintain a satisfactory level of order in halls and classrooms, negotiate with teachers over the placement of notorious student troublemakers. These pressures militate against teacher control of clientele.

As I observed the array of actors vying in the complex system of negotiation at Penrose High, I noted that teachers tend to remain in, and become identified with, one of the three categories mentioned above: the small number who manage to get most of the "top" students; the small number who habitually teach the "bottom" students; and the majority, who spend their years teaching middle-level students. In the following section I examine each of the three groups and the processes by which they gain, maintain, and lose the ability to select their clienteles.

## TEACHERS AND SELECTIVITY

### Elite Teachers: The Academic "Specialists"

Among senior teachers, a handful are recognized as having special expertise in their subjects. (A prestigious graduate degree or a publication often confers this status.) Because of their perceived expertise, members of this small elite teach mostly Advanced Placement (college-level) and Honors classes with upper-level students. To secure and maintain this position of privilege, the "specialist" must first pursue a good working relationship with the department head, generally by supporting his or her aims and policies. Second, the teacher must produce high enrollments and exceptional student performance. Finally, the teacher should, if possible, court and utilize the support of parents of superior students.

Competition from other departments as well as successful attacks from parents lobbying for the interests of average and below-average students are ever-present threats to the autonomy of these teachers and to their resulting privileged access to superior students. When, in a particular case, administrators forced a selective social studies–English program to open its doors to a random selection of students, teacher job satisfaction among the elite declined noticeably. ("Regular" teachers, who had lobbied for the change, reported increased satisfaction.)

Changes in the tracking system also pose a major threat to the quality-control strategies of elite teachers. Parents of average and below-average students persuaded the administration to reduce the number of tracks (ability levels) so that their children would have more contact with brighter students and better teachers. The morale of the "elite" teachers dropped. They complained they could not teach at the high level to which they were accustomed.

### Teachers at the Middle Level

The majority of teachers who have been at Penrose High more than three years learn and put into practice strategies for avoiding the dirtiest work (i.e., assignment to the lowest-performing classes). They cannot rise to the level of their academic-specialist colleagues and have little contact with outstanding students. There is, however, a range of "middle" students; teachers use several means to get to teach students at its upper end.

First, teachers at the same level of seniority frequently strike bargains to "take turns" with colleagues, teaching "better" classes in alternate years. Teachers feel some assurance that they will have the opportunity to teach a variety of middle-range students during their tenure at the school. Still, most teachers also want the rewarding experience of teaching some of the higher-achieving students. Those with close ties to their department heads may ask for more prestigious assignments, but mobility through this route is limited because department heads are wary of charges of favoritism.

Realizing the importance of gaining a reputation as something of a specialist fairly early in one's career, a teacher may develop a new class or a new approach to a subject. For example, one social studies teacher created a non-Western cultures class that he found very satisfying to teach. While it was not a "top-level" (or most selective) class, prerequisites eliminated the least-desirable students, and self-selection took care of a good many more in the below-average group. Developing this course gave a significant boost to the teacher's status; he is someone with a "special" class and "special" abilities to teach it. He strengthens this identity by producing "results," "good" students, and then uses this identity to try to bargain for greater selectivity next time around.

But a successful result is not automatic. Another teacher, younger and newer, developed a course in Afro-American studies. Not wanting to exclude anyone from what she thought was an important subject, she placed no restrictions on enrollment. Her class drew some top performers, but counselors also sent students who did not fit in anywhere else and needed an elective. Shortly, she began to feel that the program had become a "dumping ground," a place for unwanted students. She found in addition that, because of the disparate levels of student interest and ability, it was a difficult class to teach.

In the Penrose High system, the teacher who does not complain about teaching a few less desirable students will soon be teaching many more of them. Praise from superiors—encouragement to keep teaching "open" classes—comes quickly. Younger teachers may initially welcome such flattery, but its appeal is short-lived:

> When you teach low-ability students they give you this line: "You're so good with these kids." It's just a line to make you believe you should keep teaching them.

> If you get low-ability students they tell you you should be a specialist because you're good at teaching low-ability students. They try to flatter your ego that way, but it's really a con.

Too much interest in low-achieving students may block or delay upward career mobility. The teacher is effectively "typecast."

TEACHER: I don't want to be considered the specialist who just takes these classes. I think that's happening and that people will come to say that I'm good at low-ability but not at academic teaching.
INTERVIEWER: You think that's happened already?
TEACHER: Yes, I definitely do. I think it's happened already. As a matter of fact, someone who was pretty high up in this school, almost to the top, told me that in terms of my future career, I should stop teaching so many of these students.

Teachers' concerns to advance on the career ladder thus may conflict with the interests of department heads who are eager to identify and label "low-achiever specialists" so that they will have uncomplaining staff on whom to foist dirty work. As one department chair said:

We really need the specialists. Otherwise it would affect the morale of the department. Things would be very difficult if we had to force people to take these jobs.

In addition to developing special classes, teachers at the middle level sometimes create specialized programs. Again the goal may have more to do with skimming and dumping than education, and allies in the school administration and the public are helpful.

One program director illustrated the successful use of skimming. He developed materials and techniques for bringing students working just below par up to their grade level. He convinced the principal to give him exactly the population that he needed for his program, and the students' scores improved. Since the production of "results" looked good for the school, the principal was also able to claim credit for these achievements. Not surprisingly then, the principal continued to grant this teacher the privilege of choosing his students.

In a similar case, however, a department head actively intervened to reduce selectivity. He feared that if the program skimmed close-to-average students, other teachers would resent getting those even further below average.

A third program, an evening program for dropouts, demonstrates the substitution of dumping strategies for skimming. Despite the high status of the program director, a former principal, he could not secure the right to select students. Through persistent negotiating—in which he made use of his seniority and the success of his students in college admissions—he did gain the right to expel students who had three unexcused absences. The director was confident he could use this power to dump those with little interest or ability. Still, principals have pressured him to take in troublesome students. He feels that when he retires and is replaced by someone with less power, the program will lose all control over its clientele.

At Penrose High, all programs for middle-level students faced pressure to accept discipline problems and low achievers. An assistant principal said:

> I do not try to put acting-out kids in the programs, because they'll destroy them. But sometimes I must.

For their part, program directors and teachers fear the results. One teacher put it:

> Trying to avoid being a dumping ground is trying to avoid other people putting their problems in your classes.

The middle-level teacher who cannot maintain selectivity gets not only "problems" but also a loss of prestige.

## Teachers of the Lowest-Achieving Students

Two groups consistently are assigned primarily low-achieving students. The first is the small number of teachers who choose lower-track assignments, who believe that the teaching profession should focus on helping students who most need help. These ideological "deviants" feel they must find kindred spirits and role models among like-minded teachers at other schools, because their own colleagues at Penrose High denigrate them and their efforts. As one said:

> I tried to explain to other teachers what I was attempting to accomplish with my classes, but they still asked me how I could stand it.

According to another:

> Teachers look down on those of us who teach low-ability students as less professional. They have a snotty attitude. They don't understand it, and they think it's less professional to teach these students.

These teachers may be shunned because they remind the careerists of a more idealistic, self-sacrificing philosophy.

The other group consistently assigned low-performance students is new teachers. The stated rationale for this policy is that new teachers are not yet prepared for academically higher-level students—that it takes a teacher longer to develop the expertise for higher-level students than for lower-achieving ones. What is more likely is that schools, like many other organizations, start newcomers off with the dirty work that no one else wants. Factory workers, for example, must often spend years working on the night shift before they have earned the seniority necessary to transfer to the preferred day shift (Robboy, 1979). In many organizations, starting at the bottom is justified as a means for newcomers to "learn the ropes" and to prove their loyalty.

Some new teachers believe the school's "official" rationale; the organization can, therefore, play on their insecurities. The majority, however, readily state that the main reason new teachers are given these students is that "no one else wants them." The presence of new teachers to staff unwanted classes keeps senior teachers from having to take more of them. New teachers tolerate this situation because they expect to be tenured after three years, at which time they, too, will be able to dump undesirables on their younger colleagues.

## SUMMARY AND CONCLUSIONS

I have analyzed how teachers in one high school attempt to improve their work conditions and gain prestige and status in their school and community. The primary mechanism they use is skimming and dumping students, that is, avoiding dirty clients and dirty work. Like other professionals, teachers want to develop their own expertise based on their own image of what constitutes an ideal client, free from outside interference (Becker, 1955). Teachers accomplish skimming and dumping by foisting low-achieving students onto willing teachers or newcomers, winning political favors from department heads, developing specialized and advanced classes, and shrewdly using parental pressure.

One unintended consequence of teachers' pursuit of career advancement and job satisfaction is a low level of concern and effort for all but the highest-achieving students. Because low-achieving students are defined as dirty clients, they systematically are denied the best teachers and a proportionate share of the school's resources. This system actively creates failure: once a program or a class is labeled a dumping ground, a further denial of resources and a lowering of expectations result (Rosenthal and Jacobsen, 1966). Its teacher may be incapable of producing successes.

The practices of skimming and dumping at Penrose, or at any other high school, do not operate in isolation. They result from the norms and values of both the community and the larger society. Like most schools, Penrose High functions to socialize students to accept and perpetuate the status quo. For the most part, the high achievers are unaware of the social factors that make their successes possible. Students who are skimmed believe they are superior and more meritorious than the others. Likewise, students who are dumped in large part internalize their failures, rather than seeing sociological factors such as classism and racism as sources of their woes.

Teachers, then, pursuing what they see as their legitimate professional goals, are part of a system that insures unequal treatment for students. Aside from the schoolroom itself, does this result have other ramifications? Inasmuch as schools' sorting affects later placement in the larger society (Cicourel and Kitsuse, 1963), teachers' actions contribute to social inequality.

There is little if any evidence that the skimming and dumping procedures described at Penrose High differ from the status-attainment mechanisms employed by teachers at similar high schools throughout the United States. Approaching the issues from the students' point of view, William Chambliss's now classic study of "The Saints and the Roughnecks" (included in Part V of this book) illustrates similar institutional structures and processes in a high school in Seattle. Nationally, systems of ability tracking, specialized programs for the gifted and for the impaired, as well as narrowly focused curricula emphasizing vocational and career preparation all contribute to the reproduction of the present class structure—constraining the social actors who occupy its ranks.

From a societal point of view, Penrose High is a "rational" institution: the individuals thought to be of greatest value in perpetuating the present society benefit most. It also successfully coopts most of the teachers, administrators, and students into acting in their own self-interest at the expense of equality. Like many other institutions in contemporary society, Penrose High offers least to those who need the most.

## REFERENCES

Becker, Howard S.
   1952 "The Career of the Chicago School Teacher," *American Journal of Sociology* 57: 470–77.

   1955 "Schools and Systems of Social Status," *Phylon* 16: 159–170.

Berg, Ivan E.
   1970 *Education and Jobs: The Great Training Robbery.* New York: Praeger.

Bidwell, Charles
   1965 "The School as a Formal Organization." Pp. 972–1022 in J. G. March, ed., *Handbook of Organizations.* Chicago: Rand McNally.

Bluestone, Barry, William Murphy, and Mary Stephenson
   1975 "Education and Industry." Pp. 161–173 in Martin Cornoy, ed., *Schooling in a Corporate Society,* 2nd ed. New York: David McKay and Co.

Bowles, Samuel, and Herbert Gintis
   1976 *Schooling in Capitalist America.* New York: Basic Books.

Boudon, Raymond
   1973 *Education, Opportunity and Social Inequality.* New York: Wiley.

Callahan, Raymond
   1962 *Education and the Cult of Efficiency.* Chicago: University of Chicago Press.

Cicourel, Aaron V., and Kitsuse, John I.
   1963 *The Educational Decision-Makers.* Indianapolis: Bobbs Merrill.

Coleman, James S. et al.
1961  *The Adolescent Society*. Glencoe, Ill.: Free Press of Glencoe.

1966  *Equality of Educational Opportunity*. Washington, D.C.: United States Government Printing Office.

———, and Thomas Hoffer

1986  *Public and Private High Schools: The Impact of Communities*. New York: Basic Books.

Corwin, Ronald G.
1965  *A Sociology of Education*. New York: Appleton-Century-Crofts.

Cremin, Lawrence
1961  *The Transformation of the American School: Progressivism in American Education, 1876–1957*. New York: Vintage.

Gintis, Herbert
1971  "Education, Technology and the Characteristics of Worker Productivity," *American Economic Review* 61: 266–279.

Hughes, Everett C.
1956  "Social Role and the Division of Labor." Pp. 304–310 in Everett C. Hughes, *The Sociological Eye*. Chicago: Aldine.

Jencks, Christopher, et al.
1972  *Inequality: A Reassessment of the Effects of Family and Schooling in America*. New York: Basic Books.

1979  *Who Gets Ahead? The Determinants of Economic Success in America*. New York: Basic Books.

Karabel, Jerome
1972  "Community Colleges and Social Stratification: Submerged Class Conflict in American Higher Education," *Harvard Educational Review* 42: 521–562.

Katz, Michael
1975  *Class, Bureaucracy and Schools*. New York: Praeger.

Lightfoot, Sarah Lawrence
1978  *Worlds Apart: Relationships Between Families and Schools*. New York: Basic Books.

1983  *The Good High School: Portraits of Character and Culture*. New York: Basic Books.

Lorber, Judith, and Roberta Satow
1977  "Creating a Company of Unequals: Sources of Occupational Stratification in a Ghetto Community Mental Health Center," *Sociology of Work and Occupations* 4: 281–301.

Lortie, Dan C.
1969  "The Balance of Control and Autonomy in Elementary School Teaching." Pp. 1–53 in Amitai Etzioni, ed., *The Semi Professions and Their Organizations*. New York: Free Press.

Persell, Caroline
    1973 *The Urban School: Factory for Failure*. Cambridge, Mass.: M.I.T. Press.

    1977 *Education and Inequality*. New York: Free Press.

Rosenthal, Robert, and Lenore Jacobson
    1968 *Pygmalion in the Classroom: Teacher Expectation and Pupils' Intellectual Development*. New York: Holt, Rinehart and Winston.

Walsh, James L., and Ray H. Elling
    1968 "Professionalism and the Poor—Structural Effects and Professional Behavior," *Journal of Health and Social Behavior* 9: 16–28.

# Review Questions

1. How did the school board rate the Penrose High School teachers performance? On what bases did the teachers gain prestige and promotions?

2. How are teachers similar to and different from other occupational groups in their control of their clientele?

3. What techniques did the Penrose High teachers use to "skim" and "dump"?

4. What roles did administrators and parents play in promoting or preventing skimming and dumping?

5. How do the processes of skimming and dumping perpetuate society's stratification system?

# MAKING THE GRADE

## Howard S. Becker, Blanche Geer, and Everett C. Hughes

IN OUR STUDY, THREE OBSERVERS ([INCLUDING] BECKER [AND] GEER . . . )
spent more than two years working with students at the University of
Kansas. We went to classes with them, spent time with them in their residential units, attended formal and informal meetings of all kinds of
campus organizations, and participated in many aspects of informal
campus social life. We did not pretend to be students, nor did we assume any of the formal obligations of students; though we went to class
with them, we did not do homework or take examinations. The nature of
our fieldwork will become clear in the quotations from our field notes
that appear throughout the [article].

A fourth observer (Hughes) spent two semesters at the University as a
visiting professor and in that capacity gathered data on the perspectives
of faculty and administration. The other observers occasionally gathered
similar material and, in addition, made extensive use of documents prepared by the administration and by other organizations, largely to characterize the environment in which students act.

• • •

## GENERALIZED GOALS

[P]erspectives are modes of collective action groups develop under the
conditions set by the situations in which they have to act. The thrust of
our analysis is largely situational, emphasizing the constraints and opportunities of the [college] situation and minimizing the influence of
ideas and perspectives that students bring with them to college. Yet students do bring with them some notions about college and what they are
going to do there, and these have bearing on what actually happens,
even though they are transformed in the student's later experience.

Students have, in a rudimentary way when they enter college and in
more elaborated form afterward, a *generalized goal*,[1] a point of view about
why they have come to college and what they may reasonably expect to

Excerpted from Howard S. Becker, Blanche Geer, and Everett C. Hughes, *Making the Grade:
The Academic Side of College Life*. New York: Wiley, 1968.

get out of their stay there. Generalized goals are, when the student first enters, a mixture of vague generalities and fragmentary specific desires, between which the student dimly apprehends some kind of connection. As he goes through school, he will probably (though not necessarily) come to a more precise definition of the general goal and will discern more complicated and precise relations between it and the specific goals he develops in particular areas of college life.

•    •    •

The chief characteristic of students' generalized goal, in its fully developed form, is an emphasis on college as a place in which one grows up and achieves the status of a mature adult. To manage one's college life properly (whatever meaning is attributed to that vague statement) shows that one has what it takes to be a mature adult, for the problems of college life are seen as much more like those of the adult world than anything that has come before. To do well in college, one must have the qualities students attribute to adults: the ability to manage time and effort efficiently and wisely, to meet responsibilities to other people and to the organizations one belongs to, and to cope successfully with the work one is assigned.

•    •    •

The generalized goal students have on entering [college] may be no more than an idea that they are going to take their academic work seriously, work hard, and do well. That goal, broadened and its connections to other areas of college life made specific, exerts an influence on the perspective students develop on their academic work. It does not tell the student how to act while he is in college; it only points the direction in which an answer must be sought and specifies a criterion against which any solution to the problems of college life will have to be measured. The generalized goal does not tell students the precise perspective they should adopt toward their academic work; many perspectives might satisfy its requirements. But the generalized goal does stand ready to tell students when a potential perspective is not in keeping with their long-range aims.

## THE GRADE POINT AVERAGE PERSPECTIVE

The student's generalized goal enjoins him to be serious about college: to recognize it as a serious place where important things happen and to try to do well in all areas of college life as a sign of having achieved maturity. His perspective on academic work develops as he interacts with other students in an environment in which, as we shall see, grades are the chief form of institutionalized value and the institutional basis of punishment and reward in academic pursuits.

The perspective students develop on their academic work—we can call it the *grade point average perspective*[2]—reflects the environmental emphasis on grades. It describes the situation in which students see themselves working, the rewards they should expect from their academic work, the appropriate actions to take in various circumstances, the criteria by which people should be judged, and relevant conflicts in goals. In general, the perspective specifies the grade point average as the criterion of academic success and directs students to undertake those actions that will earn "good" or adequate grades.[3]

The main elements of the grade point average perspective are these:

*Definition of the situation*

1. The college is so organized that one can neither remain as a student nor graduate without receiving adequate grades. Furthermore, a number of other rewards that students desire cannot be achieved without sufficiently high grades.

2. A successful student, one who is achieving maturity in college, will "do well" in his academic work, however "doing well" is measured, thus demonstrating that he is capable of meeting the demands of the environment and also opening the way to success in other areas of campus life.

3. Doing well in academic work can be measured by the formal institutional rewards one wins. Since the major academic rewards are grades, success consists of getting a "good" grade point average.

4. Intellectual or other interests may suggest other rewards than grades to be sought in academic experience. Where the actions necessitated by the pursuit of grades conflict with other interests, the latter must be sacrificed.

*Actions*

5. To be successful a student should do whatever is necessary to get "good" grades, not expending effort on any other goal in the academic area until that has been achieved.

*Criteria of judgment*

6. Since any student who wants to can achieve adequate grades, failure to do so is a sign of immaturity. Grades can, therefore, be used as a basis of judging the personal worth of other students and of oneself.

7. Faculty members may be judged, among other ways, according to how difficult they make it to achieve adequate or "good" grades.

To say that student perspectives emphasize grades does not mean that there is a unitary standard for all students. What is considered "good" may vary considerably among various groups on the campus. An average of B may be considered adequate in one fraternity house but substandard in another. The grade point average that will satisfy an engineering student may not satisfy a business student or vice versa. The definition of "good" grades depends, as well, on the student's aspirations in other spheres of campus life. Failing grades are satisfactory to no one, but any other set of grades may be acceptable to some student. Although the acceptable level of grades varies from group to group and person to person, the perspective directs students to orient their activities toward getting "good" grades.

•    •    •

An analogy with a money economy . . . is instructive. Anyone participating in such an economy will want to make what might variously be described as "enough money," "good money," or "a decent living." But the conception of "enough" or "decent" will vary widely among social classes, occupations, regions—and between individuals as well. Some will be satisfied only if they are millionaires; some will settle for a bare subsistence; most are in between. Almost everyone recognizes that "money isn't everything," that one must balance the need for money against other needs which are equally important.

Similarly, students vary in the degree to which they personally accept and live according to the rules suggested by the perspective. To some it seems completely normal: "How else could things be?" Others recognize that things might, in some other institutional setting, be quite different, but find the perspective acceptable. And some are irked by it, find it constraining and uncongenial. But it has two features that cause most students to accept it, however they feel about it, as a reasonable way to view the campus world and act in it. First, it is a *realistic way to orient oneself toward the academic aspects of campus life.* To be sure, it may not be the only realistic orientation; but it takes account of what are objectively discernible features of the campus environment. For this reason, it works; a student who adopts it as a standard of action will probably not have academic troubles. Thus, even though other perspectives might produce equally acceptable results, students will probably use this one, because it has worked in the past.

Second, the grade point average perspective is *widely accepted and thus has the force of being "what everyone knows."* Most people the students come in contact with talk and act in ways congruent with it; it embodies the accepted commonsense of his world. To question it or act in ways that deny it requires the student to violate the commonsense assumptions his fellows share; it is easier and more natural to accept them.

•    •    •

Whatever the student's private reservations—and, indeed, no matter how many students may have such private reservations—the terms and assumptions of conventional discourse are those contained in the perspective. To recur to the analogy with money, an adult may feel that money is not very important and privately decide that he will ignore it; but as long as he lives in a money economy, surrounded by people and institutions that assume the importance of money, he will be constrained to accept that assumption in his dealings with them. Just so with students and grades; however the student feels privately, campus life is organized around the terms and assumptions of the grade point average perspective.

•   •   •

## THE FACULTY VIEWPOINT: AN ALTERNATIVE DEFINITION

We have described the university social structure, as students define its effects in the area of academic work, as one that emphasizes grades, grades being the chief and most important valuable. Because this is a matter on which students and faculty have widely differing viewpoints, and because we tend to give more weight to the student viewpoint than academicians commonly do, we want here to indicate what seems to us the typical faculty viewpoint and to criticize it for failing to give sufficient weight to the structural imperatives we have described.

•   •   •

Some faculty members, no doubt, believe that the grades they give accurately reflect the amount of knowledge the student has acquired and are perfectly content that students should work for grades; in doing so they will learn what they are supposed to know. Other faculty members despise grades and would like to do away with them and all the associated paraphernalia of grade point averages, cumulative averages, and the like. Still others feel great ambivalence. They find it necessary, whether out of inner conviction or because of bureaucratic rules, to give grades and try to do it in a serious and responsible way. But they do not believe that the grades they give adequately reflect student ability; there are always some students who do well on tests although their classroom performance casts doubt on their grasp of the material presented, and others who know the material but get poor grades, perhaps because of poor test-taking skill. The faculty want to reward true achievement rather than the cunning of the accomplished grade-getter.

Faculty in the last two categories probably feel that students should be concerned about grades, but not *that* concerned. In particular, they object to what they see as the student tendency to reduce everything to grades, to raise interminable questions about "what we are responsible for," about the grading system and the criteria that will be used in assigning grades, about the number of questions on the exam—all the common questions that seem to them at best extraneous to the true business of learning and at the worst a deliberate mockery of it.[4]

Faculty are usually at a loss to explain student interest in grades and see no rational basis for it. They may attribute it to misguided competitiveness or to other kinds of irrationality. They do not see its basis in the structure of campus life, do not understand that the student definition of the situation is largely based on the realities of college life.

Faculty members, in complaining about student concern with grades instead of scholarship, complain, we may argue, because they feel that student concern with "beating" the system of tests and assignments designed to test achievement interferes with the true assessment of student ability. Students have a different view. They take tests and grades at face value and see a connection between doing their academic work properly—in such a fashion as to get adequate grades—and the emphasis on maturity contained in their generalized goal. They believe that when they achieve a satisfactory GPA they have demonstrated their ability to do their work and meet their obligations to themselves . . . and their college—in short, their ability to act as responsible adults.

## THE CONFLICT BETWEEN GRADES AND LEARNING

Despite what we have just said, some students share the faculty viewpoint in part. They incorporate it into their definition of the situation as one horn of a dilemma they see the college as posing for them. They feel that the workaday world of academic requirements, which forms the basis of the GPA perspective, causes them to miss something they might otherwise get from their courses, that they must meet the requirements before they can attempt to "learn for themselves." Insofar as the dilemma reflects a persisting definition of grades as important, it does not indicate the existence of a different and alternative perspective.

We do not mean to imply that students feel the conflict most of the time or that most students do at one time or another; the implication is not necessary to our argument, which is only that where the conflict is felt it reflects the belief that grades are important. For the most part, indeed, students believe that their courses are "good"; what they are required to do to pass the course is just what they ought to do anyhow to learn the substance of that course. Even when they fail to become excited by the content they are learning, they reason that the teacher knows the subject and that what he is teaching them must be what is important to know. If one gets a good grade, one has therefore necessarily learned something worth knowing. Where students do not accept the rationale, and feel a conflict between grades and learning, we have counted the incident as evidence of the existence of the GPA perspective.

Here is an extended statement of the problem by a successful student leader who himself had very high grades:

There's an awful lot of work being done up here for the wrong reason. I don't exactly know how to put it, but people are going through here and not learning anything at all. Of course, there are a lot of your classes where you can't really learn anything at all. . . . There's a terrific pressure on everybody here to get good grades. It's very important. They tell you that when you come in, we tell our own pledges that. We have to, because it's true. And yet there are a lot of courses where you can learn what's necessary to get the grade and when you come out of the class you don't know anything at all. You haven't learned a damn thing, really.

In fact, if you try to really learn something, it would handicap you as far as getting a grade goes. And grades are important. . . .

And, you see, it says in the catalog, if you read it, that C is a satisfactory grade. Well, do they mean that or don't they. Actually it's the minimum grade here. But it's supposed to be a satisfactory grade. OK. Supposing you wanted to work on something in your own way and didn't mind if you got a C. Well, if C was really a satisfactory grade it wouldn't hurt you any. But that's not the truth. C is just barely passing. The most satisfactory thing is an A, and next is a B.

The grading systems are so cockeyed around here you can't tell what's going on. One guy does it this way and another guy does it that way and, as I say, in a lot of these courses the only thing you can do is get in there and memorize a lot of facts. I've done that myself. I've gone into classes where that's all you could do is memorize . . . memorize and memorize. And then you go in to take the final and you put it all down on the paper, everything you've memorized, and then you forget it. You walk out of the class and your mind is purged. Perfectly clean. There's nothing in it. Someone asks you the next week what you learned in the class and you couldn't tell them anything because you didn't learn anything.

There are a lot of guys around here who are very expert at doing that. They can take any course and learn what has to be learned and get through the course with an A. And yet, I don't think those guys are really that smart, not to me anyway. In my opinion there are plenty of people around here who have much greater potential and they just haven't found the classes where you can use it . . . We've got these kids coming in and I don't know what it is, they're not interested themselves in accumulating knowledge for its own sake or because it will be of any use to them. All they want to do is get a grade. Now, of course, grades are important. We tell them [pledges] to go out and get that grade. What else can you tell them? It's very important for the house and it's important for them to get the grade. They want to be offered those good jobs when they graduate. I don't blame them. I would myself. I've always tried to get high grades and I've done pretty well.

—*fraternity senior*

This articulate student has presented most of the major themes of this aspect of the perspective, themes that recur more briefly in statements by others: Grades are important, for many reasons; one can get good grades without learning; indeed, trying to learn may interfere with grade-getting; the point of view is passed on in his fraternity.

•   •   •

## INDIVIDUAL ACTIONS

Having sized up their situation by discovering what needs to be done in each of their classes and projecting their semester GPA, students take action based on their definition of the importance of grades. Specifically, they express the GPA perspective when they take actions that have as their object getting a "good" grade, a grade sufficient for them in the light of their other grades, the total GPA they desire, and their other responsibilities and desires; in short, when they set their level and direction of effort with an eye to its effect on their GPA.

Student actions designed to get desired grades can take two forms. First, students may attempt to meet the requirements presented to them: they study and try to master the materials and skills they are supposed to acquire. But they may fail in that attempt or decide that they will fail if that is all they do. Then they undertake other actions which, rather than being designed to meet the requirements, try to achieve the reward of grades through other, less legitimate means such as arguing with the instructor, "getting next to" him, or cheating. If they can do the job, they do it, putting their major efforts into academic work; if they cannot, they try to influence their grade in some other way.

Under some circumstances, students making use of the GPA perspective will, instead of raising their effort to meet requirements or looking for alternative forms of action, actually lower their level of effort substantially, leading (as we shall see) to the paradoxical result that an emphasis on grades leads to decreased effort to achieve them.

DOING THE JOB: Students study; they are supposed to. But they study harder at some times than at others, and the variation in effort is not a function of anything in the material they study itself, but rather of whether or not a term paper is due or an examination looms ahead. They study harder, too, when their GPA is lower than they would like it to be.

This may seem overly obvious and not necessarily connected with the perspective we are describing. After all, what do students come to college for if not to study? Why do we think it necessary to explain that they do so? Even if we were to grant this (ignoring the possibility that students might come to college for other reasons and have no intention of studying at all), it is still not obvious why a student should study in any particular rhythm, with peaks of effort at one time and periods of relaxation at another.

Consider the following example. A student says that his work is "piling up" on him, that he is "getting behind." Does he say this because he has come to college to study and learn and feels that he is not learning fast enough? On the contrary, he feels his work is "piling up" because he has a given amount of work to do in a specified amount of time; if he does not keep to a daily schedule, getting so much done every day, he will fall behind and have more to do on the following days.[5] He did not choose those amounts of work and time; because of the relationship of subjection in the academic area, they are set for him by the faculty. He must meet faculty demands because his grades will be based on how well he does just that.

We frequently found students who were not doing well working extremely hard. The poorer student probably studies longest; he has so much difficulty that he must devote all his time to his work. Here is an example, from a conversation with a freshman girl on the verge of flunking out:

> Well, I start studying after dinner and I study all night until midnight and sometimes until one o'clock. And sometimes I start at six o'clock and just keep going right through. And I've been getting awfully tired, I think that's why I got that cold. Last weekend I went home and I slept thirteen hours until three o'clock in the afternoon.
>
> —*freshman woman*

Most instances are less dramatic. The student indicates that he has a great deal of work to do because of previous low grades and that he is doing what he thinks will be needed to improve them:

> I said to Harry, "How are things going with you?" He immediately replied, "Oh, I got a down slip [a midterm notice that one is likely to fail a course] in one of my courses and that's what I'm studying for now. I have a test in it tomorrow. . . ." I said, "How are your other courses going?" Harry replied, "They're OK, C's and B's. I'm doing all right in those and I think if I can work a little harder on this I can get it up to at least a C by the final. . . . Of course, I have no social life this semester and about all I'm doing is studying."
>
> —*freshman independent man*

Students need not be failing to behave this way; they may simply find it necessary to devote all their time to finishing required work in time to meet a deadline. Thus a student who had previously been quite prepared to engage in long conversations with the observer said: "Gee, you've caught me at a kind of bad time. I'm just trying to finish up a paper for Soc." (*senior man, scholarship hall*). (Most of the few occasions when students were unwilling to talk to us involved similar situations; the student had too much work to do to allow him to take the time off.)

When devoting more time and effort to study does not work, students who want higher grades seek help. They may, for instance, take advantage of services organized by the faculty, such as tutorial instruction, the Reading Clinic or the University Counseling Center.

More commonly, however, students get help from other students or from files, maintained by their living group, of old examinations, term papers, and the like. During dinner at a fraternity house, an observer overheard the following:

> You know how to study for Professor Jones, now, do you? Did you follow the file? Well, if you follow that file the way the course is outlined, then you can't go wrong, because he's been giving that course in the same way for the past ten years. Just be sure that you memorize all of those definitions, just the way that they are set up in the files, and you can't go wrong, you'll be sure of an A if you do.
>
> *—junior fraternity man*

Files of old examinations and papers are a tradition on many campuses. But students rely on fellow members of their living group for more than access to already accumulated files. They also ask for help in completing current assignments:

> The observer was lounging around in a student's room in the dormitory. . . . Long said, "[Bracket is] really busy in there. He's got a theme to turn in tomorrow and I don't think he's done anything on it yet." A little later Bracket arrived saying, "Does anybody know anything about Karl Marx? I've just run out of ideas. That's all there is to it. Where is Tucker? . . . He promised to give me an old term paper of his on Karl Marx that I could use." I said, "Johnny Bracket! Don't tell me that you would turn in somebody else's term paper?" He looked around quite seriously and said, "Oh, no. I didn't mean that. I just wanted to get some ideas out of it for the last two pages of my paper. I need about two more pages." Albright said, "I see. You would just copy the last two pages, is that it?" Bracket said, "Well, I wouldn't exactly copy them."
>
> *—sophomore independent man*

The pressure of assignments and the need to get grades thus push students to do the academic work assigned them. But, if pressure supplies a motive for work, its absence makes work less necessary. If the material need not be mastered now, but can be put off until later, the student may decide to work only as much as is required and no more. If he were sincerely interested in learning for its own sake, he would presumably continue to work on a topic until he lost interest in it or felt that he had learned enough to suit his purpose. But many students do only what is required of them:

> A student described having led a very extensive social life during the last semester. I said, "Did you get pretty good grades with all that?" He said, "I can't complain, I did just about as well as I expected." I said, "What was your grade point average?" He said, "2.6" [B plus]. I said, "Wow, that's pretty

good, isn't it?'' He said, ''Yes, it is pretty good, it really could have been higher if I had applied myself more in English, but I didn't. I think 2.6 is plenty high enough. There's no harm in that. But I didn't have to apply myself to get it. And I didn't have any intention of applying myself. . . .

''I don't mean to say that it was all a breeze. I had to put myself out occasionally. I had to get all those English themes in and so on. But frankly, with the exception of English, I didn't do any work at all the whole last month of school. I was caught up on all my other courses. I had done all the work for the rest of the semester. And the only reason that I hadn't done it in English is that you couldn't tell ahead of time what kind of themes he would assign. Otherwise I would have done all of that too. I really had all the whole last month perfectly free to do whatever I wanted.''

I said, ''You might have gone out and read some things that weren't assigned. Did you do that?'' He smiled very broadly and said, ''No, sir, you don't catch me doing that. I'll do just as much as I have to to get the grades and that's all.''

*—sophomore fraternity man*

Students who take this point of view make it their business to discover just what is required so that they can do the minimum necessary for the GPA they want. As soon as they discover that some action that seems necessary for a grade in fact is not, they dispense with it, even giving up going to class when that can be managed without running afoul of rules about ''cuts'':

I don't know about these classes. I've got one class where the fellow lectured about one set of things and then gave us an exam on a completely different set of things out of the book. I really don't think I'm going to go to that class any more. I mean, what's the sense of sitting there and taking notes if he's going to ask questions straight out of the book? I might as well just read the book and let it go at that.

*—independent man, year in school unknown*

The emphasis on what is required is reflected even in the interior decoration of student rooms. We repeatedly noticed that many students' bookshelves contained nothing but textbooks. Many other students, of course, had sizable collections of books that were only distantly related, if at all, to their course work. But a substantial number of students apparently had no use for books that would not be helpful in attempting to meet requirements.[6]

ILLEGITIMATE ACTIONS: Some of the actions that students take in pursuit of grades would be regarded as illegitimate by most faculty members. Faculty believe that students should work as well as they are able, and that they will do so if the faculty member can find a way to interest them. If called on to do so, faculty tend to justify the use of grades by defining them as some kind of combined measure of ability and interest. But some student actions make a mockery of that definition, being designed to produce the end product—grades—without an appropriate input of ability, interest, and effort.

Actions designed to circumvent the ability-effort equation, then, may be regarded as illegitimate. We have already noted that students attempt to get information on instructors' prejudices and idiosyncrasies. They act on that information, and even act when they have no information and must rely on guesswork. They want to affect the instructor's judgment of their work and thus raise their grade, either by catering to his prejudices or by getting to know him personally and taking advantage of the personal acquaintance in some way.

The conception underlying such actions is embodied in the commonly used phrase "brownie points." The vulgar origins of the expression are quite lost on campus; innocent young girls and boys use it freely. One gains brownie points, of course, by "brown-nosing," by doing things that will gain the instructor's favor other than simply doing the assigned classwork. The phrase is commonly used in a half-joking way, but its import is perfectly serious. One student explained the technique in detail (though he used a more refined term):

> What I do is apple-polishing, but it's not so obvious as that. It all depends on the teacher. Mainly, I just get to know them. I go up to their offices and talk with them. [What do you talk about?] Anything, anything they feel like talking about. I might figure out a good question to ask them. That'll show them that I'm really thinking about the course. And sometimes I just go up and say hello and we sit down and start talking about things. Maybe we'll talk about new cars. I'll say I don't like the new Ford this year, what do you think of it? And he'll tell me what he thinks of it.
>
> Just different problems like that. You know, these teachers don't like to talk about their subject all the time, they get tired of it, day in, day out, the same thing. I just size them up and see what I think they will go for. Now my English teacher last year, he was a tough one to figure out the second semester. It took me almost a whole semester to figure out what to do about him. Finally, I figured it out. I praised him, that's what he liked. It paid off, too. I got my mark raised a whole grade.
>
> —*sophomore fraternity man*

One can get negative brownie points as well—lose points by doing something formally extraneous to the course work which irritates or annoys the instructor; he is thought to retaliate by lowering one's grade:

> Prentice said, "Boy, I've got minus brownie points in my speech class. I'm about 200 in the hole to her." His friend said, "What do you mean?" Prentice said, "Well, she just doesn't like me. She's got some reasons too. I mean, they're pretty good reasons." The observer said, "For instance?" Prentice said, "Well, for one thing, I didn't show up for an appointment with her, you know, it was supposed to be for my benefit. She was going to help me out. I just didn't show up, so that doesn't go over too good. And I haven't been to class in a long time."
>
> —*freshman independent men*

Students fear particularly that disagreeing with the instructor, in class or in a paper, will have bad results:

You can write a very good theme on some subject—I mean, the grammar can be perfect and the spelling and the punctuation and everything—and they'll flunk you, if you write something they don't agree with. I've seen it happen. They don't like for you to have a different interpretation than the one they think is right. You take a piece of poetry, for instance. They'll pretty much tell you what you should get out of it, how it should impress you. They'll ask you to write a theme about it. Well, you'd better get the same impressions from it that they told you you should have, or you're going to be in trouble. . . . It just doesn't pay to disagree with them, there's no point in it. The thing to do is find out what they want you to say and tell them that.

—*junior fraternity man*

•    •    •

Students also act illegitimately when they attempt to improve their grade by disputing the instructor's interpretation of a term paper or an examination question. As every faculty member knows, returning papers or exams often provokes spirited debate designed to demonstrate that the answer the teacher thought incorrect was really correct, that the paper he thought inadequate actually measured up to the requirements he had set. And, as every teacher also knows, a student can often raise his grade by such tactics; students are ingenious in discovering hidden ambiguities in examination questions and term paper assignments. Here is an example:

I had to wring a C out of the psychology man [the instructor]. I had to argue with him, you should have seen me. The thing was, on that essay question he took off because I didn't give a name [a heading] for each point. There were eight points and I got each one in the discussion but I thought I would be different and just describe it and not give the name, so he counted off two points for each one, but I made him put some back and that gives me a C.

—*junior independent woman*

Arguments over the interpretation of an answer or assignment seem illegitimate to faculty because, again, they are ways of circumventing the equation of ability and effort with grades. They turn the grade into something that can be achieved by using the academically extraneous skills of a "Philadelphia lawyer."

Some students engage in the ultimate illegitimate act—cheating. A national survey of academic dishonesty among college students suggests, however, that students and faculty differ with respect to the definition of cheating.[7] Students seldom consider that they have cheated when they consult one another about an assignment. But faculty members, who see the teacher-student relationship as a one-to-one relationship between themselves and each individual student (a dyadic model of learning), sometimes feel that if the student consults anyone else he has acted dishonestly. By doing so, he has made his grade depend in some part on the ability and effort of others. (In view of the common scholarly practice of circulating work before publication for collegial comment and criticism, this faculty notion seems unduly rigorous.)

Some acts are on the borderline. A good many students might agree with faculty members that the following chemistry "shortcut" is illegitimate:

> They give you a sample of something and you're supposed to figure out what's in it. They only give you so much of it. The idea is if you use it all up making the wrong tests then you're just out of luck, you fail on that experiment. But guys are getting another sample out of them. You know, they say that their partner knocked the jar over or that they tripped while they are carrying it and spilled it or something like that. I've seen two fellows get away with it. So I don't think it'll be all that tough, if you can get around things like that.
>
> —*sophomore fraternity man*

• • •

The same national survey reveals that grosser forms of cheating are quite widespread. Fifty percent of the students questioned admitted that they had, at least once during their college careers, copied during an examination, used crib notes, plagiarized published materials for a term paper, or turned in someone else's paper. We saw very little obvious cheating, although we saw many borderline actions. One case of copying on an examination came to our attention, and one theft of an examination from a departmental office occurred during the time we were in the field. Nevertheless, some cheating must have occurred that we did not see; the nature of the act and students' shame at engaging in it (also documented in the survey referred to) make it hard to detect.

The most important point about illegitimate actions is that *they are a consequence of the existence of a system of examinations, grades, and grade point averages*. If the faculty uses examinations and other assignments to evaluate the student's abilities or progress, some students will attempt to influence the outcome of the evaluation "illegally," by "brown-nosing," arguing, or cheating. Illegitimate actions would be foolish if nothing important could be gained from them. It is because they may be rewarded by a raised grade that students engage in them.

THE GPA AND LOWERED STUDENT EFFORT: The grade point average perspective does not always intensify student academic effort. In fact, it can depress the level of effort a student puts forth, if he feels that he is already in such serious trouble that no conceivable amount of effort will get him out; when he sees his situation this way, he may stop working altogether. If we compare students to the industrial workers studied by Donald Roy, the analogy to a monetary system is again revealing. The workers Roy studied felt that they were "entitled" to a certain hourly average when they worked on piecework. If piecework rates were set so tightly that workers could not achieve the specified amount, they then worked at well below their capacity.[8] Since they could not "make out," they might as well simply collect their hourly wage and be done with it. They saw no sense in expending effort when nothing could be gained.

College students act much the same way. When they know they cannot possibly win, they resign themselves to losing and do not throw good money after bad. Failing students refuse even to calculate their grade point average; they know that they are going to fail and are not interested in the exact degree of failure:

> Brown said, "I sure am going to have to work and pull my grade average up if I want to stay here." The observer said, "What is it now?" He laughed and said, "I haven't even figured it out. It's too awful to think about." Carlson said, "I haven't either. I don't know what I'm going to get in some of these courses, but I know it's going to be pretty bad and I don't really want to bother figuring what my average is. What good would it do? I know I've got to bring everything up."
>
> —*two independent men, freshman and sophomore*

Likewise, students who are so far behind that it seems impossible to catch up do not bother to do assigned work anymore and sometimes stop doing all schoolwork completely; they report (to the observers and to each other) that they are unable to muster the energy or spirit to do the work:

> Tucker said, "Well, you're a damn fool. You just don't even try." Long said, "Buddy, I just can't get my spirit up. I don't know what's the matter with me." Tucker said, "I know how you feel. I feel the same way. There just doesn't seem to be any point to studying. I mean, I don't feel that I can learn anything and if I did it wouldn't be worth it so the hell with it."
>
> —*three independent men, a freshman, and two juniors*

The importance students attach to grades is thus exhibited in reverse. If one has already done so poorly that nothing can be salvaged, there is no point in studying or working.

· · ·

## CONCLUSION

Grades are universally defined as important because they are institutionalized; scholarship need not be recognized as important by everyone because its status as a valuable is not ratified by a set of rules and embodied in the organization and daily routine of the college. In the same way, participants in our society may consider beauty or truth more important than money. But one can ignore beauty and truth in one's life because they are not institutionalized; no one can ignore money, no matter how unimportant he thinks it. Not to have money has consequences one must reckon with. To have grades of the wrong kind likewise has consequences one cannot ignore.

Nevertheless, just as economic achievement is not the only important thing in a man's life, so academic achievement is not the only important thing in a student's life. A certain minimum is essential in each case, because of the way the valuable is institutionalized, with other kinds of rewards contingent on reaching that minimum. But beyond the minimum, which represents the level necessary in order to have the privilege of choosing where to put one's remaining time and effort, choice becomes possible, and the person finds that he must balance the various rewards available against one another in making that choice. One may decide to sacrifice the higher grade that would come with more work in a course, choosing to devote that time instead to a political career or a girl friend.

It is at this point that both economic man and the grade-getting student achieve some measure of autonomy. To be sure, they are both captives of a system of performance and reward imposed on them by others; the student is still in a relation of subjection to faculty and administration. But, having achieved the minimum without which participation is impossible, they can then choose to go no farther, to pursue instead other valuables in other areas of life. They become, thus, men in a community, fully alive to all the possibilities available to them in that communal life. . . . [S]tudents make use of that autonomy, though not in the ways that faculty members often hope they will.

## NOTES

1. The concept of generalized goal is related to, but not the same as, the concept of long-range perspective used in Howard S. Becker, Blanche Geer, Everett C. Hughes, and Anselm L. Strauss, *Boys in White: Student Culture in Medical School* (Chicago: University of Chicago Press, 1961), pp. 35–36, 68–79. They are alike in pointing to very general definitions of the meaning of one's participation in an organization. They differ in that long-range perspective refers the meaning to some state of affairs that lies beyond the end of the period of participation, while generalized goal refers the meaning to changes that take place during participation.

For further discussion of the relation between the understanding people bring with them to a situation and those they acquire in it, see Howard S. Becker and Blanche Geer, "Latent Culture: A Note on the Theory of Latent Social Roles," *Administrative Science Quarterly*, 5 (September 1960), pp. 304–313. The question has been pursued in studies of prison culture; see, especially, John Irwin and Donald R. Cressey, "Thieves, Convicts and the Inmate Culture," *Social Problems*, 10 (Fall 1962), pp. 142–155, and David A. Ward and Gene G. Kassebaum, *Women's Prison: Sex and Social Structure* (Chicago: Aldine, 1965), pp. 56–79.

2. We occasionally shorten this, in what follows, and refer to the GPA perspective.

3. We will use the expression "good grades" to refer to the level of grades that a student finds satisfactory, given the standards that he, his living group, and his other associates have developed. Those standards will take into account the various other obligations and opportunities relevant to the achievement of a mature balancing of effort and activity. "Good grades" will thus vary among students, living groups, and possibly along other dimensions as well. In contrast, we will use the expression "adequate grades" when we wish to refer to grades that are sufficient to meet some formal requirement; unless otherwise specified, "adequate grades" will refer to the GPA necessary to remain in school. Adequate grades, of course, do not vary, except as the requirement to which they refer varies.

4. See the discussion of medical faculty views in Howard S. Becker, Blanche Geer, Everett C. Hughes, and Anselm L. Strauss, *Boys in White, op. cit.*, pp. 110 and 132–134. Several essays in Nevitt Sanford, ed., *The American College* (New York: John Wiley and Sons, 1962), give evidence of the viewpoint of college faculty members.

5. *Ibid.*, pp. 92–106.

6. We made a practice of describing in detail the student rooms we visited and were thus able to check this point in our field notes.

7. William Bowers, *Student Dishonesty and Its Control in College* (New York: Bureau of Applied Social Research, Columbia University, 1964).

8. Donald Roy, "Quota Restriction and Goldbricking in a Machine Shop," *American Journal of Sociology*, 57 (March 1952), pp. 427–442.

# Review Questions

1. Becker, Geer, and Hughes draw a parallel between "making the grade" in college and being financially successful in the larger society. What is this parallel?

2. Students come to college with generalized goals of working hard and doing well. Faculty come to class to impart knowledge and to promote critical thinking. Why and how are these two definitions of the situation subverted?

3. What techniques do students employ to "make the grade"?

4. How does the grading system of evaluating student performance sometimes boomerang, leading to a lack of motivation?

5. The students observed and interviewed by Becker, Geer, and Hughes attended college twenty years ago. Are the processes and systems which affected those students still affecting orientations for success in college in your generation? Could you devise another system for motivating and evaluating students which would promote learning rather than "making the grade"?

## Suggested Readings: Interaction in Institutional Contexts: Education

Collins, Randall. *The Credential Society: An Historical Sociology of Education and Stratification.* New York: Academic Press, 1979.

Illich, Ivan. *Deschooling Society.* New York: Harper & Row, 1971.

Larkin, Ralph. *Suburban Youth in Cultural Crisis.* New York: Oxford University Press, 1979.

Rosenthal, Robert, and Lenore Jacobson. *Pygmalion in the Classroom.* New York: Holt, Rinehart and Winston, 1968.

Waller, Willard. *The Sociology of Teaching.* New York: John Wiley, 1967.

# C. Work and Economics

W E HAVE NOTED REPEATEDLY THAT THE ECONOMIC INSTITUTION OF A SOCI-
ety—that cluster of norms and values that guides the production and distribution of food, shelter, clothing, and the host of other services and
material goods we require and want—has major consequences for all
other institutions. The rules we must follow in order to survive have
changed drastically over the past century, as agriculture gave way to industry. For one thing, we have become in large part a nation of employees, dependent not on the seasons and the climate but on the corporation, the company, the agency, or the factory. A greater *variety* of skills
are required in an industrial society, and the systems for interrelating
workers with different job descriptions are much more complicated. In a
great many instances, the organizations that hire us have adopted bureaucratic methods to coordinate work and workers.

Sociologists take a great interest in work, because it has symbolic
meaning both on a social and a personal level. Not all jobs are viewed
with equal esteem, and occupational prestige affects both one's position
in the class structure and one's self-esteem. The kind of work we do defines us to other members of society by indicating, in many cases, our
sex, the income we are likely to earn, the amount of education we are
likely to have, and the lifestyles we are likely to pursue. Being an attorney, for example, conveys a social meaning different from being a factory
worker or a housewife, meanings that are likely to affect how people interact with us in a variety of situations and how we see ourselves. The
importance of the work identity is driven home at an early age to most
children, who are repeatedly asked, "And what are you going to be
when you grow up?"

The workplace itself has also received much attention from sociologists. How do various types of formal organization affect the workers?
What informal norms and patterns of behavior emerge among workers
in the factory, the university, the corporation? What, in short, are the social processes that surround a job?

Our first selection dealing with work looks at a group of factory workers, but the processes occurring here can be recognized in other work environments, such as hospitals, prisons, and the like. Howard Robboy, in
"At Work with the Night Worker," looks at that small but significant

portion of the labor force who think of the night as a time for work rather than sleep. It would be easy to view night workers merely as deviants, but to do so would give us no clues as to why they have broken from the usual workaday pattern. Robboy shows that the incentives which motivate the night worker are both economic and social. Night workers receive a pay differential (a slightly higher hourly wage) and are free to operate businesses of their own during the day. There is, moreover, a strong sense of solidarity that is not found in the factory at other times. And because night workers do not have the multitude of bosses hovering over them that day workers do, they can claim both greater personal freedom and more control over their duties.

The issue of control over the worker's mental processes and behavior is at the core of the second article in this section, "The Managed Heart: Commercialization of Human Feeling." In this selection Arlie Russell Hochschild reports her research into the airline industry's expectations for flight attendants. She finds that industry officials and trainers define not only the specific tasks that flight attendants should accomplish, like serving meals and giving safety instructions; in addition, attendants are expected to control their own feelings and expressions in order to shape passengers' emotions, to keep them calm and happy. The airplane is to become the living room in which the attendant acts as host or hostess. Yet every set of passengers contains a few who are unpleasant, obnoxious, or unruly. The flight attendant's perpetual smile often belies real feelings of hostility or frustration.

What does this "emotional labor" cost the worker? To what degree do the job requirements impinge upon the worker's internal senses and sentiments? Hochschild's respondents voiced real concerns about wearing their false smiles and, over time, becoming divorced or alienated from their true feelings.

These concerns are not, of course, limited to flight attendants. A great number of jobs in the growing service sector of our economy—salesperson, hairdresser, teacher, nurse, shop owner, entertainer, and many more—involve considerable amounts of emotional labor. We are just beginning to recognize this fact and to study its consequences for individuals and for society as a whole.

This section of the book can by no means be said to detail all of the norms, systems, and behavior patterns pertaining to work in our society. It is our hope that the reader will begin to see how work activities can be viewed sociologically and will apply this vantage point in looking at other occupations and settings. We try to show here that work is not motivated *solely* by the promise of economic reward and that, in fact, people will often work very hard for little return or even forego income. The informal social nature of the workplace *combines* with formal structures, rules, and economic incentives to set its tone and character. We also try to indicate the variety of meanings that can be attached to economic activities and to those who perform them.

# AT WORK WITH THE NIGHT WORKER

## Howard Robboy

At 11 P.M. OR MIDNIGHT EACH NIGHT, AS MOST AMERICANS ARE EITHER asleep or thinking about going to sleep, a small but significant number of people are just beginning their night's work.

Working nights means that one's entire daily schedule is thrown out of line from the temporal flow of society. Eating, sleeping, having sexual intercourse, socializing, visiting family members, and seeing one's children must be carefully scheduled by those who work the night shift. In a sense, these people become loners. The entire family must endure the strain of living in and between two time worlds.

In this study, the focus is on married male factory workers who reside and work in central and northern New Jersey and who work at night. The question explored in this article is why these workers agree to work the night shift despite the limitations on their social, family, and personal lives.

The period defined as night—perhaps from 11 P.M. to the breaking of the dawn—exists as a unique time zone in the course of social life (Melbin, 1978). It is here that we find fewer rules governing behavior than at any other time during the twenty-four hour cycle. For example, at this time we find blinking traffic lights and no time-specific norms pertaining to dress or food preferences.

The freer atmosphere of the night is not restrained by the walls of a factory and thus permeates the work experience of those employed on the night shift. Generally, night workers speak of less pressure, less tension, and a more congenial atmosphere than exist for their counterparts on the day shift in the same organization. The more amiable atmosphere manifests itself in many subtle ways during the night workers' time on the job.

## THE FREER WORKING ATMOSPHERE ON THE NIGHT SHIFT

When a worker begins to work nights, his work experience is different from that of his counterpart on the day shift. For one thing, he finds that many of the regulations enforced on the day shift are ignored by super-

Howard Robboy, "At Work With the Night Worker," is drawn from "They Work by Night: Temporal Adaptations in an Industrial Society," unpublished doctoral dissertation, Department of Sociology, Rutgers University, 1976.

vision at night. In most cases, the workers have to report only to their foremen.[1]

The foremen are usually the only ones in charge at night and thus are themselves freed from the scrutiny of superiors. As long as the required amount of work is accomplished, they allow certain things to slide by. After all, they are working nights too.

*Case 10*

There are fewer supervisors around. The foremen are likely to overlook shop rules like going for extra coffee or goofing off. On this shift you can read or do crossword puzzles to keep your mind from getting tired. You can't do this on days.

*Case 34*

You don't have to wear safety plugs in your ears. On this job it is dangerous to wear earplugs. There is less pressure on third shift. There are no bigwigs from New York walking around. Also the supervisors don't bug you as much. There are no big shots putting pressure on them.

Having fewer supervisors gives the night worker greater control over his work. This is important for several reasons.[2] First, it means that the worker can move at his own pace while running the machines, controlling the speed at which he works, rather than following the dictum of management. It can be argued, in fact, that reports of alienated workers are less likely to come out of the night shift. It is not that night workers do less work but, rather, that they have some say about how much work will be done, and when, during their eight hours on the job.

*Case 24*

No one ever bothers me. My boss hardly ever comes to see me. As long as I do my work, things are OK.

A further consequence of working at one's own pace is that on third shift the workers don't have to "dog their job"—go through the motions of working when in fact they are not—as night-shift workers claim day shift workers do to avoid the omnipresent eye of supervision. Not having to "look busy" also lessens the night worker's role distance—there is greater correspondence between what is expected of him and what he accomplishes than is true of day workers.

*Case 12*

On third shift you don't have to dog your job because you have someone standing over you. You might do in six hours what someone else on day shift drags out to eight. If you have decent supervision they won't mind if you lie down. This is where the other shifts complain.

Third-shift workers often have the opportunity to use their own methods of operation rather than depend on procedures set by management.

In my own experience as a bull-block operator in a copper-tubing factory, I was taught that when the machines were "running good" and the copper we were using was of high quality, we were allowed to run the machines faster than permitted by management—and so achieve production bonuses. Rarely did our foreman check up on us, as we were told was done on the first shift.[3]

### Case 26

I have to carry seventy pounds of material between these two machines. It was really hard on my wrists, so I devised a little cart so I could wheel the material between the two machines. On first shift they have to carry the stuff back and forth like horses. . . . We used to have two guys who worked out a system where one of them would run two machines for an hour while the other guy took a break. They showed this to others and soon it was done on the second and third shifts. Meanwhile, on first shift they have two guys doing the job dragging their feet.

Another feature of the third shift is that workers are frequently permitted to stretch their breaks. This adds to their feeling of having greater control over their lives while on the job.

### Case 14

We get a little more wash-up time. The shifts overlap in our favor. So if we finish early we can disappear. We don't have all the snoopers around, the white shirts who are always watching over you. . . . They are more lenient about breaks. They are also this lenient on second shift, but not on first.[4]

### Case 18

We can stretch our breaks where you can't on days. We can take a walk through the locker room and talk to the guys on breaks. On first shift, if you are not at your machine, you will get caught and get yelled at.

From the literature in industrial sociology, the data reported here, and my own experiences at the copper-tubing factory, it is the bargaining–conflict model of social relationships that most clearly depicts labor–management relationships (see Shelling, 1960; Handelman, 1976). The opportunities for rule breaking by a third-shift worker, seen through this perspective, are important for several reasons. On one level, they provide outlets for worker resentment against management. By breaking the rules, the worker feels that he is getting away with something or getting back at management. When the worker is supervised closely, as he is on the day shift, few opportunities exist for the channeling of resentments. My hunch is that, if the problem of industrial sabotage were to be thoroughly investigated, one would find that it occurs more frequently on the day shift (with adjustment made, of course, for the number of the workers on each of the shifts). For if there are few outlets for a worker's resentments, one of the options remaining when conditions become intolerable is to stop the machines.

On another level, the opportunity to break the rules can be viewed as a way to humanize the workplace. The authoritarian rule of management generates the expectation that the worker is supposed to work during his eight hours on the job (except for his coffee and lunch breaks) and do nothing else. The question then raised is, how often can people realistically do only one thing for such a prolonged period of time? Night workers, because they are able to manage their own time, can, to some extent, create a more humane atmosphere in which to work.

Working nights also provides the worker with the chance to "goof off" occasionally. A colleague, Noel Byrne, relates his experiences while working nights in a mill in Northern California:

> During the night, production would stop as the workers began waging bets on forklift truck races. The forklift trucks, normally used to transport the materials used in production, would be raced against one another. One night the brakes failed on one of the trucks as it went out the door, over a ten-foot embankment and finally stopped as it went head on into a creek which ran alongside the factory. It got so bad that the vice president of the company had to come into the plant one night to stop this practice. The foremen, who normally were the only ones in charge at this time, were the ones who drove the trucks during the races.[5]

In my own experience at the copper-tubing factory, workers were constantly throwing things at the drivers of cranes that rode on monorails attached to the roof of the building. The noise level in the plant was very high, and most of the workers wore their required earplugs. Unless one looked up from his work and saw the crane approaching, it would pass unnoticed. The crane operator, however, seeing the workers below busy at their work, would throw various articles at them. This folly would continue throughout the night.

The opportunity to smoke or drink coffee while working, to control both the pace of work and the production routines, to stretch their breaks, and occasionally to "goof off" on the job becomes an important feature of work on the night shift. Such advantages, along with a quantitative and qualitative difference in supervision, greatly affect the working atmosphere.

The working conditions often give rise to a greater sense of solidarity among third shift workers than among those on other shifts. Solidarity develops not only from the looser atmosphere, which makes greater interaction among the workers possible, but from the stigma of being labeled night workers by the workers on the first and second shifts.

Although working at night doesn't lead to the formation of a deviant identity off the job, there is evidence that a deviant identity does emerge during the hours of work. Such an identity is temporally situated at the workplace and reinforced as the night workers are compared with those on the other shifts.[6] In the nonwork world night workers identify themselves, and are identified by others, as being just working men, but at work they pick up the stigmatized identity of being night workers.[7] And, as the deviance literature suggests, a deviant or stigmatized identity acts as a strong bonding mechanism.

*Case 21*

People on the third shift are much closer. They confide in each other. They help one another. There is a much closer relationship on this shift.[8]

*Case 30*

When I go on vacation, I leave the key to my toolbox in case anyone needs anything. At work we share our tools. This is not done on day shift. We share information about the different machines. On days, everyone keeps to themselves and they don't help one another. There is a rivalry between them. . . . The workers are friendlier on night shift. There is more camaraderie. If you are on days the men bitch more. On third, if you are in trouble, someone will come over. There are only eight guys on this shift and they will give you a hand. We are a close-knit group. There are more soreheads on days. On nights the guys are easygoing.

In addition to the issues already discussed, other advantages of working at night emerged during the course of the interviews.

In the summer the night worker is spared from working under the heat of the day, which, along with the heat generated from the work itself, can be oppressive. In my own work experience, bull-block operators on the day shift were issued salt tablets by the plant nurse. These were a necessity to make it through the hot, humid days of New Jersey; on the night shift, these tablets were required only occasionally.

In some cases a night worker has a greater chance of working overtime than he would if he worked days. Usually the third shift is smaller in size than the other shifts, and so the probability is increased that any one worker will get overtime work when it is available.

*Case 29*

There are fewer people on our shift, so there is a greater probability of getting overtime. I get $2,000 to $3,000 a year in overtime. There is less supervision and we can work at our own speed. We are more united, closer together than they are on the day shift.

Having a smaller number of men working at night can also result in a reduction of the overall noise level in the factory. This is cited as an advantage of the night shift.

*Case 15*

It is also quieter on nights. The noise is incredible on days if I have to stay over. At my age, more things anger you. There is less aggravation on this shift.

*Case 25*

There is no hubbub like on second or days. There are fewer bosses and fewer employees. You are closer toward your fellow employees. You don't have the cutthroat attitude like on days and second.

## SHIFT DIFFERENTIAL

All the workers interviewed in this study receive a nightshift differential in pay for working the third shift. The shift differential ranges from 12 to 71 cents an hour. Most of the workers view this as a compensation for having to work nights. A minority of the workers, those who like working nights, see the shift differential as a bonus. In any event, the shift differential allows the worker to earn an additional $5 to $28 a week and enables him to feel that he is doing better than his day-shift neighbors. Certainly such an awareness can add to his feelings of competence as a breadwinner of the family. Thus the shift differential provides a second major explanation of why workers agree to work the night shift—it can mean the difference between staying afloat financially or sinking. It can also be the difference between their being forced to work a second or third job and/or their wives being forced to seek employment.

*Case 27*

I was on day shift for two years until a few months ago. I went back on third because we needed the ten percent. The doctor told me not to work a part-time job any more. Whenever I work two jobs I wind up in the hospital. I have bronchitis, asthma, and emphysema. I got off third shift last time because my wife wanted me to. The kids were getting older and she wanted me to spend more time with them. When I was on days, she worked part-time. Then she stopped working and we needed the ten percent so I went back on third.

## MOONLIGHTING

Having the daytime hours to himself gives the night worker the opportunity to obtain a part-time job or start his own business. In his study of moonlighters, Wilensky (1964) found that 6 percent of the male labor force moonlighted.[9] In this sample of night workers, sixteen men, or 40 percent of the forty workers interviewed, either had second jobs or owned small businesses to supplement the earnings from their nightshift positions. Of the sixteen night workers reporting second sources of income, ten operated their own businesses.

*Case 16*

I work third by choice. The kids were young then and we needed the money. I always worked two jobs. I am a carpenter and a fencer. Working third gave me my days free for a second job. You only work this shift for the money.

*Case 28*

I chose to work this shift as it gives me time to do other things. I have a part-time job as a handyman as well as a catering business.

Chinoy (1955), in his study of automobile workers, reports that some of the workers considered leaving the assembly line to start their own businesses. Although they are part of the American Dream and the

Horatio Alger mystique, small businesses—the kind typically started by blue-collar workers—have a high failure rate. The night shift provides a safety valve for workers who want to set up a business of their own. They can work their night jobs and still run the business. If the business fails or doesn't produce sufficient income to support a family, they still have their jobs. Thus the night shift provides them with a trial period to get their businesses going. This is an option open to few day shift workers.

For workers with businesses of their own, the night shift can be important in other ways. Consider the following night worker who is self-employed during the day as a fence builder.

*Case 16*

I have a fence business. When someone wants a fence put around their house they want it done right away. Maybe their dog almost got run over, their kid ran out into the street, or they just had a big fight with one of their neighbors. In any case, they want you there the next day. If I was on the day shift I would have to do it on weekends or after five o'clock during the week if it is summer. If you do this, they figure they are getting a half-assed job because you are trying to moonlight. It means that you are not a regular contractor. They are paying a good buck for the work, and they want to get workman's quality. They figure that you can't do quality work at five o'clock. And on weekends they don't want to be bothered by you being there. By working nights I can be there by 9 A.M. They feel that they are getting a real contractor. This way I can charge full price and do a first-rate job. If you come in the afternoon or on a weekend, they want to pay you less because you are not a real fencer.

## THE NIGHT-WORK TRAP

A night worker can become a blue-collar entrepreneur. He can work in a factory yet be free of many of the disagreeable features of the workplace that day shift workers encounter. He can earn the shift differential and have the opportunity to hold down a second job or manage a business of his own. But it is not for these reasons that most night workers choose the third shift. More often, little choice is available when they begin employment.

One of the initial reasons why workers agree to work on the night shift is that they have little or no seniority to qualify for the preferred position on the day shift. If a young worker, newly married, wants a job at a factory, he may have to choose between the second and third shifts. He may make the selection with the idea that, once he gains sufficient seniority, he will be able to go onto the day shift. In some cases the wait can be from five to ten years.

The second shift (beginning between 3 P.M. and 4 P.M. and ending between 11 P.M. and midnight) seems to be almost as disagreeable as the night shift. A second-shift worker with a working wife may see his wife and children only on weekends. He can sleep with his wife at night, but ''night'' often begins at two or three in the morning—because many workers find that they need a few hours to unwind before they are tired enough to go to bed. Many of the workers in this study had had some work experience on the second shift and, because of the scheduling difficulties, chose to transfer to the third shift.[10]

*Case 30*

I hate second shift. All you do is eat, sleep, and work. You come home at 12:45 A.M. wide awake. When you work nine to five, you have at least four hours free before you go to bed. What do you do at 12:45 A.M.? There is no one to talk to. You watch television until six in the morning, sleep until one-thirty, and then go to work. I call second shift the get-rich shift. All you can do is work and save.

*Case 41*

I would prefer nights to the afternoon shift. You start work at 2:30 before the kids come home from school. You come home after they are in bed and wake up after they've left for school. I would like to work days. But I prefer nights to the afternoons.

Choosing to work nights with the hope of eventually accumulating enough seniority to go on the day shift is a common strategy among night-shift workers. Consider the plight of a young worker, with a wife and family, who agrees to work nights. When he gains enough seniority to bid successfully for a job on the day shift, he may be faced with a financial dilemma. To go on days would require him to forfeit not only his shift differential but his second job or small business as well. To get off the night shift would entail, then, a substantial loss in income and a corresponding drop in his family's standard of living. For the blue-collar family, whose life style is already far from extravagant, this might prove quite difficult. Thus the night-shift differential and the opportunities for moonlighting, although they are economically seductive at the outset, can prove to be a trap that makes it difficult for a worker to leave the shift.

*Case 47*

I would much prefer working days. It would be the ultimate to have a straight nine-to-five job. I could work days, but my other involvements stop it. Eventually I will go over to days. This will be when the kids are older and can take care of themselves.

## ADDITIONAL REASONS FOR WORKING THE NIGHT SHIFT

For some workers, going on nights means an advancement to a higher-paying position.

*Case 1*

I want to qualify for a foreman's job. The foreman's job includes a salary increase and job on the day shift. That is why I took this job as a mechanic. I know that if I wanted to advance, I couldn't just be an operator. A mechanic is a step to a foreman. If I knew that I would have to remain a mechanic, I would have stayed an operator and worked days.

*Case 18*

I have another five years on third in my department before I can go on days. If I switched to another department I could go on days tomorrow. Another job would mean a lower paying job, 13 cents an hour less plus the 10 percent shift differential.

During the course of the interviews, incidents were related of factories suddenly closing and workers finding themselves unemployed. With a family to support, working nights becomes attractive if it means a steady job with a secure future.

*Case 12 (Wife)*

Bud used to work at G.E. All of a sudden they moved to Texas and left us with nothing.

*Case 21*

I worked at Studebaker for two years until they closed up. So I went looking for work and I got a job in construction—building homes. This lasted for about a year, but then I got laid off when the weather got bad. I wound up in _____ on the second shift. I worked there for two years but wanted a job on days, so I went to the Mack in Plainfield to work the day shift. I was at the Mack exactly five years, because I got a five-year pin. Then Mack moved out in '61, and I went to _____again on the third shift. (*Wife*) When Mack moved out it was really hard to get a job. All those men were thrown out of work. In fact, we used up most of our savings and it was rough. We were just glad that he had a job. (*Husband*) I needed a job and I was glad to work there. When you look for a job, you try to get the most for the least. Some of the places I went to paid so little that it wouldn't cover my mortgage payments. I am very grateful for the job I do have. No one around here pays the money_____does. We also get great benefits. The hospitalization and the other benefits can't be matched. At first I didn't like the third shift. I couldn't get used to it. But I made up my mind, and I got used to it.

If a night worker doesn't have a second job or a business on the side, having the day free provides time to pursue hobbies, care for preschool children, and clean the house.

*Case 14*

I work nights for the money and to be able to babysit during the day while she is working. I am on third shift now primarily because of our youngest child. . . . I would like to go on days in a few years when my youngest child is older and can take care of herself after school. Right now our lives are set up for me on the third shift. Everything is going so well. I don't know whether I would want to go on days now. Things are going well.

*Case 41*

I have more time with my family, especially in the winter. I get up when the kids get home from school, and I am with them until they go to bed at night and I go to work.

The third shift is also advantageous for activities like shopping. The worker can leisurely shop away from the evening and weekend crowds.

### Case 4

The biggest advantage of the shift is that you can shop with no crowds. If you need a doctor's appointment, shopping, and things done around the house, it is good. You don't have to fight crowds on weekends.

Another advantage of the shift is that if the worker is not tied down by a second job, he can use some of his nonwork time for recreation and avoid the crowded periods which day shift workers utilize for leisure.

### Case 37

I love to fish and hunt. On this shift I can come home, change my clothes, and be hunting and fishing in fifteen minutes.

### Case 10

It is a perfect shift for camping. I work the Sunday to Thursday schedule and can come home Friday morning and sleep for a few hours. Then I can leave and not return until Sunday night. If I was on the regular third shift, I would have to leave Saturday morning and be back Sunday night for my wife to get to work on Monday morning.

### Case 19

During the summer, I can go to the beach during the day and not fight traffic. I can sleep on the beach, and I don't have to fight the weekend crowds.

The night shift can also provide the worker with ample time to pursue his hobbies.

### Case 17

If I could take you downstairs and show you my hobby, you would understand why I like this shift so much. I raise show parakeets, and working nights allows me time to take care of them. We also go to bird shows in New York, Boston, and Washington. If we have to go into New York for the day, I don't have to take a day off from work. I also have a greenhouse outside where I raise azaleas. On day shift you can have your evening activities, but you don't have time for a hobby.

Another feature of the night shift is that the workers save time driving to and from work because they do not have to fight rush-hour traffic. This adds to their amount of daily nonwork time.

### Case 30

I can go from here to the plant in seventeen minutes. On days it would take thirty-five to forty minutes. I save an hour this way.

One worker used his nonwork time to build a new house for himself and his family.

*Case 16*

I built this house three years ago. I saved the money from working the two jobs and from my wife working part-time. (*Wife*) We worked six hours a day on this house and in ten months we built it. He came home from work, had breakfast, and worked on the house for six hours. Then he went home and went to sleep. We now rent our old house, and that pays for the mortgage on this house. We pay the smaller mortgage on that house, and we own land in Florida. Now we don't need the money from the third shift. (*Husband*) If I had worked days, I wouldn't have been able to accomplish as much. No one helped us with this. We did it ourselves. We could not have built this house if I wasn't on third shift. I was home when the materials were delivered and could check to make sure there were no shortages or that the wrong materials weren't sent.

It should be noted that all of the "features" of the night shift cited by the workers demonstrate a degree of social isolation. Their nonwork activities act as "side bets" in embellishing their careers as loners. An element common to their remarks is that they are able to avoid crowds.

## NEGATIVE ASPECTS OF WORKING THE NIGHT SHIFT

Although the advantages of the night shift are significantly greater than the limitations, still, in the course of the interviews, the workers speak of the negative features.

One of the slang terms used for the third shift is the "dead-man's shift." The phrase symbolizes the feelings on the part of workers that management doesn't care about them or even notice their existence. The feelings manifest themselves in several ways. First, decisions about production and product development are made by management officials who work the day shift. The night workers claim that decisions are made on the basis of day-shift operations, with no consideration given to night-shift needs.

*Case 4*

You are always left out of new information or new projects being developed. Management decisions are made on the basis of the first shift and not the third. You are never noticed by anyone, so it's hard to advance. You don't get the exposure.

*Case 20*

If you get a new machine, the person on day shift will know more about the machine. If there is a question about the machine, there is no one to go to.

Night workers are also unknown to management except on paper. This factor may be significant if the worker hopes to advance to a higher position.

*Case 12*

I know a lot of young guys who are strapped and need the 10 percent. They can't get into training programs or foremanships. No one knows them. You can apply, but when they get into the office, they say, "Who is that guy?"

The night workers complain that fewer plant facilities are open at night. I experienced these difficulties. One night we were working hard trying to make production bonuses, and a 270-pound coil of hot copper tubing began falling off the conveyor belt as it approached my section of the bull block. As I grabbed the coil with my insulated gloves, a section of the tubing hit my arm. The burn wasn't serious enough to require emergency treatment in a local hospital, but a Band-Aid proved to be insufficient. Since there was no nurse on duty on the night shift, I had to wait until 7 A.M. to see the nurse, who came on duty with the day shift.

*Case 26*

On third shift you can't buy safety shoes or glasses when you want. The foreman has to do it for me. There is no nurse on duty either.

*Case 30*

On first shift they have a full cafeteria. On third they have a lunch wagon. If I have a problem, I have to see the personnel man on my own time. No one is there at 7 A.M.

## SUMMARY AND CONCLUSIONS

This research provides numerous explanations as to why married male factory workers agree to work the night shift despite serious limitations in their family, social, and private lives.

The desires for a good job, easier working conditions, control over one's work, less supervision, and a small bonus becomes immediately apparent as explanations for working this shift. As one looks at the night shift in terms of a career, however, one discovers social and economic factors that serve as traps and consequently make it difficult for a night worker to return to a normal day-shift routine if an opportunity arose.

## NOTES

1. Of all the advantages of working nights cited by the workers interviewed, having less supervision was mentioned most often. Twenty-six of the forty workers interviewed raised this issue.

2. For a further discussion of the issue of worker's control, see Gerry Hunnius, G. David Garson, and John Case, eds., *Worker's Control: A Reader on Labor and Social Change*. New York: Vintage, 1973.

3. Donald Roy, in "Efficiency and the Fix: Informal Intergroup Relations in a

Piecework Machine Shop," *American Journal of Sociology* 60, 255–266, reports a similar finding.

4. A colleague, Noel Byrne, reports the following account from his night-work job in a mill in northern California.

> One of the advantages of night work was that you didn't have to hide when you finished your work. One night it was almost time to quit when the owner of the plant who lived in Chicago made a tour. He was unknown to us as we had never seen him before. One guy was just standing around, killing time before he could punch out. The owner came up to him and said, "What are you doing?" The worker replied, "Just fucking the dog." The owner, startled, retorted with, "You're fired, because I'm the dog you are fucking."

5. Another colleague, Howard Finkelstein, verifies Byrne's experience in his account of a night shift job he held in a swimming pool factory in New Jersey.

> I worked at a place where they manufactured prefab swimming pools. We used to bust our asses getting our work done by lunch time (3:30 A.M.) so that we could goof off the rest of the night. We used to bring in gallon containers of pink lemonade and gin. Following their consumption, we used to have fork-lift truck races on the loading platforms. This practice ended one night when the brakes on one of the trucks failed, and the truck went off the loading platform into a pile of wood.

6. For a discussion of situated identities in relationship to the self, see Edward Gross and Gregory P. Stone, "Embarrassment and the Analysis of Role Requirements," *The American Journal of Sociology* 70 (July 1964): 1–15.

7. Although Pigors and Pigors (1944:3) and Sergean (1971:165) claim that there is a social stigma attached to night work, I found no evidence for this in the course of the interviews.

8. Sergean (1971), Davis (1973), and Kozak (1974) report similar findings in their studies of night workers.

9. According to Michelotti (1975:56–62), the latest statistics show that men between the ages of 25 and 54 have the highest percentage of moonlighting (between 6 and 7 percent). As expected, there is no available national data on the percentage of night workers who moonlight.

10. To complete the "picture" of the American labor force, ethnographies are needed on second and rotating shift workers. For example, the second shift has a reputation among night workers for being a haven for bad marriages. If the couple schedules it "correctly," they can see each other only on weekends, thus minimizing the friction periods when they are together. Meanwhile they can appear married to the outside world.

## REFERENCES

Becker, Howard S.
    1953–1954 "Some Contingencies of the Professional Dance Musician's Career," *Human Organization*, 12 (Spring), 22–26.
    1960 "Notes on the Concept of Commitment," *American Journal of Sociology*, 65 (July), 32–40.

Chinoy, Ely
  1955 *The Automobile Worker and the American Dream.* Garden City, N.Y.:
    Doubleday.

Davis, Murray
  1973 *Intimate Relations.* New York: Free Press.

Goffman, Erving
  1961 *Encounters.* Indianapolis: Bobbs-Merrill.

Gross, Edward and Gregory P. Stone
  1964 "Embarrassment and the Analysis of Role Relationships," *American
    Journal of Sociology*, 70 (July), 1–15.

Handleman, Don
  1976 "Rethinking Banana Time," *Urban Life*, 4 (January), 433–448.

Hunnius, G., David Garson, and John Case, eds.
  1973 *Workers Control.* New York: Vintage.

Kozak, Lola Jean
  1974 "Night People: A Study of the Social Experiences of Night Workers,"
    *Summation*, 4 (Spring/Fall), 40–61.

Melbin, Murry
  1978 "Night as Frontier," *American Sociological Review*, 43 (February), 1–22.

Michelatti, Kopp
  1975 "Multiple Jobholders in May, 1975," *Monthly Labor Review* (November),
    56–62.

Pigors, Paul and Faith Pigors
  1944 *Human Aspects of Multiple Shift Work.* Cambridge: Department of Eco-
    nomics and Social Science, Massachusetts Institute of Technology.

Roy, Donald F.
  1952 "Quota Restriction and Goldbricking in a Machine Shop," *American
    Journal of Sociology*, 57 (March), 427–442.
  1955 "Efficiency and 'The Fix': Informal Intergroup Relations in a Piecework
    Machine Shop," *American Journal of Sociology*, 60, 255–266.
  1959–60 "Banana Time," *Human Organization*, 18 (Winter), 158–168.

Sergean, Robert
  1971 *Managing Shiftwork.* London: Gower Press-Industrial Society.

Shelling, Thomas
  1960 *The Strategy of Conflict.* Cambridge, Mass.: Harvard University Press.

Shostak, Arthur
  1969 *Blue Collar Life.* New York: Random House.

Slater, Philip
  1969 *On the Pursuit of Loneliness: American Culture at the Breaking Point.* Boston:
    Beacon Press.

Stone, Gregory P.
   1971 *"American Sports: Play and Display,"* in Eric Dunning, ed., *The Sociology of Sport*. London: Frank Cass, pp. 46–65.
   1974 "Remarks," at *The Minnesota Symposium on Symbolic Interaction*. Hudson, Wis., June.

Wilensky, Harold L.
   1964 "The Moonlighter: A Product of Relative Deprivation," *Institute of Industrial Relations* (Reprint No. 219). Berkeley: University of California, pp. 105–124.

# Review Questions

1. A young married worker in need of a job accepts a position on the night shift. He or she hopes to earn enough seniority to switch to the day shift eventually. According to Robboy's study of night-shift workers, what social and economic traps might prevent an eventual switch to the day shift?

2. Robboy's research indicates that there are numerous advantages and disadvantages to working the night shift. What are they, and why do they exist on the night shift rather than on other shifts?

3. How do you explain the fact that there is less worker alienation and industrial sabotage on the night shift than on the day shift?

# THE MANAGED HEART: COMMERCIALIZATION OF HUMAN FEELING

## Arlie Russell Hochschild

W HEN RULES ABOUT HOW TO FEEL AND HOW TO EXPRESS FEELING ARE SET BY management, when workers have weaker rights to courtesy than customers do, when deep and surface acting* are forms of labor to be sold, and when private capacities for empathy and warmth are put to corporate uses, what happens to the way a person relates to her feelings or to her face? When worked-up warmth becomes an instrument of service work, what can a person learn about herself from her feelings? And when a worker abandons her work smile, what kind of tie remains between her smile and her self?

[This article examines such questions by focusing on how employers (in this case, the airline industry) require certain feelings and emotions of employees (flight attendants). Professor Hochschild's research techniques included observing and interviewing flight attendants, trainers, and supervisors at Delta Airlines in the late 1970s and early 1980s. During this period, deregulation of airline prices and a redistribution of routes were occurring. Before deregulation, airfares were fixed and service was a primary means for one airline to compete with another. After deregulation, price competition came about, fares went lower overall and varied among airlines, planes were fuller, and the clientele was less select and sophisticated. We will now see the efforts of the companies to get more and more "emotional labor" from flight attendants and the attendants' responses.]

• • •

## BEHIND THE SUPPLY OF ACTING: SELECTION

Even before an applicant for a flight attendant's job is interviewed, she is introduced to the rules of the game. Success will depend in part on whether she has a knack for perceiving the rules and taking them seriously. Applicants are urged to read a preinterview pamphlet before com-

---

*Surface acting* refers to behavior that one feels to be false. *Deep acting* is acting that convinces oneself; it begins as an act and transforms one's own feelings [Eds.].

Excerpted from Arlie Russell Hochschild, *The Managed Heart: Commercialization of Human Feeling* (Berkeley, Calif.: University of California Press, 1983).

ing in. In the 1979–1980 *Airline Guide to Stewardess and Steward Careers*, there is a section called "The Interview." Under the subheading "Appearance," the manual suggests that facial expressions should be "sincere" and "unaffected." One should have a "modest but friendly smile" and be "generally alert, attentive, not overly aggressive, but not reticent either." Under "Mannerisms," subheading "Friendliness," it is suggested that a successful candidate must be "outgoing but not effusive," "enthusiastic with calm and poise," and "vivacious but not effervescent." As the manual continues: "Maintaining eye contact with the interviewer demonstrates sincerity and confidence, but don't overdo it. Avoid cold or continuous staring." Training, it seems, begins even before recruitment.

Like company manuals, recruiters sometimes offer advice on how to appear. Usually they presume that an applicant is planning to put on a front; the question is which one. In offering tips for success, recruiters often talked in a matter-of-fact way about acting, as though assuming that it is permissible if not quite honorable to feign. As one recruiter put it, "I had to advise a lot of people who were looking for jobs, and not just at Pan Am. . . . And I'd tell them the secret to getting a job is to imagine the kind of person the company wants to hire and then become that person during the interview. The hell with your theories of what you believe in, and what your integrity is, and all that other stuff. You can project all that when you've got the job."

• • •

Different companies favor different variations of the ideal type of sociability. Veteran employees talk about differences in company personality as matter-of-factly as they talk about differences in uniform or shoe style. United Airlines, the consensus has it, is "the girl-next-door," the neighborhood babysitter grown up. Pan Am is upper class, sophisticated, and slightly reserved in its graciousness. PSA is brassy, funloving, and sexy. Some flight attendants could see a connection between the personality they were supposed to project and the market segment the company wants to attract. One United worker explained: "United wants to appeal to Ma and Pa Kettle. So it wants Caucasian girls—not so beautiful that Ma feels fat, and not so plain that Pa feels unsatisfied. It's the Ma and Pa Kettle market that's growing, so that's why they use the girl-next-door image to appeal to that market. You know, the Friendly Skies. They offer reduced rates for wives and kids. They weed out busty women because they don't fit the image, as they see it."

Recruiters understood that they were looking for "a certain Delta personality," or "a Pan Am type." The general prerequisites were a capacity to work with a team ("we don't look for chiefs, we want Indians"), interest in people, sensitivity, and emotional stamina. Trainers spoke somewhat remotely of studies that indicate that successful applicants often come from large families, had a father who enjoyed his work, and had done social volunteer work in school. Basically, however, recruiters look for someone who is smart but can also cope with being considered dumb, someone who is capable of giving emergency safety commands but can also handle people who can't take orders from a woman, and someone who is naturally empathic but can also resist the numbing effect of having that empathy engineered and continuously used by a company for its own purposes.

●  ●  ●

The trainees, it seemed to me, were also chosen for their ability to take stage directions about how to "project" an image. They were selected for being able to act well—that is, without showing the effort involved. They had to be able to appear at home on stage.

## TRAINING

The training at Delta was arduous, to a degree that surprised the trainees and inspired their respect. Most days they sat at desks from 8:30 to 4:30 listening to lectures. They studied for daily exams in the evenings and went on practice flights on weekends. There were also morning speakers to be heard before classes began. One morning at 7:45 I was with 123 trainees in the Delta Stewardess Training Center to hear a talk from the Employee Representative, a flight attendant whose regular job was to communicate rank-and-file grievances to management and report back. Her role in the training process was different, however, and her talk concerned responsibilities to the company:

> Delta does not believe in meddling in the flight attendant's personal life. But it does want the flight attendant to uphold certain Delta standards of conduct. It asks of you first that you keep your finances in order. Don't let your checks bounce. Don't spend more than you have. Second, don't drink while in uniform or enter a bar. No drinking twenty-four hours before flight time. [If you break this rule] appropriate disciplinary action, up to and including dismissal, will be taken. While on line we don't want you to engage in personal pastimes such as knitting, reading, or sleeping. Do not accept gifts. Smoking is allowed if it is done while you are seated.

The speaker paused and an expectant hush fell across the room. Then, as if in reply to it, she concluded, looking around, "That's all." There was a general ripple of relieved laughter from the trainees: so that was *all* the company was going to say about their private lives.

Of course, it was by no means all the company was going to say. The training would soon stake out a series of company claims on private territories of self. First, however, the training prepared the trainees to accept these claims. It established their vulnerability to being fired and their dependence on the company. Recruits were reminded day after day that eager competitors could easily replace them. I heard trainers refer to their "someone-else-can-fill-your-seat" talk. As one trainee put it, "They stress that there are 5,000 girls out there wanting *your* job. If you don't measure up, you're out."

Adding to the sense of dispensability was a sense of fragile placement vis-à-vis the outside world. Recruits were housed at the airport, and during the four-week training period they were not allowed to go home or to sleep anywhere but in the dormitory. At the same time they were asked to adjust to the fact that for them, home was an idea without an immediate referent. Where would the recruit be living during the next months and years? Houston? Dallas? New Orleans? Chicago? New York? As one pilot advised: Don't put down roots. You may be moved and then moved again until your seniority is established. Make sure you get along with your roommates in your apartment."

Somewhat humbled and displaced, the worker was now prepared to identify with Delta. . . . Training seemed to foster the sense that it was safe to feel dependent on the company. Temporarily rootless, the worker was encouraged to believe that this company of 36,000 employees operated as a "family." The head of the training center, a gentle, wise, authoritative figure in her fifties, appeared each morning in the auditorium; she was "mommy," the real authority on day-to-day problems. Her company superior, a slightly younger man, seemed to be "daddy." Other supervisors were introduced as concerned extensions of these initial training parents. (The vast majority of trainees were between nineteen and twenty-two years old.) As one speaker told the recruits: "Your supervisor is your friend. You can go to her and talk about anything, and I mean *anything*." The trainees were divided up into small groups; one class of 123 students (which included three males and nine blacks) was divided into four subgroups, each yielding the more intimate ties of solidarity that were to be the prototype of later bonds at work.

• • •

The company claim to emotion work was mainly insinuated by example. As living illustrations of the right kind of spirit for the job, trainers maintained a steady level of enthusiasm despite the long hours and arduous schedule. On Halloween, some teachers drew laughs by parading through the classroom dressed as pregnant, greedy, and drunk passengers. All the trainers were well liked. Through their continuous cheer they kept up a high morale for those whose job it would soon be to do the same for passengers. It worked all the better for seeming to be genuine.

Trainees must learn literally hundreds of regulations, memorize the location of safety equipment on four different airplanes, and receive instruction on passenger handling. In all their courses, they were constantly reminded that their own job security and the company's profit rode on a smiling face. A seat in a plane, they were told, "is our most perishable product—we have to keep winning our passengers back." How you do it is as important as what you do. There were many direct appeals to smile: "Really work on your smiles." "Your smile is your biggest asset—use it." In demonstrating how to deal with insistent smokers, with persons boarding the wrong plane, and with passengers who are sick or flirtatious or otherwise troublesome, a trainer held up a card that said "Relax and smile." By standing aside and laughing at the "relax and smile" training, trainers parried student resistance to it. They said, in effect, "It's incredible how much we have to smile, but there it is. We know that, but we're still doing it, and you should too."

## HOME IN THE SKY

Beyond this, there were actual appeals to modify feeling states. The deepest appeal in the Delta training program was to the trainee's capacity to act as if the airplane cabin (where she works) were her home (where she doesn't work). Trainees were asked to think of a passenger *as if* he were a "personal guest in your living room." The workers' emotional memories of offering personal hospitality were called up and put to use. . . . As one recent graduate put it:

> You think how the new person resembles someone you know. *You see your sister's eyes in someone sitting at that seat.* That makes you want to put out for them. I like to think of the cabin as the living room of my own home. When someone drops in [at home], you may not know them, but you get something for them. You put that on a grand scale—thirty-six passengers per flight attendant—but *it's the same feeling.*

On the face of it, the analogy between home and airplane cabin unites different kinds of experiences and obscures what is different about them. It can unite the empathy of friend for friend with the empathy of worker for customer, because it assumes that empathy is the *same sort of feeling* in either case. Trainees wrote in their notebooks, "Adopt the passenger's point of view," and the understanding was that this could be done in the same way one adopts a friend's point of view. The analogy between home and cabin also joins the worker to her company; just as she naturally protects members of her own family, she will naturally defend the company. Impersonal relations are to be seen *as if* they were personal. Relations based on getting and giving money are to be seen *as if* they were relations free of money. The company brilliantly extends and uses its workers' basic human empathy, all the while maintaining that it is not interfering in their "personal" lives.

•   •   •

By the same token, the injunction to act "as if it were my home" obscured crucial differences between home and airplane cabin. Home is safe. Home does not crash. It is the flight attendant's task to convey a sense of relaxed, homey coziness while at the same time, at takeoff and landing, mentally rehearsing the emergency announcement, "Cigarettes out! Grab ankles! Heads down!" in the appropriate languages. Before takeoff, safety equipment is checked. At boarding, each attendant secretly picks out a passenger she can call on for help in an emergency evacuation. Yet in order to sustain the *if*, the flight attendant must shield guests from this unhomelike feature of the party. As one flight attendant mused:

> . . . If we were going down, if we were going to make a ditching in water, the chances of our surviving are slim, even though we [the flight attendants] know exactly what to do. *But I think I would probably*—and I think I can say this for most of my fellow flight attendants—*be able to keep them from being too worried about it*. I mean my voice might quiver a little during the announcements, but somehow I feel we could get them to believe . . . the best.

Her brave defense of the "safe homey atomosphere" of the plane might keep order, but at the price of concealing the facts from passengers who might feel it their right to know what was coming.

Many flight attendants spoke of enjoying "work with people" and adopted the living room analogy as an aid in being as friendly as they wanted to be. . . . Others spoke of being frustrated when the analogy broke down, sometimes as the result of passenger impassivity. One flight attendant described a category of unresponsive passengers who kill the analogy unwittingly. She called them "teenage execs."

> Teenage execs are in their early to middle thirties. Up and coming people in large companies, computer people. They are very dehumanizing to flight attendants. You'll get to their row. You'll have a full cart of food. They will look up and then look down and keep on talking, so you have to interrupt them. They are demeaning . . . you could be R2–D2 [the robot in the film *Star Wars*]. They would like that better.

•   •   •

Despite the generous efforts of trainers and workers themselves to protect it, the living room analogy remains vulnerable on several sides. For one thing, trainees were urged to "*think* sales," not simply to act in such a way as to induce sales. Promoting sales was offered to the keepers of the living room analogy as a rationale for dozens of acts, down to apologizing for mistakes caused by passengers: "Even if it's their fault, it's very important that you don't blame the passengers. That can have a lot of impact. Imagine a businessman who rides Delta many times a year. Hundreds, maybe thousands of dollars ride on your courtesy. Don't get into a verbal war. It's not worth it. They are our lifeblood. As we say, the passenger isn't always right, but he's never wrong.''

• • •

The cabin-to-home analogy is vulnerable from another side too. The flight attendant is asked to see the passenger as a potential friend, or as like one, and to be as understanding as one would be with a good friend. The *if* personalizes an impersonal relation. On the other hand, the student is warned, the reciprocity of real friendship is not part of the *if* friendship. The passenger has no obligation to return empathy or even courtesy. As one trainer commented: ''If a passenger snaps at you and you didn't do anything wrong, just remember it's not you he is snapping at. It's your uniform, it's your role as a Delta flight attendant. Don't take it personally.'' The passenger, unlike a real friend or guest in a home, assumes a right to unsuppressed anger at irritations, having purchased that tacit right with the ticket.

• • •

It is when the going gets rough—when flights are crowded and planes are late, when babies bawl and smokers bicker noisily with nonsmokers, when the meals run out and the air conditioning fails—that maintaining the analogy to home, amid the Muzak and the drinks, becomes truly a monument to our human capacity to suppress feeling.

Under such conditions some passengers exercise the privilege of not suppressing their irritation; they become ''irates.'' When that happens, back-up analogies are brought into service. In training, the recruit was told: ''Basically, the passengers are just like children. They need attention. Sometimes first-time riders are real nervous. And some of the troublemakers really just want your attention.'' The passenger-as-child analogy was extended to cover sibling rivalry: ''You can't play cards with just one passenger because the other passengers will get jealous.'' To think of unruly passengers as ''just like children'' is to widen tolerance of them. If their needs are like those of a child, those needs are supposed to come first. The worker's right to anger is correspondingly reduced; as an adult he must work to inhibit and suppress anger at children.

Should the analogy to children fail to induce the necessary deep acting, surface-acting strategies for handling the ''irate'' can be brought into play. Attendants were urged to ''work'' the passenger's name, as in ''Yes, Mr. Jones, it's true the flight is delayed.'' This reminds the passenger that he is not anonymous, that there is at least some pretension to a personal relation and that some emotion management is owed. Again, workers were told to use terms of empathy. As one flight attendant, a veteran of fifteen years with United, recalled from her training: "Whatever happens, you're supposed to say, I know just how you feel. Lost your luggage? I know just how you feel. Late for a connection? I know just how you feel. Didn't get that steak you were counting on? I know just how you feel." Flight attendants report that such expressions of empathy are useful in convincing passengers that they have misplaced the blame and misaimed their anger.

●   ●   ●

Finally, the living room analogy is upheld by admitting that it sometimes falls down. In the Recurrent Training classes held each year for experienced flight attendants, most of the talk was about times when it feels like the party is over, or never began. In Initial Training, the focus was on the passenger's feeling; in Recurrent Training, it was on the flight attendant's feeling. In Initial Training, the focus was on the smile and the living room analogy; in Recurrent Training, it was on avoiding anger. As a Recurrent Training instructor explained: "Dealing with difficult passengers is part of the job. It makes us angry sometimes. And anger is part of stress. So that's why I'd like to talk to you about being angry. I'm not saying you should do this [work on your anger] for Delta Airlines. I'm not saying you should do it for the passengers. I'm saying do it for *yourselves.*"

From the beginning of training, managing feeling was taken as the problem. The causes of anger were not acknowledged as part of the problem. Nor were the overall conditions of work—the crew size, the virtual exclusion of blacks and men, the required accommodation to sexism, the lack of investigation into the considerable medical problems of flight attendants, and the company's rigid antiunion position. These were treated as unalterable facts of life. The only question to be seriously discussed was "How do you rid yourself of anger?"

The first recommended strategy . . . is to focus on what the *other* person might be thinking and feeling: imagine a reason that excuses his or her behavior. If this fails, fall back on the thought "I can escape." One instructor suggested, "You can say to yourself, it's half an hour to go, now it's twenty-nine minutes, now it's twenty-eight." And when anger could not be completely dispelled by any means, workers and instructors traded tips on the least offensive ways of expressing it: "I chew on ice, just crunch my anger away." "I flush the toilet repeatedly." "I think about doing something mean, like pouring Ex-Lax into his coffee." In this way a semiprivate "we-girls" right to anger and frustration was shared, in the understanding that the official ax would fall on anyone who expressed her anger in a more consequential way.

Yet for those who must live under a taboo on anger, covert ways of expressing it will be found. One flight attendant recalled with a grin:

> There was one time when I finally decided that somebody had it coming. It was a woman who complained about absolutely everything. I told her in my prettiest voice, "We're doing our best for you. I'm sorry you aren't happy with the flight time. I'm sorry you aren't happy with our service." She went on and on about how terrible the food was, how bad the flight attendants were, how bad her seat was. Then she began yelling at me and my co-worker friend, who happened to be black. "You nigger bitch!" she said. Well, that did it. I told my friend not to waste her pain. This lady asked for one more Bloody Mary. I fixed the drink, put it on a tray, and when I got to her seat, my toe somehow found a piece of carpet and I tripped—and that Bloody Mary hit that white pants suit!

Despite the company's valiant efforts to help its public-service workers offer an atmosphere perfumed with cheer, there is the occasional escapee who launders her anger, disguises it in mock courtesy, and serves it up with flair. There remains the possibility of sweet revenge.

●    ●    ●

## RESPONSES TO THE CONTRADICTION

The slowdown is a venerable tactic in the wars between industrial labor and management. Those whose work is to offer "personalized service" may also stage a slowdown, but in a necessarily different way. Since their job is to act upon a commercial stage, under managerial directors, their protest may take the form of rebelling against the costumes, the script, and the general choreography. . . .

For a decade now, flight attendants have quietly lodged a counterclaim to control over their own bodily appearance. Some crews, for example, staged "shoe-ins." ("Five of us at American just walked on the job in Famolares [low-heeled shoes] and the supervisor didn't say anything. After that we kept wearing them.") Others, individually or in groups, came to work wearing an extra piece of jewelry, a beard a trifle shaggier, a new permanent, or lighter makeup. . . . Sometimes, as in the case of body-weight regulations, the issue was taken to court. . . .

Workers have also—in varying degrees—reclaimed control of their own smiles, and their facial expressions in general. According to Webster's Dictionary, "to smile" is "to have or take on a facial expression showing pleasure, amusement, affection, friendliness, irony, derision, etc., and characterized by an upward curving of the corners of the mouth and a sparkling of the eyes." But in the flight attendant's work, smiling is separated from its usual function, which is to express a personal feeling, and attached to another one—expressing a company feeling. The company exhorts them to smile more, and "more sincerely," at an increasing number of passengers. The workers respond to the speed-up with a slowdown: they smile less broadly, with a quick release and no sparkle in the eyes, thus dimming the company's message to the people. It is a war of smiles.

●    ●    ●

The smile war has its veterans and its lore. I was told repeatedly, and with great relish, the story of one smile-fighter's victory, which goes like this. A young businessman said to a flight attendant, "Why aren't you smiling?" She put her tray back on the food cart, looked him in the eye, and said, "I'll tell you what. You smile first, then I'll smile." The businessman smiled at her. "Good," she replied. "Now freeze, and hold that for fifteen hours." Then she walked away. In one stroke, the heroine not only asserted a personal right to her facial expressions but also reversed the roles in the company script by placing the mask on a member of the audience. She challenged the company's right to imply, in its advertising, that passengers have a right to her smile. This passenger, of course, got more: an expression of her genuine feeling.

The slowdown has met resistance from all quarters and not least from passengers who "misunderstand." Because nonstop smiling had become customary before the speed-up occurred, the absence of a smile is now cause for concern. Some passengers simply feel cheated and consider unsmiling workers facial "loafers." Other passengers interpret the absence of a smile to indicate anger. As one worker put it: "When I don't smile, passengers assume I'm angry. But I'm not angry when I don't smile. I'm just not smiling."

●    ●    ●

The friction between company speed-up and worker slowdown extends beyond display to emotional labor. Many flight attendants recalled a personal breaking point. Here are three examples:

> I guess it was on a flight when a lady spat at me that I decided I'd had enough. I tried. God knows, I tried my damnedest. I went along with the program, I was being genuinely nice to people. But it didn't work. I reject what the company wants from me emotionally. The company wants me to bring the emotional part of me to work. I won't.

●    ●    ●

> The time I snapped was on a New York to Miami flight. On those flights, passengers want everything yesterday. There's a constant demand for free decks of cards. One woman fought for a free deck and groused when I told her we were all out. Finally I happened to see a deck under a seat, so I picked it up

and brought it to her. She opened her purse and there were fifteen decks inside.

• • •

I thought I'd heard them all. I had a lady tell me her doctor gave her a prescription for playing cards. I had a man ask me to tell the pilot to use the cockpit radio to reserve his Hertz car. I had a lady ask me if we gave enemas on board. But the time I finally cracked was when a lady just took her tea and threw it right on my arm. That was it.

Workers who refuse to perform emotional labor are said to "go into robot." They withhold deep acting and retreat to surface acting. They pretend to be showing feeling. Some who take this stance openly protest the need to conduct themselves in this way. "I'm not a robot," they say, meaning "I'll pretend, but I won't try to hide the fact that I'm pretending." Under the conditions of speed-up and slowdown, covering up a lack of genuine feeling is no longer considered necessary.

• • •

What is distinctive in the airline industry slowdown is the manner of protest and its locus. If a stage company were to protest against the director, the costume designer, and the author of a play, the protest would almost certainly take the form of a strike—a total refusal to act. In the airline industry the play goes on, but the costumes are gradually altered, the script is shortened little by little, and the style of acting itself is changed—at the edge of the lips, in the cheek muscles, and in the mental activities that regulate what a smile means.

The general effect of the speed-up on workers is stress. As one base manager at Delta frankly explained: "The job is getting harder, there's no question about it. We see more sick forms. We see more cases of situational depression. We see more alcoholism and drugs, more trouble sleeping and relaxing." The San Francisco base manager for United Airlines commented:

> I'd say it's since 1978, when we got the Greyhound passengers, that we've had more problems with drug and alcohol abuse, more absenteeism, more complaints generally.
>
> It's mainly our junior flight attendants and those on reserve—who never know when they will be called up—who have the most problems. The senior flight attendants can arrange to work with a friend in first class and avoid the Friendship Express altogether.

There are many specific sources of stress—notably, long shifts, disturbance in bodily rhythms, exposure to ozone, and continual social contact with a fairly high element of predictability. But there is also a general source of stress, a thread woven through the whole work experience: the task of managing an estrangement between self and feeling and between self and display.

# Review Questions

1. Hochschild contends that service jobs require *emotional labor*, or work that puts other people in a certain emotional state. Explain and give examples of how flight attendants engage in emotional labor.

2. How do flight attendants use "surface acting" and "deep acting" to manage their own emotions so they can do their emotional labor?

3. What other types of service workers do emotional labor, managing other people's emotions? In what cases is this type of labor explicitly called for in job description? In what cases is it just assumed to be part of the job?

# Suggested Readings: Interaction in Institutional Context: Work and Economics

Bigus, Odis E. "The Milkman and His Customer," *Urban Life and Culture*, 1 (July 1972): 131–165.

Lorber, Judith. *Women Physicians: Careers, Status and Power*. New York: Tavistock, 1984.

Miller, Gale. *It's a Living: Work in Modern Society*. New York: St. Martin's Press, 1981.

Reimer, Jeffery. *Hard Hats: The Work World of Construction Workers*. Beverly Hills, Calif.: Sage, 1979.

Ritzer, George, and David Walczak. *Working: Conflict and Change*, 3rd ed. Englewood Cliffs, N.J.: Prentice-Hall, 1986.

Roy, Donald F. "Quota Restriction and Goldbricking in a Machine Shop," *American Journal of Sociology* 57 (1952): 427–442.

Schrank, Robert. *Ten Thousand Working Days*. Cambridge, Mass.: The M.I.T. Press, 1979.

Sell, Ralph. "Transferred Jobs: A Neglected Aspect of Migration and Occupational Change," *Work and Occupations* 10 (1983): 179–206.

Spradley, James P., and Brenda J. Mann. *The Cocktail Waitress: Woman's Work in a Man's World*. New York: John Wiley, 1979.

Terkel, Studs. *Working*. New York: Random House, 1974.

# D. Health and Illness

In contemporary Western societies a host of spectacular medical procedures and technologies permits us to trade in our kidneys and hearts, to rejuvenate our eyes and ears, and to prolong life itself beyond the capacities of our organs. These spectacular developments overshadow many other aspects of health, illness, and treatment in our society: a large number of people have little or no access to medical treatment; a great deal of mundane, repetitive, ameliorative treatment is rendered; a wide variety of health problems is caused by medical treatment itself; and the price tag attached to staying healthy and getting treated now consumes well over 10 percent of our national economy. Sociologists looking at America's present system of defining and dealing with health and illness cannot overlook any of these issues. While some sociologists study the social consequences of kidney dialysis machinery and artificial heart implants, others inquire into the types and prevalence of medical mistakes, the implications of the medical insurance system (or "third-party payers"), and the economic benefits some people reap at the expense of the sick.

The first article in this section is an overview of many recent sociological insights about our health-and-illness system. Candace Clark's review essay, "Sickness and Social Control," summarizes a large body of research on our society's ways of defining illness and disease, the organization of medical treatment, and a process called the "medicalization of deviance." This process involves changing conceptions of what an illness is and what causes people to stray from normality, or health. Such changes have led to a shift in the locus of social control in our society. In all human groups, healers have been in charge of controlling those deviant conditions defined as illness. In the Western world, over the past century or so, more and more conditions and behaviors have come to be *interpreted* as illnesses rather than as sin, criminality, or other types of deviance. And as more deviant conditions have come to be viewed as illnesses, medical personnel have been given a larger and larger role in controlling deviance than ever before in history. Surgery, drugs, hospitalization, and other techniques of medical intervention have gained tremendously in recent years, often replacing the old techniques of social control employed by religious leaders, teachers, parents, and the courts.

The ideas in Clark's article challenge the taken-for-granted ways in which most of us think about illness and deviance, medical treatment, and social control. Since Americans have more faith and trust in the expertise and good intentions of physicians than of any other occupational group, it is often difficult for us to stand back and assess the societal functions of medical theories and treatments. Yet just because we are not used to thinking of the social-control aspects of medicine does not mean that they do not exist. If we are to understand life in the United States in the late twentieth century, we must come to grips with the expanded role of medicine in defining and enforcing our norms.

The second selection on health and illness, "Illness and the Legitimation of Failure," is by Stephen Cole and Robert Lejeune. These researchers have explored in depth one question that highlights how social the illness-definition process can be: under what conditions do people define themselves as ill? What, they ask, is the direction of the relationship between illness and deviance?

In their studies, deviance is defined as receiving public-assistance payments instead of working for pay. They base their analyses on studies of mothers who are receiving living expenses for themselves and their children from governmental agencies and who, they discovered, feel a sense of stigma for doing so.

Common sense would argue that illness or wellness would affect whether or not a person received public-assistance payments, rather than the other way around. But Cole and Lejeune present many carefully reasoned arguments that suggest the contrary. Receiving public-assistance payments, a stigmatizing occurrence, may lead people to define themselves as ill. Illness, then, provides a culturally acceptable legitimation for "failure."

# SICKNESS AND SOCIAL CONTROL

## Candace Clark

## INTRODUCTION

JUST AS EVERY SOCIETY HAS DEVELOPED A FAMILY SYSTEM AND AN ECO-
nomic system, every society known to social scientists has developed a
normative system to define, locate, and control illness (Wellin, 1978; Fábrega, 1974). What is considered illness in one society may be a mark of
health in another—that is, illness categories are devised or constructed
differently from one culture to another—yet every human group recognizes something as constituting illness and mobilizes resources in response to illness. I hope to demonstrate in this review essay that *the control of illness and sick people is one form of the more general phenomenon of
social control.* Social control, any behavior or social-structural arrangement which encourages people to conform to societal norms and values,
is an essential feature of all societies. Medical forms of social control have
increased tremendously in importance in American society over the past
century, edging aside religious, legal, educational, and familial forms
and techniques of social control. An accurate and comprehensive picture
of life and interaction in modern Western societies cannot omit the expanded role of medical models offering explanations of human experience and of medical means of transforming human behavior.

A first step in presenting this sociological view of the role of medicine
is the clarification of the key terms illness, sickness, and disease, all of
which have distinct and specific meanings here. As the terms are understood by sociologists today (Twaddle and Hessler, 1977:97), "illness"[1]
refers to the *individual's perception* or claim of a problematic physiological
experience, state, or change that he or she is feeling which is presumed
to have biological causes. By "sickness" we mean the state of being defined and reacted to by *other societal members*, including relatives, friends,
and employers, as having a problem or condition with presumed biological causes.

While all societies recognize illness and sickness, the concept of disease is a relatively new product of Western culture. "Disease" is used

This article originally appeared in print in the second edition of this reader, published in
1983.

here to refer to *whatever medical practitioners define* as a cause of illness (Freidson, 1970:206, passim). This explanation may seem overly general, but it is impossible to be more specific when the phenomena considered as disease in our society, let alone others, are as varied as bacterial infection, diabetes, alcohol "dependence," and *anorexia nervosa* (an inability or unwillingness to eat). It is commonly believed by the public that a condition seen as a disease has a known biophysiological cause and cure. There is widespread acceptance within Western biomedicine of the theory that certain bacteria produce toxic reactions in human hosts; but the causes and cures of the other conditions mentioned above are not well understood at all. With regard to alcohol dependence, there is at present no single accepted theory as to its cause, nor is there even an adequate definition of "dependence" (Conrad and Schneider, 1980:82–102). And even with the bacterium, it is not necessarily the case that a disease will be recognized.

As Dubos (1959), Freidson (1970), and Dingwall (1976) have argued, diseases do not exist "in nature," but rather are culturally created *meanings* attached to particular conditions by human beings. As Sedgwick put it, "the blight that strikes at corn or potatoes is a *human invention*, for if man wished to cultivate parasites (rather than corn or potatoes) there would be no 'blight.' " And, "the invasion of a human organism by cholera germs carries with it no more the stamp of 'illness' than the souring of milk by other forms of bacteria" (Sedgwick, 1972:211). In order for a condition to come to be seen or interpreted as a disease, *it must first be considered a problem* by many members of a society. In societies in which diarrhea is widespread, for instance, this condition may be seen as normal rather than problematic, although in our own culture it is viewed as a problem to be dealt with by medicine and, therefore, evidence of disease.

If a problematic condition is related in some way to biological functioning, and if no means of control by other than medical techniques (for instance, prayer or legal action) are considered acceptable, medical practitioners may attempt to deal with it. In some cases, a medical treatment is discovered *before* the problem comes to be seen in medical terms. For instance, the discovery that the stimulant Ritalin has a tranquilizing effect on children led to the interpretation of children's disruptive behavior, short attention span, and fidgeting as a disease called hyperkinesis. Previously, such children were simply defined as "bad" and dealt with by teachers and parents as such (Conrad, 1975). In other cases, the medical profession has come to view certain conditions as diseases even though there is little evidence as to biological causes and no medical cure or effective treatment. Such was the case with many of the conditions which have come to be seen as "mental illness" rather than as sinful or illegal behavior (Szasz, 1961, 1970; Conrad and Schneider, 1980).

The process by which a condition comes to be viewed as a disease is in some respects a political one. That is, some groups may lobby for or against a disease interpretation. In our own society, a major lobbying effort by various homosexual organizations led to the removal of homosexuality from the list of mental illnesses in 1974 (Conrad and Schneider, 1980:204–8). Pediatric radiologists lobbied to have Battered Child Syndrome seen as a mental illness of parents who use violent techniques of child-rearing (Conrad and Schneider, 1980:163–66). Such behavior was not even viewed as a "problem" two centuries ago, let alone a "disease."

The final decisions as to whether a condition will be interpreted as a disease are made by those physicians who are in charge of preparing the diagnostic manuals of the profession. The U.S. government's National Institutes of Health and the World Health Organization based in Geneva, Switzerland, are in large part responsible for the listing of diseases. There may be widespread agreement among medical practitioners as to the decisions reached by these groups, or there may be less of a consensus. In some cases, votes have been taken of medical practitioners throughout the country, with the majority view determining whether a condition is or is not a disease.

It is often difficult for us to accept the position that the diseases recognized by Western biomedicine are socially constructed, because medical models for interpreting conditions have become deeply embedded in our culture's common stock of knowledge and are now part of our taken-for-granted reality. In fact, social scientists have sometimes argued that some diseases are "real" while some (such as alcohol use, violence toward children, and *anorexia nervosa*) are "abnormal" *behaviors* which happen to have physiological consequences but which are *not* "real" diseases. In doing so, they are participating in part in our culture's taken-for-granted reality. Rather than arguing what should and should not properly be called a disease, I have adopted the view here that disease is what medical practitioners say it is. This view will allow us to focus on *how practitioners treat* those they define as diseased.

Following these three definitions, we can see that one may *define oneself* as "ill" or claim to have an illness; be *diagnosed* as having a "disease" by a medical practitioner; and/or come to be *seen as* "sick" by parents, teachers, and co-workers. A moment's reflection will illustrate that these three distinct statuses are not necessarily occupied simultaneously. For instance, one may perceive oneself to be healthy, yet be diagnosed as having a disease and come to be viewed by significant others as sick. Or, one may feel ill, but be regarded as healthy (disease free) by medical practitioners and as healthy (not sick) by one's spouse and boss. In societies such as ours where the legitimacy of medical practitioners as experts is great, definitions of disease have a strong influence on the individual's definition of him- or herself as ill and the significant others' determination of sickness.

## SICKNESS AS DEVIANCE

To understand the conceptual link between the control of sickness and social control in general, it is helpful first to come to view sickness (or impairment) as a special case or form of *deviance*, as medical sociologist Eliot Freidson argued cogently almost two decades ago (1970:205–23; see also Mechanic, 1968:44–48; Goffman, 1963; Zola, 1972; Twaddle, 1973).

### Deviance as a Label

Deviance is *not* a quality of an act or state which exists outside the confines of culture, but is rather a meaning, designation, or label which is both created by societal members and attached to particular individuals and/or to their behavior in the course of social interaction (Becker, 1973; Lemert, 1962, 1972; Katz, 1975). A behavior itself has no meaning unless societal members assign it one within their cultural framework of norms and within their understanding of situational contexts. Two individuals may engage in precisely the same behavior, yet one will be viewed as normal and the other as a criminal. The labeling process involves locating the individual within a more or less elaborate classification system as, say, a sex pervert or a check forger. In short, as situations are defined (Thomas, 1923), so are individuals—some as deviant, some as normal.

### Sickness as a Label

As implied in my introduction above, a similar labeling process occurs regarding illness, sickness, and disease. This labeling process involves the use of the culture's "common stock of knowledge" and its stock of "expert knowledge" to make sense of or interpret a societal member's problematic physiological states and experiences. It must first be determined if the individual is to be seen as healthy or unhealthy. Then the unhealthy individual is classified (by self or others) as suffering from a particular type of ill health. The problematic physiological conditions or states we experience ourselves or recognize in others are almost always *ambiguous*; that is, they could be interpreted in a number of different ways even within one culture. For example, if an individual notices some physiological change, that change may be attributed to illness or it may (1) be seen as a non-problem or (2) be seen as a consequence of tiredness, possession by the devil, laziness, or some other "cause" that is culturally acceptable. ("Is this pain 'normal,' or am I having a heart attack?," "I may be getting the flu, or I may just be working too hard,"

"I've never thought about it this way before, but maybe his behavior does indicate that he is mentally ill.")

Recent research by David Locker indicates that a general pattern often followed by lay individuals in Western societies is first to define a problematic experience tentatively as "normal" until later evidence or the input of others causes a change in interpretation (1981:87–92; see also Zola, 1973). Medical practitioners, on the other hand, tend to view even the most ambiguous symptoms as evidence of disease (Freidson, 1970: 263; Scheff, 1966:105–27; Rosenhan, 1973). Whatever the general tendencies of the parties involved in interpreting states of health, it is clear that the process of definition is a negotiated one. Our own interpretations are "validated" by checking them with others (Berger and Luckmann, 1966; Locker, 1981:62, passim). ("What do you think, Doctor? Is this sore throat serious?" "Do you think these spots are measles, Mom?" A physician says, "It doesn't *look* serious to me, but how do you *feel*?") All stages of the process of interpretation, validation, reinterpretation, and so on are rooted in interaction. The label "unhealthy" is, therefore, a negotiated social product. And the process of defining always involves comparison against a similarly socially constructed definition of "health" or "normality" (Lewis, 1953).

## Societal Reaction to Labels

The act of labeling someone as either deviant or unhealthy usually implies that some sorts of responses will be made by societal members which are different from their responses to those labeled as non-deviants or healthy. As Lennard et al. put it, labels are instructions or messages for treatment, not just descriptive categories (1971). The sick person is considered "not normal," as is the deviant; and the reactions of societal members to the mugger, to the drunk driver, to the genius, or to the sick are not the same as responses to "normal" people. Various attempts, legal or medical, are often made to return deviants and the sick to a relatively normal state of functioning and/or to protect other societal members from interaction with them. In fact, it is by viewing these societal reactions that sociologists determine whether or not deviance or sickness exists. That is, an individual can be said to be deviant or sick *when others respond as if* that person belonged in the category (Becker, 1973; Sudnow, 1967). Moreover, the sick are labeled and reacted to as deviants.

## Blame and Discreditation

To be sure, the term deviance usually carries negative connotations (except in the case of the "positive" deviant, e.g., the genius or the hero), while the term sickness may not (Locker, 1981:4–5). It is a general norm in most cultures that people viewed as sick are not to be blamed for their conditions or states (a "right"), if they act in ways that indicate their desire to improve (a "duty") (Parsons, 1951). On the other hand, those recognized as deviants are commonly felt to be able to control their actions and are therefore blamed for them (Locker, 1981:4–5). While the sick are described as "victims of" or "suffering from" diseases which they "contract," deviants presumably choose to act or think in certain ways—and are viewed by some as having more in common with disease than with the sick.

This generalization breaks down, however, when we consider the cases of venereal disease and obesity, both of which are conditions recognized as diseases that evoke blame from many members of society (Cahnman, 1979). Studies of physicians' attitudes toward those labeled as alcoholics show that the majority hold alcoholics personally responsible for drinking (Conrad and Schneider, 1980:98). It is also common for medical practitioners to complain that some of their clients "bring their illness on themselves" by their living habits or by their disregard of medically meaningful symptoms until they reach an advanced state (Millman, 1976; Locker, 1981: 138–39).[2] These practitioners are blaming the sick.

More important, there is a "moral" aspect to sickness; sickness may not evoke blame, but neither does it evoke credit. Many sicknesses call forth severe negative evaluations of the moral worth of the sick, resulting in revulsion or ostracism—as in the cases of Typhoid Mary, those with disfiguring birth defects, the mentally ill, epileptics, and lepers (Goffman, 1963). In fact, medical anthropologist Horacio Fábrega (1974) has concluded from extensive research that, in all known societies, designating an individual as sick *inevitably involves discreditation* of that person. Over and above the fact that the sick person may not be blamed for his or her condition, he or she is not viewed as being as worthy, as creditable, as reliable, or as adequate as the healthy. Thus, the amputee and the flu sufferer, the cancer patient and the mentally ill are seen (to a greater or lesser degree) as less desirable prospective interactants than the healthy—even though the sick can claim a certain amount of sympathy and attention from the healthy. Discreditation in many ways sets up barriers to routine interaction between the sick and the "normal" population in everyday life. It should come as no surprise to find that there is often some reluctance to accept the label of sickness. On the contrary, we should expect an imperfect fit between definitions of disease and sickness, on the one hand, and definitions of illness, on the other.

We now see that sickness, though unique because of its actual or presumed biological causes, has a great deal in common with what is more commonly considered deviance and can, indeed, be seen as one form of deviance. Since the mere fact of defining deviance implies social control, it follows that diagnosing and defining disease and sickness imply social control as well.

# CONTROL OF SICKNESS

What do gossip, smiles, frowns, awards, imprisonment, stares, fines, and the prescribing of antibiotics have in common? They are all behaviors or structural arrangements which serve to encourage societal members to conform to social norms—to think, to act, and indeed to look in ways which are within the culture's acceptable limits—or to discourage thinking or acting or looking outside acceptable limits. As such they constitute *social control*. Negative sanctions addressed to the deviant may induce return to normality; positive sanctions reward normality. Furthermore, negative sanctions allow those people seen as normal to view the consequences of their potential deviance, and a better understanding of what the boundaries of normality are considered to be is fostered (Dentler and Erikson, 1959).

Cultural norms, values, and beliefs tend to become manifested in our social organization and social structure. "Specialist" social statuses emerge, and patterned ways of dealing with nonconformity develop. Social-control specialists are charged with more than the ordinary degree of responsibility for exercising control, and are commensurately empowered to punish, reward, and treat. These specialists, in general, are termed *agents of social control*. Examples include teacher, judge, prison guard, child-guidance professional, advice columnist, and medical practitioner.

## Practitioners and Social Control

Assume for a moment that we are societal engineers attempting to create a system for organizing and controlling the behavior of societal members so that the group can maintain its existence into the future. One problem we would have to face would be how to insure a reasonable supply of productive members to carry out tasks which are important for societal survival. Our society could not long persist if most of its members were sick most of the time, since sickness is almost universally seen as a legitimate reason for not engaging in one's regular social functions, such as feeding and dressing oneself, going to school, going to work, and caring for others. That is, one of the norms of the sick role is that those recognized as legitimately sick should not be required to carry out their normal responsibilities (Parsons, 1951). One societal problem, then, is to guarantee that not everyone is sick—enters the sick role—at the same time.

Additionally, we may find that continual performance of social functions by our societal members, day in and day out, rain or shine, may prove difficult and stressful. An occasional release from the demands of work, family, and community roles may make it easier for our members to function—and the population easier to control—over the long run.

Thus, another problem is to provide "safety valves," occasional releases from constant drudgery, for our societal members.

As societal engineers, we might devise any number of strategies to deal with these problems. One such strategy might be to rely on medical practitioners as our agents of social control. While the process is by no means as conscious and formal as this hypothetical case makes it seem, we submit that practitioners have come to function in just such a manner in all societies.

## Treatment as Social Control

Let us take up these problems in order, beginning with supplying productive societal members. The reader will recall that the designation of sickness brings with it discreditation. It might be suggested that this discreditation, coupled with pain and suffering, could be sufficient to motivate people to return to normality or to feel inadequate enough to shun association with normal individuals. Rather than trusting solely to the motivation and abilities of the afflicted individuals to get better, however, all societies have evolved one or more "specialist" positions of medical practitioner (Hughes, 1968). Practitioners—shamans, mechanics, physicians, and the like—are relied upon by their societies to develop models or theories of what illness is, how it is caused, and how it can be eliminated or controlled, thereby contributing to the maintenance of a reasonable supply of productive societal members.

A rather small number of *techniques* of medical treatment have been devised in the course of human history. Drugs, poultices, surgery, bone setting, confinement and isolation, instrumental interventions (such as acupuncture, electric shock, or leeching), talking, ritual, magic, and appeal to the supernatural—all are techniques which have been used by medical practitioners in a wide variety of societies to control sickness and the sick. These techniques have been put to use in several *forms* or *modes* of social control: (1) returning the sick to normal functioning, (2) punishment, (3) isolation, and—occasionally—(4) altering society to prevent or alleviate sickness.

A few words are in order concerning the general implications of the disease concept of Western biomedicine for treatment in our society. Some belief systems, including Christian Science, see the causes of illness in the supernatural rather than in disease. Other systems have pointed to the social conditions of poverty and crowding as the causes of illness (Twaddle and Hessler, 1977:9–11). Our current belief system views illness as a result of foreign organisms attacking a person or an organ of a person or as a result of the malfunctioning of the body itself. In a word, we view disease as the cause of illness and as "person-centered" rather than societally, environmentally, or supernaturally centered. Our searches for cures and treatments for those conditions we interpret as disease-caused are, therefore, likely to focus on the individual level. The great success of germ theory in controlling illness related to microbial infection has probably been responsible for this thrust in Western biomedicine, although germ theory has come to be recognized as not very useful for understanding chronic, degenerative, or mental illnesses (Strauss, 1975; Twaddle and Hessler, 1977:13–15). *As a result of the person-centered disease concept, control and treatment of sickness often means control and treatment of the sick individuals, as we shall see below.*

RETURN TO NORMALITY: First, medical techniques may be used in an effort to return the sick to a level of functioning as close as possible to, or better than, that existing before the onset of sickness. (Of course, the societal expert, the medical practitioner, has a large voice in determining what is "normal.") Thus, the physician prescribes drugs in an attempt to rid the body of toxic microbes or to reduce the effects of stress, sets a broken bone, or removes abnormal tissues. The shaman or *curandero* (curer) administers herbs to try to reduce fever. Early physicians in the U.S. who viewed "Negritude" (the state of being Negro) as a disease used drugs, poultices, and the like to change blacks into whites (Szasz, 1970:153–59). All of these activities have as their goal, at least partially, the return of the sick person to "normality." This form of social control is the one which is most widely recognized as an appropriate goal of medical treatment, since it is usually assumed to be in line with the interests of the individual sufferer as well as the interests of the society.

PUNISHMENT: Second, both treatment itself and certain healers in specific may serve to punish the sick, whether the healers are conscious of this effect or not.[3] Punishment may encourage return to normality among the sick as well as signaling to the normal the consequences of their potential lapses from normality.

*Confinement* in a hospital is often deemed punishing by the hospital's clients (Roth, 1972:426–28). The restrictions and routines of the bureaucratically organized hospital demand that the client give up claims to privacy, mobility, and liberty in general. Diet and sleeping times are out of the control of the client. Even ambulatory clients are often refused permission to leave the hospital temporarily; those who do so may forfeit the benefits of medical insurance and the right to future care (Roth, 1973).

A more extreme case of this general rule applies in the case of incarceration in a mental hospital (especially involuntary incarceration). Not only are daily activities regimented, conformity to dress regulations enforced, and personal liberty circumscribed, but civil rights are forfeited (Szasz, 1970:65–66). All of these practices lead to a redefinition of self for the client (Goffman, 1961; Scheff, 1966). Additionally, non-ordinary measures are adopted in the mental hospital to ensure conformity to the bureaucratic regimen, such as routine administration of large quantities and dosages of tranquilizing drugs (Rosenhan, 1973), assignment to solitary confinement, and the use of the straitjacket. These techniques may be painful and/or dangerous, as is electroconvulsive shock, still a common form of "treatment" for the depressed which is quite often viewed explicitly as punishment by the clients. Psychiatrist Thomas Szasz has noted the punishing aspects of the treatment of mental patients, stating that "people often prefer a cure that kills to no cure at all" (1982).

Moreover, incarceration in a mental hospital produces *stigma* so great as to limit the ex-patient's ability to participate in society after his or her release (Goffman, 1961). Ex-convicts may be more readily accepted as neighbors, workers, and friends than ex-mental patients. Phillips (1963) reports that public views of the so-called mentally ill are more negative in cases where hospitalization has occurred than when less formalized treatment has been given or when no treatment at all was administered. Hospitalization, rather than the individual's behavior, elicited stigma.

Outside the realm of the hospital as well, examples of the use of medical techniques as punishment can be found. Barker-Benfield (1976) documents, for instance, the widespread practice during the late 1800s and early 1900s in the United States of performing hysterectomies and clitoroidectomies to eliminate "non-feminine" behavior in women. Sterilization operations performed on the poor and the mentally retarded (usually women) without their informed consent serve to remove the rewards of parenthood from people considered unworthy (Davis, 1974; Vaughan, 1974; Caress, 1975) as the family-planning movement of the 1960s may also have done (Kammeyer et al., 1975).

Additionally, programs to "help" handicapped or impaired populations are often punitive in their effects (Freidson, 1966; Sussman, 1966; Wiseman, 1979), a point of which many handicapped are painfully aware. Scott (1969) found that the blind, for example, very often attempted to avoid the label of blindness and the services of agencies to aid the blind. They recognized that, by accepting the label, they would be set apart from sighted society both symbolically—as when white canes and guide dogs signal a deviant condition—and physically—as a result of work and leisure activities organized for the blind only. These consequences of defining themselves as blind and accepting "help" were considered punishments by many.

In a less severe form, contacts with medical personnel in our society involve a host of other *degradations* and *inconveniences* related to the unequal distribution of power in the client-practitioner relationship. In most cases these days, the client (the sufferer) must leave his/her own surroundings and travel to receive services from the practitioner on the latter's home "turf." The cost in time and money is added to the *interactional* disadvantage to the client of trying to maintain poise in strange surroundings. As Barry Schwartz points out elsewhere in this book, the expenditure of time in waiting is a cost also borne disproportionately by the client. The use of mystifying terminology and jargon by medical personnel underscores the client's feelings of ignorance and the practitioner's status as an "insider." Outright condescension by the practitioner that challenges the client's competence may also occur (Locker, 1981: 155–65).

Although the client is the one who has the problematic condition, it is common in our society to treat the sick as though they cannot be trusted to be "in their right minds" when giving accounts of what they are experiencing. Clients' assessments of their own conditions are, therefore, often ignored or discounted, adding to their feelings of helplessness. The "good patient" is one who asks no questions, turning control over his or her fate to the practitioner (Glogow, 1973).

As if this were not enough, the client may be asked to disrobe. In most settings in our society, nudity or semi-nudity puts one at a severe interactional disadvantage. Members of what other occupational groups are allowed to remain clothed while interacting with clients who sit or lie *sans* apparel? The gynecological exam is an example of one situation fraught with embarrassment and uneasiness, in part for this reason (Emerson, 1970).

If medical treatment can be costly or punishing in terms of loss of liberty, pain, danger, stigmatization, and degradation, it is also costly in *monetary* terms in our society. The United States is one of the very few industrialized countries in the world today in which the sick person is expected to pay the costs of services as they are rendered—i.e., when he or she is ill (Waitzkin and Waterman, 1974; Navarro, 1976).[4] Other societies finance medical care with public funds, the practitioners receiving salaries or yearly "capitation" payments for each client under their care, rather than collecting a fee from the ill for each service performed (Anderson, 1972). Some segments of our population—the poor and the elderly—receive some aid with medical bills, and medical insurance (itself very costly) eases or diffuses the financial burden for many others. Still, ours is a nation in which high medical costs lead many to delay or forego treatment and in which a catastrophic condition or accident may result in severe financial difficulty for the sick and their family members. Medical costs, then, may be seen as a type of disincentive to seek treatment, or as a punishment similar to a fine levied by a judge or jury.

Closely related to the financing issue is that of *"unnecessary"* medical procedures. In essence, the practitioner in the United States can create a portion of the "demand" for his or her services by recommending that clients be observed and/or treated. The fee-for-service method of paying physicians encourages high rates of service, since procedures ranging from laboratory tests to surgery are financially beneficial to the practitioner. Some examples of commonly overrecommended procedures are hysterectomies, tonsillectomies, routine blood work, and the annual physical checkup (Scully, 1980; Millman, 1976; Freidson, 1970:257–58). The costs to the client of unnecessary procedures can be measured in terms of pain and suffering (occasionally death), money, time, and inconvenience.

Many of us are not used to thinking of medical treatment as having such a wide variety of punishing aspects. Or, we calculate the benefits of medical care as outweighing the costs. Nevertheless, medical treatment does entail costs and punishments. To the extent that these punishments encourage those who are sick to return to "normal" and those who are not sick to remain healthy, society "benefits" from them and they function as social control.

ISOLATION: A third major form of medical social control over sickness involves *protecting the healthy by removal of the sick person* from his or her normal environment. A quarantine approach such as this is based on a *contagion model* of the cause of illness, in which the removal of the "bad apple" is deemed appropriate to prevent the spread of the condition to others. It has been most often applied when evidence exists that a microbe is causing an illness. Room (1975) argues, however, that the contagion-quarantine model is the logic increasingly applied in the case of drug use (a newly recognized disease). The drug user is seen as capable of "infecting" others and thus must be removed from normal society to a special location, for the protection of the larger group. Additionally, the public relies on the staff of the mental hospital to isolate those mental patients believed to be dangerous to others. Thus, we can see that some aspects of incarcerating people in mental hospitals and segregating the handicapped, in addition to punishing them, fit with this model of protection of the healthy.

In a similar vein, medical diagnosis and treatment may serve as a sorting process for other societal institutions. By certifying who is healthy, the physician aids employers, the military, sports teams, and the like to select healthy members and reject others (Daniels, 1969; Illich, 1976: 76–77).

ALTERING SOCIETY: Fourth, and more rarely, social organization itself may be altered in order to control sickness. Stressful working conditions may be eliminated, sanitation systems may be put into operation, pollution-producing industrial practices may be controlled, and so on. (See Reverby, 1972, for further discussion of health-promoting measures as distinct from illness-response measures.) Such practices are usually regarded in our society as in the province of public health, a branch of medicine which is distinctly lower in prestige and monetary rewards than those branches which take a more person-centered approach to control. The concern is often voiced that altering societal conditions is more expensive than treating persons; yet, with more than one of every ten dollars of the total Gross National Product of the United States being spent on medicine ($425 billion, or more than $1300 per person, in 1985; *World Almanac*, 1987), it is difficult to view costs alone as the reason for the limited use of societal alterations. For whatever reasons, we see again that control of sickness is often accomplished by controlling the sick.

### Sickness As Social Control

We turn now to the issue of release from the lifelong burden of societal responsibilities. Vacations provide a degree of release (except for mothers who attend to child-care duties whether the family is at home or away). Sleep also, in addition to having physiological benefits, allows the individual to escape temporarily from the pressures of interaction (Schwartz, 1970). Another form of release occurs when one is defined as sick and enters the sick role, as Talcott Parsons noted over thirty years ago (1951). Because most conditions are temporary and self-limiting, and because the sick person is expected (1) to want to improve and (2) to cooperate with the experts in order to do so, the release associated with sickness is usually temporary and controlled. Medical practitioners, as the primary legitimate definers of sickness, serve as *gatekeepers* channeling people into the sick role. They serve as societal agents controlling "release time." The uses of treatment discussed above are then brought into play to channel the sick out of the temporary role. Thus, sickness itself, defined and controlled by medical practitioners, may serve an important social-control function for society.

The importance of the sick role as a safety valve has long been recognized by prison officials who must maintain control over their "societies of inmates." Prisoners in most penal facilities are routinely cycled through sick bay, presenting their claims of illness to practitioners who confirm or deny them (Twaddle, 1976). When prison physicians adopt get-tough policies and refuse to legitimate claims to illness, control of the prisoners often becomes difficult or impossible to accomplish (Waitzkin and Waterman, 1974:46–52).[5] In the prison context—and in the military as well (Waitzkin and Waterman, 1974:56)—allowing people to enter the sick role on a temporary basis facilitates social control in the long run. The medical practitioner may be seen as providing an important social-control service here as in the larger society.

## THE MEDICALIZATION OF SOCIAL CONTROL IN THE UNITED STATES

It should be clear by this point that medical practitioners have a great potential for wielding power to the end of social control. In our own society, that power has increased dramatically over the past half century or so, for several interrelated reasons. First, our own trust and faith in the medical profession has increased, legitimating and reinforcing the power of healers (Krause, 1977). Few question the expertise of the medical profession, the benefits of prescribed treatments, or the size of the medical bill. Medical models of defining problematic experiences and medical techniques of treating them have caught on in the lay public's consciousness and imagination. Whereas medical explanations of events—or definitions of situations—were once regarded with suspicion or hostility or amused tolerance, the medical approach has become not only accepted but also popularized and has entered the common stock of knowledge of our culture. That is, the lay public themselves increasingly invoke medical models to define situations, states, and events. Medical metaphors abound: "There is a cancer growing on the presidency." "We live in a sick world." "If you don't take that offer, you're crazy." "Surgery is required to rid ourselves of the tangle of laws governing this area." Medical diagnoses by lay persons are legion: "That's just a virus." "John has strep throat." "Of course, your headache is due to stress." Furthermore, many occupational groups such as social workers and parole officers are adopting medical and para-medical approaches to their clients, thereby borrowing a degree of prestige from medicine (Chalfant, 1977).

Second, the profession of medicine has achieved a state of professional autonomy of impressive magnitude (Freidson, 1970; Brown, 1979). Physicians, unlike most other occupational groups, control the production of new members by determining the content of medical education and the numbers and types of new recruits. Licensing of physicians also rests solely in the hands of the medical profession. Medical mistakes (deviance among the agents of social control) are dealt with mainly within the medical community, despite what the widespread publicity of some recent legal suits brought against physicians might lead us to believe (Millman, 1976). Fees for medical services are also subject to little outside regulation. The terms, hours, and content of physicians' jobs are dictated by no outside source, except perhaps the clients' willingness and ability to pay for certain types of services. Physicians enjoy a great deal of autonomy and freedom from outside intervention in their own profession, and they also exercise control and influence over other medical groups, such as nursing, pharmacy, and the like (Freidson, 1970:47–70). The trend toward group- and hospital-based practice, and especially the rise of medical "empires" connected with university research-and-teaching hospitals, have contributed to a heightening and consolidation of medical control over their own and other occupational groups (Ehrenreich and Ehrenreich, 1970).

Third, and perhaps most important, more and more conditions have come to be defined as diseases every year by the medical profession. Currently there are more than a thousand categories of disease. A large proportion of the new diseases recognized since World War II are behavioral rather than physiological in origin, and most fall into the general category of "functional" mental illness (Conrad and Schneider, 1980: 53). Hundreds of conditions have been added to the medical nosology in recent decades, including obesity, sociopathy, alcoholism, hyperactivity in children, *anorexia nervosa*, minimal brain dysfunction, and drug addiction. These conditions once were interpreted in terms of "sin" or "badness" or "illegality" but are now routinely conceived of as actual diseases. Another candidate for disease status is *hysteroid dysphoria*, a recently coined term to describe "love junkies" who feel a need to be in love. "Limerance" is another recently created term for this love obsession, although some prefer the less mystifying "lovesickness." Drug therapy is offered by some physicians for this condition (Sobel, 1980). Although *hysteroid dysphoria* may not ultimately come to be widely recognized as a disease, many other conditions undoubtedly will. Thus, the domain of medicine is expanding, and the proportion of the population subject to treatment with medical techniques is growing correspondingly. The increase in the number of disease categories explains in part the increased expenditures for medicine in our society, from about five percent of the Gross National Product in 1950 to ten percent today (Fenninger and Meeker, 1980:6).

In sum, social control can be said to be increasingly medicalized, because both the power and domain of medicine have expanded, with the blessing of the lay public.

## SOCIOLOGICAL IMPLICATIONS

In concluding, I should note a few of the implications of the increased medicalization of social control for American society which are of particular sociological importance. First, social control is achieved over many types of problems without the imposition of extreme degrees of discreditation. Since blame is often not assigned to the sick, they may receive attention and support not available under other systems of social control. Furthermore, much medical treatment is more effective and efficient than previous methods of control. In these cases, employing medical models to define and treat conditions is actually useful to individuals and/or to society. This outcome, which may be more humane than the effects of legal social control, is balanced, however, with others not as sanguine.

Second, medical treatment is less readily recognized as social control than is legal intervention. While the court and the prison are seen as overtly "on society's side," medicine is presumed (as is religion) to act in the interests of the individual. This presumption is particularly dangerous given the great power, prestige, and influence of medical practitioners vis-à-vis their clients. If the social-control functions of medical treatments are not obvious, we are less likely to provide safeguards for individual rights in this arena (Kittrie, 1971; Mechanic, 1973). Social control is not recognized as such and, in a manner of speaking, goes underground. Currently, legal and ethical debates are surfacing over the rights of clients to refuse treatment, to be informed of medical diagnoses and procedures, and to ask questions of medical practitioners regarding their bills. These debates may signal a degree of public awareness of the problems of "hidden" social control.

A third consequence of the medicalization of social control is not unique to medicine, but it is nonetheless important. The person-centered nature of much medical treatment focuses attention away from societal problems and "privatizes" them. That is to say, what *could* be viewed as a failure of societal organization and structure comes to be interpreted as the "failure" of the individual. Conrad (1975) gives a telling example to illustrate this point in his analysis of hyperactivity in children. What could have been seen as a problem of rigidly organized schools has become a disease located in the child. Treatment involves drug therapy for the individual rather than a restructuring of the school environment.

Stress provides yet another example. Stress has increasingly come to be seen as related to any manner of other problematic conditions, from digestive-tract problems to suicide to the susceptibility to influenza. Medical models of stress have tended to focus on the individual and to find solutions in psychoanalysis or tranquilizers or physical exercise. By focusing thus, attention is shifted from societal conditions—time clocks, traffic jams, deadlines, competition, rapid social change, and unemployment—to the person. Taking the opposite, society-centered approach, Brenner has found evidence for increases in suicides and heart problems corresponding to increases in unemployment (1973). Evidence such as this calls into question the usefulness of person-centered approaches to disease. That is, from the standpoint of the individual or from the standpoint of the society, medical models for defining and treating some human problems may not be useful at all, *over the long run*. The society, by not paying attention to social-structural problems, may allow them to grow to the point that they are insoluble.

## NOTES

1. Impairment and disability may also be considered as categories similar to illness (Freidson, 1966); but, for the sake of brevity, I will not make continued reference to impairment and disability.

2. Of course, clients may also be criticized for presenting themselves to their physicians with "unimportant" or "nonexistent" symptoms (Locker, 1981:62, passim)—a classic double-bind situation for the client.

3. I am ignoring in this discussion the issue of iatrogenic (treatment- or physician-produced) disease or impairment, since I assume that most cases of this

type are accidental. Nonetheless, iatrogenic conditions are a common feature of treatment. It is estimated that about 20 per cent of hospital clients leave the hospital with a problem they did not have when they entered (Roth, 1972). Illich contends that the increased tendency of the population to seek care in modern times has meant that treatment has become a considerable public-health problem (Illich, 1976:26–34, passim). To the extent that clients and potential clients are aware of the dangers involved in medical treatment, that aspect of treatment may be seen as a deterrent or punishment.

4. For a more detailed discussion of the problems inherent in the U.S. system of medical-care financing, see Fuchs (1974) and Carlson (1976).

5. Note that I am not attempting to judge whose claims are more valid, the prisoner's or the physician's. In fact, in most cases it probably makes little difference, since the power to define rests so one-sidedly with the practitioner in the prison setting.

## REFERENCES

Anderson, Odin W.
  1972 *Health Care: Can There Be Equity? The United States, Sweden and England.* New York: Wiley.

Barker-Benfield, G. J.
  1976 *The Horrors of the Half-Known Life.* New York: Harper & Row.

Becker, Howard S.
  1973 *Outsiders: Studies in the Sociology of Deviance* (2nd ed.). New York: Free Press.

Berger, Peter, and Thomas Luckmann
  1966 *The Social Construction of Reality: A Treatise in the Sociology of Knowledge.* Garden City, N.Y.: Doubleday.

Brenner, M. Harvey
  1973 *Mental Illness and the Economy.* Cambridge: Harvard University Press.

Brown, E. Richard
  1979 *Rockefeller Medicine Men: Medicine and Capitalism in America.* Berkeley: University of California Press.

Cahnman, Werner
  1979 "The Moral Treatment of Obesity." Pp. 439–54 in Howard Robboy, Sidney L. Greenblatt, and Candace Clark, eds., *Social Interaction* (1st ed.). New York: St. Martin's Press.

Caress, Barbara
  1975 "Sterilization: Fit to Be Tied," *Health/PAC Bulletin* 62:1–6, 10–13.

Carlson, Rick J.
  1976 *The End of Medicine.* New York: Wiley-Interscience.

Chalfant, Paul
  1977 "Professionalization and the Medicalization of Deviance: The Case of Probation Officers," *Offender Rehabilitation* 2:77–85.

Conrad, Peter
  1975 "The Discovery of Hyperkinesis: Notes on the Medicalization of Deviant Behavior," *Social Problems* 23:12–21.

Conrad, Peter and Joseph Schneider
  1980 *Deviance and Medicalization: From Badness to Sickness.* St. Louis: Mosby.

Daniels, Arlene Kaplan
  1969 "The Captive Professional: Bureaucratic Limitation in the Practice of Military Psychiatry," *Journal of Health and Social Behavior* 10:255–65.

Davis, Morris E.
  1974 "Involuntary Sterilization: A History of Social Control," *Journal of Black Perspectives* 1:46.

Dentler, Robert A. and Kai T. Erikson
  1959 "The Functions of Deviance in Groups," *Social Problems* 7:98–107.

Dingwall, Robert
  1976 *Aspects of Illness.* New York: St. Martin's Press.

Dubos, Rene
  1959 *Mirage of Health.* Garden City, N.Y.: Doubleday.

Ehrenreich, Barbara and John E. Ehrenreich
  1970 *The American Health Empire.* New York: Random House.

Emerson, Joan P.
  1970 "Behavior in Private Places: Sustaining Definitions of Reality in Gynecological Examinations." Pp. 74–97 in Hans P. Dreitzel, ed., *Recent Sociology No. 2.* New York: Macmillan.

Fábrega, Horacio, Jr.
  1974 *Disease and Social Behavior.* Cambridge: M.I.T. Press.

Fenninger, Randolph B. and Edward F. Meeker
  1980 "Decade of the 1970's: Window on the 1980's: A Review of Health Care Policy." Pp. 3–21 in Gerald L. Glandon and Roberta Shapiro, eds., *Profile of Medical Practice 1980.* Monroe, Wisc.: American Medical Association.

Freidson, Eliot
  1966 "Disability as Social Deviance." Pp. 71–99 in Marvin Sussman, ed., *Sociology and Rehabilitation.* Washington, D.C.: American Sociological Association.
  1970 *Profession of Medicine.* New York: Dodd, Mead.

Fuchs, Victor
  1974 *Who Shall Live? Health, Economics, and Social Choice.* New York: Basic Books.

Glogow, Eli
  1973 "The Bad Patient Gets Better Quicker," *Social Policy* 4:72–76.

Goffman, Erving
  1961 *Asylums.* Garden City, N.Y.: Doubleday.
  1963 *Stigma: Notes on the Management of a Spoiled Identity.* Englewood Cliffs, N.J.: Prentice-Hall.

Hughes, Charles C.
  1968 "Medical Care: Ethnomedicine." Pp. 87–97 in David Sills, ed., *International Encyclopedia of the Social Sciences*, Vol. 10. New York: Crowell, Collier & Macmillan.

Illich, Ivan
  1976 *Medical Nemesis: The Expropriation of Health*. New York: Pantheon.

Kammeyer, Kenneth C. W., Norman R. Yetman, and McKee J. McClendon
  1975 "Race and Public Policy: Family Planning Services and the Distribution of Black Americans." Pp. 402–21 in Norman R. Yetman and C. Hoy Steele, *Majority and Minority: The Dynamics of Racial and Ethnic Relations*, 2nd ed. Boston: Allyn & Bacon.

Katz, Jack
  1975 "Essences as Moral Identities, *American Journal of Sociology* 80:1369–90.

Kittrie, Nicholas
  1971 *The Right to Be Different: Deviance and Enforced Therapy*. Baltimore: Johns Hopkins University Press.

Krause, Elliott A.
  1977 *Power and Illness: The Political Sociology of Health and Medical Care*. New York: Elsevier.

Lemert, Edwin
  1962 "Paranoia and the Dynamics of Exclusion," *Sociometry* 25:2–20.
  1972 *Human Deviance, Social Problems, and Social Control* (2nd ed.). Englewood Cliffs, N.J.: Prentice-Hall.

Lennard, Henry, et al.
  1971 *Mystification and Drug Misuse*. New York: Perennial Library.

Lewis, Aubrey
  1953 "Health as a Social Concept," *British Journal of Sociology* 4:109–24.

Locker, David
  1981 *Symptoms and Illness: The Cognitive Organization of Disorder*. London: Tavistock.

Mechanic, David
  1968 *Medical Sociology: A Selective View*. New York: Free Press.
  1973 "Health and Illness in Technological Societies," *Hastings Center Studies* 1:7–18.

Millman, Marcia
  1976 *The Unkindest Cut: Life in the Backrooms of Medicine*. New York: Morrow.

Navarro, Vicente
  1976 *Medicine under Capitalism*. New York: Prodist.

Parsons, Talcott
  1951 *The Social System*, Chapter 10. Glencoe, Ill.: Free Press.

Phillips, Derek L.
  1963 "Rejection: A Possible Consequence of Seeking Help for Mental Disorders," *American Sociological Review* 28:963–72.

Reverby, Susan
  1972 "A Perspective on the Root Causes of Illness," *American Journal of Public Health* 62:1140–42.

Room, Robin
  1975 "The Epidemic Model and Its Assumptions," *Quarterly Journal of Studies in Alcohol* 1:16–21.

Rosenhan, David L.
  1973 "On Being Sane in Insane Places," *Science* 179:250–58.

Roth, Julius
  1972 "The Necessity and Control of Hospitalization," *Social Science and Medicine* 6:425–46.
  1973 "The Right to Quit," *Sociological Review* 21:381–96.

Scheff, Thomas
  1966 *Being Mentally Ill.* Chicago: Aldine.

Schwartz, Barry
  1970 "Notes on the Sociology of Sleep," *Sociological Quarterly* 11:485–99.

Scott, Robert A.
  1969 *The Making of Blind Men.* New York: Russell Sage.

Sobel, Dava
  1980 "In Pursuit of Love: Three Current Studies," *New York Times,* Jan. 22, III, 1; 5.

Strauss, Anselm L.
  1975 *Chronic Illness and the Quality of Life.* St. Louis: Mosby.

Sudnow, David
  1967 *Passing On: The Social Organization of Dying.* Englewood Cliffs, N.J.: Prentice-Hall.

Sussman, Marvin (ed.)
  1966 *Sociology and Rehabilitation.* Washington, D.C.: American Sociological Association.

Szasz, Thomas
  1961 *The Myth of Mental Illness.* New York: Hoeber-Harper.
  1970 *The Manufacture of Madness.* New York: Harper-Colophon.
  1982 "The Lady in the Box," editorial, *New York Times,* Feb. 16.

Thomas, W. I.
  1923 *The Unadjusted Girl.* Boston: Little, Brown.

Twaddle, Andrew C.
  1973 "Illness and Deviance," *Social Science and Medicine* 7:751–62.
  1976 "Utilization of Medical Services by a Captive Population: Analysis of Sick Call in a State Prison," *Journal of Health and Social Behavior* 17: 236–48.

Twaddle, Andrew C. and Richard M. Hessler
  1977 *A Sociology of Health.* St. Louis: Mosby.

Vaughan, Denton and Gerald Sparer
1974 "Ethnic Group and Welfare Status of Women Sterilized in Federally Funded Family Planning Programs," *Family Planning Perspectives* 6:224–229.

Waitzkin, Howard B. and Barbara Waterman
1974 *The Exploitation of Illness in Capitalist Society.* Indianapolis: BobbsMerrill.

Wellin, Edward
1978 "Theoretical Orientations in Medical Anthropology: Change and Continuity over the Past Half Century." Pp. 23–39 in Michael H. Logan and Edward E. Hunt, Jr., eds., *Health and the Human Condition: Perspectives on Medical Anthropology.* North Scituate, Mass.: Duxbury.

Wiseman, Jacqueline P.
1979 *Stations of the Lost: The Treatment of Skid Row Alcoholics.* Chicago: University of Chicago Press.

*World Almanac.*
1987 New York: Pharos Books.

Zola, Irving K.
1972 "Medicine as an Institution of Social Control," *Sociological Review* 20: 487–504.
1973 "Pathways to the Doctor: From Person to Patient," *Social Science and Medicine* 7:677–88.

# Review Questions

1. What are the distinctions among illness, sickness, and disease made by Clark?

2. How can sickness be seen as one form of deviance? Discuss situations from your own experience in which a person considered sick was treated, or reacted to, as "not normal."

3. How does the sick role contribute to social control?

4. How does medical treatment contribute to social control?

5. What are some of the consequences for society and for individuals of the medicalization of social control?

# ILLNESS AND THE LEGITIMATION OF FAILURE

## Stephen Cole and Robert Lejeune

ILLNESS EXEMPTS INDIVIDUALS FROM THEIR NORMAL ROLE OBLIGATIONS. Most of us are sick on occasion. Some, however, see themselves as permanently sick. Generally, we associate this adjustment with a serious physiological or psychological breakdown; rarely do we view sociological variables as prompting chronic illness. It is the central hypothesis of this paper[1] that people who come to view themselves as unable to fulfill their normal roles will be motivated to define themselves as permanently sick to legitimize their self-defined failure.[2]

Sociologically, a person is sick when he acts sick. Thus, the conditions that motivate people to view themselves as sick or healthy are important. Clearly, the "objective" physiological condition of one's body plays a major part in self-definition of health. Both medical doctors and social scientists, however, have become increasingly aware that physiological and social-psychological forces intertwine in determining objective and subjective states of health (Crandell and Dohrenwend 1967; Hinkle *et al*. 1956; Mechanic and Volkart 1961; Wolff 1958; Zola 1966). In this paper, we shall discuss one social-psychological determinant of one's subjective health definition. Our data treat the hypothesis that inability to fulfill their role obligations is one factor leading people to define their health as poor. To explore this hypothesis, we shall examine how definition of health relates to a mother's adjustment to being on welfare. We shall also analyze the relationship between definition of health and performance of roles as wives and mothers among a sample of working-class black women.

The data derive from three studies: The first was conducted in New York City in the summer of 1966. The National Opinion Research Center interviewed a probability sample of 2179 female heads of household receiving family public assistance in New York City in April 1966. The second study was conducted in New York City in the summer of 1968. National Analysts interviewed a quota sample of 412 working-class black mothers living in public housing projects. The final study was conducted in Camden, New Jersey, in the summer of 1969. The Center for Research

Stephen Cole and Robert Lejeune. "Illness and the Legitimation of Failure." *American Sociological Review* (June 1972): p347–356.

on the Acts of Man, University of Pennsylvania, interviewed a quota sample of 447 women recipients of Aid to Dependent Children.

The dependent variable in this study is one's subjective health definition. We asked: "In general, would you say your own health is excellent, good, fair, or poor?" A major problem in the analysis is empirically separating the physiological and social-psychological components of health definition. If people fail to fulfill their role obligations because they are physiologically ill, it would make little sense to say they are defining themselves as sick to legitimize failure. In clear-cut cases of physical breakdown such as terminal cancer, heart attacks, or tuberculosis, almost everyone will act ill. However, since practically all respondents in the three surveys are women under fifty, and most are under forty, the frequency of such illness among the respondents would not be high. In less than clear-cut cases, individuals having similar physiological conditions may behave quite differently. Most people have some health problems and some aches and pains; yet they continue to function adequately. Others magnify their aches and pains until they dominate their lives.

Even if we assume that a small minority suffered from clear-cut physiological breakdown, we are still faced with the problem of causal order. Without longitudinal data we do not know if taking the sick role proceeds [from] or precedes a self-definition of failure. Hence, our study is exploratory rather than conclusive. The best we can do to handle the problem of causal order is to show that the relationship between self-defined failure and health persists even when we control for [or hold constant] a few relatively more objective indicators of health such as symptoms, number of doctor-patients contacts, and number of reported illnesses. Our analysis begins with a discussion of the meaning of being on welfare in America.

## WELFARE AS FAILURE

. . . Americans typically see social status as a result of personal success or failure. If someone is socially mobile, it is because he is talented and works hard. If someone is not socially mobile, it is thought to be a result of his personal shortcomings. The individual's location in the social structure is not viewed as a prime determinant of his fate. It is for this reason that many Americans look down on welfare recipients. Many welfare recipients themselves believe that being on welfare signifies personal rather than societal failure.

What evidence is there that welfare recipients accept that stigma attached to their status by the dominant culture? Most welfare recipients have been repeatedly exposed to the view that they are immoral and undeserving. The data indicate that a large number of AFDC mothers share this view. Seventy-one percent of the New York welfare sample agreed with the statement, "A lot of people getting money from welfare don't deserve it." Another ten percent did not know or would not reply and only 19 percent disagreed.[3] If it is objected that some welfare mothers merely wanted to give the "expected" or "right" answer, this confirms our point: that welfare recipients know that the dominant culture defines their status as illegitimate. While we cannot tell from these replies to what extent and with what intensity welfare mothers view themselves as undeserving, they are very likely aware of the stigma attached to their status and probably prone to question the claims of need of other welfare recipients. Thus, it is not surprising that 55 percent of the New York welfare mothers agreed that "getting money from welfare makes a person feel ashamed." And fully 87 percent agreed that "people should be grateful for the money they get from welfare."

The Camden welfare mothers expressed similar views on receiving public assistance. Fifty-seven percent said it was more often true than false that "people I know look down on welfare," and 34 percent admitted that "there are times when I have been embarrassed in front of my family or friends because of being on welfare." Another indicator of whether or not the welfare mothers think of being on welfare as a type of personal failure is provided by their opinions about the conditions under which welfare should be available. For example, 84 percent of the Camden mothers believed that welfare should not be available "if there is one parent (female) and she does not try to keep up her home." We can conclude that at least a substantial proportion of mothers on welfare accept the stigma attached to the status by the general culture. . . . We wish to make explicit at this point that we do not consider welfare mothers to be failures; rather this is the view of many Americans and the data show that many welfare mothers internalize this view.

How do people who define themselves as failures cope with the knowledge of their stigma? One technique of handling this problem is to believe that things will be better in the future. Welfare clients may reduce the conflict between their need for welfare and their perception of their status as an undesirable and degrading one by believing in a welfare-free future for themsevles. Only 25 percent of the New York women thought they would "surely be on welfare" and another thirty-three percent thought that they would "probably be on welfare" a year from the time of the interview. Forty-two percent either did not know or thought they would not be on welfare.[4] Sixty-one percent said yes to the question: "Do you think you will ever (again) work for pay?" While work is not their only way to economic independence, it is certainly the most important for the majority, who are husbandless or whose husbands' earnings cannot support the family. Given the poor objective chances for most welfare mothers to succeed in an economy demanding ever higher levels of training, we would expect most of them to abandon hope. That the opposite is true attests to the continued strength of the dominant goal of success. Seventy percent of both New York and Camden welfare samples say they would rather work that remain home.

## THE LEGITIMATION OF DEPENDENCY

A woman who sees being on welfare as a personal failure but views her own welfare status as temporary may feel no need to justify her dependency; but a woman who has abandoned hope of escape from this position of self-defined failure will probably have a strong need to justify it. Thus, we hypothesize that mothers who no longer think of welfare as a temporary status will be the most likely to use illness to justify their self-defined social failure. We do not argue that welfare mothers consciously use poor health as an excuse for remaining on welfare. Although some may do this, we do not think them typical. More probably, a woman who feels the need to justify her status to herself gradually adopts the sick role. Over time, she comes to feel and act as if she were in fact sick.[5] She is likely to develop a series of psychosomatic symptoms.

Margaret Olendzki (1965), who studied 1976 applicants for public assistance in Manhattan, collected data to support this view. As part of that study, a checklist of medical conditions was presented to each applicant. The most often mentioned health complaint was "nerves," reported by 45 percent of the women respondents who were heads of families and thus correspond most closely to the respondents in our samples. We cross-tabulated the "suffering from nerves" complaint with Olendzki's question on self-defined health. It turns out that defining one's health as poor is highly associated with the presence of emotional complaints. Sixty-nine percent who said their health was poor also said they "suffered from nerves." Sixty-one percent who viewed their health as fair made the same complaint. The proportion who said they were in good and excellent health yet suffered from nerves was smaller, though not unsubstantial: 35 percent and 27 percent respectively. We conclude that welfare mothers who claim to be sick are probably so; however, sociopsychological factors may play at least as great a role as physiological factors in the development of their illness.

We can now present the data bearing on our main hypothesis—that women who have abandoned hope of getting off welfare will be more likely that those who maintain hope to define their health as poor. The New York survey showed that expectation not to work was correlated . . . with definition of health. *Women who did not expect to work were more likely to define their health as poor.* This correlation would be spurious if it disappeared when we controlled for background variables affecting work expectations such as education, age, and a more objective indicator of health. This does not happen. . . . Similarly, removing the variance due to age only slightly reduced the relationship between work expectation and definition of health. . . . Though we have no adequate measure of objective health, we did have data on the number of times the respondent reported she was ill during the preceding year. This health indicator is also a subjective measure. It is far from perfectly correlated with definition of health . . . and thus probably measures at least a different aspect of health conception. When the variance due to this variable was removed, the correlation between work expectation and health definition was hardly changed . . . [I]n each category of number of illnesses, women who do not expect to work in the future are more likely than those who do to define their health as fair or poor.

The Camden survey had similar results. Here we used two questions to measure welfare mothers' attitudes toward their health. Women not currently working were asked why. One choice was that they were "not interested in working at present time—health reason or handicap." Women who did not expect to work in the future were more likely to give this reason. . . . We also asked: "What part does your health play in your decision not to work or in the kind of work you can take?" Women who did not expect to work were more likely to say that health played a part in their decision. . . .

The Camden data allow us to test several hypothesis concerning the conditions under which welfare mothers are likely to use poor health to legitimize their dependency. We have suggested that welfare mothers view being on welfare as a type of failure and that when they give up hope of leaving welfare they develop a need to justify their permanent dependency. Some welfare recipients, however, do not accept the stigma generally attached to their positions. We would expect to find that among women who do not view welfare as a temporary status, those who accept the stigma should be more likely to take the sick role. As an indicator of attitudes toward welfare, we used the score on an index of questions concerning the conditions under which welfare should be available. Those who believe that welfare should not be available unless the recipient lives up to rigorous moral standards are more likely to define welfare as an illegitimate status. As Table 1 indicates, among mothers who expect to get off welfare, attitudes toward welfare have little effect on adopting the sick role. Among mothers not expecting to work, however, those who accept the dominant cultural view of welfare (in the table those who have "strict" attitudes toward the availability of welfare) are more likely than those who reject it (in the table those who have "lenient" attitudes toward the availability of welfare) to adopt the sick role. Clearly both conditions, defining one's status as illegitimate and viewing that status as permanent, contribute to one's adopting the sick role.

A counter theory to explain the data of Table 1 would be that poor health leads a woman to give up hope of working. Collapsing Table 1, we

**Table 1. Percentage giving health as reason for preferring not to work by attitudes toward welfare and expectation to work in the future (Camden Welfare Sample)**

| AVAILABILITY OF WELFARE | | LENIENT | | STRICT | |
|---|---|---|---|---|---|
| | | % | (n) | % | (n) |
| Expect to be working | Yes | 10 | (106) | 12 | (137) |
| in the future | No | 15 | (88) | 26 | (94) |

find that 42 percent of people with poor health and 60 percent of those without poor health expect to work. While poor health may lead women to give up hope of working, this does not explain why women who accept the dominant view of welfare are more likely to view their health as poor than those who reject that view.[6]

## FAMILY CYCLE, AGE, AND LEGITIMATION OF DEPENDENCY

Welfare mothers can use mechanisms other than illness to legitmize failure. One condition influencing the type of mechanism adopted is the family-life cycle. AFDC's primary rationale is that women without husbands should be supported so they can stay home and care for their children. A woman with a preschool child can easily legitimize her dependency. Indeed, 77 percent of the New York women who preferred not to work gave child care as a reason. It is initially surprising to find that only 19 percent of those who prefer not to work gave illness as a reason. We must remember, however, that the respondents were women. Their primary obligations center around expressive family rather than instrumental work roles.[7] We would therefore expect them to be more likely to define their health as poor when they no longer have preschool children.

In both the New York and Camden samples the age of a mother's youngest child was associated with citing health as a reason for preferring not to work. (See Table 2.) Hardly any mother with preschool children, but a substantial proportion of those with school age children, gave poor health as a reason for preferring not to work. Whereas the age of the youngest child is positively associated with giving poor health as a reason for preferring not to work, it is negatively associated with giving child care as a reason. Thus, of the Camden women not expecting to work, 72 percent with children under six and 42 percent with children six or over gave child care as their reason for preferring to stay at home. As long as a mother has young children, she can view her dependency as an objective necessity.

**Table 2. Percentage giving health reason for preferring not to work by age of youngest child (only those preferring not to work)**

| Age of youngest child | N.Y. WELFARE SAMPLE | | |
|---|---|---|---|
| | *0–5* | *6–10* | *11 or Older* |
| | 9 (401) | 20 (143) | 53 (120) |

| Age of youngest child | CAMDEN WELFARE SAMPLE | |
|---|---|---|
| | *Under 6* | *6 or Older* |
| | 14 (145) | 42 (38) |

A possible source of error in our interpretation of the data of Table 2 could be the correlation between the mother's age and the age of the youngest child. Women who have no preschool children are generally older that those who do. The results in Table 2 might be an artifact of the ''self-evident'' fact that older people are more likely to be sick and ''therefore'' less employable. Actually, ''employability'' is a culturally defined state. There are probably few disabilities which restrict work under all circumstances and in all social contexts. The sociologist must therefore view the system's classification of some welfare recipients as ''totally and permanently disabled'' as providing a socially acceptable rationale for the limited opportunities such persons have in the labor market. As in many other areas of social life the labeling process functions to tidy up the bookkeeping of a society riddled with value inconsistencies. That those excluded from participation would seek these labels is a natural outcome of the process.

As a more conclusive test of the family cycle hypothesis it is necessary to see if the relationship between age of youngest child and definition of health persists with the mother's age controlled. (See Table 3.) In Table 3, the age of the youngest child is used as an indicator of the extent of child rearing responsibilities. It turns out that even with mother's age controlled, the age of the youngest child is associated in the expected direction with giving health as a reason for preferring not to work. The association is particularly strong for those over forty. Women over 40 with no children under the age of 11 are almost three times more likely than any other group to give health reasons for preferring not to work. The decline of child-rearing functions, as one aspect of aging, leads to an increasing tendency to legitimize welfare dependency by evoking the sick role. The issue here is not whether older respondents are ''sicker'' than younger ones. Even if they were, only among those whose children are growing

**Table 3. Percentage giving health reasons for preferring not to work by age and age of youngest child (only those preferring not to work) (New York Welfare Sample)**

| AGE OF YOUNGEST CHILD | AGE | | |
|---|---|---|---|
| | *Under 30* | *30–39* | *40 and Over* |
| 0 to 5 | 8 (202) | 9 (165) | 15 (34) |
| 6 to 10 | 13  (16) | 14  (64) | 27 (63) |
| 11 or over | *  (2) | 21  (24) | 63 (94) |

*TOO FEW CASES.

up does poor health become salient as their reason for welfare dependency. We would guess that even middle-class women would be more likely to take the sick role as they age and their child-rearing function declines in significance. A middle-class woman who has devoted her life to rearing children might find poor health an acceptable way of legitimizing to herself her failure to find another socially acceptable status when her children have grown up.

Thus it is evident that though illness plays a small part in legitimizing dependency for the total family welfare population, it becomes one of the primary bases for legitimizing a claim to welfare support among women over 40 whose youngest child has reached adolescence. As these women end their child-rearing years, their chance for economic independence is highly limited. They are over forty, lack a recent job history, and have limited marketable skills. If at the same time they are black or Puerto Rican (as most are), their realistic opportunities for independence are further restricted. The sick role may provide one "substitute" status for the lack of any other socially approved positively evaluated statuses.

In Table 3 it is evident that the mother's age has a strong independent effect on adopting the sick role. Is this predominantly the result of a genuine decline in health with age, or can the finding be explained sociologically? It is necessary to separate the physiological and social components of aging. Although this is impossible given our data, we can control for some relatively more objective indicators of health. In Table 4 the relation between age and giving poor health as a reason for preferring not to work is shown, with the number of reported illnesses in the past year held constant.[8] Table 4 shows once again that with increasing age, welfare mothers are more likely to give poor health as a reason for preferring not to work. This association is found even among women who had reported earlier in the interview that they had not been sick at all in the past year. Thus, even though the number of reported illnesses in the past year may itself have been affected by subjective considerations, older respondents who by their own account had not been ill were nonetheless

**Table 4. Percentage giving health reasons for preferring not to work by age and number of illnesses in the past year (only those preferring not to work.) (New York Welfare Sample)**

| NUMBER OF ILLNESSES IN PAST YEAR: | AGE | | |
|---|---|---|---|
| | Under 30 | 30–39 | 40 and Over |
| None | 1 (86) | 3 (93) | 24 (63) |
| 1 or 2 | 4 (52) | 9 (75) | 37 (51) |
| 3 or more | 18 (80) | 21 (84) | 62 (76) |

more likely than younger respondents to give poor health as a reason for preferring not to work.

Chronological age and number of illnesses have both independent and interactive effects on mentioning poor health as a reason for preferring not to work. Thus, among women under 30, the number-of-illnesses variable accounts for a 17 percentage point difference in the first column of Table 4. There is a similar difference (18 percentage points) in the 30–39 age group. In the 40 and over group, the difference is 38 percentage points, indicating that not only illness per se but more importantly illness combined with aging increases the likelihood that illness will become a basis for legitimizing dependency. Not only does taking the sick role legitimize being on welfare, but age legitimizes taking the sick role. A young person who complains of aches and pains calls forth negative sanctions; an older person calls forth sympathy.

In Table 4, one cannot distinguish between "serious" and "nonserious" illnesses by simply counting the number of self-reported illnesses for the year. It was beyond the scope of the study to measure how seriously ill the women were. This can be approximated, however, by the number of doctor-patient contacts in the past year. We may assume that the sicker respondents would on the average contact physicians more often. Table 5 shows of those women with at least seven doctor-patient contacts in the last year, only 12 percent of the youngest and fully 66 percent of the oldest gave poor health as the reason for preferring not to work. Also, 30 percent of women over 40 who saw the doctor once or not at all during the year made the poor health claim.

## GENERALIZATION OF THE HYPOTHESIS

Thus far we have presented data illustrating how some welfare mothers use illness to legitimize self-defined failure. We believe that this practice is a widespread phenomenon in achievement-oriented societies like ours.[9] Health is perceived as physiologically determined and therefore

**Table 5. Percentage giving health reasons for preferring not to work by age and number of doctor–patient contacts in the past year (only those preferring not to work) (N.Y. Welfare Sample)**

| NUMBER OF DOCTOR–PATIENT CONTACTS IN PAST YEAR: | AGE | | |
|---|---|---|---|
| | *Under 30* | *30–39* | *40 and Over* |
| None or 1 | 5 (88) | 7 (118) | 30 (84) |
| 2 to 6 | 4 (72) | 13 (79) | 38 (69) |
| 7 or more | 12 (60) | 18 (57) | 66 (53) |

basically beyond individual control. If one fails to fulfill a socially defined role expectation, she is not to be blamed if she has poor health.

We decided to test the validity of this generalization on another set of data. We were interested in whether or not mothers and wives who defined their own role performance as below par would be more likely to define their health as poor. As part of the New York study of welfare mothers, we interviewed a "control" sample of 412 nonwelfare black mothers. These working-class women lived in several public housing projects. In this questionnaire were a series of questions designed to measure the degree of self-defined success which the women had as wives and mothers. The data are presented in Table 6. For all five questions, those women who defined themselves as relative failures in their roles as wives and mothers were more likely to define their health as fair or poor than women who felt they adequately performed these roles. For example, of those women who judged their marriage "average or unhappy," 40 percent defined their health as fair or poor; but only 22 percent of those who judged their marriage "happy" defined their health negatively. Though we have no data to measure the intervening mechanisms, we would guess that many women who view themselves as failures as mothers and wives develop a need to legitimize their failure and a substantial minority use poor health to do this.

It is, of course, possible that the associations reported in Table 6 could be spurious. It could be that women who are older, have little education, low income, and are physiologically in poor health might be more likely to see themselves as failures as wives and mothers and define their health negatively. Were we to control for these variables and eliminate the effect of self-defined role performance, then our interpretation of Table 6 would be incorrect. To analyze this possibility, we combined the answers to all five questions on role performance in an index. Women scoring high on this index (defining their role performance favorably) were least likely to define their health as fair or poor. Whereas 18 percent of

**Table 6. Percentage defining health as fair or poor by self-defined role performance (New York working-class sample)**

| | |
|---|---:|
| Compared with your friends would you say that you are an: | |
| Excellent cook | 20  (54) |
| Good cook | 31 (169) |
| Average or below cook | 33 (187) |
| How often do you feel that you can't control your children: | |
| Frequently or sometimes | 38 (125) |
| Rarely | 34  (86) |
| Never | 24 (200) |
| How often do you feel that you are not as good a mother as you would like to be: | |
| Frequently or sometimes | 38 (155) |
| Rarely | 29  (98) |
| Never | 24 (159) |
| Would you say that your marriage has been: | |
| Happy | 22 (214) |
| Average or unhappy | 40 (132) |
| Compared with your friends would you say that you and your husband get along: | |
| Very well | 23 (188) |
| About average or not so well | 36 (160) |

the high scorers defined their health as fair or poor, 45 percent of the low scorers viewed their health as fair or poor. . . . Age, education, income, and objective health were correlated with scores on the role-performance index and definition of health. The association between these latter variables could therefore be spurious. . . . Standardizing separately for age, education, and income did not substantially reduce the effect of the role-performance index on definition of health. . . . [W]e conclude that the data are supportive and the hypothesis merits further consideration.

## CONCLUSION

How people define their health influences many areas of their lives. People who think they are unhealthy act as if they were ill and may in fact become so. In this paper we analyzed some sociological determinants of definition of health. We argued that in the United States people use poor health to legitimize a sense of failure to fulfill socially prescribed roles. In America the cultural values stress the importance of maintaining economic independence and striving to move up the social hierarchy. As Merton (1957) observed, not trying to better oneself is a form of deviance.

Welfare recipients occupy a stigmatized status in America. A substantial proportion of welfare recipients themselves define being on welfare as a type of failure; yet many have given up hope of becoming independent. When people occupy a self-defined illegitimate status and have little expectation of leaving this status, they feel a need to legitimize their failure. We have shown that defining one's health as poor is one way that welfare mothers have of legitimizing their status. Drawing on data from another study, we showed that women who defined their performance as wives and mothers as being less than adequate were more likely than those who were satisfied with their performance to define their health as poor. We would hypothesize that wherever there are high rates of self-defined failure there will be high rates of self-defined poor health.

## NOTES

1. This research was in part supported by U.S. Department of Labor Contract No. 51-40-69-01, Samuel Z. Klausner, Principal Investigator, and Public Health Service Research Grant No. 7R01 CH 00369, Lawrence Podell, Principal Investigator. We thank Rose Coser and Michael Schwartz for comments on a previous draft.

2. [Over three] decades ago, Parsons, following the psychoanalytical model, noted that sick people sometimes become unconsciously motivated to retain the "privileges and exemptions of the sick role." (Parsons 1951: 437) In a subsequent examination of the problem, Parsons hypothesized that the high level of achievement demanded in America might accentuate the unconscious desire to use ill health to exempt oneself from role obligations (Parsons 1958).

3. In their responses to this question, welfare mothers may, in part, be invidiously comparing their own financial status and that of other welfare mothers. Each respondent may think that she deserves welfare more.

4. . . . . As it turned out, one year from the time of the interview, 89% of the respondents were still receiving public assistance in New York City. Furthermore, it is likely that the majority who left the rolls in the one year period—judging from case histories—will be back on again.

5. It is also possible that the poverty which attends welfare life may contribute to physiological deterioration.

6. Another plausible explanation for Table 1 would be that those who have lenient attitudes toward welfare become casual about their continuing dependence. In contrast, those who have strict attitudes are more reluctant to rely on welfare and tend to do so only when genuinely ill. We thank the ASR reader for pointing out this possibility.

7. Much ambivalence exists about the role of the working woman in America. Though women are sometimes expected to work, they are not expected to achieve too much. Whereas middle-class women may be urged to stay home and tend their children, welfare mothers are "lazy boondogglers" if they don't work. On the cultural ambivalence toward working women, see Coser and Rokoff (1971).

8. Though "the number of reported illnesses in the past year" is not an adequate measure of the "physiological component of aging," it is the best measure we have and provides at least a tentative test.

9. We do not mean that most people who define themselves as failures use ill health as a means of self-legitimation; but that a substantial minority use ill health to legitimize failure in a wide variety of situations. Clearly other techniques are used to legitimize failure. . . .

## REFERENCES

Coser, Rose Laub
   1961 *Life in the Ward*. East Lansing, Michigan: Michigan State University Press.

Coser, Rose Laub, and Gerald Rokoff
   1971 "Women in the Occupational World: Social Disruption and Conflict." *Social Problems* 18 (Spring): 535–554.

Crandell, Dewitt L., and Bruce Dohrenwend
   1967 "Some Relations Among Psychiatric Symptoms, Organic Illness and Social Class." *American Journal of Psychiatry* 123 (June): 1527–1537.

Hinkle, L. E., Jr., R. H. Pinsky, I. D. J. Bross, and N. Plummer
   1956 "The Distribution of Sickness Disability in a Homogeneous Group of 'Healthy' Adult Men." *American Journal of Hygiene* 64 (September): 220–242.

Mechanic, David, and Edmund H. Volkhart
   1961 "Stress, Illness Behavior and the Sick Role." *American Sociological Review* 26 (February): 51–58.

Merton, Robert K.
   1957 "Social Structure and Anomie." Pp. 131–160 in Robert K. Merton, *Social Theory and Social Structure*. Glencoe, Illinois: Free Press.

Olendzki, Margaret
   1965 Welfare Medical Care in New York City: A Research Study. Unpublished Ph.D. dissertation, University of London.

Parsons, Talcott
   1951 *The Social System*. Glencoe, Illinois: Free Press.
   1958 "Definitions of Health and Illness in the Light of American Values and Social Structure." Pp. 165–187 in E. Gartly Jaco (ed.), *Patients, Physicians and Illnesses*. Glencoe, Illinois: Free Press

Rosenberg, Morris
   1962–63 "Test Factor Standardization as a Method of Interpretation." *Social Forces* 41: 53–61.

Wolff, Harold
   1958 "Disease and Patterns of Behavior." Pp. 54–61 in E. Gartly Jaco (ed.), *Patients, Physicians, and Illness*. Glencoe, Illinois: Free Press

Zola, Irving Kenneth
   1966 "Culture and Symptoms: An Analysis of Patients Presenting Complaints." *American Sociological Review* 31 (October): 615–630.

# Review Questions

1. Many women in our country who receive money from the federal Aid to Families with Dependent Children program feel that they are failures. Why?
2. Cole and Lejeune present data from two studies of women receiving "welfare" payments. What did they find out about the women's own assessments of how healthy they were? What did the authors conclude about the relationship between receiving "welfare" and defining one's health?
3. Cole and Lejeune present alternatives to their own conclusions in several cases. For one of these cases, describe in detail how the authors conducted further tests to see which conclusion seemed more accurate.
4. How did the findings from the survey of married black women relate to the findings from the surveys of "welfare" mothers?

# Suggested Readings: Interaction in Institutional Context: Health and Illness

Freidson, Eliot. *Profession of Medicine*. New York: Dodd-Mead, 1970.

Millman, Marcia. *The Unkindest Cut: Life in the Backrooms of Medicine*. New York: William Morrow, 1978.

Starr, Paul. *The Social Transformation of American Medicine*. New York: Basic Books, 1982.

Strauss, Anselm L. *Chronic Illness and the Quality of Life*. St. Louis: Mosby, 1975.

# E. Religion

T HERE IS MUCH THAT IS SOCIAL ABOUT RELIGIONS. REGARDLESS OF THEIR
particular beliefs and rituals, religions emerge and flourish within societies, and nonreligious aspects of those societies affect them. Religions
generate social processes and serve social functions. They are characterized by social structures and roles. The early sociologist Emile Durkheim
noted a century ago that religion serves societal functions by bringing its
members together and providing a common element around which
group solidarity may form. Religious rituals such as weddings, bap-
tisms, and funerals give some structure to possibly disruptive events and
changes. In a country such as ours where religious diversity is a long-
standing fact of life, different kinds of issues arise. How do various ethnic groups develop styles of religious practice that are uniquely their
own? How does one's religious status affect opportunities for interacting
with other people, for marrying, for making employment contacts, and
for experiencing discrimination? What is the importance of competing
religious world views? How does one decide to change one's religious affiliation, to enter a religious career, or even to become an atheist? How
does social interaction shape the individual's religious affiliations and
beliefs?

Western societies today are, on the average, much human-centered
and less God-centered that was the case a few centuries ago. This trend
toward secular humanism has, of course, had major implications for religions and for the roles of religious leaders. The two articles in this section focus specifically on religious careers. In the first article, Sherryl
Kleinman looks at seminary students preparing to enter the ministry. In
the second, Lucinda SanGiovanni looks at former Catholic nuns who
have relinquished their religious roles. Divergent as they are, these studies both show clearly the interplay between sacred and secular worlds.

In "Equals before God: Humanistic Seminarians and New Religious
Roles," Kleinman presents a close-up look at new ministerial students in
a Midwestern Protestant seminary. When they arrive at the seminary, the
recruits are surprised by their professors' behavior, by the tenor of their
courses, and by their co-seminarians. Their prior assumptions about the
role of minister—the expected demeanor, language, piety, and purpose—
are called into question. This study shows us the marked impact that hu-

manism can have on the ministry. At the same time, it illuminates the processes that reshaped these recruits' self concepts, attitudes, and behavior.

What happens when one decides to leave a religious life and enter the secular world? As Lucinda SanGiovanni reports, in "Rediscovering Gender: The Emergent Role Passage of Ex-Nuns," many "push" and "pull" factors are at work. Rather than focusing on why nuns began leaving their convents in the mid-1960s, however, this article asks how they became reintegrated into the larger society. Since an important aspect of being a nun is a disavowal of and disattention to one's gender, reintegration requires relearning gender roles. From the accounts of ex-nuns in their in-depth interviews, we can see both the impact of their previous convent life on their modes of interaction and self-images and the impact of secular claims and social scripts in shaping new identities.

# EQUALS BEFORE GOD: HUMANISTIC SEMINARIANS AND NEW RELIGIOUS ROLES

Sherryl Kleinman

[T HIS ARTICLE REPORTS ON SIX MONTHS OF FIELD RESEARCH AT MIDWEST Seminary, a liberal Protestant theological school. The author, herself an "agnostic Jew," lived on the campus with the approximately 200 ministry students, eating in the residence hall, attending classes, and conducting interviews with students, faculty, and administrators. The focus of this article is on the re-socialization of the students. They came expecting to find restrictions, theology, and piety. They discovered, however, that the new human-centered trend in theology had created quite a different set of teachings and expectations.]

Humanistic religion is grounded in the human situation rather than in the transcendent [in the here-and-now rather than the spiritual]. In this view, the distinction between transcendent and mundane realities no longer exists, for everyday reality takes on a religious significance. Hence, humanistic religion has a this-worldly emphasis. Religion becomes a matter of human symbolism rather than a God-given truth (Gilkey 1967).

A conception of religion as symbolic, situated in time and place, and of this world suggests that religiosity is relative. Religion becomes subjective, individualized, and privatized (Lemert 1974a, 1974b; Luckmann 1967; Miller 1975). Consequently, ministers no longer set the standards for or enforce moral purity and orthodoxy (Bellah 1964). Rather, individuals become responsible, more than the Church, for their religiosity and even for determining what religious behavior is (Hiller 1969, 183). The Church simply provides an environment for the individual's spiritual growth and ministers become enablers rather than truth givers or standard setters. Consequently, the faculty at Midwest Seminary do not expect the students to be devoted to traditionally religious duties or to serve as traditional moral exemplars in the community. In addition, the subjectivizing of religion has led to a bias against intellectualizing and an emphasis on "feeling-talk."

Excerpted from Sherryl Kleinman. *Equals before God: Seminarians as Humanistic Professionals* (Chicago: University of Chicago Press, 1984), 49–62.

## WORLD-OPENNESS

In the new theology, "liberation is obtained from rigid and closed world views, and the world is accepted as sanctioned ground for action" (Hiller 1969, 80). The less rigid and closed world view tends to be associated with less rigid standards for conventional ministerial behavior. As the world becomes an open place for religiosity, ministers can participate in many activities once considered off limits for them.

Instructional personnel at Midwest Seminary do not advocate partying, smoking, drinking, and swearing, but neither do they say that such behaviors are bad. Within the humanistic framework, these behaviors become matters students should deal with themselves and do not determine whether they will become good ministers. Students discover this view when they note that the organization does not interfere in their leisure activities. Student dorm life, including parties, are not monitored by the school. Further, faculty sometimes say that behavior people usually think of as routine deviance for most people, but "real" deviance for religious people, is not necessarily bad. For example, in a class called "The Changing Conception of the Church's Self-Image" (the course title itself indicates the new orientation), the following interchange occurred:

> The professor said, "When I was younger I saw someone smoking after a revival meeting. At that time I thought that anyone who smoked or drank was a sinner. When I saw this person smoking, I thought, 'Oh, the revival didn't work.'" A male, second-year student said, "Yeah, it didn't take." The class laughed. The professor said, "We are all born into the Body of Christ, yet we set up standards for who should be let in and let out." (Field notes)

The professor implies that he used to think smoking indicated the absence of religiosity but now he knows better.

Just as the faculty do not equate abstaining from deviant activities as good, they do not emphasize participating in traditionally pious activities as the way to self-betterment. The organization institutionalizes few conventionally religious activities. One of them, a half-hour chapel service, is held twice a week. But even participation in chapel is officially and informally defined as optional. My observations indicate that the high point of chapel service for students and others is the sociability of the reception following the service. Here, students, faculty, administrators, and staff chat, drink coffee, and eat doughnuts for about fifteen minutes.

Faculty sometimes show role distance from traditional expectations of piety and respect for conventional religion in their classes. They usually do this through their jokes:

> I went with Jean over to Assessment Services. Jean said to the secretary, "I signed up for assessment last year but I couldn't take it. So I'd like to sign up again." One of the seminary faculty standing nearby said, smiling, "Isn't

there some penalty for that? Hmm, well, say 5,000 Hail Mary's." The three of us laughed. After we left, Jean decided to fill the form out right away and hand it in. She told me later, "When I handed it in, Anderson was still there. I told him it would be a good idea to hand in the form right away. He said, 'That's intelligent. Take off some Hail Mary's.' " (Field notes)

In a class on pastoral psychotherapy the instructor was discussing a "case." He then said, "I asked the client who her heroes are, maybe I should ask *you* [the class]." He then suddenly did an imitation of Christ on the Cross. Some of the class laughed nervously, others just laughed. He said, "Some of you seemed shocked at that." The third-year, male student sitting next to me smiled and said, "Only the first-years." (Field notes)

In a time-management seminar, the class was divided into groups of three in which discussed problems with their schedules. One group said their problem was having self-expectations that were too high. Someone in the class responded, "Yes, if it hurts it must be good." The instructor said, "Oh, the joy of suffering. Jesus did it, so can I." The class laughed. (Field notes)

Because faculty fail to emphasize the religious in the traditional sense but do emphasize that ministers should be egalitarian—ministers are, after all, only human—students get the idea that people who show their religiosity are using it to establish a sense of superiority and are therefore acting inappropriately. Since the conventional ministerial role is that of a superordinate, demystifying the role involves getting rid of the signs and displays of religious specialness, such as robes, the collar, talk about God, and pious behaviors. (Hence, the students had allowed me to wear traditional garb as a means to a humanistic end.) In a dorm room in which three female students were present, the following interchange took place:

One student said: "I ran into this guy I used to know, who's Fundamentalist. Anyway, he took some of us out to lunch, to McDonald's. And you know what he said? He said, 'Let's pray.' " The other student said, "Oh, gross!" I said, "What's so gross about it?" The first student said, "It's too public, it looks like he was trying to tell everyone that he's pious. It's as if he's saying, 'I'm pious, why can't you be?' It's like saying he's superior." The other students nodded in agreement. (Field notes)

Students might have challenged this man's behavior primarily on the basis of its inappropriateness for the setting—McDonald's. The fact that they challenged him on the basis of his lack of humanism is evidence for the strength of their humanistic beliefs.

The demystification of "religious people" was made explicit in the following interview with a member of the faculty.

It's in preaching that people see their prejudices, their hangups, it's a personal thing. Now some preachers don't see it that way. They gloss over what attitudes they're showing by saying, "It's the Word of God." I don't see it that way. I make the students hear and see what they're saying. That's why I use the videotape. . . . One student whose sermon I was commenting on yester-day started off the sermon by saying "There's a story about a boy who . . ." I told him it sounded like the boy was *him*—you know, the classic case of "I have a *friend* with a problem, and it's *you*." So I told him that either he should *say* the story's about him and be open about his problem; or if the person's problem is too intense or personal for the pulpit, then leave it out entirely. But why should he leave it open, why leave me with that curiosity? If it's a problem he can talk about then he *should*, because it's good for the congregation to see that even people into religion have problems.

In the lounge one evening, a former student of the seminary who had returned for a visit was speaking with one first-year female student and one second-year male student:

The returning student said, "What would you say the students are like here, pious or what?" The first-year female student said, "We're not pious at all." The former student replied, "That's good. Three years ago, we had some of those holy people around, who really could not relate to the real world. They went around like, 'I'm Christian, I'm holy, I'm happy.' They were all clean-shaven, short hair, conservative dress. I'm glad there have been some changes." The second-year student said, "The problem is we're not con-cerned with being pious at all." The female student said in a sarcastic tone, "Well, listen to him—*pious*." The second-year student replied, "I know. To you pious has a negative connotation. You think it means holier-than-thou. . . . It's as if there's an understanding that you shouldn't talk about faith here. It's un-derstood." (Field notes)

Given humanistic notions of religion, it is understandable that stu-dents did not treat me as an outsider. In their view, even a Jewish agnos-tic can become part of the minister's religious experience, for almost ev-erything and everyone is defined as part of God's reality. For example, a student I had interviewed a few days earlier came to my room and said to me:

Remember in my interview I said that I felt I had to be called to be a minister? And I've been called, I *know*, to be here *this year*, I've been called to consider the ministry. But I don't know if I've been called to be ordained. [Well, I don't think I'm qualified to . . . um] God's will is communicated through *people*, so by talking to *you*, for instance, it may help me to find God's guidance. (Field notes)

Indeed, with an understanding of religion and ministering as interper-sonal and all-inclusive, some students who thought I was a good listener suggested I become a minister.

## ANTI-INTELLECTUALISM

Most of the faculty emphasize the heart of ministry as interpersonal rather than intellectual. Intellectualizing did go on in class, but it was of-ten treated as secondary or deprecated. For example, during the break period in a small theology seminar which had had an intellectual-personal mix, one of the students asked the instructor a question about something he had written on the blackboard. The instructor looked a little embarrassed and said in an apologetic tone, "Yes, I like to keep up my image, that I'm a theological thinker." The instructor expressed role distance from the image of the "cold thinker" presumably evidenced by his having written some theological terms on the blackboard! In another class, another professor said, smiling, "Since I guess most of you expect a course on theology to talk about God, the next two sessions will be it." He then went on to emphasize the "experiential"' as the most important part of the theology. In still another class, a professor was making the point that students should refrain from using big words the congregation might not understand. He mentioned a cartoon in which the minister is speaking to a snoring congregation. He said the caption read, "Look, I know you're thinking Sabelleus, but . . . ," indicating that the minister was insensitive to the congregation's boredom at hearing an intellectual sermon.

Consequently, students believe that those few peers who engage in intellectual talk are arrogant (and therefore bad) or are defensive and need therapy. Students who tried to discuss theology in the cafeteria, for instance, made people noticeably uncomfortable and were often resented by their peers. One third-year student who attempted to intellectualize matters also recognized that by doing so he could bring out theological divisions among the students that would otherwise be left unstated:

> There's a lot of unspoken tension about faith issues . . . I mean some people should really be erupting at each other! If they knew how different they really are they should be asking, "How can we both be here and should we both be here?" And they should talk about these things, but they don't. (Interview)

This student was atypical. Most learn to refrain from intellectualizing or come to believe it is bad. For example, one student wrote the following in his ministry project:

> As I enlarge my world view, I also have found that I must look inward toward a better self-understanding. With the help of Assessment Services and new friendships, I have been made aware of the areas where I personally need to grow. I tend to intellectualize my way through emotional situations which I seem to set up for myself. . . . I use overpowerful language in order to get my point across and to break communication barriers which often should be handled more carefully. I let the debater in me come through.

In his ministry project, another student put it:

> In ministry we must give up the security of a system of verbal, intellectual formulations and enter into human relationships through love and trust.

After about three weeks in the field, I remarked to a few students that I had yet to hear a theological discussion. In response to that remark, students would now and then call me over if they were discussing anything remotely intellectual, saying things like "Quick, Sherryl, we're having a theological discussion,'' or ''Let's have a theological discussion for Sherryl.'' They were making fun of my expectation that a seminary would be pervaded by religious talk. Also, they sometimes used jokes to stop others from intellectualizing. For example, at breakfast one morning, a first-year student was discussing Zimbardo's well-known prison experiment [in which he assigned students to play the roles of inmates and guards in a mock prison] relating it to questions of human nature. Two other students continued to eat their breakfast, but didn't participate in the conversation. After about ten minutes, one of them got up to leave. She said, mocking an upper-class British accent, ''Well, thank you for this theological, spiritual, intellectual discussion.'' The other student chuckled.

Because of the new definiton of religious people as ''normal,'' or ''like everyone else,'' students come to reject their earlier expectation that a seminary should be characterized by conventional religious behavior and theological talk:

> I thought that everyone else here who came to ministry would be concerned only with religion. This is absurd, as absurd as thinking that when I was in music I would think only about music, or that you, in sociology, would be concerned only with sociology. Why I didn't grasp that before I came, I don't know. I wouldn't expect people in journalism, say, to only talk about journalism. But people expect that with religion, *even* people who come here to study. (Interview, female, first-year student)

A third-year student who had just returned from an intern year said in an interview:

> I expected the dinner table talk to be theologically oriented, you know, ''Well, did you study Martin Luther's 95 Theses today?'' And to show you how much my mind has changed on these things, well, last week I was sitting, talking to Beth [another third-year woman] across the table [in the cafeteria]. There were two guys sitting next to us—first-year students—and they were into a deep theological discussion, kind of like what I imagined would go on long ago. We just kind of looked at them and said to each other later, ''Gee, I wonder how long it's going to take them to get out of *that*?'' [laughing]. (Field notes)

## SOCIALIZATION PROBLEMS

Students initially have strong conventional expectations of religiosity, both ideologically and behaviorally. They enter the seminary expecting their peers and teachers to act in religious ways. In short, students expect an institution of religion to be a religious institution. Many of them talked about what they thought they would have to give up in seminary (partying, dancing, smoking, drinking, swearing) and what they thought they would have to do (daily devotions, talk about God, prayer groups).

I went out for dessert with four female students. After about fifteen minutes of joking around, Donna said, "Gee, I wish we could have done this last year, before coming here, then I wouldn't have worried about coming." Belle said, "You mean going out with seminary students before we became seminary students?" Donna said, "Yes, I remember talking to Nancy about that last quarter. It turns out we were both worried, before we got here, that there wouldn't be any fun people at seminary." Belle said, laughing, "Oh, but you should have realized that *you're* fun, and you're going to seminary, so there must be others—I know what you mean; I wondered about that, too." (Field notes)

It is quite common in occupational socialization settings that students' initial expectations are incorrect. In the case of the ministry, however, the students' experience is one of reality shock, for the realities of seminary life are not just different but the opposite of what they expected. For example, what was previously defined as deviant behavior (drinking, smoking, swearing) isn't, now, and what was once defined as religious behavior (piety) is now defined as deviant.

The students are in fact ambivalent about their initial conventional expectations of religiosity; they want to become ministers, but fear the "monastic" life. Their ambivalence perhaps paralleled mine. As a field worker in a seminary, I expected and was willing to make certain sacrifices, such as suspending skepticism about religion, becoming more polite, going to chapel, being proselytized, and altering other acts or attitudes. Students and I also reacted similarly to the lack of religiosity—some relief at having our tasks made easier mixed with an uneasy feeling about the legitimacy of the organization. They wonder: "Can an unconventional seminary really be a seminary?"

## STUDENTS' RESPONSES

Students largely accept the redefinition of religious deviance, acting "publicly" against traditional expectations and notions of religiosity, often through cynical remarks and jokes. Entering the seminary with traditional expectations, I, like many new recruits, was surprised at ministry students' lack of "pious" behavior. I was equally struck by the prevalence of jokes with religious content, such as making a pun on "saving a chair" for someone (and asking the chair to repent) or calling poor typing "typing in tongues." Students often point out discrepancies between their behavior and outsiders' expectations of them, saying things like, "You wouldn't know this is a seminary, right?" In light of the dominant humanistic expectations in the seminary, and the intensity of traditional expectations on the outside, this joking behavior is less surprising. Students are enacting collective role distance from traditional expectations. The behavior seems to say "We do not assume the traditional role which you outsiders are giving us." The students, like the faculty, made jokes and cynical remarks about religion among themselves.

In the evening, one male student, three female students, and I were in one of the women's rooms. There was a lull in the conversation. One of the women was leaning on the towel rack that was nailed to the closet. Suddenly the rack fell, which startled us a bit. The woman who had been leaning on it said, "Oh, it's the Holy Spirit! Wait, the Devil made me do it." We laughed. (Field notes)

After having arrived late to the party in the dorm, one of the first-year women said to me:

It's too bad you weren't here earlier. [What happened?] Oh, some of the guys were doing a mock Communion, doing it all wrong. They used pretzels. It was really funny. (Field notes)

Students often made fun of outsiders' traditional expectations of ministers. For example, the following exchange I had with a second-year student alludes to parishioners' views of ministers as asexual:

I was in Agnes' room. She said, "Do you mind if I change in front of you? I said, "No." She said, "You can put it in your study—ministers *do* have breasts." (Field notes)

The students learn that becoming a minister at Midwest Seminary means they should act counter to traditional expectations. For example, one of the new students expressed some concern about taking the vocational tests required of all members of the first-year cohort:

At breakfast Peter, the new student, said nervously, "Well, I'm off to be vocationally tested, to see that I'm not fit to be a minister." The other two second-year male students laughed. One of them said, "And that you *should* be here." (Field notes)

The new student was worried about not presenting himself as a traditional minister on the test. The veteran is telling him that he will fit in at the seminary to the extent that he doesn't fit the traditional image.

Although most of the jokes made fun of traditional religion, some of them also revealed students' skepticism about whether a humanistic seminary could really be a seminary. Some jokes suggested that the student was questioning the legitimacy of an organization that calls itself a seminary but doesn't seem religious. The students could accept their peers' remarks because they ostensibly made fun of traditional religion. But the joke may have carried another message; it also mocked the lack of religiosity. Students could questions the lack of religiosity and make fun of parishioners' "misguided" expectations at the same time:

A male seminary student walked into the cafeteria at lunch and neared our table. Ron, a first-year student, said to him, "Hi, Father. How are you doing?" The student he called Father said, "Fine, fine." I said to Ron, pretending to whisper, "Hmm, how come he's called Father?" Ron said, "Oh, I coined that because he's going to switch to an Anglican seminary and their priests are called Father. Also [smiling], he's High Church." I said, "I don't fully understand what that is." Ron said, "Oh, the service is full of liturgies, chants and praying—really structured: Not like here." I said, "You'd say this is Low Church?" Ron said, "Yeah." Eric, another first-year student, said smiling, "No. Basement Church." We laughed. (Field notes) . . .

In my interview a few months later with the student called "Father," he said, "My impression is that the school is about half liberal and half conservative. Yeah, half conservative and half . . . heretic. Yes," he said laughing, "half heretic." He then classified himself in the heretic category. The notion of heretic is not a humanistic, but a traditional word. Although this student disparaged the conservatives, his definition of the others as heretics suggests at least a slight put-down of those who are less conservative. Perhaps he used this strong language to show that he is not, as his High Church affiliation indicates to his peers, traditional. When I asked him in an interview about the High Church/Low Church distinction, he characterized his affiliation with the former as a preference or taste, rather than a matter of being essentially traditional.

> [What do people not like about High Church services?] Vestments, paraphernalia, the formalness. I do it because I like it. There's more of a celebration type atmosphere to it. Face it. We do things because we like to. And then we come up with some superstructure to back it up. And people are uncomfortable with that.

"Father," however, was not the only person who used the term "heretic" in a joking context to characterize many of the students. Other students also used the term "apostate" to describe themselves and their peers.

After two weeks in their first quarter of study, a few of the new students talked about their preconceptions of seminaries over lunch in the cafeteria:

> Others had left the cafeteria. Martin and I stayed to talk. He said, "You know what I worried the most about in coming here? What my roommate would be like. I figured I could get a really weird roommate in a seminary. I worried that I wouldn't be able to drink beer with him, in front of him. And my first night here, he not only brought in a case, but the *best*—Heineken. I'm not sure what to make of that! (Field notes)

Martin was laughing as he said this, but also fidgeted and looked a bit confused. Although questioning the legitimacy of the organization on the basis of the kind of beer students drink rather than the fact that they drink at all may seem ridiculous to an outsider, Martin is experiencing the dilemma which most students never resolve: which behavior and attitudes are definitely not "religious" and which are acceptable? Humanism does not provide the answers. . . . [T]his becomes particularly troublesome because socializers leave the question of goodness open but also lead students to expect homogeneity of "goodness" among their peers and teachers.

Students also joked and made cynical remarks about the humanistic role, and particularly the humanistic vocabulary, on occasion. For example, I was in Ellen's room (Ellen is a first-year student). Phil, a second-year student, came over. They were talking rather sarcastically about the argot of seminary students, such as "affirming" and "sharing." Ellen spoke, "Another big one is 'community.' " Phil replied, "Yes, and that means everyone knows your business." Because humanistic expectations predominate in the seminary, students made such remarks more often in small groups of close friends and outside the classroom than in large groups. Moreover, in the company of close friends, students sometimes used traditional standards to evaluate others.

Students, then, dealt with their ambivalence about humanistic religion by expressing some of those feelings in jokes with double meanings. Also, although seldom in public, students did talk and think about their faith, whether they had been called to the ministry, and their conceptions of God. However, they tended to keep these matters to themselves or discussed them in private settings with a close friend or two or with me:

> I was waiting for a phone call in the dorm hallway. I heard two students talking in the room across from the phone. One of the women left. I said, "Gee, I thought I heard the word theology in there." Kathy said, "Yes, it does happen sometimes. You have to look hard for it, though. But sometimes during the noise at lunch two people will be off in a corner discussing . . . Tillich. Or in someone's room like this, it will be going on." (Field notes)

Some students who were quite adept at making religious jokes seemed to transform in the interview situation, suddenly showing a hidden, serious, religious side. Although I do not have distributions on how many people prayed privately, I do know that some fourteen students did, alone or with a friend. However, the norms prohibiting the public display of a serious attitude toward religion often made it difficult for them to find a prayer partner:

> I had to grope a lot the first term as to praying with other persons, I mean knowing which persons would be into that sort of thing and which wouldn't. [How do you go about finding out?] Well, I was in a class last term called "Theology of Prayer." Susan was in that, so we started praying together. . . . We talked and theologized more about prayer in that class than doing it, so you could find out how people felt about it. (Interview: female, first-year student)

It is likely that more students wanted someone to pray with than looked for one. My data suggest that a situation of pluralistic ignorance may have existed: students wished at times to be "religious" with their peers but feared that they would disapprove.

# IMPLICATIONS

The esteem accorded professional knowledge in a society is partly sustained by the profession's definition of it as esoteric, either technically, intellectually, or both. As a way of establishing their turf and excluding clients from decision making, professions usually develop sets of terms, or jargon, which only those who have had the training can understand.

Religious terminology, like any professional language, can be understood only by those who learn it. In the seminary, students do learn certain terms in their theology classes that outsiders probably would not understand. But this humanistic program's client-centered emphasis downplays the importance of theological terms. Hence, technical terminology and intellectual talks about theology rarely occur in students' conversations or even in their class discussions. In fact, professors who write books and articles on theology express their distance from the scholarly role when interacting with students.

Students at Midwest Seminary do learn an argot—that of psychologizing. Although not all outside audiences understand this, it is characteristically close to the contemporary language of everyday life. The language is more expressive than many parishioners might like, but it is nevertheless easier for them to comprehend than such terms as "hermeneutics." That is the problem; the language is so common that it does not distinguish religious knowledge from everyday information and talk. As a common language, it fails to provide a sense that the ministry is distinctive and esteemed.

●  ●  ●

# REFERENCES

Bellah, Robert N.
  1964 "Religious Evolution." *American Sociological Review* 29: 358–374.

Gilkey, Langdon.
  1967 "Social and Intellectual Sources of Contemporary Protestant Theology in America." *Daedalus* 96: 69–98.

Hiller, Harry H.
  1969 "The New Theology and the Sociology of Religion." *Canadian Review of Sociology and Anthropology* 6: 179–187.

Lemert, Charles.
  1974a "Cultural Multiplexity and Religious Polytheism." *Social Compass* 21 (3): 241–253.

———.
  1974b "Sociological Theory and the Relativistic Paradigm." *Sociological Inquiry* 44: 93–104.

Luckmann, Thomas.
  1967 *The Invisible Religion*. New York: Macmillan.

Miller, Donald E.
  1975 "Religion, Social Change, and the Expansive Life Style." *International Yearbook for the Sociology of Knowledge and Religion* 9: 149–159.

# Review Questions

1. The professors at Midwest Seminary emphasize the humanistic tenet of "world-openness." What does world-openness imply for the acceptable everyday behavior of ministers (and ministerial students)?

2. What would be the reaction of professors and seminarians to students who were anti-intellectual and deported themselves informally?

3. How did the students' expectations of the seminary mesh with what they found? How did they respond?

4. What role does "psychologizing" play in the seminary's philosophy?

# REDISCOVERING GENDER: THE EMERGENT ROLE PASSAGE OF EX-NUNS

Lucinda SanGiovanni

## INTRODUCTION

Over the course of our lives as social beings we pass through many roles. Some of these personal journeys are quite familiar to us—we pass from child to teenager, from single to married, from civilian to soldier, from employed to retired. These types of *role passages* are fairly institutionalized in our society, guided by those accepted schedules, rituals, rules and meanings that facilitate our movement from certain social locations into different ones.

The aim of the present article is to explore selected dimensions of the *non*-institutionalized, or *emergent*, role passage experienced by former Roman Catholic nuns making the transition from a convent community into the secular society. One of the most astonishing events to occur in the history of American religious orders has been the large exodus of nuns from the convent during the past fifteen years. Membership began to drop dramatically in 1967 and continued to decline through the early seventies. Between 1966 and 1976, the number of nuns in the U.S. dropped from approximately 181,000 to 131,000 (Ebaugh, 1977:67–68).

The decade of the sixties was a time of crisis and change in the Roman Catholic Church and in religious orders (Kavanagh, 1967; Westhues, 1968). Nuns were questioning the authority of superiors and the hierarchical structures of religious communities. New forms of service to lay people were being suggested. The meaning of religious life and its relation to the secular society were under review. New modes of dress, new relationships, and new living arrangements were tried out.

These and a host of other improvisations in religious life were generated and sustained from two sources. One came from within the Roman Catholic Church itself. Vatican Council II, the writings and lectures of theologians and religious leaders, and the grass-roots activities of priests and nuns all came together to dramatically change the structure of religious life and the role of the nun in the modern world. A second source of change came from the larger society itself. The sixties was a decade of

This is an original article prepared for the second edition of this volume, based in part on Lucinda SanGiovanni, *Ex-Nuns: A Study in Emergent Role Passage.* (Norwood, N.J.: Ablex, 1978).

movement away from authority, hierarchy, regulation, and rationality. Criticism of conventional morality, traditional life-styles, modes of interpersonal relations, and the distribution of power gave rise to a variety of social movements that lent ideological support to the efforts at renewal within religious life.

Of course, the impact of these changes on nuns was considerable, and great numbers opted for the alternatives that were emerging in the secular society. The decision to leave the convent was a decision to leave a way of life to which one had once been committed. Being a nun was a vocation or calling to a life very different from that of most other people. It entailed rigorous training, demanded total involvement, and exerted a profound influence on identity. Thus, the decision would involve cutting oneself off from experiences, routines, relations, and self-images that were valued and comfortable while at the same time exposing the individual to new situations for which she was not accustomed or which she did not completely embrace.

Like any other major decision, this one was a consequence of both individual and social forces interacting with one another. It is not enough to *want* to leave a role or way of life. Persons must also be *aware* of alternative structural opportunities as well as coming to define themselves as *able* to make use of these opportunities. The data collected in this study reveal that these three conditions—motivation, knowledge of alternatives, and perceptions of abilities—appeared in approximately this order as the process of relinquishment unraveled itself.

## EX-NUNS: A CASE STUDY OF EMERGENT ROLE PASSAGE

This particular passage from religious to secular life presents an ideal opportunity to examine the complex processes involved in role change, because it possesses a generic character that involves a multiple transition of major roles and a fundamental transformation of personal identity. This passage entails accommodation to the basic role sequences of lay life—aging, family, work, marriage and friendship. These are, in turn, the social locations that shape the meanings and qualities in which our very self-images are grounded. In this light, then, it typifies the broad transformation of identities, behaviors and social memberships that individuals normally experience over the entire life cycle.

The choice of this passage, beyond its generic attributes, provides a chance to investigate several dimensions of role passage that have yet to receive much systematic attention in sociology. First, this passage is an *emergent* one (Glaser and Strauss, 1971:85–86) which is created, discovered and shaped by the former nuns as they go along. Few guidelines, precedents, or models are available to facilitate their transfer between roles. Although this type of role passage is seldom explored by sociologists (Clausen, 1968:189), it is becoming more and more significant as our society undergoes continuing transformations. Second, the movement from nun to lay person involves a passage through *multiple* roles. In fact, only a few transitions ever occur which entail single or isolated transfers from one to another social location. In the case of former nuns, they must simultaneously negotiate transitions to such roles as family members, workers, consumers, lovers, spouses and women. Third, this passage was a *self-initiated* one and draws attention to the often-neglected fact that individuals are active agents who make assessments of their personal and social situations and who are interested in, and capable of, exerting control over various stages of their lives. A fourth advantage of studying this particular passage derives from the fact that, by virtue of having been in religious life for some time period, former nuns do not move with their age-peers through the "typical" sequences of major roles over the life cycle. They lag behind members of their age cohort in many institutional spheres of life. Thus, this enables us to study what Glaser and Strauss (1971:31) term an *arrested passage*. Finally, as we follow women from their lives as nuns through passages to other lives, our focus is kept on the *processual* nature of role occupancy. At each phase of the former nun's passage, her problems, meanings, choices and strategies are somewhat different from earlier and subsequent phases. To grasp these essential differences it is necessary that we pan over the entire passage to underscore the fluidity of structural movement.

During the spring and summer of 1972, I conducted intensive interviews with a sample of twenty former nuns who had been members of a religious order located in a major metropolitan area on the East Coast of the United States. In order to obtain the greatest base of information, the sample included women who differed substantially from one another along the following dimensions: (1) the number of years they had spent in religious life (from 5 to 15 years or more), (2) their age at the time of leaving (from 25 to 40 years and over), (3) the type of vows they had taken (final vs. temporary vows), (4) the length of time they spent in secular life after leaving (less than 1 year to over 4 years), (5) their marital status (single vs. engaged or married), and (6) their type of occupation (academic, non-academic or unemployed).[1]

Although the in-depth interviews covered a wide range of topics, we will examine in the next section one specific passage that was negotiated by these women. This transition centers on the full resumption by former nuns of their sex role as women.

## SEX ROLES

A person's sex role as female or male is assigned by others at birth and generally is understood to be an ascribed characteristic. While sex refers to biological attributes, sex roles refer to the cluster of social expectations deemed appropriate for how women and men should behave (Chafetz,

1974:1-5). The roles of women and men and the gender definitions of their behavior as feminine and masculine are social constructions rather than biological givens. These roles and definitions are established by society and learned by individuals, beginning in infancy.

It is a basic sociological truth that all roles, including sex roles, are never static; they continue to be revised to meet changing societal and individual needs (Banton, 1965, pp. 42-67). The role of woman (and indirectly that of man) has, since the mid-sixties, been undergoing exactly such change. There is no longer any doubt that there is presently moving through our society a vigorous, determined, and ideologically informed assault on traditional sex roles (David and Brannon, 1976; Kelly and Boutilier, 1978). This changing role of woman elicits the following question in the context of our study of former nuns: What happens to people when the role that they are trying to learn, and to play with conviction, is itself undergoing profound alteration in the society at large?

All of us reading this article are, to varying degrees, grappling with the same question. But women who once were nuns are in a unique position. During much of their lives as nuns, these women subordinated their sex role to the more generalized and pervasive demands of the *religious role*. Being a nun meant being a celibate woman for whom the ordinary experiences and roles of lay women were either forbidden or unimportant.[2] Paradoxically, while a nun was discouraged—through convent laws, ideology, vows, and routines—from defining herself and acting in terms of her role as a woman, traditional feminine values and behavior were reinforced.

Over the past few years a considerable amount of literature has appeared which criticizes religion and religious organizations as sexist in consequence, if not intent (Bullough, 1973; Doely, 1970; Hageman, 1974). Theologians such as Rosemary Ruether (1974), Mary Daly (1975), and Carol P. Christ and Judith Plaskow (1979) have become well known for their feminist analyses of such questions as the ordination of women, the patriarchal underpinnings of religious traditions, the cult of Mary, and the subordinate position of women in the church. While more has been written about the Christian religions, the position of women in Judaism is also undergoing scrutiny (Koltun, 1976) as a religion grounded in patriarchal beliefs, laws, and traditions.

I believe this feminist framework is essential to understanding the paradoxical nature of the nun as woman and the consequences of the paradox for the former nun's resumption of her role as a secular woman. The culture and social organization of the Roman Catholic Church, and religious orders in particular, are permeated with sexism. The sexist imagery, symbols, language, roles and structure of authority become evident, for example, when we compare the roles of priest and nun.[3] "Father" is superior to "Sister" in authority; his major functions are "sacred" and grounded in the Sacraments, while hers are not; he can own property and have private monies, she cannot; he can drink and smoke and go out alone, she cannot; he can exercise independence, freedom of choice, and individuality, while she must always be a part of the larger "community" and subordinate herself to her order.

The process by which a woman is socialized to become a nun provides us with an unequivocal instance of conditioning women to traditional "female" attributes, virtues, skills and orientations. She is taught to be passive, subordinate, submissive, collectivity-oriented, nurturant, quiet, childlike, pure, hard-working and obedient. She is publicly a paragon of virtue—the "good Sister" who teaches the children and cares for the poor and sick; she is to be unassuming, restrained, innocent; she is to go beyond the sexuality and materialism that flaw the secular individual. She embodies, or is taught and thought to embody, the essential female complex of values, attitudes and behavior.

Thus, the nun, although living outside the mainstream of secular female culture, was nonetheless socialized to a religious role and participated in an organization that closely approximated the society's patriarchal themes. This is a crucial observation because it sheds light on the issue before us; namely, as nuns left the convent and assumed their roles as secular women they had a choice as to what kind of woman they could be. They could resume the society's more traditional female role or could opt for the emerging role of woman that was being created through the feminist movement.

In doing my research during the early seventies, the peak years of the emergent feminist consciousness, I had hypothesized that former nuns would be more likely to embrace the newer vision of women than the more traditional one. Why? My prediction was based on a certain way of looking at religious life. A religious order can be viewed as one of the rare social organizations where women freely choose to organize, staff, coordinate and play out their lives without men and motherhood—those two major coordinates that socially locate the woman in every society. Here is a genuinely radical feminist experiment: women working, eating, sleeping, creating, producing, deciding, defining, playing, praying—in sum, living by themselves with other women. If this is one's conception, and to some extent it contains much empirical validity, then one might expect former nuns to enter the secular world ready to assume the newer configuration of the role of woman. I expected them to respond favorably to this role that stressed independence, self-assertion, achievement and nonfamilistic life-style choices. The findings failed to support my hypothesized prediction. As will soon be evident, the respondents' resumption of their sex role was carried out according to the more traditional vision of women's role. Upon examining the above model of religious life, I came to see several errors in this conceptualization which help explain its failure to correctly predict the respondents' behavior.

First, as I mentioned earlier, the culture and social organization of convent life were shaped along the same patriarchal lines as those of secular institutions of the larger society. These structures, and the process of socializing women to them, were of great importance in sustaining traditional feminine behavior and values. Second, the ability to define oneself in feminist terms and to interpret one's situation within a feminist framework requires at least that one *be aware of oneself as a woman*. Regarding respondents' self-conceptions, their awareness of themselves as women was by and large suppressed under the "master status" (Hughes, 1945) of being a nun. Third, I had erroneously assumed that nuns *chose* a single, celibate, single-sexed community life-style. The fact of the matter is, however, that respondents *chose to become nuns*, and this life-style was the required condition for being officially accepted as a nun. Finally, and perhaps most important for understanding their subsequent adherence to a more traditional model of woman, I had not considered the possibility that these respondents were looking forward to the "benefits" of being women, to which they had been socialized early in their lives and which had been so long denied them while in religious life. Insofar as their goal was to become women again—in the sense in which sex role is a basic axis of self-identity and social membership—assuming the stance of a "liberated woman" could jeopardize this goal. Put bluntly, one's acceptance as a woman by others is not gained by being autonomous, competitive, rational, achieving, assertive, and the like. In most parts of society, even today, the "women's libber," as she is termed, has her credibility *as a woman* cast into doubt.[4] For former nuns, who desired acceptance as women and whose ability to make transitions to other roles was dependent on this acceptance, their choice of the traditional female role became clearly understandable.

We are now prepared to explore the process by which former nuns resumed active roles as women in secular society. One of the first strategies they employed could be called "body work"—a set of activities designed to bring the body, appearance, and overall physical impression in line with the female role. They experimented with different hairstyles, bought clothes, practiced putting on makeup, had their ears pierced, went on diets, and in various ways sought to present public images of themselves as everyday women. As Scott and Lyman (1963:33) observe, "since individuals are aware that appearances may serve to credit or discredit accounts, efforts are understandably made to control their appearances through a vast repertoire of impression management activities." One area over which my respondents had total control was precisely the area of physical impression, and much effort went into it. But even such a simple matter as this was problematic at first, as these comments reveal:

> I started to lose weight, learned how to put on makeup, which was really funny, practicing in front of a mirror; I'd dab it on and look like a clown. I also learned to set my hair, and sometimes I looked pretty awful. I worked on my clothes—a friend helped me buy shoes, clothes, jewelry. I really don't know if I could have done without that kind of help in the beginning. I really didn't know much at first.

It was really funny now when I look at it, but not then, when we had to go into the stores and of course we didn't have much money to spend and we'd go into the stores where everybody dressed in front of everybody else. (How did you feel about that?) That was a traumatic experience. I remember going into the dressing room with three or four pairs of slacks because I really didn't know what size I wore. It was pretty bad.

There were so many things I had to learn, like which styles fit me for my build and my age and which colors were flattering. My sister would go shopping with me in the beginning to help pick things out.

Ironically, at a time when many secular women were taking off their makeup, letting their hair return to natural colors and easy-to-keep styles, gaining control of their bodies through sport and other "non-feminine" activities, these women were reverting to physical activities that were targeted as "objectifications of the female" (Millum, 1975) by the feminist movement.[5] Through trial and error, observation of others, and assistance from friends and family, respondents began to shape their appearance in accord with their traditional image of themselves as women. An interesting observation made by two women suggests that some measure of their movement through transitional stages is reflected in changes in personal attire and attitudes toward one's body:

I wasn't really in tune with my body and I think it took a while. It was a very gradual thing. Like, that first summer out I got a one-piece bathing suit, last summer I had a regular two-piece bathing suit, and this summer I have a bikini, and in my own mind I see that and feel that this is my transition and I often laugh.

When I compare the type of clothes I bought when I first left and those I buy now, there's such a difference that I think it must say something about where I've come from. (Could you explain this?) Well my earlier clothes were too big for me, they were drab and in dark colors—very subdued, conservative. My style has changed, I now know what I like and I'm willing to experiment.

As a result of participating in a secular environment where being a woman is a salient feature of everyday life, respondents began to increasingly refer to *other women* for standards of evaluation. Their involvement in roles and activities which contain norms for sex-role participation made them increasingly attentive to sources for assessing their own performances as women. A respondent captures this more concentrated attention by remarking, "I'm now more likely to look at other women—how they're dressed, how they carry themselves, what they say—and compare myself to them. There was little need to do that in the convent." As time goes by, women, precisely as women, become more significant as reference points for the respondent, which helps to underscore her attachment to the female role and bring her behavior and sentiment in closer alignment with the role. A former nun who had been out for about two years compares herself now as a woman with when she was a nun and observes, "I'm not ashamed to express my emotions now. I am learning to respond more like a woman." Another suggests that, "I have become more interested in womanly things—cooking, shopping, clothes, sex—and to read and discuss these things with other women." Still another comments that "even my thinking has changed in the sense that as a nun I used to be more logical, more rational; I believe I thought like a man, and now I feel I am looking at things in more than just rational terms."

Even in the management of their other role transitions, respondents worked to integrate them into support of their role as women. Specifically, success in one role may bring confidence in playing others. Just as all roles receive social confirmation and are activated when they elicit appropriate responses from others, a major validation of being a woman in our society is to have men react in anticipated ways (Safilios-Rothschild, 1977). To be whistled at, to be told one is pretty, to be asked for a date are unequivocal signals that men see you as a woman which function to increase one's confidence in that role. Part of the motivation to date (and part of the anxiety over not dating that comes across in many interviews) is tied to this issue of wanting to validate one's claim to being a woman. This is succinctly stated by a former nun who expressed much concern with the initial absence of dating activity during the first year she was out: "I also wanted to date because it helped me know I was attractive to men—that I was a woman." Success in dating and sexual intimacy served to increase the respondent's confidence in herself as a woman and thus facilitated the resumption of her sex role.

Other respondents were also aware that what was happening in other areas of their transition—where they resided, who their friends were, where they worked—had consequences for their successful resumption of the female role:

> I wanted to get a job very badly because I knew that without it I couldn't buy clothes and things that would help me be attractive as a woman and not look like an ex-nun.

> I deliberately began to cultivate women friends who were not ex-nuns because they knew the woman's world and could help me discover it. My friends were ex-nuns; we were all in the same boat and really couldn't help each other out that much.

These activities can be seen as somewhat conscious efforts by respondents to engage in behavior that is supportive of their roles as women. By deliberately manipulating other parts of her passage—work, dating, friendship—she could strengthen her sex-role presentation.

The interview materials we have presented to illustrate ideas about sex-role accommodations can be reread to shed light on the respondents' conception of the female role. Most respondents generally accepted a traditional image of women with its emphasis on the primacy of marriage and children; the existence of "natural differences" between the sexes in terms of sentiment, modes of thinking and biological drives; and the belief that the sexes do, and should continue to, inhabit somewhat distinct spheres of existence regarding work, leisure, community participation, child-rearing, governing, and the like. Only one respondent held to a model of woman that can be called feminist, and she apparently had formulated her conception of being a woman as a result of early family socialization long before entering religious life. With the exception of agreeing to "equal work for equal pay," the majority of respondents were fairly uncritical of the content of institutionalized sex roles.

In examining the interview data I did find a few respondents who had left religious life with traditional images of the female role and had begun to *reevaluate* these ideas in the light of their immediate experiences in the secular community. These respondents were approximately thirty years old, they were single, they had been out of the convent for two to three years, they had relatively active social lives, and they expressed satisfaction with their jobs. Once these women discovered that they could, in fact, build for themselves an independent and satisfying lifestyle, the pressure they had felt earlier to follow the path of traditional women began to decrease and to be replaced by a wish to leave their present plans open-ended. These women, like the other respondents, had been very concerned about what would happen to them after leaving religious life. They keenly felt the absence of any permanent ties or plans that give most people a feeling of security for the years that stretch before them. Many of them echoed this theme by noting that "at least in the convent you knew what the rest of your life was going to be like; you had that security." It is still true today that for many, many women the life plan that is available in the female role points to marriage, children and noncareer employment. Once some of these women begin to experience success and rewards in pursuing alternate styles of existence, however, they are able to question their attachment to the ideas of what women can and should be. This reevaluation is described in dynamic terms by a very observant respondent:

> It's hard to say what factors began to influence my thinking about women's role in society. When I first left I felt I just had to find a man, get married, settle down. Maybe this was a reaction against not having the security of convent life. But really, I didn't think of any options and was pretty desperate for awhile. As I began to do things on my own and to do them—my finances, the job, new friends, and dating men—well, maybe I became more confident in myself, and more willing to think that there are options for women besides the ones we're taught by society. You come to realize that you, as a person and as a woman, can make your own way, even if it's hard at times.

These changing conceptions of woman's role seem to me to be more of a result of altered social experiences than of solely an intellectual or ideological conversion to feminism as a belief system. This implies that, for ideological shifts to occur in how women respond to roles, they must be backed up by *personal experience* that is valued and effective. Women must continue to be encouraged to play new roles, have new experiences, and join new groups so that they can test for themselves the degree of satisfaction and effectiveness possible in moving beyond the present boundaries of woman's role. Exposure to feminist ideology, either in the form of intellectual analysis or political rhetoric, is not sufficient for producing sustained change in one's personal and social life as a woman.

• • •

## NOTES

1. For a detailed discussion of the methodology used in this study see SanGiovanni (1978:13–24).

2. In a perceptive observation, Ebaugh (1977:24) interprets the fact that the novice frequently received a male name, such as Sister Mark or Sister Mary Robert, as a formal indication that ''sexual differences were no longer emphasized.''

3. Although recent changes in religious life have lessened some of these differences between priest and nun the general comparison remains valid even today.

4. This fact may help to explain such intriguing phenomena as the frequent denial by achieving women (in politics, business, the military, etc.) that they are feminist or are concerned with larger feminist issues, or the exaggerated use of ''feminine'' accoutrements (makeup, ribbons, jewelry, style of uniforms) by successful women athletes.

5. I am indebted to Mary Boutilier for this observation.

## REFERENCES

Banton, Michael. *Roles: An Introduction to the Study of Social Relations*. New York: Basic Books, 1965.

Bullough, Vern L. *The Subordinate Sex*. Champaign, Ill.: University of Illinois Press, 1973.

Chafetz, Janet S. *Masculine/feminine or human?* Itasca, Ill.: Peacock, 1974.

Christ, Carol P., and Judith Plaskow (eds.). *Womanspirit Rising*. New York: Harper & Row, 1979.

Clausen, John (ed.), *Socialization and Society*. Boston: Little, Brown, 1968.

Daly, Mary. *The Church and the Second Sex*. New York: Harper & Row, 1975.

David, Deborah S., and Robert Brannon (eds.). *The Forty-Nine Percent Majority: The Male Sex Role*. Reading, Mass.: Addison-Wesley, 1976.

Doely, Sarah B. (ed.). *Women's Liberation in the Church*. New York: Association Press, 1970.

Ebaugh, Helen R. F. *Out of the Cloister: A Study of Organizational Dilemmas.* Austin: University of Texas Press, 1977.

Glaser, Barney, and Anselm Strauss. *Status Passage*. Chicago: Aldine, 1971.

Hageman, Alice L. (ed.). *Sexist Religion and Women in the Church: No More Silence.* New York: Association Press, 1974.

Hughes, Everett C. "Dilemmas and Contradictions of Status," *American Journal of Sociology*. 50 (1945):353–59.

Kavanagh, J. *A Modern Priest Looks at His Outdated Church*. New York: Trident Press, 1967.

Kelly, Rita M., and Mary Boutilier. *The Making of Political Women*. Chicago: Nelson-Hall, 1978.

Koltun, Elizabeth (ed.). *The Jewish Woman: New Perspectives*. New York: Schocken Books, 1976.

Millum, Teresa. *Images of Women: Advertising in Women's Magazines*. London: Chatto and Windus, 1975.

Reuther, Rosemary. *Religion and Sexism: Images of Women in the Jewish and Christian Traditions*. New York: Simon and Schuster, 1974.

Safilios-Rothschild, Constantine. *Love, Sex, and Sex Roles*. Englewood Cliffs, N.J.: Prentice-Hall, 1977.

SanGiovanni, Lucinda. *Ex-Nuns: A Study of Emergent Role Passage*. Norwood, N.J.: Ablex, 1978.

Scott, Marvin B., and Stanford M. Lyman. "Accounts," *American Sociological Review*. 33 (1963), 46–62.

Westhues, K. *The Religious Community and the Secular State*. New York: Lippincott, 1968.

# Review Questions

1. How did SanGiovanni expect ex-nuns to differ from other women as a result of their experiences in the convent? Were her expectations confirmed?

2. What does the interview material in her article indicate were the typical effects of convent life on the gender-identities of nuns who are still in the convent?

3. To whom did ex-nuns look for role models and socialization agents as they adjusted to secular life?

4. How might the *seclusion* of nuns in convents reinforce their religious beliefs? Their religious identities?

## Suggested Readings: Interaction in Institutional Contexts: Religion

Bell, Daniel. "The Return of the Sacred? The Argument on the Future of Religion." *British Journal of Sociology* 28 (1977): 419–448.

Bellah, Robert N. *Habits of the Heart.* New York: Harper & Row, 1985.

Chalfant, Paul, Robert Beckley, and C. Eddie Palmer. *Religion in Contemporary Society.* Palo Alto: Mayfield Press, 1987.

Dodd, David J. "The Sweet Man of Jonestown." *New Society* 49 (September 1979): 607–610.

Lofland, John, and Rodney Stark. "Becoming a World-Saver: A Theory of Conversion to a Deviant Perspective." *American Sociological Review* 30 (1965): 862–874.

McGuire, Meredith B. *Religion: The Social Context,* 2nd ed. Belmont, Calif.: Wadsworth, 1987.

Slater, Philip. *The Wayward Gate: Science and the Supernatural.* Boston: Beacon Press, 1977.

Ward, David A. "Toward a Normative Explanation of 'Old Fashioned Revivals,' " *Qualitative Sociology* 3 (1) (spring 1980): 3–22.

# Part IX. Social and Cultural Change

SOCIAL CHANGE IS A COMPLEX, ONGOING PROCESS. ANY OR ALL OF THE ELE-ments of a culture may change—objects, ideas, beliefs, norms, values, patterns of interaction. Change may be dramatic and sudden, as in the wake of a disaster or war. Or it can occur subtly and gradually over many years.

Change may occur as the result of *formal* enactments, when those who are empowered to make laws for a nation, a state, or a company require new ways of doing things. Civil rights legislation, for example, led not only to changes in the procedures and policies of schools, businesses, hospitals, and unions, but to shifts in opinions and beliefs—some favorable to minorities and some which could be called "backlash." As the U.S. Food and Drug Administration determines which substances are dangerous to our health, even our eating habits may be altered by formal procedures.

More often, social change is not legislated or dictated but occurs at the *informal* level. Examples of such change can be found in styles of dress, technological innovations, and the declining importance of religion in everyday life. The invention of the automobile has transformed our cities, our economy, and even our courtship practices.

Informal change can also lead to formal change. This process can be seen with the gradual acceptance of marijuana smoking by middle-class society. When the editors of this book were attending college in the mid-1960s, few students were smoking marijuana at Oklahoma State University or Temple University. As marijuana smoking became part of the college experience, more and more young adults became users. Smoking soon spread to the high schools and then to the professions. As marijuana use became more extensive, the laws in many states were revised to focus on the major distributors rather than on individual smokers. Police, too, began looking the other way when college students and other adults were peacefully smoking in public.

Murray Melbin's article, "Night as Frontier," takes up the issue of gradual, unplanned, and almost unnoticed changes in social arrangements. As the geographical frontier—the American "Wild West"—filled up with people and activities, a time frontier opened during the night. Melbin traces the technological and social changes that permitted the emergence of this night frontier. He also proposes that people's behavior, activities, group affiliations, organization, and problems have turned out to be much the same in our current frontier as they were in the West a century and more ago. The implication is that, if and when this frontier is filled, new frontiers will open with some of the same social arrangements and problems.

Rarely does the alteration of one element in a culture leave the rest of the culture intact. Because social elements are intricately connected, change in one area usually affects many other areas. As women have gained equality in legal terms, for example, the rules for appropriate behavior between men and women are affected too. One pattern of coping with changed definitions and rules regarding what women can expect in male-female relationships is the subject of the first article in this section. Lynn Atwater reports here on interviews with a number of women who were having extramarital relationships (EMRs). Traditionally in our society, men "benefited" from the double standard. They were much more likely than women to have sexual encounters outside marriage. Now we see changes occurring.

As Atwater makes clear, the women in her study were seeking in relationships a kind of intimacy and acceptance that seemed to be lacking in their traditional marriages. They acquired new perceptions, of which their husbands were often unaware, of what to expect from male-female relationships. One way to have these expectations met would be to confront their husbands directly. This approach would require the renegotiation of an ongoing, taken-for-granted relationship stabilized by years of precedent. No doubt many women do this, but others may leave the relationship altogether or may maintain their traditional marriages while engaging in EMRs as well.

Some of Atwater's respondents used their EMR experiences to resocialize their husbands into becoming more satisfying spouses. In such instances, the EMR served as a rehearsal for the primary, or marital, relationship. For women who were less successful in their resocialization attempts, the EMR allowed them to continue their marriages while receiving affection and caring attention elsewhere.

A note about Atwater's methodology is in order. Because of the sensitive nature of her subject matter, acquiring a random sample was out of the question. Atwater decided that some information was better than no information, and she set about obtaining a sample from the readership of *Ms.* magazine. An innovative approach to interviewing was adopted for some of the subjects: self-administered questionnaires, the responses to which were tape-recorded. Thus, information was collected from women whose stories otherwise would not have been told. The reader should keep in mind, however, that we do not know what proportion of married women in the United States are involved in EMRs.

In part at least, we can trace the roots of a great many social and cultural changes, including alterations in women's roles, to technological changes which have affected the type of work required in our society. Put another way, the introduction of technological innovations can have much greater consequences for social change than anyone had intended or foreseen. The final article illustrates the importance of one type of technological "advancement" for the single-industry town of "Caliente." In "Death by Dieselization," W. F. Cottrell discusses the drastic consequences of the introduction of new train engines, consequences which proved to be dire for the economy and for the personal lives of the town's inhabitants.

# NIGHT AS FRONTIER

## Murray Melbin

Humans are showing a trend toward more and more wakeful activity at all hours of day and night. The activities are extremely varied. Large numbers of people are involved. And the trend is worldwide. A unifying hypothesis to account for it is that night is a frontier, that expansion into the dark hours is a continuation of the geographic migration across the face of the earth. To support this view, I will document the trend and then offer a premise about the nature of time and its relation to space. Third, I will show that social life in the nighttime has many important characteristics that resemble social life on land frontiers.[1]

## THE COURSE OF EXPANSION

We were once a diurnal species bounded by dawn and dusk in our wakeful activity. Upon mastering fire, early humans used it for cooking and also for sociable assemblies that lasted for a few hours after darkness fell. Some bustle throughout the 24-hour cycle occurred too. Over the centuries there have been fires tended in military encampments, prayer vigils in temples, midnight betrothal ceremonies, sentinels on guard duty at city gates, officer watches on ships, the curing ceremonies of Venezuelan Indians that begin at sundown and end at sunrise, innkeepers serving travelers at all hours. In the first century A.D., Rome was obliged to relieve its congestion by restricting chariot traffic to the night hours (Mumford, 1961:217).

Yet around-the-clock activity used to be a small part of the whole until the nineteenth century. Then the pace and scope of wakefulness at all hours increased smartly. William Murdock developed a feasible method of coal-gas illumination and, in 1803, arranged for the interior of the Soho works in Birmingham, England, to be lighted that way. Other mills nearby began to use gas lighting. Methods of distributing coal-gas to all buildings and street lamps in a town were introduced soon after. In 1820 Pall Mall in London became the first street to be lit by coal-gas. Artificial

Murray Melbin, "Night as Frontier," *American Sociological Review* 43, 1 (Feb. 1978): 3–22.

lighting gave great stimulus to the nighttime entertainment industry (Schlesinger, 1933:105). It also permitted multiple-shift factory operations on a broad scale. Indeed by 1867 Karl Marx (1867:chap. 10, sec. 4) was to declare that night work was a new mode of exploiting human labor.

In the closing decades of the nineteenth century two developments marked the changeover from space to time as the realm of human migration in the United States. In 1890 the Bureau of the Census announced that the *land frontier in America had come to an end*, for it was no longer possible to draw a continuous line across the map of the West to define the edge of farthest advance settlement. Meanwhile, the search for an optimum material for lantern lights, capable of being repeatedly brought to a white heat, culminated in 1885 in the *invention of the Welsbach mantle*—a chemically impregnated cotton mesh. The use of the dark hours increased thereafter, and grew further with the introduction of electric lighting.

Here and there one may find documentation of the trend. During the First World War there was selective concern, expressed by Brandeis and Goldmark (1918) in *The Case Against Night Work for Women*, about the impact of off-hours work. A decade later the National Industrial Conference Board (1927) published a comprehensive survey with an account of the characteristics of the off-hours workers.

The most systematic evidence of steadily increasing 24-hour activity in the United States is the growth of radio and television broadcasting. Broadcasters authorize surveys to learn about the market that can be reached in order to plan programs and to set advertising rates. The number of stations active at given hours and the spread of those hours around the clock reflects these research estimates of the size of the wakeful population—the potential listeners. Table 1 shows trends in the daily schedule spanning the entire periods of commercial broadcasting for both radio and television. Although not shown in the table, television hours in Boston ended at 11:30 P.M. in 1949, and then widened to include the Late Show and then the Late Late Show in the intervening years until 1974. Each medium has moved increasingly to 24-hour programming and mirrors the growth in nighttime activity.

In the [1970s] for the first time the U.S. Bureau of Labor Statistics (1976: Table 1) asked about the times of day that people worked. In 1976, of 75 million in the work force, 12 million reported they were on the job mainly after dark and 2.5 million of those persons worked a full shift beginning about midnight. Since these figures do not include *the clientele* that used such establishments as restaurants, hospital emergency wards, gambling rooms, and public transportation, these numbers are conservative estimates of how many people are up and about at night.

Today more people than ever are active outside their homes at all

**Table 1. Numbers of Radio and Television Stations and Their Hours of Broadcasting, in Boston.**[a]

|  | THE SPAN OF COMMERCIAL BROADCASTING | | | | |
|---|---|---|---|---|---|
|  | 1934 | 1944 | 1954 | 1964 | 1974 |
|  |  |  | Radio |  |  |
| Number of stations | 7 | 7 | 14 | 20 | 27 |
| Percent of stations on 24 hours | 0% | 0% | 7% | 40% | 57% |
|  |  |  | Television |  |  |
| Number of stations |  |  | 4 | 4 | 7 |
| Percent of stations on 24 hours |  |  | 0% | 0% | 14% |

[a]SOURCES: LISTINGS IN BOSTON NEWSPAPERS—*GLOBE, HERALD, RECORD,* AND *TRAVELER*—AND THE BROADCASTERS THEMSELVES. IF THE CONTENT OF A BROADCASTER'S AM AND FM RADIO PROGRAMMING OR VHF AND UHF TELEVISION PROGRAMMING DIFFERS, THAT BROADCAST IS COUNTED AS TWO STATIONS.

hours engaged in all sorts of activities. There are all-night supermarkets, bowling alleys, department stores, restaurants, cinemas, auto repair shops, taxi services, bus and airline terminals, radio and television broadcasting, rent-a-car agencies, gasoline stations. There are continuous-process refining plants, and three-shift factories, post offices, newspaper offices, hotels, and hospitals. There is unremitting provision of some utilities—electric supply, staffed turnpike toll booths, police patrolling, and telephone service. There are many emergency and repair services on-call: fire fighters, auto towing, locksmiths, suppliers of clean diapers, ambulances, bail bondsmen, insect exterminators, television repairers, plate glass installers, and funeral homes.

The trend of nighttime expansion is under way outside the United States as well. In Great Britain since the Second World War, the yearly increase in the percentage of the manual labor force on shifts in manufacturing has been about 1 percent a year, and greater increases have been noted in vehicle manufacture and in the chemical industry (Young and Willmott, 1973:175). Meier (1976:965) observes that Singapore is becoming one of the most intensive 24-hour cities. Data on around-the-clock activity in Peru, France, the U.S.S.R., and eight other nations is provided in a volume on *The Use of Time* (Szalai, 1972:appendices).

## SPACE AND TIME FRONTIERS AND SETTLEMENTS

Time, like space, is part of the ecological niche occupied by a species. Although every type exists throughout the 24-hour cycle, to reflect the way a species uses its niche we label it by *the timing of its wakeful life*. The terms *diurnal* and *nocturnal* refer to the periods the creatures are active. We improve our grasp of the ecology of a region by recognizing the nighttime activity of raccoons, owls, and rats, as well as by knowing the spatial dispersion of these and other animals. The same area of a forest or meadow or coral reef is used incessantly, with diurnal and nocturnal creatures taking their active turns. We make geographic references to humans in a similar way. We refer to an island people or a desert people, or the people of arctic lands as a means of pointing out salient features of their habitats.

This similar treatment of time and space rests on the assumption that both of them are containers for living. Consider the dictionary definition of the word *occupy*: ''2. To fill up (take time or space): *a lecture that occupied three hours*'' (*American Heritage Dictionary*, 1970:908). Geographers study activities rather than physical structures to decide whether and how people occupy space (Buttimer, 1976:286). The mere presence of buildings and related physical structures in places like Machu-Pichu, Petra, and Zimbabwe do not make us believe they are habitations now. The once-boisterous mining centers in the American West that have become ghost towns are settlements no longer. Conversely, we say a farming region in which people are active is inhabited even though buildings are few. The presence of human-built structures is not the criterion for occupying a region; it is people and their activities.

Like rural settlements, the occupation of time need not be dense. For example, London Transport lists 21 all-night bus routes. On many of these routes ''all-night'' service means no more than once an hour. Yet, even though the bus does not pass during the intervening 59 minutes, the schedule is said to be continuous. If an active moment interacts with quiet moments around it, the entire period is taken as occupied.

Of course, no time has ever been used without also using it in some place. No space has ever been used without also using it some hours of the day. Space and time together form the container of life activity. We forget this in the case of former frontiers because expansion then occurred so dramatically across the land. Less notice was paid to the 16 hours of wakefulness because the daily use of time was rather constant as the surge of geographic expansion kept on over the face of the earth. As time use remained unchanged, it was disregarded in human ecological theory. In different eras, however, expansion may proceed more rapidly in either space or time. Recently expansion is taking place in time. Since people may exploit a niche by distributing themselves and their activities over more hours of the day just as they do by dispersing in space, a frontier could occur in the time dimension too.

A *settlement* is a stable occupation of space and time by people and their activities. A *frontier* is a pattern of sparse settlement in space or time, located between a more densely settled and a practically empty region. Below a certain density of active people, a given space-time region is a wilderness. Above that point and continuing to a higher level of density, the presence of people in activities will make that area a frontier. Above that second cutoff point the further denseness of active people turns the area into a fully inhabited region. In a given historical period the frontier's boundaries may be stable or expanding. When expanding the frontier takes on the aspect of venturing into the unknown and is often accompanied by novelty and change.

## SIMILARITIES BETWEEN LAND FRONTIERS AND TIME FRONTIERS

•    •    •

There are many aspects in which social life at night is like the social life of other frontiers. [Ten such aspects will be discussed here.]

### 1. Advance Is in Stages

There is a succession of steps in colonizing any new region. People ventured into the western outskirts "in a series of waves . . . the hunter and the fur trader who pushed into the Indian country were followed by the cattle raiser and he by the pioneer farmer" (Turner, 1965:59; 1893:12, 19–20). Life-styles were distinctive in each stage as well. The hunters and trappers did not dwell like the miners who followed, and they in turn lived differently from the pioneer farmers who came later (Billington, 1949:4–5). Although living conditions were generally crude then there was a decided increase in comfort for the farmers settled in one place compared with the earlier-day trappers who were usually on the move.

There is also a succession of phases in settling the nighttime. Each stage fills the night more densely than before and uses those hours in a different way. First came isolated wanderers on the streets; then groups involved in production activities, the graveyard-shift workers. Still later those involved in consumption activities arrived, the patrons of all-night restaurants and bars, and the gamblers who now cluster regularly by midnight at the gaming table in resorts.

The rates of advance are unequal in both cases. Population gains and development are not unbroken. In the West economic growth was erratic. Periods of depression, dry seasons, and other hardships drove many people to abandon their homesteads and move back east. Similarly, during the oil embargo of 1973–1974 there was some retreat from nighttime activity, as restaurants and auto service stations and other businesses cut back hours of serving the public.

## 2. Population Is Sparse and Also More Homogenous

At first only a few people venture into the new region. . . . The demographic composition of the western frontier was mostly vigorous young males with proportionately fewer females and aged persons than found in the populations of the eastern states (Riegel, 1947:624; Godkin, 1896:13; Dick, 1937:7, 232).

This demographic picture fits the night as well. There are fewer people up and about and most of them are young males [89 percent of those observed on field visits to eight checkpoints in Boston]. . . . Estimates of the ages of passersby were also made during the field observations. . . . Whereas people of all ages were on the streets during the day, no one over 59 was seen between midnight and 5 A.M.; and from 2 to 5 A.M. no one over 41 was seen.

## 3. There Are Welcome Solitude, Fewer Social Constraints, and Less Persecution

The land frontier offered tranquillity, a place for relief from feelings of being hemmed in. "Fur traders . . . were psychological types who found forest solitudes more acceptable than the company of their fellow men" (Billington, 1949:4). It was appealing to escape into the wilderness, to leave deceit and disturbance, and vexing duties and impositions of the government behind (Robbins, 1942:148). . . . Even later the West was "a refuge . . . from the subordination of youth to age" (Turner, 1932:25). The outer fringes offered escape from persecution too. Mormons and Hutterites both made their ways westward to avoid harassment from others.

In a parallel way, many have enjoyed the experience of walking at night along a street that is ordinarily jammed during the day. Individuals who are up and about then report a feeling of relief from the crush and anonymity of daytime city life. The calm of those hours is especially appealing to young people, who come to feel that they possess the streets. (A test of this proposition must of course control for the fear of criminal assault in the dark; I will discuss this further in items 7 and 8 below.) Also, a portion of the people out at night are those avoiding social constraints and perhaps persecution. Street people and homosexuals, for example, find more peace in the dark because surveillance declines. Some night owls are urban hermits. Some individuals who are troubled or stigmatized—such as the very ugly or obese—retreat from the daytime to avoid humiliation and challenge. They stay up later, come out when most others are gone, and are more secure as they hobnob with nighttime newsdealers and porters and elevator men. In this way the night affords an outlet. Like the West it serves an insulating function that averts possible tensions from unwanted encounters.

## 4. Settlements Are Isolated

Initially migration beyond the society's active perimeter is scattered. The land frontier settlements were small and apart from one another. There was little communication across districts and much went on in each in a self-sufficient way. People in the East did not think of the relevance of borderland activities for their own existence and the pioneers were indifferent to outside society (Billington, 1949:96, 746).

As the city moves through phases of the day it switches from coordinated actions to unconnected ones. Pockets of wakeful activity are separated from one another, [these pockets] are small [in] scale compared to daytime events, and there is less communication between the pockets. The people of the daytime give little thought to those active in the dark and do not view them as part of the main community.

## 5. Government Is Initially Decentralized

Whatever high-level group may decide the laws and policies for a nation or a community, outside the purview of superiors there are subordinates who make decisions that would otherwise be the domain of the higher-ups or subject to their approval. As the land frontier moved farther from the national center of policy making, the interpretation of the law and judicial decisions were carried out by individuals who were rarely checked on and who rarely consulted with their superiors. Hollon (1973:96) notes that events took place "remote from the courts of authorities . . . [and] the frontiersmen not only enforced their own law, they chose which laws should be enforced and which should be ignored."

Today, although many organizations and cities are continually active, their primary administrators—directors, heads of departments, mayors—are generally on duty only during the daytime. At night they go to sleep and a similar decentralization of power follows. To some extent this is an explicit delegation of authority. But discretion is stretched for other reasons too. Night nurses decide not to wake up the doctor on duty because he gets annoyed at being disturbed for minor problems (Kozak, 1974:59). Shift supervisors choose not to bother the plant manager for similar reasons. Lesser officials make decisions that in the daytime are left for higher-ranking administrators. The style and content of the way the organization or the city is run at night changes accordingly. For example, for the same types of cases, decisions by police officers at night will be based less on professional role criteria and more on personal styles. This results in more extreme instances of being strict and lenient, arbitrary and humane.

## 6. New Behavioral Styles Emerge

Both land and time frontiers show more individualism because they are remote, the enviornment is unusual (compared with the centers of society), and others subjected to the same conditions are tolerant. Those who traveled to the western borders broke from ordinary society. The casual observance by others, the constituted authority, and the familiar settings and the norms they implied were gone. This left room for unconventional behavior. Easterners thought westerners were unsavory. The president of Yale College said, "The class of pioneers cannot live in regular society. They are too idle, too talkative, too passionate, too prodigal, and too shiftless to acquire either property or character" (cited in Turner, 1893:251). . . .

Deviance was also *created* out west. Many pioneer wives lived on the plains for extended periods without ordinary social contacts, especially when their husbands left on journeys for days or weeks. These women often became withdrawn and untalkative, so shy and uneasy with strangers that they would run away when one approached (Humphrey, 1931:128). From the evidence at hand, these were normal, happy women in the cities when they were growing up, but they were affected by the frontier environment. On the western boundary people were used to this behavior on the part of lonely, isolated women and accepted it. In the eastern cities the same conduct would have been taken as odd.

There is also a popular image of the night as the haunt of weirdos and strange characters, as revealed in comments like, "I don't know where they hide during the day but they sure come out after dark." Moreover, at night one can find people who, having lived normal lives, are exposed to unusual circumstances that draw them into unconventional behavior. Becker (1963:79, 97, 98) gives such an account of jazz musicians. They work late in the evening and then associate with very few daytime types in their recreation after midnight. The milieu harbors a deviant subculture that is tolerated and even expected.

## 7. There Is More Lawlessness and Violence

Both land frontier and the nighttime have reputations as regions of danger and outlawry. Interestingly, both do not live up to the myths about them, for the patterns of aggression are selective and localized.

On the one hand there is clear evidence of lawlessness and violence. Walter P. Webb observed that the West was lawless "because the law that was applied there was not made for the conditions that existed. . . . It did not fit the needs of the country, and could not be obeyed" (cited by Frantz and Choate, 1955:83). There was also a lack of policemen, and law enforcement agencies were few (Riegel, 1947: 627; Billington, 1949: 480). There was violence in the gold fields (Hollon, 1974:211). In the cow towns, mining camps and boom towns in the early days, practically everyone carried guns. Fighting words, the ring of revolvers, and groans of pain were common sounds out there. Some western settlements were renowned for concentrations of gamblers and gougers and bandits, dance-hall girls and honky-tonks and bawdy houses. Horse thieving was widespread. The stage coach was held up many times. There was habitual fear of attack from either Indians or renegades. In the face of this, the people practiced constant watchfulness and banded together for self-protection (Billington, 1954:8, Doddridge, 1912:103). Towns had vigilante groups. The covered wagons that crossed the plains were accompanied by armed convoys.

Yet the violence was concentrated in certain places; otherwise killings and mob law were remarkably infrequent. . . . [T]umult in the cow towns was seasonal, and took place when the cowboys finally reached Abilene, Ellsworth, and Dodge City after the long drive. And the mayhem was selective. Flint (1826:401) wrote, "Instances of murder, numerous and horrible in their circumstances, have occurred in my vicinity . . . in which the drunkenness, brutality, and violence were mutual. . . . [Yet] quiet and sober men would be in no danger of being involved."

• • •

Why, then, did the land frontier have the reputation of a "Wild West?" One reason may be that outlaw killers were drifters, so the same person may have contributed exploits over large areas. Another reason was boredom. The stories of violence persisted and spread because there was little to do or read about in pioneer homes. The tedium of daily life was countered by exciting stories told and retold around the stove in the general store.

• • •

The nighttime has been noted also as a place of evil. It is thought of as crime-ridden and outside of ordinary social control. Medieval and Renaissance cities had no public illumination. Assaults by ruffians and thieves were so common after dark that wayfarers took to paying others to precede them through the streets carrying lighted torches. In the seventeenth century this escort-for-hire was called a "link boy" in London, and a "falot" (lantern companion) in Paris. Deliveries of black market goods to stores, such as fuel oil to gasoline stations during the oil embargo of 1973–1974, was accomplished under cover of darkness. Lawlessness is possible then because police coverage is sparse (Boston *Globe*, 1977:1). In addition, the officers on duty make themselves unavailable by sleeping in their cars, an old custom in New York City where the practice is called "cooping" (*New York Times*, 1968). The same was informally reported to me about Boston police as well; they are found snoozing in their police cars in the Arboretum by the early morning joggers.

In Boston today, carrying arms is more common at night. For fear of mugging or rape, escort services are provided on many college campuses for women returning to their dorms at night, or for women on the evening shift going from their places of work to the parking lot or subway station. An escort is provided for nurses at Boston City Hospital because of an increase in robberies in that area. And some apartment houses, with their sentries at the door, become vertical stockades to which people in the city retreat at night.

However, like the former West, lawlessness and violence at night are concentrated in certain hours in certain places and are otherwise uncommon. Fights reach their peak about midnight . . . but are least frequent from 2:30 to 11:00 A.M. The area of Boston in which many brawls and muggings take place, where prostitution is rampant and bars and lounges feature nude go-go dancers, is called the "combat zone." A large transient population of relatively young males come into the area to patronize the moviehouses featuring X-rated films and become drunk and aggressive in bars and on the streets. Although this description may approximate what was once reported of mining towns in the West, these combat zones do not function so after 2:30 A.M. or during the daytime. In the daytime the areas are parts of business districts. Many people shop at department stores nearby, or otherwise pass through and patronize eating places and businesses there. So the combat zone designation refers to these places only at certain hours and is not true for all the city all night.

## 8. There Is More Helpfulness and Friendliness

Hollon (1974:211–2) remarks that "For every act of violence during the frontier period, there were thousands of examples of kindness, generosity, and sacrifice. . . . " He quotes an English traveler who said, " 'Even the rough western men, the hardy sons of the Indian frontier, accustomed from boyhood to fighting for existence, were hospitable and generous to a degree hard to find in more civilized life.' "

Reports of life on the land frontier are replete with accounts of warmth toward strangers, of community house building and barn raisings, and of help for those in need (Darby, 1818:400; Frantz and Choate, 1955:64; Billington, 1949:96, 167; Riegel, 1947:81). "Neighbors were ready to lend anything they possessed. No man driving along with an empty wagon on a good road would pass another on foot without inviting him to ride" (Dick, 1937:512). Travelers returning from the outskirts said they were treated more kindly than they had been in the cities (Flint, 1826:402–03; Hollon, 1974:212).

At first these stories of openhanded western hospitality may seem inconsistent in the face of the high risks of thievery and violence. But the circumstances are actually related to one another. Dick (1937:510) observed that "As the isolated settlers battled against savage men . . . and loneliness, they were drawn together in a fellowship." Billington (1972:166) added,

> Cooperation is normal within every in-group, but accentuates when the in-group is in conflict with an out-group and group solidarity is strengthened. This was the situation in frontier communities where conflicts with Indians, with raw nature, and with dominating Easterners heightened the spirit of interdependence.

That people want to affiliate under such conditions with others like themselves was demonstrated experimentally by Schachter (1959). He showed that the greater the risk people thought they were facing, the more anxious they were; and the more anxious they were, the more they wanted to be with others—even strangers—facing the same risk. Schachter (1959) concluded that being with others in the same boat served to reduce anxiety, and also provided an opportunity to appraise one's own feelings and adjust them appropriately to the risk. With less emotional uncertainty and with the knowledge that others share the circumstances, individuals feel better about confronting a stressful situation.

Because the night is a time of more violence and people feel more vulnerable then, those up and about have a similar outlook and behave toward others as pioneers did in the West. At night people are more alert to strangers when they pass on the street. Each tries to judge whether the other is potentially dangerous. Upon deciding that the other is to be trusted, one's mood shifts from vigilance to expansiveness. If not foe, then friend. Aware that they are out together in a dangerous environment, people identify with each other and become more outgoing. The sense of safety that spreads over those together at night in a diner or in a coffee shops also promotes camaraderie there.

Also, on both frontiers people may be more hospitable because they have time to devote to strangers. Pioneers had plenty to do; yet often they had nothing to do. They were not closely synchronized in daily tasks as people were in the eastern cities, and the norm of punctuality was not emphasized. One man who grew up in the West

> . . . recalled the boredom he could never escape. . . . [T]he worst time of all was Sunday afternoon, when he had nothing to do. There were no newspapers to read and no books other than the family Bible, there was no one his age to talk with, and the nearest store was miles away. (Hollon, 1974:196)

In the city during the day, the mood of pressured schedules takes hold of folk and makes their encounters specific and short. The tempo slows markedly after midnight. The few who are out then hurry less because there are fewer places to rush to. Whereas lack of time inhibits sociability and helpfulness, available time clears the way for them.

I checked on these ideas by four tests of people's helpfulness and friendliness at various times. . . . [O]ver 2,500 people were observed in various parts of central Boston throughout the 24-hour cycle and were rated on how they responded to four situations: giving directions when asked, consenting to be interviewed when asked, returning lost keys they found, and being sociable with strangers during the focused moment of paying for goods at a supermarket checkout counter. Four tests were used so that several different behaviors would help define and give face validity to what is being studied. While these do not cover the entire range of helpfulness and friendliness, showing some warmth, cooperating with another's modest appeal, and expanding the scope of interaction are the initial conditions of such relationships. [Methodological details of the four tests are given in the original article.]

• • •

There is impressive consistency for three of the tests, with nighttime scores being highest. Not only does nighttime show up best in these three cases, there is no other time of day consistently second best . . . The overall pattern supports the prediction that nighttime is a period of more helpfulness and friendliness than other portions of the day.

In that light the outcome of the key test is surprising. The night had by far the lowest rate of helpfulness. . . . This finding is so clear cut and contrary to expectations that it must be significant. Its interpretation would benefit from information still to be presented, and I will postpone comment . . . until later.

The pattern of the findings for all four tests does reject a rival hypothesis: *fear* determines people's conduct toward strangers at night. We know the night is viewed as a dangerous time to be outside one's home in the city (U.S. Office of Management and the Budget, 1974:58–9, 73). If fear of criminal assault dominated social behavior then, it should be greater in face-to-face encounters than for the passive, anonymous appeal to find a key tagged "Please return." We would expect people to be more guarded toward others at night, to shun approaches by strangers, but to be more helpful in the low-risk situation of dropping a lost key into the mailbox. . . . [J]ust the opposite happened. Nighttimers were more helpful and friendly toward strangers face to face. And yet, of the keys picked up, they returned the fewest.

## 9. Exploitation of the Basic Resource Finally Becomes National Policy

Westward expansion began long before anyone officially recognized the land frontier's possibilities for our society. It took years to realize even that the U.S. West was habitable. At one time the land west of the Missouri River was labeled on maps as the Great American Desert. Almost no one thought that some day many people would want to migrate and settle there (Hicks, 1948:508). Nor was the catch phrase "Manifest Destiny" applied to colonizing the West until 1845, centuries after the effort had been under way. In 1837 Horace Greeley introduced the slogan "Go West, Young Man, go forth into the Country." He looked upon such migration as a means of relief from the poverty and unemployment caused by the Panic of 1837. By 1854 Greeley was urging, "Make the Public Lands free in quarter-sections to Actual Settlers . . . and the earth's landless millions will no longer be orphans and mendicants" (cited in Smith, 1950:234–5). In 1862, with the passage of the Homestead Act, it became a deliberate policy of the U.S. government to use the western territory to help relieve the conditions of tenant farmers and hard-pressed city laborers. . . .

• • •

Similarly, in the first 150 years after Murdock's coal-gas illumination was introduced, there was no national consciousness in England or the United States about colonizing the nighttime. People went ahead, expanding their activities into the dark hours without declaring that a 24-hour community was being forged. Now . . . policy makers have begun talking about cheap time at night the way they once spoke of cheap western land. V. D. Patrushev (1972:429) of the Soviet Union writes that "Time . . . is a particular form of national wealth. Therefore it is imperative to plan the most efficient use of it for all members of a society." Daniel Schydlowsky (1976:5), an economist who specializes in development in Latin America and who recently ended a three-year study there, has concluded that multiple-shift work would produce remarkable gains in reducing unemployment and improve the economies of overpopulated developing cities. His claim for the use of time echoes the attitudes of nineteenth century proponents of the use of western lands as a solution for those who were out of work.

The advocates of westward expansion also saw it as a way to draw off great numbers of people from the cities and forestall crowding there (Smith, 1950:8, 238). Today Dantzig and Saaty (1973:190–3) recommend dispersing activities around the clock as a means of reducing congestion. And Meier (1976:965) writes, "Scarce land and expensive human time can also be conserved by encouraging round-the-clock operation. . . . By such means people can live densely without stepping on each other's toes."

## 10. Interest Groups Emerge

As the U.S. frontier matured, the population became more aware of its own circumstances and organized to promote its own concerns. Turner (1893:207; 1965:54) remarked that the West felt a keen sense of difference from the East . . . One hundred years ago the West gave rise to such pressure groups and farm bloc organizations as the Greenback party, the National Grange, and the Populists. The Granger movement, for example, grew with the westerners' problems with transportation in their region. . . .

The night also isolates a group from the main society. Antagonism may develop as daytimers deprecate the nighttimers and the latter resent the neglect shown by the others. People active after dark find their life-style differing from that of daytime society, become aware of having a separate identity, and evolve into interest groups. New alignments in the tradition of sectionalism begin to emerge. This has already happened for two groups usually linked with the nighttime: homosexuals and prostitutes . . . (Boston *Globe*, 1976a).

An actual day vs. night contest has already been fought in Boston. The city's airport is flanked by residential neighborhoods and its afterdark activity became a nuisance to people wanting an undisturbed night's sleep. In 1976 dwellers in those neighborhoods, as private citizens and through two organized groups—Fair Share and the Massachusettes Air Pollution and Noise Abatement Committee—made a concerted effort to stop airplane flights between 11 P.M. and 7 A.M. It led to counterarguments by the business community stressing the economic benefit of continuing the flights. The pro-nighttime group was a coalition among commercial interests, airline companies, unions, and airport employees holding jobs at night (some of whom lived in those very neighborhoods). This group argued that the curfew would result in the loss of thousands of jobs, millions of dollars in sales, and further, would discourage business investment in the New England area. Joined by the governor, the mayor, and many legislators, the coalition successfully won a decision from the Massachusettes Port Authority that the nighttime flights should be kept going. (Some proposals for noise reduction during the night accompanied the decision.) A month later, Eastern Airlines announced it was adding an airbus and expanding its staff at the airport "as a direct result of the recent decision . . . not to impose a night curfew at Logan [airport]." As one businessman put it, "The curfew decision was regarded as the shootout at the OK Corral" (Boston *Globe*, 1976b; 1976c).

## DISCUSSION

The evidence bears out the hypothesis that night is a frontier. That nighttimers are *less* likely to return the keys they find also supports the idea. While the outcome of Test 3 seems to deny the claim that more help is given on a frontier, the lost-key experiment differs from the other tests in that it is the only one in which people do not meet face to face. It is a test of anonymous helpfulness. During the nighttime, strangers identify more readily with one another. A young man told me, "At 4 A.M. if someone sees you walking the streets at the same time he does, he must think, 'Gee, this guy must be part of the brethern, because no one else is awake at these times.' '' However, if someone finds a key and does not know the owner, he would guess that everyone who passed that way is equally likely to have lost it. Nighttimers, knowing they are few, assume on the weight of numbers that the person who lost the key is a daytimer. . . . The nighttime in-group feels comradely within itself but indifferent or antagonistic toward the out-group (see Sumner, 1906:27). Whereas frontier people readily help others whom they meet on the frontier, their sense of difference from unknown daytimers leaves them less concerned about the others' plights and they do not return many lost keys. . . . [A]ssistance is given selectively to those with whom the individuals identify.

• • •

## CONCLUSION

What is the gain in thinking of the night as a frontier? A single theoretical idea gives coherence to a wide range of events: the kind of people up and about at those hours, why they differ from daytimers in their behavior, the beginnings of political efforts by night people, the slow realization among leaders that public policy might be applied to the time resource. Even the variety of endeavors becomes understandable—from metal smelting plants to miniature golf courses, to mayor's complaint offices, to eating places, to computerized banking terminals that dispense cash. The niche is being expanded. Bit by bit, all of society migrates there. To treat this as a sequel to the geographic spread of past centuries is to summarize the move within familiar ecological concepts of migration, settlement, and frontier.

Though I have reviewed materials for one period in U.S. history, these conditions are features of all frontiers. They should apply to the Russians crossing the Urals, to the Chinese entering Manchuria during the Ch'ing dynasty, to the Boers settling South Africa, to Australians venturing into the Outback, to present-day Brazilians colonizing the Amazon interior, as well as to Americans migrating into the night. . . .

We should also consider the uniqueness of this new frontier. Each settlement beyond established boundaries has its own qualities. Here are some differences between the West and the night: (1) On the land frontier settlers lived rudely with few services at hand. At night a large portion of the total range of activities is services. (2) Utilities cost more on the western fringes; at night the fees for telephone calls, electricity, and airplane travel are lower. (3) While western settlements were in remote contact with the East, day and night are joined so that either can be affected quickly by events in the other. Twenty-four hour society is more constantly adjusting, more unstable. (4) Looking westward, pioneers saw no end to the possibilities for growth, but we know that expansion into the night can only go as far as the dawn. (5) The land frontier held promise of unlimited opportunity for individuals who ventured there. Miners and pioneers endured hardships because they lived for the future. They hoped to make their fortunes, or at least a better life. At night there are large numbers of unskilled, menial, and dirty tasks; but charwoman and watchman and hospital aide and porter are dead-end jobs. Many people so employed are immigrants or members of minority groups and this expanding margin of society is a *time ghetto*. The ghetto encloses more than minorities and immigrants, for ultimate control in 24-hour organizations remains with top management in the daytime. Policy making, important decisions, employee hiring, and planning are curtailed during off-hours. Since evening and night staffs are prevented from taking many actions that would lead to the recognition of executive ability, and since their performance is not readily observable by the bosses, all have poorer chances for advancement. (6) The western frontier's natural resources were so extensive that we became wasteful and squandered them. At night there is nothing new to exploit but time itself, so we maximize the use of fixed assets and become more frugal. (7) Migrating westward called for rather significant capital investment—outlays for a covered wagon, mining equipment, cattle, the railroad. There is little extra capital required for a move to the night. Instead, the incessant organization's need for more personnel reflects a swing toward more labor-intensive operations. So the night frontier may appeal to developing countries with meager treasuries and teeming populations of unemployed.

This expansion also unusual because it happens in time rather than in space. We change from a diurnal into an incessant species. We move beyond the environmental cycle—alternating day and night—in which our biological and social life evolved, and thus force novelty on these areas. (8) In the past a single set of minds shut down an enterprise one day and started it up the next. It permitted easy continuity and orderly administration. For coverage around the clock, we introduce shifts of personnel. Several times a day another set of minds takes over the same activity and facilties. (9) A physiological upset is imposed on people who work at night and maintain ordinary recreation and social life on their days off. Each time they switch their active hours, they undergo phase shifts in body rhythms such as heartbeat, temperature, and hormonal production. The several days' malaise that results was known to such workers long before air travel across time zones popularized the phase ''jet fatigue.''

• • •

In his essay ''The Frontier in American History,'' Frederick Jackson Turner (1893:38) reviewed the impact of the advance into western lands upon our society and remarked, "And now, four centuries from the discovery of America, at the end of a hundred years of life under the constitution, the frontier has gone." But it has not gone. During the era that the settlement of our land frontier was being completed, there began—into the night—a large-scale migration of wakeful activity that continues to spread over the world.

## NOTES

1. I thank the Center for Studies of Metropolitan Problems, National Institute of Mental Health, for grant MH–22763 through which the research and the preparation of this essay was supported; and Earl Mellor of the Bureau of Labor Statistics for providing interpretive help and data tables from the 1976 Current Population Survey. I also thank my research assistants William O. Clarke, Ann Getman, Shelley Leavitt, Lee Parmenter, Alan Rubinstein, Melanie Wallace, and Marilyn Arsem for field observations at all hours in rain and bitter cold as well as mild weather; and my colleagues Paul Hollander and Anthony Harris of the University of Massachusetts at Amherst, for serving as recipients in the lost-key test.

## REFERENCES

American Heritgage Dictionary of the English Language
   1970  Boston: Houghton Mifflin.

Becker, Howard
   1963  *Outsiders: Studies in the Sociology of Deviance.* New York: Free Press.

Billington, Ray Allen
   1949  *Westward Expansion.* New York: Macmillian.
   1954  *The American Frontiersman.* London: Oxford University Press.
   1972  "Frontier democracy: social aspects." Pp. 160–84 in G. R. Taylor (ed.), *The Turner Thesis: Concerning the Role of the Frontier in American History.* 3rd ed. Lexington, Mass.: Heath.

Boston Globe
   1976a  "Prostitutes speak of pride, but they are still victims." June 25:1,10.
   1976b  "Dukakis decides to go against Logan curfew." August 12:1, 20.
   1976c  "Logan anti-noise plan offered." August 13:35.
   1977  "Boston police today." April 4:1,3.

Brandeis, Louis D., and Josephine Goldmark
   1918  *The Case Against Night Work for Women.* Rev. ed. New York: National Consumers League.

Buttimer, Anne
   1976  "Grasping the dynamism of lifeworld." *Annals of the Association of American Geographers* 66: 277–92.

Dantzig, George B. and Thomas L. Saaty
   1973  *Compact City.* San Francisco: Freeman.

Darby, William
  [1818]  "Primitivism in the lower Mississippi valley." Pp. 399–401 in M. Ridge
  1969    and R. A. Billington (eds.), *America's Frontier Story*. New York: Holt.

Dick, Everett
  [1937]  *The Sod-House Frontier, 1854–1890*. New York: Appleton-Century.
  1954

Doddridge, Joseph
  [1912]  "Life in the old west." Pp. 101–6 in M. Ridge and R. A. Billington
  1969    (eds.), *America's Frontier Story*. New York: Holt.

Flint, Timothy
  [1826]  "Frontier society in the Mississippi valley." Pp. 401–3 in M. Ridge and
  1969    R. A. Billington (eds.), *America's Frontier Story*. New York: Holt.

Frantz, J. B., and J. E. Choate
  1955  *The American Cowboy: The Myth and Reality*. Norman: University of Okla-
        homa Press.

Godkin, Edwin L.
  [1896]  "The frontier and the national character." Pp. 13–6 in M. Ridge and R.
  1969    A. Billington (eds.), *America's Frontier Story*. New York: Holt.

Hicks, John D.
  1948  *The Federal Union*. Boston: Houghton Mifflin.

Hollon, W. Eugene
  1973  "Frontier violence: another look." Pp. 86–100 in R. A. Billington (ed.),
        *People of the Plains and Mountains*. Westport, Ct.: Greenwood Press.
  1974  *Frontier Violence*. New York: Oxford University Press.

Humphrey, Seth K.
  1931  *Following the Prairie Frontier*. Minneapolis: University of Minnesota Press.

Kozak, Lola Jean
  1974  "Night people: a study of the social experiences of night workers."
        Michigan State University, *Summation* 4: 40–61.

Marx, Karl
  [1867]  *Capital*. New York: Modern Library.
  1906

Meier, Richard L.
  1976  "A stable urban ecosystem." *Science* 192: 962–8.

Mumford, Lewis
  1961  *The City in History*. New York: Harcourt Brace.

National Industrial Conference Board
  1927  *Night Work in Industry*. New York: National Industrial Conference Board.

New York Times
  1968  " 'Cooping': an old custom under fire." December, 15: Sec. 4, 6E.

Patrushev, V. D.
  1972  "Aggregate time-balances and their meaning for socio-economic plan-

ning." Pp. 429–40 in A. Szalai (ed.), *The Use of Time.* The Hague: Mouton.

Riegel, Robert E.
1947  *America Moves West.* New York: Holt.

Robbins, Roy M.
1942  *Our Landed Heritage.* Princeton: Princeton University Press.

Schachter, Stanley
1959  *The Psychology of Affiliation.* Stanford: Stanford University Press.

Schlesinger, Arthur
1933  *The Rise of the City: 1878–1895.* New York: Macmillian.

Schydlowsky, Daniel
1976  "Multiple shifts would produce 'revolutionary results' for Latin American economy." Boston University, *Spectrum* 4 (September 9): 5.

Smith, Henry Nash
[1950]  *Virgin Land.* New York: Vintage.
1957

Sumner, William Graham
[1906]  *Folkways.* New York: New American Library.
1960

Szalai, Alexander (ed.)
1972  *The Use of Time.* The Hague: Mouton.

Turner, Frederick Jackson
[1893]  *The Frontier in American History.* New York: Holt.
1920
1932  *The Significance of Sections in American History.* New York: Holt.
[1965]  *America's Great Frontiers and Sections.* Unpublished essays edited by W.
1969    R. Jacobs. Lincoln: Nebraska University Press.

U.S. Bureau of Labor Statistics
1976  Current Population Survey. Unpublished paper. May 12: Table 1. Washington, D.C.

U.S. Office of Management and Budget
1974  *Social Indicators, 1973.* Washington, D.C.: U.S. Government Printing Office.

Young, Michael, and Peter Willmott
[1973]  *The Symmetrical Family.* Harmondsworth, London: Penguin.
1975

# Review Questions

1. We usually think of a "frontier" in terms of space, or geographical areas—not in terms of time. What unique features in the history of American society have led us to adopt this view?

2. How has the use of nighttime hours changed since the Industrial Revolution?

3. What was the link between the closing of the western (geographic) frontier and the opening of the night (time) frontier?

4. Melbin discusses in some detail ten ways in which the night frontier is similar to the western frontier. He also mentions nine ways the night frontier is unique. List these similarities and differences.

5. How does this article show that a societal change has both *roots* in the larger social system and *consequences* for the future of the social system?

# WOMEN AND MARRIAGE: ADDING AN EXTRAMARITAL ROLE

Lynn Atwater

Ever larger numbers of women are becoming involved in an extramarital relationship (EMR) at some point in their married lives. The best available evidence (Bell et al., 1975; Levin, 1975) shows an increase in every age group as compared to baseline data (Kinsey et al., 1953). The change is highest for younger married women, so that the data suggest an incidence of 40–50 percent will occur as the youngest-age cohort of married women move through the life cycle. It appears that the rate for women's EMRs will approximate the rate for men's and become another area in the trend toward convergence of gender role behavior.

Much of the existing literature on women's EMR behavior was collected during an era of more traditional gender roles and tends to emphasize such reasons for involvement as unhappy marriages, falling in love with another man, or the need to compensate for loss of attractiveness due to aging (Bell, 1971; Gagnon and Simon, 1973; Hunt, 1969). Furthermore, because past studies also reflected the general cultural bias against EMRs, involvements were often seen as "sick" or "abnormal" (see Ellis, 1968, for a discussion of this point) with only negative effects on marriage and the family. Only relatively rarely did research suggest reasons as the desire for new emotional satisfaction or individual growth (Bell and Lobsenz, 1974; Hunt, 1969; Neubeck, 1969).

Because women's experience with EMRs is increasing at the same time as their gender role is undergoing much modification, it was decided to conduct a qualitative study to elicit hypotheses about the current nature of women's extramarital involvement and its integration with family life. For this purpose, exploratory research was carried out with women who were considered receptive to personal and social change.

A sample of women (N=40) was interviewed in depth about their extramarital experiences. The sample was drawn from a larger group of approximately 300 respondents to an ad in *Ms.* magazine requesting women who were involved now/recently in extramarital relationships to write the researcher. Only two women who were asked refused interviews, and no payment was made to any respondent.

All data were gathered by this researcher during 1974–1975. Inter-

This is an original article especially prepared for the first edition of this volume, based on "Women in Extra-Marital Relationships: A Case Study in Sociosexuality," Ph.D. dissertation, Department of Sociology, Rutgers University, January 1978.

views followed a nine-page interview guide prepared on the basis of previous test interviews. Questions were primarily open-ended to ensure
emphasis on the women's subjective understanding. Women were further encouraged to discuss anything they felt important that was not already the focus of a question. All interviews were tape-recorded with the
consent of the respondent.

Analytical considerations guided the selection of the sample, which
represented a range of background variables. This variation generates
the maximum number of empirical and conceptual possibilities for analysis (Glaser and Strauss, 1967). Although the use of an analytical sample
means that the findings are limited in their generalizability, the sample
fits the goals of the research in that it probably (1) reveals emergent
changes in women's EMRs, (2) suggests factors unique to the understanding of women's sexual behavior, which has consistently been different from men's (Ehrmann, 1964), and (3) uncovers possible explana-
tory hypotheses to be tested in research on representative samples.

Women who were interviewed lived primarily in urban/suburban areas in twenty-three states. They varied in age from twenty-three to fifty-
nine years and in education from high school to graduate work. The
sample somewhat overrepresents the more highly educated, middle- to
upper-middle-class woman, but these are the women more likely to be in
the vanguard of social change.

Occupationally, 30 percent of the women identified themselves as
homemakers with one-half of these working or attending school part-
time. About one-third held full-time clerical or secretarial jobs, one-third
were engaged in full-time managerial-professional employment, and the
remaining (3) were full-time students. Seventy percent (28) had children,
varying in age from infants to adults; 65 percent (26) of the marriages
were still intact at the time of the interviews; the remainder had ended in
separation, divorce, or death of the husband at some point after the first
EMR involvement.

## MEANINGS

The first observation to be made about the meanings of women's extramarital involvements is that the overwhelming majority of answers fell
into two categories, those pertaining to the characteristics of the relationship itself or those pertaining to the women's personal needs and desires. It will be noticed that there was relatively infrequent mention of
"traditional" reasons or of sex as a dominant concern, as might be expected.

> It was very important. It started off just being sexual, but changed to a more
> encompassing relationship.
>
> It makes me feel so completely a woman.

• • •

It meant learning about another person.

It was a very long-term closeness with another person. I wanted to—and it seemed very natural to—to extend that closeness to include sex.

· · ·

It was like being with a soul brother. It was nice to be able to share intellectually, sexually, emotionally.

It made me happy at a time when there wasn't a lot to be happy about.

This relationship means a great deal to me, as we explore our many differences and similarities, discuss a variety of issues, and express ourselves physically. It is a total trip, taken very slowly since we have as much time as we need to really get to know each other.

It meant I was a person, not an appendage of my husband.

It meant having another friend.

It's made me a happy person because I'm doing what I feel without worrying about someone's rules. I'm the last person that people would think would break a rule. . . . I don't believe in waking up at 65 years old and regretting the chances that you never took.

These responses reflect a distinctly modern vocabulary of meanings. Some center on the pleasures of relating interpersonally and reflect contemporary attitudes toward adding greater expressiveness to our private lives through additional primary interactions. Whether it is done in an organized fashion through encounter groups or individually through EMRs (Berger, 1966:74), it is an empirical difference of degree, not kind.

Other meanings related to self-fulfillment also embody particularly modern values, that of knowing, developing, or rewarding the self through interaction with others (Lyman and Scott, 1970:123; Berger et al., 1973:77). This is in contrast to the traditional female gender role, which emphasizes the *giving* of emotional rewards to others. The majority of these women see EMRs as an opportunity to *receive* and, therefore, to modify the definitions of the usual woman's role.

The opportunity to talk about "getting" rather than "giving" was more directly presented in the question, "What do you get from the relationship?," and the answers allow some refinement of our first observations. Here about one-half of the women talked about the pleasures of interaction as a mutual experience, but the emphasis was still on the enjoyment of communicating and relating.

I guess essentially what I get is the companionship, the closeness and the ability to communicate with a male.

The feeling of being treated as an equal; poems from him, all kinds of communication.

Mostly I get the enjoyment of really getting to know another human being, and working out the differences into a meaningful relationship. That means just knowing that he cares, without needing him to remind me often, regardless of whether he calls or not.

Essentially it was the pleasure of knowing completely a beautiful person who thought of me as being equally beautiful.

Approximately another one-quarter of the women responded to the question of "what do you get" with emphasis on the receipt of expressive rewards, for they make no reference to the relationship itself. There was, however, a distinct flavor of autonomy in the experience of getting.

I get variety. Other than that it was a real stroke, an ego boost, and one that I really needed right then, because I was doing a whole lot to hold other people together and had no support for myself—and this guy was really neat about that. Plus I knew how turned on he was to me, to my head.

It made me feel really cared for; it made me feel I was special.

I got self-confidence, a feeling of individuality, a self-reliance that I didn't have before, and understanding that I have resources and abilities, too, to meet my needs.

• • •

He was very supportive; everything I did was good—uh—and I needed it—a lot. Along with being supportive he also encouraged me to be my own person. He tried to develop that (independence) in me and he was highly successful. I was successful, but he helped me an awful lot in bringing out the independence.

The final one-quarter of cases gave answers that added the dimensions of sex, variety, and thrills that one might more typically expect although there also occurs some overlap with the previously mentioned items. It is surprising that sex was mentioned so rarely, in fact, in responses to questions about what is commonly defined as a sexual activity.

It's a thrill; it's really a thrill. Also, it's a way of knowing a serious, incredibly worthwhile person. And if I hadn't gotten involved with him, I wouldn't have known him as well. My life would be less if I had not met him and gotten to know him so well.

• • •

Well, I get a kick out of the relationship. It's a thrill for me . . . what I get out of the relationship is mostly the thrill of being with a man who wants me as a woman, in a sexy way.

Excitement, being with another man sexually.

When questioned about their feelings toward their EMR partners, approximately three-quarters of the women defined the person as a "friend" or someone they "liked." Less than one-quarter reported feelings of "love" but qualified this to mean a "human" or "person-to-person" kind of love. There was difficulty in finding the proper vocabulary to describe their feelings, suggesting a cultural lag in the development of language to express changing emotions. Only three women described themselves as being "in love" in a romantic sense.

Thus, there are a variety of subjective meanings reported to be a part of the experience of EMRs, with the major emphasis on the EMR as a social experience and the expressive pleasures of relating intimately (but not romantically) with another person. In one sense, this could be labeled a traditional meaning for women, as both sociological (Parsons and Bales, 1955) and psychological (Baken, 1966) theorists have described the female role as oriented toward expressiveness, affectivity, and concern for others. But, as we have already pointed out, these reported meanings emphasize the *mutuality* of the expressiveness or, in some cases, the *getting* instead of *giving* of emotional support, which is a significant variation on the usual female role. These women are not rejecting their interest in expressiveness but are clearly stating through their behavior and words a preference for reciprocity in the expressive dimension and, in some cases, a need, situationally or temporarily at least, for a unilateral expressiveness in which they are the recipients, rather than the donors.

These findings may be coupled with other aspects of this research in which women were questioned about their marriages and what they found particularly dissatisfying about them. The responses of thirty-eight of the forty women to this open-ended question may all be categorized as perceived deficiencies in the area of communication and expressiveness in their husbands. One solution for women with this complaint about their marital relationships is apparently found in EMRs with men who are more accomplished or egalitarian in socioemotional areas. These EMRs do not become a replacement for marriage, however, for in only one case did a woman leave her husband for her EMR partner. The important hypothesis in these data is that a strong motivation for participation in EMRs is a social one, the desire to modify the expressive dimension of the traditional female gender role from a unilateral to a mutual one. If a husband is unable or unwilling to accept such change, women may reach outside the marital framework to accomplish it.

## BEHAVIORAL CHANGE TOWARD HUSBANDS

As women's role complex has always been centered in family interaction, several queries explored how women's EMRs affect their playing of family roles. Nearly all the women (85 percent) thought that being involved with someone else had changed their behavior toward their husbands. Of this group, more than one-half characterized it as a change for the better.

> Yes, I'm not as afraid to say what I want to say, I don't think I kowtow to my husband as much as I used to, I don't let him hurt my feelings as easily as I used to 'cause I silently think that somebody else loves me. And if this man, my husband, is getting mad and raging at me, ridiculing me, then I don't bow and paw as much as I used to.

I think my EMRs have changed my behavior toward my husband. With my husband—obviously before I started these relationships I still had a dependency to meet my needs and however meager his meeting of my psychological, social and physical needs were, or how inadequate I thought they were, he still was the only one I had to meet them. So, since having the relationships and being involved in them—uh—I have no need for my husband to meet any needs of mine.

Yes, it did change my behavior toward my husband. Initially I was nicer to him because I think I was getting more than I needed and wasn't even conscious that I did need . . . I used to always, even during the first few years of my relationship with Paul, I would always give in to my husband. If he would argue with me I would always sort of in the end let him have the last word. I felt on easier ground that way. I don't do that so much anymore. I never could walk away angry but now I can. I never could go to sleep without resolving something and kissing and making up. I can do that better now and I think that's good.

Oh, yes, my behavior really did change. I bloomed. I became more interested in everything around me. I was on top of the world, and my family found me to be a much happier person, with much, much more to give to them. My God, I was alive!

Now I think I'm much nicer to my husband because I know not many husbands will accept it (her revelation of the EMR) like he did. I love my husband more because of it.

I would be divorced if it hadn't been for somebody else. I would have divorced him a hundred times over. The only thing that keeps us married is the fact that I can find sexual release outside my marriage. . . . Since I have had this second EMR ongoing, I have been able to draw my husband out more and get him to talk more and more and to be more open in expressing my feelings with him on a very gradual basis. I am slowly but surely trying to bring our relationship up to a level that meets more of my needs.

Reported improvements lie in a variety of areas. Most salient to the issue of change in gender roles is an explicit sense of an increase in wifely power and sense of autonomy in the marriage because she has an alternate source of rewards. On the other hand, some wives found that the additional rewards from outside the marriage enabled them to increase either sexual or expressive rewards to their husbands or to be more willing to try to change the marriage relationship to better meet their own needs. In one case, the husband's increase of rewards to the wife because of his acceptance of the EMR situation raised his value in her eyes (as compared to her perception of other husbands), and the woman in turn increased her rewards to him. All these situations seem to add to marital stability, at least during the time period covered by these interviews.

Of the remaining women who felt that the EMR had affected their behavior toward their husbands, ten saw it as a negative consequence and five thought there were both positive and negative effects.

The way that it did affect my behavior was to make me more hostile to him. Having to sit there and read a book or something under his watchful eyes when I knew I could have been out with someone else . . . made it even more attractive to be with the other person and made me more resentful of my husband.

Yes, I was a little strained toward him at times, but I was also mixed up about a lot of other things beside the outside relationship.

I became less tolerant of my husband. I would rather have been with Bill than at home. It did affect my relationship with my husband. I was irritable and tired.

I ignored my marriage. I let it deteriorate while I had an outside diversion.

•   •   •

Six women said their behavior toward their husbands did not change. Three possibilities suggest themselves: (1) they changed but are not conscious of it, (2) their marriages may either have been ''passive-congenial'' or ''devitalized'' (Cuber and Harroff, 1965), in which case the low frequency and intensity of marital interaction may indeed not have been affected by the EMRs, or (3) they were experts at role compartmentalization, as the following excerpt suggests.

No, it didn't, because my husband's relationship to me is in one compartment, my writing is in another, and so on and so on. My private life is in a different one completely from all else and I move within it and then come back to the house. I shut the door on it. I can do that. It works well.

## EFFECT OF EMR SEX ON MARITAL SEX

One question specifically asked was, Did the EMR sex have any effect on marital sex? Slightly over one-half (58 percent) of the women reported that it did affect their marital sex, 40 percent replied that it did not, and one woman said she did not know. Of those women who reported an effect on marital sex, only fourteen responses could be characterized as a negative impact. A few women stopped sex completely, but most reduced the frequency of or their emotional involvement in marital sexual activity.

I stopped it completely, but it had been on the wane anyway.

I probably have less sex with my husband since getting involved in an EMR. He has always wanted very little. . . . So, uhmm, you know, quite often I would be the initiator of sex, and since I'm getting all I want—well, maybe sometimes not all I want—so I don't approach him at all now.

I don't know whether it's more or less sex with him. I stopped counting. I guess it's probably pretty much the same. And—uh—I can't say that having an affair with somebody has turned me on to my husband. I think in some ways it's kind of turned me off because I know I can get it somewhere else.

Yes, it does, and as I said, I don't try to lay any trip on him anymore. And it's freed me a lot more. If I am not totally satisfied in a relationship with my husband, I have learned the masturbation in a bathtub trick. We have an old-fashioned bathtub and I can drape my legs over the end, and if he hasn't been able to finish the job, I can take care of it just very nicely in the tub.

I probably started looking for my sexual satisfaction outside the marriage. When I wasn't satisfied with my husband, I didn't even care because I knew the next night I'd be with Ed, and get satisfied.

In addition to the fact that these responses denote a basically negative impact on marital sex, a peripheral theme present was that of a decrease in some women's sexual dependence on their husbands. This finding reiterates the increased sense of autonomy women gain from perceived positive changes in the social area of marital interaction. These consequences tend to occur in situations in which women feel thwarted in making desired changes in their marriages.

The remaining nine of the twenty-three women who reported an effect in marital sex described mostly increases in sexual activity with their husbands or more enjoyment of it.

Now that the truth is out and he knows I like these things and I wouldn't be horrified, it's amazing. The whole picture's changed.

Yes, we had much more sex while I was having the relationship.

It certainly affected my sexual relationship with my husband. I became more interested in sex with him, something I really couldn't understand at the time. I was riding high, returning from a visit with my lover. All those feelings needed an outlet. At times I felt this was terribly unfair to my husband, but it was always so good between us when this happened.

One interpretation of the increase in sexual activity is that it is inspired by guilt, but this does not usually seem to be the case. Rather, it appears more frequently to be the result of an increased libido and suggests one way in which EMRs can positively affect marriage.

One curious comparison to be made in conjunction with the previous observation is that, whereas 85 percent of the sample said that their EMR affected their behavior toward their husbands, only 58 percent said that their EMR affected their sexual activity toward their husbands. Thus, the socioemotional activity in an EMR seems to have a greater impact on the woman and her treatment of her husband than the sexual activity does. Or, alternatively, women are able to compartmentalize the consequences of the sexual activity more than they can the expressive, which emphasizes the previous data that the socioemotional aspects of EMRs mean more in general to these women than the strictly sexual.

## BEHAVIORAL CHANGE TOWARD CHILDREN

Of the twenty-eight women in the sample with children, 64 percent stated that their EMR involvement affected their behavior toward their children. Two-thirds of those believing it changed their behavior saw it as a change for the better.

> With my needs being met by a man outside the home, I don't have the same dependency toward my children. And it's a good feeling, in a way. I'm reacting to the children more as people now, just for what they are. I don't have to use them any more. I am also happy to be doing things with them because I have this all freed up psychic energy and I feel good about myself; and I want to do things and I hopefully do things with my children. I think they've benefited that way.
>
> (2 children, ages 4 and 8)

> Yes, very much so, because it's put me in contact with myself in a way that was not possible with just one other person. I have opened up my feelings, in terms of my not being shocked at my own children if they should become involved premaritally, if my children decide not to marry, or decide on a lifestyle that was other than a heterosexual one. It has very much changed my whole attitude. . . . And I think if I hadn't lived the life I'm living, I think my kids would still be dependent on me; I'd be smothering them to death. And I don't think that's enhancing.
>
> (2 children, ages 18 and 13)

> With the children—you know—I had more patience with the children because I was happy and having an adult relationship and I just had—you know—a more carefree attitude.
>
> (2 children, ages 5 and 7)

•   •   •

All these comments concerning changed behavior toward children reflect the normal strains of the intensity and isolation of the maternal role in a nuclear family system. It appears that the mother's having another adult relationship helps to offset the overinvolvement and self-sacrifice that are part of the structure and ideology of American motherhood. Not that it is being suggested that women have EMRs to make themselves better mothers, but that the inherent strain in the maternal role as it is conceptualized in America (Skolnick, 1973:290–312) will have a tendency to be relieved by *any* fulfilling activity the mother pursues.

The six women who thought their treatment of their children was negatively affected seemed to focus on their absence from their children.

> Yes, but I had been irritable after my second unwanted child was born. My children would cry when I would leave for school or to go out. It used to hurt like hell. I think it's done harm. It's definitely hurt all of us.
>
> (2 children, ages 6 and 5)

Once or twice I felt bad because I put her into bed a little earlier, an hour earlier, because he was coming over. Or if I go out in the evening, sometimes, I
feel bad. I don't know if it's rationalization or what, but when I go out in the
evening to go to school, it doesn't bother me.

(1 child, age 3)

Again, these remarks evoke a belief in traditional role ideology that
mothers belong constantly with their children as well as, perhaps, guilt
over the EMR activity. In all these six cases, further questioning by the interviewer elicited information that all the children had been in the care of
their fathers or a competent baby-sitter in the mother's absence. Additionally, a number of these research interviews were conducted in the
women's houses, and there was an opportunity to do several hours' observation. In no case was there any evidence of anything other than the
kind of mother-child interaction that one can observe normally in the
course of everyday living. It is a warranted conclusion, from the evidence
in this sample, that participation in EMRs does not have any more deleterious effects on mothering than does any other activity external to family life. In other words, the maternal aspect of the female gender role
complex, if it is affected at all, is more likely to be affected positively
rather than negatively by EMR activity.

## CONCLUSION

The predominant meaning of extramarital relationships for this group of
change-oriented women lies in the opportunity to change their traditional expressive roles to be reciprocal and to become more autonomous
individuals while maintaining the marriage relationship. To the degree
that these women's experiences are representative of other women's lives
now and in the future, several conclusions are implied.

One is that the probability of maintaining a monogamous relationship
may be enhanced by fostering concurrent changes in gender roles within
marriage. The recent emphasis on modification in women's roles has resulted in a lack of integration with men's roles. Supportive methods for
achieving comparable changes in men's roles may be in the form of self-
help groups and marital counseling. Anticipatory and remedial socialization for emerging roles could also be accomplished through various
agents such as parents, peers, schools, and the mass media. Changes in
other institutional areas to support expressiveness in men and autonomy in women may also be necessary.

An alternative implication concerns the increasing number of persons
who will experience extramaritality at some point in their married lives.
The evidence suggests that many extramarital relationships do not destroy or even undermine the quality of family life. Because most EMRs in

this study did not involve the arousal of traditional romantic feelings, this is congruent with women's characterizations that EMRs mostly affect their behavior positively toward their husbands and children. The absence of conventional "in love" type of "affairs" would predictably generate a less negative impact on family life. The dissemination of information on new styles of EMRs, as well as knowledge of compartmentalization techniques, coping mechanisms, and other strategies for integrating EMRs with marriage, can only prove useful to those married persons whose lives will be touched by this phenomenon.

Finally, as has been noted in this study, variations in the numbers of persons involved in EMR behavior, their reasons for doing it, and the way in which their behavior is interpreted are constantly occurring and are a reflection of other cultural and social changes. Not only is the reality of the behavior being transformed, but the unrealistic public attitudes fostered by the low visibility of EMRs in the past may be modifying. A recent study (Bukstel et al., 1978) indicates that persons with premarital experiences project that they expect to have extramarital experiences in the future. This is an indication of a dramatic attitudinal change that could alter our perception and consciousness of what marriage is all about. For the facts are that extramarital relationships are, always have been, and will continue to be a part of the American institution of marriage.

## REFERENCES

Bakan, David, 1966, *The Duality of Human Existence*. Chicago: Rand-McNally.

Bell, Robert R., 1971a, *Social Deviance*. Homewood, Ill.: Dorsey. 1971b, *Marriage and Family Interaction*. Homewood, Ill: Dorsey.

Bell, Robert R., and Norman M. Lobsenz, 1974, "Married Sex: How Uninhibited Can a Woman Dare to Be?," *Redbook*, 143 (September), 75, 176–181.

Bell, Robert R., Stanley Turner, and Lawrence Rosen, 1975, "A Multivariate Analysis of Female Extramarital Coitus," *Journal of Marriage and the Family*, 37 (May), 375–384

Berger, Peter, Brigitte Berger, and Hansfried Kellner, 1973, *The Homeless Mind*. New York: Vintage.

Bukstel, Lee H., Gregory D. Roeder, Peter R. Kilmann, and James Laughlin, 1978, "Projected Extramarital Sexual Involvement in Unmarried College Students," *Journal of Marriage and the Family* (May), 337–340.

Cuber, John F., and Peggy B. Harroff, 1965, *The Significant Americans*. New York: Appleton-Century-Crofts.

Edwards, John N., and Alan Booth, 1976, "Sexual Behavior in and out of Marriage: An Assessment of Correlates," *Journal of Marriage and the Family*, 38, 73–81.

Ehrmann, W. W., 1964, "Marital and Nonmarital Sexual Behavior," in H. T. Christensen, ed., *Handbook of Marriage and the Family*. Chicago: Rand McNally, pp. 585–622.

Ellis, A., 1968, "Healthy and Disturbed Reasons for Having Extramarital Relations," *Journal of Human Relations*, 16, 490–501.

Gagnon, John H., and William Simon, 1973, *Sexual Conduct: The Social Sources of Human Sexuality*. Chicago: Aldine.

Glaser, Barney G., and Anselm L. Strauss, 1967, *The Discovery of Grounded Theory*. Chicago: Aldine.

Hunt, Morton M., 1969, *The Affair*. New York: New American Library. 1974, "Sexual Behavior in the 1970's. Part IV: Extramarital and Postmarital Sex," *Playboy*, 21, 60–61, 286–287.

Kinsey, Alfred C., Wardell B. Pomeroy, Clyde E. Martin, and Paul H. Gebhard, 1953, *Sexual Behavior in the Human Female*. Philadelphia: Saunders.

Levin, Robert J., 1975, "The Redbook Report on Premarital and Extramarital Sex: The End of the Double Standard?," *Redbook*, (October), 38–44, 190–192.

Lyman, Stanford M., and Marvin B. Scott, 1970, *A Sociology of the Absurd*. New York: Appleton-Century-Crofts.

Neubeck, Gerhard, ed., 1969, *Extra-Marital Relations*. Englewood Cliffs, N.J.: Prentice-Hall.

Parsons, T., and R. F. Bales, 1955, *Family, Socialization and Interaction Process*. New York: Free Press.

Skolnick, Arlene, 1973, *The Intimate Environment*. Boston: Little, Brown.

# Review Questions

1. How did women's EMRs affect their relationships with their spouses? Their children?

2. What did the women in Atwater's study gain from their EMRs that they did not have in their marriages?

3. How have changes in the norms regarding male-female relationships contributed to the rise of EMRs among women?

4. What might be the implications of changes in women's involvement in EMRs for other aspects of American life?

5. Why can't Atwater's research findings be generalized to all women in the United States? How could you design a study with a more representative sample? What problems would you encounter?

# DEATH BY DIESELIZATION: A CASE STUDY IN THE REACTION TO TECHNOLOGICAL CHANGE

## W. F. Cottrell

. . . W̶E EXAMINE [HERE] A COMMUNITY CONFRONTED WITH RADICAL change in its basic economic institution and . . . trace the effects of this change throughout the social structure. From these facts it may be possible in some degree to anticipate the resultant changing attitudes and values of the people in the community, particularly as they reveal whether or not there is a demand for modification of the social structure or a shift in function from one institution to another. Some of the implications of the facts discovered may be valuable in anticipating future social change.

The community chosen for examination has been disrupted by the dieselization of the railroads. Since the railroad is among the oldest of those industries organized around steam, and since therefore the social structure of railroad communities is a product of long-continued processes of adaptation to the technology of steam, the sharp contrast between the technological requirements of the steam engine and those of the diesel should clearly reveal the changes in social structure required. Any one of a great many railroad towns might have been chosen for examination. However, many railroad towns are only partly dependent upon the railroad for their existence. In them many of the effects which take place are blurred and not easily distinguishable by the observer. Thus, the "normal" railroad town may not be the best place to see the consequences of dieselization. For this reason a one-industry town was chosen for examination.

In a sense it is an "ideal type" railroad town, and hence not complicated by other extraneous economic factors. It lies in the desert and is here given the name "Caliente" which is the Spanish adjective for "hot." Caliente was built in a break in an eighty-mile canyon traversing the desert. Its reason for existence was to service the steam locomotive. There are few resources in the area to support it on any other basis, and such as they are they would contribute more to the growth and maintenance of other little settlements in the vicinity than to that of Caliente. So long as the steam locomotive was in use, Caliente was a necessity. With the adoption of the diesel it became obsolescent.

W. F. Cottrell, "Death by Dieselization: A Case Study in the Reaction to Technological Change," *American Sociological Review*, 16 (1951), 358–365.

This stark fact was not, however, part of the expectations of the residents of Caliente. Based upon the "certainty" of the railroad's need for Caliente, men built their homes there, frequently of concrete and brick, at the cost, in many cases, of their life savings. The water system was laid in cast iron which will last for centuries. Business men erected substantial buildings which could be paid for only by profits gained through many years of business. Four churches evidence the faith of Caliente people in the future of their community. A twenty-seven bed hospital serves the town. Those who built it thought that their investment was as well warranted as the fact of birth, sickness, accident and death. They believed in education. Their school buildings represent the investment of savings guaranteed by bonds and future taxes. There is a combined park and play field which, together with a recently modernized theatre, has been serving recreational needs. All these physical structures are material evidence of the expectations, morally and legally sanctioned and financially funded, of the people of Caliente. This is a normal and rational aspect of the culture of all "solid" and "sound" communities.

Similarly normal are the social organizations. These include Rotary, Chamber of Commerce, Masons, Odd Fellows, American Legion and the Veterans of Foreign Wars. There are the usual unions, churches, and myriad . . . clubs. . . . In short, here is the average American community with normal social life, subscribing to normal American codes. Nothing its members had been taught would indicate that the whole pattern of this normal existence depended completely upon a few elements of technology which were themselves in flux. For them the continued use of the steam engine was as "natural" a phenomenon as any other element in their physical environment. Yet suddenly their life pattern was destroyed by the announcement that the railroad was moving its division point, and with it destroying the economic basis of Caliente's existence.

Turning from this specific community for a moment, let us examine the technical changes which took place and the reasons for the change. Division points on a railroad are established by the frequency with which the rolling stock must be serviced and the operating crews changed. At the turn of the century when this particular road was built, the engines produced wet steam at low temperatures. The steel in the boilers was of comparatively low tensile strength and could not withstand the high temperatures and pressures required for the efficient use of coal and water. At intervals of roughly a hundred miles the engine had to be disconnected from the train for service. At these points the cars also were inspected and if they were found to be defective they were either removed from the train or repaired while it was standing and the new engine being coupled on. Thus the location of Caliente, as far as the railroad was concerned, was a function of boiler temperature and pressure and the resultant service requirements of the locomotive.

Following World War II, the high tensile steels developed to create superior artillery and armor were used for locomotives. As a consequence it was possible to utilize steam at higher temperatures and pressure. Speed, power, and efficiency were increased and the distance between service intervals was increased.

The "ideal distance" between freight divisions became approximately 150 to 200 miles whereas it had formerly been 100 to 150. Wherever possible, freight divisions were increased in length to that formerly used by passenger trains, and passenger divisions were lengthened from two old freight divisions to three. Thus towns located at 100 miles from a terminal became obsolescent, those at 200 became freight points only, and those at three hundred miles became passenger division points.

The increase in speed permitted the train crews to make the greater distance in the time previously required for the lesser trip, and roughly a third of the train and engine crews, car inspectors, boilermakers and machinists and other service men were dropped. The towns thus abandoned were crossed off the social record of the nation in the adjustment to these technological changes in the use of the steam locomotive. Caliente, located midway between terminals about six hundred miles apart, survived. In fact it gained, since the less frequent stops caused an increase in the service required of the maintenance crews at those points where it took place. However, the introduction of the change to diesel engines projected a very different future.

In its demands for service the diesel engine differs almost completely from a steam locomotive. It requires infrequent, highly skilled service, carried on within very close limits, in contrast to the frequent, crude adjustments required by the steam locomotive. Diesels operate at about 35 per cent efficiency, in contrast to the approximately 4 per cent efficiency of the steam locomotives in use after World War II in the United States. Hence diesels require much less frequent stops for fuel and water. These facts reduce their operating costs sufficiently to compensate for their much higher initial cost.

In spite of these reductions in operating costs the introduction of diesels ordinarily would have taken a good deal of time. The changeover would have been slowed by the high capital costs of retooling the locomotive works, the long period required to recapture the costs of existing steam locomotives, and the effective resistance of the workers. World War II altered each of these factors. The locomotive works were required to make the change in order to provide marine engines, and the costs of the change were assumed by the government. Steam engines were used up by the tremendous demand placed upon the railroads by war traffic. The costs were recaptured by shipping charges. Labor shortages were such that labor resistance was less formidable and much less acceptable to the public than it would have been in peace time. Hence the shift to diesels was greatly facilitated by the war. In consequence, every third and sometimes every second division point suddenly became technolog-ically obsolescent.

Caliente, like all other towns in similar plight, is supposed to accept its fate in the name of "progress." The general public, as shippers and con-sumers of shipped goods, reaps the harvest in better, faster service and eventually perhaps in lower charges. A few of the workers in Caliente will also share the gains, as they move to other division points, through higher wages. They will share in the higher pay, though whether this will be adequate to compensate for the costs of moving no one can say. Certain it is that their pay will not be adjusted to compensate for their specific losses. They will gain only as their seniority gives them the op-portunity to work. These are those who gain. What are the losses, and who bears them?

The railroad company can figure its losses at Caliente fairly accurately. It owns 39 private dwellings, a modern clubhouse with 116 single rooms, and a twelve-room hotel. . . . These now become useless, as does much of the fixed physical equipment used for servicing trains. Some of the machinery can be used elsewhere. Some part of the roundhouse can be used to store unused locomotives and standby equipment. The rest will be torn down to save taxes. All of these costs can be entered as capital losses on the statement which the company draws up for its stockhold-ers and for the government. . . .

What are the losses that may not be entered on the company books? The total tax assessment in Caliente was $9,946.80 for the year 1948, of which $6,103.39 represented taxes assessed on the railroad. Thus the railroad valuation was about three-fifths that of the town. This does not take into account tax-free property belonging to the churches, the schools, the hospital, or the municipality itself which included all the public utilities. Some ideas of the losses sustained by the railroad in com-parison with the losses of others can be surmised by reflecting on these figures for real estate alone. The story is an old one and often repeated in the economic history of America. It represents the "loss" side of a profit-and-loss system of adjusting to technological change. Perhaps for socio-logical purposes we need an answer to the question "just who pays?"

Probably the greatest losses are suffered by the older "non-operating" employees. Seniority among these men extends only within the local shop and craft. A man with twenty-five years' seniority at Caliente has no claim on the job of a similar craftsman at another point who has only twenty-five days' seniority. Moreover, some of the skills formerly valu-able are no longer needed. The boilermaker, for example, knows that jobs for his kind are disappearing and he must enter the ranks of the un-skilled. The protection and status offered by the union while he was em-ployed have become meaningless now that he is no longer needed. The cost of this is high both in loss of income and in personal demoralization.

Operating employees also pay. Their seniority extends over a division, which in this case includes three division points. The older members can move from Caliente and claim another job at another point, but in many cases they move leaving a good portion of their life savings behind. The younger men must abandon their stake in railroad employment. The loss may mean a new apprenticeship in another occupation, at a time in life when apprenticeship wages are not adequate to meet the obligations of mature men with families. A steam engine hauled 2,000 tons up the hill out of Caliente with the aid of two helpers. The four-unit diesel in command of one crew handles a train of 5,000 tons alone. Thus, to handle the same amount of tonnage required only about a fourth the manpower it formerly took. Three out of four men must start out anew at something else.

The local merchants pay. The boarded windows, half-empty shelves, and abandoned store buildings bear mute evidence of these costs. The older merchants stay, and pay; the younger ones, and those with no stake in the community will move; but the value of their property will in both cases largely be gone. . . .

The church will pay. The smaller congregations cannot support services as in the past. As the churchmen leave, the buildings will be abandoned.

Homeowners will pay. A hundred and thirty-five men owned homes in Caliente. . . . The least desirable homes will stand unoccupied, their value completely lost. The others must be revalued at a figure far below that at which they were formerly held.

In a word, those pay who are, by traditional American standards, *most moral*. Those who have raised children see friendships broken and neighborhoods disintegrated. The childless more freely shake the dust of Caliente from their feet. Those who built their personalities into the structure of the community watch their work destroyed. Those too wise or too selfish to have entangled themselves in community affairs suffer no such qualms. The chain store can pull down its sign, move its equipment and charge the costs off against more profitable and better located units, and against taxes. The local owner has no such alternatives. In short, "good citizens" who assumed family and community responsibility are the greatest losers. Nomads suffer least.

The people of Caliente are asked to accept as "normal" this strange inversion of their expectations. It is assumed that they will, without protest or change in sentiment, accept the dictum of the "law of supply and demand." Certainly they must comply in part with this dictum. While their behavior in part reflects this compliance, there are also other changes perhaps equally important in their attitudes and values.

The first reaction took the form of an effort at community self-preservation. Caliente became visible to its inhabitants as a real entity, as meaningful as the individual personalities which they had hitherto been taught to see as atomistic or nomadic elements. Community survival was seen as prerequisite to many of the individual values that had been given precedence in the past. The organized community made a search of new industry, citing elements of community organization themselves as reasons why industry should move to Caliente. But the conditions that led the railroad to abandon the point made the place even less attractive to new industry. . . . Yet the effort to keep the community a going concern persisted.

There was also a change in sentiment. In the past the glib assertion that progress spelled sacrifice could be offered when some distant group was a victim of technological change. There was no such reaction when the event struck home. . . .

The people of Caliente continually profess their belief in "The American Way," but . . . they criticize decisions made solely in pursuit of profit, even though these decisions grow out of a clear-cut case of technological "progress." They feel that the company should have based its decision upon consideration for loyalty, citizenship, and community morale. They assume that the company should regard the seniority rights of workers as important considerations, and that it should consider significant the effect of permanent unemployment upon old and faithful employees. They look upon community integrity as an important community asset. Caught between the support of a "rational" system of "economic" forces and laws, and sentiments which they accept as significant values, they seek a solution to their dilemma which will at once permit them to retain their expected rewards for continued adherence to past norms and to defend the social system which they have been taught to revere but which now offers them a stone instead of bread.

## IMPLICATIONS *implied meaning, logical deduction.*

We have shown that those in Caliente whose behavior most nearly approached the ideal taught are hardest hit by change. On the other hand, those seemingly farthest removed in conduct from that ideal are either rewarded or pay less of the costs of change than do those who follow the ideal more closely. Absentee owners, completely anonymous, and consumers who are not expected to cooperate to make the gains possible are rewarded most highly, while the local people who must cooperate to raise productivity pay dearly for having contributed.

In a society run through sacred mysteries . . . such incongruities may be explained away. Such a society may even provide some "explanation" which makes them seem rational. In a secular society, supposedly defended rationally upon scientific facts, in which the pragmatic test "Does it work?" is continually applied, such discrepancy between expectation and realization is difficult to reconcile.

Defense of our traditional system of assessing the costs of technological change is made on the theory that the costs of such change are more than offset by the benefits to "society as a whole." However, it is difficult to show the people of Caliente just why *they* should pay for advances made to benefit others whom they have never known and who, in their judgment, have done nothing to justify such rewards. Any action that will permit the people of Caliente to levy the costs of change upon those who will benefit from them will be morally justifiable to the people of Caliente. Appeals to the general welfare leave them cold and the compulsions of the price system are not felt to be self-justifying "natural laws" but are regarded as being the specific consequence of specific bookkeeping decisions as to what should be included in the costs of change. They seek to change these decisions through social action. They do not consider that the "American Way" consists primarily of acceptance of the market as the final arbiter of their destiny. Rather they conceive that the system as a whole exists to render "justice," and if the consequences of the price system are such as to produce what they consider to be "injustice" they proceed to use some other institution as a means to reverse or offset the effects of the price system. Like other groups faced with the same situation, those in Caliente seize upon the means available to them. The operating employees had in their unions a device to secure what they consider to be their rights. Union practices developed over the years make it possible for the organized workers to avoid some of the costs of change which they would otherwise have had to bear. Featherbed rules, make-work practices, restricted work weeks, train length legislation and other similar devices were designed to permit union members to continue work even when "efficiency" dictated that they be disemployed. Members of the "Big Four" in Caliente joined with their fellows in demanding not only the retention of previously existing rules, but the imposition of new ones such as that requiring the presence of a third man in the diesel cab. For other groups there was available only the appeal to the company that it establish some other facility at Caliente, or alternatively a demand that "government" do something. One such demand took the form of a request to the Interstate Commerce Commission that it require inspection of rolling stock at Caliente. This request was denied.

It rapidly became apparent to the people of Caliente that they could not gain their objectives by organized community action nor individual endeavor but there was hope that by adding their voices to those of others similarly injured there might be hope of solution. They began to look to the activities of the whole labor movement for succor. Union strategy which forced the transfer of control from the market to government mediation or to legislation and operation was widely approved on all sides. This was not confined to those only who were currently seeking rule changes but was equally approved by the great bulk of those in the community who had been hit by the change. Cries of public outrage at their demands for make-work rules were looked upon as coming from those at best ignorant, ill-informed or stupid, and at worst as being the hypocritical efforts of others to gain at the workers' expense. When the union threat of a national strike for rule changes was met by government seizure, Caliente workers like most of their compatriots across the country welcomed this shift in control, secure in their belief that if "justice" were done they could only be gainers by government intervention. These attitudes are not "class" phenomena purely nor are they merely occupational sentiments. They result from the fact that modern life, with the interdependence that it creates, particularly in one-industry communities, imposes penalties far beyond the membership of the groups presumably involved in industry. When make-work rules contributed to the livelihood of the community, the support of the churches, and the taxes which maintain the schools; when featherbed practices determine the standard of living, the profits of the businessman and the circulation of the press; when they contribute to the salary of the teacher and the preacher they can no longer be treated as accidental, immoral, deviant or temporary. Rather they are elevated into the position of emergent morality and law. Such practices generate a morality which serves them just as the practices in turn nourish those who participate in and preserve them. They are as firmly a part of what one "has a right to expect" from industry as are parity payments to the farmer, bonuses and pensions to the veterans, assistance to the aged, tariffs to the industrialist, or the sanctity of property to those who inherit. On the other hand, all these practices conceivably help create a structure that is particularly vulnerable to changes such as that described here.

Practices which force the company to spend in Caliente part of what has been saved through technological change, or failing that, to reward those who are forced to move by increased income for the same service, are not, by the people of Caliente, considered to be unjustifiable. Confronted by a choice between the old means and resultant "injustice" which their use entails, and the acceptance of new means which they believe will secure them the "justice" they hold to be their right, they are willing to abandon (in so far as this particular area is concerned) the liberal state and the omnicompetent market in favor of something that works to provide "justice."

The study of the politics of pressure groups will show how widely the reactions of Caliente people are paralleled by those of other groups. Amongst them it is in politics that the decisions as to who will pay and who will profit are made. Through organized political force railroaders maintain the continuance of rules which operate to their benefit rather than for "the public good" or "the general welfare." Their defense of these practices is found in the argument that only so can their rights be protected against the power of other groups who hope to gain at their expense by functioning through the corporation and the market.

We should expect that where there are other groups similarly affected by technological change, there will be similar efforts to change the operation of our institutions. The case cited is not unique. Not only is it duplicated in hundreds of railroad division points but also in other towns abandoned by management for similar reasons. Changes in the location of markets or in the method of calculating transportation costs, changes in technology making necessary the use of new materials, changes due to the exhaustion of old sources of materials, changes to avoid labor costs such as the shift of the textile industry from New England to the South, changes to expedite decentralization to avoid the consequences of bombing, or those of congested living, all give rise to the question, "Who benefits, and at whose expense?"

The accounting practices of the corporation permit the entry only of those costs which have become "legitimate" claims upon the company. But the tremendous risks borne by the workers and frequently all the members of the community in an era of technological change are real phenomena. Rapid shifts in technology which destroy the "legitimate" expectations derived from past experience force the recognition of new obligations. Such recognition may be made voluntarily as management foresees the necessity, or it may be thrust upon it by political or other action. Rigidity of property concepts, the legal structure controlling directors in what they may admit to be costs, and the stereotyped nature of the "economics" used by management make rapid change within the corporation itself difficult even in a "free democratic society." Hence while management is likely to be permitted or required to initiate technological change in the interest of profits, it may and probably will be barred from compensating for the social consequences certain to arise from those changes. Management thus shuts out the rising flood of demands in its cost accounting only to have them reappear in its tax accounts, in legal regulations or in new insistent union demands. If economics fails to provide an answer to social demands then politics will be tried.

It is clear that while traditional morality provides a means of protecting some groups from the consequences of technological change, or some method of meliorating the effects of change upon them, other large segments of the population are left unprotected. It should be equally clear that rather than a quiet acquiescence in the finality and justice of such arrangements, there is an active effort to force new devices into being which will extend protection to those hitherto expected to bear the brunt of these costs. A good proportion of these inventions increasingly call for the intervention of the state. To call such arrangements immoral, unpatriotic, socialistic or to hurl other epithets at them is not to deal effectively with them. They are as "natural" as are the "normal" reactions for which we have "rational" explanations based upon some pre-scientific generalization about human nature such as "the law of supply and demand" or "the inevitability of progress." To be dealt with effectively they will have to be understood and treated as such.

# Review Questions

1. How did World War II facilitate the shift from steam to diesel locomotives?

2. Did the people of Caliente anticipate the consequences that were to occur after the shift?

3. What groups of workers and what types of citizens suffered the most as Caliente succumbed to ''progress''?

4. How did Caliente residents' attitudes toward progress and sacrifice change after the introduction of the diesel locomotive?

5. Trace the implications of the new technology for the major social institutions of Caliente.

# Suggested Readings: Social and Cultural Change

Atwater, Lynn. *The Extramarital Connection: Sex, Intimacy, and Identity*. New York: Irvington, 1982.

Berger, Peter, Brigitte Berger, and Hansfried Kellner. *The Homeless Mind*. New York: Vintage Books, 1974.

Cohen, Yehudi A. '' 'You're O.K., How Am I?' Loneliness and Its Institutional Frames.'' In Joseph Hartog, J. Ralph Audy and Yehudi A. Cohen, eds., *The Anatomy of Loneliness*. New York: International Universities Press, 1980.

Erikson, Kai T. *Everything in Its Path*. New York: Simon & Schuster, 1976.

Lerner, David. *The Passing of Traditional Society*. New York: Free Press, 1958.

Spicer, Edward H., ed. *Human Problems in Technological Change*. New York: John Wiley, 1952.

Zurcher, Louis, and George Kirkpatrick. *Citizens for Decency: Antipornography Crusades as Status Defense*. Austin: University of Texas Press, 1976.

**Acknowledgments** (continued from p. iv)

Sandra L. Bem and Daryl J. Bem: "Case Study of a Nonconscious Ideology: Training the Woman to Know Her Place" from D.J. Bem, *Beliefs, Attitudes and Human Affairs.* Belmont, California: Brooks/Cole, 1970. Reprinted by permission of the authors.

Peter L. Berger: Excerpt from *Invitation to Sociology.* Copyright © 1963 by Peter L. Berger. Reprinted by permission of Doubleday & Company, Inc.

Peter L. Berger and Hansfried Kellner: "Marriage and the Construction of Reality," *Diogenes,* No. 46 (Summer 1964), pp. 1–24 (with deletions). Reprinted by permission of the publisher.

William Chambliss: "The Saints and the Roughnecks," *Society,* Vol. 11, No. 1 (November/December 1973), pp. 24–31. Copyright © 1973 by Transaction, Inc. Reprinted by permission of Transaction, Inc.

Candace Clark: "Sickness and Social Control" was written for this edition of *Social Interaction.*

Stephen Cole and Robert Lejeune: "Illness and the Legitimation of Failure"; *American Sociological Review;* vol. 37, pp. 347–356 (1972).

W. F. Cottrell: "Death by Dieselization: A Case Study in the Reaction to Technological Change," *American Sociological Review,* Vol. 16 (1951), pp. 358–365. Reprinted by permission of the American Sociological Association.

Charles Derber: Excerpted from "The Pursuit of Attention: Power and Individualism in Everyday Life" by Charles Derber and Yale Magrass (Oxford University Press, 1983). Reprinted by permission of Charles Derber.

G. William Domhoff: Excerpts from "The Bohemian Grove and Other Retreats". Copyright © 1974 by G. William Domhoff. Reprinted by permission of Harper and Row Publishers, Inc.

Andrea Fontana: Excerpted from "The Last Frontier," *Sage Library of Social Research,* Vol. 4, (Sage Publications, 1977), pp. 143–145, 147–167.

Charles Frazier: Excerpted from "Criminality and Emotional Ambivalence" in *Qualitative Sociology* V8-3, 1985, pp. 266–284, (Human Sciences Press, Inc.).

Erving Goffman: Excerpts from *The Presentation of Self in Everyday Life.* Copyright © 1959 by Erving Goffman. Reprinted by permission of Doubleday & Company, Inc.

Edward Gross and Gregory P. Stone: "Embarrassment and the Analysis of Role Requirements," *American Journal of Sociology,* 70 (July 1964), pp. 1–15 (with deletions). Copyright © 1964 by the University of Chicago Press. Reprinted by permission of the University of Chicago Press and the authors.

Arlie Hochschild: *The Managed Heart: Commercialization of Human Feeling,* pp. ix–x, 3–9, 11, 17–18, 24–29, 33. Copyright © 1983 The Regents of the University of California; used by permission of the University of California Press in *Social Interaction,* 3rd ed., eds. Clark and Robboy (St. Martin's).

Jennifer Hunt: Excerpted from "Police Accounts of Normal Force," *Urban Life,* Vol. 13, No. 4, (Sage Publications, January 1985), pp. 315–341.

David Karp and William C. Yoels: "The College Classroom: Some Observations on the Meanings of Student Participation," *Sociology and Social Research,* Vol. 60, No. 4, pp. 421–439. Reprinted by permission.

Sherryl Kleinman: Excerpted from "Equals Before God: Humanistic Seminarians and New Religious Roles," (University of Chicago Press, 1984), pp. 49–62.

Demie Kurz: *Skimming and Dumping at Primrose High: Career Mobility and the Perpetuation of Inequality.* Copyright © 1988 by Demie Kurz.

Janet Lever: "Games Children Play." Copyright © 1976 by The Society for the Study of Social Problems. Reprinted from *Social Problems* 23, 4, April, 1976, pp. 478–487, by permission.

Elliot Liebow: Excerpts from *Tally's Corner.* Copyright © 1967 by Little, Brown and Co. Reprinted by permission of Little, Brown and Co.

Lyn H. Lofland: "Loss and Human Connection," from W. Ickes and E.S. Knowles eds., *Personality, Roles and Social Behavior,* (Springer–Verlog, 1982), pp. 219–242.

Murray Melbin: "Night as Frontier," *American Sociological Review,* Vol. 43, No. 1 (Feb. 1978), pp. 2–22.

Marcia Millman: Selection is reprinted from *Such a Pretty Face,* "Being Fat in America" by Marcia Millman, by permission of W.W. Norton & Company, Inc. Copyright © 1980 by Marcia Millman.

Horace Miner: "Body Ritual Among the Nacirema." Reproduced by permission of the American Anthropological Association and the author from the *American Anthropologist,* 58 (1956), pp. 503–507.

Benjamin D. Paul: From "The Roles of Beliefs and Customs in Sanitation Programs," *American Journal of Public Health,* 48, pp. 1502–1506, American Public Health Association.

D. L. Rosenhan: "On Being Sane in Insane Places," *Science,* Vol. 179, No. 19 (January 1973), pp. 250–258 (with deletions). Copyright © 1973 by the American Association for the Advancement of Science. Reprinted by permission of the American Association for the Advancement of Science and the author.

Howard Robboy: "At Work with the Night Worker" is taken from the author's doctoral dissertation and was published in the first edition of *Social Interaction.*

Lucinda SanGiovanni: "Rediscovering Gender: The Emergent Role Passage of Ex-Nuns" was written for this edition of *Social Interaction.*

Barry Schwartz: "Waiting, Exchange, and Power," *American Journal of Sociology,* Vol. 79, No. 4 (January 1974), pp. 841–870 (with deletions). Copyright © 1974 by the University of Chicago Press. Reprinted by permission of the University of Chicago Press and the author.

Carol B. Stack: "Sex Roles and Survival Strategies in an Urban Black Community," from Michelle Z. Rosaldo and Louise Lamphere, *Women, Culture and Society,* Stanford University Press, 1975. Reprinted by permission of Carol B. Stack.

Anselm Strauss: From "Turning Points in Identity," *Mirrors and Masks: Transformations of Identity,* The Sociology Press, pp. 93–100.

Diane Vaughan: "Uncoupling: The Social Construction of Divorce" was written for the first edition of *Social Interaction.*

Lenore J. Weitzman: Excerpted with permission from Chapter 10 of *The Divorce Revolution: The Unexpected Social and Economic Consequences for Women and Children in America* by Dr. Lenore J. Weitzman. Copyright © 1985 by Dr. Lenore J. Weitzman. Published by The Free Press, a Division of Macmillan, Inc.

William F. Whyte: "Corner Boys: A Study of Clique Behavior," *American Journal of Sociology,* Vol. 46 (March 1941), pp. 647–664 (with deletions). Copyright © 1941 by the University of Chicago Press. Reprinted by permission of the University of Chicago Press.

Mark Zborowski: "Cultural Components in Responses to Pain," *Journal of Social Issues,* Vol. 8, No. 4 (1952), pp. 16–30. Reprinted by permission of the Society for the Psychological Study of Social Issues.

# ABOUT THE CONTRIBUTORS

**Lynn Atwater** received her Ph.D. from Rutgers University. She is currently Associate Professor of Sociology at Seton Hall University. Her book, *The Extramarital Connection: Sex, Intimacy, and Identity*, is a more comprehensive discussion of the subject presented in her article here. She is presently involved in research on children's awareness of their parents' extramarital relationships and on the social role of sibling.

**Howard S. Becker** was awarded his Ph.D. at the University of Chicago and is currently Professor of Sociology at Northwestern University. His numerous published works include *The Outsiders, Sociological Work: Method and Substance, Making the Grade: The Academic Side of College Life* (with Blanche Geer and Everett C. Hughes), *Boys in White: Student Culture in Medical School* (with Geer, Hughes, and others), and *Art Worlds*.

**Daryl J. Bem** is Professor of Psychology at Cornell University. His Ph.D. in social psychology is from the University of Michigan. He is the author of *Beliefs, Attitudes, and Human Affairs* and also of numerous articles on personality theory and on the social psychology of beliefs and attitudes.

**Sandra L. Bem** focuses her research on social-psychological aspects of gender roles. She received her Ph.D. in developmental psychology at the University of Michigan and is presently Professor of Psychology at Cornell University. Her areas of research and writing include gender, psychological androgyny, and gender-schema theory.

**Peter L. Berger** received his Ph.D. from the New School for Social Research. He taught at several institutions, including Rutgers University and Boston College, before becoming University Professor and Professor of the Sociology of Religion at Boston University. He has authored and co-authored a great number of books, including *The Social Construction of Reality* (with Thomas Luckmann), *Rumour of Angels, The Sacred Canopy, Noise of Solemn Assemblies,* and *Invitation to Sociology,* from which the first article in this volume is taken.

**William J. Chambliss**, was awarded his doctorate in sociology from the University of Indiana and also holds a law degree. He is presently Professor and Chair of the Department of Sociology at George Washington University. His many books on the sociology of law and crime include *On the Take, Crime and the Legal Process,* and *Whose Law? What Order?*

**Candace Clark** received her graduate training at the University of Chicago and Columbia University, where she was awarded the Ph.D. in sociomedical sciences. She is currently Assistant Professor of Sociology at Montclair State College. Her present research in the sociology of emotions focuses on sympathy. She is an editor of *Social Interaction*.

**Stephen Cole**, Professor of Sociology at the State University of New York at Stony Brook, earned his Ph.D. at Columbia University. He is the author of *The Sociological Method* and *The Unionization of Teachers* and co-author of *Social Stratification and Science*. He is currently engaged in research on sex roles and professional development.

**W. F. Cottrell** was Professor of Sociology at Miami University of Ohio and was associated with the Scripps Foundation at the time of his death.

**Charles Derber** received his Ph.D. from the University of Chicago and taught at Brandeis University before becoming Associate Professor of Sociology at Boston College. He is the author of two forthcoming books, *The Nuclear Seduction* and *The Role of Excerpts and Professionals in Modern Science* in addition to *The Pursuit of Attention*, which is excerpted here.

**G. William Domhoff** received his Ph.D. from the University of Miami. He is Professor of Psychology and Sociology at the University of California at Santa Cruz. His many works on social stratification include *The Higher Circles, Fat Cats and Democrats, The Powers That Be*, and *The Bohemian Grove and Other Retreats*, the latter of which is excerpted here.

**Andrea Fontana**, Professor of Sociology at the University of Nevada at Las Vegas, received his Ph.D. from the University of California at San Diego. His book *The Last Frontier* is excerpted here. In addition, he has co-authored *The Sociology of Everyday Life* and a book on social problems.

**Charles E. Frazier** is Associate Director for Research, Center for Studies in Criminology and Law, and Professor of Sociology at the University of Florida. He earned his doctorate from Southern Illinois University. His extensive writings in criminology include *Theological Approaches to Deviance*. His current research uses life-history methods to study check-forging gangs.

**Blanche Geer** earned her Ph.D. at Johns Hopkins University and is Professor Emeritus at Northeastern University. Her long-term collaboration with Howard S. Becker and Everett C. Hughes has resulted in, among other publications, *Making the Grade: The Academic Side of College Life* and *Boys in White: Student Culture in Medical School*.

**Erving Goffman** received his Ph.D. from the University of Chicago. At the time of his recent death in 1982, he was Benjamin Franklin Professor at the University of Pennsylvania and also served as president of the American Sociological Association. Goffman's unique dramaturgical perspective is reflected in his many books, including *Behavior in Public Places, Stigma, Asylums, Interaction Ritual, Frame Analysis, Gender Advertisements*, and the early *Presentation of Self in Everyday Life*, from which our selection is taken.

**Edward Gross** received his Ph.D. from the University of Chicago and is now Professor of Sociology at the University of Washington. His books include *Industry and Social Life, Work and Society*, and *University Goals and Academic Power* (co-authored with Paul Grambsch). His most recent research is in the sociology of emotions, as is the selection on embarrassment included in this volume.

**Arlie Russell Hochschild** is Professor of Sociology at the University of California at Berkeley, where she also received her Ph.D. Since 1975, she has been writing about the sociology of feelings and emotion management. Her 1983 book, *The Managed Heart: Commercialization of Human Feeling*, won the Charles Cooley Award and a *New York Times* Book of the Year award.

**Everett C. Hughes** earned a Ph.D. in social anthropology at the University of Chicago, where he taught in the Dept. of Sociology. At the time of his recent death, he was Professor Emeritus of Sociology at Boston College. Hughes was a major figure in the sociology of work and occupations and also served as president of the American Sociological Association. His many books include *Men and Their Work, The Sociological Eye, French Canada in Transition, Where People Meet: Racial and Ethnic Frontiers* (with Helen McGill Hughes), and *Making the Grade: The Academic Side of College Life* (co-authored with Howard S. Becker and Blanche Geer), which is the source of our selection in this volume.

**Jennifer Hunt** is currently Assistant Professor of Sociology at Montclair State College as well as a Research Candidate at the Psychoanalytic Institute of New York University Medical Center. She received her Ph.D. in Sociology at the City University of New York. Her research and writing focus on the police and on qualitative research techniques.

**David A. Karp**, who earned his Ph.D. from New York University, is now Professor of Sociology at Boston College. He is a co-author of *Being Urban: A Social Psychological View of City Life* (with Gregory P. Stone and William C. Yoels), *The Research Craft* (with John B. Williamson, John R. Dalphin, and others), *Experiencing the Life Cycle* (with Yoels), and *The Sociology of Everyday Life* (with Yoels).

**Hansfried Kellner** is Professor of Sociology at the University of Darmstadt in West Germany. He is a co-author of *The Homeless Mind: Modernization and Consciousness* (with Peter L. Berger and Brigitte Berger) and *Sociology Reinterpreted: An Essay on Method and Vocation* (with Peter L. Berger).

**Sherryl Kleinman** is currently Associate Professor of Sociology at the University of North Carolina at Chapel Hill. She received her Ph.D. from the University of Minnesota. She is the author of *Equals before God* excerpted here) and many articles in the field of symbolic interaction.

**Demie Kurz,** received her Ph.D. from Northwestern University. She is currently an applied sociologist at the Philadelphia Health Management Corporation and a member of the sociology faculty at the University of Pennsylvania. Her present research interests include abused women and parents as agents of emotional socialization.

**Robert Lejeune** was awarded his Ph.D. in Sociology from Columbia University. He is the author of *Class and Conflict in American Society* and has written on muggings.

**Janet Lever** received her Ph.D. from Yale University. She is currently a visiting Professor of Sociology at UCLA, having previously taught at Northwestern University and the University of California at San Diego. She is a co-author of *Women at Yale: Liberating a College Campus* (with Pepper Schwartz) and author of *Soccer Madness*.

**Elliot Liebow** is an anthropologist who earned his Ph.D. from Catholic University of America. His dissertation research resulted in the now-classic book *Tally's Corner*, from which our selection was drawn. Before becoming Professor of Anthropology at Catholic University, he served as a social anthropologist at the National Institute of Mental Health of the federal government.

**Lyn H. Lofland** has focused her recent research chiefly on the experience of grief and loss. She received her Ph.D. from the University of California at San Francisco and is currently Professor of Sociology at the University of California at Davis. Among her published works are *World of Strangers* and *Analyzing Social Settings* (with John Lofland).

**Yale Magrass** is Associate Professor of Sociology at Southeastern Massachusetts University. He obtained his Ph.D. at the University of California at Santa Barbara and is the author of *Thus Spoke the Moguls,* a study of business ideology during the New Deal.

**Thomas Meisenhelder**, Professor of Sociology at California State College of San Bernardino, received his Ph.D. from the University of Florida. He has published articles on phenomenology, popular culture, and criminology, among other topics. He has served as a visiting Fulbright Scholar in Botswana.

**Murray Melbin** is Professor of Sociology at Boston University. He obtained his Ph.D. from the University of Michigan. His recent book, *Night as Frontier,* extends the discussion of his article printed in this volume.

**Marica Millman**, Professor of Sociology at the University of California at Santa Cruz, received her Ph.D. from Brandeis University. Besides *Such a Pretty Face* (excerpted here), she is the author of *The Unkindest Cut: Life in the Backrooms of Medicine* and co-editor of *Another Voice*.

**Horace Miner** received his Ph.D. from the University of Chicago. He has long been Professor of Sociology and Anthropology at the University of Michigan.

**Benjamin D. Paul** is Professor of Anthropology at Stanford University and received his Ph.D. from the University of Chicago. He has written numerous articles on public health and culture change and edited *Health, Culture, and Community*.

**Howard Robboy** received his Ph.D. from Rutgers University and is currently Associate Professor of Sociology at Trenton State College. He has written several articles on the sociology of work and the impact of medical technology on social relationships. He is also one of the editors of *Social Interaction*.

**D. L. Rosenhan** was awarded his Ph.D. in clinical psychology at Columbia University. Currently at Stanford University, he is Professor of Psychology and Law. He is the co-editor (with Perry London) of two books: *Foundations of Abnormal Psychology* and *Theory and Research in Abnormal Psychology*.

**Lucinda SanGiovanni** received her Ph.D. from Rutgers University and is presently Professor of Sociology at Seton Hall University. In her book, *Ex-Nuns: A*

*Study in Emergent Role Passage,* she explores in more detail the ideas presented in her selection here. She has also written in the area of women and sports.

**Barry Schwartz,** Professor of Sociology at the University of Georgia, received his Ph.D. from the University of Pennsylvania. His many articles include sociological analyses of sleep and gift giving. He is the editor of *The Changing Face of the Suburbs* and the author of *Queuing and Waiting: Studies in the Social Organization of Access and Delay, Vertical Classification: A Study in Structuralism and the Sociology of Knowledge,* and a book about George Washington.

**Carol B. Stack** received her Ph.D. in anthropology from the University of Illinois. She is Associate Professor in the Institute for Policy Sciences and Public Affairs at Duke University. Her book, *All Our Kin: Strategies for Survival in a Black Community,* is a more detailed exposition of the article included here.

**Gregory P. Stone** completed his Ph.D. at the University of Chicago. He was Professor of Sociology at the University of Minnesota until his death in 1981. His many articles deal with various aspects of the sociology of everyday life. He was a co-author of *Being Urban: A Social Psychological View of City Life* (with David A. Karp and William C. Yoels), co-editor and translator of *Herman Schmalenback on Society and Experience* (with Gunther Luschen), and co-editor of *Social Psychology Through Symbolic Interaction* (with Harvey Farberman).

**Anselm Strauss,** a leading figure in symbolic interaction for many decades, is Professor of Sociology at the Medical School of the University of California at San Francisco. He is the author of *Mirrors and Masks* (excerpted here) and co-author (with Barney Glaser) of *The Discovery of Grounded Theory, Time for Dying,* and *Awareness of Dying.*

**Diane Vaughan** received her Ph.D. from Ohio State University and is currently Associate Professor of Sociology at Boston College. Her writings include *On the Social Control of Organizations* and *Uncoupling: The Social Construction of Divorce.*

**Lenore J. Weitzman** received her Ph.D. from Yale University and taught at the University of California at Davis and Stanford University before moving to Harvard University where she is Professor of Sociology. Her book, *The Divorce Revolution,* is the most recent of her writings on the social roles of women.

**William Foote Whyte,** a leading sociologist, received his Ph.D. from the University of Chicago. Now Professor of Sociology at Cornell University, he has served as president of the American Sociological Association. His books include *Men at Work, Human Relations in the Restaurant Industry, Industry and Society,* and the classic *Street Corner Society.*

**William Yoels** is Professor and Chair of the Department of Sociology at the University of Alabama at Birmingham. He received his Ph.D. from the University of Minnesota. He has co-authored *Being Urban: A Social Psychological View of City Life* (with Gregory P. Stone and David A. Karp), *Experiencing the Life Cycle* (with Karp), and *Sociology of Everyday Life* (with Karp).

**Mark Zborowski** was educated in France and is currently a medical anthropologist at the Pain Center of Mount Zion Hospital and Medical Center in San Francisco. He is also the author of *Life Is With People,* a study of Eastern European Jewish communities.